THE ILLUSTRATED ENCYCLOPEDIA OF
DESTROYERS FRIGATES & SUBMARINES

THE ILLUSTRATED ENCYCLOPEDIA OF
DESTROYERS FRIGATES & SUBMARINES

A history of destroyers, frigates and underwater vessels from around the world, including five comprehensive directories of over 380 warships and submarines

BERNARD IRELAND AND JOHN PARKER

HH
HERMES
HOUSE

This edition is published by Hermes House,
an imprint of Anness Publishing Ltd,
Blaby Road, Wigston, Leicestershire LE18 4SE
Email: info@anness.com

www.hermeshouse.com; www.annesspublishing.com

Anness Publishing has a new picture agency outlet for images for publishing, promotions or advertising. Please visit our website www.practicalpictures.com for more information.

Publisher: Joanna Lorenz
Senior Editor: Felicity Forster
Project Editor: Daniel Hurst
Copy Editors: Tim Ellerby and Will Fowler
Designer: Design Principals
Production Controller: Wendy Lawson

© Anness Publishing Ltd 2011

All rights reserved. No part of this publication may be reproduced, stored in a retrieval system, or transmitted in any way or by any means, electronic, mechanical, photocopying, recording or otherwise, without the prior written permission of the copyright holder.

Previously published in two separate volumes, *The World Encylopedia of Submarines* and *The World Encyclopedia of Destroyers and Frigates*

PAGE 1: *A Floréal-class frigate*
PAGE 2: *A Sachsen-class frigate*
PAGE 3: *USS Barb*, a Gato-class submarine
PAGE 4: A *Seawolf*-class submarine

ETHICAL TRADING POLICY
At Anness Publishing we believe that business should be conducted in an ethical and ecologically sustainable way, with respect for the environment and a proper regard to the replacement of the natural resources we employ.

As a publisher, we use a lot of wood pulp in high-quality paper for printing, and that wood commonly comes from spruce trees. We are therefore currently growing more than 750,000 trees in three Scottish forest plantations: Berrymoss (130 hectares/320 acres), West Touxhill (125 hectares/305 acres) and Deveron Forest (75 hectares/185 acres). The forests we manage contain more than 3.5 times the number of trees employed each year in making paper for the books we manufacture.

Because of this ongoing ecological investment programme, you, as our customer, can have the pleasure and reassurance of knowing that a tree is being cultivated on your behalf to naturally replace the materials used to make the book you are holding.

Our forestry programme is run in accordance with the UK Woodland Assurance Scheme (UKWAS) and will be certified by the internationally recognized Forest Stewardship Council (FSC). The FSC is a non-government organization dedicated to promoting responsible management of the world's forests. Certification ensures forests are managed in an environmentally sustainable and socially responsible way. For further information about this scheme, go to www.annesspublishing.com/trees

A CIP catalogue record for this book is available from the British Library.

PUBLISHER'S NOTE
Although the information in this book is believed to be accurate and true at the time of going to press, neither the authors nor the publisher can accept any legal responsibility or liability for any errors or omissions that may have been made.

Contents

8 Introduction

12 **PART ONE: DESTROYERS & FRIGATES**

14 **THE HISTORY OF DESTROYERS AND FRIGATES**

16 The early development of the self-propelled torpedo
18 The origins of the torpedo boat
20 The torpedo boat destroyer in the Royal Navy
22 Destroyers at the Dardanelles
24 Destroyers at Jutland
26 *Swift* and *Broke* in the Dover Patrol
28 Further developments in destroyers to 1918
30 Destroyer developments between the wars
32 Destroyers at Narvik
34 The raid on St. Nazaire
36 The "Tokyo Express"
38 The action off the North Cape
40 The sinking of the *Haguro*
42 Radar picket at Okinawa
44 The submarine threat in 1939
46 Escort vessels to World War II
48 Atlantic experience – the emergence of the frigate
50 Convoy action – Battle of the Atlantic
52 "Johnny" Walker and the Anti-submarine Support Group
54 Escort carrier Support Groups – taking the fight to the enemy
56 Improved weapons, sensors and escorts
58 The emergence of the fast frigate
60 Into the missile age
62 Frigates in the missile age

64 **DIRECTORY OF DESTROYERS: UP TO 1918**

United Kingdom
66 Early torpedo boats
67 The 27-knotters, or "A" class
68 The 30-knotters, or "B", "C" and "D" classes
69 River, or "E" class
70 Beagle, Acorn and Repeat Acorn, or "G", "H" and "I" classes
72 Tribal, or "F" class
73 Acasta, or "K" class

74 Laforey, or "L" class
75 "M" class
76 Contemporary Destroyer Leaders
77 Emergency "M" class
78 "R" and Modified "R" classes
79 "S" class
80 "V" and "W" classes

Germany
82 Early torpedo boats
83 *Divisionsboote*
84 *Grosse Torpedoboote* (1902)
85 *Grosse Torpedoboote* (1907–08)
86 *Torpedoboote* (1914–15)
87 *Torpedoboote* (1917)
88 Expropriated destroyers
89 S.113-type leaders

United States
90 Early torpedo boats
91 Bainbridge (DD.1) class
92 Smith (DD.17) and Paulding (DD.22) classes
93 Cassin (DD.43) and Tucker (DD.57) classes
94 The "Flush-Deckers"

Italy
96 Torpedo cruisers
97 High seas torpedo boats
98 Coastal torpedo boats
99 Lampo class
100 Nembo class
101 Soldati class
102 Indomito and Pilo classes
103 Sirtori and la Masa classes

France
104 Early torpedo boats
105 The "300-tonners"
106 The "450-tonners"
107 The "800-tonners"
108 Aventurier and Arabe classes

Japan
109 Early torpedo boats
110 Harusame and Asakaze classes
111 Kaba and Momo/Enoki classes

112 **DIRECTORY OF DESTROYERS: 1918 TO DATE**

United Kingdom
114 "A" to "I" classes
115 Tribal class
116 "J" to "N" classes
117 "O" and "P" classes
118 "Q" to "C" classes
119 Weapon class

120 Battle class
121 Daring class
122 County class
123 Type 82 (*Bristol*)
124 Type 42 (Sheffield) class
125 Type 45 (Daring) class

United States
126 Farragut (DD.348) class
127 Porter (DD.356) and Somers (DD.381) classes
128 Mahan (DD.364), Craven (DD.380) and Sims (DD.409) classes
129 Benson (DD.421) and Livermore (DD.429) classes
130 Fletcher (DD.445) class
131 Allen M. Sumner (DD.692) class
132 Gearing (DD.710) class
133 Forrest Sherman (DD.931) class
134 Charles F. Adams (DDG.2) class
135 Coontz (DDG.40) class
136 Leahy (DLG.16) and Belknap (DLG.26) classes
137 Spruance (DD.963) and Kidd (DDG.993) classes
138 Ticonderoga (CG.47) class
139 Arleigh Burke (DDG.51) class

Japan
140 Momi and Wakatake classes
141 Minekaze, Kamikaze and Mutsuki classes
142 Fubuki and Akatsuki classes
143 Hatsuharu and Shiratsuyu classes
144 Asashio class
145 Kagero and Yugumo classes
146 Akitsuki class
147 Yamagumo/Minegumo class
148 Takatsuki class
149 Shirane and Haruna classes
150 Tachikaze and Hatakaze classes
151 Hatsuyuki and Asagiri classes
152 Murasame and Takanami classes
153 Kongo and Improved Kongo classes

France
154 Bourrasque class
155 L'Adroit class
156 Le Hardi class
157 Chacal class
158 Guépard class
159 Aigle and Vauquelin classes
160 Le Fantasque and Mogador classes

161 Surcouf and Duperré classes
162 Suffren class
163 Tourville class
164 Georges Leygues and Cassard classes

Italy
165 Sella and Sauro classes
166 Turbine class
167 Leone and Navigatori classes
168 Dardo and Folgore classes
169 Maestrale and Oriani classes
170 Soldati class
171 Impavido class
172 Audace class
173 Durand de la Penne class

USSR
174 Skoryi class
175 Kotlin class
176 Kildin class
177 Krupny class
178 Kanin class
179 Kashin class
180 Sovremennyy class
181 Udaloy class

Germany
182 Maass and Roeder classes
183 Z23–39
184 Hamburg class

Netherlands
185 Holland/Friesland class

Sweden
186 Öland class
187 Östergötland and Halland classes

DIRECTORY OF FRIGATES

United Kingdom
190 Black Swan and Modified Black Swan classes
191 Hunt classes
192 Flower class
193 River class
194 Castle class
195 Loch and Bay classes
196 Types 15 and 16
197 Type 14
198 Types 41 and 61
199 Type 12/Leander class
200 Type 21
201 Type 22
202 Type 23

France
203 Le Corse and Le Normand classes
204 Commandant Rivière class
205 Aconit
206 D'Estienne d'Orves class
207 Floréal class
208 La Fayette class

Japan
209 Shumushu and Etorofu classes
210 Mikura and Ukuru classes
211 Kaibokan classes
212 Ikazuchi and Isuzu classes
213 Chikugo class
214 Ishikari and Yubari classes
215 Abukuma class

United States
216 Destroyer Escort (DE) classes
218 Dealey/Courtney and Claude Jones classes
219 Bronstein, Garcia and Brooke classes
220 Knox class
221 Oliver Hazard Perry class

Italy
222 Spica class
223 Ariete class
224 Pegaso and Ciclone classes
225 Albatros and de Cristofaro classes
226 Centauro class
227 Carlo Bergamini and Alpino classes
228 Lupo and Artigliere classes
229 Maestrale class
230 Minerva class

USSR/Russia
231 Kola class
232 Riga class
233 Petya and Mirka classes
234 Poti class
235 Grisha class
236 Krivak class
237 Steregushchiy class

Germany
238 Köln class
239 Thetis class
240 Bremen class
241 Brandenburg class
242 Sachsen class
243 Braunschweig class

Netherlands
244 Van Heemskerck/Kortenaer class
245 De Zeven Provinciën class
246 Karel Doorman class

Canada
247 St. Laurent class
248 Iroquois and Halifax classes

Australia/New Zealand
249 Anzac class

250 PART TWO: SUBMARINES

252 THE HISTORY OF SUBMARINES

254 Trial and error: the pioneers
256 Closer to the goal
258 Underway in the Hollands
260 Towards World War: the dash to build
262 Birth of the U-boat
264 The head to head of underwater power
266 The sinking of the *Lusitania*
268 Forcing the Dardanelles
270 Stealth and style of the Victoria Cross winners
272 A U-boat in Baltimore
274 The last vital, courageous act
276 The final reckoning
278 The "jinx" on the K boats
280 Big guns and aircraft carriers
282 Giants of the deep
284 The inter-war years
286 The Japanese story
288 The sinking and recovery of USS *Squalus*
290 The tragic loss of the *Thetis*
292 The action begins, and *Athenia* goes down
294 Mines, depth charges and leaky boats
296 Heroic work in the Mediterranean
298 "Finest work" by British submarines
300 U-boat war in the Atlantic
302 Pacific encounters of America and Japan
304 Clandestine travellers aboard
306 "The most important capture of the war"
308 Operation Mincemeat (or "The Man Who Never Was")
310 The chariots of stealth
312 Giant tasks for midget submarines
316 The cost and the legacy
318 Unfinished business: surviving a sinking
320 The Cold War: teardrops and Guppies
322 *Nautilus*, the first true submarine
324 *Skipjack* sets the standard
326 Life aboard the *Dreadnought*
328 Two lost submarines jolt the US nuclear team
330 The ballistic boomers
334 Fast and versatile: the hunter-killers
338 Sink the *Belgrano*!
340 Submarine TLAMs rain on Iraq, Belgrade and Afghanistan
342 The tragedy of the *Kursk*
344 International rescue: deep sea survival teams
346 Shaping the future

350 DIRECTORY OF SUBMARINES: 1900–45

United States
352 The *Holland*
353 A class
354 B class
355 C class
356 D class
357 E and F classes
358 G class
359 H class
360 K class
361 L class
362 M class
362 N class
363 O class
364 R class
365 S class
366 Salmon class
367 Sargo class
368 Gato class
370 Balac class
371 Tench class

United Kingdom
372 *Holland*
373 A class
374 B class
375 C class
376 D class
377 E class
378 V class (Early)
378 F class (Early)
379 G class
380 H class
381 J class
382 *Nautilus*
382 *Swordfish*
383 K class
384 L class
385 M class
386 R class (Early)
386 X1 class
387 O class
388 Parthian class
389 S class
390 T class
392 U class
393 Porpoise class
393 X-craft

Germany
394 *U1* (Early)
396 *U19*: diesel
397 *U81*
398 UB classes I, II and III
400 UC class (Minelayers)
401 U151 class
402 U classes (1939) Types IIA, B, C and D
403 U-VIIA, B and C
404 U-IX
405 U-Flak boats
406 XXI

Japan
408 KD classes
410 Type A/Type B
411 Type C
412 Type J
413 Type Sen Taka
414 Type Sen Toku

France
415 *Surcouf*
416 Redoutable class

USSR
418 Dekabrist class/Malutka class
419 Scuka class/Stalinec class

Italy
420 600 class
421 Marconi class

422 DIRECTORY OF SUBMARINES: 1945 TO DATE

United States
424 *Seawolf* SSN (Early)
425 *Triton* SSN
426 *Thresher/Permit*-class SSN
428 *George Washington* SSBN
429 *Ethan Allen* SSBN/SSN
430 *Lafayette*-class SSBN
431 *Sturgeon*-class SSN
432 *Los Angeles*-class SSN
434 *Ohio*-class SSBN
435 *Virginia*-class SSN
436 *Seawolf*-class SSN

USSR
438 *Kilo*-class SSK
439 *Victor*-classes I, II and III SSN
440 *Yankee*-class 667A SSBN
442 *Echo*-classes I and II SSN
443 *Alfa*-class SSN
444 *Delta*-classes I, II, III and IV SSBN
446 *Sierra*-class SSN
447 *Akula*-classes I and II SSN
448 *Oscar II*-class SSGN
450 *Typhoon*-class SSBN

United Kingdom
452 A-class SSK/Porpoise class (Late)
453 Explorer class
453 Oberon class
454 *Dreadnought* SSN
455 *Valiant*-class SSN
456 *Resolution*-class SSBN
458 *Churchill*-class SSN
459 *Swiftsure*-class SSN

460 *Trafalgar*-class SSN
462 *Vanguard*-class SSBN
464 *Astute*-class SSN

France
466 *Rubis-Améthyste*-class SSN
468 *L'Inflexible*-class SSBN
469 *Agosta*-class 90B SSK
470 *Le Triomphant*-class SSBN

China
472 *Xia*-class SSBN
473 *Han*-class Type 091 SSN

Germany
474 Type 212A-class SSK
475 Type 206A-class SSK/Type 214 class

Canada
476 *Victoria*-class SSK

Japan
478 *Yushio*-class SSK
479 Harushio class/*Oyashio*-class SSK

Australia
480 *Collins*-class SSK

Italy
482 *Sauro*-class SSK
483 *Salvatore Todaro*-class SSK

Spain
484 *Delfin*-class SSK
485 *Galerna*-class SSK
485 *Scorpene*-class SSK

Sweden
486 *Sodermanland*-class SSK
487 *Gotland*-class (Type A19) SSK

Pakistan
488 *Khalid*-class SSK

India
489 *Sindhu*-class SSK

Netherlands
490 Walrus II class

Brazil
491 Type 209-class SSK

Norway
492 *Ula*-class SSK

Taiwan
493 Hai Hu/Hai Lung class

494 Glossary
498 Class lists of destroyers and frigates
504 Index
512 Acknowledgements/Key to Flags

Introduction

This comprehensive volume looks closely at the progress of destroyer, frigate and submarine design through history and offers readers a fascinating historical and global insight into the intriguing world of naval vessels. It is split into two clearly defined sections: the first looking at the history and development of destroyers and frigates, and the second exploring the fascinating lineage of submarines. Each section includes a detailed history of the most important developments in mechanical design and manufacture, and a comprehensive directory, giving an extensive global and chronological view of individual vessels. Finally, there is a thorough glossary detailing the correct meanings of commonly used technical terms.

Part one: Destroyers and Frigates

On its introduction, the self-propelled torpedo made a tremendous impression on the world's navies. The measure of sea power remained the heavy-calibre gun, deployed in battleships heavily armoured to enable them to absorb damage inevitable in the gunnery exchanges that decided an encounter. Gunnery was still an art as much as a science and, with the concept of fire control still in the future, engagement ranges tended to be short. Hence the menace of the torpedo, whose effective range soon exceeded that acceptable to traditional gunnery men.

ABOVE: **Typifying World War II-built destroyers were the American Fletchers. USS *Cowell* retains her heavy surface and Anit-Submarine (AS) armament in the 1950s, but electronics are already proliferating.**

There is an old adage among designers that, to sink a ship, it is necessary to admit water. History abounds with examples of well-built ships, grievously damaged topside, that have survived through their watertight integrity remaining intact. The torpedo was invented expressly to defeat this capacity to endure such punishment, simply by delivering a powerful explosive charge beneath all protective armour and opening the hull to the sea.

In those pre-*entente cordiale* days, the French in particular saw in the torpedo an affordable means of offsetting the preponderance of British sea power. The result was a horde of torpedo boats of various sizes. As was customary, the British responded in kind.

In practice, these fragile craft, although manned by young men with boundless enthusiasm, posed little threat in a seaway but were, for instance, instrumental in obliging the British to abandon their time-honoured strategy of close blockade. Specialist yards in both Britain and France, then Germany, made a very good living as any fleet with pretentions to effectiveness felt obliged to follow suit.

INTRODUCTION

LEFT: **With the coming of missiles and helicopters, destroyers became volume-critical and rapidly increased in size. Accommodated in a Vertical Launching System (VLS), the area-defence missiles are invisible and, with just one gun, a large Spruance (USS** *Deyo***) appears underarmed.** ABOVE: **To increase numbers, the British Type 22s (***Brazen* **seen here) were designed to a budget. The result was over-tight and unsatisfactory, with later ships having to be considerably stretched.** BELOW: **Faced with tight peacetime budgets, smaller navies have the perennial choice of quality or quantity. The Italian** *Luigi Durand de la Penne* **and her sister are very capable ships but are just two.**

Concerned, however, at an obviously emerging threat to their naval dominance, the British introduced the torpedo boat destroyer. Larger, and sufficiently well-armed to run down and eliminate a torpedo boat at sea, such "destroyers" were themselves able to carry torpedoes. A new class of warship had been born.

Fast, operating in great flotillas and popularly described as "maids of all work", classic destroyers possessed innate glamour and were very popular commands for young officers keen to make their mark.

The very versatility of destroyers eventually, however, exposed their shortcomings. Modern examples were exercised endlessly in fleet escort and in flotilla torpedo attacks. In the former role they proved to be deficient against the newer threats of aircraft and submarine attack while, for all the torpedoes carried around the world's oceans, they were relatively little-used except, perhaps, in the Pacific.

Both great wars of the 20th century demonstrated the critical importance of mercantile shipping and its defence. The major threat to national security thus came, in large measure, not from the battle fleets but from submarines, natural successors to the early torpedo boats. In the absence of sufficient alternatives, older destroyers were drafted in for the vital drudgery of convoy escort. Designed for other tasks, however, they lacked the endurance, capacity and habitability inseparable from such escort duties.

For these, the simple corvette was already in production but, intended primarily for coastal duty, proved, in turn, inadequate for ocean work. Assuming a famous generic name from the days of sail, the frigate, once introduced, developed rapidly into an efficient submarine killer.

Post-war, technology advanced rapidly with fast conventional, then nuclear-propelled, submarines demanding larger frigates with stand-off weapons, notably helicopter-based. The threat from jet-propelled aircraft, themselves carrying stand-off weapons, was such that the guided missile inevitably transcended the gun.

Destroyers and frigates alike necessarily evolved from their "classic" forms in a process that remains continuous. The first half of this book endeavours to chart the full story to date. The lists of names of individual classes are so extensive as to require inclusion in a six-page section at the back of the book.

9

INTRODUCTION

Part two: Submarines

Military forces across the world witnessed some amazing developments throughout the 20th century, with each turn of events scaling up the power, death and destruction they could inflict to previously unimagined levels. Among them, the men of the Submarine Service must surely stand apart in that, when all was said and done, through two World Wars and the deadly brinkmanship of the Cold War that could have led to Armageddon, they ended that century with the future of humankind literally in their hands.

This is no overstatement. From virtually a standing start at the beginning of the 20th century, submarines were rapidly developed through the patience and ingenuity of a handful of dedicated engineers and designers who were often financially challenged, receiving little support from naval chiefs and governments. Within just a few decades of rapid progress, the so-called Silent Service became the new Navy and Masters of the Sea, culminating in an exceedingly volatile head-to-head nuclear armament. The extent of that progression is perhaps best illustrated by the size factor. In 1900, America's first submarine, the *Holland*, had a submerged weight of 76 tonnes/75 tons, carried two tiny torpedoes and a crew of nine, whereas the Russian Typhoon SSBN of the 1990s weighed in at 33,000 tonnes/32,479 tons, was crewed by 160 and carried 20 nation-obliterating ballistic missiles.

As the end of the 20th century came into view, the giant boats of the opposing forces, collectively carrying more explosive power than was unleashed in both World Wars up to and including Hiroshima, were operating in close proximity along the flashpoint sea lanes of the Cold War. It was fortunate

TOP AND ABOVE: **The progression of submarine development is perhaps no better demonstrated by the size comparison of the world's largest submarine, the Russian Typhoon class (**TOP**), crewed by 160 men and having a submerged weight of 33,787 tonnes/33,253 tons, and the first American *Holland* (**ABOVE**), which was a mere 72.83 tonnes/71.7 tons submerged and was crowded with a full crew of nine.**

for humankind that no Hitler or Stalin was around to press the button to unleash a nuclear holocaust, although the Cuban missile crisis of October 1962 presented great danger. That alone did not stop the superpowers in the continuation of their quest for domination in undersea warfare, and it remains as high a priority as ever.

Indeed, while the beginning of the 21st century marked a hundred years of incredible advances in submarine warfare, it also saw the initiation of a new era of multi-billion-dollar boats. These carry the mission forward into the next level of submarine capability, now coupled with a more diverse range of firepower to provide an effective and flexible response to the new emerging threats to national interests and the general population. The newest submarines will include technological innovations that will further enhance the advent of the true submarine, realizing the vision of Jules Verne, described in his novel *Twenty Thousand Leagues under the Sea*, as well as the ambitions of so many dedicated inventors, past and present.

INTRODUCTION

LEFT: **The mighty power of the ballistic missile-carrying submarines at the height of the Cold War is clearly evident from the open tubes of the American Polaris boat, USS *Sam Rayburn*.** ABOVE: **Despite their post-war pacifist policy, Japan maintained a small fleet of interesting boats, including this Yushio class of teardrop design introduced in 1975, although they steered clear of the nuclear-powered ambitions of other nations.** BELOW LEFT: **From the same era came the multi-faceted range of America's hunter-killer submarines, predominantly led by USS *Los Angeles*, the first of 67 that carried her class name over the two decades after her arrival in 1976.** BELOW: **The British contribution to the world power-play of SSNs included the *Trafalgar*-class boats which became the workhorses of the British fleet, and remained so as late as 2001, when one of the class fired Tomahawk cruise missiles into Afghanistan.**

The journey towards unlimited submersibility through the introduction of nuclear propulsion has been just one part – albeit the most vital – of the multi-layered and international saga of the submarine, often spurred by war and the quest for superiority, but generally advanced by building upon the dreams, ideas and inventions of a relatively small number of men of various nationalities.

The range and diversity of boats that emerged during more than a hundred years of submarine development stands as a historical tribute to those who designed, built and served on them. Furthermore, the motives and ambitions of the nations that eventually realized the potential of undersea warfare were equally varied, as demonstrated by the fact that some of the later exponents of submarine warfare, such as Britain, were initially reluctant to participate in the building of a submarine force. It is this story, regardless of the political connotations, that builds into the dramatic narrative presented in the second half of this book.

There are three chapters in this section, the first of which records some of the most important developments, plus major conflicts and incidents, in a complete history of submarines. This is followed by technical examinations in two directories, the first of which covers boats built prior to the end of World War II, the second covering submarines from 1945 to the present day.

It is also worth remembering that, although the superpowers have dominated the development of the nuclear submarine, almost all countries with sea borders do have their own submarine force, albeit largely of the diesel variety. They represent what might be viewed as the second level of a voluminous international submarine network, which is as active as ever, if substantially scaled down from the levels of earlier years when great submersible forces were built for two World Wars and, in between, general defensive operations. The past and current stock of most of these nations is also discussed in the book, along with indications of possible future flashpoints.

PART ONE:
DESTROYERS & FRIGATES

IMAGE: **The** *Shimakaze*, a Japanese Hatakaze-class ship.

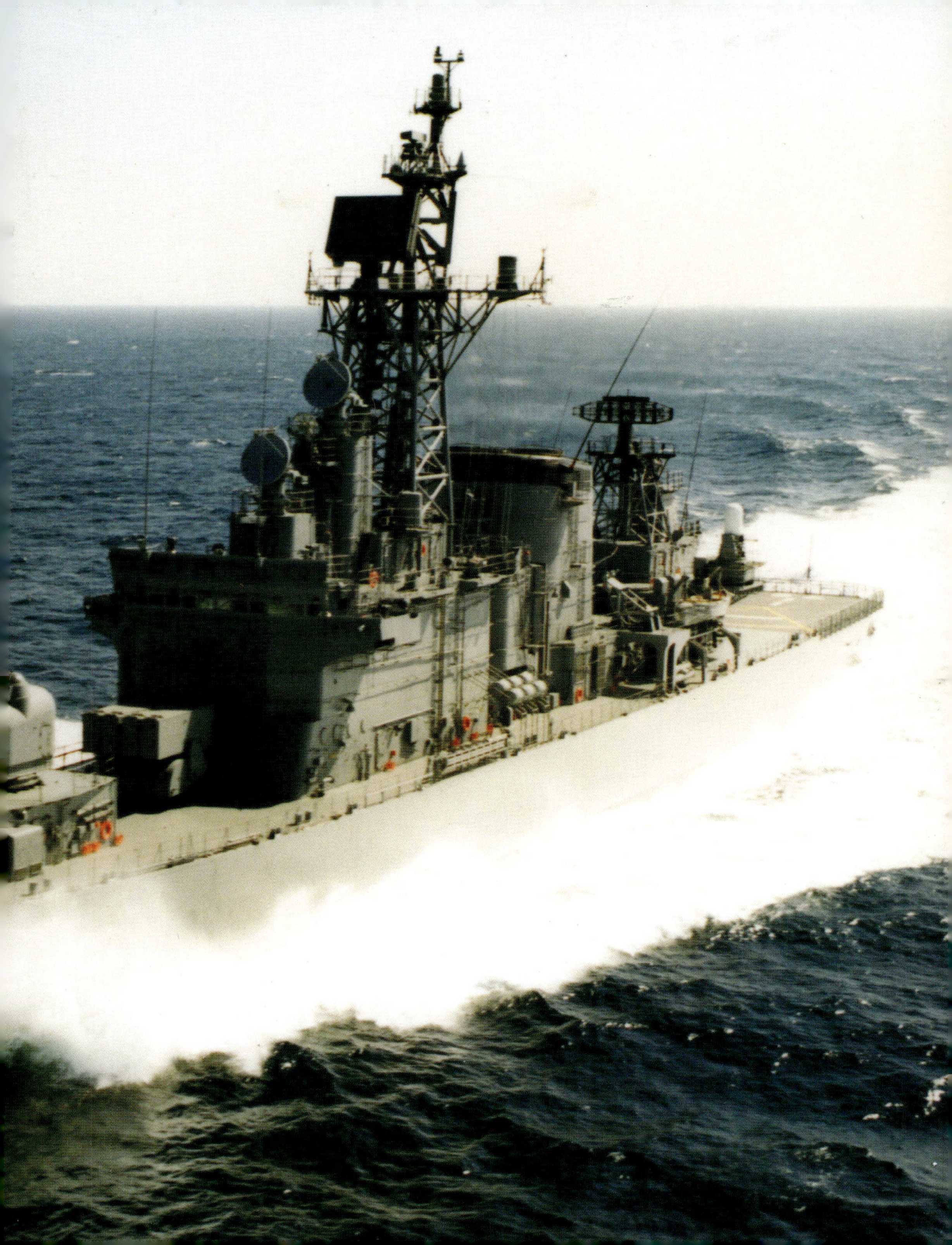

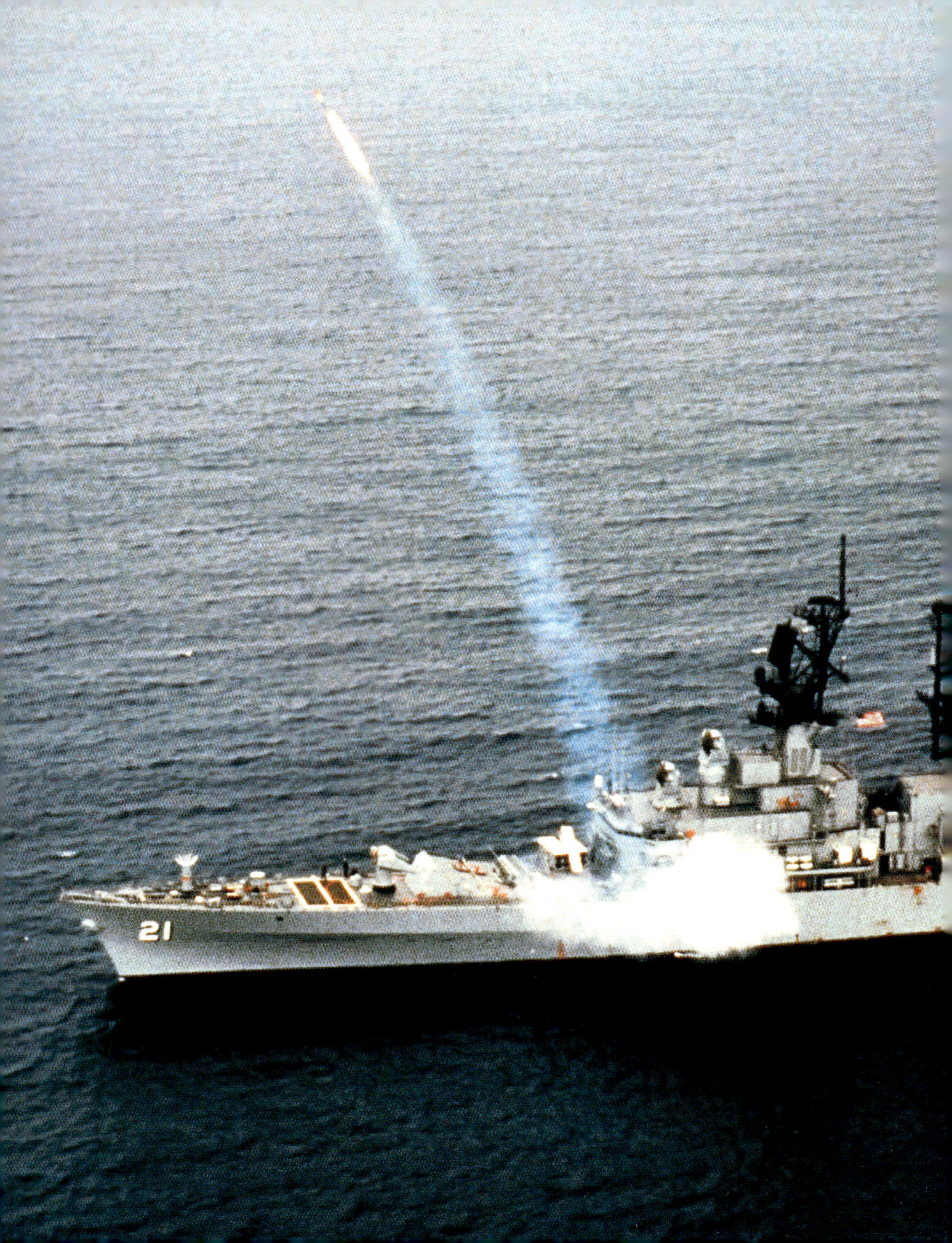
21

The History of Destroyers and Frigates

The history of war at sea is largely one of weapon and antidote. The locomotive torpedo quickly gained the status of "wonder weapon", able to strike the heaviest capital ship below its armour. Every maritime nation had to have its flotillas of torpedo boats which, themselves, were quickly eclipsed by the torpedo boat destroyer, itself a torpedo carrier.

By the end of World War II destroyers were routinely discharging salvoes of eight or more torpedoes in the course of furious, mainly nocturnal, encounters. Already, however, their effectiveness, expressed as torpedoes launched per ship sunk, was less than that for those dropped by aircraft. As the primary torpedo platform, the destroyer had already peaked, been surpassed and had begun the metamorphosis to the specialist anti-aircraft escort that she is today.

On the way, largely as a consequence of being available, destroyers had been pitted against the rapidly evolving threat of the submarine. Despite the development of sonar and depth charges, the destroyer, designed for speed, lacked the range, weapon capacity and habitability necessary for essentially low-speed convoy escort. Thus was introduced the frigate, specifically anti-submarine in concept.

LEFT: Guided missiles resulted in some confusion in categorization of escorts. The 5,670-ton, double-ended USS *Gridley*, here seen firing an Anti-Submarine Rocket missile, served 12 years as a frigate before being reclassed a cruiser.

LEFT: At what appears to be his factory at Fiume, Italy, Robert Whitehead ponders one of his experimental failures. It appears to be one of the "14-foot" weapons of 1870, the damage consistent with its having sunk beneath its crush depth.
BELOW: Better known for his successful development of the steam-driven paddle wheel, Robert Fulton also experimented with towed torpedoes, seeking patronage from both the United States and France during their wars with Britain.

The early development of the self-propelled torpedo

The *raison d'être* of the Torpedo Boat and its eventual nemesis, the Torpedo Boat Destroyer (TBD or, more simply, Destroyer), was the deployment of the torpedo, a brief look at the early development of the weapon will assist in the understanding of the craft themselves.

The American engineer Robert Fulton is generally credited with introducing the term "torpedo" during the Napoleonic Wars, its early meaning embracing any underwater explosive device intended to sink a surface ship. These could be static (later termed "mines") or mobile. The latter included "spar torpedoes" projecting ahead of steam launches or, such as the Harvey torpedo, towed like a paravane. All such variants required a human in the loop, it was a very hazardous operation in what was, unavoidably, close-quarter manoeuvring against an opponent.

About 1862, Commander Johann Luppis of the Austrian Navy built a model of a small steamboat, armed with an explosive charge and steered remotely by lines connected to its rudder. His idea was taken up by Robert Whitehead, who

"The use of the torpedo still constituted a greater danger to the man who launched it than to his enemy" — Alfred, later Grand Admiral von, Tirpitz on the Whitehead Torpedo (which he did not like) in 1877

managed an engineering concern in Fiume (now Rijeka). Whitehead saw immediately the huge potential of submerging such a vehicle, to render its approach invisible. Thus was born the idea of the Locomotive (or "Automobile") Torpedo, ancestor of all such weapons used today.

The prototype was run in 1866 and was a neutrally buoyant, spindle-shaped body with long parallel fins for longitudinal stability. It was of 14in maximum diameter and was driven by compressed air. An improved model was run two years later, incorporating Whitehead's patented arrangement of a balance chamber which, via a heavy pendulum, controlled horizontal surfaces for the maintenance of a selected depth.

In 1870, Whitehead demonstrated the weapon to British Admiralty officials. Carrying a 30kg/66lb warhead, it ran over 250m/273yd at 8 knots. The Admiralty soon afterwards bought the rights of manufacture, an endorsement that guaranteed the device's success.

Whitehead retained the patents, selling them to the French in 1873. Although the latter pronounced Whitehead's performance claims to be exaggerated, both they and the

LEFT: An early 20th-century picture of an American torpedo boat launching a "Mark 3 Whitehead". The change in shape will be evident, development being conducted independently by each purchaser of Whitehead's patent.

THE EARLY DEVELOPMENT OF THE SELF-PROPELLED TORPEDO

LEFT: **Accepted by the US Navy in 1899, the USS *Holland* successfully married the torpedo to the submersible. The round cap to the single torpedo tube is visible on the axis of the pressure hull. Above it, in the "bullnose", is the cap of a Zalinsky pneumatic dynamite gun.** ABOVE: **Between 1885 and 1889 the British carried out a protracted series of experiments, simulating the effects of exploding shells and torpedoes against the obsolete ironclad *Resistance*. Important conclusions were drawn about the use of anti-torpedo nets and watertight compartments.**

British worked independently to improve the weapon even as more fleets acquired its principles. Both worked officially on deploying it from small, semi-submersible craft similar to the "Davids" used by the Confederates during the American Civil War. The specialist British builders, Thornycroft and Yarrow, each, however, produced superior fast steam launches of conventional design.

By the late 1870s, contra-rotating propellers had been introduced, neutralizing torque effects and providing for improved straight running. This was vital to improving range, which currently stood at 1,000m/1,094yd at 7 knots, or 300m/328yd at 12 knots.

To improve directional stability the American Howell torpedo used a heavy internal flywheel, but the device was inferior to Ludwig Obry's addition of a gyroscope to directly control a pair of vertical rudders. This improvement of 1894 allowed the weapon to be increased in diameter to 45cm/18in, giving it a range of 3,000m/3,282yd with a good chance of hitting a target. As this was comparable with the effective battle ranges for gunfire at this time, the torpedo now had to be considered a real threat.

Frank Leavitt of the Bliss Company in the United States then developed the technique of burning fuel in the presence of enriched compressed air to deliver greatly increased energy. This was applied to a miniature reciprocating engine, later a turbine for smoother performance.

A torpedo was first used offensively in 1877. Its ability to be deployed from almost any type of warship, particularly small, inexpensive craft, inspired the French Admiral Théophile Aube to develop his ideas of what became known as the *Jeune École*. This propounded the concept that swarms of small, torpedo-carrying flotilla vessels could neutralize the mightiest conventional battle fleet. Although later proved specious, the philosophy led directly to the rapid development of the torpedo boat and, rather more slowly, the technologically more challenging submarine, or submersible.

ABOVE: **"Davids" of the American Civil War were not submersibles in the true sense, but were designed to be ballasted down with only the vestigial casing and funnel visible above the water. Their usual weapon was a spar torpedo.**

ABOVE: **Lieutenant William B. Cushing successfully used a spar torpedo to sink the rebel ironclad *Albemarle* in the Roanoke River on October 27, 1864. In this impression, Cushing is holding the lanyard to detonate the charge.**

17

The origins of the torpedo boat

When, in 1871, the British government purchased the rights to manufacture Whitehead's torpedo, the weapon could be launched from tubes above or below water, and under the impulse of either compressed air or a powder charge. Alternatively, it could be run-up and released from "dropping gear". To decide on how to deploy it, the Admiralty set up a Torpedo Committee. This recommended that, besides putting it aboard existing and specially designed warships, it would best be carried by ships' boats and "torpedo launches".

Larger, purpose-built warships were indeed built, but fast launches rapidly predominated in that they could be afforded in considerable numbers while, being nimble and of low profile, they were ideal for stealthy nocturnal attack. Smaller ("2nd Class") variants could even be carried aboard larger warships for both defensive and offensive purposes.

British builders, particularly Thornycroft and Yarrow, had already amassed considerable experience in constructing steel-hulled launches with compact steam machinery for private use. In 1873 Thornycroft built one, armed with a spar torpedo, for the Norwegian government and then, on approaching the British Admiralty, was rewarded with an order for a 27-tonner. About 25.6m/84ft long, she made over 19 knots on trials in 1877, whereupon she was commissioned as *Torpedo Boat No.1*. She was the first to be built specifically to deploy locomotive, as opposed to spar or towed, torpedoes.

ABOVE: The Thornycroft-built *Lightning* of 1877 was based on a river launch design. She was purchased by the Royal Navy as *1st Class Torpedo Boat No.1*, or TB No.1. In this picture, she is yet to be fitted with sided dropping gear for locomotive torpedoes. BELOW LEFT: The British Admiralty ordered from many ship yards for warship construction. The resulting non-uniformity that resulted is clear in this undated photograph. Also evident is the fine craftsmanship in their thin metal hulls. BELOW: One of a batch of 20 1st Class Torpedo Boats from Thornycroft was TB No.50, dating from 1886. Note the protected position for the helmsman, the turtledeck forward and the disproportionate size of the 18in torpedo tube.

As built, TB No.1 was equipped with two dropping frames, but these were found to be difficult to operate, requiring the craft to be slowed. They were, therefore, replaced by a single, trainable tube on the foredeck. The vessel was also renamed HMS *Lightning*.

Over the next two years, Thornycroft built 11 more, slightly longer, craft (TB Nos.2–12, not named). It is significant that similar vessels acquired by foreign navies quickly exchanged the spar-and-towed torpedoes, for which they had been designed, for Whitehead's weapons.

Lacking freeboard and superstructure, the early torpedo boats had limited seakeeping qualities. France and others were, however, also building enthusiastically, with yards such as Normand and Schichau beginning to establish reputations.

THE ORIGINS OF THE TORPEDO BOAT

ABOVE: **An important intermediate step between torpedo boat and destroyer was the 125-ton** *Swift,* **conceived by J. Samuel White and built speculatively in 1885. Purchased by the Admiralty as TB No.81, she showed superior seakeeping qualities.** RIGHT: **Instantly recognizable by her enormous goose-neck hydraulic cranes, the cruiser HMS** *Vulcan* **was designed around stowage for a flotilla of 2nd Class torpedo boats. These, armed with 14in torpedoes, were supposed to be set afloat in the vicinity of an enemy battle line.**

In 1884, J. Samuel White produced a speculative "one-off" which he named *Swift*. Displacing 125 tons and of 45.7m/150ft overall length, she showed improved seaworthiness and was acquired by the Admiralty. Renamed TB No.81 she was fitted with not only three torpedo tubes but also six 3pdr quick-firing (QF) guns. Capable of nearly 21 knots in the light conditions, she was designated a "torpedo boat catcher".

She resulted in the Admiralty building a disparate collection of boats between 41.1–44.2m/135–145ft long. Designed to have a broadly interchangeable armament of guns and torpedoes, they proved totally inadequate to the task of catching other torpedo craft. Nonetheless, this concept was also used abroad, notably in Germany, where the larger craft were termed "division boats". These were commanded by a more experienced officer, charged with maintaining order in often large flotillas of small craft, each with enthusiastic lieutenants enjoying their first command.

The French also began to construct larger and more seaworthy craft, known as "Haute Mer" torpedo boats. Their leaders, or division boats, were for a time armed with a single 14cm gun. Termed "bateaux-canon" they were intended to both lead and to support torpedo attacks but it proved impossible to fire their big gun accurately from so small and lively a platform.

To counter the threat of a flotilla of torpedo boats, the British Admiralty (still favouring the time-proven procedures of close blockade) sought a suitable design of vessel to screen major warships. These, in their evolutionary stage, were referred to variously as "catchers", "hunters" or, on occasion, "torpedo boat destroyers".

Probably inspired by the 15.24m/50ft semi-submersible "Davids", independent innovators persevered with developing an alternative form of stealthy torpedo carrier. Their endeavours would shortly produce the submersible which, with its ability to navigate both invisibly and undetectably, would become the most effective solution of all.

> "We lived on ham, sardines and tinned soups … it was as much as we could do to get a little water boiled. We had a table … but there was no point in laying it, for nothing would stay on it."
> From an account of life aboard a 33m French torpedo boat

ABOVE: **In the tranquillity of a dockyard basin an early French torpedo boat appears stylish. She proved, however, inadequate in a Mediterranean "blow". Note the pair of torpedo tubes located beneath the turtle deck forward.**
BELOW: **With only basic facilities of their own, torpedo boats depended upon their depot ships. This division of 2nd Class French boats are designed to be awash in any sea, their crews being confined largely to the light, elevated spar decks.**

FAR LEFT: **The three Hawthorne-Leslie boats of the 1898–99 Programme were highly rated, being "far superior" to the remaining 30-knotters. "Fine sea boats, combining strength, economy of coal consumption and seagoing qualities", the incomplete *Racehorse* is seen undergoing trials.** LEFT INSET: **In his various senior posts in the Admiralty, Admiral Sir John ("Jackie") Fisher may be truly said to have revolutionized the Royal Navy. As Controller and Third Sea Lord in 1892, he initiated the concept of the "torpedo boat catcher".** BELOW: **Of the first six 27-knotters, the Thornycroft pair (*Daring* seen here) were marginally the fastest. Note the pronounced tumblehome of the hull, the turtleback forecastle and the watch officer sharing the "bridge" with a 12pdr gun.**

The torpedo boat destroyer in the Royal Navy

The Torpedo Boat Destroyer (TBD) was inevitable. The torpedo boat was too small to be effective, while the larger Torpedo Gun Boats (TGBs) and their foreign equivalents, although an improvement, were still incapable of catching them.

To maintain speed in a seaway, length is the most important parameter. Having brought this fact to the attention of the Controller, then Rear Admiral John Fisher, Alfred Yarrow and John I. Thornycroft were involved in 1892 in discussions regarding larger craft. These resulted in six interested companies being invited to tender costed design proposals for a "large, seagoing torpedo boat".

The draft specification required the craft, of about 200 tons displacement, to maintain 27 knots over a three-hour trial, possible only under ideal conditions. A single 12pdr was to be carried to deal with French "haute mer" boats, in addition to a 6pdr and an 18in bow-mounted torpedo tube. Space and weight margins were to be allowed for either two more 6pdrs or a pair of deck-mounted torpedo tubes. Invitations to build were confined to private yards, as Royal Dockyards had not the expertise to design and build such lightly constructed craft.

A complication was that this was the very period in which the old-style locomotive boiler was being challenged by various types of water-tube boiler. While more compact and lighter, these still lacked the older boiler's reliability.

Before the initial order was placed – two each with Yarrow, Thornycroft and Laird – the craft, initially referred to as Torpedo Boat Catchers, had been redesignated Torpedo Boat Destroyers. Between them, they had installed three types of water-tube and one locomotive boiler for the purpose of evaluation. The six boats (like submarines, they were still commonly termed "boats") were significant in being the first real TBDs and were known officially as the A-class 27-knotters of the 1892–93 Programme.

All managed 27–27.7 knots on trials except for the locomotive-boilered *Havock*, which could make only 26.2. This obsession with high potential speed was totally academic, for even a fairly moderate sea was sufficient to cause progressively more severe damage to any TBD venturing to make better than about 15 knots. Conditions aboard remained little better than those in the torpedo boats. Vibration at speed was intense, while to hit anything with guns usually meant stopping the ship. They could, however, overhaul torpedo boats.

With the French still building numbers of large torpedo boats, the Admiralty quickly ordered six, then 30 more

> "Although the forebridge and chart house are a decided advantage, the close proximity to [the] top of [the] foremost funnel is most inconvenient ... a positive danger. Twice ... at a critical moment I was completely and suddenly enveloped in smoke and burning ashes."
> From a 1904 report by the Commanding Officer of the River-class *Itchen*

THE TORPEDO BOAT DESTROYER IN THE ROYAL NAVY

LEFT: Essentially a modified 30-knotter, the *Viper* was a testbed for Parsons' new steam turbine. She could make 36 knots with more compact machinery and with much reduced vibration. She had eight propellers on four shafts and was coal-fired. BELOW LEFT: Realistic night exercises confirmed the menace that flotillas of torpedo craft posed to capital ships. The immediate answer was additional searchlights and quick-firing guns. Jutland showed that the Germans were better prepared. BELOW: The German armoured ship *Ägir* of 1896, escorted by what appears to be a Germania-built "large torpedo boat" of 1902. With her long forecastle, the latter was much dryer than her British contemporaries and better able to maintain her speed.

27-knotters. Although also referred to as the A-class, they were of the 1893–94 Programme, with contracts being spread over no less than 14 private yards. All were in the water by the end of 1895.

The Admiralty, by now, was pressing for a minimum of 75 TBDs. Because some contractors were having difficulty reaching guaranteed performance, some earlier boats were late in delivery. This left funds available to commence work on a new class, slightly enlarged and capable of 30 knots. (Some of the A class had made 29 knots.) Known as the B, C and D classes, they were ordered under successive programmes between 1894 and 1901. They totalled 66 in all.

The expanding German fleet was now also causing concern. Between 1898 and 1901 it acquired its first true TBDs, building 12 of the Schichau-designed S.90 class. Shorter but beamier than the British 30-knotters, they were given a proper forecastle, as opposed to the British ships' very wet turtledecks. Designed less with regard to speed, they enjoyed superior seakeeping and greater endurance. Obviously better ships, they stimulated the British Admiralty to pay 40 per cent more for what became the River or E class, built between 1902–06. These followed work with several experimental turbine-driven boats, and some of the Rivers were similarly powered. Like their German peers, the Rivers traded excessive speed for a raised forecastle and an enclosed bridge structure. Seen as a great improvement, they are generally considered to have been the Royal Navy's first true destroyers.

BELOW: Yarrow's contributions to the six "special" 27-knotters of 1892–93 were the *Havock* and *Hornet*. They were similar except that *Havock*, seen here, was powered by two locomotive boilers, requiring two close-spaced funnels. BOTTOM: *Hornet* was fitted with eight, more compact water-tube boilers and four funnels. She was the first vessel to be accepted into the Royal Navy in 1894 as a torpedo boat destroyer, quickly abbreviated to TBD.

Destroyers at the Dardanelles

Although conceived for torpedo attack and defence, destroyers exhibited their versatility in other tasks during the Dardanelles operations, the first major campaign of World War I, which involved both French and British fleets.

A beguilingly simple War Council directive of January 1915 stated that the Navy would "bombard and take the Gallipoli Peninsula, with Constantinople as its objective". To achieve this aim an Anglo-French fleet would have to penetrate the 30km/18-mile long strait of the Dardanelles. Narrowing progressively from five miles to one, the waterway is subject to fierce currents. Ably assisted by their German ally, the Turks had created a near-impregnable defensive system. The ancient forts that dotted the arid and often steep shorelines were rearmed with considerable numbers of modern guns. Then lines of moored mines barred the Narrows. Fixed and mobile batteries, with searchlights, covered the minefields. Further mobile batteries ranged either shore.

Forcing a passage thus posed something of a conundrum. The considerable assembly of pre-Dreadnoughts could not transit the strait before the mines were cleared. Minesweepers, however, could not work under close-range gunfire from the numerous batteries. Top-level opinion was divided, some insisting that naval forces could do the job alone, others that military forces would need to secure the shore as the Navy advanced up the waterway by stages.

The lower, wider part of the strait, below the minefields, was largely subdued by naval bombardment, followed by landing demolition parties to destroy individual batteries.

TOP: Seen off Toulon, the Claymore-class destroyer *Massue* was one of a considerable force of French ships reinforcing the British fleet during the World War I Gallipoli campaign. Although capable of minesweeping, she was never so employed. ABOVE: Significant numbers of French and British pre-Dreadnoughts, considered expendable, were employed in the Dardanelles. The one-off French *Bouvet*, dating from 1898, hit a mine on March 18, 1915, and sank with great loss of life.

Tackling the mine barriers was, however, a different matter. With the fleet were 21 North Sea fishing trawlers, converted to sweep in pairs. Low-powered, they could manage only 5 knots with sweeps streamed and, as adverse currents could run as fast as 4 knots, they made near-stationary targets for the Turkish gunners. Sweeping was thus conducted at night, but under the glare of numerous searchlights and a hail of fire. Even with their civilian crews assisted by naval volunteers, the trawlers had little to show for numerous attempts and considerable damage. They were simply inadequate for the task.

Attending the fleet was a flotilla of 550-ton River-class destroyers. They were small ships, limited in both power and available space, but were used in pairs, linked by a cable secured to their after bitts. Thus encumbered, they preceded several major warships engaged on support duties. The wire was insufficient to cut any mine cable that it encountered but would provide warning. (It might be noted that the paravane and the serrated sweep wire were still in the future.)

> "The responsibility for the ultimate failure of the Fleet to force a passage … lies on the shoulders of those who would not allow us to accomplish our task after … efficient minesweepers [ie the destroyers] had been provided". Commodore Roger Keyes, Chief-of-Staff to the Admiral Commanding

DESTROYERS AT THE DARDANELLES

LEFT: **In the absence of proper port facilities, troop movements had to be conducted in the time-honoured fashion, using ships' boats. This picture gives an idea of the vulnerability of such craft in the face of an opposed landing.**

ABOVE: **Beaches on the Gallipoli peninsula were little more than coves backed by high ground which, once secured, gave protection from direct Turkish artillery and small-arms fire. With the eventual arrival of U-boats, ships could no longer loiter offshore.**

Fortunately for the destroyers, which were not free to manoeuvre, the larger ship following attracted the majority of the fire. The system worked well below the mine barriers, but several old British and French battleships manoeuvred out of the main stream, blundering into a hitherto unsuspected line of mines. Their loss caused despondency in the C-in-C.

Also available were two flotillas of 975-ton Beagle, or G-class, destroyers. Larger, and with 60 per cent more propulsive power, they drew considerably less water than the trawlers, giving them a good chance of being able to pass over the moored mines with impunity. With the assistance of Malta Dockyard, the Beagles were fitted to work in pairs, streaming a 2.5in steel cable. Trials showed that this could be towed at 14 knots, enabling destroyers to sweep against the tidal stream, relying on sheer power to snag a mine cable and, if not to cut it, to drag it clear.

Preliminary sweeps in the strait itself proved the efficacy of the system, but too late. To the great disappointment of the destroyer crews, they were never to have the distinction of leading the battle fleet through the Narrows. Successive C-in-Cs had been too concerned about losses, more feared than actual, and their pessimism led to the decision to take the Gallipoli peninsula by military force.

Following the landing, the Beagles were kept busy sweeping offshore on the Army's flanks, ensuring the safety from mines of fire support ships.

LEFT: **HMS *Redpole* was a 755-ton Acorn- or H-class destroyer, seen here probably at the fleet base on Mudros. She has lifelines rigged along the starboard side of the hull and has a Carley float stowed at the break of the forecastle.** ABOVE: **Destroyers, as usual, were called upon to handle all the fleet's "odd jobs". These crew members, suitably armed, are using rifle fire to explode floating mines, which posed a considerable menace in the strait.** LEFT: **Britain's then-large fishing fleet was a valuable source of modern trawlers and drifters which, with their superb seaman crews, performed as auxiliaries to the fleet. The *Seaflower*, seen here, was unusual in being owned by the Admiralty.**

23

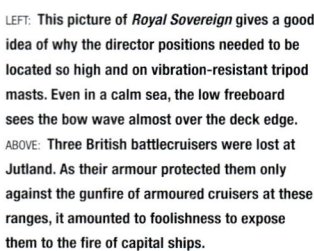

LEFT: **This picture of *Royal Sovereign* gives a good idea of why the director positions needed to be located so high and on vibration-resistant tripod masts. Even in a calm sea, the low freeboard sees the bow wave almost over the deck edge.**
ABOVE: **Three British battlecruisers were lost at Jutland. As their armour protected them only against the gunfire of armoured cruisers at these ranges, it amounted to foolishness to expose them to the fire of capital ships.**

Destroyers at Jutland

Admiral Sir John Jellicoe framed his Battle Orders around the premise that the preservation of the British Grand Fleet was more important than the destruction of the German High Seas Fleet. He forecast, correctly, that the latter, under severe pressure, would make a "battle turn away" to disengage. This would be made under cover of a smoke screen and a massed destroyer torpedo attack. It might also be to entice the Grand Fleet into a "submarine trap". Jellicoe made it clear beforehand that he would not directly follow a battle turn away but, at Jutland, this was a primary cause for the fleets to lose touch at a critical phase, just as daylight was fading.

For his destroyers (50 boats of three flotillas), Jellicoe's instructions were "not to miss a favourable opportunity for a successful [torpedo] attack on the enemy's battle fleet". Their "primary duty", however, was to prevent enemy flotillas from disturbing the Grand Fleet's gunfire. Their role was, thus, primarily defensive, with Scheer's battle fleet of secondary importance, a target of opportunity.

Not so with the destroyers (27 from four flotillas) of Vice Admiral Sir David Beatty's Battle Cruiser Fleet. Beatty believed that, by launching his torpedo attack first, he would oblige the enemy's destroyers to protect their own fleet, disrupting any plan to attack Jellicoe.

During the first phase of the battle, the battlecruisers "run to the south", the hard-pressed Beatty and his opponent, Hipper, unleashed their destroyers simultaneously. About 30 ships thus became involved in furious and confused close-range action between the lines, ended only by the sudden appearance of Scheer's main battle fleet. Each side lost two destroyers, only one to torpedo.

Most of the heavy fighting at Jutland was between the battle cruiser forces. With the second phase, the "run to the north", Beatty successfully enticed Scheer's battle fleet into Jellicoe's waiting gunnery trap. With Scheer's successful disengagement in the gathering gloom, Jellicoe eschewed the uncertainties of night action, intending to renew the action at dawn.

The main battle fleets lost touch in the darkness but British light forces fought a series of deadly skirmishes with various parts of the German line. Nineteen destroyers of the 4th Flotilla, led by the *Tipperary*, challenged strange ships, which replied with a hail of fire at close range. Unsure still of the stranger's identity, some responded with torpedoes, some held their fire. None thought it necessary to inform Jellicoe that they had discovered the position of the German main body.

LEFT: **The 14 battleships of the High Seas Fleet's 1st and 2nd Battleship Squadron drawn up in the Kiel Fiord. Closest is probably *Thüringen*, second ship of the 1st Division of the 1st Squadron. She was probably responsible for sinking the armoured cruiser *Black Prince*.**

LEFT: German destroyers steaming at high speed in quarter line. Note the day shapes on the masts; circular, triangular or rectangular in outline, they were carried in addition to painted pennant numbers on the bows. BELOW: Attached to the screen of Hood's ill-starred 3rd Battle Cruiser Squadron, the destroyer *Shark* was disabled by gunfire in a mêlée with enemy destroyers. She was torpedoed and finished off, sinking with heavy loss of life.

LEFT: German destroyers were organized in flotillas of eleven boats, comprising a leader and two "half flotillas" of five boats apiece. These were numbered in sequence so that, for instance, the 4th Flotilla (absent at Jutland) comprised the 7th and 8th Half Flotillas. BELOW: The Germania-built G.96 of 1916 was a final, modified unit of the G.85–95 batch, differing from them in that her forecastle was extended to the bridge structure. Only G.86, 87 and 88 were at Jutland, the G.96 was mined and sank off Ostend in 1917. BOTTOM: Jellicoe made clear beforehand that, in the event of a massed German destroyer torpedo attack, he would turn his battle line away, rather than towards, the enemy. He did, lost contact and valuable time, and, with it, a victory.

Several such skirmishes cost the British a further six destroyers. The nature of the actions is well borne out by the high-speed collisions between the British *Spitfire* and the German battleship *Nassau*, the British destroyers *Broke* and *Sparrowhawk*, and the German light cruiser *Elbing* and battleship *Posen*. Although reluctant to fire torpedoes in the circumstances, British destroyers succeeded in sinking the pre-Dreadnought *Pommern* and the light cruiser *Rostock*.

In the course of that night, the British light forces, including light cruiser squadrons, saw more action than the whole of Jellicoe's main body in the earlier daylight encounter. Scheer was bent on escape, while Jellicoe needed to find him in order to renew the action with daylight. One of the enduring mysteries of Jutland is how few ships with vital information felt it necessary to inform their C-in-C. This included capital ships of his main body which observed the night encounters at considerable distance without being involved. With too little information upon which to base a judgement, Jellicoe failed to re-establish contact, and Jutland was over, destined to become one of the great "what ifs" of history.

Post-battle analysis reached the conclusions that the British destroyers were organized in over-large flotillas, and were poorly trained in attack procedures. Valour and aggression were not lacking, but attacks were not co-ordinated and they were "simply overwhelmed by the enemy's searchlights, star shells … and secondary armament".

Swift and *Broke* in the Dover Patrol

With the Western Front hopelessly stagnated, the Allies could conduct operations from Dunkerque while the Germans used Ostend and Zeebrugge, the former less than 48km/30 miles up the coast. By early 1917, British shipping lost to U-boat torpedoes had reached crisis level, although the armies in France depended upon uninterrupted cross-channel shipments of troops and supplies.

The British Dover Command was thus of crucial importance, having as its main responsibilities the protection of shipping in the eastern English Channel, and the denial of U-boat's passage to the Atlantic via the shortest route.

A little over 32km/20 miles in width, the Dover Strait had been "closed" by a mine barrier. Except for shallow waters and shipping gates, mines had been laid in rows set at depths of 9–30m/30–100ft below low water. Most shipping could cross it quite safely, but submerged submarines were at great risk. Some 32km/20 miles to the north-east, a second barrier of mined nets ran between the South Goodwin and Dyck lightships, the latter near Dunkerque.

To be effective, both barriers had to be patrolled and tended by large numbers of drifters requisitioned from the fishing fleet. These unarmed craft and, indeed, the whole Command area, were subject to sudden attack by German

TOP: **An inspiration of Admiral Sir John Fisher when Controller, the *Swift* was an expensive one-off, part Scout, part Leader. The sided 4in forecastle guns, seen here, had been replaced by a single 6in by the date of the action described here.**
ABOVE: **Wreathed in steam, a 21in torpedo leaves one of *Broke*'s sided tubes. In so close a mêlée, torpedoes may not get sufficient time to arm, and may be a hazard to either side.**

destroyers, of which their Flanders Flotilla, together with coastal U-boats, were based on the inland port of Bruges. Emerging via Zeebrugge on a dark night, the destroyers could arrive at the barriers in a couple of hours. With no warning, they could not fail to encounter the drifter line, and they could operate with the confidence of knowing that every vessel met with would be hostile.

There were two leaders and sixteen destroyers attached to the Dover Command, most of the latter being older and smaller boats. These conducted deterrent patrols at irregular intervals, but had been unable to prevent several incursions by the

> "It was like an excerpt from a Marryat story, an echo of the spar-to-spar combats at Trafalgar."
> Reginal Pound, Evans's biographer

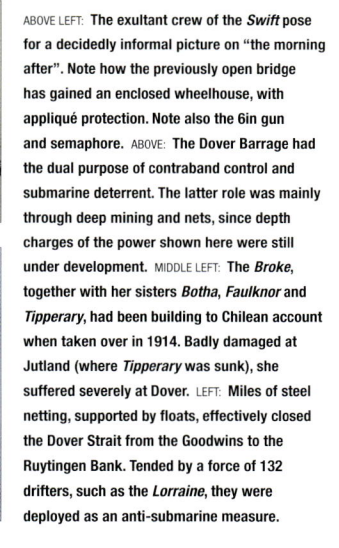

ABOVE LEFT: **The exultant crew of the *Swift* pose for a decidedly informal picture on "the morning after". Note how the previously open bridge has gained an enclosed wheelhouse, with appliqué protection. Note also the 6in gun and semaphore.** ABOVE: **The Dover Barrage had the dual purpose of contraband control and submarine deterrent. The latter role was mainly through deep mining and nets, since depth charges of the power shown here were still under development.** MIDDLE LEFT: **The *Broke*, together with her sisters *Botha*, *Faulknor* and *Tipperary*, had been building to Chilean account when taken over in 1914. Badly damaged at Jutland (where *Tipperary* was sunk), she suffered severely at Dover.** LEFT: **Miles of steel netting, supported by floats, effectively closed the Dover Strait from the Goodwins to the Ruytingen Bank. Tended by a force of 132 drifters, such as the *Lorraine*, they were deployed as an anti-submarine measure.**

Flanders Flotilla, which had sunk several ships and bombarded coastal towns before withdrawing rapidly. Public opinion over the latter activities was outraged.

In April 1917, regular rotation of Flanders Flotilla boats saw the arrival of two dozen from the High Seas Fleet. Half of these were new craft, fast and well-armed. On the night of April 20/21 six each were despatched to Calais and Dover. Both towns were briefly shelled but, on withdrawing, the Dover force ran into the two big British leaders, *Swift* and *Broke*. The Germans were in line ahead, encountering their opponents on an almost reciprocal course, port bow to port bow. Both sides opened fire, the larger British ships turning hard to ram their enemy,

It was extremely dark and, blinded by her own gun flashes, the *Swift* just missed, running close astern of the G.42, the German tail-under. Both British ships also fired a single torpedo, one of which hit the G.85, the next in line. With both ships making 30 knots, the *Broke* then slammed into the G.42. Locked together, the two swung through 180 degrees.

This brought the unfortunate G.85, already dead in the water, abeam of the *Broke*, which hit her with a second torpedo.

The *Swift* disappeared in pursuit of the four remaining enemy ships, receiving considerable punishment from their gunfire before finally having to abandon the chase.

The *Broke*, meanwhile, remained in the embrace of the stricken G.42. She was obviously settling, and her crew boldly attempted to board the *Broke*. As there had been no question of surrender, they were met with fixed bayonets, cutlasses, pistols and even "cups of hot cocoa". Also still under accurate fire from the nearby disabled G.85, *Broke* wrenched herself free and decided the issue with a third torpedo.

Her bows shattered, with just one serviceable gun remaining, the *Broke* took aboard as many survivors as she was able to locate, but had to be towed to Dover. Her commanding officer, Commander "Teddy" Evans was, thereafter, eulogized in the popular press as "Evans of the *Broke*", an incubus that he bore with good humour.

27

Further developments in destroyers to 1918

Warship development proceeded rapidly during World War I, driven by the dynamics of necessity and with the British and Germans, in particular, greatly influencing each other.

The destroyer (smaller examples of which were still termed "torpedo boats" by the Germans) was already by 1914 large enough to carry guns capable of disabling its opponents, while carrying torpedoes as the weapon of opportunity.

Torpedoes themselves were becoming more effective. The 21in "heater" torpedo, for instance, was available to the Royal Navy by 1910. It could range to 5,030m/5,500yd at 30 knots, carrying a 100kg/225lb warhead. Experimental weapons, however, were managing up to 9,144m/10,000yd at 30 knots, or 4,572m/5,000yd at 40 knots.

These increasing ranges led designers to give capital ships more powerful secondary armaments to keep destroyers beyond effective range. It seems to have been insufficiently appreciated, however, that even at 30 knots, a torpedo would take about 10 minutes to travel 9,144m/10,000yd. Its target would have moved a considerable distance in this time, making a hit by a single weapon unlikely. Only a mass torpedo attack against a battle line (so feared by Jellicoe at Jutland) would likely constitute real danger.

Pre-war French exercises suggested that close-range torpedo attack would be a different matter. This was partly confirmed at Jutland although, overall, the results here were

ABOVE: **The radiussed sheer strake on these German destroyers suggests that they are of the Vulkan-built T 150 type, although lacking a gun on the forecastle. These still have their peacetime pennant numbers painted up.**
BELOW: **The French *Commandant Bory* was one of the twelve-strong *Bouclier* class of 1911–13. Only the Bordeaux-built pair, *Bory* and *Boutefeu*, had equi-spaced funnels, the remainder having theirs in two distinct pairs.**

unspectacular (the British firing a total of 94 torpedoes for six hits, the Germans 105 for two, possibly three).

Raised forecastles greatly improved seakeeping. Having introduced the feature with the "Rivers", in 1903, the British retained it thereafter. The Germans had preceded this with a half-height forecastle in 1902 but full height only in 1908. The Americans were ambivalent, adopting it in 1909 with the *Smith* but abandoning it again, presumably to reduce topweight, in 1917. French boats carried forecastles from 1911.

The adoption of oil firing was not only a boon to weary crews, for it also influenced the size and cost of a destroyer. One ton of oil would take the ship as far as 1.32 tons of coal while occupying less space and being able to be accommodated in remote tanks. Space otherwise devoted to bunkers could be saved, although British destroyers had mediocre endurance.

> "Boats are continually out of action with minor defects due to bad materials, workmanship and inefficient personnel ... suppose due to shortage of skilled labour and good material ... more easily met if we turned out fewer destroyers." February 1918 report by Captain (D) of the 13th Flotilla on his Modified R-class boats

FURTHER DEVELOPMENTS IN DESTROYERS TO 1918

LEFT: **A British 21in torpedo, showing its contra-rotating propellers. The single tube located between second and third funnels, together with what appears to be stowage for a spare torpedo in the foreground, suggests an Acasta, or K-class boat of 1912–13.** ABOVE: **American flush-deckers were notoriously narrow aft. Note the resulting limited number of depth charges that could be accommodated and the 4in gun trained on the beam to give space in which to work.** BELOW: **The late war-built "V & Ws" introduced superimposed main armament but they were deemed large and expensive, resulting in a reversion to a Modified Trenchant, or S-class, one of 67 such actually survived until 1947.**

Steam turbines, although compact and reliable, had the drawback of driving the shafts at undesirably high revolutions. Reduction gearing was complex and expensive, first going to sea in the L-class *Leonidas* in 1913. Propulsive efficiency was, thereby, much improved and less power was required for the same speed.

Destroyers grew inexorably in size, most being better than 1,000 tons displacement by 1918. Philosophies differed somewhat, with the British tending toward superior gun armament; the Germans, torpedoes. Most war-built German boats carried six tubes of 500mm diameter. Until the Improved W-class, late in the war, British equivalents had four of 533mm. American destroyers tended to be larger, due to the oceanic conditions in which they had to operate. Their flush-deckers carried 12 tubes, but with guns limited to 4in calibre. With the Improved W-class, the British increased gun calibre from 4 to 4.7in. This increased projectile weight from 14.1 to 22.7kg/ 31 to 50lb, overtaking the Germans, most of whose war-built boats carried the 10.5cm weapon, firing a 17.3kg/38lb shell.

To save on ship length the British introduced superimposed gun positions in what became generally known as "V & Ws". In them, they had a design which, with surprisingly little modification, would serve the Royal Navy and many foreign fleets for the next 20 years.

During hostilities, the British completed no less than 28 leaders and 255 other destroyers. Experience in war showed the need for two separate types, large and long-legged for fleetwork; smaller, and more heavily gunned elsewhere. Such specialization was not possible in wartime but, with the "Hunts" of World War II, one may discern a partial realization of the ideal. British destroyers were often later criticized for their conservative structural and machinery design, but they rarely suffered major breakdown and none was lost to stress of weather.

RIGHT: **Nameship of her class of 1910, the 700-ton USS *Smith* was the first of what the Americans referred to as "flivvers". Ships of this size quickly proved to be too small, being superseded by the "thousand-tonners".**

BELOW: **Several classes of slightly enlarged leaders were built or commenced during World War I, including the eight Scotts. Note the distinguishing black top to *Stuart*'s forefunnel and the fifth 4.7in gun between the funnels.**

29

THE HISTORY OF DESTROYERS AND FRIGATES

LEFT: **Two Js and an F class at sea.** With six rather than the eight 4.7in guns, the Javelins were introduced as cheaper diminutives of the Tribals. Their main armament could elevate only to 40 degrees, saving nearly 4 tons weight per mounting.
ABOVE: Otherwise excellent ships, the Js, in common with all other British destroyers, had totally inadequate anti-aircraft firepower. Most traded their after torpedo tubes for a single 4in High-Angle (HA) whose elevated barrel is here visible.

Destroyer developments between the wars

World War I found destroyers playing roles for which they had never been designed. Catastrophic shipping losses due to the depredations of U-boats obliged a reluctant British Admiralty finally to adopt a convoy system during 1917. Where this improved matters dramatically it also gave destroyers, the only effective means to hand, a major new task as escorts.

Designed for speed rather than endurance, destroyer machinery was uneconomic and inefficient at continuous convoy speed. Depth charges, undergoing continuous improvement, accounted for 30 U-boats in the course of the war but hydrophones, as a means of detection, proved next to useless. Active sonar, then called ASDIC, was under development but, despite an enormous inter-allied effort, would not be available in practical form until the 1920s. Older destroyers, superseded for fleet work, would continue to find adequate employment as escorts.

Destroyers also found a role in offensive minelaying, although the extra topweight had often to be compensated through the temporary removal of other armament or equipment.

Replacement British destroyer construction began in 1924, the two *Amazon* prototypes being essentially 1,350-ton improvements of the war-built W-class. Conservatively, the Admiralty then kept to much the same design for more than a decade, with the A to I classes improved only in detail, their torpedo outfit increasing from six to eight, then ten.

This persistence was contrary to developments abroad, where the United States, France, Italy Japan and, later, Germany, were building larger and faster ships, with comparable torpedo armament but with guns of 5in calibre or larger. The Admiralty followed suit in 1935–36 with the Tribal (eight guns, four torpedo tubes) and several six-gun classes (J to N inclusive) with ten tubes.

To complement these expensive "fleet" destroyers the Admiralty in 1938, again identified the need for numbers of smaller and less-capable vessels. The result was the four-gun "emergency" flotillas with full destroyer specification, beginning with the O-class of 1941, together with slower "escort" destroyers with little or no torpedo armament but with a

LEFT: **Slightly enlarged versions of the war-built Admiralty Ws, the two Amazons of 1926 were designed to incorporate all wartime engineering improvements, particularly in machinery. They proved to be prototypes for the steadily evolving "A" to "I" classes, adding a flotilla annually until 1938.**

DESTROYER DEVELOPMENTS BETWEEN THE WARS

ABOVE LEFT: As built, the 16 Tribals of 1938 were held by many to be the most handsome destroyers ever. In light grey Mediterranean Fleet livery, the *Mohawk* also exhibits the red-white-blue recognition bands adopted during the Spanish Civil War. ABOVE: The USS *Maury* (DD.401) closes with battleship *South Dakota* in the Pacific. Single-funnelled, raised forecastle destroyers were unusual in the US Navy and were confined to designs of the late 1930s. LEFT: Although the British Nelsons were equipped with 24in torpedoes during the late 1920s, there was disbelief in the West, even as late as 1942, that the Japanese had brought a similar calibre into general use at the same time.

> "It is not performance on trial which is in doubt, but operational reliability at sea." Wise words from the Engineer-in-Chief to the Admiralty Board in 1931, when asked to consider new-pattern auxiliary machinery for the C-class boats

powerful dual-purpose (DP) gun battery. Begun in 1939, these became the extensive Hunt classes.

Although during the 1930s the growing potency of air attack was becoming well-recognized, destroyer armaments, British or foreign, did not reflect it. Main armaments were of insufficient elevation to engage aircraft, while multiple machine guns and "pompom" type cannon were inadequate to deter dive-bombers, which were to prove deadly against them.

Throughout the 1930s American and Japanese developments were mutually influential. As early as the late 1920s, Japanese destroyers were carrying six 5in guns and nine 21in (soon to be uprated to 24in) torpedo tubes. Although their contemporary classes were faster, the Americans had no directly comparable ships until 1939–40.

An unusual feature of Japanese boats was an armoured box, adjacent to each bank of torpedo tubes and containing a full outfit of reloads. Despite the cost of torpedoes, Japanese commanding officers were trained to use them readily and aggressively. American ten-tube destroyers were given allocated space for a few reloads but, surprisingly, no weight margins, their design already being tight.

British destroyer design remained conservative and, by not attempting too much on limited displacements, produced reliable and seaworthy ships that were also able to survive severe battle damage. German and American designers were experimenting with advanced steam conditions to produce compact but powerful machinery developing up to 52,200kW/ 70,000shp for speeds of up to a claimed 38 knots. In contrast, the six-gun British J class of 1936 had a relatively simple 29,828kW/40,000shp installation that, with little further refinement, was repeated for all war-built "emergency" flotillas. With steadily increasing deep displacements, this resulted in speeds falling off to about only 32 knots maximum. As full power was rarely used, this was adjudged a fair price to pay for reliability.

A major problem for all would be the wartime accumulation of heavy equipment (reducing stability and endurance) and the overcrowding produced by many extra personnel.

ABOVE: The German *Leberecht Maass* and her sister *Max Schultz* were sunk in error by friendly aircraft off Borkum in February 1940. There was a heavy loss of life, the incident being officially attributed to mining.

Destroyers at Narvik

Brilliantly executed, the German invasion of Norway demanded the mobilization of every available warship. Spearhead troops were landed simultaneously at Bergen, Kristiansand (South), Narvik, Oslo and Trondheim. There was considerable disparity in the length of sea passages involved and the British Home Fleet presented a major threat. Surprise was achieved, however, but, once in Norway, the German warships were open to attack.

Most remote was Narvik, over 1,609km/1,000 miles distant from Wilhelmshaven. Ten destroyers, covered by the battleships *Scharnhorst* and *Gneisenau* and transporting 20,000 troops, arrived on the evening of April 8, 1940. Alone, the destroyers then made the 160km/100-mile passage up the Vestfjord to Narvik. At dawn on the 9th they overwhelmed two elderly Norwegian warships and landed their force.

Powerful British forces were at sea and reaction was swift, Captain B. Warburton-Lee being ordered to Narvik with five destroyers of the 2nd. Flotilla. He had discretion to recapture the port but, at 16:00 on the 9th, during the long passage up the Vestfjord, he learned from Norwegian pilots that the enemy was there in strength. Warburton-Lee was, in fact, very considerably outgunned for, between them, the German ships could muster fifty 5in guns and eighty torpedoes against his twenty-one 4.7in guns and forty torpedoes. The enemy was also reported to have established shore batteries.

Screened by blindingly dense snow showers, the British arrived off Narvik at 04:30 on the 10th to find visibility there of about 1.6km/1 mile. Five enemy destroyers were present, their exact disposition not immediately obvious.

TOP: **As troops in life jackets form up prior to disembarking from the transport *Oronsay*, they are passed by one of their destroyer escort, the *Fury* of 1935. The censor has removed the pennant number from her hull but has left her flotilla markings.** ABOVE INSET: **Admiral Whitworth's decision to take the veteran battleship *Warspite* into very restricted waters for the Second Battle of Narvik was a bold one, for his reconnaissance aircraft had proven the presence of U-boats and the enemy destroyers were torpedo-armed. The loss of eight fleet destroyers at Narvik, in addition to losses and damage incurred elsewhere, would affect German surface fleet operations for the remainder of the war.**

Warburton-Lee attacked immediately with his ship, *Hardy*, leading *Hunter* and *Havock*. *Hotspur* and *Hostile* held back to engage shore defences. Totally surprised, two German ships were torpedoed alongside the pier, their commodore being among the many fatalities. The other three were damaged by gunfire before the British force rapidly drew back to regroup for a second attack. Stopping to destroy half-a-dozen enemy transports, however, they achieved little more before commencing their retirement.

It was now about 05:40 and, suddenly, the hitherto unsuspected remaining five enemy destroyers fell on the British from two directions. In a fierce manoeuvring action, swept by snow squalls, Warburton-Lee's destroyers now suffered from the Germans' heavier armament, the *Hardy* being driven ashore and the *Hunter* sunk before the three survivors escaped. In the Vesfjord, however, they encountered and destroyed a large enemy merchantman which was carrying the Narvik force's reserve ammunition. Warburton-Lee was awarded a posthumous Victoria Cross.

Only three German destroyers remained undamaged, with four more still in fighting condition. At the head of a long, many-branched fjord they were, however, trapped in a dead-end and vulnerable to further attack. This came on the 13th and in overwhelming force, the battleship *Warspite* being accompanied by nine destroyers.

Advancing up the fjord, the *Warspite* launched her Swordfish reconnaissance aircraft. This performed valuable service in warning the force of two enemy destroyers located in side fjords and positioned to ambush with torpedoes. Incredibly, the aircraft also sank one of two U-boats that had been sent in support.

The first would-be ambusher was overwhelmed without registering any torpedo hits. She did, however, raise the alarm. Of the remaining six, all but one were able to get under weigh.

Visibility was still indifferent and patchy and this, together with the destroyers' funnel and gun smoke, largely offset the value of the *Warspite*'s massive firepower. In a series of close and hard-fought exchanges the Germans, increasingly short of ammunition, were divided, confined and knocked out. Several British destroyers were hard-hit, the *Eskimo* losing her bows to a torpedo.

Without the necessary strength to reoccupy Narvik and aware of the *Warspite*'s own vulnerability, 161km/100 miles from the open sea, the Senior Naval Officer, Vice Admiral Whitworth, withdrew on the 15th. Three destroyers, particularly *Eskimo*, required temporary repair in a nearby "safe" area before their return.

The Germans retained Narvik but had lost half their fleet's total destroyer strength.

LEFT: As the background ship is the light cruiser *Emden*, these German troops must have been disembarking at Oslo. The cowl ventilators in the foreground are typically German mercantile, the vessel probably being one of two accompanying whalers. ABOVE: HMS *Hunter*, together with her sisters, *Havock*, and Captain Warburton-Lee in *Hardy*, penetrated Narvik harbour to engage enemy shipping. At point-blank range, the heavier German armaments proved decisive, *Hunter* and *Hardy* being disabled. BELOW: Warburton-Lee's ship at First Narvik was the H-class leader, *Hardy*. In this pre-war shot, she wears neutrality markings on "B" gunshield and her full leader's black forefunnel top. Leaders never painted up pennant numbers.

ABOVE: In 1940, "H" boats formed the Royal Navy's Second Destroyer Flotilla, identified by the two black bands on their after funnels. Being also a divisional, ie. half-flotilla, leader, *Hotspur* also carries a single band on her forward funnel. BELOW: The Fairey Swordfish, shown launching from a battleship catapult, could be fitted either with wheeled undercarriage or with floats. It could carry an 18in torpedo or 680kg/1,500lb of bombs. Armed with the latter, the *Warspite*'s Swordfish sank the *U-64* in the Herjangsfjord.

33

The raid on St. Nazaire

In the event that the great German battleship *Tirpitz* ventured into the Atlantic and had been damaged, the only dock available to her would have been the double-ended Normandie Lock at St. Nazaire. To reduce her options, the British Combined Operations Command was tasked with destroying the facility.

The resulting plan was to ram the outer lock gate (or "caisson") with an explosive-filled destroyer. This floating bomb would be timed to explode some 2½ hours after impact, during which time commandos would secure the immediate area while demolition squads destroyed all auxiliary machinery. Despite a 644km/400-mile passage from Falmouth and 8km/5 miles up a shoal-strewn estuary with no operative navigation aids, surprise was essential, for the port was heavily defended.

Selected for immolation was the ex-American "four-piper" *Campbeltown* (late USS *Buchanan*), prone to machinery problems and transferred to the Royal Navy in November 1940. To reduce her draught, she was stripped of all expendible weight. Three tons of explosive, in the shape of two dozen depth charges, were packed into her bows. Topside she was given light armouring and a more suitable armament of light automatic weapons. Her aftermost two funnels were removed and the forward pair given angled tops to superficially resemble those of a German Möwe-class torpedo boat, of which five were based in the port.

Two companies of commandos, totalling 268 officers and men, were to be embarked, both aboard the *Campbeltown* and on 16 Motor Launches (MLs) accompanying her. There were in addition Motor Gun Boat (MGB) 314, acting as headquarters ship, and Motor Torpedo Boat (MTB) 74, charged with torpedoing the caisson should the *Campbeltown* be sunk. Four Hunt-class destroyers were available to provide passage escort, but not participating in the raid.

TOP: **Key to the raid, the great German battleship *Tirpitz* could be accommodated in only one dry dock on the whole Atlantic seaboard of Europe. This, the Normandie dock in St. Nazaire, had to be denied her.** ABOVE: **Thoroughly wrecked, the *Campbeltown* lays with her crumpled bows overhanging the lock gate and her scuttled after end on the bottom. Apparently not having checked for explosives, a knot of Germans have gathered forward.**

Having followed a circuitous route, screened by low cloud, the little armada arrived after dark on March 27, 1942. A British submarine, posted as a navigational mark, confirmed its position and the escort left, leaving the force to head into the estuary, and the hazards of its unlit shoals.

Covered by a diversionary air raid the force was within two miles of its objective before being challenged from the shore. The correct signal was flashed back (furnished by Ultra radio decryption operations intelligence), giving a few more precious minutes before the force, in the glare of searchlights, came under fire. Light and uncertain at first, this grew to a storm of multicolour tracer as the British replied.

THE RAID ON ST. NAZAIRE

LEFT: **Awaiting transfer to the British flag are seen three of fifty vintage American destroyers. Left to right, the USSs** Buchanan, Crowninshield **and** Upshur **became** Campbeltown, Chelsea **and** Clare **respectively.** ABOVE: **Taken some weeks after the raid, this aerial reconnaissance picture shows a useless dock, empty of water again but enclosed by an earth dam. The remains of the** Campbeltown **give an idea of the installation's vast dimensions.**
BELOW: **The task of the British commandos was to hold a perimeter while demolition teams targeted and destroyed key features of the dock installation. With their means of withdrawal destroyed, the individual choice was simply between surrender or death, a choice already made by many.**

ABOVE: **A major U-boat base, St. Nazaire was powerfully garrisoned by mainly German naval personnel who proved adept at street fighting. Here, a rating with a submachine-gun guards a wounded British Commando.**

"There were tracer bullets going in every direction, a very colourful sight because the British tracers were all orange in colour and the German's were all a blue green." Lt Frank Arkle RNVR, ML177

Already badly holed, the old destroyer headed into an inferno, hitting the lock gate at 01:34 on the 28th. Her troops swarmed ashore to establish a perimeter, but those from the MLs experienced great difficulties. Their wood-built craft were literally being shot to pieces even before reaching the high walls of the dock entrance.

Expecting the Campbeltown to detonate at about 04:00, the surviving MLs and the MGB withdrew in good time, laden with wounded and any others available. Most of those ashore, however, had to be left for capture once their resistance was overcome.

Campbeltown's fuses malfunctioned. Abandoned, her stern submerged, her ruined bows rearing above the buckled caisson, she attracted the curious enemy, who were aboard in force when she exploded at 11:35. A wall of water smashed into the vast dock.

Earlier, just seven MLs cleared the estuary with the MGB to rendezvous with their waiting sea escort. They tangled briefly with German warships, which sank one, while two more and the MGB had to be scuttled. Just four MLs made it back to Plymouth, their damage bearing testimony to the action's ferocity.

Back in St. Nazaire, some 36 hours after the raid, the delayed-action torpedoes from MTB 74 exploded against the Old Entrance, causing further mayhem among the already jittery enemy garrison.

In terms of dead and missing, 24 per cent of naval and 22 per cent of total army personnel were casualties. The majority of army survivors were captured. Five Victoria Crosses, Britain and the Commonwealth's highest award for bravery, were awarded for individual and collective acts of valour. The dock remained inoperable for the remainder of the war, while the Tirpitz wasted the remainder of her short life in the North.

The "Tokyo Express"

Hot, humid and malarial, the Solomon Islands form a double-chain, aligned north-west/south-east. Some 1,086km/675 miles in length, they are separated by a channel that became known as "The Slot" to those who fought there.

During 1942 the Solomons were occupied by the Japanese who, in the July, began building an airfield on Guadalcanal. Its position flanked the vital Allied line of communication between Hawaii and Australia.

Admiral Ernest King, Chief of Naval Operations, well recognized the island's significance to the Japanese, it being their farthest point of advance through South-east Asia. Their communications and resources were already stretched, and King reasoned that an attritional campaign fought over Guadalcanal might well cost the Americans as much as their enemy, but the latter, with its greatly inferior industrial base and manpower reserves, would be less able to afford the loss. Accordingly, in their first Pacific amphibious operation, US Marines seized the still lightly defended island on August 7, 1942, in an ad hoc operation codenamed Watchtower.

The Japanese reacted quickly and effectively, badly defeating a joint Allied cruiser force off Savo Island, the first of what would be several major engagements.

> "'Tokyo Express' no longer has terminus on Guadalcanal."
> Signal from General Alexander M. Patch to
> Admiral William Halsey. February 9, 1943

ABOVE LEFT: **For the Americans, Guadalcanal was the theoretical "line in the sand", beyond which the Japanese would not be permitted to advance. This wrecked A6M2 Zero/Zeke fighter is symbolic of the gruelling campaign of attrition that followed.** ABOVE RIGHT: **Following the disastrous Battle of Savo Island, an American destroyer division weaves in tribute to lost ships and men. The reconquest of the Solomons would result in a naval war of attrition in which the Japanese were ultimately defeated.**

The Marines, nonetheless, were firmly dug in and quickly completed the half-finished airstrip, proudly renamed Henderson Field. Wildcat (F4F) fighters and Dauntless (SBD) dive-bombers were flown in by carrier, allowing the Americans local superiority by day but, as their Official Historian so well put it: "As the tropical daylight performed its quick fadeout and the pall of night fell … Allied ships cleared out like frightened children running home from the graveyard … [for] then the Japanese took over".

The night belonged to the Japanese who, immediately following the Guadalcanal landing, began nightly destroyer forays down The Slot, sometimes accompanied by the odd light cruiser. They were mounted from their base at Rabaul in New Britain, at the head of the Solomons archipelago. Their function was to run in troop detachments and supplies, and they were timed to arrive after dark, discharge rapidly and be away, beyond the 400km/250-mile range of the SBDs, by dawn. These high-speed visitations, often accompanied by bombardment, were so regular that they were known to the weary Marine defenders of Guadalcanal as the "Tokyo Express".

The Japanese were skilled night fighters, with nocturnal vision that often out-performed American radar, and with a worrying readiness to loose a salvo of their feared 24in "Long Lance" torpedoes in the direction of perceived trouble. To avoid betraying their position they were rarely first to open gunfire. New to this type of warfare, the US Navy had much to learn but, absorbing the inevitable reverses, learn it did.

Seemingly refusing to accept the strength in which the Americans held Guadalcanal, the Japanese continued to use destroyer detachments to build their numbers a few hundred at a time. Any attempt by day did, however, prove disastrous, with their opponent enjoying air superiority.

To assist in daylight air control the Americans tended to station a carrier group away to the south. This also proved to be a magnet for the Japanese, a catalyst for several major engagements that well contributed to King's philosophy of attrition – a risky philosophy in truth for the US Navy was badly short of carriers.

On Guadalcanal, too, the Americans could never quite achieve the numbers necessary for a decisive push. Despite giving the campaign the highest priority, the Japanese were likewise constricted. To escape the lash of air attack, they operated largely beneath the fetid jungle canopy, where they suffered terribly from tropical diseases and malnutrition. With the "Tokyo Express" increasingly challenged by American forces, supplies had to be dumped offshore in buoyant containers, most of which were lost.

In February 1943, having lost 23,000 men, the Japanese admitted defeat, their indefatigable destroyers spiriting away the remaining 12,000. Japan's first major setback, Guadalcanal cost either side a total of 130,000 tons of warships, a total which only the Americans could fully replace.

TOP: **American and British peacetime doctrine had been to conserve torpedoes, which were relatively expensive. It came as an unpleasant shock that the Japanese, seen here, were very ready to launch them in full salvoes and at considerable ranges.** ABOVE: **Hove-to and rescuing personnel from a stricken troop transport off Guadalcanal, the Japanese destroyer *Mutsuki* made a simple target for US Marine Corps SBDs which sank her by horizontal, rather than dive-bombing.** LEFT: **That the Japanese could dispute possession of Guadalcanal for over six months was due mainly to the valiant and persistent resupply runs made by Rear Admiral Raizo Tanaka and his light forces, whose activities instigated several actions.**

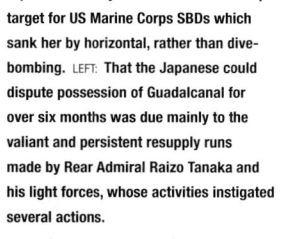

LEFT: **The first Marine Corps aircraft alighted on Guadalcanal's Henderson Field 11 days after its capture and transformation from " a wallow of viscous mud". The key construction material was the perforated steel strip known as Marston Mat.** ABOVE: **Because of the element of chance, most fleets sought to avoid night actions. The Japanese, however, positively provoked them, obliging the Americans to follow suit in what was a painful learning process.**

THE HISTORY OF DESTROYERS AND FRIGATES

LEFT: *Jamaica*, spruce again in post-war paint. Her electronic fit has been considerably augmented, "X" turret has been landed and 40mm Bofors AA gun barrels bristle her profile. She was scrapped early in 1961. ABOVE: Rear Admiral R.L. Burnett commanded the *Sheffield/Jamaica* cruiser force covering Convoy JW. 51B. In the prevailing conditions he was unaware of its precise position. Here, *Sheffield*'s bridge watch survey typical Atlantic weather.

The action off the North Cape

In addition to U-boats, Arctic convoys were menaced by heavy German surface units and air power based by the enemy in northern Norway. As far as possible, therefore, convoys were run during the dark, winter months.

Such was JW.51B, which left Loch Ewe on December 22, 1942. Its close escort comprised six (later five) destroyers and five smaller vessels.

By December 30 the convoy was at about 73 degrees North and was headed eastwards, beyond the North Cape of Norway. The senior officer of the escort, Captain R. St. V. Sherbrooke in HMS *Onslow*, had ordered that, in the event of surface attack, he would leave his older destroyer, *Achates*, to screen the convoy with smoke while, with his modern ships, he would threaten the enemy directly with torpedoes.

Alerted to a convoy in the area, the German Vice Admiral Oskar Kummetz sailed from Altenfjord the same day with the 8in cruiser *Hipper* (flag), the 11in "pocket battleship" *Lützow* and six destroyers. His intention was to run eastwards along the convoy's anticipated route and, upon locating it, split his force, the *Hipper* attacking from the left flank, the *Lützow* from the right, making use of the uncertain visibility.

Kummetz was delayed by the *Lützow* being en route to an Atlantic foray, he being ordered to decline action with equal or superior forces to avoid her incurring damage. He was also unaware that two British 6in cruisers, *Sheffield* and *Jamaica*, had left North Russia to reinforce the convoy, which they were also trying to locate. At about 08:30 on the 31st the cruisers were actually about 48km/30 miles to the north of the convoy

LEFT: **Carrying her leader's black funnel top, the** *Onslow* **is seen in northern waters. Even in a moderate sea, she is continually swept by spray, penetrating every aperture and encouraging the formation of ice topside.**

38

THE ACTION OFF THE NORTH CAPE

LEFT: **Named after the faithful friend of Aeneas, HMS *Achates* equally kept faith with her convoy. Crippled and fatally damaged by the *Hipper*'s gunfire, her commanding officer dead, she continued to shield the merchantmen with smoke until she foundered.**

when one of the latter's escort sighted three enemy destroyers crossing its wake.

Visibility was about seven miles when, shortly after 09:30, the *Hipper* made her appearance. Sherbrooke transmitted an enemy contact report and moved against Kummetz with two destroyers, while interposing two more between the enemy destroyers and the convoy, now being covered by smoke from the *Achates*.

Sherbrooke's signal had been received by Rear Admiral R.L. Burnett in the *Sheffield* and, shortly before 10:00, and already under heavy fire, the escort commander was relieved to learn that the cruisers were bending on full speed to come to his aid. Shortly afterward, the *Onslow* received four direct hits, Sherbrooke being blinded and forced to devolve command of the escort force.

With the situation on the convoy's north side looking critical, the *Lützow* group then approached from the south. The *Hipper* was concentrating on the hard-working *Achates* and had already inflicted fatal damage when suddenly, at about 11:30, she was bracketed by 6in salvoes from Burnett's cruisers. Hit badly in a boiler room and in two further places, the *Hipper* hauled off. Totally surprised, Kummetz ordered a general retirement.

The *Lützow* had barely come into the action and had succeeded in damaging only one merchant ship but the *Hipper* was already being pursued by Burnett, who sank one of his destroyers. Despite having radar, Burnett lost the enemy in deteriorating weather conditions.

Burnett's tardy intervention had retrieved an unpleasant situation but the convoy's surviving without loss had been due primarily to Kummetz's constricting orders, obliging him to attack without conviction. Despite this, the badly mauled escort had defended their charges valiantly, Sherbrooke being awarded a well-deserved Victoria Cross.

TOP: **By far the most powerful warship involved, the "pocket battleship" *Lützow* (seen here pre-war) was subordinate to Vice Admiral Kummetz's *Hipper*, and was handled with a distinct lack of determination. She was herself sunk by bombing in Kiel in April 1945.** ABOVE: **Intended as the first of a class of five, of which two were never completed, the *Admiral Hipper* differed from her sisters in her straighter bow profile. At her bows she carries the arms of her namesake, commander of the scouting forces at Jutland.**

The action had an important and unforeseen repercussion in that Hitler, on learning of the outcome, was enraged. Despite the fact that he himself had ordered that his few remaining heavy units be used with circumspection, he accused Grand Admiral Raeder of running a supine service. Raeder, who had been Commander-in-Chief for 14 years, resigned in protest when the Führer ordered the decommissioning of all remaining major warships. He was replaced by Admiral Dönitz, who would concentrate primarily on pursuing a submarine war. There was an interesting historical precedent in that the same decision resulted from the inconclusive Battle of Jutland in 1916.

The sinking of the *Haguro*

Of the 16 heavy cruisers with which the Imperial Japanese Navy went to war, just six remained by May 1945. Of these, the *Haguro* was a marked ship, having participated in the heavy Allied defeat in the Java Sea early in 1942 when the British cruiser *Exeter*, the Australian *Perth* and several other American, British and Dutch ships had been lost.

In May 1945 the British East Indies Fleet again exercised sea control in the Bay of Bengal, and the landing at Rangoon in Burma isolated Japanese garrisons in the island chains of the Andamans and Nicobars. It was known that the Japanese intended to evacuate these forces and, on May 9, signals intelligence indicated that a "Nachi-class cruiser" would depart Singapore for the Andamans on the following day. Only just returned from Rangoon, a powerful force under Vice Admiral H.T.C. Walker sailed from Trincomalee on the 10th with the intention of making an interception.

Also on the 10th, two Royal Navy submarines patrolling the Malacca Strait reported the position of the *Haguro* and her accompanying destroyer, *Kamikaze*. Both were laden with supplies for those personnel that they could not evacuate.

During the next day a Japanese reconnaissance aircraft sighted Walker's force, submarines reporting that the *Haguro* had turned back as a result. Walker deliberately altered course to give the impression that he was engaged on another mission

TOP: **HMS** *Khedive* was one of four CVEs involved in the hunt for the *Haguro*. This picture illustrates well the often windless conditions of the Indian Ocean, where heavily laden aircraft would experience difficulty in taking off.
ABOVE: *Shah*'s Avengers on this day were operating from HMS *Emperor*, as their own ship's catapult became defective. Because of the range, they were carrying no torpedoes, nor could they be supported by Hellcat fighters.

and signals intelligence duly indicated that, on May 14, the *Haguro* had sailed again.

The British had four escort carriers (CVEs) in company and, at 10:50 on the 15th, the *Haguro* was sighted by an Avenger, flying at maximum range. A small, follow-up bombing mission was unsuccessful but already Walker had sent on ahead the 26th Destroyer Flotilla, four V-class ships led by Captain M.L. Power in the *Saumarez*.

Spaced at 8km/5-mile intervals, and advancing on a line of bearing, Power's destroyers maintained 27 knots both to close their quarry and to get between him and his base. At 19:00 the *Haguro* was estimated to be 120km/75 miles distant to the north-west.

> "She was very large, and very black against a very dark monsoon cloud. An enormously impressive sight, just as a warship ought to look." Report by Lt Cdr Michael Fuller, pilot of the Avenger from HMS *Shah* which first located the *Haguro*
> [Note: The *Haguro* was actually painted pink]

THE SINKING OF THE *HAGURO*

ABOVE: *Saumarez* was, at the time, leader of the 26th Destroyer Flotilla. She had spent her earlier career with the Home Fleet, supporting Arctic convoys. Late in 1943 she was battle-damaged while participating in the sinking of the *Scharnhorst*.

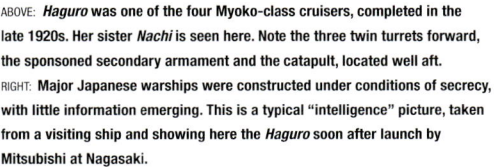

ABOVE: *Haguro* was one of the four Myoko-class cruisers, completed in the late 1920s. Her sister *Nachi* is seen here. Note the three twin turrets forward, the sponsoned secondary armament and the catapult, located well aft.

RIGHT: Major Japanese warships were constructed under conditions of secrecy, with little information emerging. This is a typical "intelligence" picture, taken from a visiting ship and showing here the *Haguro* soon after launch by Mitsubishi at Nagasaki.

All unsuspecting, the Japanese maintained a steady course and, at 22:45 and benefiting from exceptional radar conditions, the *Venus* reported a contact at 55km/34 miles. Soon after midnight the *Saumarez* acquired the target, and Power ordered a torpedo attack for 01:00, reorganizing his destroyers into a five-pointed star formation.

Just 6 minutes before the attack was due, the *Haguro* and her consort suddenly reversed course, closing the British at a relative speed of about 50 knots. The *Venus* passed within 1.6km/1 mile but was unable to retrain her torpedo tubes quickly enough to fire.

Before the British force could reorganize itself, the *Haguro* then abruptly turned eight points (i.e. 90 degrees) to port, probably to avoid torpedoes that she incorrectly assumed the *Venus* to have discharged.

Although in a position to attack, the *Saumarez* had to apply full helm to avoid the *Kamikaze*. Passing close under the latter's bow, she exchanged fire with both main battery and automatic weapons. As the *Saumarez*'s torpedo crews worked frantically to keep up with the changes of heading, their ship was suddenly brightly illuminated by a starshell from the *Haguro*, which then opened up with both main and secondary armament. The destroyer quickly took hits in the boiler space, the forecastle and through the funnel. As she lost speed, she slewed sufficiently to release a full outfit of eight torpedoes at about 1,829m/2,000yd range.

Power's dispositions had been sound for whichever way the *Haguro* headed she was menaced by torpedo. *Verulam*, undisturbed, fired at about the same time as *Saumarez* and, some ten minutes later, *Venus* and *Virago* coordinated their attack. Hit an unknown number of times, the *Haguro*, her decks cluttered with stores for the Andamans, sank at 02:09. The *Kamikaze* made good her escape as Power's destroyers, by now uncomfortably close to Japanese airfields near Penang, pulled out to the west to avoid dawn retribution.

ABOVE: Seen post-war at Malta, the *Verulam* was built by Fairfield during 1943. She is here in full destroyer configuration but would shortly be completely remodelled as a Type 15 anti-submarine frigate. BELOW: By April 1945, Japanese defences were disintegrating, and Allied warships were able to undertake direct bombardment with little risk. Here, the *Verulam* is seen within easy 4.7 range of the port of Kotaraja, now in Indonesia.

41

THE HISTORY OF DESTROYERS AND FRIGATES

LEFT: The *Laffey*'s conspicuous performance earned her a complete repair, although damage sustained would have justified writing her off as a constructive total loss. She is seen here in typical late 1950s Sumner-class configuration.
ABOVE: Struck by two enemy bombs on March 19, 1945, the USS *Franklin* survived what was reported to be the most severe fire damage experienced by any American warship. Cruisers USS *Santa Fe* and *Pittsburgh* stood by.

Radar picket at Okinawa

Despite being subjected to weeks of preliminary softening-up and attrition by American carrier-based air strikes, the Japanese air force reacted strongly and with persistence to the former's amphibious landing on Okinawa on April 1, 1945.

A mass of offshore shipping, vital to progress on the island, lay vulnerable to attack from the air. For the previous six months such orthodox attack had been supplemented with kamikaze suicide missions. At Okinawa, the Japanese went further with mass suicide attacks, called *kikusui* and involving hundreds of aircraft.

Shore airstrips not yet being properly operational, defensive aerial countermeasures had to be mounted by the Fifth Fleet Carriers. To give early warning of incoming Japanese raids, a ring of radar picket destroyers was posted. These also carried fighter control teams, which worked to such good effect that the enemy identified the pickets as primary targets. This was countered by posting the ships, where possible, in pairs, supported by Landing Craft, Support (LCS), small vessels bristling with 20 and 40mm guns and rockets.

Over the ten weeks or so of the Okinawa operation, the Japanese mounted ten kikusui, involving an incredible 1,465

ABOVE: Nimble ship handling ensured that most of the *Laffey's* kamikaze strikes were sustained well aft, while the Japanese pilot's tendency to aim for the superstructure meant that there were few solid hits to cause major failure of watertight integrity. Fires were kept well under control.

aircraft. No surprise then that the odd dozen or two could be directed at a picket destroyer, many of which suffered horrendous damage, sometimes fatal.

On April 16 the Sumner-class destroyer *Laffey* (DD.724) was just one that suffered, this in the course of the third *kikusui* onslaught. Shortly before 08:00 she easily drove off a single "bandit", only to have her radar displays suddenly saturated with 50 or more contacts, spread over a 90-degree sector. By ill fortune, the standing US Navy Combat Air Patrol (CAP) was in the process of handing over to its relief, and response to this major threat was tardy. The attackers split to approach from a variety of directions, the CAP not intercepting until they were over their target, and having to fly through

> "Stands out above the outstanding."
> *Laffey*'s performance, from the report of Rear Admiral
> C. Turner Joy, Commanding Officer of Unit Two, Task Force 54
> Gunfire and Covering Force at Okinawa

RADAR PICKET AT OKINAWA

"friendly" fire in their pursuit. They accounted for several but were defeated by sheer numbers.

Over the next 80 frantic minutes the *Laffey* underwent 22 separate attacks, was hit by six kamikaze aircraft, four bombs and thoroughly raked by strafing.

Four suiciders opened proceedings by each crashing close aboard, one grazing the ship while the blast from the explosion of another deranged her fire-control radar. The first to hit clipped the hull with a wing, spinning around into the superstructure, its fuel causing a major fire. Another, damaged, "belly flopped" before bouncing into the after 5in gun mounting. The resulting inferno acted as a magnet, an aiming point for three further bomb-armed aircraft. The *Laffey*'s whole after end was, by now, a ruin from which no gun was left firing. Surprisingly, however, the hull was not yet badly holed.

Laffey's remaining electronics were written off when a Japanese attacker, with a CAP Corsair on its tail, flew through the mast. Both aircraft spun into the sea. Now dead in the water, the *Laffey* fought back, with LCS-51 doing her utmost to defend her charge. Those aboard the destroyer who were not manning her remaining guns were engaged in rescuing their mates from the nightmare of fire and searing steam that had been their ship.

At 09:47 the ordeal ended with a Japanese attacker, already shredded with automatic fire, exploding close enough aboard to shower the ship in flaming debris. The attackers had expended an unknown number of aircraft – nobody had time to count, but the *Laffey*'s diminished gun crews claimed nine. Just four 20mm weapons remained operable.

For 3 hours damage-control parties plugged holes and shored-up straining bulkheads to save their ship while surviving engine room personnel maintained steam although, with a jammed rudder, the *Laffey* was uncontrollable.

Eventually salvage tugs arrived, pumping and towing her to a safe anchorage. She had suffered 31 dead and 72 wounded but, more fortunate than others, she eventually returned to service.

TOP: Beach Yellow 3 on Okinawa. Four Landing Craft, Tank (LCT(6)) are at the tide line, with a Landing Ship, Medium (LSM) immediately behind and a Landing Ship, Tank (LST) beyond. Visible is a bulldozer, held by Admiral Halsey to be the third most important contributor to American victory in the Pacific.

ABOVE: Covered by a Fletcher-class destroyer, two Landing Craft, Support, Large (LCS(L)) move into the Okinawa beach area, April 1945. These Mark 3s were converted from Landing Craft, Infantry, Large (LCI(L)) and were heavily armed.

BELOW: *Laffey* was sufficiently sound to serve until 1975. As with all surviving operational Sumners, she underwent a major FRAM modernization, being reconfigured as shown here. In the foreground is the 2,200-ton Coast Guard cutter *Ingham* of 1936.

43

THE HISTORY OF DESTROYERS AND FRIGATES

The submarine threat in 1939

Still, more correctly, a submersible, the submarine of 1939 spent most of its time on the surface. Conserving both power and air, it might remain submerged for 24 hours or more but would then be obliged to surface to recharge its batteries and its internal atmosphere.

Submarines were slow compared with surface ships, even though the latter were subject to weather conditions. For instance, the German Type VIIC boat, workhorse of the U-boat fleet, could make 17 knots on the surface (half the speed of a destroyer) but only 7½ knots submerged. Restraining her submerged speed to just 4 knots (a smart walking pace) she could travel a maximum of 128km/80 miles. It followed that a submerged submarine could not escape an escort by flight, only by stealth.

A further limitation of a VIIC was that she could carry only 14 torpedoes. As "spreads" were frequently launched to guarantee a hit, these could be quickly exhausted. A U-boat thus had to be resupplied at sea or spend most of her time on passage. A network of ocean re-supply ships was thus established, and these could be targeted.

To offset all these shortcomings, the submarine retained the enormous advantage of invisibility. While she could not

TOP: **A sight to stir any destroyerman's heart. Destroyers, however, were designed for fleet screening and proved to be deficient submarine hunters, being short-legged and with insufficient accommodation, particularly for equipment.** ABOVE: Woefully unprepared for submarine warfare, the Americans seemed powerless to prevent a handful of Dönitz's U-boats creating mayhem off the eastern seaboard early in 1942. Here, the tanker *Dixie Arrow* burns herself out.

be seen, she could, however, be heard. Machinery, propeller cavitation and water flow over the hull's many excrescences could, in quiet conditions, be detected on a sensitive hydrophone, the only method available during World War I. The sea, however, is never quiet, while the vessel carrying the hydrophone would, herself, generate noise. Work was already in progress in Great Britain, the United States and France to build an oscillator that would produce pulses of acoustic energy. These, transmitted through the water, would result in some of the energy being reflected from a solid body, such as a submarine. The reflected pulse would be detected by a hull-mounted hydrophone.

> "We have got to the stage when the hitherto 'undetectable craft' is detectable ... the time is coming when we shall have to re-balance our theories as to the tactical use of submarines."
> Minute by Rear Admiral Chatfield, Assistant Chief of Naval Staff, July 1921, following Asdic trials

44

THE SUBMARINE THREAT IN 1939

LEFT: **By 1945, the chance of a depth charge attack being successful had increased from five to seven per cent. Hedgehog, however, subject to less "dead time" eventually improved to about 30 per cent. Squid was even better, but arrived too late to affect the outcome.** ABOVE: **The 1930s-trained U-boat skippers were resourceful and dedicated. They enjoyed their initial "Happy Time" but, once they had been accounted for, their replacements deteriorated in quality as that of Allied escort commanders improved.**

Refinement of the system took time and the first production sets of what was termed Asdic (later Sonar) appeared in fleet destroyers only in the early 1930s. Acoustic transmission in the sea column is capricious but Asdic, in the hands of a trained operator, could determine the range and bearing of a submerged target. Importantly, however, it could not, at this stage, register its depth.

Ignoring the limitations of Asdic itself, but taking into account those of the U-boat, naval opinion, especially in Great Britain, greatly underestimated the threat that submarines again posed. This was encouraged further by Germany entering the war in 1939 with just 57 boats.

The primary anti-submarine (AS) weapon remained the depth charge, which had accounted for 30 U-boats during the earlier war. It was a simple drum, containing several hundred pounds of explosive and triggered by a hydrostatic switch at a predetermined depth.

This Asdic/depth charge combination had its own weaknesses. Fitted in a streamlined dome below a ship's forward keel, the Asdic transmitted pulses in a focused "beam", aimed downward at a fixed angle. For search purposes, it could be rotated in azimuth. Probing ahead at a fixed angle of declination, the Asdic inevitably lost contact some distance short of a submerged target. The attacker thus had to estimate the point, directly over the target, to release depth charges. Because the target's depth was not known, a "pattern" had to be dropped, set to explode at various depths. The charges themselves took time to sink and the cumulative "dead time" was sufficient to allow an astute submarine commander to manoeuvre clear of the lethal zone in good time, usually by a radical change of course.

What was required was a mortar-type weapon to project charges ahead of the ship, while the target was still "in the

ABOVE: **Early depth charges were simple cylindrical containers that sank to the required depth painfully slowly. For any chance of success they were released in "patterns", being rolled over the stern from traps and fired on the beam from projectors.** LEFT: **An excellent example of the US Navy's graphic art, but note the "handraulic" loading and enlisted men apparently in dress suits. Reality in the Atlantic is more closely portrayed by the rig of the German ratings above.**

beam". The need for this had been identified by British scientists between the wars but, due to budget restrictions, the concepts did not progress beyond the prototype stage. As a result, ahead-throwing weapons, in the shape of such as Hedgehog, Mousetrap and Parsnip, did not enter general service before the end of 1941.

45

Escort vessels to World War II

LEFT: **Although many commercial trawlers were hired by the Royal Navy, the service built several extended classes of "Admiralty Trawler", based on designs with proven seakeeping qualities. The censor has obliterated the pendant numbers of the A/S trawler** *Turquoise.* ABOVE: **In order to confuse an enemy as to her true heading, a British "Kil"-class patrol craft was given a near-symmetrical profile. The** *Kildare*, **seen here, was one of about 40 such 900-tonners, constructed during 1917–18.**

Between the wars, Great Britain was an enthusiastic supporter of naval limitation agreements even though many of the adopted clauses proved to be more detrimental to her own interests rather than to those of her peers and, increasingly, prospective enemies.

Following Jutland, the unrestricted German U-boat campaign had brought Britain to the brink of disaster before the timely institution (or, historically more correct, reinstitution) of the convoy system. The British failed, before the cessation of hostilities, to develop a viable detect-and-destroy means of countering the enemy submarines. Intense effort at the 1921–22 Washington Conference to dispose of the threat simply by banning submarine warfare was negated by late allies intent in preserving it as "the weapon of the weaker navy". In response, the British clung to the unsubstantiated belief that the introduction of Asdic (Sonar) on a general scale would remove the submarine as a major threat.

Even after the hard cull of destroyers following World War I, the Royal Navy still operated a total of 16 flotillas, or 144 ships. These were considered insufficient to both screen the battle fleet and to escort convoys, a situation made considerably worse by the London Naval Treaty of 1930, at which Britain and the United States agreed to capping global destroyer tonnage at 150,000 imperial tons apiece. Japan negotiated an improved 10:7 ratio for a total of 105,500 tons.

For the purpose of the Treaty, a "destroyer" was defined simply as having a standard displacement of less than 1,850 tons and mounting guns of under 130mm calibre. The agreed ceiling represented something like a further 25 per cent reduction in the Royal Navy's 16 flotilla establishment, exacerbating the convoy-escort situation.

ABOVE: **The German Navy continued to build both "destroyers" (for fleet work) and "torpedo boats" (effectively light destroyers) for general escort duties. Of the latter, four of the six Möwe class are seen pre-war with the two modernized Schlesiens behind.**

Fortunately, Article 8 of the Treaty stated that no limit would be placed on vessels of under 2,000 tons provided that, *inter alia*, they:
i) mounted no gun of greater than 155mm calibre;
ii) mounted no more than four of greater than 3in calibre;
iii) carried no apparatus for launching torpedoes; or
iv) were powered for no more than 20 knots' speed.

Within these stipulations are found the basic parameters of contemporary escorts ("sloops" in British parlance), particularly once (ii) was dropped at the largely ineffective Second London Naval Conference of 1936.

ESCORT VESSELS TO WORLD WAR II

Britain, still in recession, required large numbers of inexpensive convoy escorts, and divided them between trawlers, dual-role mine-sweeping sloops, (e.g. Bangor, Halcyon and Algerine classes), true sloops (Grimsby, Bittern, Black Swan) and corvettes (Flowers), of which only the Bitterns and derivatives were governed by treat limits.

Largely locked in internal rivalry, the French and Italians pursued different roles, the former opting for fewer, but larger, destroyers and the latter more numerous escort destroyers. These, confusingly, were termed Torpedo Boats (*Torpediniere*). Fast and generally below 1,000 tons, they were well-suited to Mediterranean conditions.

Through the Anglo-German Naval Agreement of 1935, the Germans were legally permitted to build to 35 per cent of current British strength. In destroyers, that represented 52,000 tons. Disturbing though German rearmament was, this total, in conjunction with the rest of their naval programme, was unattainable. The Kriegsmarine likewise opted for a mix of fleet destroyers and "torpedo boats".

With war looking inevitable by 1938 the British Admiralty looked to expand the destroyer force, complementing the large and expensive six- and eight-gun fleet destroyers with smaller vessels designed specifically for escort duties. These "Intermediate Destroyers", the extensive Hunt class, were really the equivalent to foreign torpedo boats. Like the sloops, they mounted an effective high-angle armament but had a greatly superior speed and a modest torpedo battery.

The Americans had also been looking to produce an escort destroyer but, with the US Navy's inherent dislike for small ships (which in the words of the naval historian Norman Friedman "saved very little money at a great cost in capability") made little headway until the British requested 100 hulls in June 1941, effectively crash-starting the excellent Destroyer Escort (DE) programme.

TOP: **The Italian Navy rarely receives credit for its effective AS operations, 1940–43. These Spica-class torpedo boats (*Libra* and *Climene*) were typical of those which accounted for many Malta and Gibraltar-based British submarines.**
ABOVE: **Although launched in 1921, the Italian *Generale Achille Papa* could almost pass as a three-funnelled Royal Navy "L" boat of some seven years earlier. Constructed as destroyers, the Generali were demoted to torpedo boats in 1929.** BELOW: **An early example of a "Flower" with a long forecastle, HMS *Nasturtium* was one of three ordered from the design originators, Smiths Dock, to French account but purchased by the Admiralty in June 1940.**

ABOVE: **Classed as sloops by virtue of being relatively fast and being rated anti-aircraft escorts, the Black Swans proved to be most efficient anti-submarine ships. *Starling*, seen here, sank three U-boats and participated in the destruction of eleven others.**
RIGHT: **The British equivalent of foreign torpedo boats were the very useful Hunt classes (this is the Type I *Garth*). Their dual-purpose armament made them effective against aircraft.**

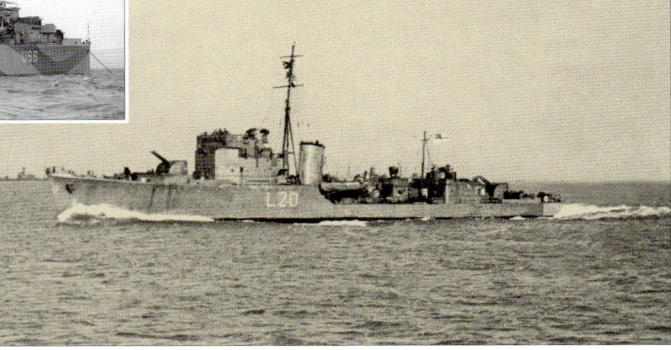

47

Atlantic experience – the emergence of the frigate

On the basis that slow-moving U-boats would waste too much time travelling to and from the deep ocean, it was assumed pre-war that they would concentrate around traffic nodal points fairly close to land. Convoy escort was, therefore, considered largely in coastal terms. Even so, restricted budgets had resulted in little being done before 1939 to develop prototypes suitable for emergency series production.

During that year an earlier proposal, to use a modified whaling ship, was reconsidered. Designed to operate independently in the Southern Ocean, these little ships were supremely seaworthy and, produced to commercial standards, were of a size that could be built by many small yards. These were not only in the United Kingdom but also in the less-developed marine industry of Canada.

In view of the looming inevitability of war as the 1930s progressed, it appears remarkable in retrospect that the orders for the first tranche of what were to become the Flowers were placed only in the late July of 1939.

In practice, Dönitz's U-boats did not operate entirely as expected, working ever further out into the Atlantic, not least to keep beyond the range of ASW aircraft. Intended for coastal escort, the Flowers thus found themselves in conditions to which they were not suited. Seaworthiness was not a problem for, although wet, a Corvette (as she became officially termed) could ride the worst of seas. In doing so, however, she had a

TOP: **By mid-1943, a high proportion of any Atlantic convoy would comprise standard, war-built ships. Laden with a low-density cargo and riding high, this unidentified Liberty ship was only one of over 2,700 built to the basic EC2-S-C1 specification.** ABOVE: **In addition to a huge Destroyer Escort (DE) programme, the Americans built about 100 Patrol Frigates (PFs) based on the British "River" design. *Anguilla* is one of 21 transferred to the Royal Navy, all of which were named after minor colonies.**

motion that induced nausea and fatigue in crews already tolerating the spartan conditions inseparable from small ship life. Mess decks were rarely dry, often flooded.

The usual track from the British west coast to the Canadian convoy terminal of Halifax was 4,023km/2,500 miles. Routed evasively to avoid known U-boat concentrations, however, a convoy could cover nearer 4,828km/3,000 miles. A slow convoy could thus be 2½ weeks in transit, while the frequency of the convoy cycle saw several on passage simultaneously. Until more ships were forthcoming, the strain on an inadequate escort force was thus considerable.

Early Asdics (Sonars) were not of great range, perhaps 1.8km/1 mile in reasonable conditions and, as the periphery of even a small convoy was considerable, the two or three

> "I was half-sitting and half-lying ... my shoulders wedged ... with the pitching of the ship, I seemed to be alternately reclining with my feet higher than my head, and then bending over so that I tended to fall forward." Alan Easton, shipper of the Canadian Flower-class corvette *Sackville*, from his autobiography *50 North*

ATLANTIC EXPERIENCE – THE EMERGENCE OF THE FRIGATE

ABOVE: **Where the 761/865-ton Type VIIC was Dönitz's general purpose, "workhorse" U-boat, the various larger Type IX were designed for lengthy patrols to say, the US eastern seaboard or the Caribbean. The ultimate IXC/40 displaced 1,144/1,257 tons.** RIGHT: **To those participating, convoys appeared to present enormous targets to enemy submarines. They were, however, mere specks in the immensity of the ocean and, with intelligence-based evasive routing, could be safely shepherded around known U-boat concentrations.**

LEFT: **Symbolically No.100, the American Destroyer Escort (DE) *Christopher* hits the Delaware River at Wilmington on June 19, 1943. Many DEs served with the Royal Navy, which considered them very satisfactory, but with a violent motion.**
BELOW: **HMCS *Sackville*, preserved as a museum ship, is the sole surviving "Flower" and fittingly commemorates the enormous contribution in men and ships that Canada made toward ultimate victory in the bitterly contested Battle of the Atlantic.**

typically available escorts had to work hard to give effective cover. This meant working at speeds considerably greater than that of their charges, consuming extra fuel and diminishing endurance as a consequence.

To extend the escorts' range, Replenishment-At-Sea (RAS) was adopted. This in turn, however, exacerbated the problems of their over-crowded accommodation, the Flowers' designed complement of 29 having grown under operational conditions to no less than 74. The extended forecastle of the modified design improved matters in terms of both space and wetness, but the steady consumption of fuel oil and of topweight, represented by sixty 136kg/300lb depth charges, served only to increase a corvette's liveliness.

Because they could be built at so many yards (a total of 23 British and 12 Canadian yards was involved), Corvettes – Flowers, Modified Flowers and, later, Castles – were being completed right up to early 1945.

Despite their numbers, however, Corvettes had effectively been superseded from April 1942, with the entry into service of the first River. Of a size and speed with a Black Swan-class sloop, this type was initially termed a Twin-screw Corvette before being reclassed as a Frigate (a title which, like Corvette, had been dormant since the days of the sailing navy). Still built to commercial standards, it was nearly half as long again as a Flower, with greatly reduced motion. Although the crew was larger, its amenities were much improved. To their considerable capacity of 150 depth charges was later added the forward-firing Hedgehog as it became available.

Operating on the surface, a U-boat could out-run a Flower, but not a 20-knot River, which also had better endurance. The simple but reliable 4-cylinder triple-expansion engine was, rather than the more complex turbine, selected for the great majority of both British- and Canadian-built escorts.

49

Convoy action – Battle of the Atlantic

Dönitz's tactics in the Atlantic included concentrating U-boats into groups or "Wolf Packs" which would form a patrol line across the anticipated track of a convoy. The boat making contact did not attack immediately but would vector-in the remainder to mount a simultaneous assault. Allied strategy, in turn, used intelligence to route convoys "evasively", around known U-boat concentrations. Although effective, this procedure did not always work.

On October 29, 1942, the 42-ship slow, east-bound SC 107 was nearing Cape Race, Newfoundland when it was seen and reported by *U-522*. The German radio intercept service had already discovered a mid-ocean rendezvous point for the convoy, and Dönitz now brought 14 boats together as Group *Veilchen* (Violet). These formed a line of search north-east of Newfoundland, awaiting the arrival of three further submarines.

On the 30th the local escort force handed responsibility for SC 107 to its ocean escort, the Canadian C-4 escort group. Even three years into the war, this comprised only one destroyer and four Flower-class corvettes, one of which was British. It was short of two units, one of which was the destroyer of the usual senior officer.

ABOVE: The Royal Navy's "C" class of 1931 was curtailed at four ships. All were transferred to the Royal Canadian Navy, the *Comet* being renamed *Restigouche*. As an Atlantic escort, she has landed "Y" gun and her after tubes. Note the High Frequency Direction Finding (HF/DF) and Type 286 air search radar antennae.

At this point, the convoy was still covered by land-based air and, working ahead, the Royal Canadian Air Force scored a notable opening success in exploiting German radio transmissions to surprise and sink the *Veilchen* boat *U-659* and the independent *U-520*.

Unfortunately, the short-range radio net used by the Allies to coordinate a convoy's defence was easily monitored by the attacking U-boats.

During the morning of November 1, SC 107 ran into the patrol line, whose *U-381* transmitted sighting reports. The escorts reacted immediately to make her submerge and to lose contact, but there were so many others in the area that, by dusk, five were in attacking positions.

German practice was to work on the surface by night, when their submarines' full speed could be utilized. The few early radar sets deployed by C-4 should have countered this, but all were unreliable or defective. Despite starshell illumination and determined intervention by individual escorts (two of whose COs had only five weeks' command experience), the enemy attacked boldly and continuously, torpedoing eight ships in 7 hours. Only one boat, *U-437*, was damaged sufficiently to oblige her retirement.

During November 2, the convoy was enveloped in thick fog and, despite being dogged by ten U-boats, lost only two further ships. A further Canadian corvette and a British destroyer arrived to buttress the escort.

LEFT: Where a convoy might advance at only 8 knots or so, its escort, in rescuing survivors or investigating contacts, might fall well behind. A fast burst of speed to regain station could greatly deplete already limited bunkers.

CONVOY ACTION – BATTLE OF THE ATLANTIC

> "Against such a scale of attack, a group of this kind cannot be expected to suffer other than heavy losses." Captain Hewlett Thebaud, US Navy, Senior Officer of US escorts based at Londonderry, commenting in writing on the report of SC 107's experience

Group *Veilchen* had not yet finished with SC 107. Attacking during the night of November 3/4, they took four more victims. One, an ammunition ship, exploded with such violence that it is believed to have destroyed her assailant, *U-132*, which disappeared without trace.

On November 4, the convoy's dedicated rescue vessel, loaded to capacity with over 300 survivors, was detached to Iceland with two escorts that were very low on fuel. One last ship was torpedoed and lost, but six U-boats had also to withdraw, themselves requiring fuel and torpedoes.

Finally having crossed the mid-Atlantic "air gap" on November 5, the convoy came under continuous air cover from Iceland, whence also arrived three American escort vessels. It proved to be the end of SC 107's travails, but the loss of 15 ships was serious and resulted in the British Admiralty, rather unfairly, severely criticizing the Canadians. SC 107's slow progress – it covered only 1,770km/1,100 miles in seven days, averaging 6 knots exposed it to a week of attack by up to 15 U-boats working together. C-4's ships were inadequate in numbers and, except for the destroyers, too slow. Their experience was limited and their defence was simply overwhelmed, just as Dönitz's tactics had intended.

The most effective procedure was to keep U-boats submerged, to prevent them using their relatively high surface speed and, thus, to lose contact. For this, more long-range maritime aircraft were urgently required.

RIGHT: **By October 1942 the battle against the U-boat was being won. Early aces such as Kretschmer (seen here), Schepke and Prien had been eliminated, and operational effectiveness was declining.**

ABOVE LEFT: **Designed as a heavy bomber, the B-24, or Consolidated Liberator, proved to be an outstanding success as a maritime patrol aircraft. Stripped to accommodate extra fuel, it could cover the notorious mid-Atlantic gap.**
ABOVE: **From a small, peacetime nucleus, the Royal Canadian Navy expanded rapidly by its own effort to become a major force in the Western Atlantic. British and American criticism of its early shortcomings was, in retrospect, unduly harsh.** BELOW: **Dönitz's single-minded objective in targeting every possible merchant ship was, militarily, a brilliant strategy. A single ship might, for instance, be carrying more armoured vehicles than could be lost in a major tank battle.**

51

"Johnny" Walker and the Anti-submarine Support Group

In September 1941, Commander Frederick J. Walker was ordered to Liverpool to take command of HM sloop *Stork*, as a senior officer of the Western Approaches Command's 36th Escort Group.

Escort groups were a comparatively new concept, possible only with increasing numbers of escorts. Ideally homogeneous in terms of ship types, groups underwent brief but intensive training at Tobermory on Mull, Scotland, thereafter being kept together to develop a high degree of mutual understanding.

The primary duty of the senior officer of a convoy escort lay in the "safe and timely arrival" of his charges. With too few escorts, each stretched to its limit, the destruction of U-boats was secondary to just "keeping them down", where their low speed prevented their further intervention. Escort groups, however, comprised about eight ships (although, at any time, two might expect to be in dock) and the odd unit or two might usually be spared to prosecute a contact to conclusion. This was made clear in the Operational Instructions issued by Walker to his commanding officers. "The particular aim of the Group", he wrote, "is ... the destruction of any enemy which attacks the convoy." Walker's preferred methods involved several ships and a generous expenditure of depth charges.

It was already recognized that the presence of an Escort Carrier (CVE) acted as a force multiplier to enable an escort force to adequately cover the long perimeter of a convoy. The prototype British CVE, HMS *Audacity*, had already made her mark when, in December 1941, she was allocated, together with Walker's group, to the Gibraltar-UK convoy HG 76.

The 32-strong convoy passed beyond Gibraltar-based air cover on December 17, and, for four days, until it came within UK-based air cover, depended upon *Audacity*'s half-dozen fighters for local support. Besides forcing U-boats to submerge, the Martlets could also direct escorts to the spot. During four days of almost continuous action, Walker's ships were able to sink five U-boats. Although the carrier, a prime target, was lost, together with a destroyer and two merchantmen, it was a decided victory for the defence. In recognition, Walker was awarded the first of his eventual four Distinguished Service Orders.

LEFT: **During one of Walker's "rolling carpet" depth charge attacks, *Starling*'s after end could be a very busy place. The rapid replenishment of 136kg/300lb depth charges required dedicated team work, although conditions here are relatively benign.** ABOVE: **Stark though it was, Liverpool's Gladstone Dock was always a welcome sight to a weary Western Approaches escort. Admiral Sir Max Horton has "cleared lower decks" to cheer in the returning *Starling*. Her upper mast detail has been censored.**

LEFT: **Built to full naval, rather than mercantile, standards, the Black Swans and their improved successors were necessarily built in fewer numbers. Conspicuous on *Starling* is the aft-mounted "lantern" of her Type 271 surface-search radar.**

ABOVE: **No "gift horse" was ever better utilized. The first British escort carrier, *Audacity*, was remodelled from the captured German merchantman *Hannover*. Her career was short but she proved the value of a CVE in the defence of convoys.**

> "No officer will ever be blamed by me for getting on with the job in hand." From Walker's Operational Instructions to the 36th Escort Group

A series of convoy actions confirmed his methods and his determination but, already exhausted when promoted Captain in July 1942, Walker was rested in a shore billet for six months. Following his repeated requests for a further sea command, however, he was given the new sloop *Starling* in January 1943, transferring to her the experienced crew of the *Stork*.

With five others of her class, *Starling* formed the Second Support Group. Support groups differed from escort groups in being intended to reinforce the escort of any convoy that found itself strongly attacked.

Besides drilling his ships into a state of high efficiency, Walker developed new attack tactics. A problem with contemporary Asdic (Sonar) was that it lost contact for the final stage of an attack approach. Depth charges were thus dropped on an estimated position, with additional error being possible through "sinking time". Walker's method was to follow the target, at the same speed and at about 1,829km/2,000yd range. Aware of his Asdic, the submarine had no immediate reason to evade. One thousand yards ahead of Walker, however, steering the same course at a silent 5 knots, and with Asdic secured, was a second sloop. Under Walker's direction, this vessel slowly overtook the unsuspecting target, rolling over a large depth charge pattern. Its detonation would be U-boat's first intimation of danger, usually too late to allow effective evasive action.

For deep-diving or "difficult" targets, a variation was to use three sloops in line abreast to release a lethal, rolling carpet of depth charges, saturating the whole target area.

Improved Sonars and ahead-throwing weapons largely cured the problem but Walker's ingenuity proved that it was possible to work effectively within the limitations of then-current equipment.

An inspirational leader, slated for flag rank but worn out by constant sea service, "Johnny" Walker collapsed and died in July 1944. He was just 48 years old.

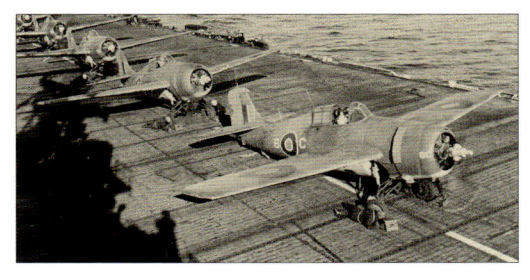

ABOVE: **Known to the US Navy as the Grumman F4F Wildcat, the Martlet entered service with the British Fleet Air Arm in 1940. Tough enough to withstand the rigours of carrier life, it served both with the fleet and, as here, on CVEs.**

LEFT: **The 2nd Escort Group seen from the *Starling*. *Loch Fada* is followed in order by *Wren*, *Dominica* and *Loch Killin*. The tall pole mast of the US-built *Dominica* contrasts with *Wren*'s tripod and the *Loch*'s sturdy lattice masts.**

Escort carrier Support Groups — taking the fight to the enemy

The first three years on the North Atlantic were all about survival, with inadequate and dangerously extended Allied AS resources covering UK-bound convoys in the face of unremitting submarine attack. This was Admiral Dönitz's chosen battleground, where his forces could destroy the greatest amount of tonnage for the least effort. Only reluctantly did he deploy extended-range boats farther afield, notably to the Caribbean and West Africa. In general, these forays resulted in fewer sinkings but were useful for their nuisance value, diverting scarce Allied defence resources.

With Allied war production getting into its stride, however, the North Atlantic and the Bay of Biscay transit area were, by mid-1943, becoming dangerous for U-boats. Dönitz responded by temporarily moving the centre of gravity of his operations southwards. Land-based aircraft from Bermuda, Morocco and Brazil proved inadequate (the Azores were not yet available) and the US Navy decided to allocate some of its earlier Escort Carriers (CVEs) to the theatre.

U-boats despatched to remote areas expended much time and fuel in transit and, to keep them on station longer, replenishment was required. It had been standard procedure for homeward-bound boats to transfer spare fuel or torpedoes to those remaining but the procedure was difficult. Special resupply submarines were thus built, notably the Type VIIF "torpedo carrier" and the Type XIV "U-tanker", which cruised the area, meeting depleted boats by appointment. They were

ABOVE: **During 1943 the US Navy formed five anti-submarine groups based on CVEs such as the *Block Island* (CVE-21). Known to the Americans as hunter-killer groups, they could operate independently by virtue of Ultra information.**

particularly valuable targets and, as their activities were frequently identified through Ultra signals intelligence, advantage was taken by the Allies now that the means had become available.

During the latter half of 1943 the US Navy created the first half-dozen "hunter-killer" groups, each based on an 18-knot CVE with about two dozen aircraft, usually Wildcats and Avengers. Four to six escorts were provided, latterly new Destroyer Escorts (DEs) but, initially, veteran "four pipers". Like the already constituted British Support Groups, the Americans were intended to reinforce dedicated convoy escorts when particularly threatened (notably on the US–Gibraltar route) but, otherwise, to seek out and destroy U-boats wherever they could be found. Before the advent of information from Ultra, such speculative hunts in a vast ocean were an impractical waste of resources but high-grade intelligence made specific targeting possible. Ultra, however, was neither guaranteed nor continuous, and the U-boats' greatest enemy continued to be the endless radio chatter generated by Dönitz's centralized control. All Allied AS vessels now sported the birdcage antenna of "Huff-Duff" (High Frequency Direction Finding, or HF/DF), which could give an accurate bearing on a transmitting boat.

ESCORT CARRIER SUPPORT GROUPS – TAKING THE FIGHT TO THE ENEMY

LEFT: **Successor to the F4F Wildcat, the F6F Hellcat became the US Navy's standard fighter from 1943. Working from CVEs, they strafed surface U-boats to suppress defensive fire while an Avenger approached with depth charges or homing torpedoes.** BELOW: **The Avenger torpedo-bomber built by Grumman was designated TBF or TBM depending upon its source of manufacture. Its cavernous ventral compartment could accommodate a full-sized 18in torpedo or 907kg/2,000lb of bombs.**

> "Presence of escort aircraft carriers with the convoys make operating conditions so difficult for the U-boats that they are not likely to meet with success." Dönitz's Command War Diary, extract from entry for July 11, 1943

First on line was American Support Group 6, comprising the carrier *Bogue* and two veteran destroyers. They were joined at intervals by further groups based on the CVEs *Card*, *Core*, *Santee*, *Croatan* and *Block Island*. Their Wildcat fighters would typically surprise and strafe a surfaced U-boat to suppress return fire for a follow-up Avenger to deliver a knockout with depth charges or, increasingly, a "Fido" homing torpedo.

Allowed to roam freely within support distance of major convoy routes, the CVE groups achieved considerable success. Submarines were frequently caught on the surface in twos, or even threes, in the process of replenishment. It was far from being a turkey shoot, however, for many U-boats were now being armed with quadruple 2cm anti-aircraft guns and, in pressing home their attacks, many aircraft were heavily damaged or destroyed. Against the AS escorts, the Germans were also deploying acoustic torpedoes.

Remarkably, the only CVE lost on these profitable operations was the *Block Island*, destroyed by *U-549* with three conventional torpedoes. With a homing weapon, the latter then blasted the stern off an escort before herself succumbing to Hedgehog salvoes. The *Block Island* group had already accounted for six U-boats.

The CVE groups exploited the technical limitations and over-tight control of U-boats which, ultimately, were responsible for the failure of their campaign.

ABOVE LEFT: **A submariner of World War I, Admiral Dönitz ran a devastating U-boat campaign against the Allies. That it was ultimately adjudged fair was illustrated by Admiral Nimitz's testimonial on Dönitz's behalf during the post-war Nuremburg Tribunal.** ABOVE RIGHT: **Caught on the surface, a Type IX is lashed as she attempts to dive. Unfortunately for her, the aircraft would follow up with a depth charge salvo or a homing torpedo just ahead of the swirl that marked her submergence.** BELOW: **The sort of rendezvous that Support Group pilots dreamed of interrupting. In order to extend their patrols, operational U-boats were directed to meet up with Type XIV resupply boats for fuel, torpedoes and fresh stores.**

55

THE HISTORY OF DESTROYERS AND FRIGATES

LEFT: **The 24 bombs of the Hedgehog were mounted on long spigots, angled so as to place the projectiles in a circular or elliptical pattern. As they exploded only on contact with a submerged target or the bottom, the bombs were not set for a specific depth.**

Improved weapons, sensors and escorts

As noted above, early Asdic (Sonar) had the unfortunate characteristic of losing contact with submerged targets at ranges below 100–150m/109–164yd. An AS vessel thus released depth charges on an estimated position, a shortcoming exacerbated by the time that the weapons took to sink to the desired depth. The result was "dead time", during which the target could take evasive action.

British Admiralty scientists were well aware of the Navy's problem, postulating that the solution lay in a mortar that could fire depth bombs ahead of a ship, while the target was still fixed in the Asdic beam.

During the 1930s a weapon was sea-tested and proved capable of throwing a small bomb up to a half-mile ahead. Although it was progressed no further, it led to proposals for two further weapons, a triple-barrelled mortar capable of firing three 200kg/440lb bombs, and a multi-way ejector throwing up to twenty smaller projectiles. From 1941 both concepts were given high priority.

The latter idea was the simpler, entering service late in 1941 as the Hedgehog. It fired 24 contact-fused bombs loaded on to spigots. Because of the powerful recoil forces, the bombs were electrically ripple-fired, the spigots aligned so as to drop them in a circle of some 35m/38yd diameter, centred

ABOVE: **Converted to a radar picket (DER), the American destroyer escort *Thomas J. Gary* retained her Hedgehog in the superfiring position forward. Further to a massive electronics upgrade, she has received an enclosed bridge and long amidships deckhouse.**

about 200m/218yd ahead of the ship. Each 30kg/65lb bomb contained half its weight of explosive, sufficient to hole a submarine hull. Somewhat more streamlined, the bomb sank twice as fast as a depth charge.

Hedgehog was initially very unpopular. Mounted on an exposed foredeck, it required constant maintenance. There was no reassuring "big bang" of a depth charge, unless the bombs actually contacted the target.

Hedgehog's first "kill", nonetheless, was in February 1942 and, by the end of the year, over 100 British ships had been so fitted. It was also adopted wholeheartedly by the US Navy.

> "Anti-Dive Bombing Equipment."
> Officially, the explanation to be given to casual enquirers of the purpose of Hedgehog during its secret introductory phase

56

IMPROVED WEAPONS, SENSORS AND ESCORTS

By the end of the war, the kill rate for Hedgehog was six times that for conventional depth charges.

Improvements to U-boats included tougher hulls for deeper diving. There began to be doubts that the Hedgehog bomb was sufficiently lethal, and work was accelerated on the triple-barrelled mortar. Called Squid, this entered service in September 1943. Like that of the Hedgehog, the launcher was roll-stabilized, and its three bombs each weighed 180kg/390lb, again half of which was explosive. The projectiles fell in an equilateral triangle of side 35m/38yd, and centred some 250m/273yd ahead of the ship. They sank four times as rapidly as depth charges.

"Double Squid" proved to be particularly effective as, in plan, the two triangles formed a six-pointed star (i.e. with a relative offset of 60 degrees), with the two salvoes separated by about 20m/65ft in depth.

Squid was teamed with new Type 147 Asdic. This generated a precise, fan-shaped beam that could be depressed through a vertical range of 45 degrees. A specially adapted pen recorder gave a visual readout of range and depth of the contact. This data was communicated directly to Squid, which was fused and aligned automatically.

By the end of the war, Double Squid's kill rate was nudging 40 per cent. It was supplied to the US Navy, which service did not pursue it, preferring to rely on Hedgehog while it developed its own weapons.

A probable reason was that the system, with its magazines and handling spaces, was too demanding in space and weight to retrofit economically into large numbers of war-built ships. A major shortcoming was the tight design of the otherwise excellent destroyer escorts (DEs), making them unsuitable for modifications to accept Squid.

ABOVE LEFT: **The American Mousetrap was Hedgehog redesigned for smaller craft. The fierce recoil forces associated with firing the Hedgehog bombs was nullified by making the Mousetrap rounds rocket-propelled** TOP: **Designed around a double Squid installation, the British Lochs were given spacious accommodation for it forward of the bridge.** Loch More **was completed just before the war's end, but the class was greatly curtailed by cancellations.** ABOVE: **Compared with that of a Loch (see above) the platform for a Castle-class single Squid was much shorter. "Castles" were too large to be built in Canada and were transferred from the Royal Navy. The Royal Canadian Navy's** Tillsonburg **was thus built as HMS** Pembroke Castle. BELOW: **The triple-barrelled Squid was built into a compact frame which allowed the weapon to be automatically roll-compensated. Barrels were angled to place the bombs in an equilateral triangle, and were lowered to the horizontal for loading.**

Fully committed to the weapon, the British designed the Loch-class frigate around the Double Squid and the Castle-class corvette around a single. Their firsts-of-class commissioned in December 1943 and September 1943 respectively. To accelerate the programme, Lochs were assembled from modules prefabricated in numerous facilities.

57

LEFT: **Type XXIs in the Blohm and Voss yard in Hamburg in May 1945. The fast electric boats, assembled from modules to production-line principles, posed a serious threat to the Allies but, fortunately, came too late to have any impact.**

ABOVE: **The head of an extensible Schnorkel for a Type XXI featured what was effectively a large ball-valve. The small stub on the top was to support a radar detector, and surfaces are meshed to reduce radar reflection and to improve flow.**

The emergence of the fast frigate

Early in 1943 the Germans acknowledged that convoy defences were getting the better of U-boats, and looked for a radical solution. The major shortcomings of existing boats were their very limited submerged endurance and speed, making it necessary to surface daily to recharge batteries, to renew the internal atmosphere, or to keep station on a convoy. Surfaced, and despite warning devices, they were vulnerable to detection and attack by increased numbers of aircraft, both shore-based and from escort carriers.

The resulting Type XXI U-boat was a major step forward in submarine design. Its large and deep hull contained three times the battery power of earlier boats while, externally, the hull was "cleaned-up" to minimize hydrodynamic drag. Schnorkel (or "Snort") was also under urgent development to permit extended submerged operation.

Tests predicted a Type XXI to be capable of submerged speeds of 18 knots for 1½ hours, or 12–14 knots for 10 hours. Hampered by surface conditions and the need to operate Asdic/Sonar, conventional convoy escorts would be unable to cope with such performance.

The Type XXI was assembled from large, prefabricated modules. These came from widely dispersed facilities and depended upon transport via inland waterways that were vulnerable to strategic bombing. This, together with acute shortages in skilled labour and materials, saw the production schedule slip to the point that the first-of-class "went operational" just four days before close of hostilities.

ABOVE: **Following the construction of two "hydrogen peroxide boats" to German principles, the Royal Navy abandoned the idea as impracticable. The ultimate goal would have been an atmosphere-independent boat, requiring no "Snort".**

Any relief at this, however, was short-lived for, with the immediate onset of the Cold War, the Soviet Union utilized captured German technology to produce a large submarine fleet of which the backbone were 236 Project 613, 644 and 665 known to NATO as the "W", or Whisky-class submarines and a near copy of the Type XXI.

Escalation to full hostilities would, once again, see Atlantic convoys as the keystone of Allied strategy, and a cash-strapped Royal Navy had to respond. The only new buildings that could be afforded were four each of Anti-Aircraft (AA) and Aircraft-Direction (AD) frigates. To provide fast frigates, capable

THE EMERGENCE OF THE FAST FRIGATE

ABOVE: **A double Limbo installation in the after well of what appears to be a British Type 12 frigate. A major difference from Squid was that the weapons, fully stabilized in both roll and pitch, lifted their bombs over the ship's superstructure.** BELOW: **Converted to a Type 15 fast frigate, the British destroyer** *Grenville* **shows her Limbo installation. She was fitted with a small flight pad for initial experiments with a helicopter, in the interests of increasing stand-off capability.**

ABOVE: **The Type 81s (Tribals) were the first British frigates designed around a shipborne helicopter. The elevated flight pad, located well forward, formed the roof of deckhouse which became, via an elevator, the hangar for the aircraft.**

> "Sometimes, the exhaust clouds would turn from grey to black and then, to the stupefaction of all who saw them, suddenly erupt into cataclysmic fireballs of smoke and flame as the oxygen in the atmosphere completed the combustion begun inside *Explorer*."
> Report of surface trials with Britain's first hydrogen peroxide-fuelled submarine HMS *Explorer* (known to the Navy as *Exploder!*), quoted in *Daily Telegraph* of November 18, 1999

of meeting the new submarine threat, it was decided to convert some of the 32-knot war-built fleet destroyers, many of which had seen little service.

Suitably strengthened, these were capable of being driven at 25 knots in Atlantic conditions, while realizing a range of 5,311km/3,300 miles at 15 knots. The full conversion (Type 15) had an AS armament including Double Squid (or its successor, Limbo) and eight fixed tubes to launch the new Mark XX homing torpedo, which could work to the limit of range of contemporary sonars. Even these ships proved to be too expensive, so a limited conversion (Type 16) was produced in parallel. About two dozen destroyers were so modified between 1950 and 1958, but proved that speed alone did not provide the complete solution.

During the war, the Germans had persevered, but failed, in their attempts to produce a hydrogen peroxide-fuelled, turbine-driven submarine capable of bursts of very high submerged speed. The Soviets had also inherited this technology. All attempts to make it work failed ultimately, due to the dangerous instability of the fuel but, from 1954, emerged the even greater threat of the nuclear attack submarine (SSN). Somewhat slower than the abortive German hydrogen peroxide-fuelled "Walter" boat, the SSN had an effectively infinite submerged endurance and posed a far more serious problem.

As no affordable AS ship could realistically hope to track an SSN bent on evasion, the adopted solution was to build a slower frigate that deployed a rapid-reaction stand-off weapon. For a ship acting alone, the range of such equipment was limited to the useful range of the ship's sonar. The US Navy opted for a rocket-propelled missile (that became ASROC) which could compensate for long-range inaccuracy by its ability to carry a small nuclear warhead. The more radical British solution was to put a light helicopter aboard the ship. Since initial trials in 1956, frigate design has become ever more driven by helicopter requirements.

59

THE HISTORY OF DESTROYERS AND FRIGATES

Into the missile age

World War II, and the ensuing Cold War, redefined the destroyer. For instance, in 1939 the Royal Navy began commissioning its J-class destroyers. Designed for surface warfare, their six 4.7s and ten torpedo tubes resulted in a 23 per cent increase in legend displacement. Their main armament, with its 40-degree elevation, could hardly be termed "high angle", however, while their few minor weapons proved to be no deterrent to a dive-bomber. Even using small patterns, their full outfit of 30 depth charges could be exhausted in prosecuting a single submarine contact.

By 1945, armaments reflected the fact that the major killers of destroyers were aircraft and submarines, not other ships. In the Royal Navy, this had brought about two, separate evolutionary lines.

Launched from 1943, the Battles were intended for Pacific operations, with about 20 per cent greater endurance than a J-class boat. Designed around the air threat, their four 4.5s were truly dual-purpose, housed in two, forward-facing gunhouses and capable of 80-degree elevation. Eight torpedo tubes were carried but the after end was dominated by two fully stabilized, twin 40mm mountings.

The second development, launched from 1945, was directed at the new threat of the fast submarine. Smaller than the Battles, the Weapons were designed around four 4in High-Angle (HA) guns and an ahead-firing Anti-Submarine (AS) mortar (first a Hedgehog, latterly a Squid). They carried a full outfit of torpedo tubes but also up to 70 conventional depth charges. "Conventional" submarines were, by now, the business of frigates but the German Type XXI "Elektroboote" were capable of bursts of submerged speed which, at that time, only a destroyer could match.

The dedicated AS destroyer proved, however, to be an evolutionary dead-end, displaced by rapidly improving frigate design. The finale of the Pacific war, meanwhile, had shown that it was not sufficient to shoot down a suicide aircraft – it had to be disintegrated, preferably at a safe distance. The one required at least 3in, proximity fused ammunition, the other a Surface-to-Air guided Missile (SAM).

With the Cold War, the Soviet Union built on captured German technology to create fleets of high-speed submarines and long-range strike aircraft, armed with ship-busting, Air-to-Surface Missiles (ASMs). These were aimed at the West's potent amphibious warfare capability and the vulnerability of still-vital convoys. They prompted development of SAM-armed escorts, deploying also stand-off AS missiles. The size of such escorts was driven by the dimensions of missile stowage and handling facilities plus the large electronic systems necessary both to "illuminate" the target and to steer the missile to interception.

TOP: **The flotilla attacks in the Surigao Strait (Leyte Gulf), and in the sinking of the *Haguro*, were effectively the last for which the classic destroyer had evolved. These three British war-built "Emergencies" were already obsolescent by 1945.**

UPPER LEFT: **With her 17-knot submerged burst speed the Type XXI U-boat arrived too late to cause problems to Allied escorts. The post-war acquisition of the technology by Soviet Russia, however, led directly to the fast escort, such as the British Type 15.**

LOWER LEFT: **The 1942 Battle class (*Cadiz* seen here) were designed to address the aerial threat. Main armament, all forward, elevated to 80 degrees. Two stabilized, radar-laid twin 40mm mountings were located aft but displacement grew to over 2,900 tons.**

INTO THE MISSILE AGE

LEFT: Despite the Terrier SAM's being successfully installed in the Gearing-class *Gyatt* as early as 1956, the series conversion of other war-vintage hulls did not prove practicable. The optimum platform proved to be the custom-designed 4,500-ton Coontz-class DLGs.

ABOVE RIGHT: The British Squid mortar proved to be a deadly killer of U-boats but, unlike the Hedgehog, was not adopted by the US Navy, which preferred to develop its own Mk.108 Weapon Able/Alfa, which could fire 12 single rounds per minute. LEFT: A shipborne helicopter has an enormous impact on ship layout and size. The DASH (Drone AS Helicopter) was a bold attempt to reduce helicopter dimensions and weight by deleting its crew. It proved to be ahead of contemporary technology. BELOW: ASROC, the US Navy's Anti-Submarine Rocket, can release a homing torpedo out to the practical range of a large sonar. All launcher versions, such as that illustrated, have been retired in favour of interchangeable vertical-launch rounds.

The US Navy had large numbers of nearly new, war-built destroyers and, to avoid block obsolescence, sought to convert them to SAM escorts. A single, prototype conversion (USS *Gyatt* in 1956) was successful in deploying a medium-range Terrier system, but no general conversion programme resulted. The destroyers were instead remodelled around the ASROC (AS Rocket) stand-off AS system. It was apparent that viable Anti-Aircraft (AA) escorts would need to be designed, bottom-up, around specific weapon systems.

With greater standardization and inter-operability becoming the norm within NATO, destroyers (in the West, at least) came to be considered primarily anti-aircraft-oriented, frigates anti-submarine. The Soviet Union then technically behind the West and still concentrating on anti-ship warfare, opted for destroyers large enough to carry large Surface-to-Surface Missiles (SSMs). As the weapons were bulky, reloading at sea was not considered practical, so more launchers were accommodated, further forcing up dimensions.

The US Navy tried to improve its AS stand-off capability with unmanned, torpedo-carrying helicopters, called DASH (Drone AS Helicopter). Ahead of its time, however, the programme failed, leading to a life-extension for ASROC and the adoption of the manned helicopter. Two of these are better than one. Each new type is larger and more capable. "Destroyers" continue to grow larger.

61

LEFT: **The superb all-round capability of large modern frigates, such as the German** *Sachsen*, **disguises their still-potent anti-submarine potential and tends to blur the distinction between destroyer and frigate as separate categories.** ABOVE: **An Australian-designed anti-submarine guided weapon, Ikara was purchased for the Royal Navy, with several Leander-class frigates being modified to deploy it. It works to maximum sonar range, releasing an American Mk 46 torpedo over the target's computed position.** BELOW: **Her duty done, the British Type 12** *Lowestoft* **is expended as a submarine target. Anti-ship torpedoes are designed, not to hit a target, but to detonate under its keel. The shock of the explosion whips the ship in a longitudinal mode, breaking its back and causing structural failure.**

Frigates in the missile age

An obvious indication that, post-war, frigates were in a new age, was the virtual disappearance of superstructure in British designs. The thinking of the early Cold War included using nuclear warheads against groups of ships such as convoys or task groups. By the late 1950s, however, the need for useful topside space ensured that superstructures returned to something like normal.

With NATO standardization, frigates became Anti-Submarine (AS) specialists and destroyers Anti-Aircraft (AA). Both types, however, were expected to contribute to the firepower of a group while being able to defend themselves.

Heavy, tube-launched AS torpedoes soon lost favour, replaced by small, lightweight weapons which could be deployed effectively by shipboard helicopter as well as by tube. The helicopter became the ship's primary AS system, directed by the ship's hull-mounted and Variable Depth Sonars (VDSs).

As a less space-consuming alternative to the helicopter, the stand-off, shipboard AS missile looked attractive. The French, Soviet Union and United States developed their own, the British adopted the Australian Ikara. With ranges of 20km/12.5 miles or more, however, such weapons worked beyond the reliable range of the ship's sonar and the helicopter, instead of being made redundant, found a necessary alternative role in carrying a dipping (or "dunking") sonar to assist in targeting. There was then, of course, immediate pressure to increase the machine's size in order to carry weapons as well, a complex data link, and a crew of two to work it all. For a submarine hunt, two helicopters are infinitely more effective, while conferring a measure of redundancy. The effect on frigate size was dramatic.

The introduction of the gas turbine as a main propulsion unit in the 1960s was a revolution. Its great advantages include its ability to start from cold in a matter of minutes, its compactness and relatively light weight. It suffers from a higher initial cost and its narrow efficiency bands, necessitating separate main and cruising turbines. Repair is by replacement, much reducing time spent in dockyard hands. An extra bonus is the reduction in engine room personnel, representing a considerable saving in through-life costs as well as in accommodation space.

FRIGATES IN THE MISSILE AGE

LEFT: **The impact of a shipborne helicopter on a frigate's design is enormous, fully 30 per cent of the *Iron Duke*'s length being devoted to the upkeep and operation of her Merlin helicopter. Fully loaded, the aircraft weighs 14.3 tons, compared with a Lynx's 4.6 tons.** ABOVE: **The current American Littoral Combat Ship project will result in an unconventional multi-purpose, high-speed vessel with interchangeable weapons systems. The General Dynamics *Independence* trimaran is shown here, one of three contenders.**

ABOVE: **One of the 46-ship Knox class of frigate, the USS *Aylwin* (FF-1081) is seen launching an ASROC missile. The 8-cell Mk.116 launcher was modified to launch Harpoon SSMs in addition, but has been superseded by Vertical Launching System (VLS).** BELOW: **The acutely raked stem of the Russian *Neustrushimyy* indicates a sizeable, low-frequency bow sonar. The hump right aft, abaft the flight pad, covers the winch and stowage for a variable-depth sonar and passive towed array. As with German frigates, freeboard is generous.**

Frigates continue to provide designers with a dilemma. Ideally, a design is compact and inexpensive, necessary for series production in an emergency. In reality, however, all modern systems are demanding in volume, driving up size and cost. The more valuable the ship, the greater the case for comprehensive "defensive armament", so space is made for up to eight canister-launched anti-ship missiles. Earlier attempts to save space by eliminating the sole remaining dual-purpose gun came to nought when, in 1982, the Falklands War was a reminder of just how indispensable it was, and remains.

Anti-ship missiles are getting ever more sophisticated and, currently, considerable effort is being devoted to "stealth" measures to reduce frigates' radar signatures. While this produces some striking designs it is possible that the effectiveness of the measures will be outweighed by their inhibiting effects on a ship's utility.

Bearing in mind that the helicopter remains the frigate's primary AS weapons and targeting platform, it makes sense to configure the ship to facilitate the operability of the aircraft across the greatest range of sea states. Since the inception of the shipborne helicopter, however, it has been the practice, almost without exception, to locate the helicopter right aft, where it is subject to the maximum accelerations and amplitude of movement. Experimental trimaran ship forms promise a steadier platform with considerable amidships deck space, hulls of reduced resistance and significantly reduced heat signatures.

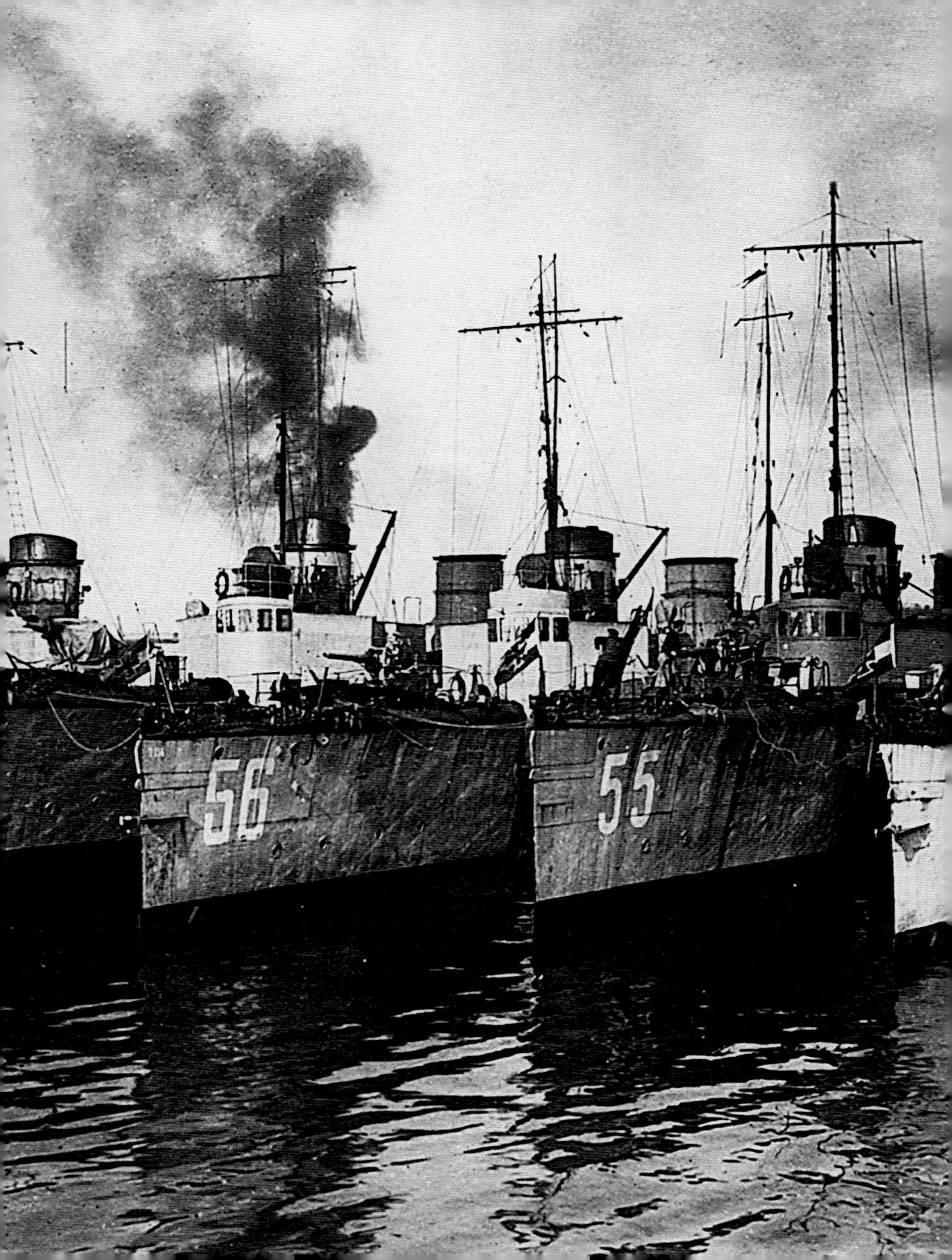

56
55

Directory of Destroyers
Up to 1918

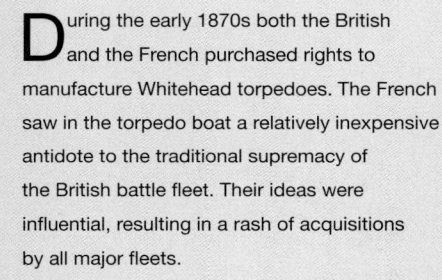

During the early 1870s both the British and the French purchased rights to manufacture Whitehead torpedoes. The French saw in the torpedo boat a relatively inexpensive antidote to the traditional supremacy of the British battle fleet. Their ideas were influential, resulting in a rash of acquisitions by all major fleets.

The American Admiral Alfred Thayer Mahan, however, in several major writings, examined the historical relationship between imperial greatness and an effective battle fleet. By thus reaffirming the pre-eminence of the capital ship, he directly influenced the ambitious German Kaiser Wilhelm II and, through him, the architect of his new navy, Admiral Alfred Tirpitz. For long, therefore, the latter pursued the gun rather than the torpedo in the developing "naval race" with the British.

Initially concerned at the threat from the French, the British Admiralty sought an antidote to the torpedo boat, finding it in the "Torpedo Boat Destroyer" (TBD). Itself little more than a large torpedo boat, its design was prioritized for seakeeping rather than for sheer speed. It could, therefore, in anything but calm sea, exploit the torpedo boat's poor seakeeping, running it down and destroying it by superior firepower.

LEFT: **A careworn pod of Vulcan-built torpedo boats in the lock at Wilhelmshaven. The bracket on the stem is for streaming paravanes. The amount of glazing to the wheelhouses is surprising, and all foremasts have been lengthened.**

DIRECTORY OF DESTROYERS: UP TO 1918

LEFT: **If this is, indeed, Thornycroft's original *Lightning*, then her riverine steam launch limitations are all too obvious. As the Royal Navy's purchased TB.1, however, she carried a single 14in torpedo tube on the foredeck, with two reloads amidships.**

Early torpedo boats

Like the static, explosive mine, the new locomotive torpedo was considered by the British Admiralty to be a weapon for a lesser fleet. Despite this element of disdain, however, it could not be ignored and considerable funds were committed to its development. The "lesser fleets" certainly seized upon the torpedo boat as an inexpensive force multiplier, in theory capable of knocking out a battleship, and companies specializing in its construction enjoyed full order books.

While mindful of the need to acquire torpedo boats to assess their value in attack, the British Admiralty was more concerned with protecting the battle fleet against such craft. Where, in 1877, it purchased its first torpedo boat in Thornycroft's *Lightning*, therefore, it was already thinking in terms of "torpedo catchers, hunters or destroyers", acquiring White's *Swift* in 1885.

Divergent evolutionary lines were, thus, already evident. The *Lightning*, or TB.1, was no more than a steam-engined river launch which, in sheltered waters, could manage barely 18 knots with torpedoes aboard. She, and her 11 sisters of 1878–79, had a single, rotatable tube on the foredeck, and "dropping gear" on either side amidships for single torpedoes.

The *Swift*, or TB.81, however, was 45.7m/150ft overall against 25.6m/84ft, enabling her to maintain speed in open water. She mounted three tubes, one in the stern and, emphasizing her "catcher" role, six 3pdrs (difficult to lay accurately in a seaway).

In an effort to produce the smallest craft with the necessary combination of speed, self-sufficiency and ability to accompany the fleet, the Admiralty evolved a 61m/200ft design, with four torpedo tubes, one 4in gun and six 3pdrs. This was the beginning of the "torpedo-gunboat" concept, which proved to be something of an evolutionary dead-end, largely because of the poor power-to-weight ratio of contemporary machinery, which was bulky and heavy.

BELOW: **Torpedo Boat No.27, or TB.27, was built in 1886, one of a group of five boats from Thornycroft. Less than a decade after the *Lightning*, displacement has more than doubled, with length increased by some 50 per cent. Already a small warship.**

Name	Builder*	Year	Displacement (tons)	Dimensions (ft)	Torpedo tubes
TB.1	T	1877	27	84.5 x 11	1
TB.21–22	T	1885	63	113 x 12.5	3
TB.41–60	T	1886	60	127.5 x 12.5	4
TB.61–79	Y	1886	75	125 x 13	5
TB.81	W	1885	125	150 x 17.5	3
TB.91–97	T, W, L	1893–94	130	140 x 15.5	3
TB.98–99	T	1901	178	160 x 17	3
TB.109–113	T	1902–03	200	166 x 17.5	3

*Builder: T= Thornycroft; Y = Yarrow; W = White; L = Laird

The 27-knotters, or "A" class

As can be seen from the data opposite, Torpedo Boats, numbered in a continuous sequence, but varying in specification, were acquired by the Admiralty until after the turn of the century. Unimpressed by their performance, particularly compared with that attributed to examples from Normand and Schichau, the Controller of the Navy, Rear Admiral John ("Jackie") Fisher, had invitations to tender sent to a group of leading builders. The requirement was simply for 27-knot craft with a substantial gun armament. The Board of Admiralty was hoping that this brief might be satisfied within a 200-ton displacement, but the three best proposals showed 240–280 tons. Orders were thus placed, early in 1893 for two Torpedo Boat Catchers from each of Yarrow, (*Havock* and *Hornet*), Thornycroft (*Daring* and *Decoy*), and Laird (*Ferret* and *Lynx*). For every quarter-knot under the stipulated 27 there was a substantial financial penalty, with rejection for less than an averaged 25 knots.

Except for widely differing funnel arrangements, the six were very similar, flush-decked with a raised, turtleback forecastle. The recessed conning position was roofed by a bandstand supporting a 12pdr gun, while a 6pdr was mounted aft.

One fixed torpedo tube was located to fire through the stem, with two rotatable single tubes being sited on the centreline aft of amidships. The latter tubes were interchangeable with two further 6pdrs. All six ships were accepted, with only *Havock* (having older-style locomotive boilers rather than water-tube) failing to make 27 knots.

ABOVE: The Fairfield-built *Hunter* made the requisite 27 knots on trials but it was some time before the Admiralty came to realize that, while high trial speeds were very expensive to attain, they were relatively unimportant compared with seakeeping.

All were now referred to as Torpedo Boat Destroyers or, simply "Destroyers".

Such was the perceived threat from France that the six prototypes, once seen as satisfactory, formed the basis for contracts for no less than 36 repeats, the orders spread among 14 yards. Officially the "A" class, but universally known as "27-knotters", all were launched in 1894–95.

Havock (27-knotters slightly larger but variable in specification)

	Built	Commissioned
Havock	Yarrow, Poplar	January 1894

Displacement: 240 tons (light); 275 tons (full load)
Length: 54.8m/180ft (bp); 56.4m/185ft (oa)
Beam: 5.6m/18ft 6in
Draught: 2.3m/7ft 6in
Armament: 1 x 12pdr gun, 3 x 6pdr guns; 3 x 18in torpedo tubes
Machinery: 2 x 3-cylinder triple-expansion engines, 2 boilers, 2 shafts
Power: 2,650kW/3,550ihp for 26.2 knots
Endurance: 47 tons coal for about 1,666km/900nm at 11 knots
Protection: None
Complement: 42

ABOVE: *Salmon*, from Earle, had an entirely different boiler/funnel layout. Note the navigating platform shared with the 12pdr gun. The airing hammocks remind of the eternal problem of wetness and condensation, a cause of major health problems in destroyermen.

LEFT: **An extra 10m/32.8ft on length certainly improved the 30-knotters' seakeeping as compared with that of the preceding class, but the turtledeck forward in no way compensated for what was inadequate freeboard. This is** Flying Fish.

ABOVE: **On the four-funnelled "B" class (**Spiteful **seen here), the two centre boilers, back-to-back, exhausted through separate uptakes. Two more Palmer's boats,** Albacore **and** Bonetta**, were the only ones to be fitted with experimental Parson's turbines.**

The 30-knotters, or "B", "C" and "D" classes

Some of the trials speeds achieved by the 27-knotters led the Admiralty to believe that 30 knots were easily attainable. The Board was anxious to acquire a force of at least 80 TBDs quickly but, lacking sufficient funds, had to delay other projects while pushing shipbuilders hard, even to bankruptcy.

The 30-knotters were built under programmes from 1894 to 1901. After 1913 they were classed according to numbers of funnels, there being 21 four-funnelled "B" class, 37 three-funnelled "C" class, and 20 two-funnelled "D" class. Builders were allowed to interpret the specification quite freely as long as their price was acceptable and certain criteria were met. Besides a 30-knot speed, the latter included a metacentric height of at least 60cm/2ft when in the deep condition, a minimum of 80 tons of coal was to be carried and, at 15 knots, a ship should steam 15nm to the ton.

In achieving these requirements, Thornycroft's D-class Desperate and Fame displaced only 310 tons on 63.4m/208ft hulls, while John Brown's C-class Thorn, Tiger and Vigilant were of 380 tons and 66.4m/218ft respectively. With no standard hull form, some builders met the speed requirement with no problem while others went bankrupt in having to undertake many expensive trials with varying loading, alternative propellers, etc., in order to have their ships accepted.

Beyond the extra length and displacement allowing for a further pair of 6pdrs to be shipped, the 30-knotters were much like the preceding "A" class. The earlier ships' stem torpedo tube was, however, abandoned as it created excessive wetness and induced a forward trim.

In full seagoing condition, no "30-knotter" ever made more than 27. High speed induced a pronounced stern trim ("squat"), shifting the centre of buoyancy aft and creating instability. Hence the requirement for a generous metacentric height.

C-class Cheerful, average for class

	Built	Commissioned
Cheerful	Hawthorn Leslie, Hebburn	June 1899

Displacement: 355 tons (light); 400 tons (full load)
Length: 64.1m/210ft 6in (bp); 65.5m/215ft (oa)
Beam: 6.4m/21ft
Draught: 2.5m/8ft 2in
Armament: 1 x 12pdr gun, 5 x 6pdr guns; 2 x 18in torpedo tubes (2x1)
Machinery: 2 x 3-cylinder triple-expansion engines, 4 boilers, 2 shafts
Power: 4,550kW/6,100ihp for 30.3 knots
Endurance: 87 tons coal for 2,400km/1,300nm at 15 knots
Protection: None
Complement: 63

LEFT: **The** Fame **and** Whiting **spent their careers in the Far East. They made their name in 1900 during the Boxer Rebellion when, following the seizure of the Taku forts by an international force, the pair cut out and captured four new German-built Chinese destroyers.**

UNITED KINGDOM

LEFT: **With the Royal Yacht on South Railway Jetty as backdrop, the *Eden* makes her way up Portsmouth Harbour. The additional freeboard conferred by the forecastle made the Rivers reportedly "wonderfully dry", but difficult to berth in a side wind.**
BELOW: **The Rivers' four water-tube boilers were accommodated in two back-to-back pairs. Deck space could thus be saved by exhausting them through just two wide funnels or two pairs of thin funnels.**

River, or "E" class

Opportunities arose during 1901 for British destroyer officers to visit their German counterparts, and their reports were full of praise for the Kaiser's ships, particularly in standards of accommodation. In British ships, "hard lying" was religion, with fatigue and cold stoically accepted, the endless wetness and commonly resulting diseases just another aspect of small-ship existence. German conditions were a revelation, relatively spacious, internally wood-lined, steam-heated, electrically lit and with real washing facilities. Worse, the ships' greater size conferred superior seakeeping and endurance.

The general specification for the next British ships, the "E" class took this to heart. Earlier structural weakness would be rectified through the greater use of high-tensile steel. A full-height forecastle would both improve seakeeping and increase internal volume. The 12pdr gun would still be located above the conning position but there would be, abaft it, an enclosed charthouse with open bridge above. Set farther aft, this benefited from reduced motion and wetness for watchkeepers.

Trials were to be run in the more realistic deep condition, with 25½ knots being stipulated. One ship, the *Eden*, was to be fitted with experimental steam turbines (she proved complex, but the fastest, at 26.23 knots). The class was spread over three programmes, the later ships being fitted for stowing oil fuel, permitting boiler room personnel to be reduced by 11.

The designers resisted burdening the larger Rivers with heavier armament, but the fact that they carried no more than their "30-knotter" predecessors attracted much adverse comment, particularly as they were 40 per cent more expensive. Their seagoing performance was, in fact, far superior and, while being popular with their crews, they are considered to have been the Royal Navy's first successful destroyers. They gave good service during World War I, some exchanging their 6pdrs for three more hard-hitting 12pdrs.

RIGHT: **Probably post-war, the *Welland* is seen in a cooler grey paint scheme, which better emphasizes detail. Note the built-up bridge structure, high mast with W/T aerials, recessed anchor bed and 6pdrs in sponsons at the break of the forecastle.**

Cherwell, average for class

	Built	Commissioned
Cherwell	Palmer, Hebburn	November 1904

Displacement: 549 tons (light); 620 tons (full load)
Length: 68.5m/225ft (bp); 70m/229ft 6in (oa)
Beam: 7.2m/23ft 6in
Draught: 3m/10ft
Armament: 1 x 12pdr gun, 5 x 6pdr guns; 2 x 18in torpedo tubes (2x1)
Machinery: 2 x 3- or 4-cylinder triple-expansion engines, 4 boilers, 2 shafts
Power: 5,222kW/7,000ihp for 25.26 knots
Endurance: 130 tons coal for 3,140km/1,700nm at 11 knots
Protection: None
Complement: 61

69

Beagle, Acorn and Repeat Acorn, or "G", "H" and "I" classes

With persistent reports of German destroyers making speeds of 33 and even 34 knots with steam turbines and coal-firing, the Beagles, like the Rivers, were influenced at an early stage. Oil-firing had been proposed but, with doubts as to its reliable supply in time of war, the Beagles stayed with coal.

This apparently simple option had considerable consequences for the ships' design. A further dozen stokers would need to be accommodated. Coal bunkers had to flank the boiler spaces to be accessible, where oil could be stowed in tanks of variable shape almost anywhere in the hull. Coal is nearly half as dense as oil. Extra space was required for stokers to work, while a coal-fired boiler developed less energy than one fed by oil. In short, the Beagles' fuel weight penalty through using coal was 45 tons, or about 5 per cent of legend displacement.

In earlier classes, builders were permitted to interpret a fairly general specification, leading to a wide variation in the appearance and, to some extent, layout of individual ships. Checking each variation imposed heavy work on the Department of Naval Construction. To reduce this, the Beagle specification was tighter, resulting in less individuality.

ABOVE: The Beagles were coal-fired (note *Racoon*'s smoke), an advantage in the Mediterranean, where oil fuel was always in rather short supply. A "first" for the class was the fitting of stockless anchors, which would stow directly against the hawse, in a much simplified procedure.

ABOVE: With the bridge structure of the early Beagles set farther forward (and correspondingly wetter) the gap between it and the forward funnel was greater, permitting the funnels to be of equal height. Note the *Pincher*'s after torpedo tube carried at the extreme after end.

ABOVE: HMS *Wolverine* is seen at Malta during World War I, with French warships in the background. The three Cammell-Laird built boats – the others being *Racoon* and *Renard* – had a pleasing (if inefficient) stern profile.

UNITED KINGDOM

LEFT: **With the Beagles came a far greater uniformity of design, with individual builders allowed less independence of Admiralty requirements. To improve their lethality against enemy torpedo boats they were the first to be given 4in guns.**

The proposed gun armament was five 12pdrs, two of which would be forecastle-mounted. In view of the German boats' 8.8cm weapons, this conservatism drew criticism, and a single forward 4in gun was substituted.

First to deploy 21in torpedoes, the Beagles had two centreline tubes, one of them right aft in a most unsatisfactory location. One spare torpedo was carried for each.

The steam turbine installation required a three-shaft arrangement, but all but one of the class comfortably exceeded the required 27-knot trial speed. All 16 Beagles were launched between October 1909 and March 1910, nine yards participating. Their final appearance varied widely.

Destroyers of this era were built in large numbers and in a rolling programme, the first of 20 follow-on Acorns going into the water just three months after the last of the Beagles. Progress will not be denied, and the principal difference was that the new ships were oil-fired. This was largely responsible for average displacement being reduced from about 950 to 760 tons, with a saving of some 12 per cent on initial cost, and with speed improved by nearly an extra knot.

"H" and "I" classes proved excellent seaboats. They served widely during World War I, particularly with the Grand Fleet and in the Mediterranean. In all, these groups totalled 59 boats yet, by the early 1920s, all had been scrapped.

ABOVE: **Like the *Larne* (above), the *Sheldrake* was actually an Acorn, or "H" class. Ships of the class were equipped with two single 21in torpedo tubes and they were oil-fired. Following only ten years of service, the class was sold as a block for scrapping.** BELOW: **The Royal Australian Navy was, at this time, dependent upon British-designed and built warships. Denny, at Dumbarton, Scotland, which had already built two Repeat Acorns and a "special", launched the similar HMAS *Yarra* in April 1910.**

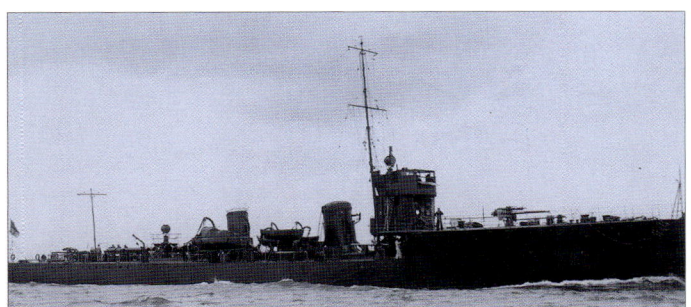

ABOVE: **To encourage innovation, the Admiralty ordered nine "specials" from three builders. One of a pair from Yarrow, the *Archer*, like the remainder, had so many contract strictures that very little improvement was effected.**

Repeat Acorn, or "I" class

Displacement: 760 tons light
Length: 73.1m/240ft (bp); 74.9m/246ft (oa)
Beam: 7.8m/25ft 8in
Draught: 2.7m/8ft 9in
Armament: 2 x 4in guns, 2 x 12pdr guns; 2 x 21in torpedo tubes (2x1)
Machinery: Direct-drive steam turbines, 3 shafts
Power: 11,040kW/14,800shp for 28 knots
Endurance: 178 tons oil for 4,260km/2,300nm at 13 knots
Protection: None
Complement: 71

71

DIRECTORY OF DESTROYERS: UP TO 1918

LEFT: Given the loose specification, and allowing seven builders considerable freedom in interpretation, while spreading the orders over three consecutive programmes, it is little wonder that the Tribals were something of a ragbag. Cammell Laird's *Cossack* is seen here. ABOVE: To achieve the requisite 33 knots, some Tribals had five boilers, others, such as the four-stack *Nubian* (seen here), six. Their puny 12pdr guns were criticized as being like "going elephant hunting with a snipe gun".

Tribal, or "F" class

Always revolutionary, Admiral Sir John Fisher, on becoming First Sea Lord in 1904, demanded big destroyers. Not only big, but fast. His requirements were stated simply – they should make 33 knots in a "moderate" sea, be oil-fired and self-sufficient for 7 days. To save weight, the heaviest guns would be 12pdrs.

Considering that yards at this time were constructing 25–26-knot Rivers of about 550 tons, this was a considerable evolutionary step. To realize the speed steam turbines, of which few builders yet had experience, were required. The necessary power demanded five or six boilers. For the sake of both speed and internal volume, a long hull was needed. For good seakeeping, a forecastle was desirable. Weight, however, was a problem, so in three cases (the seven builders were permitted considerable latitude), a turtledeck was substituted. In the remainder, forecastles were kept short and the hull scantlings very light – so light that all initial proposals were rejected pending further strengthening. Threatened with rejection for trials speeds of under 32 knots, builders' estimates were twice those for the Rivers.

The 12 hulls of what became the Tribals were launched between February 1907 and September 1909. As finished, they varied considerably, most having four funnels but one, the Palmers-built *Viking*, being the Navy's only-ever six funneller, with one for each boiler.

All exceeded 33 knots on trials, the *Tartar* actually making 35.36 knots. Their fuel economy was, however, poor, and for this reason the class found itself with the Dover Command rather than with the Grand Fleet. Here, they found themselves badly outgunned by the 10.5cm weapons of the German Flanders Flotilla. The Tribals were, therefore, upgunned to two 4in guns, although trials with a single 6in proved unsatisfactory.

Very much "specials", the nine surviving ships were quickly scrapped after the war.

ABOVE: Hawthorn Leslie's *Ghurka* was a short-hulled Tribal of the first batch. On a 6-hour trial she averaged over 33.9 knots but, as can be seen clearly, suffered excessively from "squat", which reduced speed in shallow water. She was sunk by a mine off Dungeness in February 1917.

Amazon, average for class

	Built	Commissioned
Amazon	Thornycroft	1909

Displacement: 970 tons (light)
Length: 85.4m/280ft 4in (bp)
Beam: 8.1m/26ft 8in
Draught: 3.1m/10ft 1in
Armament: 2 x 4in guns; 2 x 18in torpedo tubes (2x1)
Machinery: Direct-drive steam turbines, 6 boilers, 3 shafts
Power: 18329kW/24,570shp for 33.2 knots
Endurance: 200 tons oil for 3,890km/2,100nm at 15 knots
Protection: None
Complement: 67

UNITED KINGDOM

Acasta, or "K" class

LEFT: As the "K" class, the Acastas were intended originally to take "K" names. Thornycroft's *Porpoise* was thus allocated the name *Kennington*. Although dropped, the system was revived with the following "L" class. ABOVE: The Acastas were designed to screen the battle squadrons of the Grand Fleet. Three 4in guns were thus specified to stop enemy torpedo boats. *Unity*, here, shows the characteristic torpedo tube between second and third funnels. BELOW: The three John Brown boats could be distinguished by their shorter after funnels. *Achates* was one of the few to achieve the required 32 knots, although trials were run at displacements that varied between 903 and 1,071 tons.

Gunnery trials showed that a single hit from a 4in weapon did more damage than six from 12pdrs. One 4in gun weighed no more than two 2pdrs but required five fewer gun crew. As a single calibre also simplified logistics. The 12pdr disappeared in the Acasta class in favour of a third 4in, located between the after torpedo tube and the diminutive mainmast of the Acastas.

Experience had showed that over-running machinery through forced, rather than natural, draught for the boilers caused unreliability and mechanical failure. To achieve a required 29½ knots in the deep condition it was thus accepted that four boilers and three funnels would be necessary. The two boiler spaces were adjacent, the thicker centre funnel exhausting one boiler of each. The forward funnel was usually raised in order to keep products of combustion clear of the bridge.

Twelve Acastas (three from each of four builders) were ordered to a standard design, together with eight "specials" to allow the best builders to incorporate their own ideas. Complaints of inadequate endurance led several builders to suggest diesel engines for cruising. The extra complications – clutches, shafting, weight and cost – enthused neither the Navy's Engineer in Chief nor the Controller but, in the event, the still-nascent diesel industry proved unable to deliver what was required.

The *Ardent* was interesting in that Denny's framed her longitudinally, as opposed to the usual transverse construction. The Admiralty agreed to fund the extra work involved, the end result being a slightly lighter hull, whose enhanced stiffness reduced vibration.

During the course of World War I, several of the class surrendered an after 4in gun in favour of such as twinned torpedo tubes, anti-aircraft guns, kite-balloon arrangements or, increasingly, depth charges and throwers. Seven Acastas became war casualties.

Acasta class, standard design, as built

Displacement: 935 tons (light); 1,072 tons (full load)
Length: 79.2m/260ft (bp); 81.5m/267ft 6in (oa)
Beam: 8.2m/27ft
Draught: 2.8m/9ft 3in (deep)
Armament: 3 x 4in guns; 2 x 21in torpedo tubes (2x1)
Machinery: Direct-drive steam turbines, 4 boilers, 2 shafts
Power: 18,650kW/25,000shp for 30 knots
Endurance: 258 tons oil for 5,090km/2,750nm at 15 knots
Protection: None
Complement: 75

ABOVE: *Garland* has sent her whaler away for some rowing practice, boatwork then being more important than it is today. Note that, where her sisters here display no identifiers, *Garland* carries the "K" class letter. *Acasta* herself had "00" painted up.

73

Laforey, or "L" class

Essentially repeat Acastas, with a slightly increased beam, the 22 "L" class were still completing at the outbreak of World War I. They were the first destroyer class to adopt names based on the class letter.

In the Laforeys, No.2 4in gun was moved to an amidships position, the advantage of which is obscure, for its tubular, underdeck support now intruded into the after boiler space, while its ammunition supply had to be manhandled all the way from the forward magazine. The torpedo tubes were thus displaced farther aft and were, for the first time, twinned. No reloads were carried but all four weapons could now be fired at one time. For safety, their warheads were normally stowed below in a dedicated magazine space.

Despite the policy of greater standardization, there were still variations. Most apparent was, where the majority had three boilers and two funnels, some had four boilers and three funnels, displacing some 20 more tons on the same dimensions.

A significant technical advance lay in that two ships, *Leonidas* and *Lucifer*, had single-stage reduction gearing added downstream of their steam turbines. At normal full speed, this reduced shaft revolutions from an average of some 630rpm to about 370rmp. At lower rotational speeds, propellers can be designed for higher efficiency and the *Leonidas* was able to achieve the required trials performance while developing about 8 per cent less power. Comparative trials were run against *Lucifer*.

ABOVE: *Lucifer* was one of the class selected to trial single-stage gearing for the turbines. This nearly halved propeller speed for a significant increase in hydrodynamic efficiency. A further innovation in the Ls was twinned 21in torpedo tubes.

A further proposal, to provide a steadier fighting platform through the installation of passive, anti-roll tanks, was not progressed owing to the urgency of mobilizing the class for war.

The Laforeys saw much action, with the Harwich Force, at the Heligoland Bight, at the Dardanelles and at Jutland. Despite incurring heavy damage, however, none was lost to direct enemy action, but two to mines and one wrecked.

"L" class, average for class

Displacement: 995 tons (light); 1,115 tons (full load)
Length: 79.2m/260ft (bp); 81.9m/268ft 10in (oa)
Beam: 8.4m/27ft 8in
Draught: 2.9m/9ft 8in
Armament: 3 x 4in QF guns; 4 x 21in torpedo tubes (2x2)
Machinery: Direct-drive steam turbines, 3/4 boilers, 2 shafts
Power: 18,277kW/24,500shp for 29 knots
Endurance: 268 tons oil for 4,445km/2,400nm at 15 knots
Protection: None
Complement: 72 (3 boilers); 76 (4 boilers)

ABOVE: In other respects identical, "L" boats were either two- or three-funnelled, reflecting whether they had three or four boilers respectively. Both types had the same nominal power. *Liberty*, seen here, stemmed from J. Samuel White's yard at Cowes.

UNITED KINGDOM

"M" class

The destroyers of the 1913–14 Programme were important in that they were the last major pre-war design, greatly influencing the many war-built "standards" that followed. Again to match the reported speeds of German destroyers, they were required to make 34 knots, yet have a docking displacement small enough to allow two to be stemmed simultaneously in the Harwich floating dock.

A speed of 34 knots represented an increase of 4.5 knots on that of the still-building L-class boats, yet on a length of only about 1.2m/4ft greater and an extra 500shp. It was possible only by running trials with just 75 tons of oil (about 27 per cent) aboard, equivalent to 2½–3 knots extra.

With specifications based on those of preceding classes, three yards were building speculatively, on the understanding that orders would be forthcoming. Although they varied in length by about 0.5m/1ft 8in and in deep displacement by 172 tons, six of these boats (designated M-class "specials") were purchased by the Admiralty which went on to produce a standard M-class design, very much a mean of the above. Orders for seven of these were then placed with three builders.

The three Yarrow "specials" were, on average, the slowest of that group, but were of lighter and stiffer construction. Displacement, trim, the quality of stoking and the depth of water on the measured mile course all greatly influenced speed,

ABOVE: **The Ms were the first class since the 30-knotters to include ships with two, three or four funnels, the greater majority having three. The Admiralty "standards", such as** Murray**, had triple shafts, while the seven "specials" had twins.**

Thornycroft's *Mastiff* returning over 37 knots. The "specials" were of twin-screw design, the "standards", triple. Only one standard, *Moorsom*, bettered 34 knots.

Most boats had three boilers and three funnels. Four had four boilers, two boats having four funnels. The three Yarrow "specials" had only two funnels, that forward being heavily trunked to allow the bridge to be sited advantageously farther aft.

LEFT: **Heaviest of the first batch of Ms,** Mansfield **was a "special" from Hawthorn Leslie. Flying a Red Ensign, she is seen on trials. As with most Ms, the Admiralty's over-optimistic hopes for speed were not realized,** Mansfield **making only 33.7 knots average.**

Admiralty "standard" "M" class

Displacement: 900 tons (light); 1,150 tons (full load)
Length: 80.7m/265ft (bp); 83.3m/273ft 4in (oa)
Beam: 8.1m/26ft 8in
Draught: 2.9m/9ft 7in (deep)
Armament: 3 x 4in QF guns; 2 x 1pdr pompoms on HA mountings (2x1); 4 x 21in torpedo tubes (2x2)
Machinery: Direct-drive steam turbines, 3 boilers, 3 shafts
Power: 18,650kW/25,000shp for 34 knots
Endurance: 278 tons oil for 4,685km/2,530nm at 15 knots
Protection: None
Complement: 79

75

Contemporary Destroyer Leaders

Early Grand Fleet destroyer flotillas of World War I comprised twenty boats, organized in five divisions. Each four-boat division was divided into two subdivisions. Attached were two "scouts", 2,900-ton light cruisers with 4in armament and, usually, a Boadicea- or Gem-class light cruiser as Senior Officer's ("Captain (D)'s") ship. With the maximum speeds expected of the M-class destroyers, however, it was obvious that an attendant cruiser would be inhibiting. Designs were, therefore, called for an enlarged destroyer, not exceeding 1,800 tons but capable of over 33 knots and with an endurance superior to that of the boats that she would lead. Accommodation would be required for Captain (D) and his staff of eight or nine.

Signalling arrangements were to be the equal of those in the latest light cruisers. Four 4in guns would be supplemented by "two anti-airship pompoms".

The initial pair, at a little over 1,600 tons, were launched early in 1915. Their names, *Lightfoot* and *Marksman*, repeated the initial letters of their flotillas, but a repeat pair, *Kempenfelt* and *Nimrod*, made for an alphabetical sequence. As built, with a low bridge and four funnels of equal height, they had the purposeful appearance of miniature light cruisers, spoiled somewhat by sea experience necessitating the addition of an upper bridge and the raising in height of the forward funnel.

Before any of these ships was launched a further three were ordered,

ABOVE: *Kempenfelt* seen manoeuvring in company. Leaders were enlarged sufficiently to include accommodation for Captain (D) and his staff, an extra ten personnel. The greater size permitted increased power and a fourth main-calibre gun.

all from Cammell Laird, who were already building the *Kempenfelt*. These were given the angelic names of *Abdiel*, *Gabriel* and *Ithuriel*, and had a slightly larger displacement.

Abdiel's extra size saw her converted into a high-speed minelayer (as, later, was *Gabriel*). With torpedo tubes and two 4in guns landed, she could stow 80 contact mines on deck, although the resulting deeper draught reduced her maximum speed and endurance.

LEFT: With increasing numbers of leaders becoming available, several, including *Abdiel* (seen here), were converted to fast minelayers. To accommodate two rows, each of forty 682kg/1,500lb mines, two guns and all torpedoes had to be sacrificed.

Lightfoot class 🇬🇧

Displacement: 1,440 tons (light); 1,605 tons (full load)
Length: 96m/315ft (bp); 98.9m/324ft 10in (oa)
Beam: 9.7m/31ft 9in
Draught: 3.3m/10ft 9in (normal)
Armament: 4 x 4in QF (4x1); 2 x 2pdr pompoms (2x1); 4 x 21in torpedo tubes (2x2)
Machinery: Direct-drive steam turbines, 4 boilers, 3 shafts
Power: 26,856kW/36,000shp for 34.5 knots
Endurance: 515 tons oil for 7,960km/4,300nm at 15 knots
Protection: Thickened shell plating 11.1mm/⁷⁄₁₆in over machinery spaces
Complement: 105

UNITED KINGDOM

Emergency "M" class

The various options resulting from the 1913–14 M-class programme enabled the Admiralty to order large blocks of additional construction in order to rapidly expand the Grand Fleet destroyer force. Ninety hulls were acquired in five tranches; of these, eleven were "specials" from Thornycroft and Yarrow.

To achieve high speed, destroyers were very lightly built and, except where heavily stressed, plating was thin. Much was of only 6.35mm/¼in thickness, some even 4.76mm/³⁄₁₆in. It was essential to galvanize such plating before assembly, but war quickly brought shortages, including that of the necessary zinc. In the presence of salt water, ungalvanized 6.35mm/¼in plate could be penetrated by rust within three years. Weight considerations precluded any increase in thickness and the resulting poor condition of many destroyers by 1918 contributed to their rapid disposal.

Sixteen Admiralty "standards" and four Yarrow "specials" were ordered in September 1914. For the sake of rapid delivery, most lacked cruising turbines. The Yarrow boats had two, rather than the remainder's three, funnels, were slightly longer, and were capable of trial speeds of up to a reported 39 knots.

Nine further "standards" and one Yarrow "special" were ordered in November 1914, quickly followed by contracts for 22 more "standards". Most could, with a little coaxing, make 34 knots. Superficially, all were very similar, but the experienced eye could usually identify the products of individual builders through subtle variations in funnel section, rake of bow, stern profile, etc.

Orders for the fourth group, comprising 16 "standards" and two Thornycroft "specials" followed in February 1915, with 16 more "standards" and two each Thornycroft and Yarrow "specials" in the May. Thirteen yards were involved and all hulls bar one were in the water by November 1916.

TOP: *Orpheus* features the straight, vertical hance at the break of the forecastle, common to early destroyers. This sudden discontinuity resulted in a high-stress concentration in an already stressed shallow hull girder. ABOVE: Two of eight stemming from the Sunderland yard of Doxford, *Opal* is identical to her sister *Orpheus*. No standard pendant-numbering system existed at this time, with ships changing numbers on switching service.

Although still termed "M" class, destroyers of later groups carried names commencing "N" to "R".

Emergency, later Admiralty "standard" "M" class

Displacement: 1,025 tons (standard)
Length: 80.7m/265ft (bp); 83.4m/273ft 8in (oa)
Beam: 8.2m/26ft 10in
Draught: 2.6m/8ft 6in (light); 2.9m/9ft 6in (deep)
Armament: 3 x 4in QF guns; 1 x 2pdr pompom on HA mounting; 4 x 21in torpedo tubes (2x2)
Machinery: Direct-drive steam turbines, 3 boilers, 3 shafts
Power: 18,600kW/25,000shp for 34 knots
Endurance: 300 tons oil for 4,630km/2,500nm at 15 knots
Protection: None
Complement: 79

ABOVE: With the introduction of the blimp came aerial photography, as with this picture of *Patrician*. As a Thornycroft "special", she was given thicker, raking funnels. Note the two-stage hance, rendered less obvious by a canvas "dodger".

DIRECTORY OF DESTROYERS: UP TO 1918

"R" and Modified "R" classes

Even before hostilities commenced in 1914 the Controller, obviously concerned at the rapid growth in destroyers, and their increasing emphasis on gun, rather than torpedo, armament, proposed a smaller type of just 700 tons, with five torpedo tubes but only 12pdr guns. Essential builders were, however, desperately short of work and the quickest solution was to order further M-class vessels rather than develop a new concept.

As noted earlier in this section, two L-class destroyers had been completed with geared steam turbines. These were proving economical, so it was decided to put a similar installation into an M-type hull form, which would require only two shafts. The overall length would be slightly greater, as a slightly raked stem, combined with moderate flare and adequate freeboard, greatly improved seakeeping and dryness.

The initial order was for nineteen "standards" and seven "specials" from Thornycroft and Yarrow, the latter with direct-drive turbines proving to be faster but less efficient. All were launched in 1916–17, overlapping the orders for the second and third blocks. The second, placed in December 1915, was for eight "standards" and two "specials"; the third, of March 1916, was for twelve "standards" and three "specials".

The final block was for 11 Modified "R" class. All Rs had three boilers, necessitating one single and one double boiler space. In the modified design, these were transposed, the larger space now being the farther aft, adjacent to the engine room. This arrangement reduced survivability but, requiring only two funnels, permitted both bridge and forecastle to be located farther aft.

Despite many complaints from the crews about deteriorating standards of workmanship, which affected reliability and availability, the Rs proved to be good seaboats and were vital to the support of the battle fleet. Again somewhat perversely, the class names commenced with "R" through "U".

ABOVE: **The war-built classes were so numerous that, typically, these classes had names spanning "R", "S", "T" and even "U".** *Tyrant* **was one of seven Yarrow-built "specials" and is seen post-war, disarmed and with added structures for trials duties.**

LEFT: **The R-class** *Raider* **with pendants painted up post-war. The view emphasizes the very shallow depth of the hull. The two pairs of torpedo tubes are clearly shown, as is the afterdeck, now crowded with paravane gear and depth charges.**

Standard "R" class

Displacement: 890 tons (light); 1,223 tons (full load)
Length: 80.7m/265ft (bp); 84.1m/276ft (oa)
Beam: 8.1m/26ft 8in
Draught: 3m/9ft 10in (full load)
Armament: 3 x 4in QF guns; 1 x 2pdr pompom on HA mounting; 4 x 21in torpedo tubes (2x2)
Machinery: Single-reduction geared steam turbines, 3 boilers, 2 shafts
Power: 20,142kW/27,000shp for 36 knots
Endurance: 296 tons oil for 6,297km/3,400nm at 15 knots
Protection: None
Complement: 82

UNITED KINGDOM

LEFT: **The "S" class, whose names again commenced confusingly with either "S" or "T", marked a reversion to cheaper, simpler destroyers as an alternative to the very expensive "Admiralty Vs" then building. Note** Torbay's **long forward sheerline.** BELOW: **Not the Mediterranean of the travel brochures –** Tryphon **stranded in the Aegean during May 1919. Despite being towed to Malta, she was declared a total loss, and sold locally for scrapping.**

"S" class

Continual reports and rumours of the speed and firepower of German destroyers quickly brought about the evolution of the British "V" and "W" classes (see next pages). The Controller had earlier, but unsuccessfully, tried to revert to a simpler 700-ton boat with an enhanced torpedo armament and when, early in 1917, indications were that the enemy was, in fact, building only a few larger vessels, he proposed that Modified R-class boats would again be better value. Thus was agreed the Admiralty "S" class, a further derivative.

Sea experience with the Rs had resulted in recommendations for even higher freeboard and greater flare at the forward end. To save weight, the first was satisfied in the Ss with a sharply curved sheerline, which raised the stemhead by 61cm/2ft. To avoid the increased flare causing excessive width of forecastle deck, the sheer strake was given a distinctive radius.

Topweight being a chronic problem, the class reverted to an earlier, but lighter, mark of 4in gun. The pronounced forward sheer prevented the forecastle gun from firing in depression on forward bearings, but approval to locate it on a raised platform was refused.

The bridge structure had, by now, migrated aft to the point where it was all abaft the break of the forecastle, leaving a clear athwartship space beneath. For the high-speed, close-range encounters expected of Dover Command destroyers, two fixed 14in torpedo tubes had been shipped amidships by some. Grand Fleet boats saw little requirement for these but, nonetheless, early examples of the "S" class had two single 18in tubes sided at the break of the forecastle. They traversed through a limited angle and were in addition to the normal 21in torpedo armament.

Eleven Ss (and one R) survived to serve during World War II. Six remained in service in 1945.

LEFT: Sardonyx, **with four other Ss, survived the mass scrappings of the depression years to serve during World War II as Atlantic escorts, for which duty they were ill-suited. This 1920s picture shows her in a typical destroyer "nest".**

Admiralty-designed "S" class

Displacement: 1,075 tons (light); 1,225 tons (full load)
Length: 80.7m/265ft (bp); 84.1m/276ft (oa)
Beam: 8.1m/26ft 8in
Draught: 3.1m/10ft 4in (full load)
Armament: 3 x 4in/102mm QF guns (3x2); 1 x 2pdr pompom on HA mounting; 4 x 21in torpedo tubes (2x2); 2 x 18in torpedo tubes (2x1)
Machinery: Single-reduction geared steam turbines, 3 boilers, 2 shafts
Power: 20,142kW/27,000shp for 36 knots
Endurance: 300 tons oil for 5,090km/2,750nm at 15 knots
Protection: None
Complement: 84

79

"V" and "W" classes

By 1916 the growth of the fleet destroyer was such that yet another, even larger, leader was required. The earlier Lightfoots had been considered over-expensive, and the Admiralty now approved two, five-ship series for the purpose of comparison. Both were to prove influential.

Five (the Shakespeare class) were all by Thornycroft to their own design, which effectively set the pattern for British destroyers for nigh on two decades. Their major innovation was in the adoption of superimposed guns which, with suitable blast shielding, could be centreline-mounted, maximizing broadside fire without undue penalty in overall length.

On an identical trials displacement with the *Lightfoot*, the lead ship mounted the heavier 4.7in gun. While having a lower rate of fire, this weapon used a ship-stopping 50lb projectile in place of the 31lb shell of the 4in gun. With a fifth 4.7in carried between their two tall funnels, the Shakespeares were imposing ships, their size permitting also a single 3in

ABOVE: *Viceroy*, together with the *Viscount*, were a pair of Thornycroft "specials", recognizable through their larger after funnel. They boasted 10 per cent more power than could the Admiralty design, and were slightly beamier and deeper.

TOP: *Versatile*, marked up as a divisional leader of the then Atlantic Fleet's Fifth Destroyer Flotilla, was typical of a large number of near-identical "V & Ws", as they were invariably known. Note the minelaying track in a sponson right aft.

ABOVE: Retaining her full power but refitted with radar-equipped director, two twin 4in High-Angle (HA) mountings and multiple pompoms, *Verdun* gave valuable service to the east coast convoys as one of the "Wair" escorts.

High-Angle (HA) gun for use against aircraft or for firing starshell, and two triple banks of torpedo tubes.

More modest in scale (and 6.1m/20ft shorter on the waterline) were the five Admiralty-designed boats. Originally considered "300-foot leaders", they lost this distinction and adopted "V" names when it was decided to order 25 more. The original five were all launched between March and May 1917. They carried two pairs of superimposed 4in guns, and the two paired torpedo tubes of earlier classes.

Previous argument had revolved around the relative importance of gun and torpedo armament, but a new role had emerged in the need for anti-submarine escort. Space and weight margins thus had to be allowed, while 17 of the class were fitted for carrying over 50 mines apiece.

The initial order of "V"-named boats was followed in December 1916 by another for 21, mostly beginning with "W".

UNITED KINGDOM

The primary difference lay in their respective twinned and tripled torpedo tubes.

The "V & Ws", with their various combinations of thick and thin funnel, proved to be capable ships and, early in 1918, two blocks of what became known as "Modified V & Ws" were ordered. These differed in carrying the larger 4.7in gun. Of these later blocks, of 16 and 38 hulls respectively, only 9 and 7 were completed, the remainder being cancelled at the armistice, although many were well advanced.

Thornycroft "specials" continued to influence official opinion. Externally, they differed in having funnels of equal size, the after one flat-sided. They also had increased freeboard, although the bridge was already higher by virtue of having to maintain adequate vision over the superimposed "B" gun.

Barely a handful of the class was scrapped between the wars and when, in 1939, they entered what was for most their second war, the newest hull was 20 years old, and had deteriorated from years in reserve. No longer fleet destroyers and now, in their turn, considered small, the majority underwent conversion.

Fifteen became anti-aircraft escorts (generally known as "Wairs"), primarily to supplement the Hunts protecting the strongly contested English east coast convoys. These ships retained full propulsive power but landed at least one bank of torpedo tubes. Their four single guns were exchanged for a twin High-Angle, Dual-Purpose, (HA, DP) 4in mounting forward and aft, with multiple machine-guns or pompoms amidships. A more substantial bridge was fitted, supporting a radar-laid director, extra topweight which made for an easier roll movement.

Sixteen more of the class became long-range escorts for Atlantic convoys. The forward boiler was removed, still leaving adequate power for 24½ knots but releasing space for extra fuel tanks and accommodation for crews which, in wartime, increased from 115 to as many as 170. In this service they presented a very different appearance. The forward funnel was removed and at least one set of torpedo tubes and the two guns in "A" and "Y" positions landed. Air and surface-search radars, depth charges and throwers were added.

ABOVE: **One of the later "Repeat Ws",** *Worcester* **mounts the noticeably larger 4.7in gun. She is seen in about 1942 leading the earlier** *Walpole*; **by this time she had an enlarged bridge structure and forward funnel, even early radar.** BELOW: *Watchman* **as converted for long-range escort. Forefunnel and forward boiler have been removed. After torpedo tubes, and "A" and "Y" guns landed. Radar and "bow-chaser" added, the latter probably indicating coastal convoy attachment.**

LEFT: **Although by World War II considered small and obsolescent, the V & Ws played a noble role as Atlantic escorts, usually landing "A" and "Y" guns, together with after torpedo tubes, for increased capacity. Here, the radar-fitted** *Wanderer* **refuels at sea.**

"W" class, as built

Displacement: 1,100 tons (light); 1,460 tons (full load)
Length: 91.4m/300ft (bp); 95.1m/312ft (oa)
Beam: 9m/29ft 6in
Draught: 3.6m/11ft 8in (full load)
Armament: 4 x 4in QF guns (4x1); 1 x 3in HA gun; 6 x 21in torpedo tubes (2x3)
Machinery: Single-reduction geared steam turbines, 3 boilers, 2 shafts
Power: 20,142kW/27,000shp for 34 knots
Endurance: 370 tons oil for 4,815km/2,600nm at 15 knots
Protection: None
Complement: 115

ABOVE: **Immaculate in pre-war paint,** *Whirlwind* **has the lighter grey then worn by Mediterranean Fleet destroyers, to whose First Flotilla she is attached. Note the harbour "gash chute", rigged by the galley amidships.**

81

Early torpedo boats

Well before Tirpitz began to make his name as the architect of the Kaiser's new battle fleet, he was, as a Captain, appointed to be Inspector of Torpedo Development. At this time he was an enthusiastic supporter of the French *Jeune École* philosophy of defeating a major seapower with larger numbers of inexpensive torpedo craft. Instrumental in the establishment of a state torpedo factory and development facility, he also pressed for gun-armed "high seas" torpedo boats to be built in addition to coastal craft.

Prototype examples were obtained from domestic and foreign – including British – builders. Tirpitz's comment, on having been made responsible for developing a doctrine for their use, was that they "proved to be either unsuitable or inefficient".

Between 1890 and 1896 the Danzig firm of Schichau was given a monopoly of torpedo boat construction for the Imperial Navy, a period which saw displacements increase from generally 100 tons or less, to about 180 tons, with resulting improvements in seakeeping, in which the type was singularly deficient.

Even after other yards were permitted to build to official account, Schichau continued to turn out some of the best examples. A considerable advance over small, earlier craft was the S.67 design of 1894, of which seven were constructed, with nine improved follow-ons.

The writer Erskine Childers' description of a "low, grey rat of a vessel" in *Riddle of the Sands*, well fits the appearance of these craft, turtledeck forward with a depressed,

ABOVE: Completed in 1894, S.71 had three 45cm torpedo tubes. Later renamed T.71, she was given a second funnel and mast, serving throughout World War I as a tender and minesweeper. She was sold out in 1921. BELOW LEFT: Showing the flag on a Rhein cruise are three early Schichau torpedo boats of the numerous S.7 type, of which 50 were built. Less than 38m/124ft in length, they are fitted with a pronounced forward turtledeck.

protected conning position ahead of a single funnel. Two rotating centreline tubes aft were separated by a mast with torpedo derrick. A third tube was located in the forecastle, launching through the cutaway forefoot.

They were the last to be powered with the old-style locomotive boiler, pending the introduction of Thornycroft small-tube units.

S.67–73

Displacement: 135 tons (light); 163 tons (full load)
Length: 47.9m/157ft 3in (oa)
Beam: 5.4m/17ft 9in
Draught: 1.6m/5ft 4in (light); 2.6m/8ft 6in (full load)
Armament: 1 x 5cm gun; 3 x 45cm torpedo tubes (3x1)
Machinery: 1 x 3-cylinder triple-expansion engine, 1 boiler, 1 shaft
Power: 1,194kW/1,600ihp for 22 knots
Endurance: 30 tons coal for 2,025km/1,100nm at 15 knots
Protection: None
Complement: 21

Divisionsboote

By 1887 the Imperial German Navy had completed, or had under construction over 40 torpedo boats, with plans for many more. To control the, otherwise, unwieldy formations there was introduced the so-called "Division Boat", or flotilla leader. Although of twice the displacement of their charges, they suffered the usual shortcoming of contemporary small-scale reciprocating machinery not being capable of delivering sufficient power to make them significantly faster. Neither were they of much greater endurance.

Compare, for instance, the first, D.1, with S.41 of the same year (1887). Some 40 per cent larger, and with a second boiler, she had about 84 per cent more power yet, at 20.6 knots, had an advantage of barely half a knot. Succeeding boats, D.2–D.8, used small-tube (rather than locomotive) boilers, increasing speed by up to two knots. D.9 (1894) and D.10 (1896) were increased in size to accommodate a third boiler, the latter boat also adopting twin-screw propulsion to make 27 knots.

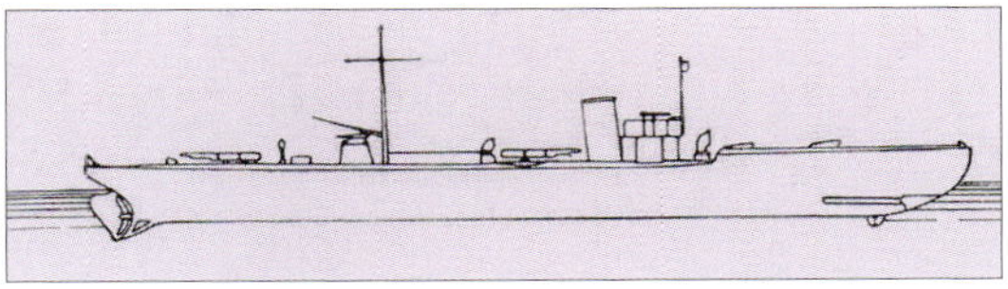

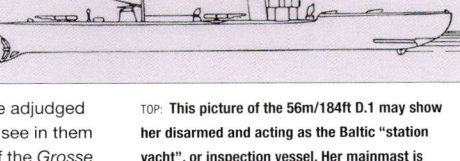

Although, as a type, Division Boats were adjudged disappointments, one can see in them quite clearly the genesis of the *Grosse Torpedoboote* (equivalent to Torpedo Boat Destroyer), which title was generally adopted after D.10.

Until D.8, Division Boats maintained the configuration of the smaller torpedo boats. Their forward turtle decks were very wet, and D.9 introduced the great improvement of a full-height forecastle. This terminated short of the bridge structure, leaving a diminutive well deck, somewhat lengthened in D.10. Their size also permitted them to carry further small-calibre guns.

In common with all early German flotilla craft, the D-boats had bow rudders, not held very effective when going ahead. All except D.1 had steel hulls, zinc-clad below water line.

As a comment on seakeeping, D.10 was known by her crew as *Schlingerpott* (roughly "rolling tub").

TOP: This picture of the 56m/184ft D.1 may show her disarmed and acting as the Baltic "station yacht", or inspection vessel. Her mainmast is unusually low and a flimsy bridge has been added.

ABOVE: D.9 dated from 1894. Note the bow torpedo tube and diminutive bow rudder. The unusual rudder arrangement was necessitated by the large-diameter single screw.

ABOVE: The Thornycroft-built D.10 shows British characteristics in appearance. The turtleback forms a low forecastle, abaft which is a gun platform which, unfortunately for the gun crews, creates an excellent breakwater.

D.10, as built

	Built	Completed
D.10	Thornycroft, Chiswick	1898

Displacement: 305 tons (light); 364 tons (full load)
Length: 64.3m/211ft 1in (wl); 66.1m/217ft (oa)
Beam: 6m/19ft 6in
Draught: 2.3m/7ft 6in (mean)
Armament: 5 x 5cm guns (5x1); 3 x 45cm torpedo tubes (3x1)
Machinery: 2 x 4-cylinder triple-expansion engines, 3 boilers, 2 shafts
Power: 4,290kW/5,750ihp for 27 knots
Endurance: 79 tons coal for 3,890km/2,100nm at 14 knots
Protection: None
Complement: 40

DIRECTORY OF DESTROYERS: UP TO 1918

LEFT: The Schichau-built S.120–124 dated from 1903–04, with S.123 seen here. Two of her three 45cm torpedo tubes were sided in the forward well deck. This arrangement allowed them to be used at finer angles on the bow. BELOW: Seen in what might be termed "fairly average" conditions for the North Sea, the Germania-built G.110 was one of a group of six built from 1900–02. Slightly larger than the S.123 (left), she was capable of the then high speed of 29.2 knots.

Grosse Torpedoboote (1902)

Good seakeeping is greatly influenced by length and by forward freeboard. Later Division Boats proved the point with short, full-height forecastles and the extra length necessary to accommodate a third boiler. They thus established the basic form of the German Large Torpedo Boat, i.e. Destroyer, which persisted through to the end of World War I.

On much the same length as a Division Boat, succeeding classes had their bridge structure moved a little farther aft. This made for drier bridges and also a forward well deck long enough to locate a single, centreline torpedo tube, capable of being trained on to either beam.

Three-boiler ships usually had two boiler spaces sited forward of the engine room, and one abaft it. There were two funnels, spaced widely to permit two more centreline tubes to be located between. The forward funnel and bridge were effectively a single structure, leading to a peculiar arrangement whereby the forward boiler exhausted via a curving trunk, which emerged from the well deck and passed beneath the bridge to join the forward funnel.

Sterns were subject to considerable variation in form in efforts to improve water flow across the propellers; "cruiser" sterns, "spoon" sterns and sloping profiles were all common.

German destroyers of this era were not named, being designated by the prefix "T" followed by a number allocated in order of construction. In general use, however, were the alternative prefixes "S", "V" or "G", denoting the major builders Schichau, Vulcan or Germania. Only the final two digits of the number were painted-up on the bows. Flotilla/division letters or numbers might be carried temporarily on the after funnel, or distinguishing day marks, e.g. triangles or rings, hoisted on the signal mast.

ABOVE: Persistent reports of 30-plus knot speeds by German torpedo boats proved to be a great spur to British development. The S.143 was one of twelve 70.7m/232ft boats dating from 1906–08, armed with 8.8cm guns and four 50cm torpedoes.

Grosse Torpedoboote, typical for type, as built

	Built	Completed
G.108–113	Germania Werft, Kiel	1902

Displacement: 324 tons (light); 432 tons (full load)
Length: 65.5m/215ft (wl); 65.8m/216ft (oa)
Beam: 6.7m/22ft
Draught: 2.3m/7ft 7in (light); 2.9m/9ft 6in (full load)
Armament: 3/4 x 5cm guns (3/4x1); 3 x 45cm torpedo tubes (3x1)
Machinery: 2 x 3-cylinder triple-expansion engines, 3 boilers, 2 shafts
Power: 4,476kW/6,000ihp for 29 knots
Endurance: 108 tons coal for 1,850km/1,000nm at 17 knots
Protection: None
Complement: 55

GERMANY

LEFT: **Vulcan at Stettin also produced many torpedo boats, including the two very similar groups V.150–155 and V.156–160, dating from 1907–08. Note how, although the bridges were well set back, they remained low to minimize silhouette.** ABOVE: **V.180 shows her generous forward freeboard. The forward well greatly reduced the amount of solid water impacting the bridge structure, though at a considerable price to the forward torpedo crews. Note the rounded, stress-reducing sheer strakes.**

Grosse Torpedoboote (1907–08)

The first destroyers to be ordered from the Vulcan yard at Stettin were V.150–161, completed in 1908. They were the last German boats to rely solely on coal-firing, while the last of the series, V.161, was the first to be propelled by steam turbines.

Similar in layout to earlier groups, they nonetheless had developed a more robust appearance. The well deck, with its single torpedo tube, was considered as a feature by the Royal Navy but was rejected on the grounds that the torpedo crew would be continuously inundated with water driving over the forecastle. Certainly the Germans tried various configurations of forecastle and breakwaters. The bridge structure, with its enclosed navigating bridge, extended the full width of the ship, its forward side slightly rounded to shed solid water the more easily. The two funnels were of large, round section, the forward one capped. Between them the hull was bare to allow the training of the two amidships torpedo tubes, themselves separated by a pair of massive engine room ventilators. A torpedo derrick was stepped on the tall mainmast, used for all flag signals. A vestigial foremast and large searchlight (the Germans took night-fighting seriously) crowned the wheelhouse roof. One 8.8cm gun was located on the forecastle, another right aft.

Spare torpedoes were often carried, unprotected, on the upper deck. Six of the class were later upgraded, the forward tube being twinned, and all changed for the heavier 50cm torpedo.

The experimental V.161 (later, T.161, all torpedo boats acquiring the standard "T" prefix) was propelled by two AEG direct-drive steam turbines. Her size and displacement were unchanged but her four boilers were of higher output, permitting speeds of up to 33 knots.

Vulcan followed up in 1909 with V.162–164, slightly enlarged and with one of their four boilers fired by diesel oil.

V.150–160, as built

	Built	Completed
V.150–160	AG Vulcan, Stettin	1907–08

Displacement: 548 tons (light); 670 tons (full load)
Length: 72.2m/237ft (wl); 72.5m/238ft (oa)
Beam: 7.8m/25ft 7in
Draught: 2.8m/9ft 3in (light); 3m/9ft 11in (full load)
Armament: 2 x 8.8cm guns (2x1); 3 x 45cm torpedo tubes (3x1)
Machinery: 2 x 3-cylinder triple-expansion engines, 4 boilers, 2 shafts
Power: 8,131kW/10,900ihp for 30 knots
Endurance: 161 tons coal for 3,700km/2,000nm at 14 knots
Protection: None
Complement: 81

ABOVE: **Still bearing her original H.190 pendant number, the Howaldt-built *Claus van Bevern* is seen as rebuilt for a "research vessel" in the late 1930s. Rearmed, she participated in the invasion of Denmark in April 1940.**

85

LEFT: The G.37 of 1915 survived what must have been a spectacular collision, not uncommon with fast-manoeuvring torpedo boats. On November 4, 1917, however, she was destroyed by a mine off the Dutch Friesian islands, and four of the crew were lost. BELOW Despite their very crowded appearance, the V.25 type (V.26 seen here) were able to accommodate 24 mines as deck load. As built, the bridge and forefunnel were considerably lower than seen here in their post-1916 reconfiguration.

Torpedoboote (1914–15)

Confusingly, all pre-1912 German torpedo boats, irrespective of builder, were renumbered in the coherent series to T.197 but, from 1912, the numbered series began again, each group assuming a prefix appropriate to one of the four major builders.

Between 1909 and 1911, successive groups had increased displacement to about 810 tons full load but the first three groups completed in 1912 (V.1–6, G.7–12 and S.13–24) retrenched to some 700 tons. All were turbine-propelled, the Schichau ships being consistently faster as well as carrying the heavier 10.5cm gun, which fired a 15kg/33lb shell.

The British Admiralty's continued concern at the reported performance of German destroyers appears well grounded for, while the Schichau boats were smaller than the contemporary Acherons, their legend speed was greater by about 5 knots. Their gun armament was also superior.

In 1914, the next group to be delivered, V.25–30, marked a further increase in size, being no less than 7m/30ft longer than the preceding class. This allowed them to carry six torpedo tubes, the after two mountings being twinned. The 8.8cm gun was, however, readopted, assisting in giving a stability margin sufficient to carry a deck load of 24 mines.

The final groups of the earlier series (T.186–191 and T.192–197) had adopted a "long forecastle" layout, the forecastle being narrowed on either side, forward of the bridge structure, sufficient to permit the location of a single torpedo tube per side, each training through a limited forward angle. This arrangement was adopted again in the 1914 Schichau boats, S.31–36. Four more, S.49–52, delivered in 1915, differed in having single-reduction geared turbines. Slightly larger than contemporary British M-class boats, they were of similar power but, reportedly, were some 2 knots faster. It is not certain, however, whether trials were conducted in the same deep condition as British ships.

V.25–30, as built

	Built	Completed
V.25–30	AG Vulcan, Stettin	1914

Displacement: 798 tons (light); 958 tons (full load)
Length: 77.8m/255ft 4in (wl); 78.5m/257ft 8in (oa)
Beam: 8.33m/27ft 4in
Draught: 3.33m/10ft 9in (light); 3.63m/11ft 11in (full load)
Armament: 3 x 8.8cm guns (3x1); 6 x 50cm torpedo tubes (2x1/2x2); 24 mines
Machinery: Direct-drive steam turbines, 3 boilers, 2 shafts
Power: 17,531kW/23,500shp for 36 knots
Endurance: 221 tons oil for 2,025km/1,100nm at 20 knots
Protection: None
Complement: 80

ABOVE: Despite her odd appearance, S.49's layout is practical. She has a short, high forecastle for dryness. The prominent casing exhausts the forward boiler and passes beneath the bridge to the forward funnel, allowing the bridge to be positioned well aft.

GERMANY

LEFT: **Howaldt at Kiel came late to German destroyer production, but their initial trio, H.145–147 completed in 1918, were among the largest. Still a new ship, H.145 was scuttled in Scapa Flow, only to be salvaged and scrapped in 1928.**

Torpedoboote (1917)

Wartime experience in the North Sea led, inevitably, to increasing destroyer size and, as in the Royal Navy, individual builders were allowed a degree of freedom to interpret a general specification in a manner totally unknown in the computer-controlled precision of today.

After 1915, Germania-built boats, e.g. G.37–42, had a loftier bridge structure, relocated to the after end of a lengthened forecastle, eliminating the forward well. The after end of the forecastle was tapered in to allow a single torpedo tube to be sited on either side. With the bridge moved, the boiler spaces were closed up and exhausted through two thicker and more closely spaced funnels. These adopted the sloped funnel cap that became a feature of German warships. All destroyers completed after 1914 were fully oil-fired.

After Jutland, in mid-1916, later German destroyers exchanged their 8.8cm guns for 10.5cm weapons carried by all new construction. This kept pace with the British, who had found that a 4in projectile was the smallest that had any chance of stopping a larger, modern destroyer.

Both pairs of torpedo tubes were now located abaft the funnels and separated by a bandstand supporting one of the three main guns. To the searchlights atop the bridge was added a second, conspicuously sited on a small house abaft the tall mainmast. Increased demands on signalling had also seen the foremast considerably heightened.

The bow rudder, a complication of doubtful utility, was being abandoned and a reasonably uniform "cruiser" stern adopted, although the form of this was often unclear due to many boats being fitted for minelaying.

Special "torpedo-boat steel" had been developed to withstand the high tensile stresses developed at sea in long, shallow hulls. Germania-built boats had double bottoms, some compartments of which were fuel tanks. It is not clear whether these could be flooded as ballast tanks.

ABOVE: **H.146 and her sister H.147 (seen here) were ceded to the French Navy post-war, becoming the *Rageot de la Touche* and *Delage* respectively and serving until 1935. The low freeboard, particularly forward, is very evident, while the bridge is located well forward.**

G.37–40, as rearmed

	Built	Completed
G.37–40	Germania Werft, Kiel	1915

Displacement: 807 tons (light); 1,031 tons (full load)
Length: 78.6m/258ft (wl); 79.5m/261ft (oa)
Beam: 8.4m/27ft 5in
Draught: 3.5m/11ft 4in (light); 3.7m/12ft 3in (full load)
Armament: 3 x 10.5cm guns (3x1); 6 x 50cm torpedo tubes (2x1/2x2); 24 mines
Machinery: Direct-drive steam turbines, 3 boilers, 2 shafts
Power: 17,904kW/24,000shp for 34.5 knots
Endurance: 295 tons oil for 3,130km/1,700nm at 17 knots
Protection: None
Complement: 84

87

DIRECTORY OF DESTROYERS: UP TO 1918

ABOVE: The six ex-Noviks, B.97–98 and B.109–112, were completed in 1915 but, in terms of armament, displacement and speed equated almost exactly to the two British Amazon prototypes, which were not launched until 1926.

RIGHT: Although wearing a naval ensign and displaying a circular flotilla day-shape at the mainmast, the B.97 appears to be unarmed in this picture. Of the six, she was the only one to have a post-war career, as the Italian *Cesare Rossarol*.

Expropriated destroyers

Warships building to foreign account are commonly taken over by governments faced with imminent hostilities. The Imperial German Navy thus benefited by the official expropriation of destroyers building for Tsarist Russia and Argentina.

Domestic classes, whether *Kleine* or *Grosse Torpedoboote*, tended to be popularly termed, simply, *Torpedoboote*. The above acquisitions were, however, so much larger that the prefix *Grosse* was invariable. They were, it could be claimed, among the German Navy's first true fleet-type destroyers.

The Hamburg yard of Blohm and Voss, not then associated with destroyer construction, had six of its own design, the Novik class, under construction at the outbreak of war. Under the German flag they were designated B.97–98 and B.109–112. All were completed in 1915 and, despite design deficiencies, emphasized the shortcomings of average size under North Sea conditions, influencing the move toward larger domestic designs. Their size permitted them to be fitted with passive, anti-rolling tanks.

Powered by four boilers, each had three, equispaced funnels, the foremost of which was later raised. As built, four 8.8cm guns were fitted, all on the centreline but in varying positions. In 1916, these were exchanged for 10.5cm weapons. All were of the short forecastle and well deck layout.

Marginally smaller were the four Argentine destroyers building at Germania. Their intended names of *Santiago*, *San Luis*, *Sante Fé* and *Tucuman* became, simply, G.101–104 on their completion in 1915. Although lacking a well deck, their forecastles were still short. They were the only wartime German destroyers with both bridge structure and forward funnel located on the forecastle deck. The navigating bridge was thus substantial and enclosed. As with the Russian boats, all were retrospectively upgunned.

Of the above twelve destroyers, no less than ten terminated their careers in the mass scuttling of the High Seas Fleet at Scapa Flow in 1919.

ABOVE: Closely resembling, in form and size, the Blohm and Voss boats (above) were the Vulcan-built pair, V.99 and V.100. V.99 was badly damaged in the Baltic, coincidentally by the existing Russian destroyer *Novik*, before sinking on mines.

B-type, average as rearmed

	Built	Completed
B.97–98 and B.109–112	Blohm and Voss, Hamburg	1915

Displacement: 1,350 tons (light); 1,812 tons (full load)
Length: 96m/315ft 2in (wl); 98m/321ft 8in (oa)
Beam: 9.4m/30ft 9in
Draught: 3.4m/11ft 2in (light); 3.8m/12ft 6in (full load)
Armament: 4 x 10.5cm guns (4x1); 6 x 50cm torpedo tubes (2x1/2x2); 24 mines
Machinery: Direct-drive steam turbines, 4 boilers, 2 shafts
Power: 29,840kW/40,000shp for 36.5 knots
Endurance: 516 tons oil for 4,815km/2,600nm at 20 knots
Protection: None
Complement: 110

88

GERMANY

LEFT: Laying astern a Bretagne-class battleship, the size of the *Amiral Sénès* ex-S.113 can be appreciated. She served as a flotilla leader in the French Navy until 1936. ABOVE: The S.113 and her completed sister V.116 introduced the 15cm gun to World War I German destroyers. In this shot, again as the French *Amiral Sénès*, her low freeboard is evident. The anchor is recessed to reduce spray.

S.113-type leaders

Launched in 1907, the British leader *Swift* proved to be an over-ambitious one-off. Her 2,200 tons and her ability to maintain 35 knots were, however, impressive. Less so was the 6in gun that she carried for a trial period.

The advantages of larger hulls were further impressed on the German Navy from 1915 in its operation of expropriated foreign destroyers. In 1916, therefore, all four major builders were each given an order for a trio of ships of exceptional size. Although most were never completed, data suggests that the builders had a degree of freedom in interpreting the specification.

Although probably intended as leaders, they attracted little priority; all were laid down in 1916 but only two were ever completed, a lead ship from each of Schichau (S.113) and Vulcan (V.116). Uniquely, they carried four single 15cm guns, one forward, one amidships and two right aft, one of which was superimposed. Large guns are notoriously difficult to lay accurately from small hulls, while manual loading of the 45kg/100lb projectiles on a lively deck would tax the best of gun crews.

Another "first" was two pairs of 60cm torpedo tubes, one mounting being located between the two funnels, the other forward of the mainmast.

They developed as much power as a contemporary light cruiser, yet failed to meet designed speed. Even without their intended deck load of mines, they were described as "crank". Both completed ships were surrendered as reparation, S.113 serving at the French *Amiral Sénès* and V.116 as the Italian *Premuda*.

LEFT: Seen at Wilhelmshaven is the 1918-completed S.131, leadship of a class of mine-destroyers that reverted to smaller dimensions and the handier 10.5cm gun. Note how the bridge is elevated to allow solid water to pass beneath.

S.113-type, as designed

Name	Builder	Displacement*	Length (oa/beam)
S.113–115	Schichau	2,372	106 x 10.2m/347ft 11in x 33ft 6in
V.116–118	AG Vulcan	2,318	107.5 x 10.4m/352ft 10in x 34ft 2in
G.119–121	Germania	2,362	107.5 x 10.3m/352ft 10in x 33ft 9in
B.122–124	Blohm and Voss	2,312	108.8 x 10.3m/357ft 2in x 33ft 9in

* Tons, full load

S.113, as designed

Displacement: 2,023 tons (light); 2,372 tons (full load)
Length: 105.4m/346ft (wl); 106m/347ft 11in (oa)
Beam: 10.2m/33ft 6in
Draught: 3.4m/11ft 2in (light); 4.8m/15ft 9in (full load)
Armament: 4 x 15cm guns (4x1); 4 x 60cm torpedo tubes (2x2); 40 mines
Machinery: Single-reduction geared steam turbines, 4 boilers, 2 shafts
Power: 33,570kW/45,000shp for nearly 37 knots
Endurance: 707 tons oil for 4,630km/2,500nm at 2 knots
Protection: None
Complement: 168

DIRECTORY OF DESTROYERS: UP TO 1918

LEFT: USS *Thornton* (TB.33) belonged to the nine-ship Shubrick class, the last torpedo boats built for the US Navy. Note that the machinery space was located between the boiler rooms. The multi-masted coastal schooners were very much a feature of the American scene. BELOW: Threatened by no foreign power, the United States showed little interest in coastal torpedo boats, the appropriately named *Cushing* (TB.1) not appearing until 1890. Although equipped with quadruple-expansion machinery, she was as frail as early European craft.

Early torpedo boats

The advisory board of the US Navy supported the acquisition of up to 150 torpedo boats for the protection of major bases and seaports. It also appreciated that an American battle fleet, operating in foreign waters, might need to defend itself against hostile torpedo attack. Also recommended, therefore, was that major warships should, themselves, carry torpedo launches, or what elsewhere would be termed Second-class Torpedo Boats.

Funds, however, were scarce, priorities laying elsewhere, and the first torpedo boat, USS *Cushing* (TB.1), was not completed until 1890. She was built largely to the ideas of her constructor, Herreshoff and, although her 23 knots were not impressive, the Navy was determined to develop domestic expertise. The department thus further developed Herreshoff's design for TB.2. Named *Ericsson*, she went to a different builder. Both craft carried three tubes to launch 18in Whitehead torpedoes.

Half a dozen yards quickly became involved each, as in Great Britain, being permitted considerable interpretation of the basic specification. In these pre-Panama Canal days, it was necessary to build ships on the east or west coast where they would serve.

A total of 35 torpedo boats was eventually built, comprising 17 separate designs. Except for the one-off *Rowan* (TB.8), which had a short, full-height forecastle, all followed the general pattern of minimum profile, with a turtledecked forward end. A displacement of 175 tons was considered optimum but, although some boats exceeded 30 knots on trials, it was thought desirable to sacrifice a little on maximum speed in order to strengthen what proved to be fragile hulls.

None had superstructures, the main features being two or three funnels and a light signal mast, all heavily raked, some collapsible. Both forward and aft were low, protected conning positions.

The nine-ship Shubrick class, the only extended group, concluded torpedo boat construction in 1901.

ABOVE: The Herreshoff-designed *Porter* (TB.6) came early in the sequence, yet it is clear that the Shubricks were only an extrapolation of her design. Despite the turtledeck forward, there is no raised forecastle, the hull having a hogged appearance.

Shubrick class, average

	Builders	Completed
TB.27–35	Various	1899–1901

Displacement: 165–220 tons
Length: 53.3m/175ft (oa)
Beam: 5.4m/17ft 9in
Draught: 2m/6ft 6in
Armament: 3 x 6pdr guns; 3 x 18in torpedo tubes (3x1)
Machinery: 4-cylinder triple-expansion engines, 2 shafts
Power: 2,238kW/3,000ihp for 25 knots
Endurance: Not known
Protection: Minimal
Complement: 28

Bainbridge (DD.1) class

With little prospect that the US battle fleet would be threatened by hostile torpedo craft, there existed no apparent requirement for the newly developing "torpedo boat destroyer". In the course of the 1898 war with Spain, however, three of the latter's destroyers steamed to Cuba, proving their capacity to cross the Atlantic. Although they were subsequently eliminated, their action was sufficient to galvanize the US Navy into acquiring its own. As politicians periodically have to relearn, warships cannot be conjured up by emergency bills, and the war was history by the time that the first American destroyer was commissioned in 1902.

The sixteen ships of the pioneer Bainbridge class (DD.1–16) comprised four distinct subgroups. The official design, to which nine were built, included a full-height forecastle to improve seakeeping. Sufficient latitude was, however, given to enable other builders to dispense with this feature in favour of a torpedo boat-style turtledeck forward. At the expense of wetness and cramped quarters, this measure saved weight which could be used to work in heavier hull scantlings.

All sixteen had four funnels. Except for those in DD.8 and 9, which were close-grouped, these were arranged in two widely spaced pairs, a visual indication of two boiler spaces separated by the engine room. The two reciprocating engines reportedly vibrated badly at high speeds; this, in conjunction with generally over-weight construction, resulted in their failing contract speed by as much as 1½ knots.

Compared with the Royal Navy's exactly contemporary "30-knotters", the Bainbridges were larger but carried the same scale of armament. Despite their disappointing maximum speed, they proved to have an unexpectedly high endurance at cruising speeds. Their extra size also conferred adequate seakeeping and this, with their robust construction, made them a suitable model for extrapolation.

ABOVE: The Spanish–American War had been fought before the US Navy received its first true destroyers. These, the 16-strong Bainbridge class, fell into four subgroups. This is *Truxtun* (DD.14). LEFT: Detail of one of *Perry*'s (DD.11) two single, revolving 18in torpedo tubes emphasizes the still-simple construction and the continuing spindle shape of the weapons themselves. The tube is located right aft. BELOW: The nine-strong "Bainbridge" group differed from the Truxtuns in having a raised forecastle. Although lighter and smaller, they were slower. The *Preble*'s (DD.12) forward 6pdrs are sided, firing ahead along the faceted sides of the forecastle.

ABOVE: This shot of *Worden* (DD.16), a sister of *Truxtun*, emphasizes the length and lack of depth of hull common to early destroyers. A corresponding lack of stiffness led to considerable deflection and "working", while machinery-induced vibration was magnified.

"Official" type

	Builders	Commissioned
DD.1–5/DD.10–13	Various	1902–03

Displacement: 414 tons (light); 450 tons (full load)
Length: 74.4m/244ft 3in (wl); 76.1m/249ft 10in (oa)
Beam: 7.1m/23ft 5in
Draught: 2.1m/6ft 9in (full load)
Armament: 2 x 3in guns; 5 x 6pdr guns; 2 x 18in torpedo tubes (2x1)
Machinery: Triple-expansion steam engines, 4 boilers, 2 shafts
Power: 5,968kW/8,000ihp for 28 knots
Bunkers: 212 tons coal
Protection: None
Complement: 71

LEFT: **Rapidly eclipsed by larger types, the very similar Smith and Paulding classes were popularly known as "Flivvers".** *Perkins* **(DD.26), like all built by Fore River, had three funnels rather than four. Note heavy W/T spreaders and World War I camouflage.**

Smith (DD.17) and Paulding (DD.22) classes

An eight-year hiatus followed completion of the Bainbridges. While this was due primarily to lack of funding, it gave the service time to evaluate what it already had, before deciding the way ahead. It was by now accepted that the battle fleet would usually have to be accompanied by destroyers. If the latter were to be asset, rather than liability, ruggedness and reliability had to be their main attributes.

A specially convened board of 1905 recommended that all future destroyers run trials in realistic loaded condition, rather than aiming simply for maximum speed. Seakeeping, strength, wetness and manoeuvrability were emphasized. For survivability, boiler spaces should be separated by the engine room.

While still effectively being stretched Bainbridges, the five Smiths (DD.17–21), authorized in 1906–07, incorporated these requirements. Their four funnels grouped distinctively by builder, the "Flivvers", as they were popularly known, emphasized gun armament at the expense of torpedoes. Of the five 3in guns, three fired forward while two were located on the centreline, aft. One centreline 18in torpedo tube was also sited well aft, with a further single tube on either side amidships. All the class were steam turbine-propelled, the resulting difficulties in designing fast-turning propellers probably accounting for the requirement for a third shaft.

A further eight units, authorized in 1908, became the Paulding (DD.22) class. Two further orders extended this class eventually to 21 ships. During "prohibition" most of these were transferred to the Coast Guard.

Although of the same basic dimensions as the Smiths, the Pauldings were some 50 tons heavier. Their resulting deeper draught was more than compensated by an increase of 20 per cent in power and an extra 1½ knots. Oil firing was also adopted. The same gun armament was carried but all three torpedo tube mountings were twinned.

ABOVE: **During "prohibition", the US Navy transferred 13 of these classes to its Coast Guard sister service. As with** *Paulding* **(DD.22), they retained names but adopted new temporary numbers. Note that she has retained the "North Atlantic" front to the bridge structure.**

Paulding class

	Built	Commissioned
DD.22–42	Various	1910–12

Displacement: 742 tons (light); 897 tons (full load)
Length: 88m/289ft (wl); 89.6m/294ft (oa)
Beam: 8m/26ft 2in
Draught: 2.5m/8ft 3in (full load)
Armament: 5 x 3in guns (5x1); 6 x 18in torpedo tubes (3x2)
Machinery: Direct-drive steam turbines, 4 boilers, 3 shafts
Power: 8,952kW/12,000shp for 29.5 knots
Endurance: 241 tons oil for 5,556km/3,000nm at 16 knots
Protection: None
Complement: 89

UNITED STATES

LEFT: *Cummings* (DD.44) of the Cassin class. These and the Tuckers were the first "Thousand Tonners". Twin-screwed, they were experimental in machinery, with geared steam turbines, some with auxiliary cruising turbines or reciprocating engines.

Cassin (DD.43) and Tucker (DD.57) classes

Even before the final "Flivvers" were completed, the characteristics of the succeeding class were being assessed. Having accepted that the very high speeds of some foreign destroyers were unnecessary, the General Board (now responsible for ship definition) looked instead for long endurance. This, ideally would match that of the capital ships that they were intended to escort. Speed (defined as 30 knots for 1 hour) was necessary in order to manoeuvre independently and to regain station, but size was a parameter that really decided a destroyer's ability to *maintain* station.

Size was also of interest in the argument (common with that in other fleets) as to whether a destroyer screen was essentially defensive (emphasizing gun armament) or offensive (torpedoes). The response was to add a further pair of torpedo tubes and to upgrade the 3in gun armament to 4in, better able to stop larger contemporary destroyers.

Problems were still being experienced with matching the high shaft speeds associated with direct-drive steam turbines with efficient propeller design. Some of the next class – the 14 Cassin (DD.43–56) – were thus given auxiliary turbines or reciprocating engines for cruising. The permanent answer lay, of course, in single-reduction gearing for the main turbines, but this was introduced only in the *Wadsworth* (DD.60), a unit of the 12-strong Tucker class (DD.57–68).

Known for obvious reasons as the "Thousand Tonners", the Cassin carried four 4in guns, two of them sided on the main deck at the break of the forecastle. The after, centreline torpedo tubes location having proved impractical, their four twin mountings were now sided farther forward.

About 3m/10ft longer, and displacing an extra 80 tons, the Tuckers differed primarily in having geared turbines and in carrying the heavier 21in torpedo. The final half-dozen of the class were given four triple mountings.

ABOVE: Taking her place in a fleet review, the *Benham* (DD.49) is seen in peacetime dark Atlantic Fleet grey. Not for the first or last time, the "Thousand Tonners" were heavily criticized as being over-large for destroyer duties, the Tuckers showing growth in size and power over the Cassins.

Tucker class

	Built	Commissioned
DD.57–68	Various	1916–17

Displacement: 911 tons (light); 1,132 tons (full load)
Length: 94.4m/310ft (wl); 96m/315ft 3in (oa)
Beam: 9.1m/29ft 10in
Draught: 2.9m/9ft 7in (full load)
Armament: 4 x 4in guns (4x1); 8/12 x 21in torpedo tubes (4x2/4x3)
Machinery: Single-reduction geared steam turbines, 4 boilers, 2 shafts
Power: 13,055kW/17,500shp for 29.5 knots
Endurance: 290 tons oil for 4,630km/2,500nm at 20 knots
Protection: None
Complement: 99

The "Flush-Deckers"

If size bought increased comfort and firepower, it failed to please all the destroyer community. They saw their role as offensive. A torpedo attack on an enemy battle line was considered so hazardous that it was likely that only one salvo could be fired before being disabled. Sided torpedo tubes, therefore (ran the argument), were less use than a powerful centreline battery. To reduce the target profile, destroyers should be *smaller*. An 800-tonner with nine centreline tubes was proposed, but the General Board refused it on the grounds that torpedoes could contact the deck edge on being fired, while the ship would be unable to carry 4in guns.

Instead, the Board proposed a ship of the same basic dimensions as the preceding Tucker class, but with a flush deck in place of a raised forecastle. The freeboard at the stem head would be similar but this would decrease in a straight sheerline to the after end, where it would be about 2m/6ft less. This conferred a much higher modulus amidships, with a cross section better suited to improved steadiness.

TOP: *Stockton* (DD.73) of the Caldwell type was one of just three of the many "Flush-Deckers" to have three funnels. She also became one of the 50 to be transferred to the Royal Navy in 1940, becoming HMS *Ludlow*. She was scrapped in 1945. ABOVE: The ambitious programme of Flush-Deckers, otherwise known as "Four Pipers" was meant to triple the US Navy's destroyer strength, but was badly delayed by a shortage of gear-cutting facilities. Converted for minelaying, the *Burns* (DD.171) was scrapped in 1932.

In keeping four, sided triple torpedo tube mountings, it was necessary to move the two 4in waist guns on to a new amidships deckhouse. As this arrangement proved to be wetter, with solid water in the waist, bulwarks were run forward from the deckhouse to meet the full-width bridge screen.

Six ships (the Caldwell class, DD.69–74) were authorized early in 1915. They had varying combinations of twin- and triple-screw propulsion, and three or four funnels.

The lead ship was launched in July 1917. By this time, the United States had entered the war, only to discover the urgent need for large numbers of Anti-Submarine (AS) ships to defeat the all-out German submarine offensive. Although not designed for this role, the *Caldwell* drawings were immediately available, a staggering 273 hulls being ordered for series production. Only six were eventually cancelled but, having been initiated so

ABOVE: During World War II, 26 Flush-Deckers were converted to Fast Transports (APDs). *Rathburne* (APD.25, ex-DD.113) shows her restyled bridge structure, just two remaining funnels, and four LCPRs (Landing Craft, Personnel, Ramped) in davits in lieu of torpedo tubes.

late in the war, the programme realized less than 40 new ships by the time of the Armistice.

The building rate was slowed through lack of gear-cutting capacity, so some ships were fitted with cruising turbines, others with direct-drive main turbines. Machinery and boilers were from a variety of sources, affecting reliability and efficiency figures. Rapid yard expansion resulted in widely varying standards of workmanship.

The first block of "flush-deckers" were known as the Wickes class (DD.75–185), which were succeeded by the Clemson type (DD.186–347), which were of higher power and which could stow one-third more fuel.

Ships were completed with a couple of 1pdr Anti-Aircraft (AA) guns, exchanged later for one 3in High-Angle (HA) weapon. Depth charges were a further new addition, their stowage ill-suited to the very narrow sterns of the ships. There were two racks and one projector, known as a "Y Gun". As many were also fitted as high-speed minesweepers, the standard canoe stern was often greatly modified.

Operating closely with their British counterparts, the flush-deckers were inevitably compared. Their crews considered them to ride better in the winter seas encountered around the British Isles, although this was really a matter of the relationship between ship length and wave length at a particular time. They appeared to be more susceptible to structural damage and were definitely less handy, having large turning circles. By 1918, too, the Royal Navy had progressed to the far superior "V & W" classes.

Although already obsolescent, new flush-deckers continued to be commissioned until 1921, their numbers guaranteeing a long domination of the US Navy's destroyer strength. Even with inter-war disposals, sufficient survived for 50 to be transferred to the British flag in 1940, a further 120 serving in the US Navy. Now referred to as "Four Pipers", about two-fifths of them were modified to non-destroyer roles, such as high-speed transports (APDs), or ocean escorts.

ABOVE: **Although completed after World War I, a sub standard block of Flush-Deckers, including the *Selfridge* (DD.320), was scrapped during the early 1930s. The unusual wave formation has probably been caused by the close proximity of another vessel.** BELOW: ***Manley* (DD.74) was the very first Flush-Decker to be completed. Here, she has landed her torpedo tubes, probably to acquire four light assault craft for a Marine company in a pre-war conversion. She became the prototype high-speed transport (APD) during 1940.**

ABOVE **Long before the days of modularization, the Mare Island Navy Yard was able to commission the *Ward* (DD.139) just 70 days after her laying-down. In sinking a Japanese midget submarine outside Pearl Harbor, she fired the first shots in the Pacific War.**

ABOVE: **Five Clemsons alongside their tender about 1930. Such a spell made a welcome break from "hard-lying". Fires could be drawn and services supplied by "Mother". There were hot baths, and hot food eaten from tables that did not roll and pitch.**

Clemson class

	Built	Commissioned
DD.186–347	Various	1918–21

Displacement: 1,125 tons (light); 1,584 tons (full load)
Length: 94.4m/310ft (wl); 95.7m/314ft 3in (oa)
Beam: 9.4m/30ft 11in
Draught: 2.9m/9ft 7in (full load)
Armament: 4 x 4in guns (4x1); 1 x 3in HA; 12 x 21in torpedo tubes (4x3)
Machinery: Single-reduction geared steam turbines, 4 boilers, 2 shafts
Power: 20,142kW/27,000shp for 35 knots
Endurance: 370 tons oil for 4,630km/2,500nm at 20 knots
Protection: None
Complement: 135

Torpedo cruisers

Pre-dating by a decade both its torpedo boats and destroyers, the so-called "torpedo cruisers" of the Italian Navy were, at a little less than 1,000 tons displacement, of about the same size as a 1917 destroyer.

The Elswick cruiser *Giovanni Bausan*, of 1885, impressed the Italians with the potential of her 17 knots and three torpedo tubes. Three domestic versions of the ship were authorized but their expense caused the then Minister of Marine, the gifted Benedetto Brin, to design the same capability into a vessel on one third the price.

His "torpedo cruiser" *Tripoli*, initially capable of 19 knots, was completed in 1886, and carried five 14in torpedo tubes. An attractive little vessel, she featured a ram bow and a mercantile-style counter stern. Her raised forecastle and long, low afterdeck, offset by two capped and boldly raked funnels, gave her a profile that anticipated by over 20 years that of a classic destroyer.

As was common, however, her high-speed reciprocating machinery was trouble-prone and, by 1897, the *Tripoli* was reduced to a minelayer.

In 1888 a class of eight follow-ons had been authorized. These, the Partenope type, were of a similar size but only one of them (*Caprera*) was built with a forecastle. Their two, heavily raked funnels were widely spaced, indicating boiler spaces separated by the engine room. They carried up to six of the heavier 17.7in torpedo tubes; four rotatable tubes were sided on the upper deck, one was fixed and fired through the stem and (in six ships only) another fired through the stern.

Still capable of only 20 knots, they were really too slow for the task and were superseded by torpedo boats. Five had been discarded by 1914 while two of these remaining had been given forecastles in the course of conversion into minelayers.

ABOVE: *Monzambano*, and her sister *Goito*, retained features of "transitional" warships in the bridge structure being amidships and in the rigging detail. The two pedestals aft support a spotlight and the magnetic compass.

LEFT: When completed in 1886, the *Tripoli*'s 19 knots was considered very fast. Reciprocating machinery does not, however, tolerate prolonged fast running, and within a decade the ship was one of many to be converted for minelaying.

ABOVE: As built, *Partenope* was flush-decked, with turtlebacked foredeck, bridge just forward of the after funnel, and two lofty masts. Converted into a minelayer from 1906–08, she gained the prominent forecastle and relocated bridge.

Partenope type, as built

Displacement: 831 tons (light); 993 tons (full load)
Length: 70m/229ft 9in (bp); 73.9m/242ft 7in (oa)
Beam: 8.2m/26ft 11in
Draught: 3.4m/10ft 2in (light); 3.7m/12ft 2in (full load)
Armament: 1 x 4.7in gun, 6 x 2.2in guns; 5/6 x 17.7in torpedo tubes (5/6x1)
Machinery: 3-cylinder triple-expansion engines, 4 boilers
Power: 2,984kW/4,000ihp for 20 knots
Endurance: 167 tons coal for 3,333km/1,800nm at 10 knots
Protection: 25–40mm/0.98–1.58in protective deck
Complement: 11

ITALY

LEFT: *Olimpia*, of the Orione class, shows her attractive lines. Abaft the breakwater is a protected conning tower and two sided torpedo tubes. A second conn and third centreline torpedo tube flank the mainmast.

High seas torpedo boats

The Italian Navy acquired a force of 29 "high seas" torpedo boats (*torpediniere d'alto mare*) in a commendably short space of time. They were led by six Saffo-class boats, designed and built by the German specialist builder Schichau. Of 206 tons and 50m/164ft on the waterline, they were all launched in 1905 and resembled closely those being built for the Imperial German Navy. Designed with the lowest possible profile, they had a single lofty funnel (necessary with natural draught), two light signal masts and a combined navigation platform and searchlight pedestal atop the low forward conning position. A second conn, also lightly protected, was located aft. A slightly raised forward turtledeck was kept largely clear of spray-inducing clutter. Only three light guns, all of 47mm calibre, were specified. Of these, one was located aft and the others were sided in the waist. The three 17.7in torpedo tubes were all centreline-mounted. The class was later remodelled around two tubes and a pair of 57mm guns.

Italy also obtained a licence to build three groups of Thornycroft-designed craft of virtually the same size as those from Schichau. Slightly finer in form, the four Pegaso type of the first group were built over much the same time scale. Externally they differed primarily in having two funnels and a much shorter turtleback. A very light navigating platform was sited just forward of the forward funnel, well back from the bows. Deck space was saved by siding the forward tubes immediately abaft the turtleback, although this reduced a torpedo salvo to only two, compared with the Schichau boat's three.

They were succeeded by eight similar Cigno (1906–09) and six Alcione (1906–07) types. All coal-burners, they were later converted to oil firing. The four domestically designed Orione type (1906–07) differed mainly in having curved stems.

ABOVE: **The eight Cigno-class torpedo boats pre-dated the Orione type and, like them, were built as coal burners. Most were later converted to oil burning, but although this reduced the crew by some 10 per cent, the programme appeared haphazard.**

RIGHT: **The first group of "high seas" torpedo boats were the six Schichau-built Saffo-class boats, which also initiated the beautiful classical/astronomical name sequences. This is *Serpente*, sunk by collision during 1916.**

Orione class, as built

Displacement: 217 tons (designed)
Length: 51m/167ft 5in (bp); 52.8m/173ft 4in (oa)
Beam: 5.8m/19ft 2in
Draught: 1.6m/5ft 4in (designed)
Armament: 3 x 47mm guns (3x1); 3 x 17.7in torpedo tubes (3x1)
Machinery: 3-cylinder triple-expansion engines, 2 boilers, 2 shafts
Power: 2,238kW/3,000ihp for 25 knots
Endurance: 44 tons coal for 1,260km/680nm at 18 knots
Protection: None
Complement: 38

97

LEFT: **The 90-plus craft built to basic Schichau design were variously known as Coastal Torpedo Boats, or Torpedo Boats 2nd Class. The identity here is uncertain but it may be 115.S, which served until after World War I.**

ABOVE: **During World War I, Italy made a large investment in coastal torpedo craft, mainly with an eye to service in the adjacent Adriatic. Although generally termed "PN" boats, i.e. Pattison, Napoli, they came from a variety of builders.**

Coastal torpedo boats

The first of Italy's very large fleet of coastal torpedo boats (*torpediniere costiere*) were one each 25-ton craft from Thornycroft and Yarrow. Named *Nibbio* and *Avvoltoio*, they were classified 4th Class and delivered in 1881. Derived from these, the first domestically designed and built 26-tonner, *Clio*, was commissioned in 1885.

At this time the two British yards were also building the 35–40-ton 3rd Class craft of the Sparviero and Aquila classes. These carried two 14in torpedoes in fixed bow tubes. Successful, they led to the slightly larger *Aldebaran*, lead ship of a class of 30, all but 11 of which were domestically constructed under licence. Now becoming too numerous to name, craft adopted sequential numbers, followed by a letter denoting the designer or builder.

In 1886, the German Schichau yard delivered the first 2nd Class boat, a 78-tonner designated 56S. Effectively a scaled-down "high seas" craft, she was the prototype for a class of nearly 100 boats (56S–154S). Built mostly in Italian yards, these were complete by 1894.

During 1887, Yarrow delivered two 100 ton, 2nd Class boats (76YA and 77YA) which were a full 3 knots better than the Schichaus' 22. They were, however, followed by only two domestically built repeats.

ABOVE: **Mediterranean-moored, stern to quay, flotillas of PN craft make a brave show in Taranto's Mare Piccolo. Despite the nature of the threat changing post-1918, these small craft were not discarded until the 1930s.**

It would be 1910 before the next extended series was commenced. Of a size with, but slightly fuller than the Yarrow design, these were the 118-ton 1st Class PN type, the letters representing the Pattison yard at Naples. Capable of 27 knots, the craft were the first coastals to feature two centreline rotatable tubes. Between 1910 and 1918 a large number was ordered in blocks from several yards – Pattison built 30 boats; Odero, Sestri Ponente (OS) built 18; Ansaldo, Genoa (AS) built 14 and Orlando, Livorno (OL) built 6. Many survived until the 1930s.

PN class, second series

Displacement: 106 tons (light); 159 tons (full load)
Length: 42.5m/139ft 6in (wl and oa)
Beam: 4.7m/15ft 3in
Draught: 1.6m/5ft 3in (full load)
Armament: 2 x 3in HA guns (2x1); 22 x 17.7in torpedo tubes (2x1)
Machinery: Triple-expansion engines, 2 boilers, 2 shafts
Power: 2,387kW/3,200ihp for 27 knots
Endurance: 23 tons oil for 1,850km/1,000nm at 14 knots
Protection: None
Complement: 30

Lampo class

Italy's first destroyer, *Fulmine*, was designed and built by Odero. Of about 300 tons (light), she was launched in 1898 and was expected to make 30 knots. Never achieving this, she was deemed a failure. Even before her completion, however, the German Schichau yard at Elbing had launched five of an order for six 320-tonners, to be known as the Lampo class.

At this time, only about 100 tons and 10m/33ft in length separated a destroyer from a "high seas" torpedo boat, but the difference in scale had a considerable effect on seakeeping and the ability to maintain speed in a seaway.

The Lampos were of typical Schichau appearance with their two large funnels of circular section. The sheer strake was radiussed to reduce stress levels in the long, shallow hull. They were given a half-height forecastle, but differed from craft in German service by having no well deck, the very light bridge structure occupying that location immediately ahead of the forward funnel. Only two 14in torpedo tubes were carried, and were located farther aft.

The class was contemporary with, and the equal of, the British 30-knotters. For their size, they were efficient little ships. Less fragile than some, they were nonetheless wet and uncomfortable, with greatly reduced effectiveness in poor conditions. Less accustomed than Northerners to heavy weather, the Italians thought them deficient.

The light navigating bridge was an advance on British practice, enabling a 3in gun to be located on the raised forecastle rather than sharing the navigating platform.

Although the class was useful during the brief war with Turkey in 1911–12, it proved inadequate to the greater demands of World War I. Used briefly for coastal escort duties, the five survivors were converted to take a deckload of 12 mines.

ABOVE: **Not 50 per cent greater in displacement than the torpedo boats, the six Schichau-built Lampos (this is *Strale*) hardly deserved the title of "destroyers". The forecastle-mounted 75mm gun did, however, have a good field of fire.**

LEFT: **This impression of a Lampo does little to refute the reputation of the class as being poor seakeepers. The ram bow was unusual in craft of this size.**

Lampo class, as built

Displacement: 314 tons (light); 348 tons (full load)
Length: 60m/197ft (bp); 62.2m/204ft 1in (oa)
Beam: 6.5m/21ft 4in
Beam: 2.6m/8ft 6in (mean)
Armament: 1 x 3in gun, 5 x 57mm guns (5x1); 2 x 14in torpedo tubes (2x1)
Machinery: Triple-expansion engines, 3 boilers, 2 shafts
Power: 4,476kW/6,000ihp for 30 knots
Endurance: 3,680km/2,000nm at 12 knots
Protection: None
Complement: 56

DIRECTORY OF DESTROYERS: UP TO 1918

LEFT: Following the loss of the *Turbine* to Austro-Hungarian forces in May 1915, the Italians gave the name to her sister *Espero* as a mark of respect.
ABOVE: As built, the Nembos were unusual in their mast/funnel arrangement. Converted to oil firing in 1908–12, they gained a third funnel, later removed along with its boiler.

Nembo class

Keen to acquire the best destroyer technology of the day, Italy followed the Schichau designed-and-built Lampo class with a further half dozen designed by Thornycroft. These, the Nembo class, were slightly larger and, as completed, had four single 14in torpedo tubes, two on the centreline, two sided. Two of the class carried a single 3in gun, the remainder an all 57mm armament.

The design reflected contemporary British practice in being flush-decked, the forward turtledeck having a diminutive breakwater to protect the light navigating bridge. This was built over the usual, lightly protected forward conning "tower", and supported a prominent searchlight platform. Another British feature was the slightly squared-off transom with the upper part of the rudder rather vulnerably exposed. As built, the ships' tall mainmast was stepped between the funnels.

Completed by Pattison, Naples in 1902–05, the ships were upgraded from 1908, with new, oil-fired boilers replacing the original coal-fired equipment. Rather than trunk the existing two funnels, a third was added. Four (later reduced to three) single 3in guns were now shipped, and the four small-bore torpedo tubes were replaced by two single 17.7in models. During World War I the side decks were fitted with rails for laying mines, of which up to 16 could be carried.

As rebuilt, the Nembos were rated fit to operate as front-line units during World War I, in the course of which three were sunk. The powerful Austro-Hungarian fleet was based just across the Adriatic, and the *Turbine* was destroyed (1915) in intercepting a hit-and-run bombardment. *Borea* was also sunk in surface action (1917) while engaged in convoy escort duty. The lead ship, *Nembo*, was destroyed (1916) by Austrian submarine torpedo, the submarine itself being lost.

ABOVE: The original *Turbine*, seen here, was caught by the scouting division of an Austro-Hungarian bombardment force. Hit in the boiler room, she had to be abandoned. As Italy had just declared war, the loss made an impression.

Nembo class, as rebuilt

Displacement: 324 tons (light); 379 tons (full load)
Length: 63.4m/208ft 2in (bp); 64m/210ft 1in (oa)
Beam: 5.9m/19ft 6in
Draught: 2.3m/7ft 7in (mean)
Armament: 4 x 3in guns (4x1); 2 x 17.7in torpedo tubes (2x1)
Machinery: Triple-expansion engines, 3 boilers, 2 shafts
Power: 3,730kW/5,000ihp for 30 knots
Endurance: 4,050km/2,200nm at 9 knots
Protection: None
Complement: 54

ITALY

LEFT: *Grantiere*'s forecastle party, precariously manning the turtleback, emphasizes just how small these "destroyers" were. Sided 75mm guns are just visible over the canvas dodgers on the bridge wings. BELOW: Another unidentified Soldati of the first, coal-burning group. Second group ships could be distinguished by their narrower-section funnels, with caps. Contemporary British Tribals were of twice their displacement.

Soldati class

In this, the first Italian Soldati class, there were 11 ships, falling into three groups. Six (*Artigliere*, *Bersagliere*, *Corazziere*, *Garibaldino*, *Granatiere* and *Lanciere*) were coal-fired; four (*Alpino*, *Carabiniere*, *Fuciliere* and *Pontiere*) were oil-fired, while one (*Ascaro*) was a hybrid, burning either. The first ten formed a homogeneous class, the major difference being due to no more than that oil was introduced during its construction. Oil reduced the complement by five, this being the saving on stokers.

The *Ascaro* was not commenced until 1911, the year following the completion of the planned ten. She was ordered to Chinese Government account but, with Italy going to war with Turkey over Tripolitania, the ship was acquired by agreement for the Italian Navy. Other than for her "dual-fuel" facility she was, in virtually every respect, another Soldato. Visually, she differed in lacking the funnel caps of the oil-fired quartette. The funnels in all eleven were unequally spaced, the forward two exhibiting the smaller gap.

Although designed and built by the Ansaldo yard at Genoa, the Soldati owed much to the just-completed, Thornycroft-designed, Nembo, with their flush-decked hull and pronounced forward turtleback.

While only 1m/3ft 3in greater in length, the Soldati carried from the outset the four 3in guns for which the Nembo were later modified. Where the latter then carried only two 17.7in torpedo tubes, the Soldati carried three, one centreline, two sided. They were also given the stability reserves to ship a deck-load of 10 mines.

It might be noted that many Italian warships had an auxiliary function in minelaying, as the constricted waters of the Mediterranean include considerable shallow areas well-suited to this form of warfare. According to Italian Navy statistics, no less than 12,293 were laid in the course of the war.

ABOVE: *Bersagliere*'s crew busying themselves in preparing to raise the old-style stocked anchor. The awnings are a reminder of what a relief it must have been to escape the Mediterranean heat at sea.

Soldati class, oil-fired

Displacement: 400 tons (light); 416 tons (full load)
Length: 64.5m/21ft 9in (bp); 65.1m/213ft 8in (oa)
Beam: 6.1m/20ft
Draught: 2.2m/7ft 2in (mean)
Armament: 4 x 3in guns (4x1); 3 x 17.7in torpedo tubes (3x1)
Machinery: 4-cylinder triple-expansion engines, 3 boilers, 2 shafts
Power: 4,476kW/6,000ihp for 28.5 knots
Endurance: 2,963km/1,600nm at 12 knots
Protection: None
Complement: 52

Indomito and Pilo classes

Laid down from 1910, the six Indomito-class destroyers represented a great advance on the preceding Soldati. They were 8m/26ft greater in length, and averaged 672 tons displacement (light). Contemporary with, but smaller than, the Royal Navy's Acastas, they superficially resembled them with a full-height forecastle that continued to be a feature of Italian boats. They were the first Italian destroyers with steam turbines and, with 11,900kW/16,000shp behind them, all bettered 33 knots on trials, being able to sustain 29.

As built by Pattison, Naples, they had a forecastle-mounted 4.7in gun, with four 3in sided farther aft. During World War I, this armament was changed to a homogeneous five 4in weapons, the two 17.7in torpedo tubes being increased to four.

Four more, similar ships were built by Orlando at Leghorn. These, the three-funnelled *Ardito* and *Ardente*, and the two-funnelled *Animoso* and *Audace* (slightly larger) appeared to have been less successful.

Following on were eight ships of the Pilo class. Although again of the same basic hull dimensions, they were of somewhat greater displacement, the resulting greater draught costing them about a knot in speed. As built, they reverted to a light armament of four 3in guns but, post-war, these were replaced by five 4in.

Completed 1915–16, the Pilos (except for the *Nievo*, disposed of in 1938) had long and often eventful lives encompassing two major wars. Three (*Abba*, *Mosto* and *Pilo*) served in a reduced minesweeping role until the 1950s. The remainder, together with the Indomito-class *Insidioso*, were lost during World War II. Two of them had the dubious distinction of changing sides twice. These, the *Bronzetti* and *Missori*, came over with the Italian Armistice but, overtaken by events, had to be scuttled at Fiume and Durazzo respectively. Salvaged by the Germans, they were destroyed in 1945.

ABOVE: *Ardito* berthed in prime position in the Taranto naval base. Completed in 1913, she has more the appearance of destroyer than torpedo boat. Here, she is still armed with her original single 4.7in gun. BELOW LEFT: The two Animosos were essentially two-funnelled versions of the Arditos. Like them, they originally mounted a forecastle 4.7, as seen here on *Animoso* at Brindisi late in 1917.

Pilo class, as rearmed

Displacement: 756 tons (light); 874 tons (full load)
Length: 72.5m/238ft 2in (bp); 73m/239ft 8in (oa)
Beam: 7.3m/24ft 1in
Draught: 2.7m/8ft 11in (mean)
Armament: 5 x 4in guns (5x1); 4 x 17.7in torpedo tubes (1x2/2x1)
Machinery: Direct-drive steam turbines, 3 boilers, 2 shafts
Power: 11,563kW/15,500shp for 30 knots
Endurance: 3,700km/2,000nm at 12 knots
Protection: None
Complement: 74

Sirtori and la Masa classes

The last destroyers completed for the Italian Navy before the cessation of hostilities were a dozen from the Odero yard at Sestri Ponente. They were effectively repeats of the preceding Pilo design and, similarly, all had three funnels. These were of unusually slender proportions, the centre one being slightly the largest. Air attack was now seen as a serious threat and some of the class had funnels fitted with umbrella-shaped, open-framed caps to prevent direct damage to the boilers. To the main armament was added two 40mm and two 6.5mm automatic weapons on High-Angle (HA) mountings. These light weapons were later replaced with a pair of 3in HAs.

There appears to be little to differentiate between the four Sirtoris and the eight la Masas which were ordered in two batches. In dimensions, displacement and power they were similar, the only significant variation being that the first group, all laid down on the same day in 1916, were completed with six 4in guns and the remainder only four. All guns were mounted singly, with two sided on the forecastle, two in the waist and two aft.

Other than the la Masa-class *Cairoli*, all survived World War I and, due to the rapid increase in the general size of destroyers, all were reclassified as torpedo boats in 1929.

During World War II the varied experience of the 11 survivors reflected the shifting political affiliations of the nation. Four were destroyed in various locations by Allied air attack and three by German bombs. One was sunk by mine; another was destroyed by her crew on Italy's capitulation in September 1943. The last two, *Carini* and *Fabrizi*, served on until the 1950s, downgraded to minesweepers and finally, in the case of the former, as a harbour training ship.

ABOVE: During World War I Italian destroyers began to carry two-letter identifiers, based on their names. These were far from standard in size or in form. This is the Sirtori-class destroyer *Giovanni Acerbi* in a dark paint scheme. LEFT: *Generale Achille Papa* seen as escort to a Cavour-class battleship. With the remainder of her class she survived to serve as a very efficient anti-submarine escort during World War II.

LEFT: This is *Angelo Bassini* of the la Masa class. Note the flimsy navigating bridge and 4in guns sided on the forecastle. Her armament was reduced to a single 4in during World War II.

la Masa class, as built

Displacement: 771 tons (light); 835 tons (full load)
Length: 72.5m/238ft 2in (bp); 73.5m/241ft 5in (oa)
Beam: 7.3m/24ft
Draught: 2.8m/9ft 2in (mean)
Armament: 4 x 4in guns (4x1); 4 x 17.7in torpedo tubes (1x2/2x1)
Machinery: Direct-drive steam turbines, 3 boilers, 2 shafts
Power: 11,563kW/15,500shp for 30 knots
Endurance: 4,444km/2,400nm at 12 knots
Protection: None
Complement: 78

DIRECTORY OF DESTROYERS: UP TO 1918

LEFT: Discovering that greater speed was possible with longer hulls, the French produced two advanced prototypes in the 27.5-knot, 43.8m *Chevalier* (foreground) and the 31-knot, 44m *Forbin*, completed in 1894 and 1896 respectively.

ABOVE: Following the poor showing of the original 35m, 58-ton torpedo boats, a large number of redesigned 37.8m, 80-ton craft, such as No.358 seen here, were built. Many served in a variety of roles until the 1920s.

Early torpedo boats

Small, unseaworthy and lacking endurance, the limitations of the torpedo boat mattered little in the days when the leading sea powers, particularly Great Britain, made close blockade a major plank of their maritime strategy, thus conveniently stationing major warships close offshore. Spar torpedoes, detonated unexpectedly against the hull of a line-of-battleships, made an appealing "David and Goliath" image and, despite the lamentable performance of large numbers of Russian craft during the war with Turkey (1877–78), French enthusiasm for the concept remained unaffected.

During the late 1870s the French acquired both spar torpedo boats and "torpedo launches", mainly of Thornycroft design, to deploy the yet unproven Whitehead automobile torpedo. With the rapid improvement of the latter came the *Jeune École* movement. Spar torpedo boats were rebuilt with torpedo tubes and, by the mid-1880s, France had not only an eclectic fleet of about 50 craft but also, in Normand, a first-class designer and builder of her own.

Developed in parallel was the "*bateau-canon*", a larger, gun-armed craft which, like a British flotilla leader or German division boat, would both direct and support torpedo craft in attack. France also experimented with the "torpedo boat carrier", transporting small torpedo craft with the fleet for the purposes of offence and defence in an action. This vessel, *Foudre*, was later converted to carry seaplanes.

By 1914, the large numbers (over 100) of 37m and 39m Normands were organized mainly in flotillas, defending ports and bases from Saigon to Dunkirk. In the English Channel the threat from the German Flanders Flotilla, based on Bruges and Zeebrugge, was very real.

The minor force was supported by a few larger craft, such as the 45m Cyclone type, which bridged the gap between the true torpedo boats and the 56m "torpedo boat destroyers" (*torpilleurs d'escadre*) which were, as elsewhere, built almost exclusively after the turn of the century.

ABOVE: Appropriately named after the renowned French corsair, the *Forbin* was a speculative example of the design genius of Jacques-Augustin Normand, whose contributions rivalled those of J.I. Thornycroft. The greatest limiting factor was reciprocating machinery.

Cyclone class, as designed

Displacement: 149 tons (light); 177 tons (full load)
Length: 45m/147ft 9in (wl); 46.5m/152ft 8in (oa)
Beam: 4.8m/15ft 9in
Draught: 1.5m/4ft 11in
Armament: 2 x 47mm guns (2x1); 2/3 x 15in torpedo tubes (2/3x1)
Machinery: Triple-expansion engines, 2 boilers, 2 shafts
Power: 2,984kW/4,000ihp for 29 knots
Endurance: 25 tons coal for 1,850km/1,000nm at 14 knots
Protection: Negligible
Complement: 29

FRANCE

The "300-tonners"

By the late 1890s the rapid development of the torpedo had left the traditional maritime strategy of close blockade untenable. Exercises convinced the French Navy that any future blockading would need to keep its distance, maintaining a visual watch using the smallest capable ships. Destroyers, recently introduced by the British, appeared ideal; they were fast and with reasonable endurance, able to threaten capital ships with torpedoes or to subdue torpedo boats with gunfire.

The French entrusted Normand with the design for what would be a considerable programme. At under 300 tons (light), the initial quartette (Durandal class, 1899–1900) were smaller than the "30-knotters" then being built for the Royal Navy. Accepting that they would be awash in maintaining speed at sea, Normand gave them a pronounced forward turtledeck. This terminated at the forward conning tower, atop which was a platform which served as a navigating bridge as well as location for a 65mm gun (later often replaced by a 75mm weapon). The heavily radiussed sheer strake was continued all the way aft and, about 1.5m/5ft above the true upper deck, there ran a light spar deck (called "duckboards" by the French) which remained tolerably dry. Three 47mm guns were spaced along either side and there were two 15in centreline torpedo tubes. The two boiler spaces were separated by the engine room.

Two more quartettes (Pique class, 1900–01 and Pertuisane, 1902–03) of these 56m/184ft craft were followed by the Arquebuse class of 20 (1902–04). By now eight yards were involved in the rapidly evolving programme.

The final groups, of 13 Claymore (1905–08) and 10 Branlebas classes (1907–08), were of 2m/6ft more on the waterline, and mounted two heavier 17.7in torpedo tubes.

TOP: **The Normand-built *Fanfare* of the Branlebas class which, at this time, were carrying experimental Italian-style identifiers. Note how the crew are standing on the light, elevated "duckboards".** ABOVE: **All named after weapons, the Claymore type preceded the Branlebas class and, while very similar, were more lightly built. At the fore the nameship is wearing the "marque distinctive" of a flag officer.**

All the so-called "300-tonners" were active during World War I but all were discarded during the 1920s.

Branlebas class

Displacement: 322 tons (standard); 338 tons (full load)
Length: 58m/190ft 4in (wl); 59.8m/196ft 4in (oa)
Beam: 6.4m/21ft
Draught: 2.4m/7ft 10in max.
Armament: 1 x 65mm gun, 6 x 47mm guns (6x1); 2 x 17.7in torpedo tubes (2x1)
Machinery: Triple-expansion engines, 2 boilers, 2 shafts
Power: 5,073kW/6,800ihp for 27.5 knots
Endurance: 30 tons coal for 2,100km/1,150nm at 14 knots
Protection: None
Complement: 60

ABOVE: **An early picture of the Arquebuse-class *Belier* with navigation still being carried out around a 65mm gun. A light bridge was later added abaft the gun. Note the height at which boats need to be carried.**

105

DIRECTORY OF DESTROYERS: UP TO 1918

LEFT: **One of four Chasseur type, the** *Janissaire* **was one of the first oil-fired French destroyers. Experimentally, the** *Janissaire* **was fitted with Foster-Wheeler boilers and Parsons direct-drive steam turbines.** ABOVE: **The Spahi class's two pairs of funnels were distinctive, but varied in proportion and spacing depending upon which of five yards was involved.** *Aspirant Herber* **came from the old naval yard at Rochefort.**

The "450-tonners"

Compared to the torpedo boats that they came to succeed, the "300-tonners" were large. In actual size, however, they were tiny, their endurance determined by their personnel as much as by mechanical limitations. Wet, uncomfortable and lively, they fatigued crews and reduced efficiency. As the torpedo boats gave way to 300-tonners, so did the latter to 450-ton craft.

A further incentive toward larger dimensions came with the steam turbine. Competent engineers, the French knew of the inefficiency of the high-revving, turbine-driven propeller at cruising speeds. For two prototype craft, therefore, built in parallel with the last of the 300-tonners, they opted for a triple-shaft arrangement with a conventional reciprocating cruise engine on the centreline shaft. For evaluation, two different French-designed turbines were directly coupled to each wing shaft. Four boilers were required, and the two ships (*Voltigeur* and *Tirailleur*), launched in 1908–09, were about 64m/210ft long.

This extra size alone made them more seaworthy, more able to maintain their speed and less wet, so that the idiosyncratic "duckboard" construction was abandoned. With four equispaced funnels, they carried a much-enhanced armament of six 65mm guns and a third torpedo tube, firing through the stem.

Again for comparison, two further groups of similarly sized destroyers were built. The seven-ship Spahi class (1908–12) also had four boilers but featured a conventional arrangement of a reciprocating engine driving each of two shafts. They were instantly recognizable with two pairs of tall funnels, widely separated about the machinery space.

The third class, comprising four ships of the Chasseur type (1909–11) were again of a size but were fitted with a British-designed Parsons turbine on each of their three shafts. They had three funnels, unequally spaced. All three classes were designed to make 28 knots on about 7,500 horsepower.

ABOVE: **The two Voltigeurs were essentially repeat Spahis but, experimentally, were fitted with reciprocating machinery on the centreline shaft and turbines on the wing shafts.** *Voltigeur* **here passes the old battleship** *Hoche***.**

Chasseur type, as built

Displacement: 442 tons (standard); 511 tons (full load)
Length: 64.3m/211ft 1in (bp)
Beam: 6.6m/21ft 8in
Draught: Not known
Armament: 6 x 65mm guns (6x1); 3 x 17.7in torpedo tubes (3x1)
Machinery: Direct-drive steam turbines, 4 boilers, 3 shafts
Power: 5,595kW/7,500shp for 28 knots
Endurance: 133 tons oil or 98 tons coal for 2,685km/1,450nm at 10 knots
Protection: None
Complement: 78

FRANCE

LEFT: The 800-tonners had a business-like raised forecastle that greatly improved seakeeping. *Cimeterre*, of the 12-strong Bouclier class, shows facets to allow waist guns to fire well forward.
ABOVE: During World War I, the *Bouclier* received a modified bridge structure which necessitated a heightened forefunnel. She has a short bulwark in the waist to improve dryness.

The "800-tonners"

During 1909 the French commenced a group of twelve 800-ton destroyers. There was considerable incentive for this increase in size, as other fleets were discovering. Vibration-free turbines, combined with compact water-tube boilers and oil firing, promised high power in moderate dimensions. Large hulls can be more efficiently driven than small, and are better able to maintain speed in adverse conditions. An obvious choice for fleet escort, large destroyers could both repel enemy craft and conduct attacks of their own.

The French naval constructive department, STCN, did not tightly define the ships' form, allowing no less than seven yards to interpret an open specification that stipulated only the target displacement, armament and type (although not manufacturer) of the main propulsion machinery.

The resulting Bouncliers, although described as a class, thus showed marked differences. All had four boilers but three or four funnels. Two had triple shafts, the remainder twin. All had full-height forecastle but, to allow waist guns to fire forward, some had faceted sides, others small sponsons. As with British experience, wide variations in hull form and propulsive efficiency resulted in trials speeds ranging from 29.3 to 35.5 knots on the same installed power.

Taking the best of the Bouclier-class characteristics, the department added a further couple of feet to the beam of the longest hull for the six more tightly defined Bisson-class ships (1912–14) and the three following Enseigne Roux type (1915–21), most of which were built in naval dockyards.

At 30–32 knots, later ships demonstrated a greater uniformity in speed, suggesting that trials were run in a more realistic loaded condition.

All groups initially had a uniform armament, including a 100mm gun at either end, four 65mm weapons in the waist and two twinned torpedo tubes. This was considerably augmented in the course of World War I.

ABOVE: *Capitaine Mehl*'s forward funnel carried a distinctive clinker screen to protect personnel on the compass platform, where a searchlight was also mounted. Aft of amidships is a canvas-shrouded Army-pattern 75mm gun.

Bisson class, as built

Displacement: 850 tons (standard); 1,000 tons (full load)
Length: 78.1m/256ft 4in (bp)
Beam: 8.6m/28ft 2in
Draught: 3.1m/10ft 2in (mean)
Armament: 2 x 100mm guns (2x1), 4 x 65mm guns (4x1); 4 x 17.7in torpedo tubes (2x2)
Machinery: Direct-drive steam turbines, 4 boilers, 2 shafts
Power: 11,190kW/15,000shp for 30 knots
Endurance: 157 tons oil for 2,500km/1,350mm at 14 knots
Protection: None
Complement: 82

DIRECTORY OF DESTROYERS: UP TO 1918

LEFT: While the French Navy was pleased to source flotilla ships in Japan, it had to revert to triple-expansion machinery and dual coal/oil firing. Even at low speed, with forecastle party drawn up, this Arabe marks her passing. ABOVE: Very tidy little ships, the Arabes showed few characteristics to betray their Japanese origins. *Sakalave*'s funnels are "not quite French", while the soft nose to the stem head was unusual at this date.

Aventurier and Arabe classes

In 1914 the Argentine government had on order four destroyers each from Germany and France. All were requisitioned, the former group becoming the German G.101–104, and the latter the French Aventurier class, which were retained post-war.

In appearance, the Aventuriers were unusual in having not only a full-height forecastle but also a half-height aftercastle, or poop. This greatly improved the officers' accommodation, but at the expense of a higher profile. Their intended armament from the United States was blocked by early neutrality laws and was replaced by four long-barrelled 100mm Canet guns and four single 450mm torpedo tubes, sided in the low waist. Later reboilered, the ships gained a fourth funnel. The four were unequal in size and spacing.

Still short of destroyers in 1917, the French Navy took the unusual step of ordering a dozen from Japan. These were near repeats of the Japanese' own Kaba class, and caused some logistics problems with their mainly British-type weapon calibres.

Known as the Arabe (or Algérien) class, they were built rapidly, one pair by each of six yards. They had a short, half-height forecastle, upon which was a single 4.7in gun. Between the break of the forecastle and the forefunnel was located, German-style a pair of torpedo tubes. These were originally of 18in calibre, as was the second pair, sited well aft. There were also four guns of 3in calibre, two sided in the waist and two on the centreline right aft. The more forward of these was mounted on a bandstand.

By coincidence, Arabes and Kabas served together on convoy escort duty in the Mediterranean at the end of World War I. Both Arabes and Aventuriers served on into the 1930s, by which time the French were building much larger destroyers for fleet work.

ABOVE: Although relatively small, the Arabes were well built and well thought of as seaboats. Post-war most served with the Atlantic fleet, based on Brest, where they are pictured here. Slow by destroyer standards, they were deleted in the 1930s.

Arabe class, as designed

Displacement: 673 tons (standard); 835 tons (full load)
Length: 79.4m/260ft 8in (wl); 83m/272ft 5in (oa)
Beam: 7.3m/24ft 1in
Draught: 2.4m/7ft 10in
Armament: 1 x 4.7in gun, 4 x 3in guns (4x1); 4 x 18in torpedo tubes (2x2)
Machinery: 4-cylinder triple-expansion engines, 4 boilers, 3 shafts
Power: 7,460kW/10,000ihp for 29 knots
Endurance: 100 tons coal and 120 tons oil for 2,963km/1,600nm at 14 knots
Protection: None
Complement: 89

FRANCE/JAPAN

Early torpedo boats

By 1904 the Imperial Japanese Navy had acquired over 90 torpedo boats and, by virtue of wars with China (1894–95), Russia (1904–05) and Germany (1914–18), was one of the few major fleets to use them in combat.

The first to enter service were four Yarrow repeats of the Royal Navy 100 footers, shipped in parts for reassembly. Delivered in 1880, they were followed by a slow trickle of larger French-built craft, many from Normand. Three became casualties when the Japanese attacked the Chinese fleet at its Wei-hei-wei anchorage in February 1895, destroying the Chinese battleship *Ting-Yen*.

The war also saw the capture of three Vulcan-built Chinese torpedo boats and the sinking of eight others, stimulating a post-war Japanese programme of 47 boats from Normand, Schichau, Yarrow and domestic yards, building under licence. All were in service by 1903 and closely reflected designs of their countries of origin.

Except for ten 46.5m/152ft Yarrow-built craft, all the foregoing were rated Second- or Third-Class. Several other First-Class boats had also been acquired, including the *Kotaka* (Yarrow 1886, 50.3m/166ft), the ex-Chinese *Fukuryu* (Germania 1886, 42.7m/140ft), *Shirataka* (Schichau 1898, 46.6m/153ft) and the four Hayabusas (Normand 1899–1901, 45.1m/148ft). The last-named were the first with 18in torpedoes.

Newly confident in domestic design and build, the Japanese now produced the 11-strong First-Class Aotaka torpedo boats. Launched in 1903–04, six were built by the Kure Naval Dockyard, the remainder by Kawasaki.

Shortly afterward, hostilities commenced with Russia. At the decisive Battle of Tsushima in May 1905, Admiral Togo used his destroyers and torpedo boats to harry his Russian opponents throughout a long night, several boats sustaining damage. Although a discontinued species, torpedo boats were still useful in the capture of the German enclave at Tsingtao in 1914.

TOP: **Designed by Normand, French yards built eleven of their 46.5m/152ft Cyclone class together with four for the Japanese, who called them the Hayabusa class. Seen newly reassembled in Japan in 1901 is the *Chidori*.** ABOVE: ***Kotaka* was a one-off from Yarrow's Poplar yard, reassembled in Japan in 1886. Her six torpedo tubes were of 15in calibre, only the two forward tubes here being apparent, splayed outward over the extraordinary stem.**

Aotaka class 🔴

Displacement: 152 tons (design)
Length: 45m/147ft 8in (bp)
Beam: 4.9m/16ft 1in
Draught: 1.5m/4ft 9in
Armament: 1 x 57mm gun, 2 x 42mm guns; 3 x 18in torpedo tubes (3x1)
Machinery: Triple-expansion engines, 2 boilers, 2 shafts
Power: 2,611kW/3,500ihp for 28 knots
Endurance: 26 tons coal for 3,700km/2,000nm at 10 knots
Protection: None
Complement: 30

Harusame and Asakaze classes

With the end of the short war with China, the Japanese ordered their first destroyers, six each from Yarrow and Thornycroft. The former (Ikazuchi class, 305 tons designed) were slightly larger than the latter (Murakumo class, 285 tons), but both approximated to the still-completing British "30-knotters". To follow on, two further boats were ordered from each yard. These, the 345-ton Shirakumos and the 360-ton Akatsukis, were slightly enlarged versions, delivered in 1902.

In the same year, seven destroyers were ordered from the Kure and Yokosuka Naval Yards. The design of these, the Harusame class, was effectively that of the Thornycroft, Shirakumo, lengthened by nearly 4m/13ft. The four funnels were similarly disposed, with the second and third more closely spaced and indicating adjacent boilers spaces, ahead of the engine room.

The hull was flush-decked, with freeboard diminishing from forward to aft. A low forward turtledeck terminated at the conning tower, topped by the usual open platform, doubling as navigating position and location for the forward 3in gun. A further 3in weapon was sited right aft. Two 6pdr guns were sided at the break of the turtledeck, with two more sided and staggered in the waist. The two single 18in torpedo tubes were set on the centreline abaft the funnels. The Harusames' machinery was less powerful than that of the earlier Thornycroft boats, costing them about 2 knots.

ABOVE: **Appearing to be on a buoy in Portsmouth, England, prior to her delivery voyage is the Thornycroft-built *Shirakumo* which, with her sister *Asashio*, was completed in 1902. They were models for the seven Japanese-built Harusames.**

By the time that the last of the class was delivered, Japan was at war with Russia. An emergency war programme thus funded no less than 32 further hulls, designated the Asakaze class. These differed mainly in having a heavier gun armament and oil sprayers to boost the performance of the coal-fired boilers. With growing expertise, eight yards were able to participate in this programme.

Asakaze class, as built

Displacement: 380 tons (standard); 450 tons (full load)
Length: 69.2m/227ft (bp); 71.3m/234ft (oa)
Beam: 6.6m/21ft 7in
Draught: 1.8m/6ft
Armament: 4 x 3in guns (4x1); 2 x 3in HA (2x1); 2 x 18in torpedo tubes (2x1)
Machinery: 4-cylinder triple-expansion engines, 4 boilers, 2 shafts
Power: 4,476kW/6,000ihp for 29 knots
Endurance: 150 tons coal and 20 tons oil for 2,220km/1,200nm at 15 knots
Protection: None
Complement: 70

ABOVE: **The Harusames carried two single 18in torpedo tubes on the centreline abaft the funnels. Although slightly larger than the Shirakumos, they could match neither their power nor speed.**

Kaba and Momo/Enoki classes

With the Anglo-Japanese alliance of 1902 bringing Japan into a mainly European war in 1914, her navy found itself short of destroyers. Two 600-ton craft, *Sakura* and *Tachibana*, had been completed by Maizuru Dockyard in 1912, and these provided the basis for the ten Kaba-class boats ordered immediately under an emergency war programme.

Contemporary with the British "M" class, they were of the same length but rather narrower. Their four boilers were housed in adjacent spaces and, by virtue of placing the centre pair back-to-back, it was possible to exhaust them through the same funnel. With only three funnels, deck space was freed, enabling a twin torpedo tube mounting to be located in the well at the break of the half-height forecastle. A second pair was sited just ahead of the mainmast.

Although the Kabas were inferior to the British Ms in having 18in, rather than 21in, torpedo tubes, they were ahead in adopting the harder-hitting 4.7in gun, one of which was carried on the forecastle. Four 3in were mounted in the waist and aft.

Japanese expertise and capacity were increasing rapidly, and they were able to build a further 12 Kabas for the French Navy. The hull had further development potential and, in the four follow-on Momo class, power was increased by about two-thirds for small increases in length and beam. By the adoption of steam turbine propulsion much weight and space was saved. Only two funnels were fitted.

The extra beam permitted three 4.7in guns to be shipped and the torpedo tubes to be tripled. Speed and range were significantly improved.

Six more hulls were completed in 1918 as the Enoki class. They were essentially repeat Momos but with a 10 per cent increase in power.

ABOVE LEFT: *Tsubaki* was of the Enoki class, which were virtual repeats of the preceding Momo type. The forward triple torpedo tubes abaft the break of the short forecastle oblige the bridge to be located uncomfortably far forward. ABOVE: Launched in a very advanced stage of completion, *Kaba*, first of ten, is named with full ceremony. In a neat example of pupil teaching master, 12 more were built for France as the Arabe class.

ABOVE: In a clear profile, the layout of this Momo-class destroyer can be readily discerned. Seaboats, frequently carried away by heavy rolling, are carried high. Roman letter identifiers indicate Mediterranean service.

ABOVE: The 21 Momi-class boats were built post-war, and were developed directly from the Momos. They were the first with 21in torpedoes and, like the *Osu* (ex-*Kaki*) seen here, served throughout World War II.

Enoki class, as built

Displacement: 850 tons (standard); 1,100 tons (full load)
Length: 83.8m/275ft (bp); 85.8m/281ft 8in (oa)
Beam: 7.7m/25ft 4in
Draught: 2.4m/7ft 9in
Armament: 3 x 4.7in guns (3x1); 6 x 18in torpedo tubes (2x3)
Machinery: Direct-drive steam turbines, 4 boilers, 2 shafts
Power: 13,055kW/17,500shp for 31.5 knots
Endurance: 98 tons coal and 210 tons oil for 4,445km/2,400nm at 15 knots
Protection: None
Complement: 110

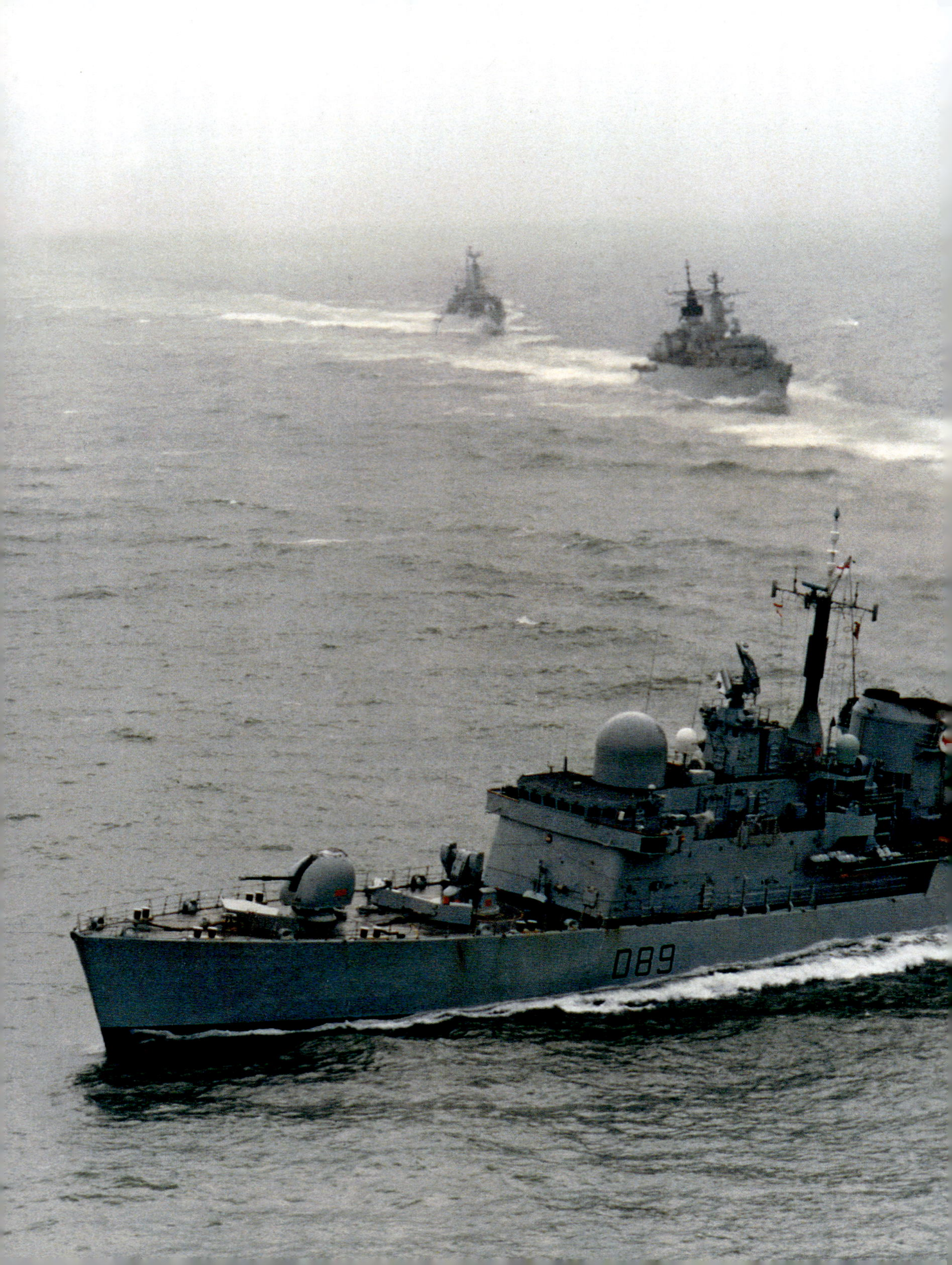
D89

Directory of Destroyers
1918 to Date

By 1918 the destroyer had progressed to the classic layout of gun and torpedo armament that, with minor variations, would last until the 1950s. World War II, however, saw the destroyer necessarily adapt to the new roles of anti-submarine and anti-aircraft escort. Rapid wartime development of both submarine and aircraft, together with the lack of opportunity for torpedo attack, found the destroyer form increasingly inadequate, resulting firstly in the introduction of the specialist frigate and, post-war, in a renaissance around the imperatives of guided missiles and helicopters. Such fast-reaction, stand-off weapon systems made very high ship speeds unnecessary, while the gas turbine's supersession of steam machinery resulted in considerable reduction in complement. Today's "destroyer" embraces a wide variety of forms, but is usually configured primarily for area defence against aircraft and missile attack.

The following directory takes the destroyer story from the ship designed for high-speed flotilla torpedo attack against a battle line to a multi-purpose anti-aircraft escort, often the size of an earlier light cruiser. Although the listing is comprehensive, space forbids the inclusion of every class. If selected examples here tend to favour major combatants, it is they that are subject to the greatest evolutionary forces.

LEFT: **A typical modern destroyer, the British Type 42** *Exeter* **is configured around an area-defence SAM system combined with good anti-submarine capability.**

DIRECTORY OF DESTROYERS: 1918 TO DATE

LEFT: In light, pre-war Mediterranean grey, and with awnings rigged, the *Brilliant*, launched in 1930, gives an impression of the standards maintained by the then-Royal Navy, still a major force. ABOVE: The *Electra* of 1934 is seen in the darker "Home Fleet" grey that was less flattering than the paler livery. Sent to the Far East, she was lost in the Java Sea battle.

"A" to "I" classes

With a surfeit of war-built tonnage, Britain built no more destroyers until a pair of "specials", designed in the mid-1920s by Yarrow and Thornycroft. *Amazon* and *Ambuscade* were essentially "W"-class boats, some 3m/10ft longer and incorporating the latest refinements in steam technology and fire control.

Based on these, tenders for a flotilla of eight, plus a leader, were sought in 1927. These, the "A" class, were all launched in 1929, the leader being larger and with a fifth gun between the funnels. All carried quadrupled torpedo tubes.

Nine flotillas were built, roughly one per year, with names commencing "A" to "I". The Cs were restricted to a half-flotilla. Over this period, there were minor variations, which are summarized in the table (right).

Quintuple torpedo tubes were introduced in the "I" class, but it will be noticed that, with the Gs, there was an effort to arrest the progressive growth in size and power.

Originally criticized for its size, the basic, long-forecastle design proved to have excellent seakeeping and handling. With World War II and the commissioning of larger destroyers, most were converted to long-range, anti-submarine escorts.

Flotilla	Launch date	Standard displacement (tons)	Dimensions (LWLxB) (ft)	Designed power (shp)	Designed speed (knots)
A	1929	1,330	320x32.25	34,000	31.25
B	1929	1,360	320x32.25	34,000	31.25
C	1931	1,375	326x33	36,000	32
D	1932	1,375	326x33	36,000	32
E	1934	1,405	326x33.25	36,000	31.5
F	1934	1,405	326x33.75	36,000	31.5
G	1935	1,350	320x33	34,000	31.5
H	1936	1,340	320x33	34,000	31.5
I	1936–37	1,370	320x33	34,000	31.5

One or two 4.7in guns were landed and the after torpedo tubes replaced by a 3in high-angle gun. To reduce topweight for greater depth charge capacity, the mainmast was removed and the after funnel shortened.

ABOVE: The "I" class of 1936 were the last of a continuous line of development that began with the "V & Ws". *Ilex* is seen here as built, marked up as a unit of the 3rd Destroyer Flotilla of the Mediterranean Fleet. She was transferred to Greece in 1945.

"E" class, as designed

Displacement: 1,405 tons (standard); 1,940 tons (full load)
Length: 99.3m/326ft (wl); 100.2m/329ft (oa)
Beam: 10.1m/33ft 3in
Draught: 3.5m/11ft 5in (standard)
Armament: 44 x 4.7in guns (4x1); 8 x 21in torpedo tubes (2x4)
Machinery: Single-reduction steam turbines; 3 boilers, 2 shafts
Power: 26,856kW/36,000shp for 31.5 knots
Endurance: 470 tons oil for 11,765km/6,350nm at 15 knots
Protection: None
Complement: 145

UNITED KINGDOM

LEFT: **Only four of the original 16 Royal Navy Tribals survived World War II. Immediately post-war,** *Tartar* **is seen here in her hostilities paint scheme. Note the addition of radar, lattice masts and a twin 4in gun mounting in "X" position.** ABOVE: **A rather nice impression of** *Arunta*, **one of the three Tribals built in Sydney for the Royal Australian Navy. These served alongside the US Navy in the Pacific War. Of the eight Canadian Tribals, four were constructed in Halifax, Nova Scotia.**

Tribal class

The London Naval Treaty of 1930 restricted the Royal Navy to a global limit of 150,000 destroyer tons. No individual ship could exceed 1,500 tons (standard), but 16 per cent of tonnage could be allocated to "leaders" not exceeding 1,850 tons. There was concern that large foreign destroyers were being armed with guns of up to the permitted maximum calibre of 130mm. The "A" to "I" flotillas had emphasized torpedo armament and it was now decided to build a double flotilla of primarily gun-armed leaders. Trials with 70lb, 130mm projectiles proved that their weight would slow the rate of fire, so the 4.7in gun with its 50lb shell was retained.

Designed to the 1,850-ton limit, the new Tribals carried eight guns, in two twin-shielded mountings, at either end. Only one quadruple set of torpedo tubes was shipped. The aerial threat was recognized with the requirement for 40 degrees of main battery elevation for long-range barrage fire. Two single-barrelled pompoms and two four-barrelled 0.5in machine-guns were also specified, although still inadequate.

The sheer beauty of the Tribal design was marred by wartime modifications, the most useful of which was the provision of a 4in twin high-angle mounting in lieu of "X" guns. Later, survivors were given a lattice foremast.

Tight design limitations caused the Tribals to be highly stressed and, as they were hard-driven, they tended to suffer bottom damage, which required additional stiffening. They also had a naturally high centre of gravity, giving them a slow, high amplitude roll that could prove unnerving for the uninitiated.

With excellent endurance, seakeeping and armament, the Tribals were very heavily used during World War II. Seldom out of the limelight they lost no less than 12 of their original 16. Eight more were built by or for the Canadians and three by the Australians.

The Tribal design evolved to counter the specific threat posed by foreign destroyers and was far too expensive to be built in large numbers.

ABOVE: *Mashona* **shows the classic Tribal appearance as originally built, with two light tripod masts. The new curved bow profile was adopted not for cosmetic reasons but to increase forecastle deck area without increasing waterline length.**

Tribal class, as built

Displacement: 1,854 tons (standard); 1,959 tons (full load)
Length: 111.1m/364ft 8in (wl); 114.9m/377ft (oa)
Beam: 11.1m/36ft 6in
Draught: 3.3m/10ft 9in (standard)
Armament: 8 x 4.7in guns (4x2); 2 x 2pdr pompom (2x1); 4 x 21in torpedo tubes (1x4)
Machinery: Single-reduction steam turbines, 3 boilers, 2 shafts
Power: 32,824kW/44,000shp for 32.5 knots
Endurance: 525 tons oil for 10,556km/5,700nm at 15 knots
Protection: None
Complement: 195

DIRECTORY OF DESTROYERS: 1918 TO DATE

LEFT: Cheaper and smaller than a Tribal, the "J" type re-emphasized torpedo armament at the expense of guns. The *Kashmir* shows how the mainmast has been suppressed in order to give the after guns uninterrupted firing arcs.
ABOVE: Unlike half the Ls, all of the M class received their designed armament. *Matchless* is shown here in her 1945 paint scheme, and has already acquired a lattice mast. Post-war, she was sold to Turkey.

"J" to "N" classes

For a smaller and cheaper destroyer to succeed the Tribals, a 10-tube torpedo battery was required, as was a dual-purpose main armament. At the desired elevation of 70 degrees, however, projectiles could not be hand-loaded. The arrangement also set the breech uncomfortably high for low-angle use. Three Tribal-type mountings were thus specified, with no guns in "Y" position. A quadruple 2pdr pompom occupied a bandstand immediately abaft the large single funnel. Sufficient power could be generated by two boilers and, by placing these back-to-back, they could be exhausted through a single large funnel casing.

The speed of these, the "J" and "K" classes, was 32 knots in the deep condition but this was criticized in view of the increasing speeds of capital ships and, indeed, foreign destroyers. The following two flotillas, the "L" and "M"s, were thus designed for a continuous speed of 33 knots. They were given large, fully enclosed twin gunhouses, whose 4.7in weapons were capable of 50-degree elevation while firing a heavier 62lb shell.

The new gun mountings were not an unqualified success, while their extra weight was compensated by the readoption of quadruple torpedo tubes. Slow delivery of the gun mountings also resulted in four L-class boats being fitted instead with four twin 4in HA apiece, and being reclassed as anti-aircraft destroyers.

In 1939, the next flotilla ordered reverted to a repeat of the J/K class, presumably because of the increasing tempo of warship construction. Only one of the "N" class served during hostilities with a British crew. Four were Australian-manned, two Dutch and one Polish (as was one "M").

Several ships of these classes substituted a 4in HA for the after torpedo tube but losses, particularly from air attack, were high, comprising six Js, six Ks, seven Ls, three Ms and one N.

ABOVE: The extra 50 tons of the L-class's enclosed gunhouses required an extra 0.4m/16in of beam compared with a "J", together with eight torpedo tubes rather than ten. The weather-worn *Lookout* has a Bay-class frigate on her far side.

"N" class, as designed

Displacement: 1,775 tons (standard); 2,385 tons (full load)
Length: 106m/348ft (wl); 108.6in/356ft 6in (oa)
Beam: 10.9m/35ft 8in
Draught: 4.2m/13ft 9in (standard)
Armament: 6 x 4.7in guns (3x2); 4 x 2pdr pompoms (1x4); 10 x 21in torpedo tubes (2x5)
Machinery: Single-reduction steam turbines, 2 boilers, 2 shafts
Power: 29,840kW/40,000shp for 32 knots
Endurance: 490 tons oil for 10,190km/5,500nm at 15 knots
Protection: None
Complement: 183

UNITED KINGDOM

LEFT: **Both "O" and "P" classes were instantly recognizable because of their 4in armament and the sharper sheerline at the extreme bow. There were exceptions, the non-minelayers being equipped with 4.7in guns, and** *Petard* **(shown here) gaining two 4in HA in 1945.**

"O" and "P" classes

The cost, complexity and large complements of recent classes resulted in a requirement for a new-style destroyer with a specification between those of the "I" and "J" classes, and leading to its becoming known as the Intermediate Type. Torpedo armament and speed were to be retained but air defence emphasized. Heavy projectiles (and, thus, a slow rate of fire) and ship movement led to a true dual-purpose armament being thought impracticable. The older 4.7in gun, with a 23kg/50lb shell, was thus specified for the first two groups. These, the "O" and "P" classes, were ordered in September and October 1939 as the First and Second Emergency Flotillas respectively.

None had yet been launched when the experience of Norway and Dunkirk in 1940 highlighted the true level of the air threat, particularly from dive-bombing. The first four of the Os were fitted with four 4.7in guns apiece, as planned, but the second division received four single 4in HAs. With the "Y" gun removed they could also carry a deck load of 60 mines. The second flotilla (i.e. "P" class) might have received twin 4in HA mountings, had production permitted. All, however, were completed with singles, capable of 80 degrees elevation.

With the same machinery as the "J" class the O/P classes were slower, their shorter hulls being hydrodynamically less efficient. Inferior speed and broadside excepted, the ships were well praised for their handling and seakeeping, although progressive weight accumulation necessitated some ballasting in order to restore an acceptable stability range.

The Os, particularly, behaved extremely well when escorting Arctic convoys but, as the first to be constructed to reduced war standards, they showed high rates of deterioration if maintenance was allowed to slip. Despite this, surviving P-class hulls were the oldest to be converted in the crash post-war AS frigate programme.

ABOVE: *Opportune* **(seen here) and three sisters were fitted as minelayers. Their normal armament in this role was three 4in weapons, but here "A" gun has been landed. Sixty mines could be carried, laid over the mine chutes visible right aft.**

ABOVE: **An end-of-war picture of** *Offa* **which, despite not being fitted for minelaying, has landed her torpedo tubes in addition to "A" and "Y" gun mountings. In 1949 she was transferred to the Pakistan flag.**

"P" class, as built

Displacement: 1,550 tons (standard); 2,250 tons (full load)
Length: 102.7m/337ft (wl); 105.1m/345ft (oa)
Beam: 10.7m/35ft
Draught: 4.1m/13ft 6in (standard)
Armament: 4 x 4in guns (4x1); 1 x 2pdr pompom; 8 x 21in torpedo tubes (2x4)
Machinery: Single-reduction steam turbines, 2 boilers, 2 shafts
Power: 29,840kW/40,000shp for 32.25 knots (deep)
Endurance: 475 tons oil for 7,130km/3,850nm at 20 knots
Protection: None
Complement: 175

117

DIRECTORY OF DESTROYERS: 1918 TO DATE

LEFT: With the "S" class came the new 55-degree 4.7in mounting, seen here in the similar *Ulster*. *Savage* trialled a new twin 4.5in 85-degree mounting intended for the Battles. **ABOVE:** All eight Cr-class ships found themselves under foreign flags. Four went to the Royal Norwegian Navy, the *Cromwell* (seen here) becoming the *Bergen*. Of the remainder, two each went to Canada and Pakistan.

"Q" to "C" classes

The Third to Fourteenth Emergency Flotillas comprised 96 ships of identical hull dimensions, in 8-ship flotillas without additional leaders. Their conservative, but reliable, steam plant was heavy and bulky and, when it was thought imperative to increase endurance with the Qs, a magazine had to be sacrificed for extra fuel capacity. Endurance was now calculated at 20 knots, common for fleet operations.

Hydrodynamic efficiency was improved by the adoption of a squared-off transom. Adequate margin was left for progressive weight accumulation, making them initially exceedingly stable.

The "Q" and "R" classes retained the 40-degree 4.7in gun, succeeded by the 55-degree model from the "S" class. The *Savage* trialled a new twin 4.5in gunhouse for later use on the larger Battle class. Too large for Emergency Flotillas, it did introduce the new 4.5in calibre which, in a 55-degree shielded mounting, was standard from the "Z" class onwards.

Close-range armament was steadily improved, with 40mm Bofors taking the place of pompoms and 20mm Oerlikons replacing 0.5in machine guns. Radar now demanded pride of place at the foremast head, necessitating the reinstatement of a mainmast to support the vital HF/DF antenna. This did nothing to improve arcs, made worse when, with even more topweight, short lattice masts began to displace tripods, which had been standard since the "J" class.

Although of the same dimensions, the final four flotillas (Ca, Ch, Co and Cr classes) showed a growth of 100 tons on deep displacement. Their number included the *Contest*, the first all-welded British destroyer.

To reduce wetness, the sharply sheered bows of the "O" to "R" classes were modified and flattened, but seaworthiness of all flotillas attracted favourable comment. All were designed to be able to remove "Y" gun to convert rapidly for minesweeping or extra depth charge capacity.

Ca class, as built

Displacement: 1,825 tons (standard); 2,535 tons (full load)
Length: 106.1m/348ft (wl); 110.6m/362ft 9in (oa)
Beam: 10.9m/35ft 8in
Draught: 4.4m/14ft 3in (standard)
Armament: 4 x 4.5in guns (4x1); 2 x 40mm Bofors (1x2); 8 x 21in torpedo tubes (2x4)
Machinery: Single-reduction geared steam turbines, 2 boilers, 2 shafts
Power: 29,840kW/40,000shp for 32.25 knots (deep)
Endurance: 615 tons oil for 8,610km/4,650nm at 20 knots
Protection: None
Complement: 190

ABOVE: With rigged awnings obscuring some detail, the T-class leader *Troubridge* enters Grand Harbour. She was rebuilt as a Type 15 frigate in 1955–57, but the remaining seven Ts were given limited conversion to Type 16s, giving them a five-year shorter lifespan.

UNITED KINGDOM

ABOVE: Only four of a planned 20 Weapons were completed. Their sole anti-surface ship armament was their ten torpedo tubes, and they sacrificed these during the 1950s in order to ship a new mast and Type 965 long-range, air-search radar. This is *Battleaxe* at recommissioning.

Weapon class

In 1942, it was decided that all new-design destroyers should have a High-Angle (HA) armament, capable of 80-degree elevation. The Weapons were the first class to be affected but, owing to the typically three-year construction span, none was completed before the cessation of hostilities.

The hull was little larger than that of the "intermediates", dimensioned so as to utilize very narrow slips or even to be built two to a slip. For main armament the ubiquitous 4in twin mounting was selected. Simple, robust and relatively light, its rate of fire made it suitable for long-range barrage fire against aircraft, yet it was just heavy enough to deal with the thick hide of a surfaced submarine.

Weapons were intended to act in the role of either fleet destroyer or of anti-submarine (AS) escort. For the former, they would carry six 4in guns, eight torpedo tubes and a Hedgehog spigot mortar. Otherwise, four 4in guns would be supplemented by ten tubes and a double Squid mortar. All would be equipped with stabilized High Angle/Low Angle (HA/LA) directors and 40mm mountings, both twin and single.

For greater survivability, machinery was laid out on the unit system, with alternate boiler and engine rooms. This resulted in two widely spaced funnels, but deck space was conserved by leading the forefunnel up the inside of the lattice foremast. More advanced steam conditions reduced machinery size somewhat, and topside weight was reduced by incorporating some aluminium alloy into the superstructure (offset somewhat by the addition of patches of quarter-inch steel splinter protection).

Orders for 19 hulls were placed in April 1943, but the first of 15 cancellations occurred as early as September 1944.

From the late 1950s all four surviving ships served as radar pickets, their torpedoes having been traded for a large, amidships lattice mast bearing a single-mattress Type 965 antenna to extend the fleet's radar horizon.

LEFT: *Crossbow* demonstrates the major characteristics of a radar picket Weapon-class 4in HA armament, all forward; forward boiler exhausting via foremast; amidships mast for 965 antenna; double Squid; and 40mm battery aft.

Weapon class, as AS escorts

Displacement: 1,955 tons (standard); 2,825 tons (full load)
Length: 106.8m/350ft (wl); 111.3m/365ft (oa)
Beam: 11.6m/38ft
Draught: 4.4m/14ft 4in (standard)
Armament: 4 x 4in HA guns (2x2), 6 x 40mm guns (2x2/2x1); 10 x 21in torpedo tubes (2x5)
Machinery: Single-reduction steam turbines, 2 boilers, 2 shafts
Power: 29,840kW/40,000shp for 30 knots (deep)
Endurance: 630 tons for 9,260km/5,000nm at 20 knots
Protection: Negligible
Complement: 234

Battle class

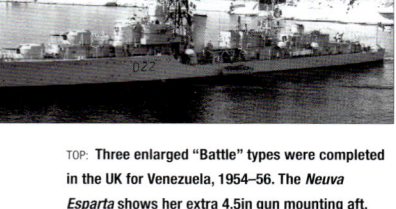

Known as the "1942 Design" the early Battle-class were true fleet destroyers with heavier firepower than the Weapons yet all of it high angle. Their new Mk.IV twin 4.5in gunhouse, with 80 degrees of elevation, had been extensively trialled aboard the *Savage*. The so-called "between decks" mounting required space in the level below. It was heavy and was power-driven to follow the director. With pronounced ship movement this implied constant correction and consequent wear. Anti-roll stabilizers were thus specified, but quickly cancelled when it was decided that their weight/space allocation was better invested in 60 extra tons of oil fuel.

An intended third 4.5in mounting aft was never fitted, the whole after end being given to four twin 40mm mountings, individually stabilized and extremely complex.

Back-to-back boilers required only a single funnel, abaft which was a bandstand supporting a single 4in starshell gun. Two quadruple sets of torpedo tubes were fitted.

Criticism attended both the unconventional armament layout and the ships' size, although the latter was the smallest that could accommodate all the Fleet's requirements.

Orders for 24 were placed March–June 1943. Of these, only 16 were completed to the original "1942 Design", the last being launched as late as September 1945.

The final eight, of the "1943 Design", had an American Mk 37 director, topped by the same pair of nascelles, associated with the British Type 275 radar. Beam was slightly increased, the single 4in upgraded to a fifth 4.5in, and the torpedo tubes to quintuples. The considerable depth charge capacity was rearranged around a single Squid AS mortar on the quarterdeck. Increasing weight saw an enforced reduction of one twin 40mm mount, compensated somewhat by exchanging the effectively redundant starshell gun for two single 40mm.

In total, 24 Battles were completed and 16 cancelled, some well advanced.

TOP: Three enlarged "Battle" types were completed in the UK for Venezuela, 1954–56. The *Neuva Esparta* shows her extra 4.5in gun mounting aft, and depth charges in lieu of Squid. There was only one triple torpedo tube mounting, permitting more spacious accommodation. ABOVE: Four later Battles were converted to full radar picket configuration. *Aisne* shows her "Double 965" on a new foremast and an associated Type 278 height-finder aft. The after 40mm mountings have been replaced by Seacat SAM.

1943 Battle class, as built

Displacement: 2,460 tons (standard); 3,420 tons (full load)
Length: 111m/364ft (wl); 115.6m/379ft (oa)
Beam: 12.4m/40ft 6in
Draught: 4.7m/15ft 4in (standard)
Armament: 5 x 4.5in guns (2x2/1x1), 8 x 40mm guns (3x2/2x1); 10 x 21in torpedo tubes (2x5)
Machinery: Single-reduction steam turbines, 2 boilers, 2 shafts
Power: 37,300kW/50,000shp for 31.25 knots (deep)
Endurance: 765 tons oil for 8,150km/4,400nm at 20 knots
Protection: Negligible
Complement: 251

ABOVE: *Trafalgar* was an earlier (1942) "Battle", and is seen in her original configuration. The main armament, located all-forward, was a direct result of the enhanced anti-aircraft battery, but it attracted much adverse comment. Unusually, as a leader, she has her pendants painted up.

UNITED KINGDOM

LEFT: The *Daring* was the logical three-mounting extension of the "Battle" design but, in meeting the declared deficiencies of a Battle, it became, in the opinion of most destroyer officers, too large. It was considered too valuable to hunt submarines.
BELOW: The *Diamond* shows the massive profile resulting from the large gunhouses. In place of the Battles' handsome soft-nose bow, the Darings reverted to a bar stem, given a somewhat unappealing curved profile.

Daring class

The Battles were disappointing – insufficient firepower, low rate of fire, too slow. A new, lightweight twin 4.5in mounting, the Mk VI, was under development and, in contrast to the Battles' Mk IVs, it was an above-deck mounting, the penalty for which (given its 80-degree elevation) was a very high profile. This increased the height of the navigating bridge.

One Mk VI forward and one aft were planned for a new "Intermediate" destroyer (the aborted "G" class) but for the "1944 Battle", which became the Daring, three mountings were required. This, and a readoption of unit machinery layout (one boiler and one turbine in each of two separated compartments) increased hull length, but a politically acceptable displacement of 2,750 tons had to be observed. This caused design problems because the Admiralty Board also wanted two quadruple sets of torpedo tubes (quintuples were actually fitted), three twin 40mm stablized mountings and a Squid AS mortar in lieu of depth charges. With faster submarines, the latter were obsolescent, while a Daring was considered too valuable to hunt submarines as a primary requirement.

With participation in the Pacific war an increasing likelihood, a third set of torpedoes was proposed and rejected, but facilities for fighter direction were incorporated. For air-dependent operations, such as those in the Pacific, these were essential.

The Darings were the first British destroyers to be designed for assembly from all-welded modules. Improved methods of stress analysis prompted a greatly increased degree of strengthening at the discontinuity of the break of the forecastle. So heavy was this that a long-forecastle version would have been lighter, but would have raised the centre of gravity unacceptably.

Only eight of the 16 planned Darings were ever completed, and these well after the war. Not their least problem was their 330 complement. They marked the end of the gun and torpedo-armed "conventional" destroyers in the Royal Navy.

RIGHT: The space-saving concept of the forefunnel being enclosed within the foremast was borrowed from the Weapons. *Dainty*, here, retains her original Mk VI director, in contrast to *Diamond*'s (above right) newer MRS.3.

Daring class, as built 🇬🇧

Displacement: 2,610 tons (standard); 3,350 tons (full load)
Length: 114.4m/375ft (wl); 119m/390ft (oa)
Beam: 13.1m/43ft
Draught: 3.4m/11ft standard
Armament: 6 x 4.5in guns (3x2), 6 x 40mm guns (3x2); 10 x 21in torpedo tubes (2x5)
Machinery: Double-reduction steam turbines, 2 boilers, 2 shafts
Power: 40,284kW/54,000shp for 31 knots (deep)
Endurance: 580 tons oil for 8,150km/4,400nm at 20 knots
Protection: Nominal
Complement: 329

121

County class

By 1952–53, when the Darings were completed, the Cold War was firmly established and the threat greatly changed. The Soviet Union appeared quite prepared to use tactical nuclear weapons and, deficient herself in naval terms, she was developing weapons and delivery platforms aimed at offsetting the West's pre-eminence in aircraft carrier and amphibious warfare groups. Her counter centred on Air-to-Surface Missiles (ASMs), launched from specialist bombers, and Surface-to-Surface Missiles (SSMs) deployed by small craft, destroyers and submarines.

The West focussed mainly on the ASM threat, developing Surface-to-Air Missiles (SAMs) and their complex guidance systems. These were so bulky that that the host ship was necessarily designed around them.

The Royal Navy's Seaslug had been under development since 1947. It was 6.1m/20ft long and weighed 2,000kg/4,400lb at launch. It could intercept at a slant range of up to 27,430m/30,000yd and altitudes to 15,240m/50,000ft. Eschewing the US Navy's space-saving "Coke-Bottle"-type vertical stowage, British designers stowed the missiles horizontally in a long, centreline, upper deck magazine, a feature which dictated the distinctive, high-freeboard hull of the County-class "destroyer" built to deploy it.

The ships carried a helicopter, rather than a Squid/Limbo, for AS operations. Their COmbined Steam And Gas turbines (COSAG) propulsion system was primarily steam, but supplemented by gas turbines for rapid start-up from cold or for boosting sprint speed.

The second quartette of the eight Counties built was an improved type, with superior electronics and a Mk II Seaslug, capable of carrying a nuclear-tipped warhead and with improved capability against surface targets.

All eight ships were designed with two Mk VI 4.5in twin gun mountings forward. On the last four of the second group "B" mounting was exchanged for four Exocet MM38 SSMs in unreloadable canister launchers.

TOP: Chile purchased the second quartet of "Counties" during the 1980s. Their obsolete Seaslug systems were replaced by hangar and flight pad for two large helicopters. Finally retired in 2003, *Blanco Encalada* was originally HMS *Fife*.

ABOVE: The four Batch I Counties carried two twin 4.5in gun mountings forward and a single Type 965 mattress. One deck in depth, the Seaslug magazine ran as far forward as the foremast, despite which only 20 missiles could be carried.

LEFT: In their original configurations, *Norfolk*, *Antrim* and *London* steam in formation. Note that the forward funnel exhausts the steam plant, the after the gas turbines. Unusually, the helicopter was moved athwartships in and out of its hangar.

First group, as designed 🇬🇧

Displacement: 5,250 tons (standard); 6,150 tons (full load)
Length: 154m/505ft (wl); 158.8m/520ft 6in (oa)
Beam: 16.5m/54ft
Draught: 4.7m/15.7in (standard)
Armament: 4 x 4.5in guns (2x2); 1 x twin Seaslug launcher; 1 x quadruple Seacat SAM launcher
Machinery: Double-reduction steam turbines and gas turbines (4), 2 boilers, 2 shafts
Power: 30,000shp/22,380kW plus 30,000shp/22,380kW for 31.5 knots (deep)
Endurance: 780 tons fuel (total) for 6,440km/3,500nm at 20 knots
Protection: Nominal
Complement: 460

UNITED KINGDOM

LEFT: Larger than many earlier cruisers, the *Bristol* was a "destroyer" by virtue of her status as a primarily anti-aircraft carrier escort. Her size was driven largely by the decision to accommodate both Sea Dart SAM and Ikara ASM systems.
ABOVE: No helicopter facilities were provided beyond a flight pad. The cumbersome twin-armed Sea Dart launcher is located forward of this. The radome of the after Type 909 missile director and the split uptakes from the gas turbine spaces are visible.

Type 82 (*Bristol*)

In 1966 CVA-01, Britain's first post-World War II aircraft carrier, was cancelled. With her went the Type 82s, her dedicated escorts. So many novel systems were involved, however, that it was decided to construct one already designed Type 82 as a trials ship. She was launched in 1969 as HMS *Bristol*.

Her primary area air-defence system was Sea Dart. More compact than Seaslug, its missiles were fed vertically to the twin launcher from a rotating drum. Their maximum slant range was 27,430m/30,000yd at an altitude of 19,800m/65,000ft. Optimistically, it was hoped that Sea Dart would fit into a "frigate-sized" ship, the reason why the "Type 82" class identifier was from the frigate numbering sequence.

Bristol's Sea Dart was located aft, controlled by two Type 909 illuminator/tracker radars, sited forward and aft under large radomes. Forward, she carried Ikara, a stand-off (9,140m/10,000yd) AS weapon comprising a fully controllable torpedo-carrying, rocket-propelled vehicle. Right forward was the new single Mk VIII 4.5in mounting. Fully automatic, this was adopted as the Royal Navy's standard gun, serving long and reliably.

Because the T82 was designed to work with a carrier, no helicopter facilities, beyond a pad, were included.

Yet another intended new system was the Type 988 Anglo-Dutch "Broomstick" surveillance radar, whose antenna would have been housed within a very large radome atop the bridge structure. With this project's cancellation, a double Type 965 was substituted, later updated to a Type 1022.

An improved COSAG propulsion system was specified. Its Olympus gas turbines were repair-by-replacement, necessitating split after uptakes to facilitate engine changes.

The *Bristol*'s all-round capability resulted in such a large and expensive ship that it is doubtful whether the planned eight would ever have been approved. Since 1991 she was served as static harbour training/accommodation ship, a function that she still fulfils at the time of writing.

ABOVE: *Bristol*'s Ikara launcher was housed in the "zareba" abaft the single 4.5in gun. Its missile was controlled by radars located under small domes flanking the bridge front. Note that the large radome over the forward Type 909 is removed in this view.

Type 82, as built

Displacement: 6,300 tons (standard); 7,100 tons (full load)
Length: 149.5m/490ft (wl); 154.6m/507ft (oa)
Beam: 16.8m/55ft
Draught: 5.1m/16ft 7in (full load)
Armament: 1 x 4.5in gun; 1 x twin Sea Dart SAM launcher; 1 x Ikara AS launcher
Machinery: Double-reduction steam turbines (2) and Olympus gas turbines (2), 2 boilers, 2 shafts
Power: 22,380kW/30,000shp plus 33,272kW/44,600shp for 30 knots
Endurance: 9,260km/5,000nm at 18 knots
Protection: Nominal
Complement: 407

Type 42 (Sheffield) class

Politics left their mark heavily on the Type 42s. Built at a rate of barely one per year and to tight cost and displacement limits, most were completed "for but not with" essential systems. The intention was to house all of the T82 *Bristol's* systems (less Ikara but with a Lynx helicopter) in a hull of little more than half the displacement. The designers succeeded, but at the cost of a cramped, wet ship.

In saving weight, Batch 1 units proved inadequately stiff, resulting in the later ships being heavily reinforced along the sheer strake.

The short forecastle of the 125.7m/412ft overall Batch 1 and 2 ships put their single 4.5in gun in a very wet position and left the twin-arm Sea Dart launcher in a cramped situation between it and the bridge front.

Externally, the earlier T42s were dominated by the two Type 909 Sea Dart control radars, the double Type 965 surveillance radar atop the bridge structure, and the outsized funnel casing which exhausted the all-gas turbine drive of two Olympus and two Tynes, the latter used for cruising.

All four surviving Batch 1s were expected to have been deleted by the end of 2006, Batch 2s by 2012.

Already a tight design, the T42s gained further, post-Falklands War topweight in Vulcan Phalanx CIWS and 20mm cannon, a Type 1022 radar in place of the 965, and improved electronics. Seaboats and triple AS torpedo tubes were landed as partial compensation.

The inadequacy of the basic Type 42 design was recognized by the insertion of a considerable 15.6m/51ft section in

LEFT: **Although lengthened by over 16m/52.4ft overall to improve seakeeping, endurance and habitability, the Batch 3 Type 42s, such as** *Gloucester*, **retain the same armament. Note the heavy strakes added amidships to reduce longitudinal stress levels.**

ABOVE LEFT: **The cramped arrangements of the earlier Type 42s is well evident in this shot of** *Exeter*. **Experience in the Falklands War dictated the addition of the waist CIWS systems, installed at the expense of the original seaboats on davits.**
ABOVE: **Even the lengthened Batch 3** *Manchester* **can still ship solid water forward, alleviated somewhat in her sister ship** *Edinburgh* **by the addition of a bulwark. The low-freeboard quarter deck is also prone to wetness.**

the forward hull of the four Batch 3s. The length of the entry, plus bow bulwarks, makes for greatly improved dryness and extra missile stowage. Better lines also give an extra 1.5 knots for the same power.

Batch 3 units

Displacement: 3,810 tons (standard); 5,075 tons (full load)
Length: 132.3m/434ft 3in (wl); 141.1m/463ft 2in (oa)
Beam: 14.9m/49ft
Draught: 5.8m/19ft (maximum)
Armament: 1 x 4.5in gun; 1 x twin Sea Dart launcher; 2 x 20mm Vulcan Phalanx CIWS
Machinery: 2 Olympus and 2 Tyne gas turbines, 2 shafts
Power: 40,582kW/54,400shp or 7,967kW/10,680shp for 29.5 or 18 knots
Endurance: 600 tons fuel for 8,800km/4,750nm at 18 knots
Protection: Nominal
Complement: 285

UNITED KINGDOM

Type 45 (Daring) class

During 1995 the British, French and Italians formed a consortium to define a destroyer of a common form suitable to each. Although the British left the ship group four years later they remained committed to the French missile system. There remains also a strong family resemblance between the resulting ships – the six British Daring class, three French Forbin type and two, possibly four, Italian Bergamini.

The British ships are replacements for the rapidly aging T42s and a second set of six will be a necessity but, inevitably, their fate will be bound up with that of the Royal Navy's two projected fleet carriers, long a political football. Despite sharp lessons of the past, we once again see plans to commission ships fitted "for, but not with".

Displacing half as much again as a T42, the Darings are of a sharply sculpted, radar signature-reducing design, but laid out much like a T23 frigate. A single 4.5in gun in a new "Mod 1" enclosure is located forward of a 48-cell Vertical Launch System (VLS) containing 16 long-range Aster 30 and 32 medium-range Aster 15 Surface-to-Air Missiles (SAMs).

Despite the hugely expensive development of the capable Merlin helicopter, reports speak of the Daring "making do" with Lynxes on grounds of economy. As the ships lack any anti-ship missiles they will need to rely on the Lynx for delivery of Sea Skua ASMs as well as AS torpedoes. Neither does the ship carry a CIWS.

Two shafts are driven directly by reversible electric motors, speed-controllable over their full range. Power for them is generated by two new Anglo-American WR-21 gas turbines or, for ultra-quiet navigation, two vibration-isolated diesel alternators.

ABOVE: **First-of-class *Daring* undergoing an extended period of acceptance trials. Between the low bridge and the "Mod 1" gun mounting is the VLS housing. This may later include cells for Tomahawk cruise missiles.** LEFT: **Although all hull and superstructure modules are built in covered facilities, they are assembled and launched into the Clyde from a traditional slipway. This is *Diamond*, already in an advanced state of fitting out.**

Assembled from modules built both in Portsmouth and on the Clyde, the Daring class has been subjected to many changes and delays as naval funding becomes ever tighter.

Type 45, as projected

Displacement: 7,350 tons (full load)
Length: 152.4m/500ft (wl)
Beam: 21.2m/69ft 7in (at upper deck); 18m/59ft 1in (at wl)
Draught: Not known
Armament: 1 x 4.5in gun; 16 x Aster 30 and 32 x Aster 15 SAM; 2 x 30mm cannon (2x1)
Machinery: Gas turbine/electric, 2 shafts
Power: 40,000kW/53,650shp for 29 knots (or 4,000kW/5,365shp for quiet drive)
Endurance: 12,965km/7,000nm at 18 knots
Protection: Nominal
Complement: 190

LEFT: **Compared with the pre-war picture of** *Farragut* **(below), the** *Macdonough* **(DD.351) has shipped much extra topweight during the Pacific war, compensated by little except the loss of the mainmast and the amidships 5in gun.**

Farragut (DD.348) class

Following World War I, the US Navy had large numbers of new flush-decked destroyers, but lacked suitable flotilla leaders. Larger destroyers were favoured over light cruisers, but numerous 1920s design studies resulted in no actual ships. The London Naval Treaty of 1930 then defined maximum individual and global displacements, establishing also that gun calibres should not exceed 130mm.

Future destroyers, it was decided, should be of two basic types, designed either to screen the battle fleet or to operate offensively in independent, torpedo-centred strike squadrons.

Bethlehem Steel, a specialist destroyer yard, produced the design that resulted in the "1,500-ton" Farragut class of the early 1930s. The general layout accorded closely with that already well-established by the Royal Navy, but with displacement and 5in guns pushing more closely at Treaty-agreed maxima.

Far less conservative than the British in machinery practice, American plant had far higher power-to-weight ratios, the Farraguts being designed for a respectable maximum speed of 36.5 knots. The two closely spaced funnels indicated adjacent boiler spaces, the thicker after funnel exhausting boilers in each of the spaces.

Readopting a half-height forecastle for improved seakeeping, the Farraguts were designed with five single 5in guns, two superimposed at either end and a fifth on a bandstand immediately abaft the after funnel. The bridge was set well back to improve dryness and to reduce the blast effect of "B" gun mounting. Above it was a substantial dual-function director. There were two quadruple banks of torpedo tubes.

The design proved to be weight-critical and, in order to acquire an adequate AA armament during World War II, the ships lost their amidships 5in gun mount, the shields of the after 5in guns, the mainmast and one or more boats. Two of the class capsized during the 1944 typhoon, unable to utilize their depleted fuel tanks for water ballast.

ABOVE: **In this 1930s photograph, the Bethlehem-designed** *Farragut* **(DD.348) shows well the influence of the classic British layout. Although a considerable advance on the preceding flush-deckers, the design was regarded as "tight". The "E" is for "Excellent", an accolade earned over a specific period.**

Farragut, as designed 🇺🇸

Displacement: 1,360 tons (standard); 1,585 tons (full load)
Length: 101.9m/334ft (wl); 104.2m/341ft 6in (oa)
Beam: 10.5m/34ft 3in
Draught: 2.9m/9ft 8in (deep)
Armament: 5 x 5in guns (5x1); 8 x 21in torpedo tubes (2x4)
Machinery: Single-reduction steam turbines, 4 boilers, 2 shafts
Power: 31,930kW/42,800shp for 36.5 knots
Endurance: 200 tons oil for 12,965km/7,000nm at 12 knots
Protection: None
Complement: 160

UNITED STATES

LEFT: As built, the 1,850-tonners had massive tripod masts. These were removed, as seen here on *Phelps* (DD.360), along with the twin 5in mountings in "B" and "X" positions. A single 5in was substituted at "X", together with eight 40mm weapons. ABOVE: An early wartime picture of *Somers* (DD.381), lead ship of an improved Porter type. Inherently overweight, she has shed some after superstructure but still retains her original 5in mountings and rather odd, box-like director.

Porter (DD.356) and Somers (DD.381) classes

Following on from the Farragut, the "1,850-ton" Porters were built to the treaty limit on displacement. Described as "leaders", they were intended to be large enough to act offensively. To this end, they carried eight 5in 38-calibre ("5-inch 38") guns in four twin gunhouses, superimposed at either end. While having no more torpedo tubes than the Farragut, they carried a reload for each.

Imposing in appearance, the Porters had a full-height forecastle, bulky superstructure, topped off by low-angle directors forward and aft, and substantial tripod masts. The mainmast supported an elevated platform bearing two searchlights. Superfiring "B" and "X" positions were quadruple 1.1in anti-aircraft cannon.

Unofficial policy was to build to treaty limits, with capacity to add further weight in an emergency. Even without such as depth charges and arrangements being included, however, the class was overweight (cf British Tribal). With war they landed "B" and "X" mountings, acquiring a single in "X" position. Pole masts replaced tripods and the after director was landed. Reload torpedoes were abandoned in favour of a third quadruple bank.

The five Somer class ships of the following year's (i.e. 1934's) programme were described as Improved Porter. Their machinery was completely redesigned, generating a further 1,492kW/2,000shp. This alone could drive a destroyer at 15 knots, but already on the steep part of the speed/resistance curve, it was good

for only an extra half knot. A single trunked funnel served both boiler spaces. The third set of tubes was included, with the suppression of after director and tripod masts contributing to the saving of topweight. With war, however, main armament was likewise reduced to five 5in guns in order to acquire eight 40mm anti-aircraft weapons.

Only 2 of the 13 were lost, the *Porter* to a Japanese torpedo off Guadalcanal, the *Warrington* (DD.383) foundering in a Caribbean hurricane.

RIGHT: *Porter* (DD.356) in an interim wartime condition. Compared with *Phelps* (above), she has not received 5in 38 Dual Purpose (DP) mountings, has had her original director radar-fitted and retains her original funnel profiles. The bulwark amidships is an addition.

Somers class, as designed

Displacement: 2,010 tons (standard); 2,765 tons (full load)
Length: 113.3m/371ft 6in (wl); 116.4m/381ft 6in (oa)
Beam: 11.2m/36ft 10in
Draught: 4.1m/13ft 5in (full load)
Armament: 8 x 5in guns (4x2); 12 x 21in torpedo tubes (3x4)
Machinery: Single-reduction steam turbines, 4 boilers, 2 shafts
Power: 38,792kW/52,000shp for 37.5 knots
Endurance: 620 tons oil for 7,870km/4,250nm at 20 knots
Protection: None
Complement: 235

LEFT: **As designed, the 1,570-ton Sims class –** *Anderson* **(DD.411) seen here as built – packed a maximum of five 5in guns and twelve torpedo tubes, one quad on the centreline and one each beam. Note the heavy after superstructure, with boats under derricks.** BELOW: **In Pearl Harbor, December 1941,** *Downes* **(DD.375) is shown supporting the near-submerged** *Cassin* **(DD.372) in a flooded drydock. In a gesture of pride, the US Navy salvaged the machinery of both, installing it in new hulls, bearing identical names and numbers.**

Mahan (DD.364), Craven (DD.380) and Sims (DD.409) classes

Built to replace aging flush-deckers, the "1500-tonners" of the 1930s followed the Japanese lead in favouring torpedoes over gun batteries. Tactics called for high speeds, leading American practice to successively higher steam pressure and temperatures. Simpler and lighter turbines rotated at higher speeds, but with the penalty of two-stage reduction gearing. Improved power-to-weight ratios and fuel economy came at the cost of increasingly cramped machinery spaces.

Launched 1935–36, the 18 Mahans were a development of the Farraguts. Their foremasts were designed as tripods, the extra stiffness reducing rigging, which adversely affected fields of fire. It was ironic, therefore, that they were later exchanged for stayed pole masts when the acquisition of more light weapons demanded economies in topweight.

Designed for five 5in 38s, they were reduced to four, with the forward mountings in shields, the after ones unprotected. Separate funnels served the two boiler spaces. Between them was an elevated quadruple torpedo bank; two more were sided further aft.

With the 22 Cravens (otherwise termed Gridleys or Bagleys) that followed, a single, very large, trunked funnel served all four boilers. Saving both topweight and deckspace, it also removed the smoke nuisance further from the bridge. By reducing the main battery to four 5in weapons, a fourth quadruple torpedo tube bank was possible. All were sided.

As the waist abaft the break of the forecastle tended to be very wet, bulwarks were added, extending as far aft as the forward tubes.

The final dozen of the series (sometimes referred to as the Benham subgroup) had only three boilers, resulting in a considerably smaller funnel.

The final group of single-stackers was the 12-strong Sims class. These were much the same but readopted the fifth gun (landed in wartime), with only three quadruple torpedo tube banks.

ABOVE: **Lead ship of 22, the** *Craven* **(DD.380) carried only four main-battery guns to compensate for a massive complement of twelve torpedo tubes, with two triples on either side. Note the prominently trunked funnel and lack of shields to after guns.**

Sims class, as built

Displacement: 1,760 tons (standard); 2,290 tons (full load)
Length: 104m/341ft (wl); 106.1m/347ft 9in (oa)
Beam: 11m/36ft 2in
Draught: 3.9m/12ft 9in (full load)
Armament: 5 x 5in guns (5x1); 12 x 21in torpedo tubes (3x4)
Machinery: Double-reduction steam turbines, 3 boilers, 2 shafts
Power: 37,300kW/50,000shp for 35 knots
Endurance: 444 tons fuel for 6,720km/3,650nm at 20 knots
Protection: Nominal
Complement: 192

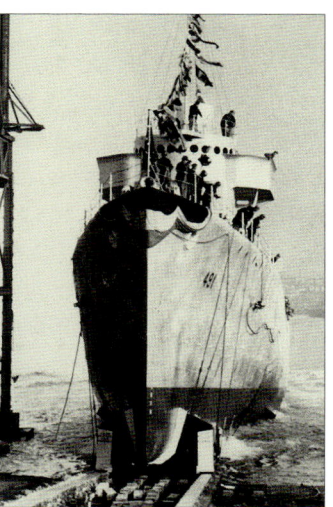

Benson (DD.421) and Livermore (DD.429) classes

The single-funnelled classes evolved a multi-purpose destroyer design that provided the basis for a huge replacement programme begun in 1937. The previous design displacement of 1,500 tons had proved over-constricting and the new ships, nominally at least, would be of 1,630 tons, treaty restrictions by now being effectively a dead letter. The smaller ships were known as the Benson class, the larger as the Livermore. Externally, their funnels differed, the Livermore being round, the Benson slab-sided.

At the time of the programme's instigation a theoretical Pacific war dominated the ship's specification. By the time of the early deliveries the Atlantic war was a reality and, although neutral until late 1941, the United States became increasingly involved through the president's "Short of War" policy.

Early units commissioned with five 5in guns and ten torpedo tubes. Escorting convoys in the western Atlantic, however, required large outfits of depth charges. Following British experience, therefore, destroyers landed one gun and one bank of tubes in order to ship not only depth charges but also a respectable anti-aircraft armament.

More compact boilers allowed the Benson/Livermore class to adopt a unit machinery layout. Two each alternate boiler and engine rooms necessitated two thin, but nicely proportioned, funnels. Acceptance of centreline torpedo tubes gave the same broadside for half the weight, a bonus being the adoption of quintuple mounts.

Reduction in weight elsewhere and modifications such as lowering the director tower permitted the fitting of two twin 40mm Bofors and four 20mm Oerlikons. These complemented the main battery guns, which were Dual-Purpose (DP). Because of supply bottlenecks, however, there was a wide variety of armament fits at any time. By the end of World War II, what with acquisitions of electronics, further armament and crew, many units were running at an extra 300 tons deep, a problem common to most destroyers.

ABOVE LEFT: **Although the majority of the Bensons were given only one quintuple bank of torpedo tubes and four main-battery guns, they still came out considerably overweight. Some of the slightly enlarged Livermores took the designed five guns and ten tubes.** ABOVE: **The Benson-class *Farenholt* (DD.491) is launched from Bethlehem Steel's Staten Island yard on November 19, 1941. Typical of so many destroyers, she enjoyed barely 4 years of active service, followed by 25 years in reserve before being scrapped.**

LEFT: **Following President Roosevelt's "Short of War" directive, US Navy destroyers aggressively escorted North Atlantic convoys. On October 17, 1941, *Kearny* (DD.342) survived torpedoing by *U-568*, incurring the first fatal casualties of the US Navy's war.**

Benson class, average, as built

Displacement: 1,910 tons (standard); 2,475 tons (full load)
Length: 104.1m/341ft 3in (wl); 106.1m/348ft (oa)
Beam: 11.1m/36ft 3in
Draught: 4.2m/13ft 9in (full load)
Armament: 4 x 5in guns (4x1); 5 x 21in torpedo tubes (1x5); 4 x 40mm (2x2) guns; 4/6 x 20mm guns (4/6x1)
Machinery: Double-reduction steam turbines, 4 boilers, 2 shafts
Power: 37,300kW/50,000shp for 35 knots
Endurance: 450 tons oil for 7,223km/3,900nm at 20 knots
Protection: Nominal
Complement: 191

Fletcher (DD.445) class

The scale of American destroyer programmes meant considerable overlap in classes, with the first of 175 Fletchers commissioning long before many of the preceding Livermores. Where the latter were, nominally at least, treaty-constructed, the Fletcher located the same five 5in/ten tube outfit in a hull that was comfortable and not overloaded. Unfortunately, spare capacity always appears to be something of a challenge to evolution.

At the outset, the design successfully combined the specified main armament with Anti-Aircraft (AA) weapons, a five-pattern depth charge capacity, sufficient endurance and a sustained speed of better than 35 knots. Standard displacement as designed, however, increased from some 2,100 tons to about 2,275 tons.

Once again, designers opted for a flush-decked hull. This avoided the obvious stress concentration caused by the discontinuity at the break of the forecastle and also better suited the longitudinal framing chosen for series production. The resulting continuous sheerline gave a greater depth of hull amidships, increasing strength. Wetness remained a problem, however, the waist bulwark being retained.

Progressive weight acquisition saw some units displacing over 3,000 tons (deep) by 1944. Designed AA batteries of two 40mm and six 20mm had grown by up to ten 40mm and seven 20mm, director controlled and most in splinter-proof tubs. Superstructures that had been designed to incorporate a degree of aluminium alloy for lightness had already been worked in steel because of shortages of raw materials; these had now acquired further areas of light steel protection, 12.5–19mm/½–¾in in thickness. Complements increased from a designed 273 to about 300, putting increasing pressure on accommodation.

ABOVE LEFT: **No longer constrained by treaty restrictions, the Fletchers grew to a size well capable of carrying a five-gun, ten-tube armament. Modernized, as seen here, the *Cowell* (DD.547) was transferred to Argentina in 1971, serving until the mid-1980s.** ABOVE: **A foredeck shot of *Fletcher* (DD.445), as delivered. She is fitted with the original pole mast, topped with its SC-2 air-search radar antenna, seen near end-on. Despite their size, they were soon more than 200 tons overweight.**

Together with considerable topside electronic additions, these changes were paid for in reduced stability, greater draught and lower speed. Despite all, however, (including their enormous turning circle), the Fletchers were considered very successful.

LEFT: **A total of 39 Fletchers, including *The Sullivans* (DD.537), were modernized after the Korean War. The tripod mast supports the large SPS-6B air-search radar, the after funnel a spreader with domes for radar direction finders.**

Fletcher class, as designed

Displacement: 2,110 tons (standard); 2,700 tons (full load)
Length: 112.5m/369ft (wl); 114.8m/376ft 6in (oa)
Beam: 12.2m/39ft 9in
Draught: 4m/13ft 3in (full load)
Armament: 5 x 5in guns (5x1); 10 x 21in torpedo tubes (2x5)
Machinery: Double-reduction steam turbines, 4 boilers, 2 shafts
Power: 44,760kW/60,000shp for 35 knots
Endurance: 491 tons oil for 6,450km/3,500nm at 20 knots
Protection: Nominal
Complement: 273

UNITED STATES

Allen M. Sumner (DD.692) class

In formulating the specification for the Sumners, the successors to the Fletchers, the US Navy took account of the battle experience of the already heavily engaged Royal Navy. Torpedoes appeared to have been of far less application than an effective, dual-purpose armament. In the interests of standardization, machinery and hull length would not be changed but beam would need to be increased, at consequent cost to speed.

The Fletchers' high profile had attracted criticism, leading to the development of a twin 5in 38 gunhouse and the likely intention of siting one forward and one aft. Immediately, however, a four-gun forward battery was thought desirable and, as the arrangement of the forthcoming British 1942 Battle did not enthuse, a third mounting was sited aft in the "Y" position. For little increase in weight a further gun had been added while precious centreline space had been saved in using three mountings in place of five. The bridge was lowered one level and, on some, opened to allow better all-round visibility in the event of air attack.

Where the Fletchers' two torpedo tube banks bracketed the after funnel, the after set in the Sumners was moved aft to a location just forward of "Y" mounting. In many units, it was later exchanged for a further quadruple 40mm mounting. Two more of these were sited in staggered, sided tubs, with singles or twins also mounted on the box-like wings which added space to the bridge structure.

The Sumners were improved but overloaded; Fletchers were a half-way house to the stretched, follow-on Gearings. They had, by virtue of twin rudders, improved manoeuvrability but, due to the extra weight forward, were notably wet.

Backbone of the post-war US Navy's destroyer fleet, both Sumners and Gearings would be subjected to comprehensive modernization programmes.

ABOVE LEFT: **Built for gun and torpedo attack, American destroyers had to be remodelled for Cold War anti-submarine operations by 1960.** *Allen M. Sumner* **(DD.692) thus underwent Fleet Rehabilitation And Modernization (FRAM).** ABOVE: **The Sumner-class** *Walke* **(DD.723) lays outboard of the Fletcher-class** *Halford* **(DD. 480) at the Mare Island Navy Yard in March 1945. Note the latter's temporary bows.**
BELOW LEFT: **The FRAM-ed** *Strong* **(DD.758) was transferred to Brazil in 1973 as the** *Rio Grande do Norte.* **Although she has retained the updated electronics and DASH facilities, she has lost the large VDS visible on** *Sumner* **(above left).**

Sumner class, as designed

Displacement: 2,535 tons (standard); 3,150 tons (full load)
Length: 112.5m/369ft (wl); 114.8m/376ft 6in (oa)
Beam: 12.5m/41ft
Draught: 4.3m/14ft 1in (full load)
Armament: 6 x 5in guns (3x2), 12 x 40mm guns (2x2/2x4); 10 x 21in torpedo tubes (2x5)
Machinery: Double-reduction steam turbines, 4 boilers, 2 shafts
Power: 44,760kW/60,000shp for 35 knots
Endurance: 504 tons oil for 6,020km/3,250nm at 20 knots
Protection: Nominal
Complement: 336

Gearing (DD.710) class

Only 58 Sumners were built (12 of them modified for minelaying) before 4.3m/14ft was added to the length to accommodate the obvious overloading. The transition was smooth, many ships ordered as Sumner being delivered as the longer Gearing. Ninety-nine of these were completed, many others being cancelled with the close of hostilities.

Although parallel construction programmes were producing large numbers of Destroyer Escorts (DEs) for Anti-Submarine (AS) operations, some Fletchers were modified post-war to Escort Destroyers (DDEs) with enhanced depth charge capacity and a full Hedgehog in place of "B" mounting. (The US Navy never adopted the more deadly Squid.) Most Fletchers, however, had short lives, although some were reactivated for the Korean War. Others exchanged their remaining torpedo tubes for two twin 3in in the waist to engage Japanese kamikaze suicide aircraft.

By the late 1950s, however, the US Navy was faced with block obsolescence of its destroyer force. As an alternative to a prohibitively expensive replacement programme, the Navy embarked on the so-called FRAM (Fleet Rehabilitation And Modernization) option. This was undertaken at three levels: FRAM I conversions, applied to 49 Gearings, were effectively total rebuilds; FRAM II, equivalent to a half-life refit, affected 113 destroyers, mostly Sumners; and FRAM III, involving only eight Sumners, replaced specific on-board systems.

By now, the fast nuclear submarine was a reality, and FRAM I ships received the ASROC (Anti-Submarine Rocket) stand-off weapon together with the ultimately abortive DASH (Drone AS Helicopter) system. They retained four 5in guns, but FRAM II conversions kept all six, receiving Variable-Depth Sonar (VDS) in addition to both long and short AS torpedo tubes. Topside, both types were notable for a mass of newly acquired electronics, including Electronic Countermeasures (ECM) to defeat incoming anti-ship missiles.

ABOVE: *Fiske* (DD.842) is seen here in the early 1950s as a DDR, i.e. radar picket, conversion. She retains her original main armament but has gained the very heavy SPS-8 height-finding radar on the after superstructure. BELOW: Steaming at high speed into a calm swell, *Rowan* (DD.782) is seen here before her FRAM I conversion. The broad, flat fronts of the twin 5in gunhouses could cause deck cracking when impacted by heavy seas.

LEFT: As the bulk of the US Navy's destroyers dated from 1943–45, in the early 1960s the service was faced with the huge problem of block obsolescence. The FRAM I modernization, seen here on *Rowan* (DD.782), extended useful life by an estimated eight years.

Gearing class, as designed

Displacement: 2,635 tons (standard); 3,480 tons (full load)
Length: 116.8m/383ft (wl); 119.3m/392ft (oa)
Beam: 12.4m/40ft 9in
Draught: 4.4m/14ft 5in (full load)
Armament: 6 x 5in guns (3x2), 16 x 40mm (2x2/2 or 3x4) guns; 5 or 10 x 21in torpedo tubes (1 or 2x5)
Machinery: Double-reduction steam turbines, 4 boilers, 2 shafts
Power: 44,760kW/60,000shp for 34.5 knots
Endurance: 740 tons oil for 8,056km/4,350nm at 20 knots
Protection: Nominal
Complement: 336

UNITED STATES

Forrest Sherman (DD.931) class

First post-war attempts to produce the ideal fleet destroyer, based on recent experience, resulted in the one-off, 5,600-ton *Norfolk* of 1951 and the four 3,675-ton Mitschers of 1952. Too large and expensive, both types were classified, firstly as "frigates", latterly as "leaders". The Mitschers, however, had advanced steam machinery which, although initially trouble-prone, was scaled-down successfully to suit the succeeding class, the Forrest Shermans.

Destroyers had, by now, moved away from their classic role in torpedo attack to become escorts capable of protecting a surface group against air and submarine attack. The Forrest Shermans, of which the nameship was laid down in October 1953, were the last gun-armed destroyers and, 7.3m/24ft longer than a Gearing, looked decidedly under-armed.

In place of the earlier twin 5in 38 gunhouses, they carried three of the new 5in, 54-calibre weapons in single, automatic mountings, one forward, two aft. The 54s had, however, twice the rate of fire and considerably greater range. At both ends they were superfired by a twin 3in 70. Flanking "B" position forward were two half-Hedgehogs. Four tubes for launching heavyweight AS torpedoes were sited in the waist, but these were later removed.

In the course of the 18-ship programme, the forward freeboard was twice increased to improve dryness. Much aluminium alloy, not then appreciated as a potential hazard, was incorporated in the superstructure.

By late 1958, when the last units commissioned, rapid advances in Surface-to-Air Missile (SAM) technology had already rendered them obsolescent. In 1967–68, therefore, four were converted to Guided-Missile Destroyers (DDGs), exchanging their after armament for a Tartar SAM system and an ASROC launcher. Eight more surrendered "X" gun, the 3in mountings and Hedgehogs in favour of ASROC, VDS and lightweight AS torpedo tubes. The class was scrapped during the 1980s.

ABOVE: **Transitional between the classic gunned destroyer and the current all-missile ships, the Forrest Shermans (the nameship shown here) had the power and seakeeping required to escort the new generation of large carriers.** BELOW: **During the late 1960s, four of the class were converted to Tartar-equipped DDGs. This is *Parsons*, originally DD.949, renumbered DDG.33. Note that she has landed her after guns for conversion but has gained an ASROC launcher amidships.**

RIGHT: **Nearing the end of her career, the *Dupont* (DD.941) is seen here in 1982, following her major anti-submarine modernization. She has gained a full-width deckhouse aft with ASROC at O1 level. Right aft is a variable-depth sonar.**

Forrest Sherman class, as designed 🇺🇸

Displacement: 2,850 tons (standard); 4,750 tons (full load)
Length: 124.1m/407ft (wl); 127.6m/418ft 6in (oa)
Beam: 13.7m/45ft
Draught: 4.6m/15ft (full load)
Armament: 3 x 5in guns (3x1), 4 x 3in guns (2x2); 4 x 21in torpedo tubes (2x2)
Machinery: Double-reduction steam turbines, 4 boilers, 2 shafts
Power: 52,220kW/70,000shp for 33 knots
Endurance: 8,335km/4,500nm at 20 knots
Protection: Nominal
Complement: 337

133

Charles F. Adams (DDG.2) class

Between 1956 and 1962, the Gearing-class destroyer *Gyatt* (DD.712) served as a testbed to prove the possibility of converting conventional destroyers to SAM escorts. Although feasible, it proved uneconomical. For the duration, *Gyatt* was designated DDG.1, so that the Adams, the first group of designed-to-task GM destroyers, commenced with DDG.2

Gyatt deployed the nuclear-capable Terrier missile, but the Tartar, derived from it, was built into the Adams. Each carried 42 rounds of the 32.19km/ 20-mile ranged weapon.

Cut by budget restrictions, the Adams class ran to 23 units. Although about 4m/13ft longer, the hull was basically that of a Forrest Sherman, as was the propulsion machinery. The extra length eased constrictions in the machinery spaces and permitted an amidships ASROC launcher. The ships remained cramped, however, which militated against subsequent major modernizations. They thus received only limited upgrading.

The final five units were fitted with the large SQS-23 sonar. Located in a forward bulb, this necessitated a more heavily raked bow and a stem anchor.

The Tartar launcher (twin-arm in the first 13 units, single-arm in the remainder) was located aft, atop a cylindrical structure that contained magazine and loading gear. Sited abaft the after 5in 54, it restricted the gun's firing arcs at lower elevations. The missile system was later modified to launch either Harpoon SSMs or Standard SM-1 MR SAMs.

ABOVE LEFT: *Charles F. Adams* (DDG.2) was lead ship for a class of 23 dating from the late 1950s. They featured a lengthened Forrest Sherman hull, with greater forward freeboard, but retaining the same machinery. ABOVE: Later units of the class were completed with improvements. The *Tattnall* (DDG.19), seen here in the Suez Canal, has the later single-arm Mk 13 launcher replacing the twin-arm Mk 11 and uprated SPS-40 air-search radar.

Two directors for target acquisition and illumination were situated abaft the after funnel. As these precluded the addition of a mainmast, the heavy, stabilized antenna for the tracking radar had to be supported on the after funnel The class was deleted during the 1990s, outlived somewhat by three modified versions built for each of the Royal Australian and German navies (*Brisbane*, *Hobart* and *Perth*, and *Lütjens*, *Mölders* and *Rommel* respectively).

LEFT: *Waddell* (DDG.24) was the last of the US Navy's Adams, a further six being built to foreign account. This photograph well portrays the powerful sheerline and modified bow associated with the later ships' bow-mounted SQS-23 sonars.
ABOVE: A Tartar missile blasts off from the single-arm Mk 13 launcher of the *Berkeley* (DDG.15). Ever-demanding of space, the revised launch system was later modified to fire the derived Standard SM-1 MR as well as Harpoon.

Adam class, as built 🇺🇸

Displacement: 3,275 tons (standard); 4,525 tons (full load)
Length: 128.1m/420ft (wl); 133.3m/437ft (oa)
Beam: 14.3m/47ft
Draught: 5.8m/19ft (full load)
Armament: 2 x 5in guns (2x1), 0/4 x 3in guns (0/2x2); Single/twin-armed Tartar SAM launcher; 8-cell ASROC launcher
Machinery: Double-reduction steam turbines, 4 boilers, 2 shafts
Power: 52,220kW/70,000shp for 31.5 knots
Endurance: 900 tons oil for 8,335km/4,500nm at 20 knots
Protection: Nominal
Complement: 345

UNITED STATES

LEFT: Superficially similar in appearance to an Adams, the larger Coontz type could be instantly differentiated through the considerable lattice structure before the after funnel. Ex-DLG.9 *Coontz* here shows her revised DDG.40 pendant number.
BELOW: With uprating from Terrier to Standard SM-2 ER missiles, the original two twin 3in gun mountings had to be sacrificed. The sole remaining anti-surface ships capability left to the *Luce* (DDG.38) is her single 5in gun.

Coontz (DDG.40) class

Clearly from the same stable as the Adams class, which was built in parallel, the Coontz (otherwise Farragut) class ships were an imposing 21.4m/70ft longer on the waterline. Comparable with earlier gun-armed Mitschers, the ten ships were initially classified DLG.6–15, i.e. "missile-armed destroyer leaders". In 1975, however, they were regraded as "GM destroyers", or DDG, and were renumbered DDG.37–46.

Designed for the area air defence of carrier groups, the class was designed around the Terrier III SAM. This was later uprated to the ER, or Extended Range, version of the Standard SM-1 (cf the Adams' MR, or Medium Range, version). Unlike the Adams', the Coontz-class launcher was located abaft the 40-round, flat-roofed missile magazine.

Only one 5in gun was fitted. This was in "A" position, superfired by an eight-cell ASROC launcher. As built, the class had a twin 3in 70 mounting on either side in the waist but, during the 1970s modernization, exchanged these for two, quadruple Harpoon SSM launchers. With the Standard missiles having terminal-phase homing, ship-end guidance electronics became simplified.

Operating facilities for a shipborne helicopter were not provided, although a touch-down pad was available right aft. Defensive armament lacking, a Close-In Weapon System (CIWS) such as Vulcan Phalanx was considered but not pursued, due to considerations of weight, cost and age.

Larger, but similar in profile to an Adams, a Coontz could be instantly differentiated by the tower-like lattice mainmast forward of the after funnel. To serve the ASROC, all had a hull-mounted (as opposed to bow-mounted) SQS-23 sonar. Later experience showed that sonars could be located within bulbous bows that could be designed to actually improve a ship's hydrodynamic performance over a given speed range. The by-now obsolete Coontz class was discarded during the 1990s.

ABOVE: Quadruple Harpoon SSMs, visible by the *Mahan*'s (DDG.42's) after funnel, redressed the earlier deficiency. The 40-round Standard magazine is contained within the flat structure forward of the launcher.

Coontz class, as completed

Displacement: 4,175 tons (standard); 5,650 tons (full load)
Length: 149.5m/490ft (wl); 156.3m/512ft 6in (oa)
Beam: 16m/52ft 4in
Draught: 5.4m/17ft 9in
Armament: 1 x 5in, 4 x 3in guns (2x2); 1 x twin Terrier SAM launcher, 8-cell ASROC launcher
Machinery: Double-reduction steam turbines, 4 boilers, 2 shafts
Power: 63,410kW/85,000shp for 32.5 knots
Endurance: 900 tons oil for 9,250km/5,000nm at 20 knots
Protection: Nominal
Complement: 365

Leahy (DLG.16) and Belknap (DLG.26) classes

To boost the area air defence of high-value surface groups, the "double-ended" escort was introduced with the nine Leahy. They were completed (1962–64) with a twin-arm Terrier SAM launcher at either end. An ASROC launcher was also located forward, with AS torpedo tubes in the waist. The only medium-calibre guns were paired 3in 70s on either side of amidships.

As with the preceding Coontz class, the Leahy were initially classified DLG but, in the general 1975 reclassification were, because of their size and capability, revised upward to "GM cruisers" DLG.16–24 thus became CG.16–24.

Even on a 162.6m/533ft hull, centreline space was at a premium not least because of the necessity for a pair of missile control radars at either end. A palliative was to combine masts and funnels into so-called "macks" (i.e. mast/stacks).

A second block of DLGs, the nine Belknaps, followed on immediately. Yet another 4.3m/14ft on the waterline, they had a more balanced armament. The forward launcher could handle either Terrier or ASROC rounds. In place of an after SAM system was a hangar and pad for the ultimately aborted DASH (Drone AS Helicopter). The old missile stowage and handling area provided further much-needed accommodation while a single 5in 54 occupied the space otherwise occupied by the launcher. Commissioned as DLG.26–34, the Belknaps subsequently became CG.26–34.

Modernization during the 1970s saw both classes exchange their waist 3in mountings for two quadruple Harpoon SSM launchers. Their SAM systems were upgraded; the Leahy class to five Standard SM-1 ER, the Belknaps to the improved SM-2 ER. The old DASH facilities in the latter were remodelled to accommodate the manned LAMPS (Light Airborne Multi-Purpose System) helicopter. Both classes were stricken and scrapped about the turn of the century.

ABOVE LEFT: **Like the Coontz-class ships, Leahys (nameship seen here) and Belknaps were originally categorized "Guided-Missile Destroyer Leaders" or DLGs. With the 1975 rationalization, however, they were upgraded to "Guided-Missile Cruisers", or CGs.**

ABOVE: **For improved seakeeping, both classes adopted a higher-freeboard, long-forecastle-style hull with a pronounced knuckle.** *England* **(CG.22) shows double-ended Standard SAM systems, Harpoon SSM and an ASROC launcher, but no gun.**

LEFT: **Although very similar to a Leahy from this angle, the Belknap-class** *Josephus Daniels* **(CG.27) is "single-ended", her after end being occupied by a single 5in gun and full facilities for a LAMPS (Light Airborne Multi-Purpose System) manned helicopter.**

Leahy class, as built

Displacement: 5,150 tons (standard); 7,600 tons (full load)
Length: 155.6m/510ft (wl); 162.6m/533ft (oa)
Beam: 16.3m/53ft 6in
Draught: 5.8m/19ft (full load)
Armament: 4 x 3in guns (2x2); 2 x twin Terrier SAM launchers, 8-cell ASROC launcher
Machinery: Double-reduction steam turbines, 4 boilers, 2 shafts
Power: 63,410kW/85,000shp for 32 knots
Endurance: 1,800 tons oil for 12,590km/6,800nm at 20 knots
Protection: Nominal
Complement: 396

UNITED STATES

Spruance (DD.963) and Kidd (DDG.993) classes

The 31-strong Spruance class was built by a single contractor (Litton), who was charged with producing a design to suit the requirements of the US Navy's Ship Characteristics Board (SCB) as well as setting up the associated building facility. Most unusually, the ship was specified over-large to facilitate later modernization.

Being multi-purpose, the Spruances also bucked the trend of destroyers being area air-defence platforms. Missile systems are demanding on volume and the final result appeared superficially to be under-armed.

A single 5in 54 was provided at either end. Abaft the forward gun was an eight-cell ASROC launcher. The after gun, located on a short, low quarterdeck, was superfired by a Sea Sparrow launcher. Designed for "point defence", this has a best range of 12.87km/8 miles. Forward of this were spacious facilities for a LAMPS-I (later a LAMPS-III) helicopter. An early addition was two Vulcan Phalanx CIWS, mounted high on the superstructure, forward and aft.

Propulsion was by gas turbine, two to a shaft. Machinery spaces were staggered, it being convenient to locate the enormous funnel casings to the sides of the ship. They were topped by eductors, the purpose of which was to reduce exhaust temperatures and, hence, Infra-Red (IR) signature.

Later additions added considerable, but greatly variable, weight. Most received a Vertical Launch System (VLS) forward, capable of handling both ASROC and the Tomahawk cruise missile in its anti-ship and land-attack versions. Considerable quantities of Kevlar "plastic armour" have been added to protect vital spaces.

Four modified Spruances were built to Iranian account. Completed 1981–82, they were never delivered, due to the Islamic Revolution. They were, therefore, assimilated into the US Navy as the Kidd class (DDG.993–996), their "DDG" classification resulting from their having the Standard SM-1 (later SM-2) system.

Only a handful of Spruances remain at the time of writing, mostly in reserve.

ABOVE LEFT: **Much-criticized for their apparent dearth of armament, the Spruances and Kidds were large enough to have their helicopter platform at the point of minimum accelerations.** *Chandler* **(DDG.996) is a double-ender of the Kidd quartet, designed for Iran.**
ABOVE: **The massive, featureless bridge front and navigating bridge of the** *Comte de Grasse* **(DD.974) would do credit to a cruise ship but, despite its bland appearance, it pre-dates the application of Aegis fixed array radar to destroyers.** LEFT: *Deyo* **(DD.989) here shows her attractive hull lines and low-visibility number. The installation of a VLS has gathered ASROC and Tomahawk missiles together. Two quadruple Harpoons are located amidships, with Sea Sparrow aft. Note CIWS atop the bridge.**

Spruance class, as built

Displacement: 5,830 tons (standard); 7,800 tons (full load)
Length: 161.3m/529ft (wl); 171.8m/563ft 4in (oa)
Beam: 16.8m/55ft
Draught: 6.3m/20ft 6in (full load)
Armament: 2 x 5in guns (2x1); 2 Vulcan Phalanx CIWS; 1 x 8-cell ASROC launcher; 1 x Sea Sparrow launcher
Machinery: 4 gas turbines, 2 shafts
Power: 59,680kW/80,000shp for 30 knots
Endurance: 1,600 tons fuel for 11,112km/6,000nm at 20 knots
Protection: Kevlar patches
Complement: 296

Ticonderoga (CG.47) class

Using the same hull and propulsion system as the Spruances, the Ticonderogas are complementary in providing the specialized air-defence component that the multi-purpose Spruances lacked. This was recognized in 1980 by elevating their category from DDG to CG.

Designed for future updating, the Spruances gained an average 1,850 tons over their lifetime. Beginning near the Spruance maximum displacement, the Ticonderogas have already gained a further average of 500 tons. The Spruance deep draught of 6.3m/20.5ft has thus increased to a Ticonderoga's 7.5m/24ft 6in, at a cost of over 2 knots in speed and reduced freeboard, evidenced by the addition of a forward bulwark to decrease wetness.

A major threat to a surface group is saturation missile attack using air, surface and sub-surface platforms in coordination. The Ticonderogas' phased-array radar was designed to cope with multitude simultaneous threats, its electronic scanning being more flexible than conventional rotating scanners. Her boxy superstructure is arranged around the four fixed arrays of the SPY-1A/B radar, to which are slaved four illuminators which, it is claimed, can control over a dozen ship-launched missiles simultaneously. Ship-end response has been speeded by retro-fitting two Vertical Launch Systems (VLS) in place of the earlier twin-arm launchers. VLS can handle Standard SM-2 MR, Tomahawk or ASROC, while Harpoons can be fired from two quadruple mountings located right aft.

ASROC can be targeted by the ship's LAMPS-III helicopter or by sonars, both hull-mounted and towed array. Lightweight AS torpedo tubes are located within the hull, launching through shutters. Two Vulcan Phalanx CIWS are located high in the superstructure.

ABOVE LEFT: *Mobile Bay* (CG.53) and *Leyte Gulf* (CG.55) clearly show their Spruance parentage. On the same hull they have greater displacement, reducing freeboard and requiring a bulwark forward to alleviate the consequent wetness.

ABOVE: The four-quadrant "billboard" arrays of the SPY1A/B 3-D radar are split between the forward and after superstructures. Early units were originally equipped with Mk 26 launchers forward and aft. *Anzio* (CG.68) is shown here.

An essential element of a coordinated area air-defence system is the ability to share real-time data between ships, the function of the so-called Tactical Distribution Link.

The first five ships of the class have already been retired.

LEFT: The helicopter platform and after VLS are visible on this view of *San Jacinto* (CG.56). On the "fantail", a further level lower, are located the after 5in gun and two quadruple Harpoons. Note the staggered funnels.

Ticonderoga class, as built

Displacement: 6,600 tons (standard); 8,900 tons (full load)
Length: 161.3m/529ft (wl); 171.7m/563ft (oa)
Beam: 16.8m/55ft
Draught: 7.5m/24ft 6in (full load)
Armament: 2 x 5in guns (2x1); 2 x Vulcan Phalanx CIWS; 2 x quadruple Harpoon SSM launchers, 2 x VLS with Standard SAM, ASROC AS and Tomahawk TLAM
Machinery: 4 gas turbines, 2 shafts
Power: 59,680kW/80,000shp for 30+ knots
Endurance: 2,000 tons fuel for 11,112km/6,000nm at 20 knots
Protection: Kevlar patches
Complement: 347

UNITED STATES

LEFT: Note the beamy hull of *Curtis Wilbur* (DDG.54), whose L/B ratio is only 7.89 compared with a *Ticonderoga*'s slender 9.62. The neat octagonal forward superstructure accommodates all four fixed arrays of the SPY 1/D Aegis system.

ABOVE: Flight II units, such as *McFaul* (DDG.74), are indistinguishable externally from Flight Is like the *Curtis Wilbur*. The differences lay in the electronics fit.

Arleigh Burke (DDG.51) class

A design objective for the Burke was to combine, as far as was possible, the capability of a Ticonderoga with the versatility of a Spruance. The result in two main versions, appears to be a reasonable compromise, with the added advantage of the deletion of structural aluminium alloy and the addition of a reported 130 tons of Kevlar splinter protection. Much of the structure, including the robust tripod mast, has been configured to reduce radar signature, the resulting appearance being less extreme than that of some foreign examples.

The hull form reflects an interest in the "short-fat" principle, with its generous waterplanes. Compared with a Spruance's orthodox Length-on-Breadth (L/B) ratio of 9.62, a Burke is only 7.89. The choice appears to favour volumetric capacity and ship movement.

DDG.51–71 inclusive are termed "Flight I" ships. Externally identical, "Flight II" units (DDG.72–78) have more advanced data links and Electronic Countermeasures (ECM). They are also fitted "for but not with" the ER (Extended Range) version of the Standard SM-2.

The bridge structure is a truncated, irregular octagon, whose angled faces incorporate the four fixed arrays of a modified Aegis system. This controls three illuminators. There is a 61-cell VLS aft and a 29-cell VLS forward (64 and 32 respectively in DDG.79 onwards). These can launch Standard SM-2 MR, ASROC or Tomahawk missiles. There are two quadruple Harpoon launchers, two Vulcan Phalanx CIWS and a single 5in 54-calibre gun. No helicopter is carried but a large pad and basic facilities are provided on the afterdeck.

In "Flight IIA" ships, i.e. DDG.79 onwards, the after superstructure is extended full width in order to provide a double hangar for LAMPS-III helicopters. Unusually, no Harpoons are currently carried but Sea Sparrow Basic Point Defence SAMs have been added to the VLS inventory.

ABOVE: The smaller forward extension of the bridge structure and the full-width helicopter hangar aft mark *Shoup* (DDG.86) as a "Flight IIA" unit. These are also 1.52m/5ft longer.

ABOVE: *Mustin* (DDG.89), seen early in 2007, shows less-prominent eductors atop the funnel casings. The large, low structure aft accommodates a VLS as well as a double helicopter hangar.

Flight I, as built

Displacement: 6,820 tons (standard); 8,940 tons (full load)
Length: 142m/466ft 2in (wl); 153.8m/504ft 10in (oa)
Beam: 18m/59ft 1in on waterline
Draught: 6.3m/20ft 9in hull (full load)
Armament: 1 x 5in gun; 2 x Vulcan Phalanx CIWS; 2 x quadruple Harpoon launchers; 2 x VLS with Standard SM-2 MR, ASROC AS and Tomahawk TLAM
Machinery: 4 gas turbines, 2 shafts
Power: 67,140kW/90,000shp for 31.5 knots
Endurance: 8,150km/4,400nm at 20 knots
Protection: Kevlar patches
Complement: 337

139

LEFT: **As war reparation, the Japanese Navy was awarded a group of ex-German destroyers. From these it adopted the practice of locating torpedo tubes forward of the bridge. This is** *Kaki* **of the Momi class, as she was in the 1920s.**

Momi and Wakatake classes

Although the Imperial Japanese Navy (IJN) worked closely with the British as an ally during World War I, even operating some Royal Navy destroyers on loan, it continued with an essentially German layout in its first post-war programmes. Development built on the preceding Enoki and Momo types, with some influence from a handful of ex-German boats awarded as reparation.

Twenty-one Momi-class destroyers were built in three consecutive batches. They were the first Japanese boats to deploy 21in torpedoes, for which two twin-tube mountings were carried. The forward of these was located in a well, abaft a short, full-height forecastle. The bridge structure was now resited abaft these tubes, a dryer location for the bridge personnel, but at the expense of the forward torpedomen, regularly inundated by green water coming over the forecastle.

Three 4.7in guns were again carried, the forward one on the forecastle, the amidships and after one being elevated on bandstands for dryness. The curved, boat-shaped bow profile had now also become a distinctive feature of Japanese construction.

Completed 1919–23, the Momis were followed immediately by the 12-strong Wakatake class, of which five were cancelled. Of the same length and layout, they were given an extra 15cm/6in beam to compensate for a further 50 tons of displacement. They were also fitted to both lay and sweep mines. Not alone among Japanese warships of the time, their stability was always suspect, evidenced in 1932 by the loss of *Sawarabi* in a storm.

Both classes were active during uncontested operations in Chinese waters during the 1930s. In 1940, however, tubes, one 4.7in gun and all mine-related gear were removed in favour of depth charges, added in their conversion to convoy escorts.

Seventeen Momi served 1941–45, only seven surviving. All six of the participating Wakatakes were destroyed.

Wakatake class, as built

Displacement: 900 tons (standard); 1,100 tons (full load)
Length: 83.9m/275ft (bp); 85.4m/280ft (wl)
Beam: 8.1m/26ft 6in
Draught: 2.6m/8ft 6in (standard)
Armament: 3 x 4.7in guns (3x1); 4 x 21in torpedo tubes (2x2)
Machinery: Direct-drive steam turbines, 3 boilers, 2 shafts
Power: 16,040kW/21,500shp for 36 knots
Endurance: 275 tons oil for 5,560km/3,000nm at 15 knots
Protection: None
Complement: 110

ABOVE: **Despite their apparent size, the Wakatake-class destroyers had a standard displacement of only about 900 tons, and mounted only twin torpedo tubes forward and aft. They were reckoned "Second Class" destroyers.**

JAPAN

ABOVE: **Effectively lengthened Momis, the 15 Minekaze class represented a great step forward. Note that the four 4.7in guns were all at an equal height. A third pair of torpedo tubes was preferred to tripling the existing two mountings.**
LEFT: ***Mutsuki*, the nameship of a class of 12, was the ultimate development of the Momi type. Otherwise similar to the preceding Kamikaze class, the Momis mounted the 24in torpedo and were given a distinctive bow profile.**

Minekaze, Kamikaze and Mutsuki classes

Complementary to the Second Class Momis, and built in parallel were the 15 First Class Minekaze-type destroyers. Scaled-up, their extra length permitted a third pair of torpedo tubes and a fourth 4.7in gun. The latter was mounted abaft the after funnel in some, on the after deckhouse in others.

Length-on-Breadth (L/B) ratios were exceptionally fine, the earlier Wakatake 10.6 being exceeded by the Minekaze 11.0. The latter were the first Japanese boats with geared turbines and returned high trial speeds.

The nine follow-on Kamikaze class, completed between 1922 and 1925, were virtual repeats. All carried two single 4.7in guns on the after deckhouse. Their bridge structure was more substantial and the hull had a nominal increase in beam as compensation for topweight.

Considered successful, the design was developed further with the 12 Mutsuki, completed 1925–27. Their recognition feature was a bow of the new "double-curvature" profile.

This class introduced the 24in torpedo, which would develop into a much-respected weapon. These early versions were driven by compressed air (rather than oxygen) but already carried a 50 per cent heavier warhead half as far again as a standard 21in torpedo.

LEFT: ***Shimakaze* was a further unit of the Minekaze class. In this rather touched-up view, she carries no pendant number forward but, as was general between the wars, has her name in Japanese characters amidships.**

The Mutsukis' six tubes were better organized in two triple mountings, thus saving precious centreline space. Four reload torpedoes could be carried or, alternatively, 16 mines. Again, all carried their two after 4.7in guns on the after deckhouse all guns being located at the same height above the upper deck.

Japanese fleet destroyers were very hard-worked during World War II and, typically, ships of all three of these classes surrendered one or two 4.7in guns, some a set of torpedo tubes, in order to ship up to ten small automatic weapons and large outfits of depth charges. Widely used as transports, supporting island garrisons, they paid a high attritional price, only 7 out of 34 surviving the war, most of them damaged.

Mutsuki class, as built 🔴

Displacement: 1,315 tons (standard); 1,775 tons (full load)
Length: 97.6m/320ft (bp); 103.1m/338ft (wl)
Beam: 9.2m/30ft
Draught: 3m/9ft 9in
Armament: 4 x 4.7in guns (4x1); 6 x 24in torpedo tubes (2x3)
Machinery: Geared steam turbines, 4 boilers, 2 shafts
Power: 28,720kW/38,500shp for 37 knots
Endurance: 420 tons oil for 7,400km/4,000nm at 15 knots
Protection: None
Complement: 150

141

Fubuki and Akatsuki classes

Treated unfairly, as they saw it, by the 1921–22 Washington Conference, the Japanese sought to compensate for insufficient capital ship tonnage by building some of the world's most formidable cruisers and destroyers. Of the latter, the Fubuki class, commenced under the 1923 Programme, set a new benchmark, causing foreign fleets to upgrade their own specifications.

Over 15.2m/50ft longer than the still-building Matsukis, these "special-type" destroyers were designed for attack rather than for screening. They mounted a third triple set of 24in torpedo tubes. These were later fitted with splinter-proof shields and modified for the improved, oxygen-fuelled version of the torpedo.

One reload, housed in protective casings, was provided for each of the nine tubes.

A heavier 5in calibre gun was also introduced with the class. Six were housed in three twin, fully enclosed gunhouses, another world "first". Bearing in mind British problems with introducing a High-Angle, Dual-Purpose (HA/DP) armament, it is noteworthy that the Japanese in the later Fubukis, mounted weapons of 55 degrees' elevation in 1930.

Also with a very slender hull (L/B about 11.13) the design proved to be tender. Stability was restored only by lowering funnels and bridge structure, together with substantial ballasting. This cost 4 knots in speed.

ABOVE: **When they appeared in the late 1920s, the Fubukis set a new world standard for destroyers. At the price of considerable size, they combined high speed with a heavy gun and torpedo armament. This picture shows** *Uranami*.

For the final four units of the class only three, improved boilers were fitted, in place of the earlier four. With only one boiler to exhaust, the forward funnel could be considerably, and distinctively, reduced in girth. The shorter forward boiler space also meant that the hull itself could be shortened by some 5.2m/17ft. These were termed the Akatsuki class.

With war, both classes landed "X" mounting and three spare torpedoes in favour of automatic weapons and depth charges. Just one ship of each type survived, both in a damaged condition.

ABOVE: **Generally similar to the Fubukis were the four follow-on Akatsukis, of which the** *Ikazuchi* **is seen here. Note the thinner forefunnel, the 5in guns twinned in enclosed gunhouses, and long forecastle. Nine 24in torpedo tubes were carried in triples.**

Fubuki class, as built

Displacement: 1,750 tons (standard); 2,090 tons (full load)
Length: 111.9m/367ft (bp); 118.5m/388ft 6in (oa)
Beam: 10.4m/34ft
Draught: 3.2m/10ft 6in
Armament: 6 x 5in guns (3x2); 9 x 24in torpedo tubes (3x3)
Machinery: Geared steam turbines, 4 boilers, 2 shafts
Power: 37,300kW/50,000shp for 38 knots
Endurance: 500 tons oil for 8,700km/4,700nm at 15 knots
Protection: None
Complement: 200

Hatsuharu and Shiratsuyu classes

Previously unrestricted, destroyers became limited by the 1930 London Treaty to a standard displacement of 1,850 tons. The still-completing Akatsukis, once necessarily ballasted, displaced 1,980 tons and, for Japanese designers already loading destroyers to the limit, a shift to smaller dimensions did not come easily. All-welded construction was already, however, saving considerable weight.

The 1931 Programme provided for the six Hatsuharus which, while about 7.9m/26ft shorter than an Akatsuki, contrived to carry the same armament, less one 5in gun. As built, they had a twin 5in gunhouse at either end, the forward one superfired by a single. In order to accommodate three triple 24in torpedo tube banks and their reloads the fore- and aftermost were elevated, permitting some overlap, while the after funnel was offset to starboard.

With two ships completed, stability proved deficient, necessitating the lowering of funnels and bridge structure. The aftermost tubes and reload facility were landed, enabling "B" gun to be relocated one level down, back-to-back with the after twin.

Considerable ballast was also added although the final displacement, officially at least, remained under treaty limits. Delayed by the modifications, the class overlapped the succeeding Shiratsuyus.

These ten ships, nominally of the same dimensions, took the same battery layout. To compensate for the loss of one set of tubes, the remaining two were made quadruples, the after bank reloading from the after deckhouse, the forward from a pair of angled box containers flanking the after funnel.

The class maintained an L/B ratio of 10.82 and, considering its tenderness,

TOP: *Nenohi* and *Hatsuharu* were completed in 1933 as lead ships for the class, but were found to be critically unstable. This picture shows *Nenohi* as completed, before drastic weight reduction was undertaken. ABOVE: Heavily used, the Japanese destroyer force took terrible losses, including all ten Shiratsuyus. The *Yamakaze*, here, was torpedoed by the US submarine *Nautilus* on June 25, 1942. Note the recognition panel on the turret roof.

it is surprising that a slightly lower top speed was not accepted in exchange for a further foot of beam. Wartime modifications included removal of the single 5in gun and all torpedo reloads. All 16 ships of these classes became war losses, mostly to air and submarine attack.

Shiratsuyu, as built

Displacement: 1,820 tons (standard); 2,150 tons (full load)
Length: 103.6m/339ft 7in (bp); 111.3m/365ft (oa)
Beam: 9.9m/32ft 6in
Draught: 3.5m/11ft 6in (full load)
Armament: 5 x 5in guns (2x2/1x1); 8 x 24in torpedo tubes (2x4)
Machinery: Geared steam turbines, 3 boilers, 2 shafts
Power: 31,332kW/42,000shp for 34 knots
Endurance: 500 tons oil for 11,110km/6,000nm at 15 knots
Protection: None
Complement: 180

ABOVE: The Shiratsuyus were redesigned to reduce topweight. Note *Kawakaze*'s third turret carried at upper deck level, aft. The bridge structure has been greatly reduced, but the massive quadruple 24in torpedo tube mountings have been retained, still comprising the major weapon system.

Asashio class

In order to adequately accommodate a six-gun main battery, the ten Asashios, commenced in 1935, were over 7.6m/26ft longer than the preceding Sharatsuyu. Although larger, a compensating near-20 per cent greater installed power gave them an extra knot.

Because the twin 5in gunhouses were too heavy to permit a superimposed "B" mounting, two were located aft in "X" and "Y" positions. With just one forward mounting, it was possible to maintain a useful gap between it and the bridge front, allowing it to fire on a considerable after bearing without damage to the bridge structure.

Two quadruple torpedo tube banks were now accepted as a practical maximum. By the mid-1930s, the 24in torpedo was energized by fuel burned in an atmosphere of pure oxygen. Weighing 2,700kg/5,940lb at launch, it could carry a 490kg/1,078lb warhead to a distance of 40km/25 miles at a speed of 36 knots. Although not kept particularly secret, its performance came as something of an unpleasant surprise to the Allies during the Pacific war. Also ready to use torpedoes in large numbers, Japanese destroyers continued to be designed to carry a full set of reloads. The after deckhouse was asymmetrical in plan to accommodate four spare torpedoes, while two were stowed in each of two protected boxes flanking the forward funnel.

A simplified bridge structure, with a measure of streamlining, pointed to efforts at reducing topweight. The class introduced a new 25mm Type 96 Hotchkiss-type Anti-Aircraft (AA) gun, with a dedicated director.

With war, the usual deletion of "X" gun mounting and all spare torpedoes enabled up to 28 of the 25mm weapons to be carried, together with depth charges sufficient for six 6-charge patterns. Heavily used, every one of the class was lost.

ABOVE: **In order to return to a full six-gun 5in armament with one superimposed turret, the *Arashio* required an increase in displacement of about 25 per cent. "X" gunhouse was, nonetheless, later removed. Weight-saving measures have resulted in a "monoblock" bridge structure and very light masting.**

ABOVE: ***Arashio*, nameship of the class, in an as-completed condition. Note the Anti-Aircraft (AA) director immediately abaft the after funnel and the large, twinned 5in "X" mounting, later landed in favour of more light automatic weapons. Up to 28 25mm guns were added, at the expense of all reload torpedoes.**

Asashio class, as built

Displacement: 2,070 tons (standard); 2,530 tons (full load)
Length: 111.1m/364ft 2in (bp); 118.3m/388ft (oa)
Beam: 10.4m/34ft
Draught: 3.7m/12ft (full load)
Armament: 6 x 5in guns (3x2); 8 x 24in torpedo tubes (2x4)
Machinery: Geared steam turbines, 3 boilers, 2 shafts
Power: 37,300kW/50,000shp for 35 knots
Endurance: 500 tons oil for 8,700km/4,700nm at 15 knots
Protection: None
Complement: 200

JAPAN

LEFT: **Essentially modified Asashios, the *Kagero* class is represented here by *Shiranui*.** As in many Japanese destroyers, the galley funnel, snaking from bridge structure to forward funnel, and crowned with a "Charlie Noble", is an art form in itself.

Kagero and Yugumo classes

With the *Asashio*, the IJN had a destroyer design suitable both for its requirements and for series production. That it was still considered deficient in stability, however, is apparent in that the 18 follow-on Kagero-class boats, although nominally of the same length, were given an extra 50cm/20in of beam. Treaty limitations now abandoned, the Japanese recognized the inexorable increases of displacement in referring to the Kageros as a "cruiser" type, a reference to size rather than to function.

To reduce the size and bulk of machinery, the Japanese were using advanced steam conditions. There were mechanical problems but, also, those of stability. This was because machinery weight saved from low in the ship was immediately replaced by further topside equipment and weaponry.

One weight-saving feature was the exceptionally light tripod masts, yet even these were replaced by fragile, stayed pole masts in some destroyers. Radar, when it was introduced, require antennae separated on to both fore- and mainmasts, so that the latter had to be retained. Neither radar nor sonar was particularly effective, a situation not helped by the general attitude that their use was "defensive", opposing the fiercely "offensive" ethic of the IJN.

Up to eighteen 25mm weapons were later added – forward of and flanking the bridge structure, immediately abaft the after funnel, and on two levels atop the after deckhouse in place of the 5in "X" mounting, which was landed.

Considerably out-classing the contemporary American Benson, the Kageros were completed by mid-1944, the series continuing with the Yugumos, of slightly modified design but near identical in appearance. Although 28 of the latter were authorized, only 20 were actually built.

The 38 ships of these classes saw action throughout the theatre. Only one survived the war, the remaining laying in waters from Japan to the Philippines, from China to New Guinea.

ABOVE: **An interesting late picture shows the Kagero-class *Nowaki* stemmed in dry dock.** Note the wartime additions of heavy degaussing cable, showing as a dark line around the hull, and the added twin AA mounting forward of the bridge.

Yugumo class, as built

Displacement: 2,220 tons (standard); 2,690 tons (full load)
Length: 111.6m/366ft (bp); 119.3m/391ft (oa)
Beam: 10.8m/35ft 5in
Draught: 3.8m/12ft 6in
Armament: 6 x 5in guns (3x2); 8 x 24in torpedo tubes (2x4)
Machinery: Geared steam turbines, 3 boilers, 2 shafts
Power: 38,792kW/52,000shp for 35 knots
Endurance: 9,260km/5,000nm at 18 knots (Kagero class)
Protection: None
Complement: 230

ABOVE: **The Yugumo-class *Kiyoshimo* as completed, with additional AA guns forward but still in possession of "X" mounting.** The gantries facilitating the reloading of the heavy 24in torpedoes are becoming prominent features. Throughout the war, the Japanese regarded the torpedo as the weapon of choice.

145

Akitsuki class

During the late 1930s the major fleets became aware that the likely scale of air attack on a surface group would be such as to require dedicated Anti-Aircraft (AA) escorts. Both the Americans and British built small cruisers in response (Atlanta and Dido classes respectively), but neither was fully satisfactory in that their main calibre weapons were too heavy to enjoy the required rate of fire, yet too light for ships of their size.

A better British solution was the conversion of 20-year old, 4,290-ton C-class cruisers to carry eight or ten 4in high-angle guns with efficient direction. These could well have influenced the IJN in its choice of small AA cruiser form. The Akizukis were 3.4m/11ft 3in shorter than the elderly British ships, but considerably narrower.

They carried four twin, fully enclosed 3.9in gunhouses. The guns themselves were 65-calibre models with high muzzle velocity. With a raised forecastle and two superimposed mountings at either end, the ships certainly looked like destroyers.

Also not overloaded, it was hardly surprising that a single quadruple 24in torpedo mounting was added, together with reloads. Seventy-two depth charges and their projectors completed the transformation from cruiser to destroyer.

They were instantly distinguishable from earlier Japanese destroyers by their single funnel, heavily trunked to exhaust both boiler spaces. The single casing saved a little weight and offered less obstacle to AA weapons while keeping smoke clear of the bridge structure.

Being more closely associated with battle fleet operations, the Akitsukis probably found themselves less called upon to perform the high-attrition, maid-of-all-work tasks that fell to other fleet destroyers, accounting for their relatively high 50 per cent survival rate.

Twenty-six more destroyers of the same size were cancelled or never completed, while sixteen planned larger versions were never commenced, due to a dearth of raw materials.

TOP: **To meet the requirement for more fleet AA escorts, the Akitsuki class was designed with four twin 3.9in gun mountings. Only one quadruple torpedo tube bank could be accommodated. This is** *Harutsuki*, **which survived the war.** ABOVE: *Yoitsuki* **also avoided destruction by being under repair. Here, she awaits disarmament post-war, prior to being used for repatriation duties. Following these, she was ceded to China. Note the class's very fine lines.**

LEFT: **The Akitsukis were well designed for their task. This is** *Terutsuki*, **sunk by US torpedo boats in December 1942. Note the gap between the forward armament and the bridge to permit maximum clear firing arcs.**

Akitsuki class, as built

Displacement: 2,700 tons (standard); 3,700 tons (full load)
Length: 126.1m/413ft 4in (bp); 134.3m/440ft 3in (oa)
Beam: 11.6m/38ft 1in
Draught: 4.1m/13ft 7in
Armament: 8 x 3.9in guns (4x2); 4 x 24in torpedo tubes (1x4)
Machinery: Geared steam turbines, 3 boilers, 2 shafts
Power: 38,792kW/52,000shp for 33 knots
Endurance: 1,100 tons oil for 15,270km/8,300nm at 18 knots
Protection: None
Complement: 290

Yamagumo/Minegumo class

Restyled the Japanese Maritime Self-Defence Force, the Japanese Navy began building destroyers in 1953. All weaponry was now American-supplied and the first pair of ships, the 1,700-ton Harukaze class, were of typical US flush-decked design.

They were followed by seven Ayanami class (1957–60), three Murasames (1958–59) and two Akizukis (1959), all of long forecastle design. Their widely spaced funnels indicated adoption of unit machinery layout, but the one-forward, two-aft gun disposition was inherited from earlier practice.

More original were the nine Yamagumos/Minegumos of 1965–77. Well removed from the classic destroyer concept, they featured advanced Anti-Submarine (AS) equipment and light, Dual-Purpose (DP) guns in place of the earlier heavy gun and torpedo batteries. With their change in function, high speed was no longer necessary, propulsion being by three diesels coupled to each of two shafts. The ships' ASW bias reflected the fact that, during the Cold War, the Japanese were the West's closest allies to the submarines of the Soviet Pacific Fleet.

Three Yamagumos, launched 1965–66, began the series. They were designed around an ASROC system, whose launcher was located amidships for minimum ship movement. A quadruple-barrelled Bofors AS mortar was carried forward and triple AS torpedo tubes sided in the after waist. Their six diesel engines were divided between two, widely separated compartments.

The following trio, termed the Minegumos (1967–69), were modelled around the abortive Drone Anti-Submarine Helicopter (DASH) system. This necessitated a compact superstructure and single funnel, with a DASH hangar and flight pad sited aft. From 1979 ASROC was retro-fitted in lieu.

DASH was already proving technically inadequate when the decision was made to complete the final group of three to the original Yamagumo design.

All hulls were identical except that the final six had knuckles forward. One ship, Yugumo, still exists, in a training role.

ABOVE: Although of the same basic design as Yamagumo (below left), the Minegumo was one of three remodelled around the abortive DASH system, whose small hangar can be seen aft, adjacent to the eight-celled ASROC launcher.

ABOVE: The eight Yamagumo variants had their machinery divided around the ASROC arrangement amidships. With no helicopter, some had their after end raised to accommodate a Variable-Depth Sonar (VDS) installation. Note the two funnels.

Yamagumo, as built

Displacement: 2,150 tons (normal); 2,700 tons (full load)
Length: 114.9m/377ft 2in (wl)
Beam: 11.8m/38ft 9in
Draught: 4m/13ft 2in
Armament: 4 x 3in guns (2x2); 1 x 8-cell ASROC AS launcher; 1 x 4-barrelled Bofors 375mm AS mortar; 6 x 12.7in AS torpedo tubes (2x3)
Machinery: Six 12-cylinder diesel engines, 2 shafts
Power: 19,769kW/26,500bhp for 27 knots
Endurance: 12,965km/7,000nm at 20 knots
Protection: None
Complement: 215

LEFT: **This early picture of** *Kikusuki* **shows her with her name painted up amidships and her after end still configured to operate DASH. The flight pad was later used for a Sea Sparrow SAM launcher, superfired by a Phalanx Close-In Weapon System (CIWS).**

Takatsuki class

Contemporary with the first group of Yamagumos, the four Takatsukis were larger and steam-propelled. Again, they had a strong ASW bias. Their flush-decked hulls, with long, sweeping sheerline, continued a more uniform "American" appearance. Superstructure was divided between two blocks with deck space being conserved by combining masts and funnels in so-called "macks".

As completed, the after end was dedicated to facilities for no less than three DASH helicopters. Forward of the bridge structure was the ASROC launcher, right forward a Bofors AS mortar. In the waist were triple tubes on either side for AS torpedoes. Bow sonar was fitted in two, VDS in the others. Except for the dual-purpose capability of the two 5in 54s, air defence, for such valuable ships, appeared deficient.

DASH was removed from 1977, along with the after 5in gun located on the hangar roof. The space so freed was used to greatly improve the ships' defensive armament. On what had been the flight deck was mounted an 8-cell launcher for the Sea Sparrow, a point-defence SAM system effective out to 12.8km/8 miles. In place of the after gun, a lofty structure was added to accommodate associated acquisition and guidance electronics.

Superfiring Sea Sparrow was added a self-contained Vulcan Phalanx, Gatling-style 20mm CIWS. Its inbuilt radars track both target and projectile stream to bring them coincident. Its range is about 1.7km/1 mile (5 seconds for a trans-sonic missile).

Between the new director tower and the after funnel was added two quadruple Harpoon canister launchers. Although this SSM has a reported range of better than 96.5km/60 miles the ships, sans helicopter, would require third party assistance to realize its full potential.

To improve the potential of the ASROC, the class was also fitted with passive towed arrays. Now specialist in neither AAW nor ASW, and with no reloads for ASROC or Harpoon, the remaining class life was limited.

ABOVE: *Takatsuki*, nameship for the class, appears rather under-armed in the original configuration. She and *Nagatsuki* differed in having a mainmast, topped with a Tactical Air Navigation (TACAN) beacon. Note the triple ASW torpedo tubes amidships. Modernization saw the addition of Sea Sparrow and Harpoon.

Takatsuki class, as built

Displacement: 3,200 tons (normal); 4,500 tons (full load)
Length: 136m/446ft 5in (wl)
Beam: 13.4m/44ft
Draught: 4.4m/14ft 5in
Armament: 2 x 5in guns (2x1); 1 x 8-cell ASROC AS launcher; 1 x 4-barrelled Bofors 375mm AS mortar; 6 x 12.7in AS torpedo tubes (2x3)
Machinery: Geared steam turbines, 2 boilers, 2 shafts
Power: 44,760kW/60,000shp for 32 knots
Endurance: 900 tons oil for 12,965km/7,000nm at 20 knots
Protection: None
Complement: 270

Shirane and Haruna classes

With the demise of DASH, there was an urgent requirement to get manned helicopters to sea. Where the latter had the disadvantage of extra bulk and weight they were, once equipped with an efficient data link, an intelligent extension to the ship herself. Two or more helicopters are more efficient in a submarine hunt, while also conferring a measure of redundancy.

The two Harunas (launched 1972–73), although looking very different, were logical rearrangements of the Takatsukis, with ASROC and both 5in guns forward, but without the AS mortar. Greater size was driven by the dimensions of an enormous hangar, suitable for three aircraft. Originally these were HSS-2 Sea Kings, replaced latterly by the more effective SH-60J version of the LAMPS-III Seahawk.

Launched in 1978–79, the two Shiranes are improved Harunas, some 6.1m/20ft greater in length. All four have a knuckle running the full length of the hull, to maximize deck width without increasing beam at the waterline. Both types are designed to achieve 32 knots on a relatively modest 52,220kW/70,000shp. All are steam-turbine propelled, the Haruna having one huge "mack", the *Shirane* two smaller. Uptakes on both are offset from the centreline to better utilize space.

As both types had the size to act as flagships, they were extensively modernized during the 1980s, with superstructures enlarged and electronics renewed and extended. Earlier deficient in AA defence, both gained a Sea Sparrow launcher on the hangar roof and a pair of Vulcan Phalanx CIWS high on the superstructure. Active stabilizers have been added to facilitate flying operations in adverse conditions and right aft, below the flight deck, is a passive towed array.

With the oldest now over 33 years in service, all four ships are due for replacement, their successors likely to be up to four 13,500-tonners with through flight decks.

ABOVE: *Shirane's* flight deck, appearing foreshortened here, occupies, with the hangar, 50 per cent of the ship's length. A helicopter dominates the layout. Note the full-length knuckle, a device to increase width at upper deck level. LEFT: A pretty photograph of *Kurama* leaving Yokosuka. Although she carries a modern range of electronics, she is still fitted with the old-style ASROC launcher forward, and remains essentially an ASW ship. The two funnels give the appearance of a single structure.

Shirane class, as modernized

Displacement: 5,200 tons (normal); 6,800 tons (full load)
Length: 158.8m/521ft 3in (wl)
Beam: 17.5m/57ft 5in
Draught: 5.3m/17ft 5in
Armament: 2 x 5in guns (2x1); 1 x 8-cell ASROC IAS launcher; 1 x 8-cell Sea Sparrow SAM launcher; 2 x 20mm Vulcan Phalanx CIWS; 6 x 12.7in AS torpedo tubes (2x3)
Machinery: Geared steam turbines, 2 boilers, 2 shafts
Power: 52,220kW/70,000shp for 32 knots
Endurance: Not known
Protection: Nominal
Complement: 360

DIRECTORY OF DESTROYERS: 1918 TO DATE

ABOVE: **Imposing ships for their size, the three Tachikazes are now dated, but are too elderly to be modified for a multi-purpose Vertical Launch System (VLS). Note the Mk 13 Mod 4 Standard SM-1 MR system aft. Harpoon is not being carried here by** Sawakaze. RIGHT: **Slightly longer and beamier, the two Hatakazes have their armament rearranged in order to provide a helicopter flight pad aft. The knuckle appears effective in this shot of** Shimakaze, **deflecting water from the hull as she proceeds at high speed.**

Tachikaze and Hatakaze classes

With the *Amatsukaze*, launched in 1963, the Japanese acquired their first Guided Missile Destroyer, or DDG. A single-arm launcher for Standard SM-1 MR occupied the whole after end, while the associated directors and electronics gave the ship a lofty, almost stately, appearance that made her look far larger than her 3,050 tons.

It would be a decade and more before she was followed by further DDGs in the three Tachikazes (1974–81). ASROC, located amidships in the *Amatsukaze*, was resited forward while a 5in 54, forward and aft, gave the ships more credible firepower than the earlier ship's four 3in weapons. Their launcher was later modified to fire Harpoon SSMs as an alternative, the missile total remaining a maximum 40.

Slightly lengthened, their hull forms were shared with the earlier Takatsukis, the forward sections being particularly elegant. Serving steam turbine propulsive machinery, the two widely spaced funnels were again combined with heavy, electronics-laden masts.

Again, it would be a decade before further DDGs were built. The two Hatakazes (launched 1984–87) in turn shared a lengthened hull with much the same form as the preceding Hatsuyuki-class AS destroyers.

Gas-turbine propulsion had, by now, superseded steam, greatly reducing machinery weight and bulk, and the number of engine-room personnel. They assumed the proven combination of two Olympus and two Speys, exhausted via a single large funnel.

The Standard launcher was moved forward, sharing the foredeck with one of the two 5in guns and ASROC. A forward bulwark and knuckle testify to forward wetness, the entry being fine.

Two quadruple Harpoon canister launchers are located abaft the *Hatakaze*'s funnels, allowing the full 40-round Standard outfit to be carried. Two Vulcan Phalanx CIWS have been added, but no Sea Sparrow. None of the DDGs carries a helicopter.

Hatakaze class

Displacement: 4,650 tons (normal); 5,600 tons (full load)
Length: 150m/492ft 4in (wl)
Beam: 16.4m/53ft 10in
Draught: 4.8m/15ft 9in
Armament: 2 x 5in guns (2x1); 1 x single-arm launcher Standard SM-1MR SAM; 1 x 8-cell ASROC launcher; 2 x quadruple Harpoon launchers; 2 x 20mm Vulcan Phalanx CIWS; 6 x 12.7in AS torpedo tubes (2x3)
Machinery: 2 Olympus gas turbines and 2 Spey gas turbines, 2 shafts
Power: Olympus each 18,426kW/24,700hp; Spey each 9,940kW/13,325hp, in COGAG format; 56,700kW/76,000hp for 32 knots
Endurance: Not known
Protection: Nominal
Complement: 260

LEFT: **This against-the-light image gives an excellent view of** Hatakaze's **layout. She has manned ship, has her stem anchor "a-cockbill" and has sternway. An American tug is in the foreground.**

JAPAN

LEFT: The combined mass of funnel and helicopter hangar gives the *Shimayuki* a distinctive "hump-backed" appearance. To reduce the effects of ship movement, the flight pad is located more forward than usual and is elevated one level. ABOVE: *Hatsuyuki*, nameship of a class of 12. The hull has no knuckle but has a slight crank level with the helicopter pad. Note the smaller 76mm gun forward. The conspicuous white dome covers the radar control for Sea Sparrow, located right aft.

Hatsuyuki and Asagiri classes

General Purpose Destroyers (DDK) but heavily biased toward AS operations, the 12 Hatsuyukis carry a heavy equipment load on a modest displacement. Their bulky topsides were designed around the HSS-2 Sea King, now being replaced by the marginally smaller SH-60J Seahawk. Two Olympus gas turbines deliver the power for sprint speed but, for cruising, the smaller and more appropriate Tyne has been specified.

Forward, the ships mount ASROC; amidships, AS torpedo tubes. Aft, they can deploy a passive towed array to complement the hull-mounted sonar. The helicopter can deploy dipping sonar, sonobuoys and AS torpedoes.

Conventional firepower has been scaled down to a single OTO-Melara 76mm gun forward. Quadruple Harpoon SSM launchers flank the funnel, although, as is common, the full outfit appears not to be usually carried.

Defensively, a Sea Sparrow launcher is mounted aft, its director protected by the conspicuous white radome atop the hangar. Vulcan Phalanx CIWS flank the bridge structure.

Described as Improved Hatsuyukis, the eight Asagiris followed on immediately. They carry the same weapon and sonar fits, and in the same basic layout, but are approximately 5m/16ft 5in longer and 1m/3ft 2in broader. They also look very different.

The Hatsuyukis are COGOG (Combined Gas Or Gas), meaning that they can run on Olympus or Tyne, but not together. The Asagiris have adopted four Speys in a COGAG (Combined Gas And Gas), where either one or two engines can power each shaft. Here, they have been divided between two separated machinery spaces. The two funnels, Spruance-style, are offset, the forward to port, the after to starboard. Their appearance from one quarter thus differs from that from the other.

A knuckle has been added forward, suggesting that the earlier ships were wet. Proliferating electronic systems, an increasing proportion of which are domestically produced, have necessitated the addition of a substantial mainmast of complex lattice construction.

LEFT: Only 5m/16ft 5in longer, but looking larger, the six Asagiris have four similar Spey gas turbines. Separated into two spaces, they require a second offset funnel. Note the unoccupied Harpoon cradles by the after funnel and the reversion to a forward knuckle.

Asagiri class

Displacement: 3,500 tons (normal); 4,300 tons (full load)
Length: 136.5m/448ft 1in (wl)
Beam: 14.6m/47ft 11in
Draught: 4.5m/14ft 9in
Armament: 1 x 76mm gun; 2 x quadruple Harpoon SSM launchers; 1 x 8-cell ASROC launcher; 1 x 8-cell Sea Sparrow launcher; 2 x 20mm Vulcan Phalanx CIWS; 6 x 12.7in AS torpedo tubes (2x3)
Machinery: 4 Spey gas turbines, 2 shafts
Power: 40,209kW/53,900hp for 30 knots
Endurance: Not known
Protection: Nominal
Complement: 220

151

Murasame and Takanami classes

LEFT: The nine Murasames (this is *Samidare*) may easily be confused with American Arleigh Burkes, but they are not fitted with Aegis radar and can immediately be differentiated by the substantial lattice mast. ABOVE: Two VLSs are visible on *Harusame*, that abaft the gun for ASROC and that between the funnels for Sea Sparrow. Note that the stem anchor is housed in an extension to the hawsepipe, indicating a very large bow sonar.

Some 15m/50ft longer than the Asagiri design from which they were derived, the nine Murasames have an extremely capable range of weaponry.

Amidships, the two quadruple canister launchers fire not Harpoon but the new Japanese-built SSM-1B, an interim model capable of a range of 150km/93 miles. Another innovation is the inclusion of two Vertical Launch Systems (VLSs). The VLS immediately abaft the 76mm OTO-Melara gun contains 16 ASROC missiles, doubling earlier capacity. It is scheduled to be modified to fire also the Standard SM-2 MR SAM. Although without additional magazine capacity, this will allow the ships to be armed according to mission.

The second VLS, ahead of the after funnel, loads 16 Sea Sparrow SAM, obviating the need to reload under conditions of saturation attack. Sea Sparrow, too, is due to be superseded by a domestically developed derivative. The two Vulcan Phalanx CIWS are located on the centreline, forward and aft, improving their arcs of fire.

The gas turbine combination continues to change, the Murasames having two British-designed Speys and two American-designed LM-2500s.

Major electronics are concentrated on a single, very tall and heavily braced lattice mast, but separate directors, forward and aft, provide redundant control for both gun and Sea Sparrow.

LEFT: *Takanami* shows her differences with the Murasame class. Both ASROC and Sea Sparrow are located in a single VLS forward. An OTO-Melara 5in gun has replaced the 76mm while, not fitted, a new-style SSM has been preferred to Harpoon.

Still under construction at the time of writing, the eight Takanami-class ships are modified Murasames, sharing the same hull but with a 250-ton greater displacement. The same gas turbine fit also has a similar power rating and so, on a deeper draught, a slightly reduced speed has been accepted.

The major difference is that the two VLSs of the earlier class have been combined in one of twice the capacity. This is located in a forward extension of the bridge structure. The gun has also been uprated to a 5in, but of OTO-Melara, rather than of American pattern. All carry a Seahawk helicopter.

Takanami class

Displacement: 4,650 tons (normal); c.5,350 tons (full load)
Length: 145m/476ft (wl); 151m/495ft 8in (oa)
Beam: 17.4m/57ft 2in
Draught: 5.3m/17ft 5in
Armament: 1 x 5in gun; 2 x quadruple SSM-1B launchers; 1 x 32-cell VLS with variable mix of Standard SM-2 MR and ASROC; 2 x Vulcan Phalanx CIWS; 6 x 12.7in AS torpedo tubes (2x3)
Machinery: 2 LM-2500 gas turbines for sprint, 2 Spey gas turbines for cruising, 2 shafts
Power: 44,760kW/60,000hp for 32 knots
Endurance: 8,335km/4,500nm at 18 knots (*Murasame*)
Protection: Nominal
Complement: 170

JAPAN

LEFT: Two of a kind, the Japanese Aegis destroyer *Myoko* in company with the American Aegis cruiser *Shiloh* (CG.67). Measures to reduce radar signature are less extreme than those in the West, the masts being particularly substantial.
BELOW: The VLS on the afterdeck of the *Kirishima* houses her Standard SM-2 MR system, whose twin directors appear beyond. Despite the space aft, helicopters may only touch down, there being no accommodation for them.

Kongo and Improved Kongo classes

The four Kongos immediately invite comparison with the slightly smaller Flight I DDGs of the US Navy. Externally similar, they can be differentiated by their lattice masts and flush-decked hull, the helicopter pad right aft being one level higher.

With its octagonal plan, the bridge structure is similar, the fixed, phased arrays of the Aegis system occupying the oblique faces. Capable of undertaking long-range air search, target tracking and missile guidance an Aegis ship can, with suitable data links, control a surface group, assessing threats, selecting priority targets and, if required, launching and guiding missiles from accompanying vessels. As their Standard MRs are reputedly capable of intercepting ballistic missiles, the ships are reckoned to be part of the Japanese national defence plan, being deployed accordingly.

Vertical Launch Systems (VLSs) are fitted forward and aft, their total capacity being 90 missiles, either Standard SM-2 MR or ASROC. There is no separate Sea Sparrow point defence system, but Vulcan Phalanx CIWS are located at either end of the superstructure. The two quadruple Harpoon launchers, sited amidships, are likely to be replaced by the domestically built SSM-1B.

The single 5in gun is of OTO-Melara manufacture, favoured apparently for a higher rate of fire than the standard American Mk 42. The Improved Kongos will be slightly larger, normally displacing a further 450 tons. They, too, will have their VLS split between a 32-cell unit forward and a 64-cell unit aft. The latter will lay between the hangars provided for a pair of Seahawk (or, possibly, EH.101/Merlin) helicopters.

Both classes have bow- and hull-mounted sonars, together with passive towed arrays. Beside ASROC and Standard missiles, the improved ships' VLS can launch Sea Sparrow.

Propulsion in all is by four, licence-built LM-2500 gas turbines. Visually the improved ships differ in their solid masts and bulkier after superstructure.

LEFT: Completed in 2007, the *Atago* was the first Improved Kongo. The two main features in which they differ from the first group are visible here: the solid mast and the larger after superstructure incorporating double hangars.

Kongo class

Displacement: 7,250 tons (normal); 9,485 tons (full load)
Length: 150.5m/494ft (bp); 161m/528ft 6in (oa)
Beam: 20m/65ft 8in
Draught: 6.2m/20ft 4in
Armament: 1 x 5in gun; 2 x quadruple Harpoon SSM launchers; 2 x VLS with 90 Standard SM-2 MR and ASROC; 2 x Vulcan Phalanx CIWS; 6 x 12.7in AS torpedo tubes (2x3)
Machinery: 4 LM-2500 gas turbines, 2 shafts
Power: 74,600kW/100,000hp for 30+ knots
Endurance: 1,000 tons fuel for 8,335km/4,500nm at 20 knots
Protection: Nominal
Complement: 310

LEFT: Looking very sleek for a 1920s design, the *Bourrasque* was lead ship of a class that began a series of very fine French destroyers, fated never to demonstrate their potential. Evacuating 600 troops, she was sunk by a French mine at Dunkirk.

ABOVE: A pre-war rendering of *Siroco* with French neutrality markings on "X" gunshield. She was another Dunkirk casualty, sunk by E-boat torpedoes while evacuating 770 troops. Of more than 900 aboard, only 252 survived.

Bourrasque class

When French destroyer construction was resumed after World War I, it was divided primarily between the large *Contre-torpilleurs*, or Torpedo Boat Destroyers, and the medium-sized and more affordable *Torpilleurs d'Escadre*, or Flotilla Destroyers.

The first of the latter type, the 12-strong Bourrasque class, were of a design that owed less to earlier French practice than to contemporary British, with long-full-height forecastles, superimposed guns forward and aft, and two sets of centreline torpedo tubes.

As usual, the French adopted their own calibres for weaponry. Their 130mm gun fired a 32kg/70.4lb projectile and when the limits of destroyer specifications were eventually set by the 1930 London Naval Conference, this calibre was made the destroyer maximum. Torpedoes, too, were of an odd 550mm diameter that differed but marginally from the 533mm used almost universally elsewhere.

In profile, the Bourrasque presented a more rakish appearance than their British peers. The stem was sharply curved rather than raked, and the funnels were prominently capped. A very French feature was the provision of one funnel for each of the three boilers. The after pair of these were installed back-to-back in a single space, resulting in the funnels being unequally spaced. Speed in deep condition could be only 28 knots.

Those that survived to fight an active war underwent the usual modifications of landing "X" gun and one set of tubes in favour of further automatic weapons and depth charges. Mainmasts were removed and the foremast reduced in height, in some braced as a tripod.

With the division of France in 1940, the fortunes of the class were varied. Three were sunk during the Dunkirk evacuation; two more, rearmed, fought subsequently with the Royal Navy. Two, were destroyed by British action at Mers-el-Kebir. Three were variously scuttled, one later being salvaged and serving briefly under the Italian flag.

LEFT: An interesting shot of two French destroyer flotillas swinging into a line-ahead formation. Note the two apertures for depth charges, set into the sloping, rounded stern, and the prominent range clock above "X" gun.

Bourrasque class, as built

Displacement: 1,320 tons (standard); 1,900 tons (full load)
Length: 105.8m/347ft 2in (oa)
Beam: 9.6m/31ft 8in
Draught: 4.2m/13ft 9in
Armament: 4 x 130mm guns (4x1); 1 x 75mm HA gun; 6 x 550mm torpedo tubes (2x3)
Machinery: Geared steam turbines, 3 boilers, 2 shafts
Power: 23,126kW/31,000shp for 33 knots
Endurance: 2,780km/1,500nm at 15 knots
Protection: None
Complement: 138

L'Adroit class

ABOVE: **With the rugged ridge of Mont Faron in the background, the l'Adroit-class destroyer *la Palme* steams in company off Toulon, where she was to be scuttled in 1942. Note the later-model 130mm guns as compared with the Bourrasques.**

As is customary, the Bourrasque design was an armament and speed specification that fitted into the smallest envelope which satisfied seakeeping and cost criteria. Almost inevitably, the compression was somewhat overdone, the end result being cramped and liable to roll heavily. A little extra length assists in the maintenance of speed at sea, while a slightly increased beam makes a marked difference in stability and steadiness. For a given power, a longer ship is potentially faster, a wider ship slower. Having lengthened and widened his original design in order to improve it, a designer will often see his efforts nullified by the larger vessel immediately being burdened with more equipment.

The 14-ship l'Adroit class, which succeeded the Bourrasque, carried the same armament (although with a newer-model 130mm gun) but were given about 1.5m/5ft more in length and 16cm/6in in beam. To maintain the same speed, however, power was necessarily increased by 10 per cent.

The unusual, pronounced forward slope of the stern made gravity release of depth charges from the quarter deck traps difficult. The charges thus fell through apertures, being guided clear by rails protruding from the counter.

The 75mm anti-aircraft gun, fitted abaft the funnels and replaced in war by two single 37mm weapons, was a modified army field artillery gun on a high-angle mounting.

Ten of the class became war losses. Two joined the long list of casualties attendant upon the Dunkirk evacuation. The considerable French force based on Casablanca was loyal to the Vichy administration and allowed some freedom under the agreed Franco-German armistice conditions. In resisting the Allied invasion of November 1942, four more of the class were lost there. Following attempted German seizure, the mass scuttling of the main body claimed three more at Toulon.

ABOVE: **Manning ship, *l'Alcyon* steams by in review. French flotilla markings were unusual, here denoting that *l'Alcyon* was the second ship in the Eleventh Flotilla. Despite the ship's apparent size, only triple torpedo tubes were carried. The general appearance suggests that topweight was always a problem.**

L'Adroit class, as built

Displacement: 1,380 tons (standard); 2,000 tons (full load)
Length: 107.2m/351ft 10in (oa)
Beam: 9.8m/32ft 2in
Draught: 4.3m/14ft 1in
Armament: 4 x 130mm guns (4x1); 1 x 75mm HA gun; 6 x 550mm torpedo tubes (2x3)
Machinery: Geared steam turbines, 3 boilers, 2 shafts
Power: 25,364kW/34,000shp for 33 knots
Endurance: 2,780km/1,500nm at 15 knots
Protection: None
Complement: 138

ABOVE LEFT: Moored to a buoy, *le Hardi* presents her magnificent profile. Note the torpedo tube layout, with a triple between the funnels and twins sided farther aft. Both gunnery rangefinders are trained on the beam. ABOVE: Although having seen less than three years service, it was the fate of these fine ships to be scuttled with the Mediterranean Fleet at Toulon in November 1942. This is the bridge front of *Mameluck*. LEFT: Completed at la Seyne, near Toulon, in June 1940, the *Fleuret* is probably seen here soon after handing over. She was almost immediately renamed *Foudroyant*.

Le Hardi class

Having built several classes of large destroyer, the French increased the size of their next flotilla boats to meet the limits allowed by treaty. At a time when the Royal Navy was still building the four-gun "I" class of 1,370 tons, the new French le Hardi type mounted six of greater calibre on a standard displacement of (officially) 1,775 tons. They were a major factor in the British adopting the six-gun "J" type.

Nearly 19m/62ft longer than the contemporary "I" class, the French ships had four boilers in separate spaces to develop the power for a sustained 37 knots. They did, in fact, develop 7.5 per cent more power than the British Darings of 15 years later, and the largest conventional destroyers ever built for the Royal Navy.

The French gun was a new-model 130mm, dual purpose but, reportedly, unreliable. Six were mounted in three gunhouses, one forward on the raised forecastle, two superfiring aft. Abaft and above the forward mounting were located the two 37mm automatic weapons that comprised the main anti-aircraft defence. Four single 13.2mm machine guns were mounted aft. To improve fields of fire there was no mainmast, aerials being strung to a substantial frame on the after funnel. The resulting profile was handsome.

An unusual seven torpedo tubes were fitted, a triple mount on the centreline between the two funnels, and two twins sided abaft the after funnel.

Of the 12 planned ships, only 8 were complete or mobile in June 1940. All were at Toulon and scuttled in November 1942. They were subsequently salvaged by the Italians and, in slow time, were being refurbished when, in September 1943, the Armistice saw the Germans take them over. None of them was yet operational when the Germans scuttled them, finally, a second time. All were scrapped post-war.

LEFT: With the sinking of *l'Adroit* at Dunkirk in June 1940, the new *l'Epeé*, completing at Bordeaux, assumed the name. Although salvaged by the Germans and repaired, the ship saw no further action.

Le Hardi class, as built

Displacement: 1,775 tons (standard); 2,420 tons (full load)
Length: 118.8m/390ft (bp)
Beam: 11.9m/39ft 1in
Draught: 3.6m/11ft 10in (standard)
Armament: 6 x 130mm guns (3x2); 7 x 550mm torpedo tubes (1x3/2x2)
Machinery: Geared steam turbines, 4 boilers, 2 shafts
Power: 43,268kW/58,000shp for 37 knots
Endurance: 470 tons oil for 5,090km/2,750nm at 20 knots
Protection: None
Complement: 187

FRANCE

LEFT: **A feature of the big French destroyers was their generous freeboard, as seen here with** *Chacal*. **This facilitated their maintaining high speed in poor conditions. The distinctive tripod mainmast was removed in surviving ships.** ABOVE: *Chacal* **again, here under the lowering skies of Portsmouth, England. Note the fifth gun amidships and the distinctive, forward-sloped profile of the stern. The horizontal bar amidships is a furled awning.**

Chacal class

The multi-national agreement resulting in the Washington Treaty of 1921–22 concealed considerable repressed resentments. Not only did Japan feel slighted by being allowed only a 5:3 ratio in capital ships compared with Britain and the United States, but France also maintained that, as she had more colonies than Italy, she should have had greater than parity. In truth, both France and Italy already had as many capital ships as either needed or, indeed, could afford, but pride and rivalry now saw them start to compete in cruisers and destroyers, of which the latter were not yet subject to limitation.

Several ex-German destroyers had been acquired by France in 1920. Larger than the war-built norm, they underlined the advantages of size in terms of speed, seakeeping and firepower.

The six-ship Chacal class were, accordingly, commenced in 1922. By the new Washington "standard" reckoning, they displaced 2,125 tons, but it was nearer 2,700 tons in seagoing trim. Although Britain had not yet recommenced destroyer construction, these "super destroyers" were far and away superior to anything being planned for the post-war fleet.

Their hulls were long in order to accommodate five boilers. The forward of these exhausted through the thin forward funnel; the others, arranged back-to-back in pairs, required two more funnels of greater girth.

Two 130mm guns were superimposed at either end, a fifth being located immediately abaft the after funnel. Two 75mm anti-aircraft guns were carried and two triple centreline torpedo tube mountings.

Two were lost at Dunkirk and two scuttled at Toulon. Another was taken intact from Toulon but, following the Italian capitulation, was returned to the French. She, together with the *Tigre*, then joined the *Léopard* as an Allied long-range escort, in which role main armament was reduced and the forward funnel and boiler removed in favour of extra fuel tanks.

ABOVE: **Carrying the coveted "11" pendants the** *Tigre* **is seen here probably as a new ship in 1926. Captured in June 1940, she operated under the Italian flag until October 1943. Returned to France, she served, modernized, in their post-war fleet with a modified profile, having lost her forefunnel.**

Chacal class, as built
Displacement: 2,125 tons (standard); 3,000 tons (full load)
Length: 126.8m/416ft 3in (oa)
Beam: 11.4m/37ft 5in
Draught: 4.1m/13ft 5in (standard)
Armament: 5 x 130mm guns (5x1), 2 x 75mm HA guns (2x1); 6 x 550mm torpedo tubes (2x3)
Machinery: Geared steam turbines, 5 boilers, 2 shafts
Power: 37,300kW/50,000shp for 35.5 knots
Endurance: 530 tons oil for 3,700km/2,000nm at 20 knots
Protection: None
Complement: 195

157

DIRECTORY OF DESTROYERS: 1918 TO DATE

Guépard class

LEFT: Not usually formed into flotillas, the large French "super destroyers" normally carried individual pendant numbers, as on *Verdun*. She is moored to a buoy, with her motor boat riding to the boat boom; there is a Bretagne-class battleship in the background.
ABOVE: "Chamfered-up" for the occasion, the *Bison* presents immaculately clear decks. The picture is, however, dominated by the extraordinary twin 203mm pressure-tight gun mounting of the "Corsair" submarine *Surcouf*. Note the *Bison*'s boat cranes.

A logical derivative of the Chacal design, the six Guépards which followed four years later were larger again, with main battery guns increased to 138.6mm. The distinction between these "super destroyers" and light cruisers now began to became somewhat blurred, not least because France, piqued at some aspects of the Washington Treaty, would refuse to accept the full limitations on the types, soon to be agreed at the 1930 London Naval Treaty.

At 130.2m/427ft 4in overall, and armed with five 138mm guns, a Guépard compared favourably with a British C-class cruiser of only ten years earlier. These mounted five 6in weapons on a length of 137.7m/451ft 6in.

Compared with a Chacal, the most obvious difference was in the adoption of two pairs of funnels. Four boilers of larger capacity were specified, with machinery arranged on the unit system for improved survivability, two pairs of adjacent boiler spaces being separated by the engine room. The 64,000 designed horsepower (60 per cent more than that of a C-class cruiser) drove the Guépards at some impressive trials speeds, several reputedly exceeding 40 knots, for a sustained speed of 35.5.

Layout was similar to that of the Chacals, with the addition of a second range finder aft. The earlier class's tripod mainmast was suppressed in favour of funnel-mounted W/T aerial spreaders.

With plenty of freeboard, the ships could maintain their speed, and the two based on Beirut during the 1942 Syrian campaign proved more that a match for the British H and J-class destroyers that tried to contain them. One of these two, before the division of France, had operated successfully with the Royal Navy. Another of the class was lost during the 1940 Norwegian campaign. The five surviving boats were scuttled at Toulon in 1942. Super destroyers had come and gone without ever proving themselves.

MIDDLE: A pre-war picture of *Guépard* at speed. The overall impression is one of low, spare superstructure and very light masting. As was common at the time, there is no evidence of anti-aircraft guns. Her "2" pendant is at the dip. ABOVE: *Guépard*, wearing the flag of a rear admiral. Supporting the Allies early in 1940, *Guépard* and *Valmy* sank a German U-boat. Post-June 1940, and now siding with the Vichy government, the pair fought an action with British destroyers off Syria.

Guépard class

Displacement: 2,435 tons (standard); 3,200 tons (full load)
Length: 130.2m/427ft 4in (oa)
Beam: 11.8m/38ft 8in
Draught: 4.7m/15ft 5in (standard)
Armament: 5 x 138mm guns (5x1); 6 x 550mm torpedo tubes (2x3)
Machinery: Geared steam turbines, 4 boilers, 2 shafts
Power: 47,744kW/64,000shp for 35.5 knots
Endurance: 580 tons oil for 4,075km/2,200nm at 20 knots
Protection: None
Complement: 230

FRANCE

Aigle and Vauquelin classes

Despite the usual "class" grouping of the previous "super destroyers", they were officially grouped in series, each with homogeneous names. Thus, Series A (animals) were *Bison*, *Guépard* and *Lion*; Series B ("V") were *Valmy*, *Vauban* and *Verdun*; while Series C (birds) were *Aigle*, *Albatros*, *Gerfaut* and *Vautour*. Superficial differences, as detailed, ran however in sequence, and were confined more to the "classes" (as described) rather than to "series" (as above).

To confuse matters further, neither Series D (*Milan* and *Epervier*) nor Series E (*Cassard*, *Chevalier Paul*, *Kersaint*, *Maillé Brézé*, *Tartu* and *Vauquelin*) conform. Alike, they all had a cruiser stern in place of the forward-sloped, "bevelled" arrangement of the earlier ships. Their wheelhouse was also rounded where others were angular.

Their torpedo outfit was also increased to seven, with twin mountings sided between the two pairs of funnels and a triple centreline mounting farther aft.

Most of the D and E series post-dated the 1930 London Naval Treaty, which France did not ratify. The agreed destroyer upper limit of 1,850 tons standard displacement and a maximum of 130mm guns was, therefore, ignored.

British-made Asdic (Sonar) was added only in 1940, together with depth charge throwers, but the small depth charge capacity was not much improved. Neither was the ship's inadequate anti-aircraft armament.

These fine ships also suffered a war of divided loyalties. Of the Series E ships, one (*Chevalier Paul*) was sunk by British torpedo aircraft off Syria while

ABOVE: The six Aigle-class destroyers were virtual repeats of the Guépards, the *Gerfaut* differing only slightly in detail of the bridge front and counter. In this pre-radar age, designers could produce ships of classic, uncluttered beauty.

another (*Maillé Brézé*), which sailed alongside the Royal Navy under the Free French flag, was destroyed by a torpedo explosion in the Clyde.

The remaining four were scuttled by their crews at Toulon in November 1942, to prevent them, as part of the French Mediterranean Fleet, from falling into German hands. None was salvaged in usable condition, although most were flooded rather than destroyed.

Series E ships, as completed

Displacement: 2,441 tons (standard); 3,140 tons (full load)
Length: 122.4m/401ft 9in (bp); 129.3m/424ft 5in (oa)
Beam: 11.7m/38ft 5in
Draught: 5m/16ft 5in (full load)
Armament: 5 x 138mm guns (5x1); 7 x 550mm torpedo tubes (1x3/2x2)
Machinery: Geared steam turbines, 4 boilers, 2 shafts
Power: 47,744kW/64,000shp for 36 knots
Endurance: 585 tons oil for 5,555km/3,000nm at 20 knots
Protection: None
Complement: 230

ABOVE: The Vauquelin-class *Maillé Brézé* as a leader at about 1939. Note the modified stern profile. In a freak accident in 1940, the ship was destroyed by a torpedo fired inadvertently along her upper deck.

Le Fantasque and Mogador classes

ABOVE LEFT: By 1936, when *le Fantasque* was completed, French and Italian superstructure design had begun to develop some "Odeon" characteristics, the hull remaining as pretty as ever. Note the main battery disposition, echoed in the later American Fletchers. ABOVE: *Le Fantasque* following her US refit of 1943. The great increase in Anti-Aircraft (AA) armament and electronics was compensated partially by landing one torpedo tube mounting. Despite extra topweight, she looks remarkably steady on a fast turn.

Following criticism of the high silhouette of preceding classes, the six Fantasques, commenced in 1931, were redesigned internally. By locating their boilers in two, back-to-back pairs, the distinctive four funnels could be reduced to two short stacks of considerably greater girth. Boiler and machinery spaces were again alternated. The earlier tripod mast was reduced to a slender vertical pole, crossed with cruciform yards. The bridge front was rounded to make it difficult to estimate the ships' heading.

Five 138mm guns were again carried, the earlier amidships mounting being moved to the after deckhouse, not least to improve ammunition supply. By tripling all three torpedo mountings, the outfit was increased to nine.

The Fantasques had a standard displacement of 2,570 tons, but were hardly in the water when the first of six planned Mogadors of 2,885 tons was commenced. These were over 5m/16ft 5in longer and, by virtue of higher steam conditions, developed about 13 per cent more power. Like the Italians, the French ran trials in a very light condition, often without armament. Speeds returned were, nonetheless, impressive with some ships maintaining over 43 knots for 8 hours (at which speed their range was 700 nautical miles, or barely 16 hours' steaming). Endurance was regulated largely by Mediterranean operations.

The Mogadors were armed with four twin 138mm gun mountings. They had ten torpedo tubes, arranged in two triple and two twin mountings, all sided.

Probably due to shortcomings in main battery design, only two of the projected six were actually built.

Unusually, four of the Fantasques survived to serve eventually alongside Allied forces during World War II. In the process of American refits, they were much modified to achieve logistic compatibility and to permit replenishment at sea. With added radar, sonar and much improved anti-aircraft armament, they went on to serve until 1955, still impressive, but obsolete.

LEFT: The ultimate expression of French "super-destroyer" design were the Mogadors. This illustration highlights the major external differences, i.e. four twin 138mm gunhouses and ten torpedo tubes, with a twin and a triple on either side.

Mogador class

Displacement: 2,885 tons (standard); 4,020 tons (full load)
Length: 137.5m/451ft 4in (oa)
Beam: 12.7m/41ft 8in
Draught: 6.6m/21ft 8in
Armament: 8 x 138mm guns (4x2); 10 x 550mm torpedo tubes (2x3/2x2)
Machinery: Geared steam turbines, 4 boilers, 2 shafts
Power: 68,632kW/92,000shp for 3 knots
Endurance: 710 tons for 5,555km/3,000nm at 20 knots
Protection: None
Complement: 264

Surcouf and Duperré classes

World War II drastically changed the role of the classic destroyer and, although still of conventional long forecastle design, France's first post-war ships, authorized in 1949, were rather smaller. The 12-strong Surcouf, or T47, class were categorized as "Fast AAW Escorts" rather than "Destroyers".

A major change was the adoption of the 5in gun calibre, reflecting American assistance through then-membership of NATO. Three twin 5in Dual-Purpose (DP) and fully automatic mountings were carried, one forward and two aft.

France preferred the heavier 57mm to the near-universal 40mm, although both were Bofors-designed weapons. One twin 57mm occupied "B" position with two more sided in the waist.

Four triple torpedo tube mountings were carried. All were of the standard French 550mm calibre, but six tubes were reserved for AS torpedoes of domestic manufacture. Main and secondary gun directors were backed by comprehensive air-and surface-search radars. Braced tripod masts for these were located near amidships to minimize effects of ship motion.

The five T53R Duperré-class ships were very similar to the above but, with even more comprehensive radar, were fitted for command and aircraft direction roles. Six tubes were sacrificed, the remainder being dual-function. A sextuple 375mm Bofors AS rocket launcher was added, as destroyers' role moved away from surface attack.

All were extensively modified during long careers. During the 1960s, four T47s exchanged their 5in gun batteries and four 57mm for an aft-mounted Tartar/Standard SM-1 system. A Bofors AS launcher was added forward. Others had their after ends heavily modified with various combinations of fixed and folding helicopter hangars and flight pads.

France rapidly developed a capable defence electronics industry and an extra ship, the T56 *la Galissonnière*, was trials vessel for an AS system incorporating a powerful Variable Depth Sonar (VDS) and the new Malafon Stand-off weapon. Several of the classes served into the 1990s.

ABOVE: *Cassard* was one of three Surcoufs to be converted to "command ships". The twin 57mm in "B" position has been sacrificed for an accommodation extension, and only six lightweight AS torpedo tubes are carried.

LEFT: Much modified by the end of her career, *Duperré* has landed her conventional after armament in favour of full helicopter facilities, a large Variable Depth Sonar (VDS) installation and four MM38 Exocet SSMs in the waist.

Surcouf class, as built

Displacement: 2,7500 tons (standard); 3,750 tons (full load)
Length: 128.7m/422ft (oa)
Beam: 12.7m/42ft 8in
Draught: 5m/16ft 6in
Armament: 6 x 5in guns (3x2), 6 x 57mm guns (3x2); 12 x 550mm torpedo tubes (4x3)
Machinery: Geared steam turbines, 4 boilers, 2 shafts
Power: 47,000kW/63,000shp for 34 knots
Endurance: 700 tons oil for 9,260km/5,000nm at 18 knots
Protection: None
Complement: 347

Suffren class

The difficulty of pigeon-holing modern warships was amply illustrated by the two Suffrens, whose initial prestige saw them ordered as "Guided Missile (GM) cruisers", completed as the then-current "GM frigates" before serving, more realistically, as "GM destroyers". Their significance rested in their affirmation of French independence in every aspect of ship, weapons and electronics. The distinctive radome protecting the antenna of the DBRI-23 three-dimensional air search radar could give rise to superficial confusion with the two Dutch Tromps (of a rather later date) but closer comparison reveals little further resemblance.

The ship's major system was the Masurca SAM, whose twin-arm launcher and paired tracker/illuminators were located aft. A large, stern-mounted VDS and a bow sonar provided, in the absence of a helicopter, data for targeting the Malafon stand-off AS weapon. Four launchers were mounted for domestically designed AS torpedoes. Four canister launchers for MM38 Exocet SSM were paired amidships. Forward were two single 100mm automatic guns, which calibre had replaced the 5in as standard. Both ships were fitted with the latest SENIT combat data system, enabling them to act as force flagships.

Heat and smoke from the boilers were exhausted clear of electronics via a lofty, streamlined casing that acted also as a basis for the foremast. To steady the ships as weapons platforms,

ABOVE: Completed in 1967, The *Suffren* typifies the "new generation" destroyer, built around a 3-D air search radar and area-defence SAM, here the French-built Masurca, aft. Amidships is the Malafon stand-off AS weapon, served by the VDS.

three pair of active stabilizers were fitted. Being designed at the height of the Cold War, with nuclear exchanges a very real possibility, the ships had hulls devoid of scuttles, all living and working spaces being air-conditioned and slightly pressurized against ingress.

At the time of writing, both ships still exist, although the nameship has been in low-category reserve for some years. Both their major weapon systems have long been superseded and are no longer supported.

ABOVE: This later view of *Duquesne* shows the Exocet SSMs added to supplement anti-surface ship armament. Not the large towfish of the DUBV 43 Variable Depth Sonar (VDS). She is flying a Dutch courtesy flag and her four-character international "number".

Suffren class

Displacement: 5,335 tons (standard); 6,785 tons (full load)
Length: 148m/485ft 10in (bp); 157.6m/517ft 4in (oa)
Beam: 15.5m/51ft
Draught: 7.3m/23ft 9in maximum
Armament: 2 x 100mm guns (2x1); 1 x Masurca SAM system; 1 x Malafon AS system; 4 x MM38 Exocet SSM launchers
Machinery: Geared steam turbines, 4 boilers, 2 shafts
Power: 54,085kW/72,500shp for 34 knots
Endurance: 8,280km/4,500nm at 20 knots
Protection: Nominal
Complement: 349

FRANCE

Tourville class

In March 1970 the French launched a one-off, general-purpose "corvette" *Aconit*. Her speciality was ASW, for which purpose she carried Malafon, a quadruple mortar and AS torpedoes, supported by VDS and bow sonar. For her size, she carried also a sophisticated air surveillance radar. At 3,500 tons, she was a large corvette but was apparently felt to be limited by her size and lack of helicopter. Her builders, Lorient Dockyard, then produced an enlarged version in the trio of Tourvilles, also commenced in 1970.

Smaller than the Suffrens, they have a similar tall, tapered funnel/mainmast combination. This leaves clear arcs behind for the octuple Crotale point-defence SAM launcher, and ahead for Malafon. As the latter required a steady platform, ships so fitted exhibited a characteristic gap amidships, where its launcher was located. Now obsolete, the system has been removed from all three ships.

With their extra length, they are able to accommodate hangar and flight pad for a Lynx helicopter (or, at a squeeze, two) which constitutes a potent AS system in itself when sharing tracking and targeting data with the ship.

Where the *Aconit* was a 27-knot single-shaft vessel, the Tourvilles have reverted to relatively high power on two shafts for a more destroyer-like 32 knots.

Like the Suffrens, their low quarterdeck is dedicated to the substantial Variable Depth Sonar (VDS) towed body and its handling gear. Its bistatic sonar is the active component, "illuminating" a submerged target for the ship-end passive sonar.

During major refits, all three ships have been stiffened by the addition of a substantial external longitudinal, fitted along either sheer strake.

Duguay-Trouin, never fully modernized, has already spent some years in low category reserve. Her two sisters are planned to pay off before 2010.

ABOVE: **The effectiveness of the Tourvilles as AS ships was increased by adding the full helicopter facilities to the Malafon/VDS combination. Lacking area defence, she is more truly a frigate, but is powered for 32 knots.**

ABOVE: Like the *Tourville* (above), the *Duguay-Trouin* is pictured in the mid-1970s, before the after 100mm gun was replaced by a short-range Crotale SAM system. Note the triple Exocet SSMs, sided abaft the bridge structure. The line of the hull is particularly pleasing.

Tourville, as built

Displacement: 4,580 tons (standard); 5,745 tons (full load)
Length: 142m/466ft 2in (bp); 152.8m/501ft 7in (oa)
Beam: 15.3m/50ft 2in
Draught: 5.7m/18ft 9in
Armament: 2 x 100mm guns (2x1); 1 x Malafon AS system; 6 x MM38 Exocet SSM launchers; 1 x Crotale point-defence SAM system
Machinery: Geared steam turbines, 4 boilers, 2 shafts
Power: 40,582kW/54,400shp for 32 knots
Endurance: 6,667km/3,600nm at 20 knots
Protection: Nominal
Complement: 298

163

DIRECTORY OF DESTROYERS: 1918 TO DATE

FAR LEFT: A small ship to accommodate a full Standard SM-1 MR system, the *Jean Bart* emerges atmospherically into an early sun. She has space for only one 100mm gun forward and a small helicopter aft. ABOVE INSET: The *Cassard* shows her unusual layout. The narrow hangar is flanked by Sadral point-defence SAM mountings. Forward of this is a gap accommodating the Standard SAM launcher. Note the offset diesel exhaust and uncovered air-search antenna.

Georges Leygues and Cassard classes

Currently the backbone of the French *Force d'Action Navale*, the seven Leygues and two Cassards share a common hull form, the former being F70-type ASW and the latter C70 AAW escorts. All carry destroyer pendants. The F70s are CODOG-propelled (Combined Diesel Or Gas), using gas turbines for high (30 knots) speed or diesels (21 knots) for AS operations. The C70s are, unusually, of all diesel configuration for 29.5 knots.

Externally, the major difference is in the replacement of the F70s' large funnel casing with diesel exhaust in the C70s surmounted by the radome-protected, air-search radar associated with the single-arm, launcher for Standard SM-1 MR missiles. Flanking the C70s' helicopter hangar are sextuple launchers for the Sadral point-defence SAM system. Amidships are two quadruple canister launchers for the MM40 version of the Exocet SSM.

With no area-defence SAM system, the F70s have more space for the helicopter facilities, and both VDS and towed-array sonars. Both classes have a large, low-frequency bow sonar. As on other examples, the relatively shallow, highly stressed hull has exhibited fatigue cracking in service, requiring heavy remedial reinforcement along the sheer strakes. The extra topweight involved required compensatory ballast, increasing displacement by some 330 tons. This would have increased draught by nearly 50cm/20in, affecting maximum speed.

Both C70 and F70 are due for replacement, the former by the French variant of the Horizon frigate. At the time of writing, three of these have been authorized, of which the first two will resurrect the names *Forbin* and *Chevalier Paul*, and be in service by 2008.

A Franco-Italian project will produce the 4,500-ton Aquitaine class to replace the F70s. Built in both ASW and land-attack versions, they will also replace the Tourvilles.

ABOVE: The Georges Leygues class are AS (Anti-Submarine) ships sharing a common hull with the Cassards. That of the *Dupleix*, seen here, has since been stiffened with a heavy sheer strake. Note the CODOG (Combined Diesel Or Gas) funnel/intakes, Crotale SAM, larger hangar and Variable Depth Sonar (VDS).

Georges Leygues (F70) type, as built

Displacement: 3,830 tons (standard); 4,170 tons (full load)
Length: 129m/423ft 5in (bp); 139m/456ft 3in (oa)
Beam: 14m/46ft
Draught: 5.6m/18ft 4in
Armament: 1 x 100mm gun; 4 x MM38 Exocet SSM launchers; 1 x Crotale point-defence SAM system
Machinery: 2 Olympus gas turbines (sprint) or 2 medium speed diesel engines (loiter/cruising)
Power: 34,316kW/46,000shp for 30 knots, or 7,982kW/10,700bhp for 21 knots
Endurance: 600 tons fuel for 18,400km/10,000nm at 15 knots (on diesel engines)
Protection: Nominal
Complement: 216

Sella and Sauro classes

Following World War I, new Italian construction first favoured what were, for the time, very large destroyers, classed as "scouts". Exceeding 1,750 tons standard displacement, the Mirabello and Leone classes carried eight guns but only four torpedo tubes. Such large and expensive craft were unsuitable for flotilla attack on an enemy line, for which smaller and more nimble craft were required.

Launched by the Pattison yard in Naples during 1925, the four Sella-class ships were thus of less than 1,000 tons. They were of orthodox design, with two closely spaced funnels. Unusually, the forecastle extended to a point between the funnels, increasing accommodation.

As with British destroyers, Italian ships carried guns of 120mm/4.7in calibre. As built, the Sellas carried a single on the forecastle and a twin mounting on the after deckhouse. Besides being a drier location, this located all weapons on a common horizontal datum, simplifying gunlaying. Shortly after their completion, their forward mountings were also twinned.

Two pairs of torpedo tubes were carried, sited back-to-back on the centreline. All units, as was customary, were fitted for minelaying, to a maximum of 32 apiece.

The Sellas were quickly followed by the four Sauros. At nearly 5m/16ft 6in longer, these were able to accommodate tripled torpedo tubes and a larger mine capacity of 52.

Very similar to the earlier ships, they could be distinguished by the profile of the hance at the break of the forecastle.

ABOVE: **Although fitted with very early examples of twinned gun mountings, the Sauros were of simple design. The bridge structure remains flimsy. Unusual features of the *Cesare Battisti* are very long forecastle and a stern modified for an alternative minelaying role.**

They later had a heavier director tower atop the bridge structure, together with a secondary director located between the banks of torpedo tubes.

Two of the Sellas (*Ricasoli* and *Nicotera*) were sold to Sweden in 1940. Following the Italian capitulation in September 1943 the *Crispi* was taken under the German flag, being sunk by British aircraft. Her sister *Sella* was sunk by a German torpedo boat. With hostilities, all four Sauros were isolated in their Red Sea bases and inevitably destroyed.

ABOVE: ***Francesco Crispi*** of the earlier Sella class. Note the funnels of near-equal height, a later and improved bridge, fragile masting and different hance profile. Operated by the Germans, she was sunk by British aircraft. Early in 1940, two sister ships were acquired by the Swedish Navy.

Sauro class

Displacement: 1,060 tons (standard); 1,600 tons (full load)
Length: 89.6m/294ft 1in (bp); 90.1m/296ft (oa)
Beam: 9.2m/30ft 2in
Draught: 2.9m/9ft 6in
Armament: 4 x 120mm guns (2x2), 2 x 40mm guns (2x1); 6 x 533mm torpedo tubes (2x3)
Machinery: Geared steam turbines, 2 shafts
Power: 26,856kW/36,000shp for 35 knots
Endurance: Not known
Protection: None
Complement: 155

Turbine class

With the Sauros, the Italians had produced a useful small destroyer which would provide the basic form for succeeding classes. It is natural law of ship design, however, that a few extra metres will solve the problems encountered with any class. The result is inevitably a creeping escalation in size. Thus, although carrying the same armament, the eight *Turbine*-class destroyers were 3m/10ft longer than the Sauros which, with the same layout, had been 5m/16ft 5in longer than the preceding Sellas. Greater length also confers improved seakeeping, manifested as reduced wetness and the ability to maintain speed in adverse conditions. The greater steadiness also makes the ship a better gun platform.

Masting was very light and not reduced during hostilities. The bridge structure appeared massive, the large tubular director tower at its forward end being overlooked by a higher observation platform, surmounted in turn by a large searchlight.

Identification of Italian destroyers was by pairs of letters rather than the more usual pendant numbers. At 2m/6ft 6in high, they were indicative of a ship's name, the surname in the cases of those named after people (e.g. the full name of *Sauro* was *Nazario Sauro*, but she carried the identifier "SU"). The Turbines were named after winds. With the outbreak of war, Italian destroyers adopted bold disruptive camouflage paint schemes to make difficult the estimation of their heading, and the hitherto black characters of their identifiers was changed to a softer red. Numbers were adopted when Italy joined NATO.

ABOVE: **Slightly enlarged Sauros, four Turbines of the Italian Prima Squadriglia are seen "Mediterranean moored", stern to jetty. Named after winds, they are (from left to right)** *Espero*, *Zeffiro*, *Borea* **and** *Ostro*. **All four came from the Ansaldo yard.**

The Italian destroyer force suffered badly during World War II. Six of the eight Turbines were lost in the first three months. Their poor anti-aircraft armament made them vulnerable to British torpedo aircraft, which claimed three

Following the 1943 Italian Armistice the *Euro*, under the Italian colours, was destroyed by German aircraft, while the *Turbine*, in a reversal of fortune, was appropriated by the Germans and sunk by American aircraft.

LEFT: **An earlier shot of** *Ostro*, **which here lacks the after fire control visible in the top picture. Note the moderate flare, which would have increased pitch amplitude but hopefully reduced pitch accelerations, making a steadier gun platform.**

Turbine class, as built

Displacement: 1,090 tons (standard); 1,700 tons (full load)
Length: 92.6m/304ft 1in (bp); 93.2m/305ft 11in (oa)
Beam: 9.2m/30ft 2in
Draught: 3m/9ft 10in
Armament: 4 x 120mm guns (2x2), 2 x 40mm guns (2x1); 6 x 533mm torpedo tubes (2x3)
Machinery: Geared steam turbines, 2 shafts
Power: 29,840kW/40,000shp for 36 knots
Endurance: Not known
Protection: None
Complement: 179

Leone and Navigatori classes

In 1909 the British completed the experimental one-off "flotilla leader" Swift. A 35-knotter of 2,170 tons, she was enormous for her day and was meant to replace the light cruiser customarily dedicated to leading a 16-strong destroyer flotilla. She was not considered a success, but her size and duty saw her armed, not with the usual 12pdrs, but with a single forecastle-mounted 6in gun and with two single 4in secondary weapons.

Although the Swift proved to be an evolutionary dead end for the Royal Navy, it is interesting that the Italians commenced work on three 1,810-tonners in 1914. These, the Mirabellos, carried a single 150mm and up to seven 100mm. Again, the experiment was not repeated, but the obvious advantages of size led to the launch in 1923–24 of the three Leone-class scouts, later classed simply "destroyers". At 1,745 tons these carried a homogeneous battery of eight 120mm guns, in twin mountings, at a moderate 34 knots.

It was no coincidence that the French, even before the Leone launch, laid down their initial class of large contre torpilleur (Chacal). Larger, faster, more heavily armed they, too, carried "big cat" names, with the pointed omission of Lion, retained for use in the following (Guépard) class. These, laid down in 1927, were immediately matched by the 12 Italian Navigatori.

The latter's six 120mm threw a broadside of 139kg/306lb against a Guépard 202kg/445lb, but with a superior range and rate of fire. Although smaller than the French, the Italian boats well exceeded 40 knots on trials, but were very wet until their bows were modified with increased freeboard and flare.

The Navigatori class's third twin 120mm mounting was carried amidships. Machinery spaces were separated on the unit system. Torpedo tubes were mostly removed during the war, which claimed every one of the class except Nicoloso da Recco.

ABOVE: Of nearly twice the displacement of preceding destroyers, the Navigatori were built as scouts. They were credited with very high trial speeds, and the two widely spaced funnels attest to the length of the machinery spaces.

Navigatori class, as built

Displacement: 1,944 tons (standard); 2,580 tons (full load)
Length: 107m/351ft 3in (bp); 107.7m/353ft 3in (oa)
Beam: 10.2m/33ft 6in
Draught: 3.4m/11ft 2in
Armament: 6 x 120mm guns (3x2), 2/3 x 37mm guns (2/3x1); 4/6 x 450mm or 533mm torpedo tubes (2x2/3)
Machinery: Geared steam turbines, 2 shafts
Power: 37,300kW/50,000shp for 38 knots
Endurance: Not known
Protection: None
Complement: 224

ABOVE: Of a size, but slower than the Navigatori, the three Leones were an earlier type of scout. Their four twin 120mm guns were spaced along the ship and these, together with their four torpedo tubes, equalled the armament of a British Tribal of 14 years later.

Dardo and Folgore classes

The four Dardos followed immediately upon the completion of the Turbine-class flotilla destroyers and, like them, were designed by Odero. Not surprisingly, therefore, there was not great change, with much the same outfit on a hull a little over three metres more in length.

Claimed to be the first-ever destroyers designed with a single funnel, they achieved this with close-spaced boilers, whose uptakes were directed into a rectangular upper deck casing upon which stood the funnel proper. This was not trunked. Surprisingly, an increase of just 10 per cent in installed power was expected to realise a further two knots in maximum speed.

A new-style director tower was less bulky than its predecessor, but the bridge structure, considered as a whole, still presented a very high profile. This contrasted with the Dardos' very low-freeboard after end. The wetness of this was underlined by after twin 120mm mounting being located atop the after superstructure, and the two triple torpedo tube banks on high turntables.

The overall appearance of the class was pleasing, assisted by the adoption of a slightly raked bow with a soft nose. This was raked slightly more in the four Folgore-class boats which continued the series and which, otherwise, showed little significant external difference.

ABOVE LEFT: With their large, single funnel and bold, clean styling, the Dardos set the pattern for Italian flotilla ships for the following 15 years. Common Italian practice, the after awning is extended to screen the accommodation ladder.
ABOVE: Concerns about topside weight are apparent in this photograph of the Dardo-class *Strale*, which has had the shields removed from her twin 120mm guns. Note the very clear side decks for the stowage of up to 54 mines.

Although of the same length as the Dardos, the Folgores were more than 50cm/20in less in beam. It may be assumed that this, most unusual, step was part of a refinement of hull lines to actually make the 38 knots' service speed which the Dardo class reportedly had difficulty in achieving.

None of either class survived World War II. Like their merchant fleet, many Italian warships were sunk in the resupply of Axis armies in North Africa. All four Folgores were lost in surface combat while escorting convoys.

MIDDLE: The *Lampo* on a picturesque port visit. As is here seen, the bow profile and anchor stowage of the Folgores differed from that of the Dardos. The angular casing is clearly visible, gathering the boiler uptakes into the single funnel. ABOVE: Except for the angled funnel cap, the follow-on Folgore-class boats were virtually identical to the Dardos. The after freeboard is very limited, and the torpedo tubes and after guns are located relatively high. This photograph is of *Folgore* herself.

Folgore class

Displacement: 1,240 tons (standard); 2,090 tons (full load)
Length: 94.3m/309ft 6in (bp); 96m/315ft 2in (oa)
Beam: 9.2m/30ft 2in
Draught: 3.3m/10ft 10in
Armament: 4 x 120mm guns (2x2), 2 x 37mm guns (2x1); 6 x 533mm torpedo tubes (2x3)
Machinery: Geared steam turbines, 2 shafts
Power: 32,824kW/44,000shp for 38 knots
Endurance: Not known
Protection: None
Complement: 182

ITALY

LEFT: One of the very few Italian destroyers to survive World War II, the *Grecale* is seen as modernized, with a rebuilt bridge structure, tripod foremast and electronics, and new armament. Italy now being a NATO partner, she bears new-style pendant numbers. BELOW: An impression of the Oriani-class *Vincenzo Gioberti*, which usually carried the designators "GB". The class had a fifth 120mm gun amidships for starshell illumination and stowed anchors at the deck edge to reduce spray-making.

Maestrale and Oriani classes

These handsome classes, each of four ships, differed only in the latter displacing an extra 75 tons. The small extra draught was more than compensated by a 9 per cent increase in installed power, giving it a legend increase of an extra knot's maximum speed, an unsustainable 39 knots.

Unlike earlier classes, they were of commercial design and, although considerably larger than the preceding Folgores, carried the same four-gun, six-tube main armament. It might be noted that, commencing with the Navigatori, their 120mm guns were of a new 50-calibre type, throwing a slightly heavier round to an improved range of 22,000m/24,060yd. Their maximum elevation, however, was only 45 degrees, so anti-aircraft defence depended upon Italian-pattern 20mm and (in the Orianis) 37mm weapons. Both classes carried one/two short-barrelled 120mm high-angle guns dedicated to firing starshell. (This was of some irony in the case of the latter-class *Alfieri* and *Carducci*, overwhelmed by British destroyers in the night action off Cape Matapan.)

Something of an Italian trademark of the 1930s, the single funnel was prominently trunked, both to reduce topweight and to set it back somewhat from the bridge structure. A further characteristic design feature, first seen in the Navigatori, was to house anchors at the level of the deck edge, rather than in conventional hawse pipes, probably to reduce pounding and spray-making.

The Maestrale-class *Scirocco* foundered during the violent storm that was rising on March 22, 1942, at the Second Battle of Sirte.

Her sister *Libeccio* had been sunk on controversial circumstances about four months earlier. She had been engaged in rescuing survivors from the badly mauled "Duisburg convoy" when torpedoed by a Malta-based submarine, following a deliberate decision.

ABOVE: Reduced to reserve, this Oriani has had her identifiers painted out. Note that the tall mainmast has been struck. *Alfredo Oriani*, the lead ship, survived to be ceded to the French Navy in 1948, serving for a further six years as the fast escort *d'Estaing*.

Oriani class, as built

Displacement: 1,715 tons (standard); 2,290 tons (full load)
Length: 104.4m/341ft 4in (bp); 106.7m/350ft 4in (oa)
Beam: 10.2m/33ft 6in
Draught: 3.4m/11ft 2in
Armament: 4 x 120mm guns (2x2), 2 x 37mm guns (2x1); 6 x 533mm torpedo tubes (2x3)
Machinery: Geared steam turbines, 2 shafts
Power: 35,808kW/48,000shp for 39 knots
Endurance: Not known
Protection: None
Complement: 206

169

LEFT: *Carabiniere*, of the first set of 12 Soldatis, undertakes a jackstay transfer. The early electronic additions suggest a late-1940s date. She has had an open bridge added above the wheelhouse and a breakwater about the forward gun mounting.
BELOW: **A pretty view of *Geniere*,** a light following wind lifting a haze of funnel smoke. She was nearly destroyed in March 1943 in dry dock at Palermo, when the caisson was breached during a heavy bombing raid. She was salvaged.

Soldati class

With the obvious approach of war, the launch of the final Oriani, late in 1936, was followed by the commencement of 12 further hulls of identical size. Completed by May 1939, this group apparently satisfied the Italian Navy's requirements, for it was not until the nation's rather unanticipated entry into World War II in June 1940 that a further seven units were ordered. With shipyards already busy, the last of these was not even commenced until September 1941.

The two series differed little and were named after specialist military units, hence "Soldati". For a 1,700-tonner, an Oriani, with four guns and six torpedo tubes, was quite lightly armed. Eight of the first series were given the same outfit, the last four gaining a fifth gun, located on a bandstand between the sets of tubes. All the second group were so armed but, as some were reduced to three tubes while others lost their secondary director to ship extra automatic weapons and/or depth charges, it suggests that the displacement (grown to 1,850 tons from an Oriani 1,715) had reached a safe maximum.

When, early in 1943, Italy belatedly began to replace her considerable losses, it was with a 2,100-tonner. Named after "Gold Medal" naval heroes, twenty of these were ordered; nine were actually laid down but none ever completed. Of 120.7m/396ft 2in length, these would have rivalled the French destroyers, carrying four single 135mm guns of the type mounted also in the *Capitani Romani* light cruiser/scouts.

Of the 17 Soldatis actually completed, ten were sunk. One, *Lanciere*, foundered in the same storm that sank the *Scirocco*. Two, incomplete, were taken by the Germans at the Armistice, but destroyed. Of those remaining, three were ceded to France and two to Soviet Russia. *Carabiniere* and *Granatiere* served under the Italian flag post-war.

Soldati, second series

Displacement: 1,845 tons (standard); 2,500 tons (full load)
Length: 104m/341ft 4in (bp); 106.7m/350ft 4in (oa)
Beam: 10.2m/33ft 6in
Draught: 3.6m/11ft 10in
Armament: 5 x 120mm guns (2x2/1x1), 2/3 x 37mm guns (2/3x1); 3/6 x 533mm torpedo tubes (1/2x3)
Machinery: Geared steam turbines, 2 shafts
Power: 37,300kW/50,000shp for 39 knots
Endurance: Not known
Protection: None
Complement: 217

ABOVE: **A comparative view of *Carabiniere*** as rebuilt into a fast AS escort during the early 1950s. Torpedo tubes have been landed and a single 120mm gun has replaced the earlier twin mounting forward. Note the remodelled bridge structure, depicted in better detail on *Grecale* (see previous page).

Impavido class

Somewhat reminiscent of the contemporary American Coontz class, the two Impavidos ushered in the missile age for the Italian Navy, narrowly ahead of the more handsome Andrea Doria-class GM cruisers that they were designed to complement. Their strongly "vertical" look, shared with their American peer, was due to the single-arm Tartar SAM launcher being mounted aft. In order to "gather" the missile on launch, it was necessary to locate the two SPG-51 tracker-illuminator radars just ahead, clear of the smoke resulting from launch. To carry hot exhaust gases over these, the after funnel needed to be even higher. The system's associated SPS-39 height-finding radar had then to be located on a rigid, lattice mast, to site it above the funnel exhaust.

The flush-decked hull, with its long, sweeping sheerline, also echoed American practice. Shorter-range air defence was vested in four single OTO-Melara 76mm mountings, sided in the waist. They, and the twin 5in 38-calibre, US-pattern gunhouse forward had a bridge-mounted director, with secondary directors amidships. Active fin stabilizers were added to the specification to improve system accuracies.

Both ships were equipped with American sonar and had a flight pad aft for a light AB 204 ASW helicopter, carried only until the 1970s. Triple light-weight AS torpedo tubes flanked the bridge structure. With the emphasis on

ABOVE: **Although somewhat smaller, the Impavidos share some of the lofty appearance of the American Coontz type, with which they might be superficially confused. The US-sourced Tartar SAM system contrasts with the elderly twin 5in 38 gun mounting of World War II vintage.**

stand-off weaponry, speed was no longer of primary importance.

A mid-1970s upgrade saw the SAM system adapted to fire Standard SM-1 MR missiles, housed again in the large, flat structure immediately ahead of the launcher. Domestically built surface-search radar and Selenia/Elsag gun director radars also replaced existing obsolescent equipment.

Dating from an age that showed a strong reliance on American-sourced technologies, the two Impavidos were replaced in the early 1990s by the pair of de la Penne-class GM destroyers.

ABOVE: **This view gives a good idea of the *Intrepido*'s layout. Much deck area is absorbed by the missile magazine structure ahead of the launcher. Although there is a spacious helicopter pad, there are therefore no hangar facilities.**

Impavido class, as built

Displacement: 3,200 tons (standard); 3,940 tons (full load)
Length: 131.1m/430ft 4in (oa)
Beam: 13.6m/44ft 8in
Draught: 4.4m/14ft 5in
Armament: 2 x 5in guns (1x2), 4 x 76mm guns (4x1); 1 x Tartar SAM system
Machinery: Double-reduction geared steam turbines, 4 boilers, 2 shafts
Power: 52,220kW/70,000shp for 33.5 knots
Endurance: 650 tons oil for 6,110km/3,300nm at 20 knots
Protection: Nominal
Complement: 238

LEFT: *Audace*, as built, carried two 127mm OTO-Melara single guns, seen here. During the 1980s, "B" mounting was landed in favour of an Albatros/Aspide point-defence SAM launcher. Note the distinctive humped profile of the helicopter hangar aft. ABOVE: A close-up of the starboard waist gun mountings visible in the overall view at left. These are the 76mm 62-calibre OTO-Melara guns that have enjoyed remarkable export sales. The quoted rate of fire is 85 rounds per minute.

Audace class

It would be a further nine years before the two Impavidos were joined by the pair of slightly larger Audaces which, from the outset, were designed around the Standard SM-1 MR SAM system. Although this was again located aft, the overall ship length was more compact, giving the appearance of being smaller. The funnels were less dominant, the forward one being also a structure supporting the foremast, while the after, of strangely cranked shape, provided support for the SPS-52 three-dimensional, height-finding radar.

Flanking the distinctive gap between the two main superstructure blocks were four single OTO-Melara 76mm guns. Originally of the new, fully automatic Compatto type, these were later upgraded to the "Super Rapid" variant. The gap itself was later occupied by eight canister launchers for the Italian-built Teseo/Otomat SSM, an active radar homer capable of a theoretical range of about 185km/115 miles.

The after end of the ships was better utilized than those of the Impavidos, with hangar and flight pad for two AB-212 helicopters. Four aft-facing torpedo tubes were added subsequently beneath the flight pad, firing wire-guided, heavyweight torpedoes. These were later removed, their use impeding free movement of the parent ship.

As built, two OTO-Melara 127mm dual-purpose guns occupied "A" and "B" positions. With modernization, "B" gun was landed in favour of an 8-cell launcher for the Aspide point-defence SAM system. This is an Italian-manufactured variant on the widely used NATO Sea Sparrow.

As is usual in Italian destroyers, the hull and bridge structure was devoid of scuttles as an NBCD measure. The hull itself readopted a forward knuckle to reduce wetness.

Superseded by the pair of de la Pennes and with the "Horizon" destroyers due in the short term, both Audaces are bound for retirement at the time of writing.

ABOVE: A low morning light emphasizes the detail of *Audace*'s hull. Having sailed, she lowers her four-character "number" but retains her anchor "a-cockbill", i.e. ready to release. This is again a 1980s photograph, the ship lacking both Aspide and the Teseo SSM launchers amidships.

Audace class, as built

Displacement: 3,950 tons (standard); 4,550 tons (full load)
Length: 140.7m/461ft 10in (oa)
Beam: 14.7m/48ft 2in
Draught: 4.6m/15ft 1in
Armament: 2 x 127mm guns (2x1), 4 x 76mm guns (4x1); 1 x Standard SM-1 MR system; 4 x 533mm torpedo tubes (4x1); 6 x 324mm AS torpedo tubes (2x3)
Machinery: Geared steam turbines, 4 boilers, 2 shafts
Power: 54,458kW/73,000shp for 33 knots
Endurance: 7,410km/4,000nm at 25 knots
Protection: Nominal
Complement: 380

ITALY

Durand de la Penne class

Ordered as the *Animoso* and *Ardimentoso*, this pair of GM destroyers was, while under construction, renamed for two naval heroes of World War II. The considerable rearrangement of the two Audaces, completed in 1988, left them as near diminutives of the new vessels, upon which work had recently commenced. These are a generous 7m/23ft greater in length, not least to accommodate an EH.101 helicopter.

Similar to the Royal Navy's Merlin, their aircraft weighs more than two AB-212s together, and has a rotor diameter some 4m/13ft greater. In accordance with the general realignment of western fleets toward "littoral" warfare, only half of them will be ASW-specialist. Four more are due to be equipped with Marte air-to-surface (i.e. anti-ship) missiles and their associated search and targeting radar, while four/eight more will be configured as "assault transports". The five-hour endurance of the aircraft, together with its ability to target both its own and its ship's weapons, makes it an effective "force multiplier".

A major departure for the de la Penne is the adoption of CODOG propulsion. Two cruising-diesel engines exhaust through the centreline forward funnel, while a pair of licence-built LM-2500 gas turbines exhaust through casings angled out on either side of the Standard SM-1 MR fire control radars. The latter's associated SPS-52 3-D air-search radar has a proper mainmast to support it (the arrangement on the Audaces required later strengthening). Again, eight SSMs are located amidships, but one of the earlier four 76mm Super-Rapids has been made unnecessary by mounting one weapon centreline on the hangar roof.

The ships are shortly to be complemented by a first pair of "Horizon" frigates, closely related to the British Daring-class T45s. As the Bergamini class, they will probably more closely resemble the French *Forbin*.

ABOVE LEFT: *Francesco Mimbelli*, with *Aviere* on her quarter and the two San Giorgio LPDs in the distance. Both foreground ships have 127mm guns superfired by Albatros/Aspide launchers. Note *Mimbelli*'s angled gas turbine exhaust casing. ABOVE: Here, both Durand de la Pennes are followed in line by a pair of Artiglieres and both San Giorgios. Note the paired directors for the Aspide missile control above the wheelhouse. The crowded electronics environment requires careful arrangement. BELOW LEFT: *Luigi Durand de la Penne*'s forward funnel indicates that she is proceeding under diesel power. In a CODOG system the two types of prime mover cannot be used together. This picture pre-dates the 2005–07 upgrades, the ship lacking IRST domes.

Durand de la Penne class

Displacement: 4,500 tons (standard); 5,400 tons (full load)
Length: 135.6m/445ft 1in (bp); 147.7m/484ft 10in (oa)
Beam: 15.9m/49ft 3in
Draught: 5.1m/16ft 9in
Armament: 1 x 127mm gun, 3 x 76mm guns (3x1); 1 x Standard SM-1 MR system; 1 x 8-cell Albatros point-defence SAM system; 6 x 324mm AS torpedo tubes (2x3)
Machinery: 2 gas turbines and 2 cruising diesels in CODOG configuration
Power: 41,030kW/55,000shp for 31.5 knots or 9,400kW/12,600bhp for 21 knots
Endurance: 12,965km/7,000nm at 18 knots (on diesels alone)
Protection: Mirex/Kevlar patches
Complement: 375

173

Skoryi class

Following World War II, the Soviet Union used captured German expertise and resources to develop new weapons and technologies. Until these came "on line", however, the supposed threat posed by the Western powers had to be met by conventional means. Ambitious programmes of cruisers, destroyers and submarines were, therefore, put in train. For rapid production standardization was essential.

The adopted design of destroyer was the Skoryi (or Skory), based on a pre-war class, but further influenced by German ships acquired as reparation. Not surprisingly, given the climatic conditions in which they would have to operate, the ships were large, their 2,600 tons and 121m/397ft overall length exceeding even the 2,425 tons and 119m/390ft 6in of an American Gearing. With the common occurrence of heavy topside ice accumulation, the Skoryi was less burdened with weaponry, notably carrying only two twin gunhouses to the American's three. Masting, however, was substantial and well braced.

As designed, the Skoryi profile was not unpleasing, with a conventional raised forecastle and two quintuple torpedo tube banks alternating with two squat funnels. Gunhouses, each of two 130mm guns, were fully enclosed and mounted at different levels, one forward, one aft. Superfiring the after gunhouse was a twin 85mm high-angle mounting. Manually operated, this was probably too heavy to be effective as an anti-aircraft weapon, being often replaced by 37mm weapons, of which four twins were already usually carried.

A rather Germanic, broad transom stern was fitted, improving reserve buoyancy at the after end and facilitating minelaying. Two tracks, with a capacity of about 70 mines, ran much of the length of the after deck.

Probably 64 of a planned 80 Skoryis were completed. Modest modernization was begun in the late 1950s but quickly discontinued. Upgraded units could be identified through their larger funnel caps and heavier mainmasts.

ABOVE: A Skoryi (sometimes rendered Skory) in her original classic form, whose design dated from the 1940s. The broad transom with minelaying apertures echoes German wartime practice. The after 130mm guns are superfired by a twin 85mm mounting.

ABOVE: Another Skoryi in its original form. Note the two sets of torpedo tubes and long, parallel afterbody. The platform forward of the bridge was later widened to accommodate sided MBU-2500 AS rocket projectors, the forward tubes landed and Anti-Aircraft (AA) armament enhanced.

Skoryi class, as designed

Displacement: 2,600 tons (standard); 3,500 tons (full load)
Length: 121.5m/398ft 10in (oa)
Beam: 12m/39ft 4in
Draught: 4.5m/14ft 9in
Armament: 4 x 130mm guns (2x2), 2 x 85mm guns (1x2), 7/8 x 37mm guns (7x1 or 4x2); 10 x 533mm torpedo tubes (2x5)
Machinery: Geared steam turbines, 4 boilers, 2 shafts
Power: 44,760kW/60,000shp for 36 knots
Endurance: 790 tons oil for 8,520km/4,600nm at 18 knots
Protection: None
Complement: 260

USSR

Kotlin class

During the course of the Skoryi programme, the Russians built a prototype destroyer leader. Launched in 1953, the *Neustrashimy* (NATO reporting name *Tallinn*) was an enormous 3,200-ton flush-decker, but carrying little more effective armament than a Skoryi. The proposed series was terminated at this one ship, but she acted as test-bed for advanced steam machinery and new stabilized gunhouses.

The Kotlins were Tallinn diminutives, wide-transomed, flush-decked and with a long, sweeping forward sheerline. Machinery was arranged on the unit system, with the resulting wide-spaced funnels alternating with quintuple torpedo tube mountings. Like the Skoryis, the heavily braced tripod mainmast was stepped between the funnels to give the anti-aircraft armament clear arcs. This powerful secondary battery comprised four quadruple 57mm mountings. Of these, one superfired the main gunhouse at either end. The other two were sided, flanking the mainmast. Separate secondary directors were provided, forward and aft.

Most units later landed the after set of torpedo tubes in favour of more superstructure and a brace of forward-firing MBU-2500 type, 12-railed AS rocket projectors.

It is believed that 28 of a planned 36 Kotlins were completed as what were probably the last-ever classic destroyers. Eight, possibly nine, of those were converted to carry the 25km/16-mile ranged, SA-N-1 (NATO reporting name "Goa") SAM system. Known as "Kotlin-SAMs", these ships sacrificed their after tubes and gun armament for a large magazine/deckhouse upon which was mounted the twin-armed launcher. Their after funnel was moved farther aft to accommodate a pyramidal "mainmast" bearing the guidance radar.

In lieu of the waist 57mm AA guns, some ships gained four of the new helmet-like, twin 30mm mountings, fully automatic and controlled in pairs by adjacent "Drum Tilt" directors. The SAM conversions lost the 70-mine capacity of the remainder.

ABOVE: **A nice view of a Kotlin as originally built. The massive enclosed twin 130mm gun mountings are fully stabilized, as are the four quadruple 57mm weapons, two of which are sided amidships. The after torpedo tubes were later removed.**

RIGHT: **During the 1960s, several Kotlins were rebuilt aft in order to accommodate the pioneer SA-N-1 ("Goa") SAM system, whose twin-armed launcher is located here on the large 20-round magazine, added aft. Note the new pyramidal mainmast.**

Kotlin class, as designed

Displacement: 2,850 tons (standard); 3,880 tons (full load)
Length: 128m/420ft 2in
Beam: 13m/42ft 8in
Draught: 5m/16ft 5in
Armament: 4 x 130mm guns (2x2), 16 x 57mm guns (4x4); 10 x 533m torpedo tubes (2x5)
Machinery: Geared steam turbines, 4 boilers, 2 shafts
Power: 53,712kW/72,000shp for 36 knots
Endurance: 850 tons oil for 7,410km/4,000nm at 18 knots
Protection: None
Complement: 325

175

Kildin class

To deal with the supposed threat from the West's carrier and amphibious forces, the Soviet Union early developed two large Ship-to-Ship Missiles (SSM). These were known to NATO as the SS-N-1 (NATO name "Scrubber") and the rather smaller SS-N-2A ("Styx"). Both were effective to horizon range, although the former, based on the German V-1 flying bomb design of World War II, had a maximum range of about 160km/ 100 miles. The Styx was deployed in the many minor war vessels intended to deal with amphibious forces, but the Scrubber first went to sea on four Kotlin-class conversions. The first of these was modified for the task, the others being especially built. They were known as the Kildin-class and, by pre-dating the Kotlin SAMs, were reputedly the world's first GM destroyers.

As modified, the ships retained their basic Kotlin appearance but with the afterdeck now occupied by the cumbersome, twin-rail launcher for the SS-N-1, which weighed over 3 tons at launch. Between the launcher and the after funnel was a single-level deckhouse, topped with a magazine containing two reloads.

With the necessarily more comprehensive electronics fit, masting was on a much heavier scale than that of the Kotlins. No main battery 130mm mountings were carried but the sixteen 57mm guns were retained. Two quadruple mountings were located in the centreline "A" and "B" positions, with two more flanking the mainmast. Only four torpedo tubes were shipped, these being paired on either side in the waist.

During the 1970s the Kildins were upgraded to deploy the SS-N-2C, an improved Styx. These were accommodated in canister launchers, elevated at a fixed angle and sited, two per side, abreast the after funnel. There were no reloads. Without the requirement for the earlier magazine and launcher, two 130mm gun mountings were reinstated aft.

ABOVE: **The Kildins were the world's first true guided-missile destroyers but, with the discontinuation of the SS-N-1, some were given four canister-launched SS-N-11. This photograph probably shows *Bedovy*. Note the 57mm quads forward and amidships, and the 76mm twins aft.**

ABOVE: **This Kildin had a machinery fire while in the Mediterranean, but the obsessively secretive Soviet Navy refused all offers of assistance. Note the size of the twin SS-N-1 launcher aft, with its magazine reportedly containing four reloads. Compare the layout with the later version (top).**

Kildin class, as built

Displacement: 3,000 tons (standard); 4,000 tons (full load)
Length: 128m/420ft 2in (oa)
Beam: 13m/42ft 8in
Draft: 5m/16ft 5in
Armament: 16 x 57mm guns (4x4); 1 x SS-N-1 SSM launcher; 4 x 533mm torpedo tubes (2x2); 2 x 12-rail MBU-2500 AS rocket launchers
Machinery: Geared steam turbines, 4 boilers, 2 shafts
Power: 53,712kW/72,000shp for 36 knots
Protection: None
Complement: 350

Krupny class

The single-ended Kildin conversions could launch only two missiles before having to reload, a process which appeared to be critically time-consuming under operational conditions. Their major function was to knock out hostile aircraft carriers and, as SSMs would need to be launched in pairs to give one of them a reasonable chance of a hit, a rapid follow-up with a second pair was obviously of advantage. The eight Krupny-class double-enders were thus a logical development.

For the sake of urgency, the long-suffering Kotlin hull form was not only lengthened by 10m/33ft but also "kippered" and widened by 1.6m/15ft 3in. This increased the Length-on-Breadth (L/B) ratio somewhat, making for a more stable weapon platform but at the cost of hydrodynamic efficiency. The resulting ships, although of higher power, were thus somewhat slower.

An interesting innovation, right aft, was a helicopter platform. The SS-N-1 had the potential to hit a target at about 160km/100 miles, but lacked the necessary on-board intelligence. A helicopter, pre-positioned beyond the horizon, would be able to order a mid-course correction sufficient to bring the missile within its own active homing range of the target.

Even 160km/100 miles is a suicidally close range to approach a carrier and, while reloading the four repeat rounds, a Krupny could expect to be under heavy air attack. Even if accompanied by a Kotlin SAM, she would need all of her sixteen 57mm anti-aircraft weapons to survive. Having exhausted her eight (although possibly more) SSMs, she would be reduced to torpedo attack, for which purpose two triple mountings were sided in the waist.

As a weapons system, the SS-N-1 failed to impress and, by 1968, a programme was initiated to convert six of the Krupnys to Kanins.

ABOVE: **A good view of a Krupny at a 1962 review. As hull numbers were constantly changed, individual identities are never certain. Note the World War II vintage "Wasp Head" director. The large gun mountings are twin 57mm.** LEFT: **There were probably no more than a couple of double-ended Krupnys created from stretched Kotlin hulls. Despite the space required by the SS-N-1 systems, this one retains her waist torpedo tubes and has a helicopter pad right aft.**

Krupny class

Displacement: 3,650 tons (standard); 4,600 tons (full load)
Length: 138m/452ft 11in (oa)
Beam: 14.6m/47ft 11in
Draught: 5m/16ft 5in
Armament: 16 x 57mm guns (4x4); 2 x SS-N-1 SSM launchers; 6 x 533mm torpedo tubes (2x3); 2 x 12-rail MBU-2500 AS rocket launchers
Machinery: Geared steam turbines, 4 boilers, 2 shafts
Power: 59,680kW/80,000shp for 34 knots
Endurance: 900 tons oil for 8,280km/4,500nm at 18 knots
Protection: None
Complement: 360

DIRECTORY OF DESTROYERS: 1918 TO DATE

LEFT: **Late in the 1960s, the Krupnys' obsolete SS-N-1s were stripped out and the ships, now known to the West as Kanins, were rebuilt around the SA-N-1 SAM system. Note the bow profile, altered for a new sonar installation.**

Kanin class

Efforts to improve the SS-N-1 SSM continued until 1966, at which point the even larger SS-N-3 (NATO name "Shaddock") assumed the primary anti-surface ship role. The double-ended Krupnys were then taken in hand for conversion to area air defence escorts. In this guise they were redesignated Kanin by NATO.

On what had been the after SS-N-1 magazine structure was mounted the twin-armed launcher of a SA-N-1 ("Goa") SAM system. The magazine beneath stowed a reported 22 missiles. Forward of the after funnel was erected a pyramidal "mainmast" bearing the massive "Peel Group" control radar associated with the SA-N-1. Its heavy "Head Net-C" search radar antenna topped the foremast.

Forward, two quadruple 57mm gun mountings now occupied centreline "A" and "B" positions. A new structure around the after funnel supported four 30mm automatic twins, each pair of mountings being controlled by a dedicated "Drum Tilt" radar located on the mainmast. The two quintuple torpedo tube groups, sided in the waist, represented the Kanins' only defence against surface ships.

Anti-submarine capability was considerably improved. Three MBU-2500A 12-round AS rocket projectors were carried, one in a very exposed location on the foredeck, the others sided on raised platforms in the waist. A new, low-frequency bow sonar was added, necessitating an extended and more heavily raked bow to enable ground tackle to drop clear of the bulb. This added a further 1.5m/5ft to the length of the hull.

Right aft, the helicopter platform could be moved somewhat farther forward, thus reducing the amplitudes and accelerations of ship motion experienced by the aircraft. There was no hangar, the ships presumably acting as platforms for shared Kamov KA-25 "Hormone" ASW helicopters.

Apparently effective in their new role, the Kanins remained on the inventory until the 1990s. Like most Soviet warships, they occasionally changed their hull numbers. The reasons for these changes were never quite clear.

LEFT: **Soviet Black Sea units habitually spent long periods at anchor in remote offshore Mediterranean anchorages. The twin-arm SA-N-1 launcher is clearly visible here. Note the forward 57mm mounting, tracking the photographer's aircraft and the four 30mm "Dalek" mounts.**

Kanin class

Displacement: 3,675 tons (standard); 4,550 tons (full load)
Length: 139.5m/457ft 10in (oa)
Beam: 14.6m/47ft 11in
Draught: 5m/16ft 5in
Armament: 8 x 57mm guns (2x4), 8 x 30mm guns (4x2); 1 x SA-N-1 SAM launcher; 10 x 533mm torpedo tubes (2x5); 3 x 12-rail MBU-2500A AS rocket launchers
Machinery: Geared steam turbines, 4 boilers, 2 shafts
Power: 59,680kW/80,000shp for 34 knots
Endurance: 900 tons oil for 8,280km/4,500nm at 18 knots
Protection: Nominal
Complement: 350

178

LEFT: **An earlier Kashin with her entire above-surface armament trained on the port beam. Note the size of the 25.7km/16-mile-range SA-N-1 SAMs on the launcher rails. A total of 22 missives were accommodated in each of the two magazines.**

Kashin class

As the Soviet fleet's first gas-turbine destroyers, the Kashins were all gas, not being combined with steam or diesel power. Probably lacking the range of engines available in the West, the designers opted for four identical M-8E units, each rated at some 18,000kW maximum. Although the ships had a distinctly "Soviet" profile, they were instantly, identifiable by their massive split funnel casings, angled to eject exhaust gases clear of electronics. These gases were first cooled to reduce the ships' Infra-Red (IR) signature, while structural surfaces also were subtly angled to reduce radar return.

The Kashins were designed as "double-ended" SAM escorts, having two SA-N-1 systems. These required two "Peel Group" control radars, one atop the strangely truncated bridge structure, the other on a short tower ahead of the after funnels. Long-range, three-dimensional air search/warning was provided by two complementary systems, known as Head Net (A or C) and Big Net, whose large and weighty antennas were located on high and substantial lattice masts.

Forward and aft were sited twin 76mm dual purpose guns, a new calibre of weapon in fully stabilized mountings, each with its own director. Only one quintuple torpedo tube mount was carried, located amidships on the centreline. A helicopter pad, again without hangar, was provided on the quarterdeck.

Twenty Kashins were built, of which eight were converted during the 1970s to more capable Kashin-Mods. Variable-Depth Sonar (VDS) was added aft, necessitating elevating the helicopter platform by one level. The earlier lack of close-in AA defence was rectified by the addition of four Gatling-type 30mm cannon, grouped with their directors forward of the after funnels. Sided abaft these were four canister launchers for SS-N-11 SSMs (essentially an improved variant of the SS-N-2C).

By 2007 no fully operational Kashins or Kashin-Mods remained on the inventory, joining the very considerable drawdown in the strength of the Russian fleet.

LEFT: **The Modified Kashins, as seen here, were retro-fitted with canister launchers for four SS-N-11s, here flanking the after SA-N-1 launcher. The split uptakes for the gas turbines are evident, as is the quintuple torpedo tube bank amidships.**

Kashin class, as built

Displacement: 3,750 tons (standard); 4,750 tons (full load)
Length: 144m/472ft 8in
Beam: 15.8m/51ft 10in
Draught: 4.8m/15ft 9in
Armament: 4 x 76mm guns (2x2); 2 x SA-N-1 SAM launchers; 5 x 533mm torpedo tubes (1x5); 2 x 6-rail MBU-1000 AS rocket launchers
Machinery: 4 gas turbines (COGAG), 2 shafts
Power: 71,616kW/96,000shp for 36 knots
Endurance: 940 tons oil for 5,556km/3,000nm at 20 knots
Protection: Nominal
Complement: 285

DIRECTORY OF DESTROYERS: 1918 TO DATE

Sovremennyy class

The planned programme for these formidable-looking 8,000-tonners fell into complete disarray due to uncertain funding following the collapse of the Soviet Union. Of the original 28, only 10 are active under Russian Federation colours. Two, possibly four, have been sold to China. Some languish incomplete, others have been prematurely scrapped.

In function, the Sovremnnyys are intended primarily for surface action and area air defence, having only basic ASW capacity. Of almost twice the displacement of a Kashin, they reverted to steam turbine propulsion in order to generate a one-third increase in sustained power.

The hull has also reverted to a raised-forecastle which, like that of a Kashin, has a gentle knuckle running almost full length. A new-style 54-calibre, 130mm gun has been introduced. Fully automatic and dual-purpose, it appears in twin mountings, forward and aft. There are also four 30mm Gatlings, two forward and two aft.

Superfiring each main gun mounting is an SA-N-7 ("Gadfly") SAM launcher. First trialled on a Kashin, the weapon has a reported range of 25km/15 miles. Flanking the massive bridge structure are eight canister launchers for SS-N-22 ("Sunburn") SSMs, manoeuvrable and with a putative range of 101km/63 miles. Targetting for these is facilitated by the "Bandstand" radar within the conspicuous dome atop the bridge block, alternative targeting assistance being possible through the ship's Ka-27 ("Helix") helicopter. This is carried high on the after superstructure and is provided with a light, telescoping hangar.

The helicopter can also be used defensively against submarines, for which purpose the ship is also equipped with bow sonar and two rocket projectors. Unlike Western equivalents,

LEFT: Mutual interest; the Northern Fleet's *Rastoropnyy* encounters the American Spruance-class *O'Bannon*. The Russian ship is not carrying her helicopter, for which the telescoping hangar has been stowed. The hull is subtly knuckled to reduce radar signature.

ABOVE LEFT: Many modern warships appear under-armed; not so the Russians. Here, the *Nastoychivyy* fairly bristles. The SA-N-7 ("Gadfly") launchers forward and aft are complemented by eight canister/launchers for the 101km/63-mile SS-N-22 ("Sunburn") SSMs. ABOVE: Forward and aft the *Otchayannyy* is equipped with twin, 130mm guns which, as can be seen, are capable of local control. CIWS Gatling-type guns flank the wheelhouse and also the elevated helicopter pad, three-quarters aft.

the Sovremennyys retain heavyweight torpedo tubes which, presumably, could accommodate either anti-ship or anti-submarine weapons.

Finally, these very capable ships can carry up to 40 mines.

Sovremennyy class

Displacement: 7,950 tons (normal); 8,500 tons (full load)
Length: 145m/475ft 11in (wl); 156m/513ft 4in (oa)
Beam: 16.3m/53ft 6in
Draught: 6m/19ft 8in
Armament: 4 x 130mm guns (2x2), 4 x 30mm Gatling guns (4x1); 2 x SA-N-7 SAM launchers; 8 x SS-N-22 SSM launchers; 4 x 533m torpedo tubes (2x2); 2 x 6-rail MBU-1000 AS rocket launchers
Machinery: Geared steam turbines, 4 boilers, 2 shafts
Power: 82,060kW/110,000shp for 33 knots
Endurance: 1,740 tons oil for 6,480km/3,500nm at 20 knots
Protection: Nominal
Complement: 296

Udaloy class

Also affected by the distintegration of the Soviet Union were the Udaloy-class ASW destroyers. Ten are in service but at least four appear to have been cancelled, scrapped or cannibalized. The latter course is not unusual as now-separate republics bargain over single-sourced technologies.

Slightly larger than a Sovremennyy, an Udaloy is easily differentiated by her long-forecastle hull form and two paired funnel casings that indicate her gas turbine propulsion. Two boost engines and two cruise units are arranged in COGAG configuration but, even run together, develop less power than is customary in Russian ships.

The exaggerated bow overhang results from a complex bow bulb, arranged around several acoustically based systems, but adversely affecting resistance and manoeuvring. Two Ka-27 "Helix A" ASW helicopters are accommodated in hangars but the Udaloy main combat system is the SS-N-14 "Silex" missile, whose quadruple canister launchers flank the bridge structure. The 50km/31-mile weapon may be configured either to release an AS torpedo over a submerged target, or fitted with a warhead to counter surface targets, probably with mid-course correction.

To two 100mm and four 30mm Gatling guns the ships add the SA-N-9 ("Gauntlet") vertically launched SAM. Eight 8-round silos for these are divided between the forecastle and the after superstructure, each group having its own distinctive "Cross Sword" directors.

Short-range AS weapons comprise a pair of MBU-6000 rocket launchers and two quadruple banks of heavyweight torpedo tubes. Although massive in appearance, the ships are contoured to reduce radar signature.

LEFT: **The Udaloys have twinned helicopter hangars of compact design. Between them is an unoccupied "Bandstand" for the Kinzhal SAM system, presumably not fitted. Note the large stern door, through which the towed VDS is deployed.**

ABOVE: **The Udaloy-class destroyers have an unmistakably "chunky" appearance and are unusual these days in having superimposed gun mountings forward. The quadruple canisters are for the SS-N-14 ("Silex") anti-ship/anti-submarine SSM.**

Of the ten extant Udaloys, one (*Admiral Chabanenko*) varies sufficiently to be classed separately as an Udaloy-II. Probably designed for the former KGB, she has an even longer forecastle, necessitating the heavy torpedo tubes being carried behind shutters. Her major weapon has been changed to eight SS-N-22 "Sunburn" anti-ship missiles, while a twin 130mm mounting replaces the single 100mms.

Udaloy class

Displacement: 6,940 tons (standard); 8,400 tons (full load)
Length: 145m/476ft (wl); 163.5m/536ft 8in (oa)
Beam: 17.2m/56ft 6in
Draught: 5.2m/17ft 1in
Armament: 2 x 100mm guns (2x1); 4 x 30mm Gatling guns (4x1); 8 x SS-N-14 SSM/AS launchers; 8 x 8-cell SA-N-9 SAM launchers; 8 x 533mm torpedo tubes (2x4); 2 x 12-rail MBU-6000 AS rocket launchers
Machinery: 2 boost and 2 cruise gas turbines, 2 shafts
Power: 2 x 16,7985kW/22,500shp and 2 x 5,595kW/7,500shp for 29.5 knots
Endurance: 1,500 tons fuel for 13,890km/7,500nm at 18 knots
Protection: Nominal
Complement: 220

LEFT: **More correctly "Z10", the *Hans Lody* was of the original Maass type. Designed for high speed and maximum firepower, these lacked the range for oceanic operations. Note the lack of forward sheer, contributing to wetness.** ABOVE: **By virtue of the incorrect funnel proportions, this impression of *Max Schultz* (Z3) gives more the appearance of a light cruiser. She also had a straight stem and rounded sheer strake to the forecastle.**

Maass and Roeder classes

A large German naval construction programme followed the naval agreement with Britain in 1935. As destroyers were required to conform to the generally adopted maxima of the London Naval Treaty of 1930, the large majority were limited to a standard displacement of 1,500 tons and a number of guns not exceeding 130mm (German 13cm) in calibre.

Twenty-two were laid down 1934–38, comprising four Type 34s and twelve Type 34As (collectively the Leberecht Maass class), followed by the six Type 36s, or Diether von Roeder, class. Their design brief emphasized seaworthiness, hull strength, speed, endurance and firepower, a conflicting set of ideals which, not surprisingly, inflated their reported displacements to well beyond the 2,000-ton treaty limit.

Types 34 and 34A differed primarily in the latter having a new bow configuration to improve seakindliness. The Type 36s were somewhat longer and beamier, otherwise not dissimilar.

All were of orthodox layout, with a raised forecastle and five 12.7cm guns in single open mountings, two forward, three aft. Masting was light, the foremast bearing a distinctive cruciform yard. Tophamper otherwise was heavy, particularly forward, making earlier units very wet. The after funnel was located between two quadruple banks of torpedo tubes, and sided mine rails ran most of the length of the afterdeck. Funnels were heavily capped.

The most contentious element in their design was the adoption of yet-untried steam conditions, far and away in advance of anything used in other major navies. The objective of compact, but powerful, plant was achieved at the cost of endless mechanical problems.

Unlike British equivalents, German destroyers never saved topweight by landing one set of torpedo tubes and when, in 1944, surviving units were given comprehensively improved "flak" defences, they became even more heavily loaded.

Although ten of the twenty-two had been destroyed by April 1940, seven succeeded in surviving hostilities.

ABOVE: **Derived directly from the Maass, or Type 34/34A, were the six Type 36 units, usually referred to as the Diether von Roeder class. *Hans Lüdemann* (Z18) shows their shorter funnels and bows with greater sheer and flare.**

Types 34 and 34A

Displacement: 2,220 tons (standard); 3,155 tons (full load)
Length: 115m/377ft 6in (bp); 120m/393ft 11in (oa)
Beam: 11.3m/37ft 1in
Draught: 4m/13ft 2in
Armament: 5 x 12.7cm guns (5x1), 4 x 3.7cm guns (2x2); 8 x 53.3cm torpedo tubes (2x4)
Machinery: Geared steam turbines, 6 boilers, 2 shafts
Power: 52,220kW/70,000shp for 36 knots
Endurance: 715 tons oil for 3.312km/1,800nm at 19 knots
Protection: None
Complement: 325

GERMANY

LEFT: The 12 ships of the Z23 type were war-built, officially of the Type 36A class. They can be recognized by the twin gunhouse forward with no superfiring "B" gun, strongly curved bow profile and tripod mast. ABOVE: Contrasting with the French post-war paint scheme (left), this Type 36A (Mob) in Norwegian waters carries a disruptive pattern. Note the large search radar antenna.

Z23–39

Unique in bearing names, the previous German destroyers were also allocated pendant numbers, prefixed "Z" (*Zerstörer*/Destroyer). Types 34 and 34A were thus also Z1–16, and Type 36 Z17–22 inclusive. Subsequent war-built destroyers reverted to the earlier convention of numbers only.

Concerned that large foreign destroyers, notably French, still outgunned its ships, the German Fleet Command wanted new construction to mount 15cm guns rather than 12.7cm. Throwing a much heavier projectile (45.3kg/100lb against 28kg/62lb), it was also a much heavier gun. Following various permutations of layout, and bearing in mind the need to reduce weight forward, it was decided to specify an enclosed twin gunhouse forward and three open, single mountings aft.

Together with two quadruple banks of torpedo tubes, this would demand no more than a couple of metres on length, together with a small increase in beam to maintain stability.

The resulting eight Type 36A ships, numbered Z23–30 inclusive, were completed 1940–41. Their twin gunhouses being delayed, all were completed with a fourth open single mounting forward. Their appearance otherwise was similar to that of earlier vessels except for tripod foremasts, markedly greater forward sheer and curved bow profiles.

When, in 1942, a first twin 15cm mounting became available, it was fitted to Z23. It caused the ship to plunge heavily in adverse conditions and proved unreliable because of resulting water ingress.

The next group, known as Type 36A (Mob), comprised Z31–34 and Z37–39 inclusive. Retaining four guns, they differed internally.

With the 15cm gun continuing to cause problems, a batch of seven Type 36Bs, with five 12.7cm weapons was ordered in February 1941. Of this group, only Z35–36 and, eventually, Z43 were ever completed.

Plans for destroyers propelled by multiple diesel engines ended with the destruction by bombing of the prototype Z51. She was lead ship for the projected eight-strong Type 42 (Z51–58).

Type 36A

Displacement: 2,600 tons (standard); 3,580 tons (full load)
Length: 121.9m/400ft 2in (bp); 127m/416ft 10in (oa)
Beam: 12m/39ft 3in
Draught: 3.9m/12ft 10in
Armament: 4/5 x 15cm guns (4x1 or 1x2/3x1), 4 x 3.7cm guns (2x2); 8 x 53.3cm torpedo tubes (2x4)
Machinery: Geared steam turbines, 6 boilers, 2 shafts
Power: 52,220kW/70,000shp for 36 knots
Endurance: 775 tons oil for 4,075km/2,200nm at 19 knots
Protection: Nominal
Complement: 318

ABOVE: Reversion to smaller gun mountings, in combination with a tripod foremast, mark this unidentified unit as a Type 36B, i.e. either Z35 or Z36. Both ships were destroyed in a German minefield in the Gulf of Finland, December 1944.

183

LEFT: The significance of then-West Germany's first post-war destroyers was emphasized by their adoption of names of provinces. This fine shot of *Schleswig-Holstein* well portrays the class's main impression of bulk. ABOVE: Despite being well sheered both forward and aft, the hull of *Hessen* appears to lack adequate freeboard. The size of the bridge structure and full-width deckhouse suggests a strong training role.

Hamburg class

While still the Federal Republic, or West, Germany became a member of NATO, and its first post-war destroyers were both named and given "D" pendant numbers. For their category, the four Hamburgs had a massive profile. A flush-decked hull form was readopted, somewhat disguised by the full-width lower levels of the bridge block. The bow section, with its prominent sheer and knuckle, and anchors stowed at the deck edge, was reminiscent of later war-built German destroyers. Indeed the whole hull appeared to be an extrapolation of that of the slightly earlier Köln-class frigates, which stemmed from the same yard.

For their bulk, the Hamburgs always gave the impression of being under-armed. As built, they carried four French-pattern, single 10cm guns in enclosed mountings. In the course of a major 1970s refit, "C" mounting was landed in favour of four, forward-angled MM38 Exocet canister launchers.

Five 53.3cm torpedo tubes were built into the hull, three firing forward through the stem head, and two aft through the transom. These were all removed during the 1970s refit, at which time the bridge structure was also remodelled.

The main ASW weapons were a pair of Bofors four-barrelled projectors, sited immediately forward of the bridge front, and two lightweight torpedo tubes in the waist. With the removal of the hull-mounted tubes, the latter were replaced with sided pairs of heavyweight tubes.

Masting was also heavy, bearing an array of mainly British-and-Dutch-sourced electronics. The aftermost of the three original masts was later removed. Funnels were large and heavily capped. The inadequate anti-aircraft armament of four paired 40mm Bofors weapons was later supplemented with launchers for the Rolling-Airframe Missile (RAM). All four were scrapped in the late 1990s.

LEFT: *Bayern*'s large funnel caps were intended to protect electronics from hot, corrosive stack gases. Her "X" gun has here been landed in favour of four MM38 Exocets. The wide transom was designed to accommodate minelaying.

Hamburg class, as built

Displacement: 3,500 tons (standard); 4,700 tons (full load)
Length: 128m/420ft 2in (bp); 133.7m/438ft 10in (oa)
Beam: 13.4m/44ft
Draught: 5.2m/17ft 1in
Armament: 4 x 10cm guns (4x1); 5 x 53.3cm torpedo tubes (5x1); 2 x AS torpedo tubes (2x1); 2 x 37.5cm Bofors AS rocket launchers (2x4)
Machinery: Geared steam turbines, 4 boilers, 2 shafts
Power: 50,728kW/68,000shp for 35 knots
Endurance: 810 tons oil for 6,297km/3,400nm at 18 knots
Protection: Nominal
Complement: 276

… GERMANY/NETHERLANDS

Holland/Friesland class

Four new destroyers, closely following classic British (Yarrow) design, were under construction in Dutch yards when the nation was invaded in 1940, Two were completed, one by the British, one by the Germans, and two were scrapped. This might have been the end of what would have been the Callenburgh class, except that four complete sets of Parsons-designed machinery, intended for them, surprisingly survived the war. Designed to deliver a continuous 33,570kW/ 45,020shp, these would drive the 1,600-ton Callenburgh at 36 knots. Post-war, however, they were used to power the four-ship Holland class which, at 2,215 tons, longer and beamier, could make only 32 knots.

Unusual in having a light protective belt over the length of their machinery space, the Holland were otherwise of conventional raised forecastle design.

No anti-surface ship torpedo tubes were carried (although heavyweight AS tubes were unsuccessfully trialled early in their careers), destroyers by now having evolved into primarily fast AA/AS escorts.

The main gun battery was fully automatic and dual purpose, comprising two twin Bofors 120mm gunhouses, one mounted forward, one aft. There were also six 40mm Bofors weapons. Several directors were backed by a comprehensive radar fit. Beyond depth charges, AS armament consisted of two 4-barrelled, 375mm rocket projectors, also from Bofors. These fired forward from a location ahead of the bridge front. As a space-saving measure, the forward funnel was built into the foremast, as on a British Daring.

The requirement for a dozen destroyers was met by building eight more to the same basic design but with slightly enlarged dimensions to

ABOVE: **Built post-World War II, the Frieslands were designed to counter aircraft and submarines rather than surface ships.** *Rotterdam*, here, and others, if ever fitted with 21in torpedo tubes, quickly had them removed. BELOW LEFT: *Amsterdam*, another of the Frieslands, differed slightly in machinery and hull dimensions from the Hollands. Note the two Bofors AS rocket launchers in "B" position. Guns are also of Bofors pattern but major electronics are of Dutch design; the topmast is British.

accommodate more powerful machinery, reportedly similar to that specified for the American Gearing. Appreciably faster, the eight were termed the Friesland class, also named after provinces.

Following the disposal of the Holland, the seven surviving Frieslands were sold to Peru in the early 1980s.

Friesland class, as built

Displacement: 2,500 tons (standard); 3,075 tons (full load)
Length: 112.8m/370ft 3in (bp); 116m/380ft 9in (oa)
Beam: 11.8m/38ft 9in
Draught: 5.2m/17ft 1in
Armament: 4 x 120mm guns (2x2);
 2 x 4-barrelled 375mm AS rocket launchers
Machinery: Geared steam turbines,
 4 boilers, 2 shafts
Power: 44,760kW/60,000shp at 36 knots
Endurance: 6,110kW/3,300nm for 22 knots
Protection: Light vertical belt over machinery spaces
Complement: 285

Öland class

The two Ölands evolved from the Göteborgs of the late 1930s. Of only 1,140 tons, these six were orthodox destroyers with two funnels and two triple sets of torpedo tubes. One of their three single 120mm guns was located amidships. Their dominant feature was a monolithic bridge block, extending the full width of the ship.

To ensure her neutrality during World War II, Sweden expanded her small fleet. The four Visbys were slightly enlarged Göteborgs differing in having two, close-set funnels of unequal size, and the third gun moved aft to a superfiring position.

Swedish warships, not intended for blue water operation, tend to have limited endurance and, post-war, both these classes were remodelled as anti-submarine frigates.

The succeeding Ölands were also a wartime design but, incomplete in 1945, were finished in slow time. Although obviously derived from the *Visby*, they were a considerable 13.6m/44ft 7in greater in length. Where the preceding classes emphasized speed, the Ölands were powered for a more moderate 35 knots.

Their armament was designed for maximum anti-aircraft capability. At either end was a twin Bofors 120mm mounting – fully enclosed, semi-automatic and with an 80-degree elevation. Both uptakes were trunked into a single large funnel casing and the massive bridge, subsequently rebuilt, supported a stubby pole mast. As built, the ships had a seventh 40mm Bofors located right forward in the "bow-chaser" position favoured by contemporary British Hunt-class ships that frequently engaged fast enemy torpedo boats. Exposed, and with no peacetime application, these were later removed, their bases remaining.

ABOVE: At the outbreak of World War II, Sweden acquired a couple of Italian-built torpedo boats, effectively light destroyers. Their influence on layout may be discerned in the *Öland*. The ring, right forward, supports a 40mm "bow chaser" gun, when fitted. BELOW LEFT: *Uppland* at speed. Note how the depth of hull is varied to reflect bending moments. The profile is exceptionally low, Swedish ships sometimes being berthed in bomb-proof chambers hewn into solid rock.

Although not rerated as frigates, at least one of the Ölands was modified to carry a helicopter, as were some of their smaller destroyers. As part of a general drawdown of larger Swedish combatants, all three of these classes had been discarded by 1981.

Öland class, as built

Displacement: 1,880 tons (standard); 2,400 tons (full load)
Length: 107m/351ft (bp); 111.1m/364ft 2in (oa)
Beam: 11.2m/36ft 9in
Draught: 3.4m/11ft 3in
Armament: 4 x 120mm guns (2x2); 6 x 533mm torpedo tubes (2x3)
Machinery: Geared steam turbines, 2 boilers, 2 shafts
Power: 32,824kW/44,000shp for 35 knots
Endurance: 300 tons oil for 4,630km/2,500nm at 20 knots
Protection: Splinter protection
Complement: 200

SWEDEN

LEFT: The two Hallands were of an age with the Dutch Frieslands, and it will be noticed how the twin 120mm Bofors mountings and Dutch LW 02/03 air-search radar are common to both types. BELOW: Unusually, the four Östergötlands showed a reduction in size compared with the preceding Hallands. This is the nameship, breasting the wake of another vessel. Note how she lacks the twin 57mm guns in "B" position.

Östergötland and Halland classes

Completed in 1955–56, the two Hallands must be contenders for the most handsome destroyers ever. Their two funnels were slightly tapered and well proportioned, their profiles complemented by the angled front and back faces of the otherwise monolithic bridge block.

The first Swedish destroyers of post-war design, they had raised forecastles and a fully automatic, dual-purpose, twin 120mm Bofors mounting at either end. The forward mounting was superfired by a twin 57mm, also by Bofors. The same company also supplied the two four-barrelled AS launchers on the foredeck and that for the early RB O8 SSM, located abaft the funnels. One quintuple and one triple torpedo tube mounting was also fitted. Modernization saw them acquire a large air/surface-search radar on the mainmast, and a four-rail Seacat point-defence SAM.

Two sister ships were cancelled, but were probably subsumed into the four-ship Östergötland class which followed on. Almost uniquely, these were smaller than the ships from which they were derived. Chunky and powerful looking, they lacked the classic elegance of the Halland.

The Östergötland differed primarily in having a flush-decked hull form, while their diminutive mainmast was stepped before the after funnel. The 57mm twin mounting was omitted, the forward 120mm being superfired by two of the seven single 40mm weapons that were carried. These too, were later supported by a Seacat system. No SSM was carried, and only one bank of torpedo tubes, a probably unique sextuple.

Sweden's long coastline, shallow offshore, lends itself to defensive mine warfare, and all destroyers had considerable minelaying capacity.

Geography determines that Swedish waters could be dominated by hostile, land-based air power, leading to the conclusion that major surface combatants were over-vulnerable. All were thus paid off by the early 1980s in favour of smaller, more agile warships which could be readily concealed.

Östergötland class, as built

Displacement: 2,050 tons (standard); 2,600 tons (full load)
Length: 112.1m/367ft 6in (bp); 115.9m/380ft (oa)
Beam: 11.2m/36ft 9in
Draught: 3.7m/12ft
Armament: 4 x 120mm guns (2x2); 6 x 533mm torpedo tubes (1x6); 2 x 4-barrelled 375mm AS rocket projectors
Machinery: Geared steam turbines, 2 boilers, 2 shafts
Power: 29,840kW/40,000shp for 35 knots
Endurance: 330 tons oil for 4,075km/2,200nm at 20 knots
Protection: Some; extent not known
Complement: 210

ABOVE: The *Halland* shows her complex superstructure. Note the enclosed bridge structure, with few apertures, and the transom, configured for minelaying. Abaft the after funnel is the inclined launcher for the Bofors RB 08 anti-ship missile, unique to Swedish ships.

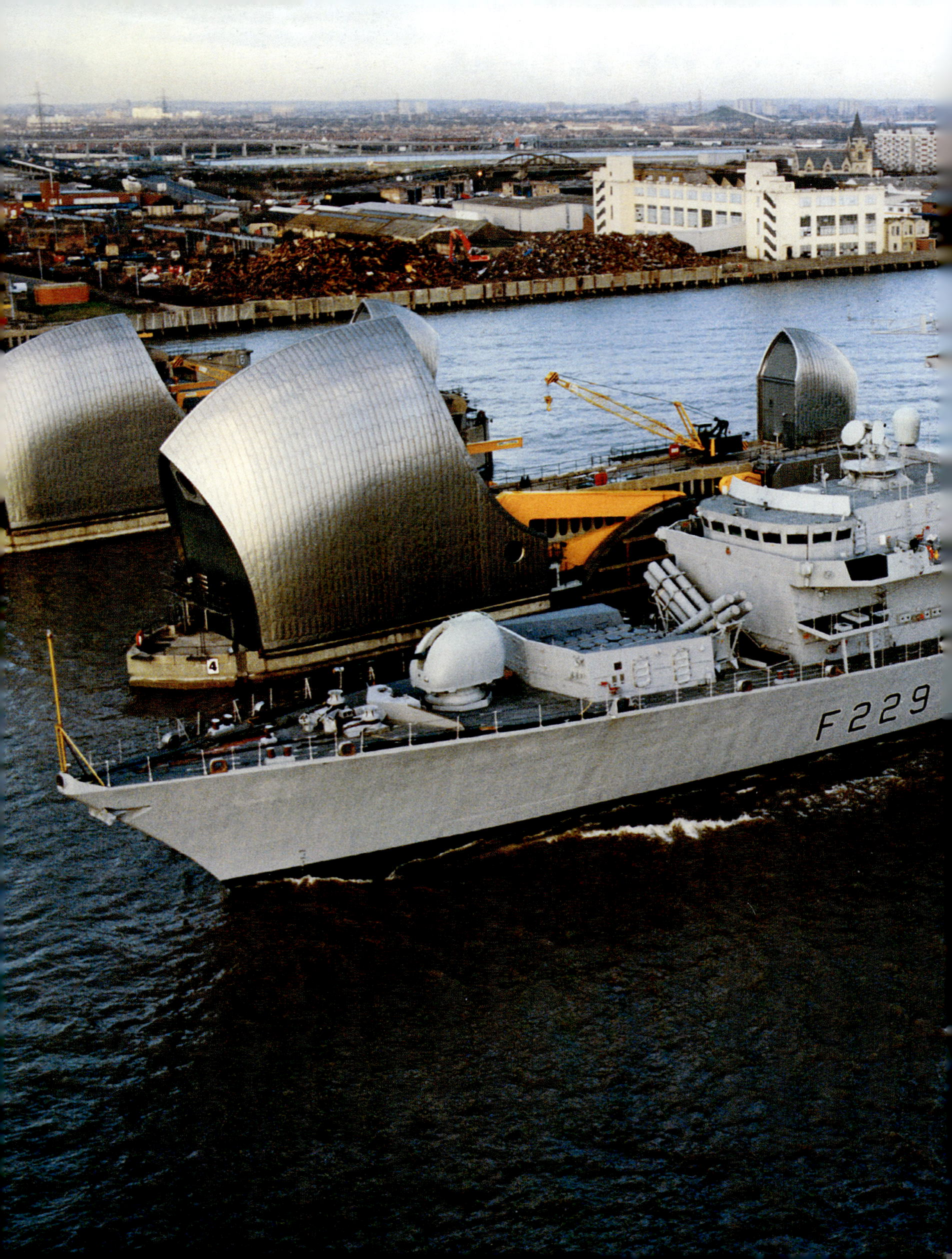
F229
4

Directory of Frigates

For the purposes of this book, the term "frigate" is synonymous with "escort", including as it does the various sloops, corvettes, torpedo boats/escort destroyers/ destroyer escorts that were concerned primarily with the safe passage of commerce and, by extension, taking the war to the submarines bent on its destruction. Space, regrettably, forbids the inclusion of the considerable classes of ocean minesweeper and "Admiralty trawler" which, although performing admirably as escorts, cannot be considered frigates.

The eventual employment of convoy during World War I resulted in the development of the first dedicated escorts, uncomplicated ships designed for humdrum routine, releasing destroyers to the business for which they were better suited. The Battle of the Atlantic underlined the need for "large corvettes", combining range and capacity with seaworthiness, simplicity and cheapness. Thus emerged the frigate, a further feature of which was its suitability to be series-built in large numbers.

With the formation of NATO, all primarily Anti-Submarine (AS) escorts became generically termed "frigates", in contradistinction to "destroyers", which were now configured primarily around Anti-Aircraft Warfare (AAW).

LEFT: HMS *Lancaster*, a Type 23 frigate, passes the Thames flood barrier on a port visit to London. As a general-purpose frigate, her AS capacity resides in her helicopter and shipboard torpedo tubes. Note the Harpoon and Sea Wolf VLS forward.

DIRECTORY OF FRIGATES

LEFT: **In a distinctive Western Approaches camouflage scheme, *Crane* is seen here "swinging compasses". The censor has deleted the HF/DF antenna at the masthead, the communications antenna at the yardarm extremities and the pendant number.** BELOW: **Badly shot-up during the "Yangtze Incident", *Amethyst* was repaired in time to participate in the Korean War. Bridge personnel and gun crews, clad in anti-flash gear, stand by in anticipation of yet another bombardment detail.**

Black Swan and Modified Black Swan classes

Fine ships, the Black Swan sloops tended to be built by destroyer yards. They were designed for the AA protection of convoys, for which they carried the very effective twin 4in high-angle (HA) Mk X1X mounting, four in the earliest examples, three in the remainder, with a quadruple 2pdr pompom in lieu of "Y" guns. Together with full director control, this amounted to a considerable aggregation of topweight and this, with the requirement for a slow, easy roll (to make a good gun platform) gave designers a challenging stability problem. Active fin stabilizers, not yet very effective, were fitted but hostilities saw a creeping increase in complement and topweight, necessitating an extra 30cm/1ft of beam in the "modified" subclass, with the omission of splinter protection and some boats.

Extra weight included a proliferation of light, automatic weapons and a lattice mainmast bearing the "lantern" of the Type 271/272 surface warning radar. Depth charge capacity also increased, from 40 with two projectors in early units to 110 and eight respectively.

The design did not readily lend itself to later modification for a forward-firing Squid mortar, taking instead a split Hedgehog, located either side of "B" mounting. Despite this, the Black Swans were deadly submarine hunters. Based mainly at Liverpool and Greenock, they were fully or partly responsible for 28 kills, many by Captain "Johnny" Walker's redoubtable 2nd Escort Group. Afterdeck arrangements were cramped by the Admiralty requirement that a proportion of the class should be capable of minesweeping.

Steam-turbine propelled, they had good acceleration and were handy in manoeuvring. At "convoy" speeds, they had an endurance of about 13,800km/7,500nm.

Thirteen original and twenty-four modified Black Swans were built, six to Indian account. Five were cancelled and, although hard-worked, only four were lost.

LEFT: **Seen shortly after World War II, the Modified Black Swan *Peacock* enters Grand Harbour, Malta. She retains her old-style "U" flag superior and the original depth charge arrangements. Split Hedgehog was carried forward but the class did not get Squid.**

Modified Black Swan class, as designed 🇬🇧
Displacement: 1,350 tons (standard); 1,960 tons (full load)
Length: 86.3m/283ft (bp); 91.3m/299ft 6in (oa)
Beam: 11.7m/38ft 6in
Draught: 3.5m/11ft 4in
Armament: 6 x 4in guns (3x2), 4/6 x 40mm guns (2x2/2x1)
Machinery: Geared steam turbines, 2 boilers, 2 shafts
Power: 3,208kW/4,300shp for 19.5 knots
Endurance: 420 tons for 11,220km/6,100nm at 15 knots
Protection: Nominal
Complement: 210

Hunt classes

The Black Swans were officially termed Convoy Escorts; the Hunts, Fast Escorts. Where the sloops traded speed for capacity, the Fast Escorts were small destroyers, smaller but considerably faster than the sloops, carrying the same powerful AA battery but lacking their great endurance. They were intended to undertake all destroyer activities short of fleet work.

Over-worked constructive staff unfortunately made a fundamental error in stability calculation. On being inclined, the first-of-class was obliged to land "X" gun mounting, shorten the funnel and to reduce the upper structure. These measures, together with 50 tons of permanent ballast, were sufficient, and 22 of these Type I Hunts were built.

The Type Is were seen as deficient in armament, however, so that follow-on Type IIs were made a considerable 76cm/30in beamier. This cost about three knots in speed, but allowed the reinstatement of the third mounting and an improved bridge layout. This programme ran to 34 units.

As the war obliged Hunts to undertake duties for which they were not intended, torpedo tubes were demanded. This resulted in the 28 Type IIIs, with a twin 21in torpedo tube mounting, but reverting to only two twin 4in mountings, in "A" and "X" positions. Funnel and masts were set vertically, without rake.

The two Type IVs were not related, being Thornycroft "specials", Nearly 5m/16ft 5in longer, and beamier, they

ABOVE: **Steaming past an interned Italian battleship in Malta, the *Tanatside* shows the characteristics of the Type III Hunts, vertical funnel and mast, "Y" gun mounting suppressed, but with a twin torpedo tube mounting added amidships.**

could carry the full specified six-gun AA battery and three of the desired four torpedo tubes. With similar machinery, however, they were slower. Their major innovation was to continue the forecastle deck three-quarters aft, making for a stronger and more comfortable (if hotter) ship. The pronounced forward knuckle was not successful.

The Hunts performed very effectively, particularly in support of English East Coast and Mediterranean convoys. Nearly one in four was lost.

ABOVE: **The Type I Hunts, typified by *Meynell*, came out badly overweight. Torpedo tubes and "X" 4in gun mounting were sacrificed, funnel shortened and director lowered. Although employed on the East Coast, she has the Type 271 radar lantern and the "Huff-Duff" aerial of an ocean escort.**

Type II Hunt class, as built

Displacement: 1,050 tons (standard); 1,420 tons (full load)
Length: 80.6m/264ft 3in (bp); 85.4m/280ft (oa)
Beam: 9.6m/31ft 6in
Draught: 3.4m/11ft (mean)
Armament: 6 x 4in guns (3x2); 1 x quadruple 2pdr pompom
Machinery: Geared steam turbines, 2 boilers, 2 shafts
Power: 14,174kW/19,000shp for 25.5 knots
Endurance: 277 tons fuel for 4,630km/2,500nm at 20 knots
Protection: Nominal
Complement: 164

DIRECTORY OF FRIGATES

LEFT: **Still looking very "mercantile", the 1941-built** *Jasmine* **has been given a long forecastle but still has the original flimsy bridge structure and mast ahead of it. Engaged in convoy escort, she has her whaler griped but turned out for instant use.**

Flower class

Although immortalized by their role in the Battle of the Atlantic, the Flowers were intended to be coastal escorts. Built largely to mercantile, rather than Admiralty standards, their hull was based on a stretched version of a Smiths Dock whale catcher. Their size and class meant that they could be built by many yards, British and Canadian, with no previous experience of warship construction. Already in production, they were involved in ocean warfare in the absence of anything more suitable.

Expected also to double as minesweepers, early examples had a short forecastle, with a single bandstand-mounted 4in gun. The after sheer was pronounced; the forward, less so. Like trawlers, they had a deeper after draught to give the hull "bite" and the single, large-diameter propeller adequate immersion. Propulsion was by a simple steam reciprocating engine, but lacking both redundancy and size, a Flower could not expect to survive torpedo damage.

There was a distinctly mercantile air about early Flowers, with their cowl ventilators, flimsy glazed wood wheelhouse and foremast ahead of it. Later ships were improved with much longer forecastles, modified forward sections and an "Admiralty" bridge.

They were amazingly seaworthy little ships but had a rapid and pronounced movement that fatigued the best of crews. Living conditions, already spartan, were frequently made worse by flooding.

Flowers were built in yards ranging from the mighty Harland & Wolff to tiny slips up obscure Canadian creeks.

ABOVE: *Vetch*, **as shown in 1942, has gained a more "naval" bridge structure, radar and a relocated mast. She carries her escort group number on her funnel. The 2pdr gun has a good all-round arc of fire.**

With little shipbuilding tradition, the contribution of Canada to the Atlantic battle is worthy of great credit, their 121 (many improved) Flowers being just one element. The many British yards involved constructed a further 145. Most were completed by 1942, with construction moving on to frigates and the improved Castle-class corvette. Flowers are credited with sinking 53 enemy submarines; 35 became war losses.

LEFT: **HMCS** *Oakville* **is a reminder of the great contribution made by the Canadians to victory in the Battle of the Atlantic. In total, 121 Flowers stemmed from Canadian yards. Note the American-sourced anchor.**

Flower class, with long forecastles 🇬🇧

Displacement: 1,015 tons (standard); 1,220 tons (full load)
Length: 58.9m/193ft (bp); 63.5m/208ft 4in (oa)
Beam: 10.1m/33ft 1in
Draught: 4.2m/13ft 9in (mean)
Armament: 1 x 4in gun; 1 x Hedgehog AS spigot mortar (later)
Machinery: 1 x 4-cylinder triple-expansion steam engine, 2 boilers, 1 shaft
Power: 2,052kW/2,750ihp for 16 knots
Endurance: 230 tons oil for 6,480km/3,500nm at 12 knots
Protection: None
Complement: 85

UNITED KINGDOM

LEFT: **The numerical "2" on the nearest River proclaims her as French. She is ex-HMS *Windrush*, now *la Découverte*, berthed in the Penfeld at Brest. Post-war, all three have gained the heavy dish of the Type 277 radar.** BELOW: ***Swale*, producing the spray that constantly washed down ship and crew. Completed in 1942, she is still armed with Hedgehog. Squid might later have been accommodated had not the Lochs been coming into service by then.**

River class

Even as the Flowers first demonstrated their limitations under ocean conditions, a more appropriate type was under development. To pursue a surfaced submarine, or to quickly regain station, an escort really required 22 knots rather than the Flowers' 16. As this would require steam turbine propulsion, however, it was decided to compromise with a "twin-screw corvette", capable of 20 knots with a Flower-type reciprocating engine on each shaft. Only in 1942 was their extra speed and capability recognized by recoining the historic term "frigate".

Even 20 knots demanded an increase of nearly 50 per cent in hull length, so that many of the small, corvette builders could not construct the new ships, all named after British rivers. This was remedied, however, by the United States building the design as its Patrol Frigate (PF). Of these, 21 were transferred to the Royal Navy as the Colony class.

Dimensioned around full minesweeping gear, the Rivers' spacious afterdeck was able to accommodate over 200 depth charges. A full Hedgehog was carried forward, but very exposed. Later fitting of a double Squid was intended, but eventually applied to just one ship.

Larger escorts such as frigates were also expected to contribute to the AA defence of a convoy. To the single 4in low-angle guns of the surface armament was thus added an eclectic range of automatic weapons. The mix depended upon availability but only latterly included 40mm Bofors to replace pompoms and Oerlikons.

In addition to the universal "Huff-Duff" direction-finding antenna, all sported the Type 271 "lantern", later superseded by the tilting "dish" antenna of the improved Type 277.

In all, there were 57 British-built Rivers, 45 Canadian and 22 Australian. There were 77 American PFs. Five Rivers were lost, but accounted for 18 submarines.

River class, as designed 🇬🇧

Displacement: 1,400 tons (standard); 1,925 tons (full load)
Length: 86.3m/283ft (bp); 91.9m/301ft 4in (oa)
Beam: 11.1m/36ft 6in
Draught: 3.9m/12ft 10in (mean)
Armament: 2 x 4in guns (2x1/1x2); 1 x Hedgehog AS mortar
Machinery: 2 x 4-cylinder triple-expansion steam reciprocating engines, 2 boilers, 2 shafts
Power: 4,103kW/5,500ihp for 20 knots
Endurance: 646 tons for 13,335km/7,200nm at 12 knots
Protection: Nominal
Complement: 114

RIGHT: ***Antigonish* was one of 70 Rivers built in Canada. Following post-war modification, she has been built up aft to create a well for Squid, has a twin 4in gun forward and an enclosed bridge, more appropriate to Canadian weather conditions.**

193

DIRECTORY OF FRIGATES

LEFT: In a late World War II paint scheme, *Leeds Castle* shows her clear Flower ancestry. With a full frigate-type bridge structure and long, easy sheer, there is little "mercantile" left except, perhaps, the cowl ventilators over the machinery space. ABOVE: It is 1946, but *Bamborough Castle* still looks weather-worn and carries her wartime-style pendant number. The robust lattice mast still supports a Type 272, where *Leeds Castle* (left) has a later Type 277, its dish laid horizontally.

Castle class

Designed to rectify the shortcomings of the Flowers, the Castles were some 15m/50ft longer, placing them halfway between a Flower and a River. Still to be built by many small, unsophisticated yards, they were designed for construction by traditional methods, rather than by the pre-fabrication then becoming general.

Dating from late 1942, the Castle design was able to incorporate features proven by early Rivers. The forward end had a sweeping flare and sheer, with the forecastle deck continued well aft. The quarterdeck, made more spacious by an adaptation of the Rivers' triangular transom, was enclosed by a solid bulwark. There was a full naval bridge structure, and an amidships lattice mast supporting the Type 272 (later 277) radar antenna at an effective height. Visually, the Castles were very attractive.

The class was designed around the new Squid mortar, the *Hadleigh Castle* being the first to take it to sea operationally, in August 1943. Only a single Squid could be accommodated, located in the elevated "B" position and superfiring an improved single 4in gun. Because of the (fully justified) confidence placed in Squid, the depth charge arrangements were much reduced.

Unseen, the Castles accommodated their major advantage, the Type 147Q Asdic (Sonar) that could continuously feed the Squid system with range, bearing and depth, "holding" a submerged target up to the mount of firing three, fast-sinking bombs.

For simplicity of production, the propulsion unit was the same type of reciprocating engine that powered both the Flowers and Rivers, though with improved, water-tube boilers.

Maturing rather late in the war, the Castle programme was drastically curtailed, only 39 being completed as corvettes. Fifteen from British yards were cancelled, as were all thirty-six ordered from Canadian yards. Twelve British-built Castles were transferred to Canada, and one to the Norwegian flag.

ABOVE: *Hadleigh Castle* as a new ship in late 1943. The single Squid, on the platform forward of the bridge, is not obvious. Although few depth charges needed to be carried, she had a wide, uncluttered afterdeck.

Castle class

Displacement: 1,080 tons (standard); 1,580 tons (full load)
Length: 68.6m/225ft (bp); 76.9m/252ft (oa)
Beam: 11.1m/36ft 6in
Draught: 4.1m/13ft 6in (mean)
Armament: 1 x 4in gun; 1 x 3-barrelled Squid AS mortar
Machinery: 1 x 4-cylinder triple-expansion, steam-reciprocating engine, 2 boilers, 1 shaft
Power: 2,051kW/2,750ihp for 16.5 knots
Endurance: 480 tons oil for 11,480km/6,200nm at 15 knots
Protection: Nominal
Complement: 100

194

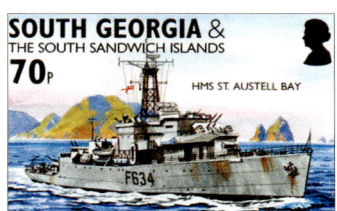

UNITED KINGDOM

ABOVE LEFT: **This picture of** *Loch Killisport* **shows that only a single 4in gun is carried, located on a bandstand. There is no director, but a quadruple 2pdr pompom is sited aft.** ABOVE: **For philatelic artwork, this rendering of** *St. Austell Bay* **is surprisingly accurate. It indicates well the crank level with the bridge at the commencement of the straight line sheer. Lapped plates are, however, shown where the hull was, in fact, all-welded.**
LEFT: **The Bays were AA variants of the Lochs. As can be seen here on** *Mounts Bay*, **the double Squid was suppressed in favour of a Hedgehog in "A" position. Two twin 4in guns are carried, together with full director control and Type 293 radar.**

Loch and Bay classes

The Rivers confirmed the optimum size for a North Atlantic escort, but there continued to exist the urgent need for numbers. These could be produced only by redesigning for construction from prefabricated modules, fitted out to rigidly standard specification. The resulting Loch-class frigates thus comprised large numbers of elements, none heavier than 3 tons, produced by non-shipbuilding concerns and transported to dedicated assembly and fitting-out facilities. Complex curvature was avoided, the result retaining River-class characteristics but with greater sheer and flare forward.

Larger, of course, than a Castle (to which there was a distinct resemblance), a Loch could accommodate a double Squid in the elevated "B" position. The associated Asdic, which made the system so deadly, was situated adjacently, in an office extending from the bridge front. As the depth charge outfit was, again, much reduced, it left adequate space aft for the first crude countermeasures ("Foxers"), designed to meet the threat of the acoustic torpedoes with which U-boats were now targeting convoy escorts specifically.

Only one 4in gun was carried, on a bandstand where it could be depressed easily to engage very close-range targets. The after centreline position was occupied by a quadruple 2pdr pompom with an excellent field of fire.

By the time that the first-of-class, *Loch Fada*, was completed at the end of 1943, the conventional U-boat was a spent force. Only 31 hulls were, therefore, completed as Lochs but, despite their limited numbers, they still accounted for 16 of the enemy.

With emphasis shifting to Pacific operations, the next 19 hulls were completed as Bay-class AA escorts, with Squids suppressed in favour of a Hedgehog, but with a twin 4in mounting at either end and two sided twin 40mm Bofors. These proved their worth during the Korean War, which involved considerable bombardment details.

Loch class, as built

Displacement: 1,430 tons (standard); 2,260 tons (full load)
Length: 87.2m/286ft (bp); 93.7m/307ft 4in (oa)
Beam: 11.7m/38ft 6in
Draught: 3.8m/12ft 4in (mean)
Armament: 1 x 4in gun; 1 x quadruple 2pdr pompom; 2 x 3-barrelled Squid AS mortars
Machinery: 2 x 4-cylinder triple-expansion, steam-reciprocating engines, 2 boilers, 2 shafts
Power: 4,103kW/5,500ihp for 19.5 knots
Endurance: 725 tons oil for 12,965km/7,000nm at 15 knots
Protection: Nominal
Complement: 114

ABOVE: **Six surplus Lochs were acquired by the Royal New Zealand Navy in 1948. Here, a pristine** *Rotoiti* **retains her original Royal Navy pendant number as** *Loch Katrine*. **Post-war, all frigates took on an "F" flag superior.**

195

Types 15 and 16

Although the German fast submarine programme was delayed sufficiently for it to have little effect on World War II, the Soviet Union's acquisition and exploitation of the associated technology posed a new threat, the more real with the outbreak of the Korean War. Faced again with the prospect of general war, the Royal Navy needed a new generation of escort, fast enough to deal with high-speed submarines. Funds, however, were sufficient only for the conversion of war-built fleet destroyers to "fast AS frigates".

Full conversions, eventually numbering 23, were known as Type 15s, the programme running from 1949 to 1956. Remodelling was very thorough, the selected hulls being razed to upper-deck level. To tolerate the requirement of being driven into a head sea at 25 knots, the bow section was stiffened and the forecastle extended to over 80 per cent aft. At its after end were two staggered pockets housing Squid AS mortars, later replaced by Limbos.

The Bikini A-bomb trials had highlighted the effect of nuclear blast, so superstructure was restricted to just one level above the forecastle deck. All needed to be enclosed, causing bridge personnel difficulties in navigation.

Cleared of all except anchor gear, foredecks were given two breakwaters and a curved bridge front. Armament was reduced to a twin 4in mounting aft and a twin 40mm Bofors atop the bridge. Ships were fitted for, rarely with, up to eight sided tubes for homing torpedoes. Much of the new topside structure was in aluminium alloy. The original machinery and funnel were retained.

Less thoroughly rebuilt were the ten Type 16s. These had higher, frigate-style bridges and a twin 4in in "B" position. Their forecastles were not extended, the original forward set of tubes being retained for AS torpedoes. Two Squids were located aft.

ABOVE: AS high-speed convoy escorts, the Type 15s were designed to co-operate with aircraft in countering the fast submarine. *Wakeful* here, has the full standard outfit. Note how the line of the original destroyer hull can be clearly discerned.

LEFT: An ice-dusted *Virago* is seen in the Arctic during the 1950s. The conditions point to the weakness of having the wheelhouse set so low. A double Squid and twin 4in guns were located aft, with only a twin 40mm gun forward.

ABOVE: The Type 16 limited conversions were just that. The ships retained their destroyer-like characteristics being able, as this picture of *Termagent* shows, even to remount their torpedo tubes. Gun armament has, however, been drastically reduced, the after deckhouse accommodating a Double Squid.

U-class destroyer, as Type 15 AS frigate 🇬🇧

Displacement: 2,200 tons (standard); 2,700 tons (full load)
Length: 103.5m/339ft 6in (bp); 110.6m/362ft 9in (oa)
Beam: 10.9m/35ft 9in
Draught: 4.9m/16ft
Armament: 2 x 4in guns (1x2); 2 x 3-barrelled Limbo AS mortars; 8 x heavyweight (8x1) or 6 x lightweight (2x3) AS torpedo tubes
Machinery: Geared steam turbines, 2 boilers, 2 shafts
Power: 29,840kW/40,000shp for 36.5 knots
Endurance: 585 tons for 5,370km/2,900nm at 20 knots
Protection: Nominal
Complement: 185

UNITED KINGDOM

LEFT: **Termed "Second Rate" frigates to differentiate them from such as the big Type 12s, the Type 14s (or Blackwoods)** were really an updated and (relatively) cheap corvette. Despite single screw and rudder, *Hardy* shows her manoeuvring qualities. ABOVE: **The Type 14s were often criticized for being under-armed and,** as this picture of *Duncan* shows, there was little to see beyond the two Limbo mortars. Disposal of a damaged, surfaced submarine would have been a problem.

Type 14

Budgets boosted by the threat posed by the Korean War, the Royal Navy embarked on a relatively ambitious frigate building programme during the 1950s. To the "de luxe", but stop-gap, Type 15/16s needed to be added a simple convoy AS escort, capable of being produced in quantity in emergency. Earlier, the Type 14 or Blackwood, would have been called a "corvette"; in new terminology, it was classed a Second-Rate Frigate.

Designed to a cost limit, the Type 14 was the smallest that could accommodate a double Limbo and full sonar outfit, while being large and fast enough to deploy them effectively against a 17-knot (submerged) submarine. The result looked, and was, utilitarian.

A raised forecastle extended 50 per cent of her length, topped by a full-width house upon which was set the diminutive bridge. This arrangement resulted in a two-level transition to the bridge deck, which made the after end appear to lack freeboard. A single, vertical funnel served to two boilers of the half-frigate propulsion plant. For compactness, diesel engines were considered, but rejected on cost grounds. There was a single shaft and rudder.

The two Limbos, which occupied the after end, were protected by bulwarks and deckhouse, but wetness was such that an overhead catwalk connected after superstructure and forecastle, while a solid bulwark was provided right forward. Anchors were recessed.

Controversially, the Type 14s did not carry a medium-calibre gun. Submarines forced to the surface would thus need to be finished by torpedo, for which paired tubes, unusually of large calibre, were sided in the waist.

Although only 12 of a planned 23 were built, they were deemed successful although, by today's standards, service aboard was spartan. Fine-lined and fast, if somewhat fragile, they made their mark in fishery protection.

LEFT: **In the late 1960s,** *Exmouth* **was converted into a trials ship for gas turbine propulsion. One sprint Olympus and two cruise Proteus were installed COGOG fashion. Note how the ducting dominated the topsides of so small a ship.**

Type 14, as designed

Displacement: 1,100 tons (standard); 1,460 tons (full load)
Length: 91.5m/300ft (bp); 94.6m/310ft (oa)
Beam: 10.1m/33ft
Draught: 3.1m/10ft
Armament: 3 x 40mm guns (3x1); 2 x 3-barrelled Limbo AS mortars; 4 x 21in AS torpedo tubes (2x2)
Machinery: Geared steam turbines, 2 boilers, 1 shaft
Power: 11,190kW/15,000shp for 24.5 knots
Endurance: 260 tons oil for 8,335km/4,500nm at 12 knots
Protection: None
Complement: 111

197

DIRECTORY OF FRIGATES

LEFT: Types 41 and 61 shared a common hull, being fitted out either for anti-aircraft (Type 41) or aircraft-direction duties. Designed for convoy duties, both were diesel-propelled. *Salisbury*, a Type 61, shows her comprehensive electronics fit.

Types 41 and 61

Even with the end of hostilities in 1945, the defence of trade, specifically convoys, still loomed large with the Admiralty Board. The dual-function Loch/Bay programme had impressed, producing numerous hulls quickly and relatively cheaply. They had, however, already been rendered obsolete by the arrival of the fast submarine and jet aircraft. ASW would need to be addressed by faster ships, but the Board also required a hull that could be fitted out for AAW or for the control of carrier-borne or shore-based aircraft. As both of these functions were aimed primarily at the defence of convoys, a 25-knot maximum speed would suffice, with emphasis being placed instead on endurance and good seakeeping.

Endurance was conferred with diesel propulsion. Three machinery spaces accommodated no less than ten engines, four of which could be coupled to each of two shafts. The remaining pair powered generators.

A high-freeboard hull took the forecastle deck right aft to a point just forward of a short quarterdeck. Forward of the break was a pocket containing a single Squid. The chosen medium-calibre weapon was the new Mk VI twin 4.5in gun. The size and weight of this mounting resulted in the unusually cranked forward sheerline. This gave the required freeboard while lowering the weight of the gunhouse in relation to the hull for stability purposes. It also allowed the personnel in the new-style, low-level bridge to see over it. There were no conventional funnels, the diesel exhausts led up the inside of the lattice masts.

Only four of each type were built for the Royal Navy. The AAW version (Type 41/Leopard class) was roll-stabilized with two twin 4.5in guns. The AD (Aircraft-Direction Type 61/Salisbury class) had half the firepower but an impressive array of electronics, later extensively modernized.

LEFT: This is the Type 41 *Puma*, as completed, with a second twin 4.5in gunhouse aft. The mainmast was later plated-in to support a single 965 radar. Note the "two ball" daymark to indicate that she is engaged in towage.

Type 41

Displacement: 2,225 tons (standard); 2,525 tons (full load)
Length: 100.7m/330ft (wl); 103.7m/339ft 11in (oa)
Beam: 12.2m/40ft
Draught: 3.3m/10ft 10in (mean)
Armament: 4 x 4.5in guns (2x2); 1 x 3-barrelled Squid AS mortar
Machinery: 8 diesel engines, 2 shafts
Power: 11,190kW/15,000bhp for 23 knots
Endurance: 230 tons fuel for 8,335km/4,500nm at 15 knots
Protection: Nominal
Complement: 221

198

UNITED KINGDOM

INSET RIGHT: **Built as essentially general-purpose frigates, the Leanders were also given major conversions for specialization in either surface or AS warfare. Here,** *Penelope* **of the former group shows Exocets and a shrouded Sea Wolf launcher.** RIGHT: **The basic Leander design, an Improved Type 12, sold well for export. Here, the Royal New Zealand Navy's** *Wellington* **prepares to refuel from the replenishment tanker** *Endeavour***. Note her sister** *Canterbury* **in the background.**

Type 12/Leander class

To run alongside the Types 41/61 frigates, a new ASW ship was required, fast enough to counter the expected Soviet HTP (High Test Peroxide) closed-cycle submarines. The best compromise was the 28-knot Type 12, essentially a similar hull form, but with an extended and fine-sectioned bow. Steam-driven with a standardized and compact machinery outfit, these required a conventional funnel, initially thin and vertical, later, and less successfully, larger.

Excellent Sonar was teamed with two Limbos, located in a deep pocket where the long forecastle terminated, well aft. Sided in the waist were, initially, no less than 12 heavyweight AS torpedo tubes but, with the failure of the weapon itself, these were replaced by tripled small-calibre tubes, not always carried.

From 1966 the Wasp helicopter became the delivery platform for highspeed, stand-off reaction to submerged contacts. The Type 12's forward Limbo was landed and part of the well decked-over to provide a flight deck. The after superstructure was converted to a hangar and topped with the four-rail Sea Cat point-defence SAM, a not-too successful replacement for the 40mm Bofors.

The Improved Type 12, or Leander, class used the same hull form (later units were given 61cm/2ft more beam) and machinery. Full freeboard extended right aft, but with a transom notch for VDS. A solid, compact superstructure had plated-in masts, the mainmast supporting a "single bedstead" of the Type 965 air warning radar. A small helicopter, Sea Cat and a single Limbo were incorporated from the outset.

Of the twenty-six Leanders built for the Royal Navy, eight were later converted to deploy the Australian Ikara stand-off AS missile. Seven more were remodelled around the MM38 Exocet SSM, with a further five taking both Exocet and the Sea Wolf point-defence SAM.

Magnificent seaboats, the Leanders also sold well abroad.

Leander class, as designed

Displacement: 2,305 tons (standard); 2,875 tons (full load)
Length: 109.8m/360ft (wl); 112.9m/370ft (oa)
Beam: 12.5m/41ft
Draught: 4.1m/13ft 4in (mean)
Armament: 2 x 4.5in guns (1x2); 2 x Sea Cat 4-rail SAM launchers; 6 x 325mm AS torpedo tubes (2x3)
Machinery: Geared steam turbines, 2 boilers, 2 shafts
Power: 22,380kW/30,000shp for 28 knots
Endurance: 480 tons oil for 8,335km/4,500nm at 12 knots
Protection: Nominal
Complement: 258

ABOVE: **An early Type 12,** *Scarborough***, with the original small funnel. To minimize the effects of nuclear blast, the upperworks were deliberately made very low. The long, high-freeboard bow design made them magnificent seaboats. She is seen at Malta with an American Coontz-class DDG.**

199

DIRECTORY OF FRIGATES

Type 21

The Admiralty's own resources being at full stretch, Vosper-Thornycroft's gas turbine Mark 5 frigates, built for Iran, were made the starting point for the new Type 21, intended as a replacement for the aging Types 41 and 61 and, possibly as a follow-on to the Leanders. The Admiralty Board was convinced that it could thus acquire a cheaper, but equally capable, ship. It couldn't, but the reduced complement resulting from gas-turbine propulsion certainly effected a real through-life saving.

Two Olympus engines were supplied for sprint speeds, and two Tynes for cruising. Even derated, the former delivered power for an unusually high speed of 30 knots. The forward end, otherwise conventional, was thus given a pronounced knuckle to throw water clear, while the anchors were set high and in pockets.

Rakish rather than handsome, the Type 21s had a full-width superstructure deck which dropped to a broad-transomed afterdeck, giving relatively generous space for a small helicopter. Much of the superstructure was of load-bearing aluminium alloy which, in service, proved liable to fatigue cracking, weakening the hull girder.

Forward was a single 4.5in gun of the new fully automatic Mk VIII design. Superfiring it, on most of the eight ships, were four MM38 Exocet SSM launchers. On the hangar roof was a quadruple Sea Cat SAM launcher. The primary ASW system was the Lynx helicopter, capable of carrying a limited combination of weapons, sensors and datalink. It was supported by its ship's sonar and two sets of AS torpedo tubes.

A single, plated-in mast was located amidships and the after superstructure was dominated by the single large funnel and its associated downtakes. Accommodations were spacious, adding to the ships' popularity.

The design proved to have little margin for updating, and all six survivors were sold to Pakistan in 1993–94.

ABOVE: **Safeguarding vital tanker traffic during the Iran–Iraq War was but one of the Royal Navy's duties, discharged here by** *Active.* **The controversial industry-designed Type 21s were the first British all-gas turbine frigates.**

LEFT: **The class lead ship,** *Amazon,* **replenishes at sea. Four Exocets superfire the forward 4.5in gun, and the Sea Cat mounting is visible aft. All structure above upper deck level was of aluminium alloy, the hull requiring subsequent stiffening.**

Type 21, as designed 🇬🇧

Displacement: 2,750 tons (standard); 3,250 tons (full load)
Length: 109.8m/360ft (wl); 117.1m/384ft (oa)
Beam: 12.7m/41ft 8in
Draught: 5.9m/19ft 6in (maximum)
Armament: 1 x 4.5in gun; 4 x Exocet MM38 SSMs (4x1); 1 x quadruple Sea Cat SAM; 6 x 325mm AS torpedo tubes (2x3)
Machinery: 2 Olympus and 2 Tyne gas turbines, 2 shafts
Power: 37,300kW/50,000shp for 30 knots
Endurance: 7,410km/4,000nm at 17 knots
Protection: Nominal
Complement: 175

200

UNITED KINGDOM

LEFT: **One of the Batch I Type 22s, *Brazen*'s dimensions were limited by home dockyard covered facilities. Designed as successors to the Leanders, they were gas-turbine driven and carried fewer crew members, but were considerably larger.** BELOW: **Built as a replacement for Falklands War losses, *London* was a Batch II ship whose major differences, besides upgraded electronics, were a remodelled bow section to accommodate improved sonar, and facilities for a larger helicopter. Note the lack of a gun.**

Type 22

Originally as Anglo-Dutch project, from which the Dutch withdrew, the Type 22 was intended as close escort for high-value vessels. The hull was designed around the two 45.8x3.1m/150x10ft arrays of the Type 2016 sonar, one of which was located on either side of the keel. The primary AS weapons delivery system was the helicopter (one/two Lynx or one Sea King), backed by shipboard AS torpedo tubes.

At either end was a Sea Wolf point-defence SAM system, capable of engaging incoming missiles as well as aircraft. There was no space for a medium-calibre gun but four MM38 Exocets were located forward.

Two Olympus and two Tyne gas turbines were again arranged COGOG fashion, exhausting through a single funnel of considerable dimensions.

Only four of these "Batch I" units were built before it was decided to significantly upgrade capability by adding both towed array and new (Type 2015) bow-mounted Sonars. The former required a widened transom, enabling helicopter facilities to be extended, possibly for the future Merlin. The bow Sonar dictated a heavily raked bow profile and stem anchor.

Electronic Counter and Support Measures (ECM/ESM) were also greatly improved. The machinery fit was changed to a more economic pair of Spey gas turbines for sprint with two Tynes retained for cruising. Termed "Batch IIs", six were built.

Following the loss of two Type 42s and two Type 21s during the Falklands War, four further Type 22s were built as replacements. These, known as "Batch IIIs", added a 4.5in gun (found indispensable in the shore support role) and Harpoon SSMs in place of Exocets. These were relocated amidships.

Only the Batch IIIs remain in the Royal Navy. The four Batch Is were sold to Brazil and two Batch IIs each to Chile and Romania. One has been scrapped and one expended as a target.

Type 22, Batch III

Displacement: 4,280 tons (standard); 4,850 tons (full load)
Length: 135.7m/445ft 4in (bp); 148.1m/486ft 2in (oa)
Beam: 14.8m/48ft 5in
Draught: 6.4m/21ft (max)
Armament: 1 x 4.5in gun; 8 x Harpoon SSM (2x4); 2 x sextuple Sea Wolf SAM; 1 x 30mm Goalkeeper CIWS; 6 x 325mm AS torpedo tubes (2x3)
Machinery: 2 Spey and 2 Tyne gas turbines (COGOG), 2 shafts
Power: 35,957kW/48,200shp for 30 knots.
Endurance: 700 tons fuel for 12,965km/7,000nm at 18 knots
Protection: Nominal
Complement: 232

ABOVE: **Sharing a common hull form with the Batch IIs, the Batch III *Cornwall* has been given a 4.5in gun. Exocets have been replaced by Harpoon, relocated abaft the bridge and thus releasing valuable space on the foredeck. The carrier is the American CVN.74 *John C. Stennis*.**

201

DIRECTORY OF FRIGATES

LEFT: Designed for quiet operation, the Type 23 is driven by electric motors coupled directly to the shafts, eliminating gearing. Power for the motors is generated by separate vibration-isolated units. This is *Northumberland*. ABOVE: The class lead ship, *Norfolk*, on builders' trials, and wearing Red Ensign and Yarrow's flag. Forward, she has a 4.5in gun, a VLS for Sea Wolf SAM and eight Harpoon SSMs, the latter missing on the *Northumberland* (left).

Type 23

The Type 23 began as an austere vessel, designed around the major task of deploying a passive towed array sonar for sustained periods. Such has been the pace of the Royal Navy's retrenchment, however, that the design grew into a full-specification frigate, necessarily filling the gap left by Leander disposals. Size and cost escalation nonetheless demanded that, where there were 26 Leanders, there were but 16 Type 23s. These were launched over a 13-year period, with early units being sold abroad just five years after the last ones hit the water.

The remainder are capable, multi-purpose frigates whose subtle, signature-reducing features have resulted in an appearance both pleasing and business-like. Their major combat system is the Merlin ASW helicopter, whose size demands a generously dimensioned flight pad, from beneath which the towed array is streamed. Anti-submarine torpedo tubes are carried, as is an active, bow-mounted sonar.

The single 4.5in dual-purpose gun forward is backed by eight Harpoon SSMs, sited forward of the bridge. Between is the Vertical-Launch System (VLS) containing 32 Sea Wolf point-defence SAMs, whose all-round control is exercised by directors both forward and aft. Two 30mm cannon flank the structure forward of the large, angular funnel, which is wider than it is long.

Two Spey gas turbines drive generators to provide the power for the electric propulsion motors built around the shafts. Emergency, get-you-home power may also be diverted from the ships' four diesel generators. Because the electric propulsion units may be reversed, variable-pitch propellers are not necessary, their fixed-pitch alternatives being optimized to run most quietly over the ships' most sensitive speed range. The final ten of the class have a 25 per cent greater propulsion power, increasing speed by possibly 2 knots. Every effort has been made to minimize crew strength.

ABOVE: Type 23s have a much-reduced radar signature, even to giving the hull a flare over its full length. *Lancaster* has the well-tried Mk VIII 4.5in gun, but all will receive the new Mod. 1 version with the "radar-reduced" angular shield. These will be issued to all units as they come to major refit.

Final ten of Type 23 class

Displacement: 3,600 tons (standard); 4,300 tons (full load)
Length: 123m/403ft 9in (bp); 133m/436ft 7in (oa)
Beam: 15m/49ft 3in
Draught: 5.5m/18ft 1in (maximum)
Armament: 1 x 4.5in gun; 8 x Harpoon SSM (2x4); 1 x 32-cell Sea Wolf SAM VLS; 6 x 325mm AS torpedo tubes (2x3)
Machinery: 2 Spey gas turbine/generators driving electric propulsion motors, 2 shafts
Power: 39,015kW/52,300shp for 30 knots
Endurance: 800 tons fuel for 14,445km/7,800nm at 17 knots
Protection: Nominal
Complement: 185

202

UNITED KINGDOM/FRANCE

LEFT: **During the course of their careers, the E50s and E52s underwent so many modifications that they became difficult to differentiate.** *Le Corse*, **here, shows the E50s' early "trademark" of four triple AS torpedo tubes forward.**

Le Corse and Le Normand classes

Much of a size with the British-sourced River-class frigates that they superseded, these were the first significant post-war classes built by the French with funding supplied partially by the Americans under their Mutual Defence Assistance Programme.

The four le Corse (E50) types and the 14 le Normands (E52) had a common hull and machinery fit, differing only in their armament disposition. Both types were classified "fast escorts" and carried both AA and AS outfits of considerable potency for the size of ship.

Their hulls were flush-decked, with pronounced forward sheer, a form possibly influenced by the ex-American Destroyer Escorts (DEs) which were also still serving under French colours. In line with the then-current assumptions on the likelihood of nuclear exchanges, neither the monolithic bridge structure nor the hulls were pierced for scuttles.

Besides a quadruple or sextuple mortar (two in the E50s) the major AS weapons resided in four triple torpedo tube mountings. In the E50s, these were all forward of the bridge at 01 level, backing on to structures containing reloads. The E52s carried theirs in a more orthodox arrangement, sided in the waist. This created space for a forward-mounted mortar.

Both classes carried three twin 57mm dual-purpose gun mountings, one forward and two in superfiring arrangement aft. Steam turbine propulsion gave a good turn of speed, and the taller, prominently capped funnel located close to the mast differentiated them immediately from Commandant Rivière-class frigates with which they could be confused.

During 20 years of service, individual units began to differ widely in detail, *le Brestois* for instance acting as trials ship for the single 100mm gun that went on to be widely adopted in French warships, and *l'Agenais* trialling a large VDS installation in lieu of the after guns.

By 1981, none of either class remained on the active list.

ABOVE: *Le Picard* **was an E52, this photograph showing clearly that the four triple AS torpedo tubes are located in more protected positions, sided in the after waist. Note the sextuple AS launcher forward. The 57mm armament was effective only against aircraft.**

E52 type, as built

Displacement: 1,295 tons (standard); 1,795 tons (full load)
Length: 95m/311ft 10in (bp); 99.3m/325ft 11in (oa)
Beam: 10.3m/33ft 10in
Draught: 4.1m/13ft 6in (maximum)
Armament: 6 x 57mm guns (3x2);
 1 x 4- or 6-barrelled 305mm AS mortar;
 12 x AS torpedo tubes (4x3)
Machinery: Geared steam turbines,
 2 boilers, 2 shafts
Power: 14,920kW/20,000shp for 28.5 knots
Endurance: 310 tons oil for 8,335km/4,500nm at 12 knots
Protection: Nominal
Complement: 175

203

DIRECTORY OF FRIGATES

FAR LEFT: The *Commandant Rivière* class followed the E52s quickly and, while only slightly larger, differed considerably. The dual-purpose 100mm guns were effective against aircraft and surface craft, while diesel propulsion conferred greater range. ABOVE: During the early 1970s, the *Balny* acted as the trials ship for gas turbine propulsion. Although echoing *Exmouth*'s role in the Royal Navy, she had a gas turbine and diesel (COGAD) arrangement as opposed to the British ship's COGOG.

Commandant Rivière class

Specialist in series small-ship production, Lorient naval dockyard, which had built eight of the E50/52s, went on to construct all nine of the Commandant Rivière-type follow-ons.

The later ships were to act in peace time as "avisos", station ships in the still-numerous French colonies. In this sense, they were the lineal descendants of the colonial cruisers, the sailing corvettes of a different era.

For the sake of required speed, the E50/52s were relatively fine, while their pronounced forward sheer would have translated somewhat uncomfortably to the accommodation deck below. The Rivières' hull was made about 4m/13ft 2in longer but proportionately more beamy. Unlike that of the preceding class, the deckhouse extended to the ships' sides, the foredock accommodating a 100mm gun. The extra space was required to transport and support up to 80 troops, for whom two small Landing Craft, Personnel (LCP) could be carried under davits.

Essential to colonial duty was extended endurance and reliability. For this reason, they were powered by four medium-speed diesel engines. These were coupled two to a shaft, making it possible to run with any combination of one to four units. Any could thus be taken off-line for routine maintenance while, together, they could power the ships for 25.5 knots, sufficient for them to act as useful escorts in wartime.

The *Commandant Bory* and *Balny* performed the same role as the *Exmouth* of the Royal Navy in being trials platforms for gas turbine propulsion. Work concluded, they were refitted with standard diesel units.

As built, the Rivières had three of the new 100mm guns, in single, automatic, enclosed mountings, in place of the earlier ships' twin 57mm mountings. From the late 1970s most exchanged "X" gun for four MM38 Exocet SSMs. An enclosed quadruple AS mortar occupied "B" position. The class was scrapped during 1988–92.

MIDDLE: *Doudart de Lagrée* at her full 25-knot speed. Note the "X" gun replaced by four Exocets, the French-built quadruple AS mortar and reload facility in "B" position, and the triple AS torpedo tubes sided abaft the funnel. ABOVE: Oblique lighting picks out the effects of years of stress on the hull of *Enseigne de Vaisseau Henry*. The large full-width deckhouse allows the carriage of an 80-man marine unit or, in their absence, spacious accommodation, welcome on what frequently acted as station ships.

Commandant Rivière class, as designed

Displacement: 1,750 tons (standard); 2,250 tons (full load)
Length: 98m/321ft 8in (bp); 103.7m/340ft 4in (oa)
Beam: 11.6m/38ft 1in
Draught: 4.6m/15ft 2in (maximum)
Armament: 3 x 100mm guns (3x1); 1 x 4-barrelled 305mm AS mortar; 6 x AS torpedo tubes (2x3)
Machinery: 4 diesel engines, 2 shafts
Power: 11,936kW/16,000bhp for 25.5 knots
Endurance: 210 tons for 13,890km/7,500nm at 16 knots
Protection: Nominal
Complement: 166

FRANCE

LEFT: **A one-off, the *Aconit* was very unusual for a ship of her size in having single-shaft propulsion. In this early picture she mounts an AS projector forward of the bridge and Malafon (not visible) amidships.**

Aconit

Her original status indicated by her name, one of the British-built Flower-class corvettes manned by Free French crews, the *Aconit* nonetheless carried full frigate capability, indicated by an "F" identifier. Despite her single shaft and anti-submarine configuration, however, she looked more like a destroyer, and soon adopted a "D" flag superior. Her task was, primarily, to act as a trials platform for the larger Tourville-class destroyers then building.

Aconit's hull was flush-decked, dropping one level to a short afterdeck, whereon was accommodated the large winch/towfish assembly of the DUBV 43 Variable Depth Sonar (VDS). The bows showed the pronounced overhang associated with a large bow sonar, also incorporating the flattened sheerline that enabled the forward gun to work at slight depression for close ranges.

She was the first to be designed around the Malafon AS stand-off system, following its satisfactory trials in the converted destroyer *La Galissonnière*. Destined for the new Tourville and Suffren classes, Malafon was a small, rocket-propelled, aerodynamic vehicle that could release a homing torpedo on coordinates determined by the ship's sonars.

For self-defence, *Aconit* had launchers for AS torpedoes and, forward of the bridge, an enclosed quadruple AS mortar. The latter was removed during the early 1980s in favour of eight updated MM40 Exocet SSMs, grouped in two quadruple protective boxes.

Although lacking an AA missile system, the *Aconit* was dominated by the large tower and dome associated with the DRBV 13 (later DRBV 15) surveillance radar, and the antenna of the DRBV 22A targeting radar on the lattice mast on the after superstructure.

Being steam propelled, *Aconit* had a conventional funnel although, in order to conserve centreline deck space, this had to support a lofty, and complex foremast, an ungainly arrangement.

Along with the Malafon system itself, the *Aconit* was retired in the mid-1990s, her name being quickly reassigned to a La Fayette-class frigate, perpetuating a unique Anglo-French naval link.

LEFT: **With modernization during 1984–85, the *Aconit* had eight MM40 Exocets fitted, visible here inside protective boxes. Malafon remained as there was no helicopter, but a new VDS and passive towed array were installed aft.**

Aconit, as built

Displacement: 3,500 tons (standard); 3,840 tons (full load)
Length: 127m/416ft 10in (oa)
Beam: 13.4m/44ft
Draught: 5.5m/18ft 1in (maximum)
Armament: 2 x 100mm guns (2x1); 1 x Malafon AS stand-off system; 1 x quadruple 305mm AS mortar; 2 x launchers for AS torpedoes
Machinery: Geared steam turbines, 2 boilers, 1 shaft
Power: 21,373kW/28,650shp for 27 knots
Endurance: 9,260km/5,000nm at 18 knots
Protection: Nominal
Complement: 255

DIRECTORY OF FRIGATES

D'Estienne d'Orves class

Although twin-screwed and carrying "F" pendants, the d'Estienne d'Orves, or A69, class are strictly corvettes, designed for inshore AS operations. They began to commission in 1976 as the first E50/52s reached about 21 years of age and, thereafter, replaced them on a near one-for-one basis. Considerably smaller, however, they are also less capable, their design being strongly driven by the requirement for economical operation. Through-life costs have been reduced considerably by their diesel propulsion and a crew of only 100. Classed as "avisos", their lack of size has, nevertheless, been a drawback in that their additional full 18-man military detachment apparently cannot, in practice, be supported.

Compact little ships, their single 100mm gun looks disproportionately large. The low bridge structure is integral with a long, full-width deckhouse. Not having space for a helicopter, their AS capability is, by current standards, weak.

Four fixed AS torpedo tubes are built into the after superstructure, but the quadruple AS mortar on top has now been removed in favour of light AA missiles, either the capable Crotale or the much lighter, two-rail Simbad. Only one, hull-mounted sonar is fitted.

Originally termed A70s, some units were fitted with two MM38 Exocets. This variant disappeared as all were gradually fitted for, but not always with, two of the later MM40s which would, however, require a third party in order to realize their full over-the-horizon potential. This greater emphasis on light escort ("*frégate légère*") function is underlined by the addition of defensive anti-missile and anti-torpedo decoy systems.

TOP: **An early picture of *d'Estienne d'Orves*, lead ship of an excellent class of twin-screw corvette. The 100mm gun was standard throughout the French Navy and was a useful yardstick in estimating a ship's size.** ABOVE: **Unusually carrying no pendant number, the nameship here looks more weatherworn and retains her short funnel. Note the caps of the AS torpedo tubes in the after deckhouse, atop which is a sextuple Bofors-pattern AS rocket launcher.**

Ordered originally by South Africa, two more units were purchased by Argentina, which then built a third. Seven have now been retired and one transferred to Turkey. All of the remainder are due to be paid off by 2016.

A69, as built

Displacement: 1,050 tons (standard); 1,250 tons (full load)
Length: 76m/249ft 6in (bp); 80m/262ft 7in (oa)
Beam: 10.3m/33ft 10in
Draught: 5.3m/17ft 4in (maximum)
Armament: 1 x 100mm gun; 1 x quadruple/sextuple AS mortar; 4 x fixed AS torpedo tubes
Machinery: 2 diesel engines, 2 shafts
Power: 8,335kW/12,000bhp for 23 knots
Endurance: 8,280km/4,500nm at 15 knots
Protection: Nominal
Complement: 100

ABOVE: **During Operation "Desert Shield" in 1990, the *Commandant Ducuing* is seen with the later raised funnel and mast. She lays alongside repair ship *Jules Verne*, with a Durance AOR beyond (right) and Clemenceau carrier (left). In Gulf conditions, large-ship facilities are welcome to small-ship crews.**

FRANCE

LEFT: Larger and more comfortable for lengthy seatime than the d'Estienne d'Orves type, the Floréal-class corvettes are designed more as offshore patrol vessels. The Moroccan *Mohammed V* was one of two built to a reduced export specification. ABOVE: Here, the Moroccan *Mohammed V* is led by her sister the *Hassan II*. In armament and electronics, they have a lower capability than the French Floréals but are similar otherwise. Note the 76mm guns and rather dated WM-25 fire control.

Floréal class

With ever-fewer front-line warships available, their use can no longer be justified for low-risk duties such as fishery protection or colonial policing. Rather limited as "avisos", the A69s were more useful as escorts in the Mediterranean. The Floréals, which effectively replaced them in patrolling the overseas territories, were built more cheaply to mercantile standards, constructed at St. Nazaire but fitted with their military equipment in the Lorient naval dockyard. Named after months of the New Revolutionary Calendar, all were commissioned in 1992–94.

In length, the Floréals are pitched between the A69s and the E50/52s that preceded them in colonial duties. Being designed for only 20 knots, however, they are relatively beamy (L/B 6.09 compared with the 23-knot A69's 7.38 and the 26-knot E50's 8.31), with a capacious hull. This allows the A69's major shortcomings to be addressed. Up to 24 military personnel may be carried, along with an LCP under davits. Where smaller, utility helicopters are usually deployed, the hangar has the capacity to accommodate either an AS.332 Super Puma transport helicopter or, if required, an NH-90 AS machine. The ships are not fitted with sonar or AS weapons but can carry two MM38 Exocets and a Simbad/Mistral SAM system.

The aircraft hangar runs forward between the sided uptakes which have mercantile-style tops. The hull is flush-decked, a form much disguised by the long, full-width "centre-castle". This terminates short of the stern, suggesting that, in emergency, the ships could be fitted with a large towed array passive Sonar for surveillance purposes. Forward, the rather limited freeboard is compensated by a pronounced flare. Active stabilizers reduce ship motion.

All six carry a single 100mm automatic gun with optronic fire control. They are fitted to ship two MM38 Exocets and/or one Simbad/Mistral point-defence SAM mounting.

ABOVE: "Regular" Floréals carry a 100mm gun, more modern electronics and are fitted for, but not necessarily with, two Exocet SSMs. Their considerable internal space results in a bulky hull that gives the effect of low-freeboard bows. This is *Prairial*, the "month of meadows" and ninth in the New Calendar.

Floréal class, as built

Displacement: 2,600 tons (standard); 2,950 tons (full load)
Length: 85.2m/279ft 8in (bp); 93.5m/306ft 11in (oa)
Beam: 14m/45ft 11in
Draught: 4.4m/14ft 5in
Armament: 1 x 100mm gun; 2 x MM38 Exocet SSM; 1 x twin-rail Simbad SAM
Machinery: 4 diesel engines, 2 shafts
Power: 6,565kW/8,800shp for 20 knots
Endurance: 390 tons fuel for 18,520km/10,000nm at 15 knots
Protection: Nominal
Complement: 83

207

DIRECTORY OF FRIGATES

LEFT: Lead ship of the class, *la Fayette* has lowered shutters covering the mooring ports forward. The boat aperture may also be screened. A pair of Exocets are visible amidships and, to their left, the launcher for the Crotale point-defence SAM.

ABOVE: The latest of many French warships to bear the name *Surcouf* is seen in the Gulf in 2002, serving as part of a multinational force. Note how the hull and upperworks are not pierced with scuttles, and also the newly profiled 100mm gunhouse.

La Fayette class

Although much of a size with a British Type 42, a la Fayette appears somewhat smaller by virtue of her radically different appearance and lack of detail. There had been a growing trend toward inclining surfaces in order to reduce radar return, particularly to defeat the active homing radar of anti-ship missiles. The la Fayettes took the concept a stage further, with an outer shell configured to screen all the many minor protuberances that, collectively, define a ship's radar signature. Their hulls have a continuous flare and the extensive inclined planes of the superstructure are fabricated from a radar-absorbent sandwich. All apertures, such as those for access, for boat stowage, anchor pockets, etc are covered by flush-fitting doors as tightly engineered as those of an automobile, and likely as vulnerable to contact damage.

Diesel propulsion has again been specified, considerably simplifying problems associated with hot exhaust emissions while improving both economy and endurance. The cost, however, is a mediocre maximum speed.

Like the smaller Floréals, the la Fayettes normally carry no AS sensors or armament. They can accommodate a 25-strong military detachment and are fitted for colonial duties. Current peacetime armament comprises a 100mm gun forward (its enclosure reconfigured to further reduce reflection), two quadruple MM40 Exocet SSM launchers (behind deep bulwarks amidships) and an 8-cell Crotale point-defence SAM mounting on the hangar roof. A Panther multi-purpose helicopter is normally carried, but facilities are adequate to accommodate the larger NH-90 AS helicopter if required for specific tasking.

The half deck between gun and bridge front marks a covered cavity into which can be slotted a double 8-cell VLS for the smaller type of ASTER SAMs, probably not normally fitted.

Six modified and more heavily armed versions were built for Taiwan (1994–96) and three for Saudi Arabia (2000–02).

ABOVE: Model-like in her simplicity of form, the *la Fayette* sheers away from the American Fast Combat Support Ship *Seattle* (AOE.3). Her low radar signature is to fool incoming SSMs as much as to avoid detection.

La Fayette class, as built

Displacement: 3,200 tons (standard); 3,600 tons (full load)
Length: 115m/377ft 6in (bp); 124.2m/407ft 8in (oa)
Beam: 13.6m/44ft 8in
Draught: 4.8m/15ft 9in (maximum)
Armament: 1 x 100mm gun; 8 x MM40 Exocet SSM (2x4); 1 x 8-cell Crotale SAM launcher
Machinery: 4 diesel engines, 2 shafts
Power: 15,666kW/21,000bhp for 25 knots
Endurance: 350 tons fuel for 12,965km/7,000nm at 15 knots
Protection: Nominal
Complement: 153

FRANCE/JAPAN

LEFT: **A good beam shot of *Manju* of the Etorofu class, whose elegant destroyer-like hull belies her humbler status. Later units had hulls almost devoid of double-curvature plating. Her low-elevation 4.7in guns date from World War I.**

Shumushu and Etorofu classes

Although the Imperial Japanese Navy viewed convoy as "defensive" and, therefore, of low priority, it did produce during the late 1930s the four-strong Shumushu (or Shimushu) class of general-purpose escorts. Basically of sound design, they proved suitable for later series production and for further development. With some uncertainty as to their exact role, they were fitted initially for minesweeping.

Unlike the British and American navies, which disliked diesel propulsion (not least because it was then very noisy in an AS escort, which needed to minimize self-generated noise), the Japanese adopted it readily. Its advantages included compactness and few engine room staff, against which it required highly refined fuel, which would become difficult to obtain.

In length comparable with a British Castle-class corvette, a Shumushu was somewhat narrower, with a 3-knot speed advantage. Like a small destroyer, with no torpedo tubes, she had a very short forecastle which terminated short of the simple bridge structure, reminiscent of German World War I practice, illustrated elsewhere.

For their size, these escorts were relatively heavily gunned, i.e. with an eye to resisting surface attack rather than the threat from submarine and aircraft which actually developed. Both the Shumushus and the 14 virtually identical Etorofu type, that followed somewhat later, carried three single 4.7in guns, one forward, two aft. All were on low elevation mountings removed from destroyers scrapped after World War I.

As built, the early ships carried only a handful of automatic weapons and a dozen depth charges (without associated sound equipment) but, under pressure of combat experience, minesweeping gear

ABOVE: **The Etorofus (Type A) were the first derivative class, similar but of slightly greater displacement. This is *Kasodo* at an unknown date, fitted with a temporary bow, not an unfamiliar sight in the Pacific.**

and other topweight was landed in favour of up to 60 depth charges and a dozen or more 25mm automatic weapons. They also gained sonar and radar although, at this time, these were of indifferent quality.

Etorofu class, as built 🔴

Displacement: 870 tons (standard); 1,020 tons (standard)
Length: 73m/239ft 7in (bp); 77.5m/254ft 4in (oa)
Beam: 9.5m/31ft 10in
Draught: 3.1m/10ft
Armament: 3 x 4.7in guns (3x1)
Machinery: Geared diesel engines, 2 shafts
Power: 3,133kW/4,200bhp for 19.5 knots
Endurance: 14,816km/8,000nm at 16 knots
Protection: None
Complement: 147

ABOVE: **Although having the appearance of a wartime emergency design, the four Shumushus were completed pre-war. They were successful, and provided the basis for the extended classes of anti-submarine escorts that succeeded them.**

LEFT: Where the earlier classes had been configured as general-purpose escorts with minesweeping gear, the Mikuras (Type B) were fitted primarily for AS duties. This is *Awaji*, early in 1944, with reduced surface armament and clear quarterdeck.

Mikura and Ukuru classes

A major weakness of the Japanese high command was its inflexible attitude to planning so that, as the Pacific war developed into a protracted test of attrition, it was unwilling to adapt. Because a short war had been hypothesized, escorts came low on the construction priority list. This remained the case even when the Japanese merchant marine, upon which the sustenance of the newly acquired empire depended, was targeted by a growing infestation of American submarines. Thus, although the four Shumushus were launched in 1939–40, it would be late in 1942 before the first of the follow-on Etorofus entered the water. This class of 14 was then launched over a 14-month period with apparently little urgency even though, up to December 1943, over 2.9 million tons of mostly unconvoyed shipping had been lost.

From October 1943 the yet-incomplete Etorofu programme overlapped that for the eight Mikura type, modified and slightly enlarged. Their forecastles extended aft to the bridge block and the funnel was placed much farther aft. Although configured primarily for AS operations, with a 120 depth charge capacity and sonar gear, they were still burdened with three 4.7in guns, the after weapons in an open twin mounting. An interesting response to the lack of a purpose-designed, ahead-throwing weapon was to mount a 75mm Army-pattern mortar ahead of the bridge. Again, AA weaponry was augmented as opportunity offered.

The Mikuras, launched between July 1943 and February 1944, could be built in as little as six months. During this period, however, mercantile losses were causing some concern. The Mikura design was thus redrawn to cut out all complex, or double, curvature, even deck camber, in order to facilitate construction through the assembly of prefabricated modules. Thirty-three of these Ukuru-class variants were built.

ABOVE: Later versions of the Mikuras were known as the Ukuru class, or Modified Type B. Of similar design, they began to incorporate single-curvature plating, as apparent in the bow section of the *Ukuru* herself, seen here post-war.

Ukuru type, as built

Displacement: 940 tons (standard); 1,020 tons (full load)
Length: 72m/236ft 4in (bp); 78m/256ft (oa)
Beam: 9m/29ft 7in
Draught: 3.1m/10ft
Armament: 3 x 4.7in guns (1x2/1x1); 1 x 75mm mortar
Machinery: Geared diesel engines, 2 shafts
Power: 3,133kW/4,200bhp for 19.5 knots
Endurance: 9,260km/5,000nm at 16 knots
Protection: None
Complement: 150

JAPAN

LEFT: Far too late, the Japanese began series production of escorts to screen their fast-diminishing merchant marine. The Kaibokans were smaller versions of the preceding classes. This example is a diesel-propelled Type C.
ABOVE: The Kaibokans were much smaller than Western AS escorts, and this unidentified Type D has succumbed quickly to the mining effect of several near missiles. As she rolls over, her crew can be seen evacuating.

Kaibokan classes

Far too late, the Kaikobans were the major series-built, emergency escorts. They were known commonly as "Type C", Types "A" and "B" being the Shumushu/Etorofu and Mikura/Ukuru classes respectively. Although the "Type C" design was approved early in 1943, production began only late in that year. Despite its being given higher priority, the programme suffered from the generally poor organization and decision-making process that was a feature of a Japan unready for an extended war. There was a chronic lack of skilled workers and increasing shortages of essential, imported raw materials.

Types "A" and "B" were of about 78m/256ft overall length, their production confined to just five yards. The emergency Kaikoban programme involved an initial order of over 130 hulls. Many more yards needed to be involved, and it was probably to utilize smaller facilities that the "Type C" design was limited to 67.5m/221ft 6in. Less just one medium-calibre gun, however, they carried the same armament as the still-building "Type Bs".

Apparently too numerous to name, Kaikoban were simply numbered. With diesel engine production inadequate, some later units were given steam turbine propulsion. Twin-shaft, diesel-driven units (odd numbers) remained "Type C" but the slightly larger, single-shaft, turbine-driven ships (even numbers) were known as "Type Ds". Externally, these differed in having a taller, more slender funnel of round section, placed further forward than the hexagonal-sectioned stacks of the diesel ships.

Building times varied between three and eight months, and the programme was successful in that upwards of 90 units were definitively completed, many others existing as partly assembled modules. Although even the oldest saw barely a year of hostilities, it bears testimony to the, by then, overwhelming superiority of the Americans by sea and air that 55 of them became war losses. Orders for hundreds more, many half-complete, were cancelled.

ABOVE: Due to a dearth of suitable diesel engines, the Type D Kaikobans were fitted with single-screw steam turbine machinery, evidenced by the smoke and taller funnel of this example, known simply as "No. 8".

Type C, as built

Displacement: 745 tons (standard); 810 tons (full load)
Length: 63m/206ft 7in (bp); 67.5m/221ft 7in (oa)
Beam: 8.5m/27ft 10in
Draught: 2.9m/9ft 6in
Armament: 2 x 4.7in guns (2x1); 1 x 75mm mortar
Machinery: Geared diesel engines, 2 shafts
Power: 1,417kW/1,900bhp for 16.5 knots
Endurance: 12,040km/6,500nm at 14 knots
Protection: None
Complement: 136

211

DIRECTORY OF FRIGATES

LEFT: **This view of the** *Oi* **emphasizes the high forward freeboard of the Isuzu design. Anchors are partly recessed to reduce slamming and spray-making. Note the Bofors-type AB rocket launcher.**

Ikazuchi and Isuzu classes

Reconstructed as the Japanese Maritime Self-Defence Force (JMSDF), the Japanese navy was, during the early 1950s, permitted to build its first new ships. Closely controlling Japan's regeneration, the United States was also concerned at Soviet Russia's naval building in the Pacific. Japan's ability to defend herself, or even act as an ally, was to be encouraged.

A major perceived threat was from Russian high-speed conventional submarines, derived from captured German technology. These were capable of bursts of 15 to 17 knots submerged and, to engage them, it was reckoned that contemporary escorts needed to have a 10-knot speed advantage.

In December 1954 Japan laid down her first trio of new frigates. The Ikazuchis were smaller than the ex-American escorts that the JMSDF was already running, but showed the latter's influence in that armament and electronics were all American sourced. Unambitious, flush-decked vessels, they were armed with a pair of 3in guns, a Hedgehog and depth charges. There was a single, braced tripod mast, replaced by a lattice on the Isuzus.

All were twin-screwed, but *Akebono* (slightly the largest and with two funnels) was steam-turbine propelled, while the other single-funnelled pair had diesel engines, Mitsubishi in *Ikazuchi* and Mitsui/B&W in *Inazuma*.

Although the 28-knot *Akebono* was a clear 3 knots faster, she also required 30 more crew, and diesel propulsion was selected for the four Isuzus, launched in two pairs in 1961 and 1963. All four had differing types of diesel engine layout.

As long as a DE, but narrower, the Isuzu was an obvious derivative of the Ikazuchi, but differed in having fore- and mainmasts, both of lattice construction. Four 76mm/3in guns were carried, in twin mountings forward and aft. There was a forward-firing Bofors-type quadruple AS mortar and, later, AS torpedo tubes and VDS. They were very dependent upon standard American equipment but although capable, would have had difficulty in tackling a fast submarine.

LEFT: **Inheriting the name of a notable heavy cruiser of World War II, the** *Mogami* **shows her deck layout. Of an essentially simple design, suitable for series production, she carries her name amidships, a custom briefly revived post-war.**

Isuzu class, as built

Displacement: 1,490 tons (standard); 1,700 tons (full load)
Length: 94m/308ft 6in (oa)
Beam: 10.4m/34ft 2in
Draught: 3.5m/11ft 6in (mean)
Armament: 4 x 3in guns (2x2); 1 x quadruple AS mortar
Machinery: 4 diesel engines, 2 shafts
Power: 11,936kW/16,000bhp for 25 knots
Endurance: Not known
Protection: None
Complement: 180

JAPAN

LEFT: Japan's increasing value as a Western ally was evident in the further sophistication of transferred weapons technology. Acquisition of ASROC was a major step forward, *Ayase* of the Chikugos being among the smallest vessels to deploy it. ABOVE: The Chikugo design – this is *Chitose* – was of a size with the Isuzus and directly derived from them. The layout appears less cluttered, but the bridge structure is, in proportion, rather more bulky.

Chikugo class

Developed Isuzus, the Chikugos followed after a lapse of seven years. They were slightly shorter, but beamier, continuing the trend to the deployment of increasingly sophisticated sensors and weaponry. From the Ikazuchis' already out-moded Hedgehog, the Isuzus tried the Americans Mk 108 launcher (Weapon Able) before adopting the Bofors quadruple mortar. With the Chikugos came ASROC, they being reputedly the smallest ships to carry it. Previous weapons had been forward-firing, and were located in "B" position, forward of the bridge. Depending upon sonar conditions, ASROC could range effectively to 9.6km/6 miles and could, therefore, be mounted aft of amidships where its large Mk 16, 8-cell launcher was better protected, dominating the ship's profile. ASROC could deliver either a homing torpedo or a nuclear depth charge, although the latter are most likely never to have been supplied.

In layout, the Chikugos closely followed that of the Isuzus but, in overall appearance, had lost some of the latter's Japanese characteristics. The sharply cut-off funnel was replaced by a more conventional "flower-pot", while the traditional curved stem profile gave way to the heavily overhung, straight stem and anchor that advertised the bow-mounted sonar which necessarily complemented the ASROC. Later, the class would gain also a towed VDS, located in a well in the transom, offset to starboard. In order to reduce wetness, the forward hull had a long knuckle, a feature then used extensively in the US Navy and, for designers, of debatable effectiveness.

Diesel propulsion was again specified and, once again, was sourced from two separate manufacturers. To reduce radiated noise, diesel engines were, by this time, being raft-mounted and supported on flexible mounts to decouple their noise and vibration from a ship's hull. AS torpedo tubes could also be shipped but, otherwise, the Chikugos were weakly armed.

All 11 were discarded between 1996 and 2003.

ABOVE: Lacking a helicopter for targeting, the *Chikugo*'s ASROC depended upon another ship or her own sonar to supply coordinates. A medium-frequency Variable Depth Sonar (VDS) is installed aft and a lower-frequency unit under the sharply raked bows.

Chikugo class, as designed

Displacement: 1,510 tons (standard); 1,760 tons (full load)
Length: 93m/305ft 3in (oa)
Beam: 10.8m/35ft 5in
Draught: 3.5m/11ft 6in (mean)
Armament: 2 x 3in guns (1x2); 1 x 8-cell ASROC launcher; 6 x 324mm AS torpedo tubes (2x3)
Machinery: 4 diesels, 2 shafts
Power: 11,936kW/16,000bhp for 25 knots
Endurance: 19,816km/10,700nm at 12 knots
Protection: Nominal
Complement: 165

213

DIRECTORY OF FRIGATES

LEFT: *Ishikari* was lead ship for a class of small multi-purpose frigates which, apparently, proved to be too small to meet their designated requirements. Note the Harpoon SSMs aft and a reversion to the Bofors pattern AS rocket launcher forward.

Ishikari and Yubari classes

By virtue of not being designed to operate shipborne helicopters, Japanese frigates tend to be small and compact but, by the standards of their peers, are more general-purpose combatants than specialist anti-submarine escorts. A Chikugo was less than half the displacement of, say, a British Type 23 but at 93m/305ft was obviously thought over-large, for the one-off *Ishikari*, launched in 1980, was a considerable 8.5m/27ft 10in shorter.

A consistent feature of Japanese frigates was a 25-knot maximum speed, achieved in the *Ishikari* with a Combined Diesel Or Gas (CODOG) turbine installation. Her two shafts are driven from a common gearbox, powered either by a single diesel (for cruising speeds up to 19 knots) or by a single, licence-built Olympus gas turbine. Although more compact, the arrangement lacks to a degree the versatility.

Externally, a major departure was to increase internal volume by the addition of a long, full-width deckhouse of an otherwise flush-decked hull. The bridge-mast-funnel arrangement is much the same, the large funnel casing resulting from the requirement of the gas turbine.

A considerable amount of aluminium alloy is reportedly incorporated in the upper structure. As such alloys can melt and fail in the event of a serious fire, this is not considered very good practice.

Apparently over-compact, the *Ishikari* was followed by the two Yubaris, near-identical but some 6.5m/21ft greater in length. Like her, their AS capability is limited to small-calibre torpedo tubes and a Bofors quadruple mortar. There is no bow sonar.

The gun calibre remains the same, but firepower is limited to a single weapon of OTO-Melara manufacture. A planned Vulcan/Phalanx CIWS appears never to have been fitted. There being no VDS, the low afterdeck is occupied by four to eight Harpoon SSMs.

LEFT: *Yubetsu* was the second of a pair of slightly enlarged Ishikari derivatives. The gearing arrangements were such that both shafts could be powered by either a single gas turbine or a single diesel engine.

Yubari type

Displacement: 1,470 tons (standard); 1,760 tons (full load)
Length: 91m/298ft 8in (oa)
Beam: 10.8m/35ft 5in
Draught: 3.6m/11ft 10in (mean)
Armament: 1 x 76mm gun; 4/8 x Harpoon SSM; 1 x quadruple 375mm AS mortar; 6 x 324mm AS torpedo tubes (2x3)
Machinery: 1 Olympus gas turbine and 1 diesel engine, 2 shafts
Power: 21,179kW/28,390shp for 25 knots or 3,730kW/5,000bhp for 19 knots
Endurance: Not known
Protection: Nominal
Complement: 98

Abukuma class

Terminated at just two units, the Yubari type was probably an exercise in producing a lean-crewed, small escort that could be series-built in an emergency. Too limited for peacetime activities, it was succeeded by the Abukuma class, six units that harked back to the earlier Chikugos.

The most important influence on the Abukumas was the decision to increase maximum speed to 27 knots. This required an increase in length, a full 16m/52ft 5in greater than that of a Chikugo. A necessary two-thirds increase in power is developed by a pair of Spey SM-1C gas turbines, whose size gives them a more economical operating range than the larger Olympus. For cruising, there are two diesel engines. Arranged CODOG-fashion, each shaft can be driven by one gas turbine or one diesel. The machinery is located in two, well-separated spaces, each served by a large, square-sectioned funnel.

The hull is of the long forecastle type, without a forward knuckle. The upper deck is continued right aft, over the short, open afterdeck. This gives the impression that the ships have both VDS and a helicopter pad. The former, however, is only a possible future option, while a helicopter can only be "vertically replenished" (VERTREP) while hovering.

The space between the funnels is occupied by an 8-cell ASROC launcher. ASROC rounds are now launched more commonly from a Vertical Launch System (VLS). The considerable space between the bridge front and the gun suggests that a small VLS could well be another future option.

Ahead of the VERTREP area are two pairs of Harpoon SSMs and a Vulcan/Phalanx CIWS. Lack of a second CIWS and the usual complement of SSMs suggests topweight problems. The foremast is a truly massive lattice structure and there had yet appeared few concessions to radar invisibility.

ABOVE: **Unusual in modern frigates, the Abukumas have no shipborne helicopter. The area right aft, abaft** Chikuma's **Phalanx CIWS, is fitted for the "vertical replenishment" (VERTREP) of helicopters, which have to remain on the hover.** BELOW RIGHT: **The large gap between** Chikuma's **gun and the bridge front suggests that space has been reserved for the later addition of a small Vertical-Launch System (VLS). At present, ASROC is launched from an amidships Mk 112 mounting.**

ABOVE: *Oyodo* is seen fitted with two pairs of Harpoon SSMa aft, whereas *Chikuma* (top) has only empty cradles. It is now unusual for such small ships to be fitted with two funnels, whose black caps are something of a Japanese trademark.

Abukuma class, as built

Displacement: 2,050 tons (standard); 2,550 tons (full load)
Length: 109m/357ft 10in (oa)
Beam: 13.4m/44ft
Draught: 3.8m/12ft 6in (mean)
Armament: 1 x 76mm gun; 4 x Harpoon SSMs (2x2); 1 x 8-cell ASROC launcher; 1 x Vulcan/Phalanx CIWS; 6 x 324mm AS torpedo tubes (2x3)
Machinery: 2 gas turbines, 2 diesel engines, 2 shafts
Power: 20,142kW/27,000shp for 27 knots or 7,460kW/10,000shp for 19 knots
Endurance: Not known
Protection: Nominal
Complement: 115

DIRECTORY OF FRIGATES

LEFT: **Of 268 Rudderow type ordered, only 81 were actually completed, the programme being curtailed by the war's end. Compared with the Buckleys' 3in guns, the Rudderows' 5in 38 at either end look somewhat outsized.**
ABOVE: **No less than 152 Buckleys were completed, this being** *Wilmarth* **(DE.638). One of the "long-hull" types, the Buckleys accommodated machinery for a respectable 24 knots. Note the prominent trunking to the funnel and the triple-torpedo tubes, carried high.**

Destroyer Escort (DE) classes

As early as 1939 the US Navy was considering specifications for an escort vessel suitable for production in large numbers, which would release destroyers for the duties for which they had been designed. Protracted consideration of the conflicting merits of speed and armament, endurance and seakeeping indicated, however, that a larger number of standard destroyers would be better value.

A near-moribund project was then kick-started in June 1941 by an urgent request for escorts from a hard-pressed British Admiralty. All the necessary design work had been done for a small, destroyer-like vessel of some 91.5m/300ft overall, about the same size as a River-class frigate. Like British corvettes, these new "Destroyer Escorts", or DEs, would be built in yards not used to naval orders, although naval standards would apply.

The US Navy, now itself at war, realized the utility of DEs and the numbers involved became staggering. Over 1,000 were ordered, of which about 450 were eventually cancelled. Of 565 actually completed, 90 were transferred during hostilities, 78 of them to the Royal Navy.

The DEs' flush-decked hulls, with their pronounced forward sheer, were diminutives of those of American destroyers. The open-topped bridge, with its all-round visibility, was adopted from British practice. They were excellent seaboats but, designed with an unusually large metacentric height, they had a rapid and vicious motion until extra weight was moved topside and larger bilge keels fitted to dampen rolling.

US Navy practice stressed relatively high speeds, the DE's specification calling for steam turbines and 24 knots. With the numbers involved, machinery production could not keep pace, necessitating some

ABOVE: **DEs were transferred widely with the end of World War II, the French-flag** *Touareg* **being one of 14 acquired in two batches. One of the 21-knot diesel-electric Bostwick type, she served originally as the USS** *Bright* **(DE.747).**

units being diesel powered. Various combinations of machinery were used, resulting in six major variants of DE being recognized.

Experience with British Hunt classes had demonstrated the occasional value of torpedo tubes, and a triple bank was fitted to the Edsall, Buckley and Bostwick classes. In those transferred to the Royal Navy, all of the Evarts and Buckley types, the extra speed and tight turning circle were much appreciated (as were the relatively high-class accommodation and facilities). Although an excellent dual-purpose weapon, the 3in gun was considered by the British to be inadequate to quickly dispose of a surfaced submarine.

Type	Length (oa) (m/ft)	Beam (m/ft)	Propulsion type	Power (kW/h)	Speed (knots)	Armament
Evarts	88.3/289.5	10.7/35	Diesel-electric	4,476/6,000	21	3 x 3in
Edsall	93.3/306	11.3/37	Geared diesel	4,476/6,000	21	3 x 3in
Buckley	93.3/306	10.7/35	Turbo-electric	8,952/12,000	24	3 x 3in
Bostwick	93.3/306	10.7/35	Diesel-electric	4,476/6,000	21	3 x 3in
Butler	93.3/306	10.7/35	Turbo-electric	8,952/12,000	24	2 x 5in
Rudderow	93.3/306	10.7/35	Turbo-electric	8,952/12,000	24	2 x 5in

UNITED STATES

Two 3in guns were superimposed forward, "A" gun being very wet in a seaway. Abaft "B" gun was a full Hedgehog. Effective in its day, it proved to be the DE's weakness in that the highly efficient Squid (never adopted by the US Navy) could not be retro-fitted. The slower, but more roomy, British Lochs thus became the better U-boat killers.

The adoption of diesel drive was expedited by utilizing the standard 1,500hp diesel generator/motor combination already used in submarines. No less than eight of the sets were to have been installed to generate the required 12,000shp but, owing to conflicting demands of submarine and amphibious craft programmes, only four diesel engines per ship could be spared. Diesel-powered ships thus enjoyed only half the propulsive power of steamers, the speed penalty being 3 knots. In the Edsalls (only) diesels drove the shafts through gearing rather than electrically.

Post-war, 94 DEs were converted to high-speed transports (APDs), with accommodation for 162 troops and their equipment, with four LCVPs under davits. About 45 more became radar pickets, both types reflecting experience gained in the Pacific war. Many were transferred abroad post-war, some serving into the 1960s.

ABOVE LEFT: Resulting from the massed air attacks of World War II, the US Navy modified considerable numbers of destroyers and DEs to Radar Pickets for the purposes of providing early warning. *Calcaterra* (DER.390) was one of 34 Edsall-class conversions. ABOVE RIGHT: *Sellstrom* (DER.255) was another Edsall-class conversion. Note the full-width amidships deckhouse and modified bridge. She has been given an unshielded, twin 3in 50 forward and retains her Hedgehog, here uncovered. BELOW: During the south-west Pacific campaign, suitably modified "four-pipers", then DEs, proved to be invaluable as fast transports/troop carriers (APDs). *Ruchamkin* (APD.89) shows her assault landing craft and 5in gun for supporting fire.

LEFT: The diesel-electric *Dobler* (DE.48) of the short-hulled Evarts type was one of the original large British order that was retained by the US Navy. Two forward guns were appreciated, but at the cost of a very wet "A" position.

Buckley type, as built

Displacement: 1,400 tons (standard); 1,685 tons (full load)
Length: 91.5m/300ft (wl); 93.3m/306ft (oa)
Beam: 10.7m/35ft
Draught: 3.2m/10ft 6in (maximum)
Armament: 3 x 3in guns (3x1); 3 x 21in torpedo tubes (1x3); 1 x Hedgehog AS mortar
Machinery: Turbo-electric, 2 boilers, 2 shafts
Power: 8,952kW/12,000shp for 24 knots
Endurance: 11,112km/6,000nm at 12 knots
Protection: Nominal
Complement: 213

217

DIRECTORY OF FRIGATES

Dealey/Courtney and Claude Jones classes

Built to rigid standard specification in order to facilitate series production, DEs faced mass obsolescence by 1945 because of the rapid parallel advance of the fast, deep-diving submarine. As early as 1947, studies began for a DE replacement. Again, it had to be inexpensive and suitable for series production in an emergency.

A 27-knot speed, together with good seakeeping, demanded a hull of comparable dimensions. Because of the limited training angles of ahead-throwing weapons, a fast helm response and tight tactical diameter were important. In this respect, the US Navy favoured its Weapon Able (or Alfa) over the British Squid.

Based on the reasonable argument that wartime experience demonstrated that damaged ships survived by circumstance rather than by redundancy, single-screw propulsion was chosen, necessitating only one set of machinery and fewer personnel.

Not surprisingly, the indistinguishable Dealey and Courtney classes closely resembled earlier DEs, but with twin 3in 50s forward and aft, and a Weapon Able forward. A substantial lattice mast supported a comprehensive range of electronics, while much of the upper structure was in aluminium alloy. All 13 of the class were completed between 1954 and 1958, subsequent to the Korean War.

Some of the class were later converted to deploy the ultimately abortive DASH (Drone Anti-Submarine Helicopter) system but, even without this failure, they had been less than impressive with their high cost and insufficient range.

A long-forecastle, diesel-driven variant was thus developed in the four-ship Claude Jones class, completed 1958–60. These had four diesels, two shafts and two funnels. A 21.5 knot maximum was offset by an extra 1,852km/1,000nm endurance at the range of speed normally expected of a convoy escort. With very similar salient-dimensions, they had a reduced specification of two single 3in guns, two trainable Hedgehogs and two triple AS torpedo tubes. All four were transferred to Indonesia in 1973–74.

ABOVE LEFT: **Because of priorities in machinery production, many of the war-built DEs were powered for only 21 knots. They were, nonetheless, so valuable that the DE concept was updated post-war. This is the 25-knot** *Courtney* **(DE.1021).** ABOVE: **The post-war DE design proved to be useful for construction by allied NATO navies, the Portuguese building three Dealeys with mainly US offshore funding.** *Almirante Gago Coutinho* **has twin Bofors AS launchers in place of the usual Mk 108, Weapon "Able".**

LEFT: **The four Claud Jones-class DEs were a post-war attempt to produce an inexpensive, diesel-driven escort. They proved to be too small and were transferred to Indonesia. This is the nameship** *Monginsidi*. **Note the two funnels.**

Dealey class, as built

Displacement: 1,450 tons (standard); 1,880 tons (full load)
Length: 93.9m/308ft (wl); 96.1m/325ft (oa)
Beam: 11.2m/36ft 8in
Draught: 3.7m/12ft
Armament: 4 x 3in (2x2); 1 x Able AS rocket launcher; 6 x AS torpedo tubes (2x3)
Machinery: Geared steam turbines, 2 boilers, 1 shaft
Power: 14,920kW/20,000shp for 25 knots
Endurance: 400 tons oil for 11,112km/6,000nm at 12 knots
Protection: Nominal
Complement: 173

UNITED STATES

Bronstein, Garcia and Brooke classes

With the introduction of the nuclear submarine came the requirement for a new type of escort, fast enough to be able to screen a task group, and capable of detecting and engaging a submerged target at a safe range. The key element for this was the low frequency SQS-26 sonar, necessarily housed in a large bulbous forefoot that required a telltale overhung bow profile.

The resulting sonar data would be used to control a Drone Anti-Submarine Helicopter (DASH). Theoretically, this could place a homing torpedo over a target at out to 9,144m/10,000yd but, proving unreliable, was effectively abandoned in 1968 in favour of the LAMPS (Light Airborne Multi-Purpose System) manned helicopter. This left the escorts with only ASROC, which had only half the range but which had the option of compensating for its lack of accuracy by carrying a nuclear warhead, capable of "sanitizing" a considerable area.

Completed in 1963, the two prototype Bronsteins were designed with the smallest hull that could efficiently accommodate a SQS-26 system. Even powered with only 20,000shp, they were some 21.3m/70ft longer than earlier DEs. With adequate freeboard, their long forecastle-deck hulls did not require a pronounced forward sheer. A "mack" exhausted boiler uptakes via a plated-in mast and a generously dimensioned helipad was located about three-quarters aft. The 8-cell ASROC launcher was sited forward of the bridge.

The Bronstein design proved to be too tight and the derived Garica class were a further 13.1m/43ft longer. Guns were upgraded from four 3in to two 5in, the DASH facility being moved right aft. In the six-ship Brooke subgroup the amidships 5in gun was exchanged for a modified Tartar SAM system. All had 35,000shp, but still with a single shaft. ASROCs were reloadable and heavy, wire-guided torpedoes could be launched through the transom.

ABOVE LEFT: **The two Bronsteins (this is the *McCloy*)** were the forerunners of a second-generation DE designed around the new ASROC stand-off missile. Larger and more expensive, they could target ASROC with both low-frequency bow sonar or helicopter-deployed sensors. ABOVE: *Albert David* **(DE.1050) of the Garcia class executing a tight turn. Derived directly from the Bronsteins, the Garcias are significantly longer by virtue of shipping two 5in 38 guns and being equipped with a helicopter hangar, initially for the aborted DASH.** LEFT: *Bronstein* **(DE.1037) quietly proceeding at listening speed. The sheer size of her bow-mounted sonar dome requires her bower anchor to be stowed nearly abreast the 3in 50 gun mounting. Note that there is no hangar or ASROC reload facility.**

Garcia class, as designed

Displacement: 2,625 tons (standard); 3,480 tons (full load)
Length: 121.8m/400ft (wl); 126.3m/414ft 8in (oa)
Beam: 13.5m/44ft 3in
Draught: 7.9m/25ft 11in (maximum)
Armament: 2 x 5in guns (2x1); 1 x 8-cell ASROC launcher; 4 x AS torpedo tubes (2x2); 2 x 21in torpedo tubes (2x1)
Machinery: Geared steam turbine, 2 boilers, 1 shaft
Power: 26,110kW/35,000shp for 27+ knots
Endurance: 600 tons oil for 7,410km/4,000nm at 20 knots
Protection: Nominal
Complement: 209

ABOVE: *Talbot* **(FFG.4) was one of the six Garcia-class derivatives which exchanged the amidships 5in mounting for a Mk 22 launcher, intended for Standard SM-1 MR (Medium-Range) SSM.**

DIRECTORY OF FRIGATES

Knox class

The cost differential between the Tartar-armed Brooke-class DEGs and the non-missile, but otherwise similar, Garcia-class DEs was considerable and, for the planned successors, would be higher, To reduce unit cost in order to obtain the numbers required, the Knox-class ships did not receive an area defence SAM. Their programme overlapped that of the Garcias and, resulting from considerable effort to clean up the rather "bitty" appearance of earlier ships, they were reasonably handsome, if functional.

The truncated conical "mack" was located exactly amidships to minimize ship motion, bearing as it did a short lattice mast supporting the ships' electronics. Earlier classes carried a stem anchor, with the second stowed, submarine-style, in the keel. The Knoxes were given a keel and a port-side anchor, the latter of Danforth pattern. It appears improbable that this feature created the wetness for which the class was noted, but both spray rails and bow bulwarks were added to most.

By the time that the lead ship entered service in 1969, DASH was a dead letter, the class being adapted for LAMPS. Its helipad was sited slightly forward of the after end and, to economize on length, was fitted with a telescopic hangar.

Much of the superstructure was made full width to increase internal volume. Forward was a 5in gun of the new, 54-calibre, type. The adjacent 8-cell ASROC launcher could be reloaded from a facility in the bridge front. Two cells were adapted to launch Harpoon SSMs as an option. Right aft, the originally fitted Sea Sparrow point-defence launcher was replaced by a single Vulcan-Phalanx CIWS. The large bow

LEFT: **The Knox class quickly acquired a reputation for wetness, and each was fitted with forward bulwarks and spray rail, as seen here on** *Aylwin* **(FF.1081). Note the CIWS added aft. Two cells of the ASROC launcher have been modified to launch Harpoon SSMs.**

ABOVE LEFT: **The Knox-class ships took the title "frigate" and designator "FF", FF.1054 being the** *Gray*, **seen here leading a Newport-class Tank Landing Ship. Her sonar dome, visible through the clear water, is smaller than those on preceding classes.** ABOVE: **The Knox class ran to 46 units, more than could usefully be employed in a peacetime navy, and many quickly found themselves reduced to reserve fleet status. Seven, showing remarkably few preservation measures, lay here alongside the veteran battleship** *New Jersey*.

sonar was complemented by VDS and/or towed array sonars.

The class extended to a respectable 46 units, all of which were disposed of by the mid-1990s. At the time of writing, a dozen or more are still serving under foreign flags.

Knox class, as designed

Displacement: 3,075 tons (standard); 4,070 tons (full load)
Length: 126.6m/415ft (wl); 133.6m/438ft (oa)
Beam: 14.3m/47ft
Draught: 7.6m/24ft (maximum)
Armament: 1 x 5in gun; 1 x 8-cell ASROC/Harpoon launcher; 1 x Sea Sparrow BPDMS; 4 x fixed AS torpedo tubes; 2 x fixed 21in torpedo tubes (2x1)
Machinery: Geared steam turbine, 2 boilers, 1 shaft
Power: 35,000shp/26,110kW for 27+ knots
Endurance: 750 tons oil for 8,100km/4,400nm at 20 knots
Protection: Nominal
Complement: 224

UNITED STATES

LEFT: **Derived directly from the Knox design, the Perrys differ in being built around a Standard/Harpoon system forward (relying on a single launcher) and facilities aft for a LAMPS-III helicopter and TACTASS towed array. They are classified "FFG".** BELOW: **Executing a zig-zag trials manoeuvre,** Kauffman **(FFG.59) shows her layout. Note the squat, round funnel casing exhausting the gas turbines, the single 76mm gun amidships and CIWS aft.**

Oliver Hazard Perry class

By 1970, the US Navy was faced with the mass retirement of modernized, war-built hulls. To maintain the required number of hulls, it appeared an attractive option to build "for but not with", creating a pool which could, at a later date, be fitted out specifically for AAW, ASW or surface warfare. The resulting 51 Perry-class missile frigates (FFG) were considerably upgraded Knoxes.

Procured under the strictest of cash-control regimes, the ships have a bow form capable of accepting a large Sonar, which never materialized. The hull itself is Knox-like, but topped by a continuous, two-level boxy superstructure. Its after end extends full-width to provide a hangar for a pair of LAMPS-III, SH-60B Seahawk helicopters, not always carried. Their required operating area, however, necessitated the transom to be given a pronounced rake.

Because of the effectiveness of a double LAMPS-III, ASROC is not provided. All were fitted originally with a single-arm Mk 13 launcher forward, giving them "FFG" status. The launcher could handle Standard SM-1 MR SAMs or Harpoon SSMs. With the demise of the former in 2003, however, the launcher was removed. Not replaced with a VLS, the class has been downgraded to "FF" and 18 of the earlier units sold out to friendly flags.

Despite their capacious appearance, Perrys have little reserve capacity and are now up to 500 tons overweight. Despite this, they are criticized (unreasonably) for their under-armed appearance, not helped by the adoption of a single 76mm OTO Melara for general-purpose firepower. Most have received a Vulcan Phalanx CIWS in addition. Some have their hull sonar complemented by a towed array.

The single shaft is driven by a pair of LM-2500 gas turbines, a pair of azimuth thrusters providing a measure of "get-you-home" redundancy.

A modernization programme for the 24 newest units has been proposed.

LEFT: **The SM-1 version of the Standard SAM having reached retirement, the Perrys had the Mk 13 launcher removed, as in this photograph of** Elrod **(FFG.55). The newest 24 units are slated to receive an extensive modernization.**

Earlier units, as designed

Displacement: 2,770 tons (standard); 3,660 tons (full load)
Length: 124.4m/408ft (wl); 135.7m/445ft (oa), or later 138.8m/455ft 7in (oa)
Beam: 15.2m/50ft
Draught: 8.6m/28ft 3in (maximum)
Armament: 1 x 76mm gun; 1 x standard SAM/Harpoon SSM launcher; 1 x Vulcan-Phalanx CIWS; 2 x AS torpedo tubes (2x1)
Machinery: 2 gas turbines (COGAG), 1 shaft
Power: 29,840kW/40,000shp for 29 knots
Endurance: 587 tons fuel for 7,730km/4,200nm at 20 knots
Protection: Splinter protection over vital spaces
Complement: 176 (now up to 225)

221

DIRECTORY OF FRIGATES

Spica class

The category of "torpedo boat", as opposed to "destroyer" was, as in the German Navy, only a matter of scale. Italian destroyers built during the early 1920s were of a maximum 876 tons and, being greatly outclassed by the 1,640-tonners of the mid-1930s, were downgraded to torpedo boats.

For the relatively short distances involved in Mediterranean operations, ships of this size were useful and, after over a decade's lapse, the 32-strong 800-ton Spica class were laid down from 1934. They resembled the contemporary Oriani-class fleet destroyers but could be quickly differentiated by their smaller, capped funnel, that of an Oriani being broad, trunked and not capped. The Italian love of 1930s streamlining was evident in the compact bridge structure and funnel being combined in a single entity, teardrop-shaped in plan.

They were not over-gunned, their three 100mm weapons being split between one on the forecastle and two superfiring aft. As built, some had four, sided 450mm torpedo tubes, each provided with a deck-mounted reload. Others had one centreline twin and two, sided reloadable tubes. During World War II all are believed to have had two twin centreline mountings. Heavily used as convoy escorts, particularly on the bitterly contested North Africa route, they were also fitted with shields on "A" and "Y" guns, their 20mm armament being increased to 16 barrels. They could carry up to 20 mines or their equivalent weight in depth charges.

LEFT: **One of the 16-strong Alcione type, *Libra*** is seen here raising steam during World War II. Note the paravane, deployed by a powered davit. Three read-use depth charges are in the trap, while, forward of the canvas dodger, are two loaded throwers with reloads.

ABOVE: ***Cassiopea*** belonged to the Climene subgroup of the Spica class. She is seen here in the early 1950s, modified with a new bridge structure, as a "fast corvette". The attractive lines of her light destroyer pedigree remain in evidence.

With twin-shaft, steam turbine propulsion, the Spicas could, with a clean hull and calm conditions, raise 34 knots but their speed fell off rapidly in the "deep and dirty" condition.

Two of the class were sold to Sweden in 1940 and 23 more were to become war losses. Survivors served as "fast corvettes" until the late 1950s, armed with Hedgehog but no torpedo tubes.

Spica class, as built

Displacement: 794 tons (standard); 1,020 tons (full load)
Length: 78.5m/257ft 8in (bp); 83.5m/274ft 1in (oa)
Beam: 8.1m/26ft 10in
Draught: 2.6m/8ft 6in
Armament: 3 x 100mm guns (3x1); 4 x 450mm torpedo tubes (4x1)
Machinery: Geared steam turbines, 2 boilers, 2 shafts
Power: 14,174kW/19,000shp for 34 knots
Endurance: 215 tons oil for 3,520km/1,900nm at 15 knots
Protection: None
Complement: 99

Ariete class

War estimates provided for no less than 42 Improved Spica, or Ariete, class torpedo boats. Italy's ability to carry through her emergency programmes was, however, already badly eroded and, by January 1942 when the first keel was laid, ten of the earlier class had already been lost. Only three yards were involved, all situated in the north and farthest removed from Allied interference. Despite this, only 16 had been laid down by September 1943, when Italy negotiated an armistice.

Ansaldo at Genoa had laid down its full six-ship allocation on the same day in July 1942. The two furthest advanced, *Ariete* and *Arturo*, were launched during March 1943, the former being delivered in the August. Ten more were launched and fitting out, but the *Ariete* would be the only one to serve in the Italian Navy.

Because of the remoteness of the yards from the battle front, the Germans succeeded in completing the remainder. They thus became war losses under the German flag. Only the *Ariete*, together with two damaged on the slip, survived the war, all three being ceded to the fleet of then-Yugoslavia.

The Arietes differed little from the original Spica class. The bridge front was squared-off rather than rounded. With 100mm guns in "A" and "X" positions only, and a larger, uncapped funnel, they could easily be confused visually with a fleet destroyer. A minesweeping winch and two sets of permanent minelaying rails were provided aft.

The main deck was no longer pierced for scuttles. This was probably a damage-control feature.

The class was officially referred to as "attack torpedo boats", a reference presumably to their two triple 450mm torpedo tube mountings and the 16 per cent increase in installed power, providing for a sustained sea speed of 31.5 knots.

TOP: **The Italian port of Fiume was incorporated into post-war Yugoslavia as Rijeka. The incomplete hull of the *Balestra*, already renamed TA 47 by the Germans, was captured there. She was completed as the Yugoslav *Ucka* to a modified design.** ABOVE: **As the only unit of the class to be completed for the Italian Navy, the *Ariete* is seen here in the original form. Note the ungainly squared-off bridge structure and lack of main deck scuttles, as compared with *Ucka* (above).**

Ariete class, as designed

Displacement: 757 tons (standard); 1,127 tons (full load)
Length: 81.1m/266ft 3in (bp); 83.5m/274ft 1in (oa)
Beam: 8.6m/28ft 3in
Draught: 3.1m/10ft 2in (mean)
Armament: 2 x 100mm guns (2x1); 6 x 450mm torpedo tubes (2x3)
Machinery: Geared steam turbines, 2 boilers, 2 shafts
Power: 16,412kW/22,000shp for 31.5 knots
Endurance: 214 tons oil for 2,780km/1,500nm at 16 knots
Protection: None
Complement: 150

DIRECTORY OF FRIGATES

LEFT: Completed only shortly before the Italian capitulation, *Aliseo* survived only to be ceded to Yugoslavia. As can be seen, the Ciclone/Animosos lowered the silhouette and landed "Y" gun for an increased depth charge capacity.

Pegaso and Ciclone classes

A further variant of the Spica design was that of the four-strong Pegaso class. Although of much the same dimensions and appearance, the hulls were refined hydrodynamically for improved seakeeping and endurance. A small bulbous forefoot, common on Italian cruisers, was designed for optimal flow conditions over a specific speed band, allowing either higher speed for the same power, or greater economy at the same speed.

Instead of the Spicas' flattish cut-up, under the after end, typical of current destroyer practice, the Pegasos had a "cruiser" stern. Besides giving more buoyancy right aft, this would probably have given a more uniform flow over the propeller disc, reducing vibration and increasing propeller efficiency. Forward, a slight knuckle was introduced to reduce wetness. Very wet aft, the Spicas had a centreline catwalk connecting the forecastle deck to the light automatic gun positions and "X" gun. On the Pegasos, the underside of this was filled in to create safe fore-and-aft access at upper deck level. Because of this, the two twin torpedo tube mountings had to be sided, halving the maximum salvo. Three depth charge projectors were provided on either side.

The 16 Ciclone-class "destroyer escorts" (*torpediniere di scorta*) were derived directly from the Pegasos.

LEFT: *Pegaso*, one of four, has had a second depth charge trap added, forward of the propeller guard, allowing for larger patterns. The small crane, right aft, was a feature of these classes, and was provided to assist recovery of the paravanes.

Mostly laid down before disruption and shortages bit too hard, most were completed before the armistice.

Looking similar to Pegasos but, in some cases, with a third 100mm gun added amidships, the Ciclones in general arrived too late to experience the worst of the North African convoy run. The only ones, therefore, to be lost in surface action with Allied forces were two of the three commandeered by the Germans following the separate Italian Armistice. With three being ceded to Soviet Russia and two to then-Yugoslavia none remained to Italy post-war.

LEFT: Already in an advanced state of completion, the Ciclone-class *Monsone* is seen here on the slip at Castellammare di Stabia. Note the adoption of a knuckle forward and the aftward extension of the forecastle deck.

Pegaso class, as designed

Displacement: 855 tons (standard); 1,600 tons (full load)
Length: 82.5m/270ft 1in (bp); 89.3m/293ft 2in (oa)
Beam: 9.7m/31ft 10in
Draught: 3.7m/12ft 2in (full load)
Armament: 2 x 100mm guns (2x1); 4 x 450mm torpedo tubes (2x2)
Machinery: Geared steam turbines, 2 boilers, 2 shafts
Power: 11,936kW/16,000shp for 28 knots
Endurance: 390 tons oil for 9,385km/5,100nm at 14 knots
Protection: None
Complement: 154

Albatros and de Cristofaro classes

ABOVE: **With a 19-knot speed and dimensions significantly less than those of war-built escorts, the Albatros class was near the bottom end of capability for an AS corvette.** *Albatros* **herself shows her Italian ancestry in "boat" bow and anchor stowage.**

In the early 1950s, the Italian Navy's escort forces comprised World War II survivors and three ex-American DEs, transferred under the Mutual Defence Assistance Programme. This last arrangement also funded Italy's first post-war corvettes, a series of eight providing much-needed employment.

Only three of these (the Albatros class) were to Italian account, four going to Denmark and one to the Netherlands. The Dutch, with limited use for a one-off, transferred theirs back to Italy after five years, when she was renamed *Aquila*.

Perhaps with a nod toward its source of funding, the Albatroses' hull abandoned the more usual Italian raised-forecastle arrangement in favour of a flush-deck with a pronounced forward sheer. The compact superstructure was based on a full-width amidships deckhouse and there was a transom stern. No funnel was provided, the relatively low-power diesels exhausting through the hull.

Not much admired, the quartette were nonetheless useful 21-knot AS escorts, carrying two Hedgehogs and two 76mm guns (later replaced by 40mm weapons). Modest though they were, it would be seven years from their completion before Italy could embark on an improved version in the de Cristofaros, of which a fifth planned unit was cancelled.

About 4m/13ft longer, the hull of the de Cristofaros reverted to a raised forecastle design, the hance at the break of the forecastle being very long to increase the modulus at the hull discontinuity. A retained feature was the unusual "boat" bow profile. The higher-powered diesel engines exhausted through a small, tapered pot of a funnel. The two 76mm guns also gained a proper director.

The out-dated Hedgehogs and depth charges of the earlier class were here replaced by tripled AS torpedo tubes and a domestically developed, single-barrelled "Menon" AS mortar. VDS was added to a hull-mounted sonar.

ABOVE: **A decade later, but little larger, the four de Cristofaros were higher-powered and faster, with two improved 76mm guns and an Italian-designed Menon single-barrelled AS launcher in place of the Albatroses' two Hedgehogs. Note the reinstatement of a raised forecastle.**

de Cristofaro class

Displacement: 850 tons (standard); 1,020 tons (full load)
Length: 75m/246ft 2in (bp); 80.3m/263ft 7in (oa)
Beam: 10.3m/33ft 9in
Draught: 2.8m/9ft 2in
Armament: 2 x 76mm guns (2x1); 1 x 305mm Menon AS mortar; 6 x 324mm AS torpedo tubes (2x3)
Machinery: 2 diesel engines, 2 shafts
Power: 6,266kW/8,400bhp for 23 knots
Endurance: 100 tons fuel for 7,410km/4,000nm at 18 knots
Protection: None
Complement: 130

DIRECTORY OF FRIGATES

LEFT: **Nameship of the class,** *Centauro* **is seen here as originally completed with a unique but trouble-prone solution to twin 76mm gun mountings. She has American electronics but no modern director. The tripod and topmast are an interesting combination.**

Centauro class

Also funded by the American mutual defence "offshore" programme were the four ships of the Centauro class. As ordered, they carried numbers from the US Navy DE series, starting with DE.1020, but, looking like destroyers, they took "D" pendant numbers on completion. With a speed of only 25 knots and no anti-surface ship torpedo tubes, however, they were later reclassified with "F" identifiers.

Although exceeding 1,800 tons displacement, they had features in common with the Albatros type, the hull being flush-decked, with a triangular, flat transom. Because of the greater length, the forward sheer did not appear to be so pronounced.

Since the early 1930s, Italian destroyers had been designed with adjacent boiler spaces and a single, large, trunked funnel. The arrangement was compact but vulnerable to a single hit. Since 1951, the Italians had been operating two ex-American destroyers. Their boiler spaces were separated for survivability, resulting in two funnels, with the Centauros following suit.

Forward and aft, the Centauros carried a totally new style of 76mm gun mounting, with two barrels arranged in a common vertical plane and elevating together. Although credited with a high rate of fire they proved to be over-complex and were replaced by a simpler single mounting.

Two paired 40mm mountings originally flanked the superfiring "X" position, their firing arcs reduced somewhat by the rather superfluous pole mainmast. Both mast and 40mm were later suppressed in favour of a third 76mm gun.

In addition to an American-sourced sonar, there were two large-diameter AS torpedo tubes and depth charges, with a triple-barrelled Menon AS mortar in "B" position. This triple-barrelled version also proved to be relatively short-lived.

Not lending themselves easily to economical conversion to true AS frigates, the class began the process of disposal in 1980 with the sale of *Castore*.

ABOVE: **Modernization saw the Centauro class receive more orthodox single 76mm guns with proper director control. Further electronics tried the mast's stiffness, resulting in the addition of cross-bracing. Note that** *Canopo*'s **flag superior has been changed from "D" to "F".**

Centauro class, as designed

Displacement: 1,680 tons (standard); 2,120 tons (full load)
Length: 96.9m/317ft 8in (bp); 103.2m/338ft 4in (oa)
Beam: 11.6m/38ft
Draught: 3.5m/11ft 6in
Armament: 4 x 76mm guns (2x2); 2 x 21in torpedo tubes; 1 x 3-barrelled AS mortar
Machinery: Geared steam turbines, 2 boilers, 2 shafts
Power: 16,412kW/22,000shp for 25 knots
Endurance: 360 tons oil for 6,760km/3,650nm at 20 knots
Protection: None
Complement: 207

ITALY

LEFT: *Alpino* (seen here) and her sister *Carabiniere* were developments of the Centauro design and, indeed, were originally to have taken "C" names. They have diesel engines of far higher output than their predecessor's steam plant, two helicopters and six 76mm guns.

ABOVE: The four Bergaminis show a different and cheaper line of development from the Centauro design. They have two 76mm guns and a mortar forward, like the Alpinos, but just one helicopter and half the engine power. This is *Luigi Rizzo*.

Carlo Bergamini and Alpino classes

Launched in 1960, the four Bergaminis were frigate versions of the de Cristofaro corvettes. For an extra 10m/33ft, they shipped a helicopter and a third gun, and gained 2.5 knots.

Again, a flush-decked hull was topped with a full-width deckhouse, now supporting at its after end a telescopic hangar for a small Agusta-Bell 47 helicopter. A light, elevated extension of the 01 level served as a flight pad. Active fin stabilizers were fitted to assist flight operations through roll reduction.

During the late 1960s, helicopter facilities were upgraded for the more capable AB.212. A larger hangar and extended flight pad meant the landing of the after 76mm guns and a single-barrelled Menon AS launcher. The uptakes from the four diesels exhausted via a funnel/mast combination. Beyond further upgrading, the Bergaminis were discarded in the early 1980s.

Some 20m/65ft 7in longer than the Bergaminis, the two Alpinos took the concept a stage further. This pair were to have been named *Circe* and *Climene*, continuing the astronomical names associated with torpedo boats. Before launch, however, they took *Alpino* and *Carabiniere*, old destroyer names that better reflected their size.

Their propulsion was by two small gas turbines and four diesels in CODAG combination. The resulting large funnel had proportions which greatly enhanced the ships' appearance. To the usual Menon launcher and two 76mm guns mounted forward were added four more 76mms, sided along the superstructure. Accommodation, originally for two small AB 204B helicopters, was later adequate for a single AB.212.

Two further units were cancelled but both Alpinos still exist (at the time of writing) as special-purpose auxiliaries and trials ships. They have been reduced to diesel propulsion only and their armament cut to three guns and their helicopter. Both now carry "A", auxiliary pendant numbers.

Alpino class, as designed

Displacement: 2,000 tons (standard); 2,690 tons (full load)
Length: 106.4m/349ft 3in (bp); 113.3m/371ft 10in (oa)
Beam: 13.3m/43ft 8in
Draught: 3.8m/12ft 5in
Armament: 6 x 76mm guns (6x1); 1 x single-barrelled AS mortar; 6 x 324mm AS torpedo tubes (2x3)
Machinery: 2 gas turbines, 4 diesels, 2 shafts
Power: 11,488kW/15,400hp plus 12,533kW/16,800bhp for 28 knots
Endurance: 275 tons fuel for 7,780km/4,200nm at 17 knots
Protection: Nominal
Complement: 247

ABOVE: Lead ship *Carlo Bergamini* in historic surroundings. Her small helicopter is demanding on space, which has been economized by the combination of mast and funnel, and a telescopic hangar. The flight pad is well forward to minimize movement and accelerations.

DIRECTORY OF FRIGATES

LEFT: **With massive gas turbine sprint power in a relatively small hull, the Lupos had an un-frigate-like 35-knot top speed, but cruised on diesel engines.** *Sagittario*'s **four starboard-side Otomat SSM cradles are unoccupied.**

Lupo and Artigliere classes

Although of the same length as the preceding Alpinos, the Lupos, most unusually, were significantly narrower. The reason, probably, lay in the adoption of CODOG (as opposed to CODAG) propulsion. Two diesel engines were installed for cruising (up to 20 knots) but, for sprint power, there were two licence-built LM-2500 gas turbines, capable of a joint 37,300kW/50,000hp output. This represented a 25 per cent increase in propulsive power compared with an *Alpino*, and which, with an improved hull form, translated into a 4-knot increase in sustained speed.

Some sacrifice was necessary in topweight and a single 127mm gun, and tube- and helicopter-launched topedoes were able to replace the earlier six 76mm weapons and Menon AS launcher, now obsolete. Modern missile systems are bulky but not heavy, the Lupos carrying both an 8-cell Sea Sparrow point defence SAM and eight canister-launchers for Otomat SSMs.

That the Lupo design was too tight was evident in the class being curtailed in favour of the longer Maestrale type, all being scrapped by 2003. Handsome ships, they sold well for export, however, with six being built to Venezuelan account and four each to Peru and Iraq. The last named, laid down 1981–84, ran foul of a generally imposed embargo on West-supplied war materials. With no potential buyers, they were taken into the Italian Navy as the Artigliere class.

All remain on the inventory and are effectively identical with the late Lupo class, with the important difference that acceptance was conditional upon all ASW weaponry and sensors being removed. This was presumably a budgetary manoeuvre, the ships being officially "Fleet Patrol Ships" rather than frigates. To compensate for their lack of ASW armament (which, presumably, could be added), their helicopters have enhanced capability for over-the-horizon direction for the ships' SSMs.

LEFT: **Between 1980 and 1982, Italy completed six standard Lupos for Venezuela. Here, the** *Mariscal Antonio José de Sucre* **crosses the stern of the stationary** *General Bartolomé Salom***. Both are carrying their full outfit of Otomat SSMs.**

Lupo class, as designed

Displacement: 2,210 tons (standard); 2,525 tons (full load)
Length: 106m/347ft 11in (bp); 113.6m/372ft 10in (oa)
Beam: 12m/39ft 4in
Draught: 3.5m/11ft 7in
Armament: 1 x 127mm gun; 8 x Otomat SSM (8x1); 1 x 8-cell Sea Sparrow SAM launcher; 6 x 324mm AS torpedo tubes (2x3)
Machinery: 2 gas turbines, 2 diesels, 2 shafts
Power: 37,300kW/50,000hp or 5,968kW/8,000bhp for 35 or 20 knots
Endurance: 8,060km/4,350nm at 16 knots
Protection: Nominal
Complement: 194

ITALY

Maestrale class

The limitations of the Lupo design were recognized early, for the first half-dozen of the improved version, the Maestrales, were ordered nine months before the lead ship, *Lupo*, even commissioned. Although 10m/33ft longer, they were even finer (L/B *Lupo* 8.83; *Maestrale* 9.04) and further reduction of weapon topweight was evident. A Lupo's Sea Sparrow launcher and its director were mounted on the hangar roof at 02 level. On a Maestrale the launcher has been moved to 01 level, superfiring the 127mm gun from "B" position. The compact Italian-built RTN-30X director above the bridge serves both weapons. A Lupo carried eight Otomat SSMs at 01 level. A Maestrale carries only four, in a less cramped 02 location, a net gain offset by the shift of the two twin 40mm mountings from main deck to 01 level.

The small increase in beam allowed the hangar to be widened sufficiently to accommodate a second helicopter. For ASW, these work in conjunction with the ships' VDS and towed array, deployed from a handling deck and well situated beneath the flight deck.

Although rather more powerful cruising diesels are fitted, higher speeds remain dependent upon a pair of LM-2500 gas turbines. Given the greater length it is, perhaps, surprising that they are credited with being upwards of 2 knots slower than a Lupo.

It is reported that the Maestrales were designed with no capacity for mid-life modernization and that their retirement is planned for 2011–15. The planned replacement for both the Maestrales and the already defunct Lupos is a new ten-ship class of general-purpose frigate, the lead ship of which will be named, rather confusingly, *Carlo Bergamini*. At 5,000 tons displacement and 135m/443ft 2in overall length, these will mark a considerable advance in size, capability and adaptability. They will be similar to the projected French Aquitaine class.

ABOVE LEFT: **Easily mistaken for a Lupo (opposite), a Maestrale differs primarily in having her SAM launcher forward of the bridge and in having a distinct gap between funnel casing and mainmast. This is *Libeccio*.** ABOVE: **This overhead view of *Maestrale* emphasizes the complexity of the modern funnel, whose contents are critical to the functioning of the ship's gas turbines as well as exhausting the cruising diesels and auxiliaries. It needs to be carefully cooled.**

LEFT: **In the later stages of fitting out, *Grecale* presents her unusual stern configuration. The transom, very wide to support the helicopter deck above, is deeply notched to facilitate deployment of the variable depth sonar.**

Maestrale class, as designed

Displacement: 2,700 tons (standard); 3,040 tons (full load)
Length: 116.4m/382ft 1in (bp); 122.7m/402ft 10in (oa)
Beam: 12.9m/42ft 4in
Draught: 6m/19ft 6in (maximum)
Armament: 1 x 127mm gun; 4 x Teseo/Otomat SSM (4x1); 1 x 8-cell Aspide/Sea Sparrow SAM launcher; 2 x 533mm AS torpedo tubes (2x1); 6 x 324mm AS torpedo tubes (2x3)
Machinery: 2 gas turbines, 2 diesels, 2 shafts
Power: 37,300kW/50,000hp or 7,572kW/10,150bhp for 33 or 21 knots
Endurance: 11,110km/6,000nm at 15 knots
Protection: Nominal
Complement: 225

DIRECTORY OF FRIGATES

LEFT: Rather like a cut-down Maestrale in appearance, the *Minerva* differs in having a low afterdeck not overlaid with the helicopter flight pad. The practice of painting discharge areas black gives a rather tatty appearance. ABOVE: *Fenice* is seen here with the original lower funnel, which affected helicopter operation. The latter's pad has been moved forward to reduce the effect of ship motion, itself reduced by active stabilizers.

Minerva class

Classed officially as "light frigates" (FFL), the Minervas, slightly larger than a torpedo boat (light destroyer) of World War II, are configured as general-purpose escorts. Their hulls have relatively high freeboard and are of long forecastle type with a knuckle forward. Although the bridge structure is of full width, it is not elongated as in earlier classes. Forward is a single 76mm OTO-Melara Super Rapid gun, a dual-purpose weapon supported by an 8-cell Sea Sparrow/Aspide SAM launcher, a point-defence weapon that occupies premium space on the low afterdeck. Standard AS capability is thus limited to small-calibre torpedo tubes and a keel-mounted sonar. Space, however, has been allocated for the addition of a VDS.

Conflicting priorities are evident in that four units have landed their SAM system and torpedo tubes in favour of a projected helicopter facility. A helicopter and VDS would greatly enhance the AS qualities of the ships, but at the expense of self-defence (or that of any vessel under escort).

A further designed option is to ship both SAM system and a reload facility, together with four Otomat/Teseo SSMs, giving flexibility for fitting out according to likely operational requirements.

Between 2002 and 2004 were completed six more corvettes classed, probably for funding purposes, as patrol ships (Sirio class) or EEZ patrol ships (Fulgosi class). Built on a common, 88.4 x 12.2m/290 x 40ft hull, they are slightly longer than a Minerva but proportionately beamier. Their hulls follow contemporary fashion, with highly sculpted, low-signature features. As patrol vessels, most have a reduced armament.

Where the Sirio type is powered for only 22 knots, the Fulgosis are as fast as a Minerva (although requiring 58 per cent more installed power due to a fuller hull form). Both types already carry a 76mm gun and facilities (with telescopic hangar) for a large helicopter.

ABOVE: Like most of the class, *Urania* is operating without either helicopter or Aspide/Albatros launcher which, if shipped, are alternatives. The ships are at the low end of displacement to effectively operate either.

Minerva class, as designed

Displacement: 1,030 tons (standard); 1,285 tons (full load)
Length: 80m/262ft 7in (bp); 86.6m/284ft 3in (oa)
Beam: 10.5m/34ft 6in
Draught: 4.8m/15ft 9in (maximum)
Armament: 1 x 76mm gun; 1 x 8-cell Aspide/Sea Sparrow SAM launcher; 6 x 324mm AS torpedo tubes (2x3)
Machinery: 2 diesel engines, 2 shafts
Power: 8,206kW/11,000bhp for 25 knots
Endurance: 6,480km/3,500nm at 18 knots
Protection: Nominal
Complement: 133

Kola class

Designed shortly after World War II, the Kola-class fast escorts remained on the active list until the late 1970s. Between six and ten were built, their design borrowing features from German fleet torpedo boats (light destroyers), particularly the T25–36 group of 1941–42, commonly known as Elbings, and of much the same size. The low-set, spray-deflecting knuckle forward was typically German, as was the configuration of the wide transom stern. The latter was specifically to facilitate the laying of mines, tracks for which extended on either side as far as the forward funnel.

The profile of a Kola was pleasing, with two single 100mm guns in open mountings superimposed at either end. Two well-separated, strongly raked and capped funnels indicated boiler spaces divided by the engine room. Between the funnels was a centreline, triple torpedo tube mounting. Grouped around the after funnel were four twin automatic gun mountings, two of 37mm, two of 25mm. That most units appeared to lack two of these, together with the usual MBU AS rocket launchers, reinforced the general suspicion that the design was rather tender. Certainly, the dangers of ice accretion and extreme weather were avoided by assigning the class generally to the Black Sea fleet.

The length of the permanent mine rails suggested a capacity of at least 80. This considerable extra load could have been accepted only at the expense of landing other armament to compensate.

A feature of the main gun disposition was the lack of protection for the crews of "A" and "Y" guns, exposed to the muzzle blast from "B" and "X" guns.

The comparatively large, enclosed bridge structure was topped by a heavy "Wasp Head" director (derived from the stabilized German "Wackeltopf") to the front of which was attached the "Sun Visor" radar antenna. Only one triple 21in mounting was ever fitted.

ABOVE: **With the Soviet system then at its most secretive, good photographs of Kolas are scarce, identities of individual vessels rendered uncertain through change of pendant numbers. The Kolas' light armament classed them as "escorts" rather than destroyers.**

LEFT: **Although heavily retouched, this image of a Kola shows her major features, particularly the long, unobstructed side decks and wide transom associated with minelaying. The flush deck reduces stress concentrations in the hull.**

Kola class, as designed

Displacement: 1,500 tons (standard); 1,900 tons (full load)
Length: 96m/315ft 2in (oa)
Beam: 10.4m/34ft 2in
Draught: 3.5m/11ft 6in
Armament: 4 x 100mm guns (4x1); 3 x 21in torpedo tubes (1x3); 2 x quadruple MBU-900 AS rocket launchers
Machinery: Geared steam turbines, 2 boilers, 2 shafts
Power: 22,380kW/30,000shp for 30.5 knots
Endurance: 300 tons oil for 6,480km/3,500nm at 12 knots
Protection: Not known
Complement: 190

DIRECTORY OF FRIGATES

Riga class

With more the characteristics of destroyers than the escorts that were required, the Kolas were too much configured for speed and insufficiently for capacity. Their programme was thus curtailed in favour of the Riga, a more frigate-like type whose design was, in many respects, a reduced Kola.

Overall length was reduced by 4.5m/14ft 9in, but the beam was little changed. By accepting a 28 knot (as opposed to 30.5 knot) speed, installed power could be reduced by one third. The shorter hull required the boilers to be located in adjacent spaces, reducing survivability but requiring only one large funnel to exhaust both.

Although it retained the broad, minelayer's transom, the Riga hull already showed more "Russian" characteristics, flush-decked with a long, sweeping sheerline, the anchor pocket set well back. There was no knuckle but an enhanced flare. To further reduce wetness, a short bulwark was added right forward and an American-style, full-width screen abreast "B" gun. A solid bulwark ran from the screen to the funnel; with the 01 level continued to the ship's sides, this created a covered way.

Three 100mm guns were fitted, two superimposed forward, one aft at upper deck level. Two MBU AS rocket launchers, of various types, flanked "B" mounting at 01 level. Immediately abaft the funnel was a triple torpedo tube mounting. Permanent rails ran along either side as far forward as the funnel, their capacity about 50 mines if the tubes were landed as partial compensation.

ABOVE: **Finland acquired two Rigas from the Soviet Union in 1964. This is the *Hameenmaa*. Note the height of the 100mm guns in their trunions, indicating high elevation angles.**

Originally fitted with braced tripod masts, Rigas eventually gained a lattice structure to support increased electronic equipment.

Roughly equivalent to a British Hunt, the Riga proved to be rugged and seaworthy. Sixty-six were reportedly built, of which sixteen were transferred to including states from Finland to Indonesia. Some, fitted for intelligence gathering, gained a stub mainmast. All were discarded by the late 1980s, some having served for over 30 years.

Riga class

Displacement: 1,080 tons (standard); 1,400 tons (full load)
Length: 91.5m/300ft 4in (oa)
Beam: 10.1m/33ft 2in
Draught: 3.3m/10ft 10in
Armament: 3 x 100mm guns (3x1); 3 x 21in torpedo tubes (1x3); 2 x MBU-2500 AS rocket launchers
Machinery: Geared steam turbines, 2 boilers, 2 shafts
Power: 14,920kW/20,000shp for 28 knots
Endurance: 230 tons oil for 4,075km/2,200nm at 15 knots
Protection: Not known
Complement: 177

ABOVE: **In an attitude typical of the Cold War era, the Wasp Head director and "A" gun of this unidentified Riga are tracking the photographer's aircraft, although the gun crews are not closed up. Note the broad transom and clear side decks. The funnel casing is louvred to direct gases away from the electronics.**

USSR

LEFT: **Designed for coastal escort duties, this Petya I shows her broad range of armament: two enclosed twin 76mm gun mountings, two shrouded MBU-2500 AS rocket launchers forward of the bridge and two aft, and a covered quintuple torpedo tube bank amidships.** ABOVE: **An interesting close-up of a Petya fitted with two of the later MBU-2500A AS weapons. The bowl over the bridge is the Hawk Screech fire control radar for the 76mm guns. The casual "rig of the day" suggests that she is a Black Sea unit.**

Petya and Mirka classes

Produced in parallel with the Poti programme were 46 of the larger and more capable Petya class. Multi-role craft, they were triple-screwed, the centreline shaft being driven by two cruising diesels, and each wing shaft by a gas turbine. The hull was flush-decked, with marked forward sheer and a forward bulwark. Mine rails terminated at the broad transom.

As designed, Petyas had an enclosed twin 76mm gun mounting forward and aft, a quintuple 400mm AS torpedo tube bank abaft the low, square stack, and four of the flat-form MBU-2500s AS rocket launchers. Two of these were located aft and two on the bridge structure in a position that appeared perilously close to the wheelhouse windows.

Later units, known as Petya IIs, exchanged the after MBU-2500s for a second quintuple torpedo tube mounting, the bridge-mounted launchers being upgraded to the round-form MBU-2500-A.

A third variant, known variously as a Modified Petya I, or a Petya III, landed the after torpedo tubes in favour of various configurations of deckhouse, enclosing a VDS.

Of virtually the same size as a Petya, the succeeding Mirka varied mainly in its propulsion system. Two shafts were each usually powered by a cruising diesel engine. The propellers ran in tunnels, configured to as to act also as water jets when powered by the alternative gas turbines. The latter were housed, Poti-style, in the raised after end of the hull. Lacking a funnel, the Mirka had their lattice mast relocated amidships to minimize motion.

The raised after end prevented Mirkas being mine-capable, but two MBU-2500-As were sided both forward and aft. A Mirka II variant, however, exchanged the after pair for a second quintuple set of torpedo tubes. Nine of each type were constructed.

Some Petyas were transferred, but no Mirka. Units of both classes served into the 1990s.

Mirka II

Displacement: 950 tons (standard); 1,120 tons (full load)
Length: 78m/256ft (bp); 82.4m/270ft 6in (oa)
Beam: 9.2m/30ft 2in
Draught: 2.9m/9ft 6in
Armament: 4 x 76mm guns (2x2); 10 x 400mm AS torpedo tubes (2x5); 2 x MBU-2500-A AS rocket launchers
Machinery: 2 gas turbines, 2 diesel engines, 2 shafts
Power: 22,380kW/30,000shp for 33 knots or 8,952kW/12,000bhp for 20 knots
Endurance: 150 tons fuel for 5,555km/3,000nm at 20 knots
Protection: None
Complement: 92

ABOVE: **Successors to the Petyas, the Mirkas had their gas turbines relocated right aft. Note the raised deckline and large air intakes. This is a Mirka II, with two quintuple torpedo tubes but no MBUs aft.**

233

DIRECTORY OF FRIGATES

LEFT: **A slightly confusing picture with the two Potis overlapping. Their flat 16-barrelled MBU-2500 projectors are also staggered, the forward one to port, the superimposed one to starboard. The hump over the gas turbine space is even more pronounced.**

Poti class

Although, in the early 1960s, Soviet Russia posed an enormous threat to the West through its considerable submarine fleet, the Russians themselves faced a similar threat. This ranged from nuclear attack boats, and SSBNs deploying the Polaris ICBM, to conventional diesel-electric boats, and resulted in a range of specialist Russian ASW vessels, varying in size from large helicopter carriers to corvette-sized craft designed for inshore AS operations.

Smallest of the latter type, and surely among the least attractive warships of all time, were the Poti class. Slightly smaller than a British Flower-class corvette of World War II, the Potis had CODAG propulsion with two diesel engines ahead, and two small gas turbines. Each drives a separate shaft, partly enclosed within tunnels. With all four engines coupled, the top speed was probably nearer 30, rather than the 34 knots sometimes claimed. The latter figure appears excessive for a small, non-planing hull.

Otherwise flush-decked, with marked sheer, the hull had a raised after section to accommodate the air ingestion units for the gas turbines, whose large, shrouded intakes were arranged in tandem. An unintentional bonus was that the odd profile made it, from a distance, difficult to estimate the ship's heading.

On two levels forward, and staggered about the centreline, were two MBU-2500A AS rocket launchers. Looking outsize on so small a ship, these could lay six-or-twelve bomb salvoes out to about 6.4km/4 miles' range. In the waist, firing outboard at fixed angles to the centreline, were four long, medium-calibre tubes for the launching of wire-guided AS torpedoes.

For self-defence a Poti depended upon the radar-directed, twin 57mm mounting amidships.

Over 60 Poti were believed built, several being transferred within the Warsaw Pact navies. Most served well into the 1980s.

ABOVE: **With its darkly painted after end, this Poti looks distinctly ungainly, but paint schemes varied from ship to ship. Visible amidships is the twin 57mm gun mounting with its associated Muff Cob director. To its left can be seen the two starboard 400mm torpedo tubes.**

Poti class

Displacement: 530 tons (standard); 615 tons (full load)
Length: 60.7m/199ft 3in (oa)
Beam: 8.2m/26ft 11in
Draught: 2.9m/9ft 6in
Armament: 2 x 57mm guns (1x2); 4 x 400mm AS torpedo tubes (4x1); 2 x MBU-2500-A AS rocket launchers
Machinery: 2 gas turbines, 2 diesel engines, 4 shafts
Power: 17,904kW/24,000shp plus 5,968kW/8,000bhp for 30+ knots
Endurance: 125 tons fuel for 4,815km/2,600nm at 16 knots
Protection: None
Complement: 80

USSR

LEFT: **At about 71.5m/234ft 7in, a Grisha lies somewhere between a Poti and a Mirka, but is a much neater design. This unit, the Lithuanian-flag *Aukstaitis*, was one of two acquired from Russia in 1992. Note the NATO-style number.** ABOVE: ***Aukstaitis*** **again. This variant is termed a Grisha III, which appears to vary only in the addition of a six-barrelled, Gatling-type 23mm gun, whose helmet-like containment is visible between the after 57mm gun mounting and its director.** BELOW: **A late-model Grisha V. The circular cover on the forecastle screens a "pop-up" SA-N-4 ("Gecko") SAM launcher, whose control is through the Pop Group director atop the bridge. Her main surface/air search radar is an updated Half Plate-B.**

Grisha class

At around 1,000 tons full load displacement, the Grishas are considered corvettes. They were built in considerable numbers, probably about 70 in all. While they were follow-ons to the Poti class, they are 11m/36t longer and constitute a new design rather than a derivative.

The hull has the same pronounced sheerline, but here flattened somewhat right forward to allow any forward guns to depress. The bridge structure is based on a full-width deckhouse, abaft which is a low, square-sectioned funnel, offset slightly to port and exhausting both the gas turbine and the two diesels of the CODAG propulsion system. Broad after waterplanes permit mine rails to run along either side from the after superstructure to the wide transom.

Grishas are, depending upon armament fit, divided into several sub-types. Grisha I had a retractable SA-N-4 ("Gecko") twin SAM launcher on the foredeck, superfired by two MBU-6000 12-barrelled AS rocket launchers. Sided in the waist were twin heavyweight torpedo tubes, and aft there was a twin 57mm gun mounting. Grisha IIs differed in having a second twin 57mm forward in place of the SA-N-4. All surviving examples of Types I and II reportedly serve with the Federal Border Guard in its large quasi-military fleet.

Grisha IIIs replicate Type Is but have a modified after deckhouse, which accommodates a VDS system and supports a six-barrelled 30mm Gatling. Grisha IVs appear never to have existed, the follow-ons being Grisha V. Probably 20 of these are still active. They have improved electronics while, aft, the twin 57mm mounting has been replaced by a single 76.2mm. Only one MBU-6000 is carried forward, indicating possible topside weight limitation.

The defensive firepower of all surviving Grishas has been augmented significantly by their being equipped with shoulder-launched Strela-3 close-range SAMs. Despite considerable variation, the Grisha classes are collectively termed MPK, an acronym for "Small AS Ship".

Grisha V

Displacement: 880 tons (standard); 1,030 tons (full load)
Length: 66.9m/219ft 4in (wl); 71.2m/233ft 5in (oa)
Beam: 9.5m/31ft 2in
Draught: 3.6m/11ft 9in
Armament: 1 x 76.2mm gun; 1 x 6-barrelled 30mm Gatling; 1 x SA-N-4 twin SAM launcher; 2 x shoulder-launched SA-N-8; 4 x 533mm torpedo tubes (2x2); 1 x MBU-6000 AS rocket launcher
Machinery: 1 gas turbine, 2 diesels, 3 shafts
Power: Gas turbine 13,428kW/18,000shp; diesels 7,460kW/10,000bhp each; total CODAG configuration 28,348kW/38,000shp for 32 knots
Endurance: 143 tons fuel for 4,630km/2,500nm at 14 knots
Protection: Nominal
Complement: 86

235

Krivak class

Powerfully armed for their size and often categorized as "destroyers", the Krivaks were built for the Soviet Navy as "large anti-submarine ships" and are, therefore, more correctly frigates.

The Krivak hull is of long forecastle type, with adequate freeboard. A slight knuckle over the centre section results from a gentle flare at the waterline. The sharply overhung stem betokens provision for a large bow sonar. On the low afterdeck a centreline casing covers a VDS, flanked by the usual mine rails.

The bridge structure is sited to place both it and the major electronics close to amidships, to minimize the effects of ship motion. The foredeck is dominated by a quadruple SS-N-14 ("Silex") launcher. This missile is dual purpose, capable of being fitted to carry either warhead or torpedo, for use against surface ship or submarine out to a 50km/31 mile range. With no embarked helicopter, the ship may require assistance in targeting.

Forward and aft are the unobtrusive silos for the pop-up SA-N-4 ("Gecko") launcher. Each has its own director. Forward of the bridge are the usual pair of MBU-6000 AS rocket launchers, while at the break of the forecastle deck are superimposed gun mountings, twin 76.2mm in Krivak Is and single 100mm in Krivak IIs. Forward of the stumpy funnel is a square deckhouse supporting radar directors for both the guns and the after SA-N-4. Sided abreast the amidships gap are quadruple heavyweight torpedo tubes. Propulsion is by gas turbine, cruise and boost units being run in COGAG configuration for maximum output on two shafts.

Of about 34 Krivaks built, probably only ten remain operational at the time of writing. At least four were late new-builds for Border Guard service. Known as Krivak IIIs, these have a single 100mm gun forward and helicopter facilities aft.

ABOVE: **A Krivak I identifiable by her 76mm gun mountings aft. She has no helicopter, relying on the VDS (located in the low housing right aft) and bow sonar to provide long-range targeting data for the SS-N-14 ("Silex") AS missiles in the launchers forward.**
LEFT: **In what appears to be a joint Baltic exercise, a German Bremen-class frigate lays astern of a Krivak I. SA-N-4 SAM launchers are housed forward and aft, the directors for each being visible. The SS-N-14 also has an anti-ship capability.**

Krivak II, as built

Displacement: 3,075 tons (standard); 3,500 tons (full load)
Length: 113m/370ft 11in (wl); 123.1m/403ft 7in (oa)
Beam: 13.2m/43ft 3in
Draught: 4.6m/15ft 1in
Armament: 2 x 100mm guns (2x1); 1 xquadruple SS-N-14 SSM launcher; 2 x twin SA-N-4 SAM launchers; 8 x 533m torpedo tubes (2x4); 2 x MBU-6000 AS rocket launchers
Machinery: 2 boost gas turbines, 2 cruise gas turbines, 2 shafts
Power: 2 x 14,920kW/20,000shp and 2 x 5,595kW/7,500shp maximum; 41,030kW/55,000shp for 30.5 knots
Endurance: 7,220kW/3,900nm at 20 knots
Protection: Nominal
Complement: 210

USSR/RUSSIA

LEFT: **The radar-signature reduction features of *Steregushchiy* combine to make her appear larger than her true size. Note how the masting arrangements on the ship vary from those on the official model (below).**

Steregushchiy class

Following the collapse of the Soviet Union, cuts in defence funding saw the apparent abandonment of several interesting warship classes. These included a helicopter-equipped Krivak replacement in the 3,200-ton Neustrashimyy type, of which only two appear to have been completed, and the 1,600-ton Gepard-class "utility frigate", a concept reminiscent of the British Type 14s and also curtailed at two units.

Looking rather more hopeful, with plans for 10, even 25, ships is the slightly larger Steregushchiy type, which appears to have been aimed at the export market. About 250 tons greater than a Gepard, it can operate a helicopter of the size of a Kamov Ka-27 (Helix A), for which a permanent hangar is provided.

The hull is of the long forecastle type, the low afterdeck being occupied largely by an enclosed VDS, which is roofed over to full hull width by the helipad. The VDS is complemented by a large, low-frequency sonar at the forefoot (of a size that could cause headaches when stemming the vessel in a small dry dock).

Backing up the helicopter for AS operations, the ship carries two twin heavyweight torpedo tubes, reportedly able to launch the Type 84R Vodopad-NK anti-submarine missile as well as wire-guided torpedoes.

The earlier planned large funnel has been reduced to a stump. A single, dual-purpose 100mm gun is mounted forward. Between it and the bridge front is a low casing which can accommodate a VLS for eight SS-N-25 ("Switchblade") SSMs or a gun/missile CIWS.

Unobtrusively recessed into the deck adjacent to the hangar are silo-housed SA-N-11 ("Grison") close-in anti-aircraft missiles, apparently optional, while flanking the after superstructure are two six-barrelled 30mm Gatling-type weapons.

ABOVE: **Virtually complete, the *Steregushchiy* presents a workmanlike appearance. Note the Kortik-M CIWS fitted abaft the gun in place of the reported VLS. This may indicate an export version.**

Armament and electronics fits appear to be flexible, while models indicate optional redesigned upperworks for signature reduction.

LEFT: **Although there are minor differences, the appearance of the official model is true to that of the ship herself. The very deep fairing around the bow sonar results in deep submergence and a reduced liability to damaging slamming.**

Steregushchiy class

Displacement: 1,850 tons (standard); 2,100 tons (full load)
Length: 111.6m/365ft 10in (oa)
Beam: 14m/45ft 10in
Draught: 3.7m/12ft 2in
Armament: 1 x 100mm gun; 2 x 30mm Gatling guns; 8 x SS-N-25 SSM; 64 x SA-N-11 CIWS SAM; 4 x 533mm torpedo tubes (4x1)
Machinery: 4 diesel engines, 2 shafts
Power: 24,767kW/33,200bhp for 26 knots
Endurance: 6,667km/3,600nm at 15 knots
Protection: Not known
Complement: 100

DIRECTORY OF FRIGATES

LEFT: **Like their Italian counterparts, German designers preferred a flush-decked small frigate with accommodation gained by a full-width, non-structural deckhouse. Amidships,** *Augsburg* **is dominated by gas turbine requirements, with outsize funnel and casings.**

Köln class

Products of the same yard as the Hamburg-class destroyers, the six Köln were, in basic respects, diminutives of them. They were the first domestically built fast escorts permitted after 1945, and their designers naturally drew on their earlier experience, both types featuring bow sections remarkably similar to those of post-1943 torpedo boats and destroyers – sharply flared and knuckled, with anchors stowed high up at the deck edge to reduce impact and spray formation.

The Kölns were contemporary with the British Type 81s ("Tribal") and, like them, incorporated the still-new technology of gas-turbine propulsion. Of lower power, the single-screwed British ships cruised on steam, using the gas turbine (which represented only 37.5 per cent of installed power) in COSAG combination only for high-speed boost and getting under weigh from cold. The Germans installed a CODAG arrangement, coupling a pair of diesel engines and a gas turbine, singly or in combination, to either shaft. The gas turbines here generated some 68 per cent of maximum combined power. The four diesels resulted in somewhat complex gearing arrangements for either shaft but probably were the best available choice from a still-recovering heavy manufacturing industry.

The Kölns' hull was flush-decked, with full-width deckhouse, a form that was repeated with reduced crew on the Hamburgs. A French-sourced single 100mm dual-purpose gun was located at either end, the forward mounting superfired by two quadruple Bofors AS rocket launchers, sited immediately forward of the bridge.

Although fast, bettering 30 knots in service, the Kölns were cramped and had no scope for the addition of a helicopter. With the new Bremen-class frigates entering service from 1982 (confusingly with some repeated names) the Kölns began to be retired. *Karlsruhe* and *Emden* were acquired by Turkey; *Augsburg* and *Lübeck* served into the 1990s. The MEKO frigates that superseded them began an entirely new trend.

LEFT: **Portland, Dorset, where** *Lübeck* **is seen pierside in company with a British Hecla-class survey ship, a gun-armed Leander and a distant Type 42. Portland long served as a working-up base for newly commissioned European-NATO warships.**

Köln class, as built

Displacement: 2,150 tons (standard); 2,620 tons (full load)
Length: 105m/344ft 3in (bp); 109.9m/360ft 4in (oa)
Beam: 10.8m/35ft 5in
Draught: 3.6m/11ft 6in
Armament: 2 x 100mm guns (2x1); 2 x 4-barrelled 375mm AS rocket launchers; 4 x 533mm torpedo tubes (4x1)
Machinery: 2 gas turbines, 4 diesels, 2 shafts
Power: 2 x 9,698kW/13,000bhp and 4 x 2,238kW/3,000bhp; maximum in CODAG combination; 28,348kW/38,000shp for 30 knots
Endurance: 330 tons fuel for 5,370km/2,900mm at 22 knots
Protection: Nominal
Complement: 210

GERMANY

LEFT: **Best described as corvettes, the five Thetis-class AS vessels were built at Bremen during 1961–63. All, including *Najade* seen here, carried the patrol-craft "P" flag superior. A funnel would appear unusual on a diesel-propelled craft of this size.** BELOW: **Designed for shallow-water anti-submarine operations, the *Najade* has a four-barrelled Bofors-type AS launcher on the foredeck and four sided heavy torpedo tubes, two of which are visible abaft the bridge structure.**

Thetis class

German waters are notable for their shallowness, limiting the size of ships intended to operate specifically within them. This is particularly true of the Baltic, something of a maritime backwater except that during the early 1960s, the Cold War was at its height. For the not-inconsiderable Soviet naval force based on Leningrad/Kronstadt, the Baltic exits represented the only route to the open sea, and control of the Belts separating the Danish islands could expect to be contested. Considerable numbers of German wooden-hulled minesweepers were under construction (these shallow waters being ideal for mining) but further, offensively armed, units were required to dispute the passage of hostile surface ships and submarines, and for the escort of friendly traffic. Surface-to-surface missiles (once available) and torpedoes were weapons of choice to counter the former, and would eventually be deployed on large numbers of steel- and later composite-hulled fast patrol boats. These, however, were still in the future when the Thetis class was built to address the shallow-water anti-submarine requirement.

As was usual at the time, all five were contracted with a single yard. Again, the design featured the flush-decked hull, full-width deck house and knuckled forward sections that were common to most types of German warships of the period. The flat bridge front was extended in some to provide additional space for the operations room.

No medium-calibre gun was carried. The foredeck was occupied by a quadruple Bofors AS rocket launcher. Four single, heavyweight torpedo tubes were sided abaft the main superstructure, while either depth charges or mines could be accommodated aft. Defensive armament was limited to a twin 40mm mounting, located aft with its control system.

Useful as multi-purpose ships in peacetime, the Thetis class served through to the 1990s.

ABOVE: **Rather late in her career, *Triton* has been renumbered for patrol craft duties. She retains the twin 40mm mountings in the elevated aft position, but has landed her torpedo tubes. Note the broad, flat hull form.**

Thetis class

Displacement: 575 tons (standard); 660 tons (full load)
Length: 65.5m/214ft 9in (bp); 69.8m/228ft 10in (oa)
Beam: 8.2m/26ft 22in
Draught: 2.7m/8ft 10in
Armament: 2 x 40mm guns (1x2); 1 x Bofors 375mm quadruple AS rocket launcher; 4 x 533mm torpedo tubes (4x1)
Machinery: 2 diesel engines, 2 shafts
Power: 5,073kW/6,800bhp for 23.5 knots
Endurance: 78 tons oil for 5,090km/2,750nm at 15 knots
Protection: Nominal
Complement: 48

239

Bremen class

Known officially as Type 122s when built, but Type 122As since modernization, the Bremen resulted from a co-operative venture with the Dutch, the latter building the Kortenaer in parallel. While there are external similarities, the Bremens differ in their masting, notably with the lofty "Eiffel Tower" construction in place of the Kortenaers' rather bare pole mainmast. Dutch ancestry is evident also in the flush-decked hull, with its long, double-curvature sheer, where succeeding German design favours a raised forecastle, having adequate freeboard with little or no sheer.

The Bremens are of orthodox layout, with distinct gaps between the three (i.e. bridge, funnel-mainmast and hangar) superstructure blocks. Forward of the bridge is a single OTO-Melara 76mm gun, superfired by the rectangular NATO Sea Sparrow SAM launcher. Prominent atop the bridge are the WM-25 and optical/infra-red fire control system. Immediately abaft the bridge block, two quadruple Harpoon SSM launchers are aligned athwartships.

Where the Kortenaer are all-gas-turbine propelled, the Bremen cruise on diesel engines. The Dutch have Rolls-Royce gas turbines, the Germans Fiat-built American LM 2500s.

Together with a full updating of electronics, the 1990s modernizations saw two fast-reaction RAM (Rolling Airframe Missile) point-defence launchers added to the corners of the hangar roof, the space shared with the low structure supporting the air-search radar antenna. Conspicuous, the full-width hangar is configured for a pair of Super Lynx helicopters. Their airborne "dunking" sonars are complemented by a large,

LEFT: **Except for their masting, the Bremens closely resemble the Dutch Kortenaers, built as a cooperative venture. Unlike earlier classes, the Type 122/Bremens stemmed from five different yards. This photograph is of the nameship.**

ABOVE: **A later addition to *Lübeck*'s armament was the two 21-cell RAM launchers prominent atop the hangar. The slightly longer-ranged Sea Sparrow is seen forward, and one of two quadruple Harpoon launchers abaft the bridge structure.**

low-frequency unit at the ships' forefoot. There is also, reportedly, a mine-detecting sonar capability.

To the helicopters' AS torpedoes can be added those from four, fixed 324mm tubes aboard the ships.

No further modernization being considered practical, the Bremens will be retired from 2010.

Type 122A

Displacement: 2,950 tons (standard); 3,800 tons (full load)
Length: 121.8m/399ft 4in (wl); 130m/426ft 3in (oa)
Beam: 14.4m/47ft 3in
Draught: 4.3m/14ft 1in
Armament: 1 x 76mm gun; 8 x Harpoon SSM launchers (2x4); 1 x 8-cell launcher for Sea Sparrow SAM; 2 x 21-round RAM launchers; 4 x 324mm AS torpedo tubes
Machinery: 2 gas turbines, 2 diesels, 2 shafts
Power: 38,046kW/51,000shp or 8,206kW/11,000bhp for 30 knots
Endurance: 610 tons fuel for 10,555km/5,700nm at 17 knots
Protection: Nominal
Complement: 200

GERMANY

LEFT: *Schleswig-Holstein* (left) makes an interesting contrast with the rather smaller Spanish Knox-class *Estremadura* (centre) and an unidentified Perry-class frigate (right). The German's powerful shoulders and high freeboard are evident. ABOVE: *Brandenburg* shows her speed. Note how Sea Sparrow is now accommodated in a VLS forward, abaft the RAM launcher which superfires the gun.

Brandenburg class

The four Brandenburgs were designed in accordance with the MEKO principles developed by Blohm and Voss, whose yard led the construction consortium. MEKO (MEhrzweck KOmbination or, roughly, multi-purpose) see as many armament and electronics systems as possible modularized into discrete blocks which can, literally, be dropped into a ship's pre-wired system, being added or removed as required. Ships are thus delivered "for", but not necessarily "with", and can be, in theory at least, outfitted for specific missions.

An obvious drawback is that, with so much of the structure removable, the remaining hull requires to be rather more capacious, and compensated to maintain structural strength. Not surprisingly, therefore, the Brandenburgs, with much the same specification as the preceding Bremens, are of about 25 per cent greater displacement, and are proportionately more beamy to compensate for greater topweight and future growth.

The overall result is a ship which is not only structurally strong but, with its considerable depth, looks it. Freeboard is such that sheer is not required and, as a "stealth" measure, the hull has two gentle knuckles running along the greater part of the length.

The foredeck 76mm gun is superfired by one of the two RAM launchers. Between this and the bridge is a VLS with 16 Sea Sparrow SAM cells. Space is reserved to double this number.

Between the bridge block and the divided uptakes of the CODOG propulsion system are, surprisingly, four MM38 Exocet SSM launchers. A second RAM launcher is located atop the hangar roof, while two fixed AS torpedo tubes fire obliquely through apertures on either side of the hull at upper deck level. There are two Super Lynx helicopters.

Officially termed Type 123s, the Brandenburg are all named after German provinces, or *Länder*, with town/city names now apparently being reserved for smaller vessels such as corvettes.

LEFT: *Brandenburg*'s hull, built to MEKO principles, maintains its high freeboard over the greater part of its length, contrasting with the more traditional form of the Bremens (opposite). Note the torpedo tube aperture amidships.

Brandenburg class

Displacement: 3,600 tons (standard); 4,490 tons (full load)
Length: 126.9m/416ft 1in (bp); 138.9m/455ft 4in (oa)
Beam: 15.7m/51ft 6in
Draught: 4.4m/14ft 5in
Armament: 1 x 76mm gun; 4 x Exocet SSM launchers (4x1); 1 x VLS launcher for Sea Sparrow SAM; 2 x 21-round RAM launchers; 4 x 324mm AS torpedo tubes (2x2)
Machinery: 2 gas turbines, 2 diesels, 2 shafts
Power: 38,046kW/51,000shp or 8,206kW/11,000bhp 29.5 knots
Endurance: Over 7,410km/4,000nm at 18 knots
Protection: Nominal
Complement: 219

241

DIRECTORY OF FRIGATES

Sachsen class

Slightly larger than the Brandenburgs, the Type 124, or Sachsen, class share maximum commonality. Enclosed space has been gained by extending both bridge block and hangar to the deck edge. These now complement the subtly angled planes of the shell plating to give a very low radar return. To this end, the apertures for boats, torpedo tubes and accommodation ladders can be blanked off. The process is continued with the carefully configured "masts" supporting the advanced electronics which, for the first time, include three-dimensional, phased-array target designation and tracking radar with four-quadrant fixed antennas.

Although a 155mm modularized gun has been trial-fitted, a 76mm weapon is currently carried forward. Abaft it is the forward RAM mounting and a VLS with a mixed load-out of 24 Standard SM-2 and 32 Sea Sparrow SAMs. Amidships, the Sachsens have reverted to eight Harpoon SSMs. AS torpedo tubes have been tripled and are above deck.

Two Super Lynxes are currently carried, but the hangar is dimensioned to accept the larger NH-90 helicopter flown by the French and Italians.

The machinery layout has been considerably revised to a CODAG configuration, with two diesel engines but only one gas turbine. The diesels now account for about 30 per cent of total power and are used to supplement the gas turbine at maximum speed as well as for cruising.

Active fin stabilizers were fitted in the Brandenburgs, but the Sachsens use actively controlled rudders for the purpose. This is likely to lead to increased wear of steering mechanism and rudder bearings.

ABOVE LEFT: The sculpted form of the tower bearing the four faces of the APAR radar immediately identify a Sachsen, or Type 124, frigate. Unusually, the faces are orientated along the main axes rather than at 45 degrees. ABOVE: On diesels alone, the Sachsens can maintain 18 knots. The machinery configuration is CODAG, i.e. combined diesel and gas turbine. With the latter on-line in combination, 29 knots can be exceeded.

Probably another "first" for the Sachsens is the provision of dedicated accommodation for female crew members, a measure which, taken to its logical conclusion, will be a major contributor to the increase of warship size and, inevitably, expense.

German frigates work in four-ship squadrons but the fourth Sachsen (*Thüringen*) is yet to be ordered.

LEFT: In peacetime, port visits, naval occasions and generally "showing the flag" occupy a considerable part of a warship's schedule, and here *Hessen* is dressing overall. The light clearly shows the subtle planes of the hull plating.

Sachsen class

Displacement: 4,500 tons (standard); 5,690 tons (full load)
Length: 132.2m/433ft 3in (wl); 143m/468ft 10in (oa)
Beam: 16.7m/54ft 9in
Draught: 5m/16ft 4in
Armament: 1 x 76mm gun; 8 x Harpoon SSMs (2x4); 1 x VLS launcher for Standarad SM-2 and Sea Sparrow SAMs; 2 x 21-round RAM launchers; 6 x 324mm AS torpedo tubes (2x3)
Machinery: 1 gas turbine, 2 diesels, 2 shafts
Power: 23,500kW/31,500shp and 15,000kW/20,100bhp for 29.5 knots
Endurance: Over 7,360km/4,000nm at 18 knots
Protection: Nominal
Complement: 242

GERMANY

LEFT: The diesel-propelled *Braunschweig* has dispensed with a funnel, always a potential target for an IR seeker. Exhaust in early trials, however, has blackened the hull, resulting in a panel being painted black, as seen on the right.
BELOW: The class has adopted the Pool-type high holding power anchor. Although lighter, it is stowed low down and is not pocketed. Even in a calm sea, as shown here, it is the cause of spray formation. This, again, is *Braunschweig*.

Braunschweig class

Now firmly established as both a European and a NATO power, a united Germany is increasing its profile at a global level, her navy consequently undertaking more foreign deployments. Its large, capable, and very expensive frigates are its new capital ships, and there is room for smaller and simpler general-purpose vessels. The considerable flotillas of missile-armed fast patrol boats, built primarily to contest the Baltic exits have, with the relaxation of East–West tensions, lost much of their major role. The newest is also 25 years of age, old for a minor warship. Their replacements, not surprisingly, are light frigates/corvettes of considerably greater size and capability, a consequence of which has already been the reduction of the programme from a planned 15 units to just 5.

The early design favoured the flexibility of the MEKO concept but, on so small a scale, the weight penalty was excessive. The Braunschweig, or Type 130, hull is of long forecastle type, the low afterdeck forming a helipad large enough to handle a Lynx or NH-90, but with only basic facilities. Hangar space is provided only for two drone helicopters, used primarily in surveillance.

Seemingly unsettled in their choice of SSM, the Germans, having already deployed Exocet and Harpoon on their frigates, have specified the 100km/62-mile Saab RBS-15 for the Braunschweigs. Dynamically programmable, this weapon is virtually a cruise missile, and can be used in land attack against designated targets.

A 76mm gun and a pair of RAM launchers are common with larger ships, but, for propulsion, the Type 130s are all-diesel, with one engine on either shaft. There is no funnel, exhaust gases being sea water-cooled to reduce IR signature.

The data stream from the drone helicopters is fused with that from the shipboard electronics systems for target designation and guidance.

ABOVE: *Erfurt* is seen here fitting out alongside at her Emden builders. Although classed as corvettes, ships of this class are very capable. They can deploy a Lynx-sized helicopter but can hangar only two small drone machines.

Braunschweig class

Displacement: 1,690 tons (full load)
Length: 82.8m/271ft 6in (bp); 88.8m/290ft 11in (oa)
Beam: Not known
Draught: Not known
Armament: 1 x 76mm gun; 4/12 x Saab RBS-15 SSMs; 2 x 21-round RAM launchers
Machinery: 2 diesel engines, 2 shafts
Power: 14,920kW/20,000bhp for 26.5 knots
Endurance: Over 7,410km/4,000nm at 15 knots
Protection: Nominal
Complement: 65

243

Van Heemskerck/Kortenaer class

As already noted, the Kortenaer had a common ancestry with the German Bremens but differed visually, particularly in having a pole mainmast and a solid pyramid supporting the fire control radar atop the bridge. Both classes had gas turbine main machinery, but where the Bremens cruised on diesels, the Kortenaers used Tyne gas turbines, with the machinery arranged COGOG fashion.

The Dutch do not use the RAM point-defence system favoured by the Germans. Complementing the Sea Sparrow launcher in "B" position, the earlier Kortenaers had a second 76mm gun on the hangar roof. Later ships had light automatic weapons until Goalkeeper 30mm CIWS was acquired and fitted throughout the class. Eight Harpoon SSMs were located immediately abaft the bridge and four lightweight AS torpedo tubes could be shipped when required.

Two Lynx-sized helicopters could be accommodated in the full-width hangar, upon whose roof was located the conspicuous antenna of the long range air search radar.

Two of the ten Kortenaers were sold new to Greece in 1981 and were replaced by *Jacob van Heemskerck* and *Witte de With*, completed to a modified specification as guided-missile frigates, commissioning several years after the remainder of their near-sisters.

The van Heemskercks sacrificed their AS air component for a Standard SM-1 area defence SAM system, whose launcher is located atop the long, low superstructure that replaced the hangar. No 76mm gun is carried, while the Goalkeeper has been relocated right aft. In contrast with the standard Kortenaers, the stern is fully plated-in.

Between 1993 and 2002, the remaining eight Kortenaers were also acquired by Greece and a current rolling modernization programme seeks to extent their lives by 15 years. It was speculated that the two Heemskercks, retired early, would follow the remainder of the class, but they were acquired by Chile complete with Standard.

ABOVE LEFT: **The Kortenaers were of compact but pleasing appearance, dominated aft by a large, near full-width hangar, upon whose roof** *Abraham Crijnssen* **has a Goalkeeper CIWS. Harpoon is just visible forward of the funnel.** ABOVE: **Two Kortenaers were completed as Guided Missile Frigates. The Standard SM-1 MR magazine and launcher have here replaced the helicopter hangar and flight pad on** *Witte de With*. **She lacks a 76mm gun forward but has CIWS aft.**

LEFT: *Jacob van Heemskerck* **has a more complex electronics fit than a standard Kortenaer. The larger dishes forward and aft are for Standard SM-1 control, while the smaller dish on the "foremast" gives guidance for the adjacent Sea Sparrow.**

Kortenaer class, final specification

Displacement: 3,000 tons (standard); 3,785 tons (full load)
Length: 121.8m/399ft 4in (bp); 130.2m/426ft 10in (oa)
Beam: 14.4m/47ft 3in
Draught: 4.4m/14ft 5in
Armament: 1 x 76mm gun; 8 x Harpoon SSM launchers (2x4); 1 x 8-cell Sea Sparrow SAM launcher; 4 x 324mm AS torpedo tubes (2x2)
Machinery: 2 Olympus gas turbines, 2 Tyne cruise gas turbines, 2 shafts
Power: 38,494kW/51,600shp for 30 knots or 7,311kW/9,800shp for 20 knots
Endurance: 8,705km/4,700nm at 16 knots
Protection: Nominal
Complement: 200

NETHERLANDS

De Zeven Provinciën class

The gradual transfer of Kortenaers to Greece was offset by the construction of the six Karel Doorman general-purpose frigates and four larger Zeven Provinciëns, described as Air Defence and Command Frigates.
The latter were to have been another co-operative project with Germany, in this case joined by Spain. The latter partner withdrew, although the resulting four Alvaro de Bazan class obviously owe much to work already done, but are heavily influenced by American Aegis technology. Germany then pulled out, her four Sachsens being based on preferred MEKO principles. Where both classes have a recognizable common ancestry with the Dutch ships, the latter reflect current French practice.

The Zeven Provinciëns are of long forecastle design, but this is not immediately apparent as the extremities are linked by a continuous knuckle, whose elegant curve divides the slight outward flare of the hull plating from the inwardly inclined, and virtually unbroken, sides of the superstructure blocks. These signature-reducing measures are continued in every "vertical" surface, and particularly in the towers incorporating the APAR phased-array radar and SMART-L early warning radar, both products of Dutch technology.

Somewhat hindered in depression by an inclined forward bulwark, the gun has been upgraded to a 127mm OTO-Melara weapon, abaft which are the flush-fitting covers of a 40-cell Vertical Launch System (VLS), designed for mixed load-outs of Standard SM-2 and Improved Sea Sparrow SAMs.

Equally unobtrusive are the eight Harpoon SSMs, concealed amidships behind inclined panels. One Goalkeeper CIWS is located over the bridge, another aft on the hangar roof.

Paired AS torpedo tubes fire through small apertures in the shell plating immediately forward of the hangar,

LEFT: **The distinctive faceted tower housing the APAR three-dimensional, phased-array, target designation and tracking radar dominates *Tromp*'s profile. Abaft the 127mm gun she is fitted with a 40-cell VLS.**

ABOVE LEFT: **Frigate designers are currently suffering from a bad attack of "radar invisibility", resulting in ships of closely similar appearance. Although a trifle bland, *de Zeven Provinciën*'s sharply sculpted form is still quite pleasing.** ABOVE: **A study in shapes: in the foreground, the elegant lines of the US Aegis cruiser *Normandy* framing the Dutch *Evertsen*, and beyond, a Danish Niels Juel corvette. The inclined black rectangle of *Evertsen*'s SMART-L radar also appears on British Darings.**

which is dimensioned to accommodate a single NH-90 helicopter.

Propulsion is of CODAG configuration, the ships cruising on diesels but using a pair of Spey gas turbines for high speed.

De Zeven Provinciën class

Displacement: 5,870 tons (standard); 6,050 tons (full load)
Length: 130.2m/426ft 11in (bp); 144.2m/472ft 11in (oa)
Beam: 17.2m/56ft 4in
Draught: 5.2m/17ft 1in
Armament: 1 x 127mm gun; 8 x Harpoon SSM launchers (2x4); 1 x 40-cell VLS for Standard SM-2 and Improved Sea Sparrow SAMs; 2 x 30mm Goalkeeper CIWS; 4 x 324mm AS torpedo tubes (2x2)
Machinery: 2 gas turbines, 2 diesels, 2 shafts
Power: 39,000kW/52,280shp for 30 knots or 8,400kW/11,260bhp for 19 knots
Endurance: 9,260km/5,000nm at 18 knots
Protection: Nominal
Complement: 202

Karel Doorman class

Representing the "Lo" end of the "Hi-Lo" frigate force were the eight so-called "M"-class ships, effectively scaled-down Kortenaers. In service, they adopted the name of the lead ship. As in the UK, government policy is to reduce naval strength while having to recognize that the rump of a great shipbuilding industry no longer has work sufficient to justify its existence. The Ms, therefore, were ordered ahead of schedule, which served only to accelerate the disposal of the Kortenaers in compensation. At the time of writing, the Ms – the latest just 13 years in service – are themselves slated for transfer abroad.

Pre-dating the more capable de Zeven Provinciën class by some years, the Doormans lack the extreme profiling adopted to reduce radar and IR signatures. The hull has a gentle knuckle, running the greater part of its length, but the superstructure, despite its "vertical" surfaces being slightly inclined, remains conventional in layout.

The solidly plated mast is unusually tall, and is flanked by two prominent radomes for SATCOM antennas. There is a 76mm gun forward and, abaft the funnel, space for two quadruple Harpoon SSMs, rarely carried. Within the after superstructure are two pairs of lightweight AS torpedo tubes.

The hangar is dimensioned for only one Lynx-sized helicopter as it is flanked by eight Sea Sparrow launcher cells on either side. There is no capacity for Standard SM-2 missiles. This after superstructure is dominant, bearing on its roof the large standard antenna of the Dutch-built LW-08 early warning radar and, on its starboard after corner, a single Goalkeeper CIWS, again not always fitted. Later units can deploy towed array passive sonars.

Currently, two of the class are to be transferred to each of Belgium, Chile and Portugal. The remaining pair will undoubtedly follow.

ABOVE: Originally termed M-class frigates, the Karel Doormans have an unusual Sea Sparrow SAM arrangement, 16 missiles being located in pairs on the port side of the hangar. *Van Amstel* has hers partly concealed by a radar-reflecting panel.

LEFT: Only 12 years of age, *Abraham van der Hulst* was one of two M-class ships sold to Chile in 2004. Unchanged except for modified helicopter arrangements, she is seen here en route to a new career in South America as the *Almirante Blanco Encalada*.

Karel Doorman class

Displacement: 2,800 tons (standard); 3,320 tons (full load)
Length: 114.4m/375ft 1in (bp); 122.2m/400ft 9in (oa)
Beam: 13.1m/43ft
Draught: 4.3m/14ft 1in
Armament: 1 x 76mm gun; 8 x Harpoon SSM launchers (2x4); 2 x 8-cell VLS launchers for Improved Sea Sparrow SAM; 1 x 30mm Goalkeeper CIWS; 4 x 324mm AS torpedo tubes (2x2)
Machinery: 2 gas turbines, 2 diesels, 2 shafts
Power: 36,000kW/48,257shp for 29 knots or 6,300kW/8,450bhp for 21 knots
Endurance: Over 9,260km/5,000nm at 18 knots
Protection: Nominal
Complement: 154

NETHERLANDS/CANADA

St. Laurent class

ABOVE LEFT: *Fraser* shows something of the St. Laurents' magnificent seakeeping qualities in a short Atlantic swell. Her 3in gun mounting is trained aft to minimize water ingress. She was remodelled in the early 1980s to operate a large AS helicopter. ABOVE: *Terra Nova* of the Restigouche group has retained much of her original configuration, but with an ASROC (not visible here) replacing one of her Limbo mortars. Note the unusually lofty mast and the anchor pocket shuttered to reduce spray formation.

This extended class of 20 frigates replaced the last of the war-built anti-submarine force. Their enclosed design emphasized operations in hostile northern waters and low temperatures. The hull was flush-decked and of high freeboard, the after end encompassing a long, open well containing two Limbo mortars and, with later modernization, a VDS. Except in way of the full-width deckhouse under the bridge, the sheerstrake was radiused over the entire length of the ship. Most of the anchor gear was located below the forecastle deck, clear of ice formation. The anchors themselves were recessed into pockets, with covers to reduce spray formation and further ice accretion. As this can add dangerously to topweight, this may have influenced the decision to construct the superstructure mainly in aluminium alloy.

As designed, the ships mounted two 3in 50 mountings, but the after one was landed during later modifications. The forward mounting was situated on a low, raised platform, behind a breakwater.

The extended timescale, with construction shared between six yards, saw modifications introduced to the extent that few ships were alike, and these quickly changed with further updates during their long careers.

In the original Limbo-armed version there was a single, tapered funnel and a short, plated-in mast with lattice extensions. Some later landed one Limbo, along with the after gun mounting, in order to accommodate an 8-cell ASROC launcher amidships. Half the class lost both Limbos, the well being covered with an elevated flight pad for a single Sea King helicopter. The provision of its amidships hangar required the uptakes to be split, with a separate casing on either side. To the helicopter's "dunking" sonar and AS torpedoes, the ship added VDS and six AS torpedo tubes.

The ships proved to be remarkably durable, most serving into the 1990s.

ABOVE: Following her 1980s DELEX modernization, *Restigouche* has acquired a reloadable ASROC installation. Most of her Limbo well has been plated-over, but her stern has been modified to accept a large American VDS. During their long careers, the ships acquired many individual characteristics.

St. Laurent class, as designed

Displacement: 2,260 tons (standard); 2,800 tons (full load)
Length: 111.6m/366ft (oa)
Beam: 12.8m/42ft
Draught: 4m/13ft 3in
Armament: 4 x 3in guns (2x2); 2 x Limbo 3-barrelled AS mortars
Machinery: Geared steam turbines, 2 boilers, 2 shafts
Power: 22,380kW/30,000shp for 28.5 knots
Endurance: 8,800km/4,750nm at 14 knots
Protection: None
Complement: 230

247

DIRECTORY OF FRIGATES

LEFT: Very considerably modernized during the early 1990s, the Iroquois class emerged as capable ships. *Algonquin*'s VLS, visible forward of the 76mm gun, is configured for Standard SM-2 SAMs. CIWS is atop the hangar and AS torpedo tubes are abreast the flight pad.
BELOW: The Halifax class is fitted with a Bofors 57mm gun forward. Visible abreast of the funnel of *Charlottetown* is the port side, vertical-launch Sea Sparrow installation, obscuring the Harpoon launchers.

Iroquois and Halifax classes

Carrying some of the "Tribal" names made famous during World War II, the four Iroquois of the early 1970s introduced gas turbine propulsion to the Royal Canadian Navy. Considerably larger than the St. Laurents, more heavily armed and with some command facilities, they were classed as destroyers, although still primarily AS vessels.

Their dimensions were driven by the then-bold decision to accommodate two large, Sea King-sized helicopters. Hulls were sufficiently spacious to install a passive anti-rolling system, effective at low speeds when there is inadequate flow over active stabilizing fins.

During the 1990s they were considerably updated. In place of the 5in gun appeared a recessed VLS, accommodating 29 Standard SM-2 SAMs, superfired by a 76mm OTO-Melara weapon. Cruising gas turbines were upgraded and the split exhaust casings replaced by a single large funnel. A Vulcan Phalanx CIWS was installed atop the hangar and a VDS aft.

Meanwhile, the 12-strong Halifax class was built to replace the aging St. Laurents. Despite their "frigate" label, they carry only one helicopter but are as large, and virtually as fast, as the Iroquois. They also carry Harpoon SSMs and, given small differences in layout, are comparable with the Royal Navy's Type 23s.

For improved physical protection, the Harpoons are located immediately forward of the hangar, while the VLS for the Sea Sparrow SAMs is a split, above-deck installation, flanking the enormous funnel, screened by a reflective panel.

The main propulsion units have been changed from the Iroquois' Pratt & Whitneys to the more widely used General Electric LM-2500 while, in CODOG configuration, a medium-speed diesel is used for cruising. Despite budget cuts, the class is due for thorough upgrading, including the addition of a Dutch-sourced three-dimensional search radar and an active/passive towed array sonar.

Halifax class, as built

Displacement: 4,300 tons (standard); 4,760 tons (full load)
Length: 124.5m/408ft 2in (bp); 135.5m/444ft 3in (oa)
Beam: 14.8m/48ft 6in
Draught: 4.9m/16ft 1in
Armament: 1 x 57mm gun; 8 x Harpoon SSM launchers (2x4); 2 x 8-cell VLS for Sea Sparrow SAM; 1 x Vulcan Phalanx CIWS; 4 x 324mm AS torpedo tubes (2x2)
Machinery: 2 gas turbines, 1 diesel, 2 shafts
Power: 35,435kW/47,500shp for 29 plus knots or 6,472kW/8,675shp for 18 knots
Endurance: 550 tons fuel for 8,335km/4,500nm at 20 knots
Protection: Nominal
Complement: 224

248

CANADA/AUSTRALIA/NEW ZEALAND

LEFT: **Nameship of an eight-strong class, *Anzac* is seen off a Gulf oil terminal, her MEKO 200 origin clearly recognizable. She is fitted with two quadruple Harpoon SSM forward and abaft the funnels, a VLS for Sea Sparrow.** ABOVE: ***Anzac* again, this time leaving Portsmouth, England, without Harpoon and the Vulcan Phalanx CIWS on the hangar roof. Electronics are a Franco-British/German/Swedish/American mix.**

Anzac class

Previously dependent upon British and American designs, Australia and New Zealand turned to Germany for the Anzacs. These were intended to replace both Adams-class destroyers and River-class (i.e. modified Type 12/Leander) frigates, two very different types of ship. Their role could be high-risk as part of a multinational force, or low-risk in policing very long coastlines and large areas of ocean. Although Australia currently faces no obvious external threat, she is increasingly prepared to shoulder the responsibilities of regional power.

Short-listed for consideration were the German MEKO 200 (of which three had been recently and fortuitously completed for Portugal), the Dutch Karel Doorman and the "Yarrow frigate". The first-named won because of its "for, but not with" design, making it capable of being fitted for specific missions. Australia contracted for eight units, with New Zealand opting for just a pair. All were Australian-built.

On a more limited scale, the Anzacs follow the general MEKO principles featured above in the Germany section. It is worth remembering that a module for, say, a 5in 54 gun is as large for a 3,300-tonner as it is for a ship of 5,700 tons.

As delivered, the ships for both navies were similarly equipped. Forward is a 5in gun, abaft the split funnel an 8-cell VLS for Sea Sparrow SAMs. For these, space is allocated for a second 8-cell block. Margins are also provided for both eight Harpoon SSMs and a Vulcan Phalanx CIWS. Only the New Zealanders currently carry the latter.

All carry an American Super Sea Sprite LAMPS helicopter but, currently, no AS torpedo tubes. For economy, only one LM-2500 gas turbine is fitted for boost, limiting maximum speed to about 27 knots.

ABOVE: **Australian-built in the same series were two near-identical Anzacs for New Zealand. This is *Te Kaha*, with NATO-series numbering, in contrast to the Australian's US Navy style.**

Anzac class, with full planned outfit

Displacement: 3,250 tons (standard); 3,550 tons (full load)
Length: 109.5m/359ft (bp); 117.5m/385ft 3in (oa)
Beam: 13.8m/45ft 3in
Draught: 4.2m/13ft 9in
Armament: 1 x 5in gun; 8 x Harpoon SSMs (2x4); 1 x 8-cell VLS for Imp. Sea Sparrow; 1 x Vulcan Phalanx CIWS; 6 x 324mm AS torpedo tubes (2x3)
Machinery: 1 gas turbine, 2 diesels, 2 shafts
Power: 22,500kW/30,160shp for over 27 knots or 6,600kW/8,847bhp for 20 knots
Endurance: 423 tons fuel for 11,040km/6,000nm at 18 knots
Protection: Nominal
Complement: 148

PART TWO:
SUBMARINES

IMAGE: **The** *Los Angeles,* leader of the largest class of SSNs produced by the US Navy.

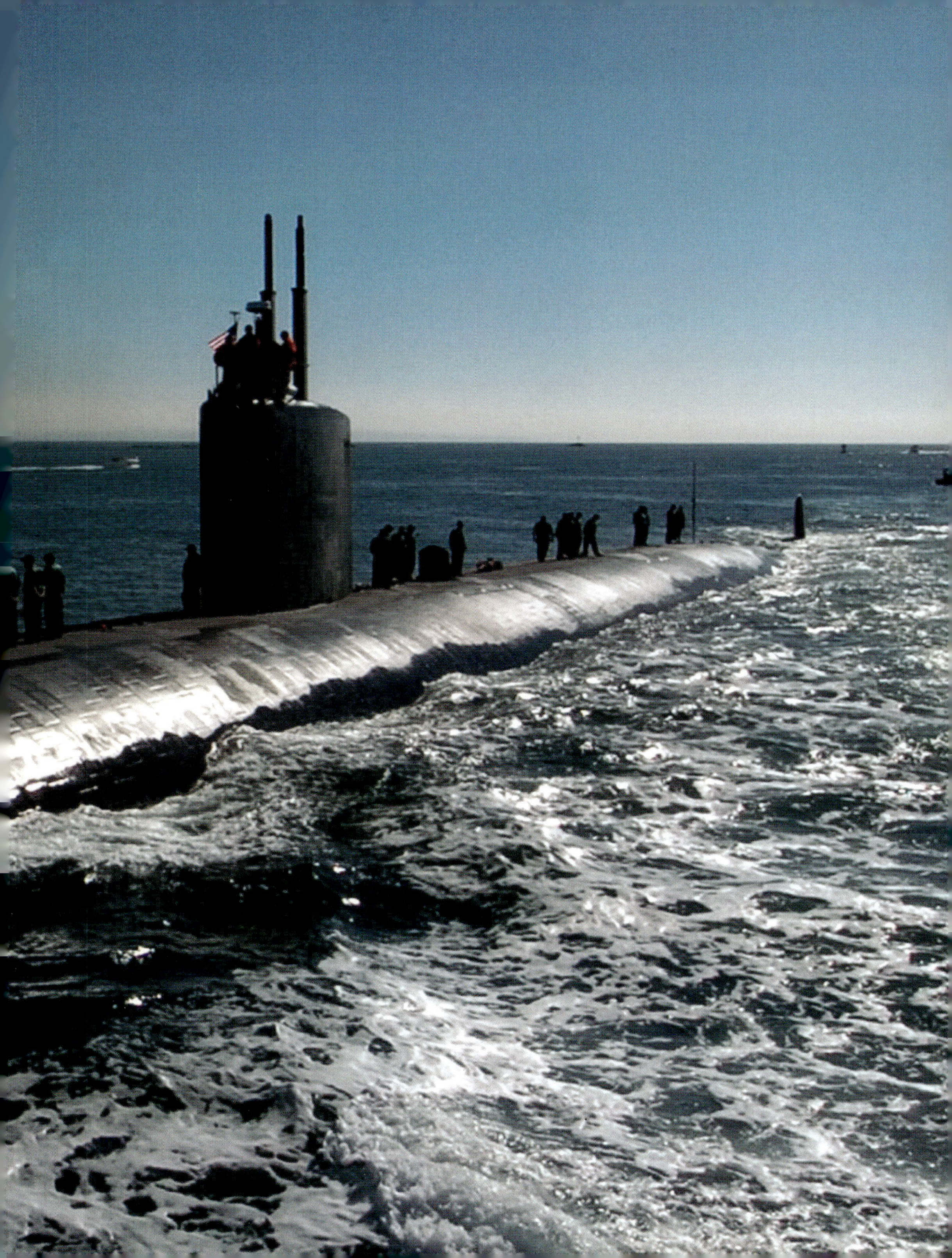

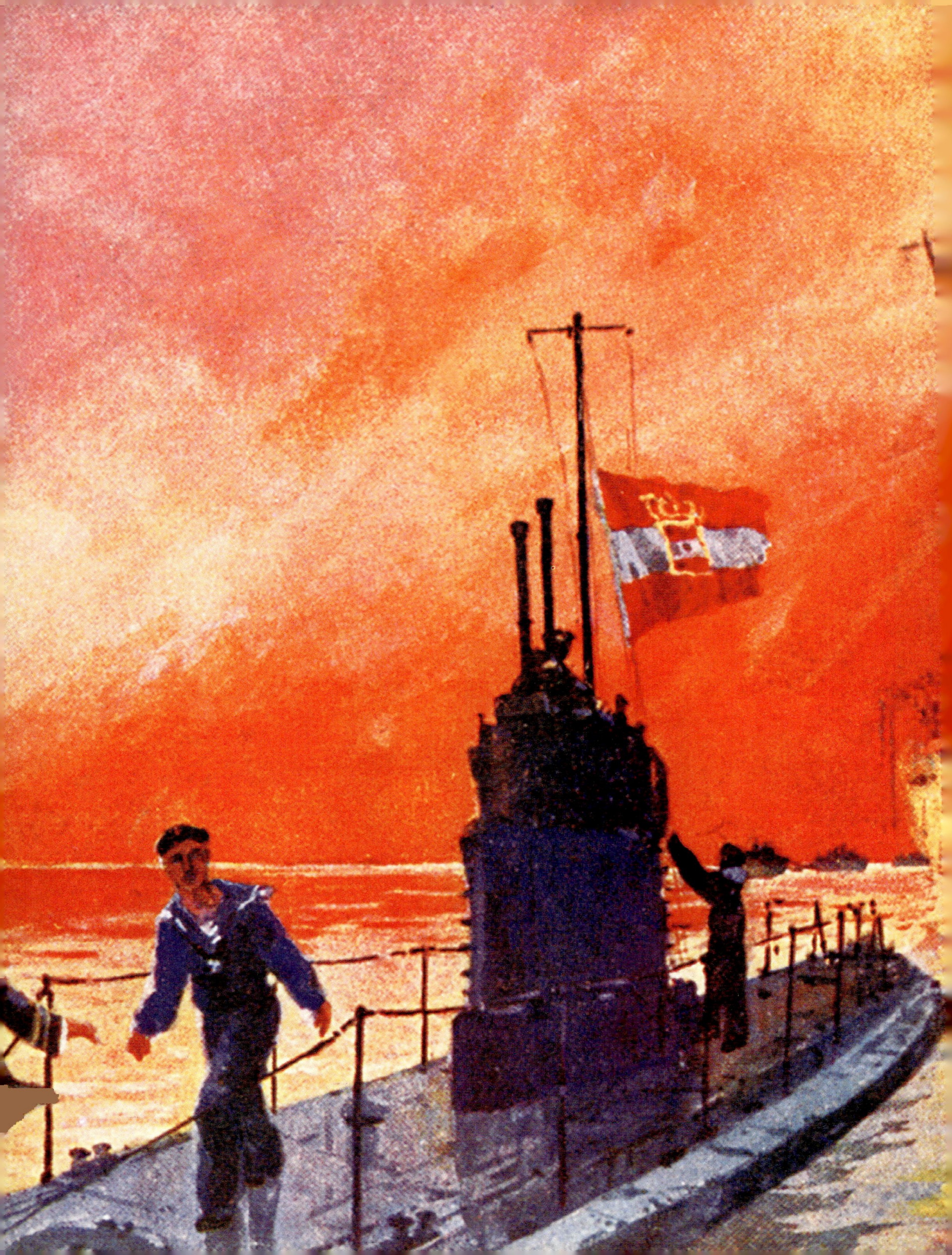

The History of Submarines

Submariners will say that, notwithstanding the risks, there is a certain romanticism connected with submarines. After years of trial, error and often fatal attraction, a handful of men emerged in the late 1800s who were clearly making progress towards the realization of the dream, often in the face of adversity and controversy. Traditionalists among the naval hierarchies of several nations – including Britain – fought a bitter struggle to have the submarine banned, but gradually the experimental vessels produced by men such as J.P. Holland and Simon Lake began to show remarkable promise, in spite of the volatile nature and foul conditions inside the boats.

Winston Churchill described submarine development as the most dangerous of all occupations: "Of all the branches of men in the forces there is none which shows more devotion and faces grimmer perils than the submariners." Yet emerging submarine services of nations around the world never lacked volunteers. Indeed, as will be seen, this book tells a very human story, highlighting some of the outstanding events from the very early days to the present, with many tales of courage, drama and quite astounding invention.

LEFT: **In the line of fire: the assassination of Archduke Franz Ferdinand of Austria sent that nation's U-boats, along with those of Germany, into the first major conflict involving submarines, depicted here against a French merchant ship.**

THE HISTORY OF SUBMARINES

LEFT: **The Confederates' *Hunley*, which sank four times during trials, twice killing all her crew. She was raised each time and sent back into commission, and on her fifth voyage torpedoed and sank the Union warship *Housatonic* off South Carolina, but in doing so went to the bottom with her victim.** BELOW: **David Bushnell's *Turtle* which moved perfectly and with amazing accuracy but failed in its attempts to attach a mine to British ships in New York harbour in 1776. He had more success with his "drifting" mines which harassed the British fleet.**

Trial and error: the pioneers

Through the ages, inventors and sailors alike sought to find the technology that would allow the construction of boats that could travel under water. Since Alexander the Great was lowered to the bottom of the sea in a glass barrel in 337BC, attempts at such endeavour failed to make any progress until the 16th century. Then, in 1578, the principles of creating a truly submersible craft appeared in the writings of Englishman William Bourne and, although he never actually built one, his ideas were pursued by others.

Among them was Dutch scientist Cornelius Drebbel, who was best known at the time for his perpetual-motion machine, a golden globe mounted on pillars which told the time, date and season. By 1620, his work having attracted the interest of dignitaries across Europe, he began work on designs for his submarine. It was a simple construction akin to a rowing boat with raised sides, made water-tight with a greased leather covering and propelled by four oarsmen. A larger model was later demonstrated to King James I, who was reportedly given a submerged trip along the Thames from Westminster to Greenwich.

The fascination with underwater travel gripped the imagination of the inventors, but naval commanders showed little enthusiasm until the American War of Independence (1775–83), when a young Yale graduate named David Bushnell designed a one-man submarine, which he called *Turtle*. Built from wood in the shape of an egg, his machine was powered by a hand-cranked propeller. Its sole purpose was to damage the British fleet during its blockade of New York harbour in 1776.

The next step forward came in 1800, when Robert Fulton, a brilliant American artist and inventor, of quite recent Irish descent, built the *Nautilus*, a copper-covered submersible with a collapsible sail. Born in Little Britain township (now Fulton), Pennsylvania, he went to England as a young man to study painting. His thoughts quickly turned from art to draughtsmanship, concentrating on canal navigation and, eventually, submersible boats. In 1796 he travelled to France where, in due course, Napoleon commissioned Fulton to build his submarine, 6.4m/21ft long and shaped like a bullet. Fulton and three mechanics descended to a depth of 7.5m/24ft 7in, and later he added a detachable mine to demonstrate his theory of carrying out clandestine attacks on surface ships. The latter part of the equation failed and Napoleon lost interest. Fulton returned to England and managed to bring his invention to the attention of the British government but the Admiralty rejected his plans with a damning condemnation of submarines that was to remain their policy for the remainder of the 19th century. Back in the

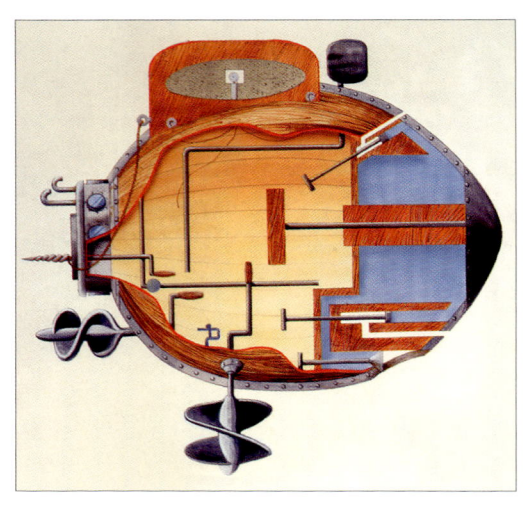

TRIAL AND ERROR: THE PIONEERS

United States, he enjoyed success with steam-powered navigation, and was still working on a new version of his submarine when he died in 1815.

Other attempts at submarine construction met with modest success, including that of a former Germany artillery sergeant, Wilhelm Bauer. He was sponsored to build a submarine, which he called *Fire Diver*, in 1850, but it sank after only two outings. The German Navy was quietly pleased, although Bauer did eventually build an ambitious 16m/52ft 6in submarine for the Imperial Russian Navy, which was known to have completed at least 120 successful dives.

The historical turning point came during the American Civil War (1861–65) when the Confederacy used the first true submarine to sink an enemy ship in war. It was a massive cigar-shaped boat, 18.25m/59ft 11in in length. Named the *Hunley* after one of the three designers who drew up the blueprint for the Confederates' secret weapon, the boat was powered, when submerged, by a manual crankshaft requiring eight members of the crew to propel it at six knots. During trials, the *Hunley* sank four times, twice killing all her crew. Even so, she was raised and sent back into commission. On her fifth journey in 1864, she carried a torpedo to sink the Union warship *Housatonic* off the coast of South Carolina but, in doing so, went to the bottom with her victim. All aboard perished.

The Union, meanwhile, had less success. What is now officially classed as the American Navy's first submarine, USS *Alligator* was designed and built by French diver and inventor Brutus de Villeroi in 1861. Fabricated from riveted iron plates and originally powered by a system of oars, *Alligator* was constructed and tested at Philadelphia on the Delaware River. Later, a hand-cranked screw propeller was added but while being towed to launch an attack on Charleston Harbour in April 1863, the *Alligator* sank somewhere off Cape Hatteras, North Carolina.

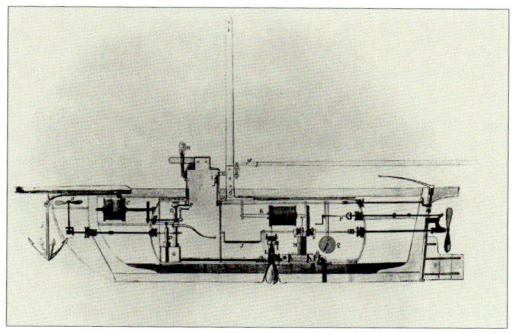

TOP: **CSS *David*, a cigar-shaped 15.2m/50ft steam torpedo boat built at Charleston, South Carolina, in 1863 by David C. Ebaugh, was used by the Confederates in a daring attack on Federal ships in 1863.** ABOVE: **A copy of the original blueprint of H.L. Hunley's submarine, which became the first in history to sink a ship.** BELOW LEFT: **The *Pioneer*, a successful hand-cranked submarine built by two wealthy New Orleans engineers in 1862 for the Confederates, but sunk by them to prevent it falling into enemy hands.** BELOW: **Partially submerged incendiary and gun ships attracted the attention of inventors in the 19th century, and this one, designed by Scottish engineer James Nasmyth in 1853, was described as an anti-invasion floating mortar.**

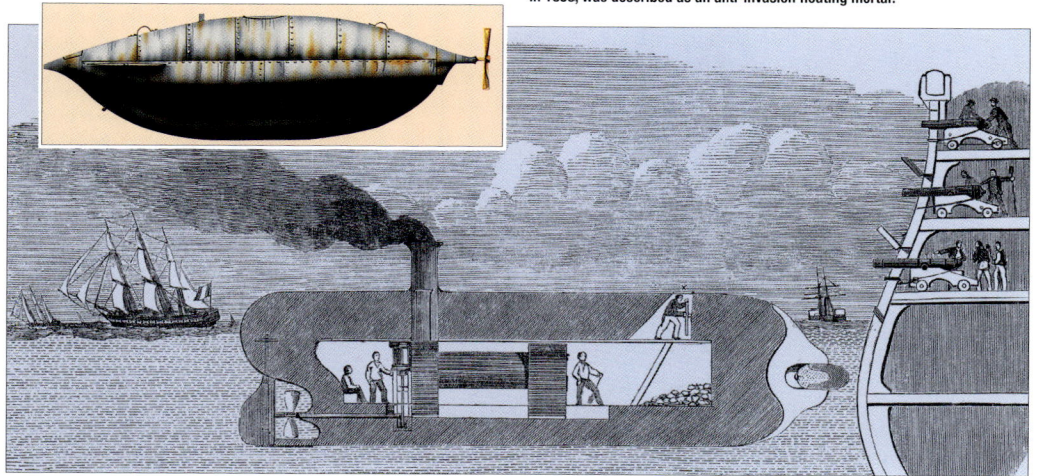

255

Closer to the goal

Early setbacks did not deter a worldwide search for a successful design that overcame the most difficult challenge of all, which was to find a workable means of propulsion under water. Another experimental American project involved a boat called the *Intelligent Whale*, a hand-cranked submarine that could stay submerged for ten hours. This was built on the design of Scovel S. Meriam in 1863 by Augustus Price and Cornelius S. Bushnell. The American Submarine Co. was formed to take over production, but this interesting project became bogged down by years of litigation as to who actually owned the rights. When title was established, the *Intelligent Whale* was bought by the US Navy and subsequently abandoned after unreliable trials, eventually being consigned to the Navy Museum, Washington, D.C.

That these difficulties would eventually be overcome was foreshadowed by the appearance in 1870 of the latest novel by Jules Verne, *Twenty Thousand Leagues under the Sea*, the story of Captain Nemo who cruises beneath the oceans in a submarine. It was the inspiration for the Reverend George Garrett, a determined young scholar who had followed his father into the Church but had his heart set on other things. After an education that took him to Trinity College, Cambridge, his interest in mechanical science consumed him. At the age of 26, he produced detailed plans for a bullet-shaped submarine he called *Resurgam* ("rise again"). He raised more than £1,500 and had the submarine built on the banks of the Mersey.

Garrett decided to sail the submarine around the coast to Portsmouth for the ceremonial Spithead Review and set off on December, 10, 1879, with *Resurgam* under tow, crewed by two men while Garrett directed operations from the yacht. The submarine was powered by a coal-fired, single-cylinder steam engine for surface travel, which had to be shut down shortly before the submarine submerged. In theory, residual heat from the engine would keep the vessel under way for about an hour before the need to surface again. It was a dangerous and overpowering contraption, giving off strong carbon monoxide fumes. The crew avoided death from poisoning by wearing a breathing device Garrett himself had invented, although this was not entirely efficient, and lighting was by candles in a craft virtually devoid of instruments.

On February 25, 1880, after a break in the journey at Rhyl, *Resurgam* set off again under tow behind the steam yacht. The weather took a turn for the worse with a heavy swell, and the hawser connecting the yacht to the submarine suddenly went slack. *Resurgam* had gone to the bottom and efforts to find her were unsuccessful. The submarine was to remain undiscovered for more than a century. As for Garrett, he never did get to give the British Navy a demonstration, although a second submarine designed by him and of sleek, revolutionary design did achieve attention.

ABOVE: The *Intelligent Whale*, a hand-cranked submarine built by Augustus Price and Cornelius S. Bushnell in 1862, was eventually sold to the US Navy, subject to the completion of successful trials. However, the first trial failed to impress naval engineers and the project was abandoned without further payment. LEFT: *Resurgam*, the coal-fired and steam-powered submarine built by the Reverend George Garrett in 1879, was originally designed to penetrate the chain netting placed around ships' hulls to defend against attack by torpedo vessels.

LEFT: **Simon Lake, one of America's first pioneers of submarine development, produced this early boat, *Protector*, in 1901, but it was rejected by the US Navy and sold to Russia in 1904.**

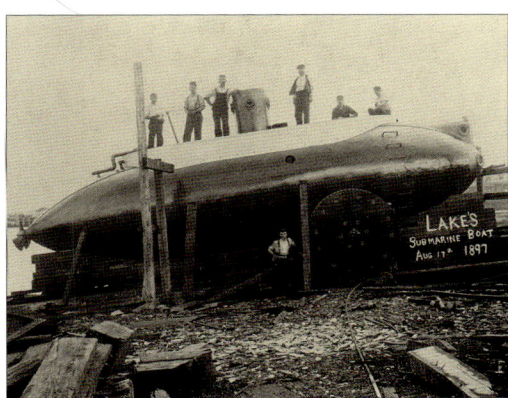

ABOVE RIGHT: **The spacious interior of Simon Lake's first submarine, *Argonaut*, built in 1895 with innovative design features including the ability to stay submerged for 24 hours.** LEFT: **The distinctive wheels of *Argonaut*, added for bottom crawling, and a diver's air-lock hatch, are clearly visible.** BELOW: **Flying the flag, but *Argonaut* was rejected by the US Navy in favour of the *Holland* and Lake began designing submarines for the Austro-Hungarian Navy, although he subsequently built 24 boats for the US Navy during and after World War I.**

Named the *Nordenfelt*, two were built, one in Stockholm and a second at Barrow-in-Furness. Turkey bought the first and awarded Garrett the title of Pasha Garrett. The second, an incredible 36.75m/120ft 7in long and displacing 230 tonnes/226 tons, sank during the delivery voyage to Russia. Garrett, dismayed at his lack of success, emigrated to America to become a farmer, went bankrupt, and ended up in the US army. In 1995 trawlerman Dennis Hunt was fishing off Rhyl when his nets became snagged. A diver friend, Keith Hurley, came out to free his nets and became the first person to lay eyes on *Resurgam* since February 1880.

Back in America towards the end of the 19th century, Simon Lake, a name now synonymous with submarine development in the US, came to the fore – also carrying a copy of Jules Verne's novel under his arm. Lake was born in Pleasantville, New Jersey in 1866, the son of Christopher J. Lake, whose father was the Honourable Simon Lake, one of the founders of Atlantic City. Simon began work at his father's foundry and machine shop in New Jersey, and the prototype *Argonaut Junior*, constructed in wood, was successfully demonstrated.

The success led to the formation of the Lake Submarine Company of New Jersey in 1895, which built the *Argonaut*, the first submarine to operate successfully in the open sea in 1898, and which subsequently drew a congratulatory telegram from Jules Verne.

Even so, Russia – not America – gave Simon Lake his first contract to built submarines. The US Navy ran a competition for best design for a revolutionary new submarine. Simon Lake came second, and was snapped up by the Tsar's Royal Navy, moving temporarily to St Petersburg to begin production. The Americans – followed soon afterwards by the British – chose to award their contract to Lake's closest rival, the Irish-American inventor J.P. Holland, who became the primary figure in the next stage of the development of the submarine.

257

Underway in the Hollands

When Irish-American pioneer John Philip Holland (1841–1914) won the American competition for submarine designs, the British Royal Navy at last began to take a real interest, given that France, Germany, Russia and Italy were all entering the field. It was Holland's version that became the model for the first submarines to be built for the fleets of both Britain and America, which was rather ironic. Holland was born in County Clare, Ireland, where he joined a religious order in Cork at the age of 17, but other ideas distracted him from a spiritual calling, and he began to draw sketches of submersible boats. He left the order to join the exodus to America, and in 1873 submitted his drawings to the US Navy, which rejected them. However, the American branch of the Irish patriots, the Fenian Society, heard about Holland's work and gave him $6,000 to build two submarines, which they planned to use against the British Navy.

The Fenian brotherhood was founded in New York by veterans of the 1848 Irish uprising to raise funds for the recruitment and training of exiles to fight the British for Irish independence. Holland, desperate for funds, was not in the least restrained by the possibility that his boats might be turned on British shipping because he, too, harboured strong anti-British feelings.

His first submarine was tested with mixed results in the Passaic River in 1878. She sank on her first outing because of loose-fitting plugs and had to be hauled back from the seabed. Holland himself took the controls on his second trip, and it was a successful run, although still leaky. His second submarine, *Fenian Ram*, was launched in 1881. Powered by one of the earliest internal-combustion engines, the boat was 9.5m/31ft 2in long and displaced 19 tonnes/18.7 tons. She went through a series of successful trials in the lower Hudson River and became the subject of close scrutiny by British spies, aware

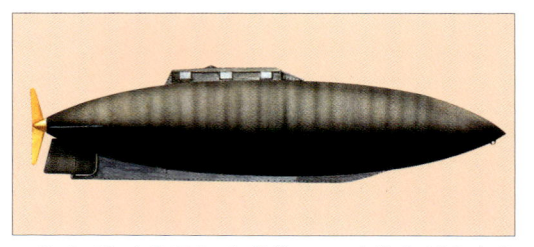

TOP: **The Royal Navy's First Submarine Flotilla, commanded by Captain Reginald Bacon arrived in Portsmouth in 1902, consisting of two completed Holland boats. Five were built at a cost of £35,000 each and Bacon reported: "Even these little boats would be a terror to any ship attempting to remain or pass near a harbour holding them."** ABOVE: **J.P. Holland's first submarine, the *Fenian Ram*, built in 1878 and funded by a brotherhood of American Irish patriots with the aim of attacking British shipping. The first Holland boats contained many of the original design features.**

of the Fenian connection. Holland's backers, meanwhile, were becoming impatient and demanded action. When he persisted in continuing his rigorous trials they "stole" the boat, which they said was rightfully theirs anyway, and towed it to New Haven, ready to begin blitzing British shipping. After several attempts to master the controls, however, they gave up and washed their hands of submarines.

Holland came to the attention of a businessman named Isaac Rice, a magazine publisher and industrialist who had already established a monopoly in the American storage battery industry. Rice financed the creation of the Holland Torpedo Boat Company and correctly assessed that this time Holland had come up with a winner. The boat was 17m/55ft 9in long and was powered by a petrol engine on the surface and an electric motor when submerged. The United States

UNDERWAY IN THE HOLLANDS

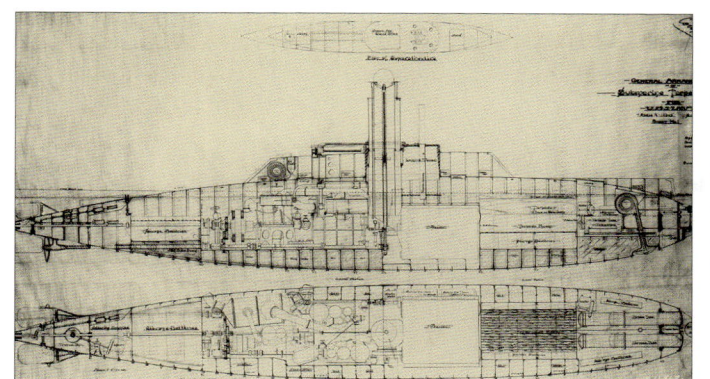

ABOVE: **Drawings for the first of the Holland boats to be bought by the US Navy, the ill-fated *Plunger*, built in 1897 but doomed to failure because US Navy officials insisted on tinkering with Holland's design.**

ABOVE RIGHT: **The famous image of J.P. Holland in his submarine that provided the prototype for the American and British navies.** BELOW: **USS *Holland*, the 65 tonne/64 ton initiator of the US submarine force, successfully completed trials in 1899.** BOTTOM: **The *Fulton* (Holland VII-type design) built by the Electric Boat Company in 1901. The *Fulton* itself was sold to Russia along with another five, and the US Navy also bought five.**

government finally agreed, in April 1900, to purchase the prototype for $165,000 from the renamed Electric Boat Company, and the craft was commissioned as the USS *Holland*.

Rice then travelled to London, armed with the knowledge of highly successful trials in the USA, where the *Holland* had "sunk" a battleship in fleet exercises, and the Admiralty decided that it, too, must finally join the submarine age. The British agreed to buy five improved Hollands, capable of carrying a crew of seven and able to withstand pressure down to 30m/98ft 5in. Each one cost £35,000 to build, although Holland himself saw little profit from his invention. Rice had taken the precaution of including the designs and patents when he established his company, and eventually Holland resigned. Blocked by legal ties from utilizing his designs again, he died in obscurity while his Electric Boat Company went on to become one of the world's foremost manufacturers of submarines, celebrating its centennial in 1999. Therefore, finally, the British were to get a submarine fleet, although the Admiralty stressed to newspapers at the time that the craft were for experimental purposes only. Lord Selborne, First Lord of the Admiralty, would only go as far as to say in his estimates to the Commons, "What future value these boats may have in naval warfare can only be a matter of conjecture".

This negative view at the Admiralty changed virtually overnight. In July 1901, newspaper reports from France brought a graphic account of dramatic developments. A dummy torpedo struck a French battleship as she left Ajaccio harbour during naval manoeuvres. It had been fired from a brand new French submarine, *Gustav Zede*, which had secretly been sent from Toulon for the express purpose of demonstrating to the navies of the world that the French had exceeded every one of them. For Britain, at a time when France, rather than Germany, was considered an "enemy", this was stern news indeed. The race to form submarine fleets was on, across the world.

259

Towards World War: the dash to build

To many British and American naval chiefs at the start of the 20th century, submarines were a "cursed invention". The very idea of dark, shadowy vessels lurking unseen beneath the waves, waiting to sink their magnificent and beloved capital ships, was simply unthinkable. Sir Arthur Wilson, Third Sea Lord in the British Admiralty, best summed up their view when he described submarines as being "underwater, underhand and damned unEnglish…certainly no occupation for a gentleman. Submarine crews, if captured, should be hanged as pirates".

The Germans, similarly proud of their naval heritage, felt the same. Admiral Alfred von Tirpitz, said "The submarine is, at present, of no great value in war at sea. We have no money to waste on experimental vessels." The Americans were in no hurry to equip either, in spite of their own history of experiments with underwater warfare. However, the new century was barely months old before the great and the good among the naval fraternity were forced to change their tune. The greater urgency emerged after the French – historically Britain's main enemy before *entente cordiale* — launched a competition for the design of a submarine of 200 tonnes/ 197 tons, with a range of 161km/100 miles on the surface, and received some startling new ideas, notably Laubeuf's 1899 double-hulled *Narval*, which used steam propulsion for surface work and batteries when submerged.

In 1900, the Americans bought the Holland prototype, commissioned USS *Holland* for immediate operations and began building more. The British introduced their own class, the A boats, the first of which (*A1*) was put through her paces with the five Hollands for the first-ever fleet exercise involving

TOP: After utilizing the Holland boats as a starting point and thereafter, principally for experimental and training purposes, the Royal Navy initiated its own A class, British designed and built, 12.2m/40ft longer than the Hollands, and at 193 tonnes/190 tons surface displacement was almost a third heavier. Thirteen boats of the class were completed. ABOVE: The US equivalent was the Adder class, also an enlarged production version of the original *Holland*, with a more powerful petrol engine.

submarines, off the south coast of England in 1904. Although based on the *Holland*, *A1* was 12.2m/40ft longer and 203 tonnes/ 200 tons heavier and was accepted with pride by the Royal Navy. Unfortunately, she did not survive the exhibition. George, Prince of Wales (later King George V), himself a sailor, was aboard for the demonstration, but was called home because of the death of the Duke of Cambridge. Soon after he left, *A1* submerged to continue her trials, and never came back.

The passenger steamer, SS *Berwick Castle*, reported having struck something below the surface. The following day, divers

TOWARDS WORLD WAR: THE DASH TO BUILD

LEFT: **The French were at the forefront of submarine design. The attractive *Anguilla*, in the Naiade class, was a single hull boat with a surface displacement of 71.6 tonnes/70.5 tons, carried a crew of 12 and had a range of 370km/ 200 nautical miles.**

ABOVE: **Another French boat that looked well ahead of her time was the *Narval*, built by Laubeuf in 1899. It was the winner of a government-sponsored competition for the best design: a massive 33.8m/111ft long and with a displacement of 170.7 tonnes/168 tons.**

ABOVE: **The race towards submarine power was spurred on by another French development, the *Gustav Zede*, which became the first boat to successfully fire a dummy torpedo, aimed at a French battleship in Ajaccio harbour in 1901.**

BELOW: **The D-letter in Britain's fast track to a major submarine fleet was reached in 1907 and the class had far better endurance than any previous boat. The D class was also regarded as the first UK submarine to have a proper patrol capability.**

went down at the spot, and found *A1* on her side in 13m/ 42ft 8in of water. All on board were lost. Five more A class vessels were hit by misfortune, resulting in deaths of crew members. Conditions for the dozen crew members in the early models were dire and cramped. There were no toilet facilities in the early boats. Crews used buckets, which were emptied over the side, and when the air – poisoned by the fumes, toilet buckets and mere body odour – became too overpowering, compressed air bottles were tapped to refresh the atmosphere.

In Britain, the A class was followed by new, improved and larger designs: B, C, D and E classes progressively took the experimentation and improvements at a quite exceptional pace, indeed well in time for the early battles of World War I. Despite this, as late as 1912, senior officials were still rejecting the notion that submarines posed a serious threat to the British fleet.

The era of petrol-driven engines was also thankfully coming to an end. For the British, this was signalled with the arrival of the D-class boats, with *D1* becoming the prototype for diesel-driven power, albeit invented by Rudolph Diesel of Germany. She was also the first British submarine with twin propellers, and her ballast tanks were not inside the hull but fitted on the outside as "saddle tanks". The D boats were also the first submarines to have a wireless, and with their greater endurance level, became ocean-going submarines with a range of more than 4,023km/2,500 miles. A two-pounder gun became standard with *D4*. Eight D boats were in commission by the start of World War I, and along with the other classes, Britain could muster 55 submarines as the conflict began.

France, well ahead in terms of numbers, had a creditable total of 62 very decent submarines. The Germans, latecomers to the race for a submarine stock, had fewer boats than Britain and France. In 1914, they could muster just 28 boats, with a further 17 under construction, but their technology was advancing in new directions that others would copy.

261

Birth of the U-boat

Germany's early reluctance to join the race in submarine development was only overcome as other nations around the world – France and Britain in particular – began to take up the challenge. In fact, when Germany's history of submarine building began in 1904, it was inspired, curiously enough, not by the country's own navy. Russia ordered three *Karp*-class vessels, which were duly delivered two years before the arrival of the first German submarine, *U1*, which itself was a full six years behind the first British and French boats. The first U (for *Unterseeboot*) boat, also initially designed for coastal work, was larger than British and American A boats, with a double hull and twin screws, and came with a powerful electric motor for faster speeds submerged. The 298kW/400hp engines used heavy oil rather than petrol, although they did have the drawback of emitting very visible smoke and sparks from the upper deck exhaust system. German designers were therefore encouraged to press ahead with diesel-fuelled engines, which they first produced in 1910.

Even so, *U1* produced impressive trial results, and her first major endurance test from the German port of Wilhelmshaven, passing around Denmark and back to Kiel in northern Germany – a distance of 1,087km/587 nautical miles – was noted with concern by competing nations. There was another major difference in the German boats in that from the outset they possessed real fighting qualities, which were quickly enhanced through the early stages of development. It was a capability that Winston Churchill noted on his appointment as First Lord of the Admiralty in 1910: "The whole character of the German fleet shows that it is designed for aggressive and offensive action of the largest possible character in the North Sea and the North Atlantic." Armed initially with a single torpedo tube at the bow, *U2* was further enlarged and came with four tubes, two bow and two stern, ahead of the first British D class carrying four tubes.

U1, the pacesetter for fast and capable boats, showed its mettle from the beginning, survived the war, and was eventually moved to a museum in Munich, where she is retained to this day. At the outbreak of war in August 1914, Germany had around 20 operational U-boats assigned to its High Seas Fleet, working from a fortified forward base on the island of Heligoland. When hostilities with Russia began, they combined to form a defensive screen in the North Sea, and when Britain and France declared war on Germany, ten U-boats set out to make a bold surprise move against the British Grand Fleet, at its supposedly secure base at Scapa Flow. This first outing in wartime proved disappointing for the Germans. Two of the boats had to turn back, one was lost en route, and one, *U15*,

ABOVE: *U1* was launched at Keil in 1906 to become a trial and evaluation boat for the German Imperial Navy. She was much larger than the British A class, possessed an exemplary electric motor, and had an endurance of 1,087km/587 nautical miles.

BELOW: **The results of what became an all too familiar attack on British merchant shipping in the U-boat campaigns of World War I.**

LEFT: *U35* was the most successful German submarine in World War I, sinking 224 vessels (excluding warships) during 17 patrols from November 1914 and remaining in action to the very last, when she was surrendered and broken up at Blyth.

was sunk by HMS *Birmingham*. The remainder failed to score any hits, let alone penetrate the British base, although the latter was finally achieved in November 1914, when *U18* under the command of Captain Hans von Hennig gained entry, only to be spotted and sunk. Although this mass attack on the British fleet achieved little, it came as a wake-up call to all opposing nations, and the British in particular. This was reinforced one month later when *U21*, which had taken part in the move on Scapa Flow, became the first submarine since the American *Hunley* to sink a ship in wartime, sending the British cruiser *Pathfinder* to the bottom with a single torpedo hit.

This was indeed a shocking event, analysed with great concern by the seafaring nations of the world, given that the time which elapsed from the launch of the torpedo to the disappearance of the cruiser was a mere four minutes. Only nine of the 268 crew survived the attack. Undoubtedly the most significant development in submarine warfare to date came on September 22, 1914, when a relatively old boat, *U9*, under the command of Lt Otto Weddigen, sank no fewer than three British cruisers – the *Aboukir*, *Hogue* and *Cressy* – within a 40-minute timeframe, taking down almost 1,400 men. As naval analysts pored over the details, it did not escape anyone's attention that on July 16, 1914, the crew of *U9* had performed the task of reloading torpedoes while submerged, the first time ever that this had been recorded. One further milestone in German submarine history came one month later, when *U17* became the first submarine in history to sink a merchantman. In fact, the boat went on to sink 11 other non-combatant ships.

ABOVE: The crew of *U9*, then captained by Otto Weddigen, made history by performing the task of reloading torpedoes while submerged. Using this process, Weddigen sank three British cruisers in under an hour in September 1914, with the loss of almost 1,400 men. The captain would himself perish with his *U29* later in the war. RIGHT: An interior view of *U9*.

THE HISTORY OF SUBMARINES

The head to head of underwater power

The submarines of World War I were engaged in vast arenas of sea warfare, and the crews of these early, technically deprived small boats were relied upon well into the conflict, taking on challenges way beyond the true level of their capabilities and endurance. Furthermore, the sheer numbers of boats in any fleet did not compensate for deficiencies in the infant submarine technology, although the rate of improvement on that score was dramatic. The British Navy was far greater in both experience and numbers, while the newly equipped German fleet was lean, hungry and thoroughly modern.

ABOVE: In 1915, a new class of efficient German minelayers came into service around coastal waters. Ironically, the class leader *UC1* was sunk by a mine off Nieuport two years later with all 17 hands lost. BELOW LEFT: Some of the targets of extensive German minelaying were the new British E-class boats, which began a daring and highly successful campaign in the Baltic and elsewhere as they emerged to fight in the front line of the war at sea.

On paper, the submarine stock of Britain and France looked healthy as Europe inched towards World War I. However, well over half the boats were of such vintage as to be virtually useless other than for coastal patrols, and to use them – as the British did – on more demanding tasks presented their crews with exceptional challenges that they met with considerable aplomb.

But other developments were already in the pipeline, and by the end of the war the Royal Navy's submarine fleet would extend across a confusing range of 20 different designs and classes. The star of the British submarine fleet was the versatile E class, with boats being launched by the week to match Germany's massively increased production schedule. Additional types F, G and H classes were scheduled to begin rolling out of the production pens from 1915.

In early action, the Heligoland Bight region remained the key to Germany's ability to set forth, so German commanders sealed the route to the Baltic from the North Sea. This area became an early flashpoint as Britain's C, D and E boats made

THE HEAD TO HEAD OF UNDERWATER POWER

LEFT: **E1 was the first of 56 E-class boats which came on stream between 1911 and 1917, built in three groups at an average cost of £105,000 each. Sadly, to avoid capture after a successful campaign, E1 was scuttled off Helsinki in April 1918, along with E8, E9 and E19.** BELOW LEFT: **E32 was among just 25 E boats that survived World War I, and was sold in 1922.**

constant forays into the region. The problems of going to war in craft with, as yet, still unsophisticated communications soon became apparent. Boats went out of wireless range and, in place, intelligence messages were sent back using homing pigeons, which were usually kept in the forward peak of the boats. Usually, important messages were sent in triplicate – using three pigeons.

Britain's first major sortie was led by Lt Commander Max Horton who went on to become an acclaimed hero in British submarine history. His E9 sank an old German cruiser, the *Hela*, on the approaches to Heligoland and then scored a direct hit on a German destroyer in the North Sea in mid-September 1914. The euphoria of these first submarine successes was to be short-lived, however. A reversal quickly followed, and another "first" in the history of submarine warfare – the first submarine to be sunk by another submarine. The victim was the British *E3*, which was sighted cruising on the surface in the Heligoland Bight by the *U27* captain, Lt Bernhard Wegener. In the weeks and months that followed, the British 8th Flotilla, operating off the east coast, suffered five further losses, although the German fleet was sufficiently harassed to pull back into the comparative safety of the Baltic Sea.

As well as giving trouble to the German fleet in the Baltic, British submarines had the equally important task of interrupting shipments of iron ore from Sweden to Germany. This was eventually achieved, although in terms of attacks on ships, successes were initially few, partly because the British submarines had been placed under inefficient Russian control. The German propaganda machine complained bitterly of the "underhand and criminal methods of the British pirate submarines" in the Baltic.

ABOVE: **The famous U-boat poster, one of many produced by Hans Rudi Erdt for the German government in World War I, this one to publicize a film, *U-boats Out!* on submarine warfare.** BELOW: **Lt Commander Martin Nasmith's *E11*, which began its so-called "career of destruction" against enemy shipping in the Baltic in October 1914. Also in this photograph is Admiral Sir Roger Keyes, who later planned the famous raid on the German submarine base at Zeebrugge.**

265

LEFT: **The sinking of the passenger liner** Lusitania **by** U20 **in February 1915, with the loss of 1,195 lives, brought allegations that the boat laid in wait for the ship as part of a policy of unrestricted warfare, although Lt Commander Walther Schweiger denied it.**
BELOW: **The sinking of the great ship undoubtedly inspired what a German newspaper described as "national pride", and a special medal was cast for the submariners involved.**

The sinking of the *Lusitania*

Battle for control of the high seas intensified by the day, eventually resorting to what many described as "sheer bloody murder" on February 4, 1915. On that day, Germany declared that the international waters around the coasts of Great Britain and Ireland would henceforth become a war zone. Ships sailing under the British flag would be sunk on sight, and the Germans said they could not guarantee the safety of ships from neutral countries because of the difficulty of identifying flags at a distance or in fog.

On May 7, the threat became a reality. *U20*, under Lt Commander Walther Schweiger, was – according to the German version of events – heading home at the end of a week-long patrol off the south coast of Ireland, having sunk two small steamers and one sailing boat. Schweiger was travelling west from Waterford at 13:20 hours when he saw a very large passenger liner steaming into view, sailing eastwards. It was the *Lusitania*, a magnificent vessel of 31,500 tonnes/31,003 tons, carrying 1,257 passengers and 702 crew. As the liner came closer and closer, she was an unmissable target. Schweiger ordered his crew to battle stations, took aim and at 14:09 hours gave the order to fire.

From a range of less than 730m/798yds, there was no chance of avoidance, no chance of a miss and no chance of escape for the hundreds of men, women and children on board. The torpedo struck amidships. Within 20 minutes, the great liner lurched beneath the waves in a great mass of white foam. Schweiger had sunk the pride of the Cunard Line, and in doing so, 1,195 passengers perished. He watched them as hundreds scrambled to save themselves, and made the following note in his war diary:

An unusually heavy explosion takes place with a very strong explosion cloud (cloud reaches far beyond front funnel). The explosion of the torpedo must have been followed by a second one (boiler or coal or powder?). The superstructure right above the point of impact and the bridge are torn asunder, fire breaks out, and smoke envelops the high bridge. The ship stops immediately and heels over to starboard very quickly, immersing simultaneously at the bow. It appears as if the ship were going to capsize very shortly. Great confusion ensues on board; the boats are made clear and some of them are lowered to the water with either stem or stern first and founder immediately. On the port side fewer boats are made clear than on the starboard side on account of the ship's list. The ship blows off [steam]; on the bow the name Lusitania *becomes visible in golden letters. The funnels were painted black, no flag was set astern. Ship was running twenty knots. Since it seems as if the steamer will keep above water only a short time, we*

THE SINKING OF THE *LUSITANIA*

LEFT: Although America had not yet entered the war, the sinking of the *Lusitania* finally brought home to Atlantic travellers the potential of the German U-boat campaign against shipping, given that there were many US passengers among the casualties, whose bodies were carried ashore covered in the national flag. BELOW: The famous ship depicted on a postcard of the day.

dived to a depth of twenty-four meters and ran out to sea. It would have been impossible for me, anyhow, to fire a second torpedo into this crowd of people struggling to save their lives.

Many claimed that Schwieger added the last sentence after the voyage, after the world became shocked by the sinking. Indeed, the reaction was one of stunned disbelief, but not in Germany. Naval chief Admiral von Tirpitz received hundreds of telegrams congratulating him. An article in an influential German newspaper summed up the "national pride" with the comment that "the news will be received by the German people with unanimous satisfaction since it proves to England and the whole of the world that Germany is quite in earnest in regard to her submarine warfare". Despite the fact that 124 Americans were among the passengers who died, "riotous scenes" were reported in New York's German clubs and restaurants. Elsewhere, of course, the monstrous crime was universally condemned, and few believed that it was a coincidence that Schwieger just happened upon the *Lusitania* but, more likely, had been lying in wait. That view was reinforced when it became known that the German ambassador to the United States had published a warning to those intending to embark on the *Lusitania*, days before she sailed.

Meanwhile, the deadlocked war of attrition in the trenches and Germany's home-front crisis of shortages of food and supplies through the blockade being waged by the British fleet turned the Germans towards a merciless campaign on the high seas in which submarines were to spearhead a blockade of the British Isles. In spite of the international protests in the wake of the *Lusitania* calamity, Germany began to focus U-boat attention on unarmed merchant shipping in addition, of course, to any British fleet ships they might come upon. In spite of the assurances given to America, in August 1915 *U24* torpedoed and sank the small White Star liner *Arabic* and in early 1916 the French steamer *Sussex*, with the loss of American lives.

ABOVE: A steamer is torpedoed when, convinced they could starve Britain into submission, the Germans began an all-out U-boat war against merchant shipping. By the autumn of 1916, British and Allied vessels sunk by the Germans reached a staggering 300,000 tonnes/295,262 tons a month, double the totals reached in the summer months. BELOW: Nor were attacks limited to below the surface, as demonstrated here, when a U-boat crew launches a surface assault using their powerful deck guns.

The famous naval confrontation, the Battle of Jutland, waged on May 31 and June 1, 1916, between the British Grand Fleet and the German High Seas Fleet, resolved nothing. British losses in both ships and human lives were greater than Germany's. Even so, Germany's capital ships returned to home ports and did not venture to give battle again during the war. The battle on the high seas was handed over to the U-boat commanders, convinced that they could starve the British into submission.

Forcing the Dardanelles

Apart from the war in the main European waters, there were battles elsewhere that brought praise and tragedy in equal measure for the British and Allied submariners. The most famous of all came in the Gallipoli campaign against Turkey, as the Royal Navy was tasked with forcing the Dardanelles straits. From the outset, this was to become a life or death mission for many submarine crews when the waterway became bitterly contested as soon as Turkey sided with Germany in the autumn of 1914. In return, the Turks received German military advisers, military hardware and two brand-new ships, the *Breslau*, a light cruiser, and the *Goeben*, a battlecruiser. The two ships were stabled at Constantinople (Istanbul), on the northern coast of the Sea of Marmara, from where the Turks unleashed them to bombard Russian Black Sea ports. In December 1914, Britain's War Council decided to attack Turkey to neutralize the attacks on Russia. Among the advance party in this mission was the submarine service.

For centuries, the Dardanelles had provided the Turks with a natural defence to their capital city. Running south out of the Sea of Marmara past the Gallipoli Peninsula into the Aegean and on to the Mediterranean, the straits are 45km/28 miles long and contained many hazards. Although 6.4km/4 miles from shore to shore at its widest points, there was a rat-run 19.3km/12 miles upstream, known as the Narrows, reducing to just over 1.6km/1 mile in width, and notorious for unpredictable currents. The rocky banks of the straits bristled with forts, guns, torpedo launchers and mobile howitzers, while below the water there were floating and fixed minefields and anti-submarine nets. In December 1914, well before the infamous invasion of the Gallipoli Peninsula began, the French and the British sent a large flotilla of ships of all kinds to settle in the wide harbour of Moudros on the Greek island of Limnos. Among them were

TOP: **The British and French sent many submarines into the costly attempt to take control of the Dardanelles, in conjunction with the ill-fated Gallipoli campaign. These submarines included some of the earliest and most basic boats, such as the** *B11*, **which undertook heroic efforts to force a path through the deadly minefields.** ABOVE: **The crew of** *B11*, **with their skipper, Lt Commander Norman Holbrook – early heroes in the battle for control of the Dardanelle straits.**

six submarines, including three small and very basic British B-class boats, *B9*, *B10* and *B11*, all hankering to have a shot at forcing the straits. Lt Norman Holbrook in *B11* was the first to try. On the morning of December 13, 1914, having warned his crew of the dangers, they set off and covered 19.3km/12 miles before the boat reached minefields at Sari Siglar Bay. There, the Turkish battleship *Messudieh* was spotted at anchor. Holbrook dived his vessel under five rows of mines and torpedoed the battleship. He then managed to turn around and bring the *B11* safely back, although assailed by gunfire and torpedo boats, having been submerged on one occasion for nine hours.

The operation brought great acclaim in Britain, and Holbrook was awarded the Victoria Cross, thus becoming the first submariner to be so honoured. The dangers were re-emphasized on January 14, 1915, when the French submarine *Saphir* attempted to get through but was lost with all hands just beyond the Narrows. Naval commanders called for help from the larger E boats, which were promptly despatched from England.

The E boats began arriving in March, ahead of the planned invasion of Allied ground forces scheduled for April 25. The first to try to run the gauntlet of the Dardanelles was *E15*, under the command of Lt Commander Theodore Brodie. In dodging the minefields, his boat was caught by the infamous current and ran aground directly below heavy guns that opened fire immediately. The boat was hit twice, killing Brodie himself, and the crew had no alternative but to surrender.

The next boat to make the attempt was Australia's *AE2*, which began the journey through the straits in the early hours of April 25, the same day that ANZAC troops landed on the beaches at Gallipoli. Lt Commander Hew Stoker, the Irish-born captain of *AE2*, set off steadily on the surface under a moonless sky until searchlights suddenly swept his boat. The shellfire that quickly followed forced him to dive, and as he did so, he ran straight into a minefield. Stoker was forced to keep his boat on the bottom for 13 hours, with barely enough air to sustain life. Finally, he was able to move forward, and at 07:30 hours on April 26, the jubilant skipper signalled that *AE2* had entered the Sea of Marmara. In spite of the somewhat fragile state of his boat, and without a gun, Hew Stoker and his crew immediately began to wreak havoc. Virtually overnight, enemy shipping was curtailed substantially.

Lt Commander Edward Courtney Boyle was dispatched in *E14* to join Stoker. He, too, successfully negotiated the Dardanelles, to enter the Marmara on April 29, and rendezvous with Stoker in Atarki Bay to discuss a plan of action. The following day, *AE2* was shelled by a Turkish torpedo boat and went down, although all hands escaped before the boat sank, and became prisoners of war. Boyle, in *E14*, carried on as planned, carrying out a series of remarkable and daring raids, dodging the Turks hunting for him and sinking several ships before returning to base on May 15, to discover that he too had been awarded the Victoria Cross for his "conspicuous bravery".

ABOVE: **A depiction of one of the most acclaimed events of the Gallipoli campaign, when *B11* negotiated a treacherous minefield five rows deep to torpedo and sink the Turkish battleship *Messudieh*, for which Holbrook was subsequently awarded the Victoria Cross.** BELOW: **The French Navy had numerous submarines in the Allied assault on the Dardanelles, including the *Saphir*, which was lost with all hands in January 1915.**

ABOVE: **Another French casualty was the hefty and very visible *Mariotte*, sunk by murderous Turkish shoreline gunfire after being trapped in anti-submarine nets in the Dardanelles on July 27, 1915.** LEFT: **One of the hero boats of World War I was the Austrialian *AE2*, here in the Suez Canal en route to the Dardanelles, where, after a successful opening sortie, she was sunk by Turkish torpedo boats. All hands escaped, only to be taken prisoner.**

269

Stealth and style of the Victoria Cross winners

There were yet other VCs to be won in the dramatic sequence of events that set in stone the stealth, style and drama of British submariners operating in the Dardanelles, and in particular the adventures of *E11*, captained by Lt Commander Martin Nasmith. The exploits of this boat, and others of the period, were to become the stuff of legend, winning worldwide acclaim. Nasmith began his journey through the Dardanelles on the night of May 18, 1915, emerging 16 hours later into the Sea of Marmara. There he and his crew began a remarkable run of success. First, they seized a Turkish vessel and strapped her to the landward side of the submarine to serve as a disguise as she passed shore observers, and using this disguise, *E11* torpedoed a Turkish gunboat and sank several smaller craft. On May 23, a Turkish transport ship, the *Nagara*, which was heading for the Dardanelles, came into view.

E11 surfaced close by and Nasmith appeared in the conning tower and warned that he was going to sink the ship. When all crew and passengers were safely aboard lifeboats, an *E11* boarding party carried explosives to the Turkish ship. As *E11* sailed away, the *Nagara* blew up in a sheet of flame. She had been carrying ammunition. *E11* now headed for Constantinople itself, where another audacious scheme was hatched. Nasmith planned to deliver an assault on the harbour that supposedly could never be attacked from the sea: his first torpedo smashed into the sea wall and the second sank a moored Turkish gunboat.

The city flew into panic, convinced that a group of British enemy submarines were in the Marmara. Nasmith continued on, diving and surfacing around the approaches to Constantinople, replenishing his own supplies of food, fuel and water from craft his men boarded, and in this way kept on the move for an incredible three weeks before arriving back on June 6, 1915, to the news that he too had been awarded the Victoria Cross. This ongoing campaign was handed over to Edward Courtney Boyle in *E14*, which returned to the Marmara to keep up the pressure, and was joined eight days later by Lt Commander Ken Bruce in *E12*. Nasmith also returned to the fray in July, and literally within minutes of entering the Marmara he had sunk a transport. The next day he sank another transport and then while on the surface shot up a column of Turkish troops, passing along a coast road with his brand new 12-pounder gun. His greatest triumph came just before dawn on August 8, when Nasmith found the Turkish battleship *Hayreddin Barbarossa* in his sights. He stalked the ship for 20 minutes before firing a single torpedo. It scored a direct hit, followed soon afterwards by a massive explosion when the magazine went up. The battleship sank within minutes.

Nasmith and Boyle continued their patrols, sinking ships and bombarding troops on the coast road well into the autumn. They were joined in September 1915 by Lt Commander Archie Cochrane, 33-year-old captain of *E7*, making his second tour of the Marmara. But bad luck dogged Cochrane from the outset. First, he discovered that a second anti-submarine net had been positioned in the Narrows and, as he tried to break through, part of the metal entwined around his propeller. Repeated attempts to free the boat failed, and the Turks, spotting the commotion, began dropping depth mines. When the boat had been submerged for almost 13 hours he decided to surrender to ensure his men's safety. He asked for full astern and managed to surface promptly in the midst of an array of enemy craft waiting to shell him. Amid a hail of gunfire, Lt John Scaife scrambled on deck to surrender the crew. Two motorboats manned by German submarine crews came alongside and took the men off. Cochrane himself

ABOVE: **Light cruiser *Breslau*, one of two warships supplied to the Turks by Germany for the Dardanelles campaign, ran straight into a minefield in the Aegean in January 1918, and was sunk.**
RIGHT: **The wreck of hero boat *E15*, which ran aground en route to the sea of Mamara directly under the fire of defensive batteries, which killed Lt Commander T.S. Brodie and six crew. The remainder were captured and five more died in prison camps.**

270

ABOVE: *E11* 1st/Lt Guy D'Oyley-Hughes swam ashore pushing a platform packed with explosives to blow up a railway line that was out of reach of shells. RIGHT: Returning safely home, VC winner Lt Commander Martin Nasmith, aged 32, and his crew of *E11* following their action-packed campaign in the Dardanelles, sinking a record 122 enemy vessels, mostly in the harbour of Constantinople, a tally achieved by no other submarine.

was the last to leave, and as the rescue boats cleared the stricken submarine a time-fuse explosive set by Cochrane before he left was detonated, returning *E7* quickly to the bottom. Cochrane joined Hew Stoker in the prisoner-of-war camp at Yozgat.

Back in the Marmara, Nasmith continued his operations which he now extended to include a number of onshore sabotage missions. He remained operational for an incredible 47 days, a record equalled by no other commander in World War I. During that time, the crew of *E11* sank 11 steamers, 5 large sailing vessels and 30 small sailing vessels. By then, the need for such daring assaults was diminishing rapidly as the land battles around Gallipoli were firmly entrenched in a hopeless stalemate from which there seemed no respite from the daily sacrifice of human life. That one battle zone had engaged more than a million men from the two sides, half of whom became casualties. Early in December 1915, the Allies finally decided to call a halt and to withdraw. In the final days of the campaign, *E14*, now under the command of Lt Commander Geoffrey White, was severely damaged. White gave the order to surface in the hope of making a final dash to safety but immediately came under heavy fire from the shore batteries. With no hope of escape, White altered course towards the shore to give his crew a chance of safety, but was

ABOVE: **Through the guile and daring of their skippers, the British E class became one of the most successful boats in early British submarine history, with a significant tally that included seven U-boats. They were fast, versatile and safe and much loved by their crews, but the cost was high, with almost half of the 56 E boats built being lost to enemy action.** RIGHT: **Hovering, to keep a low profile.**

himself killed shortly before *E14* sank. Geoffrey White, who had two sons and a daughter he had never seen, was posthumously awarded the Victoria Cross, received by his widow at Buckingham Palace on July 2, her late husband's birthday. Nonetheless, the statistics for the Dardanelles campaign told their own story: 13 Allied submarines completed 27 successful passages through the straits. Seven were sunk, but the scorecard was somewhat uneven. The Turks lost 2 battleships, 1 destroyer, 5 gunboats, 11 transports, 44 steamers and 148 sailing boats.

THE HISTORY OF SUBMARINES

A U-boat in Baltimore

Of all the major seafaring nations of the Western world, the United States Navy was slow in equipping itself with a submarine force, for which it would later become renowned. America did not enter World War I until April 6, 1917, at which time her navy possessed a mere 24 diesel-powered submarines that had been used to patrol the waters off the east coast. Until that date, U-boats had been visiting the US since mid-1916 for trading purposes, as well as operating unhindered in the western Atlantic. In July that year, *Deutschland,* a large German cargo-carrying submarine, broke through the British Atlantic blockade by submerging to avoid British patrols. She arrived in the American port of Baltimore with a shipment of chemicals and dyestuffs, which were traded for a quantity of strategic war materials to be carried back to Germany. The boat, capable of carrying 711 tonnes/700 tons of cargo, made another round trip in November, although the next time the boat travelled the Atlantic, she had been converted to a combatant role.

When America entered the war, US submarines were deployed overseas to the British territory of the Azores and also around the coast of Ireland. Their primary mission was to assist in countering the U-boat threat to Allied shipping, although there were to be no confirmed sinkings of U-boats by American submarines. Back in the territorial waters of the United States, the US Navy began dispatching its submarines as far afield as the Panama Canal Zone and the Philippines, as well as mounting numerous defensive patrols along the east

TOP: **A depiction of one of the epic escapes of World War I, when the passenger line USS *President Lincoln,* which transported 23,000 American troops across the Atlantic, was torpedoed by the German submarine *U90* on May 29, 1918, and sank with the loss of only 26 of the more than 700 personnel on board.** ABOVE: **An interior view of *Deutschland* at the end of the war, when she was in French hands.**

coast, where there was significant concern about U-boat attacks on American shipping.

The threat was very real. Germany had by then created the ultimate World War I U-boat – a true long-range submarine cruiser. These boats were 70.1m/230ft long, with a speed of 15.3 knots on the surface, and an incredible range of 20,326km/12,630 miles at eight knots. They were heavily armed, with twin 15cm/5.9in deck guns for which 1,600 rounds of ammunition were carried along with 19 torpedoes, manned by a crew of 56 with room for 20 more if needed for special missions. Although 47 boats were ordered, only nine were in service before the war ended, six of them deploying to the east coast of the United States, where they laid mines and sank 174 ships, mostly smaller vessels without radios which could

ABOVE: **The compartmentalized *Deutschland*, one of the first of the UA-class boats. These appeared in 1916 and were considered to be the ultimate long-range submarine cruisers. They were 70m/230ft long, 1,524 tonnes/1500 tons, had a speed of 15.3 knots on the surface, a range of 20,326km/12,630 miles at 8 knots, and carried a crew of 56. *Deutschland*, specifically built as a blockade-breaking civilian cargo submarine, with a carrying capacity of 711 tonnes/ 700 tons, caused an uproar among the Allied nations in Europe when the US government allowed her access to US ports, carrying dyestuff and gemstones to America and returning with a cargo of nickel, tin and rubber. She made two trips in civilian mode before being converted for hostilities.** BELOW: **Fully flagged and impressively majestic, the largest of the German submarines of that era, pictured in civilian mode, was clearly a model for future developments.**

neither be warned or give warning. They proved emphatically that submarines could operate with ease 6,437km/4,000 miles from their home base.

By comparison, the dozen submarines that America sent to the Azores and Ireland had little or no effect on the outcome of the war, in that they existed mainly to provide an anti-submarine patrol for the trans-Atlantic convoys, using L-class boats that were no match for German submarines. One statistic alone proved the point: the L boats took almost two-and-a-half-minutes to dive, whereas the U-boats were out of sight in less than half a minute.

One of the most successful boats in the cruiser flotilla was *U151*, which left Kiel in mid-April 1918 and mined the entrances to Chesapeake and Delaware Bays and severed several telegraph cables near New York. During a career of four major patrols, the boat sank 51 ships totalling 140,503 tonnes/138,284 tons – excluding warships. Of these, 23 totalling 61,979 tonnes/61,000 tons were sunk off New Jersey and North Carolina in a seven week onslaught in the summer of 1918. The most notorious became known locally as Black Sunday – June 2, 1918. On that day, *U151* destroyed six American vessels, including the passenger liner SS *Carolina* en route to New York from San Juan with 217 passengers and 113 crew aboard. Although the U-boat captain observed the rules, and allowed all aboard to take to the lifeboats before sinking her, 13 passengers were drowned.

These seemingly fearless German long-range boats also sank or damaged several major American warships. It was a stark lesson for the Americans, as the Germans had convincingly demonstrated that modern submarines could operate with ease over transoceanic distances.

When the war ended, the US Navy had 74 submarines in commission, with another 59 under construction. Except for two submarines sunk in accidents, the US Navy lost no submarines to enemy action, and by early February 1919, all the boats that had served in the Azores and Ireland had returned to the United States. America knew by then that her submarine resources were insufficient compared to those of Europe, and set about developing a world-class force that began to emerge in the late 1920s and beyond.

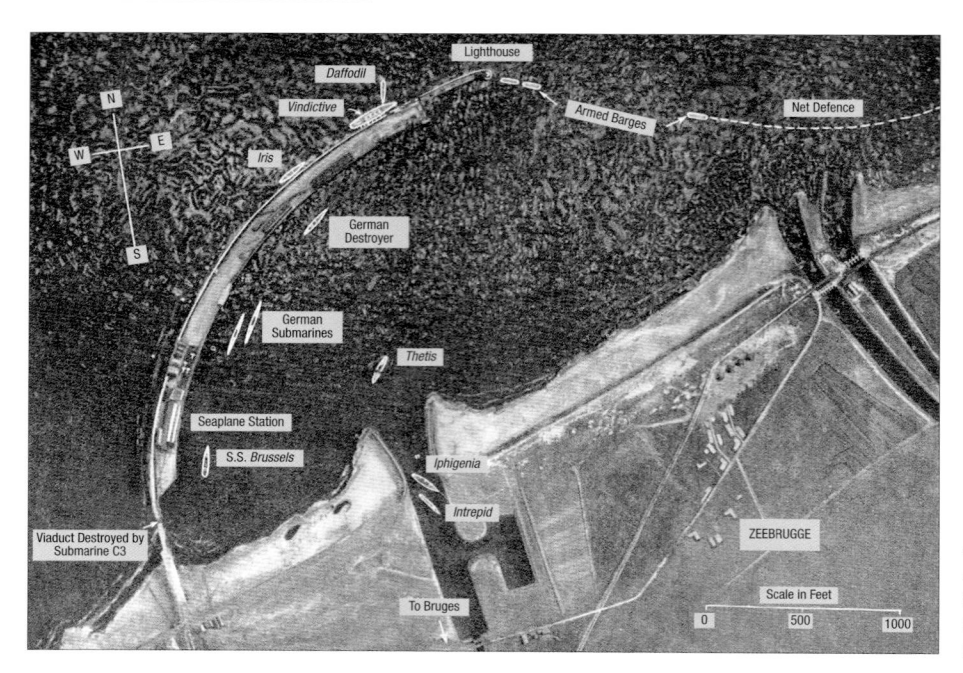

LEFT: An aerial view of the waterway to be attacked and blocked.

The last vital, courageous act

Many of the U-boats that caused so much damage in the Atlantic had been based at Bruges, in Belgium, following its capture by German land forces. It was because of this forward position from which the U-boats were able to operate that the system of convoying fleets of merchant ships was introduced. Warships stood guard, seaplanes spotted the submarines and depth bombs or charges were available for destroying them. By the beginning of 1918, the convoy system allowed the Allies to begin to regain the momentum, but the U-boat base remained a major thorn in their side. Finally, in the spring of that year, one major, daring operation was planned to directly attack the U-boat campaign at its source.

The U-boats' safe haven was strongly defended, allowing boats to come and go with comparative ease. Their hideaway was 13km/8 miles from the open sea and accessed through two canals, one via Ostend and the other through Zeebrugge. A joint operation was planned utilizing air, land and sea units to block the canals and force the U-boats to use the more dangerous northerly route, where the British could attack them. It was proposed that old ships could be sailed to the canal entrances and then sunk, a task that the Royal Navy undertook with relish with the Royal Marines in a large military operation involving 1,760 men and numerous vessels.

A crucial element of the main operation was handed to the 6th Submarine Flotilla. It entailed blowing up a viaduct connecting the Zeebrugge mole to the mainland to stop troop

ABOVE: The vintage submarine *C3*, one of the two boats packed with explosives to be rammed into the viaduct while the block ships were being put into position. Unfortunately, the second boat, *C1*, broke down and it was left to some heroic work by the five-man crew of *C3* to ensure her deadly cargo was positioned and time-fuses set before they made their escape.

reinforcements being brought to the scene at the time of the raid. Two older-type submarines, *C1* and *C3*, were nominated for duty. Six tonnes/5.9 tons of explosives were packed into the bows, and it was planned to ram the submarines under the viaduct using an automatic pilot. In theory, the crew would make a quick getaway in a motor skiff 1.6km/1 mile from the target, and they would hopefully be well clear when the time-fuse blew everything up.

Only unmarried volunteers were accepted, and the crew was stripped to a bare minimum of two officers and four ratings. Lt Aubrey Newbold was already captain of *C1*, while Lt Richard Sandford, who had just reached his 26th birthday, took

THE LAST VITAL, COURAGEOUS ACT

LEFT: **The ancient cruiser HMS *Vindictive* was one of the principal ships carrying the diversionary raiding parties of Royal Marines who swarmed ashore at Zeebrugge to engage the German defenders until the block ships had been manoeuvred into position and scuttled** (ABOVE). **These were to block the entrance to the harbour used by U-boats for their forays into the Atlantic. While the Marines dashed ashore, the ship's gunners bombarded the German emplacements on the mole. Even so, she remained an easy target for the incoming shells and took a number of severe hits. *Vindictive* managed to get away when the task was complete, albeit with heavy casualties.**

command of *C3*. The task force moved out after dark on April 22, with the two submarines towed by destroyers towards a rendezvous point 8km/5 miles from the viaduct. *C1* never made it, having been delayed by mechanical trouble en route, and Sandford took *C3* into attack alone, but made a significant deviation from the original plan. He was to have set the submarine on automatic pilot for the final stages of the journey, thus allowing him and his crew to abandon the submarine at a safe distance. However, having lost his companion boat, he decided to manually steer right to the last. German gun emplacements were firing all around, while star shells bursting directly overhead brought fake daylight for the gunners to take a range and fire. Sandford held course and made it to the target, ramming the bow of the submarine into the side of the masonry. Overhead, there were howls of laughter as German troops mistakenly believed a British submarine had become stuck.

Even so, as Sandford led his five crew members out after setting the time-fuse, the Germans opened fire. Their little motor skiff was badly shot up and the engine was useless, so they had to row. As they pushed off, two of them were hit, then Sandford himself took two bullets. Four of the six were wounded, but they managed to keep rowing until they were rescued by a picket boat, driven by Sandford's brother, from their destroyer. As they climbed aboard, the sound of a terrific explosion from the place they had just vacated confirmed that the job was done – and, indeed the viaduct was missing a very large chunk in the middle of the run. All who took part in the operation received medals, and Sandford was among eight officers involved who were awarded Victoria Crosses. His citation read:

ABOVE: **The results of the explosion can be clearly seen – a gaping stretch of broken masonry after the submarine exploded.**

"He eagerly undertook this hazardous enterprise, although well aware (as were all his crew) that if the means of rescue failed and he or any of his crew were in the water at the moment of the explosion, they could be killed outright by the force of such explosion. Yet Lieutenant Sandford disdained to use the gyro steering, which would have enabled him and his crew to abandon the submarine at a safe distance, and preferred to make sure, as far as humanly possible, of the accomplishment of his duty."

This was represented at the time as a tremendous British victory by Allied propaganda with the consequence that its devisor, the Navy's youngest admiral Sir Roger Keyes, was ennobled. Conversely, the Germans cited it as a demonstration of their success by holding the two ports. In reality, the Zeebrugge raid did not hinder German operations from either port for more than a few days. Some 500 British casualties were incurred during the operation, of which approximately 200 were fatalities.

The final reckoning

The threat of what could have been a massive U-boat offensive against the Allies was only revealed at the end of the war. While talk of mutiny and rebellion among the German Navy matched the mood of many of the nation's citizens, the submarine service remained loyal to the last, with 176 U-boats still in operation and another 200 or so still under construction. However, there was no role for them, at least not in the foreseeable future. Under the Treaty of Versailles, Germany was hammered into straitjacket surrender terms, and in addition was to have her fleet confiscated and her government was barred from keeping, buying or building any submarines whatsoever.

The Germans were forced to hand over the bulk of their ships to the Allies, comprising 10 battleships, 17 cruisers, 50 torpedo boats and 176 submarines. Most of the fleet, with the exception of the submarines, was interned at Scapa Flow in November 1918, where many were scuttled by their own crews under the very noses of their British guards. All operational U-boats were delivered into the hands of the Royal Navy initially at the port of Harwich, temporarily giving the British the largest submarine fleet in the world. In fact, the spoils were shared among the Allies and some even ended up in Japan, allowing naval architects and scientists to copy the technology.

Most were eventually scrapped, and 250 damaged or unfinished U-boats were also destroyed where they lay in the German shipyards. It seemed an appalling waste, but in reality this was trifling when set against the cost of the war itself to all the belligerents, amounting in total to about $186 billion. Casualties in the land forces amounted to more than 37 million men, with almost 10 million deaths among the civilian populations caused indirectly by the war. Famously talked of as "the war to end all wars", which would bring permanent world peace, quite the reverse would result.

TOP: **The image that came to signify the horror of the mounting U-boat attacks among the Allied fleets, a fate that befell 6,596 merchant ships totalling 13,006,146 tonnes/12,800,733 tons during the war years.** ABOVE: **To the Germans, their submariners were heroes, and there are numerous memorials to them, such as this one, which mentions the U-boat flotillas in the Aegean and Mediterranean seas.**

From the British standpoint, the only salvation was that the nation had not fallen to defeat at sea at the hands of the U-boat commanders, although it had been a very close contest. Even so, the nation's near bankruptcy as the war ended more or less forced the British government to embark on a major culling programme of its own, scrapping and selling dozens of submarines, many of which had seen little service and some not even commissioned. At the end of the war, Britain's submarine stock included 10 out of the original 13 A boats, 9 of 11 Bs, 27 of 38 Cs and 3 of the 9 Ds remaining in service. All were scrapped, as were the following:

E class: These boats had seen terrific service during the war years but were all destined for the breaker's yard. Twenty-seven

THE FINAL RECKONING

had been sunk in enemy action, mined, scuttled or lost for reasons unknown. The remaining 30 were all scrapped by 1924.

F class: Only three were built; all were used for training and then scrapped.

G class: Designed initially as an overseas patrol boat, with powerful engines and long endurance submerged, the G class also had the distinction of being the first to carry a 533mm/21in torpedo as well as two 457mm/18in tubes on both bow and beam. Fourteen were built, and four were lost during the war, including *G67*, the last submarine lost to enemy action, sunk in the North Sea on November 1, 1918. The remaining ten were to be sold or scrapped.

H class: Forty-three were built between 1914 and 1918; this was another workhorse of the period. Eight were lost, 18 were scrapped or sold in the 1920s and the remainder were kept in service for several years hence; some still active in World War II.

J class: Seven were launched, one lost and the remainder transferred to Australia in 1919.

L class: Another major production schedule produced this class from midway through the war. The design was based on an elongated E class; 34 were ordered, although only 27 were commissioned. They were of variable designs to provide boats for basic torpedo armament, as minelayers, and later all carried a 102mm/4in gun mounted on the superstructure. Three were lost (two accidentally) during the war and another sank with all 40 hands in 1924. The rest remained in service until the 1930s, when most were sold, although a handful was still in service at the beginning of World War II.

R class: Ten were launched in 1918, but few were commissioned before the war's end. They were notable for their very attractive streamlined hull design, which produced a fast underwater speed capability. They were designed specifically as attack boats and had a huge firepower of six 457mm/18in torpedo tubes. Since most of them were launched when the need for attack boats had virtually passed, they saw little in the way of active service and were all scrapped in 1923. Two more, known as the second R class, with various amendments, were built in 1930.

ABOVE LEFT: **Under the terms of the Armistice at the end of World War I, Germany was required to surrender her submarines to the Allied nations. Britain received a large number at the east coast port of Harwich and these two, *U124* and *U164*, were almost brand new.** ABOVE: ***U117* was among the boats surrendered to the USA and was subsequently used for naval exhibitions along the Atlantic coast before she sank in June 1921 off Virginia during tests.**

ABOVE: ***U120* had been operational for only two months prior to the end of the war and was one of the boats surrendered to Italy for inspection by their own designers and engineers before being broken up at La Spezia in April 1919.** BELOW: **The continuing stream of forlorn U-boat commanders and skeleton crews who surrendered vessels allotted to Britain at the end the war, coming ashore at Harwich in 1919.**

The "jinx" on the K boats

Among the boats retained for post-war service by the Royal Navy were those in the experimental K class, a steam-driven fleet submarine, hugely impressive in appearance and, at the time of their first commissioning in 1916, the largest and fastest submarines in the world, bar none. Unfortunately, their performance and stability did not live up to the great expectations surrounding them, and after a succession of disasters, the tag of "jinxed" was soon assigned.

Their design called for steam engines, which had never been completely successful in submarines, not least because they required funnels. They were 103m/337ft 11in in length, with a surface displacement of 1,850 tonnes/1,821 tons and 2,450 tonnes/2,411 tons submerged, driven by a pair of massive steam turbines powered by oil-fired boilers which could produce a speed of 23 knots on the surface and 10 knots dived from four electric motors. There were eight 457mm/18in torpedo tubes on the bow and beam and a crew of 55.

However, steam power had a number of drawbacks. The boilers had to be shut down on the command of "Dive!" a process that took up to five minutes. The funnels had to be retracted into their housings and covered by watertight shutters. Four mushroom-shaped ventilators that took heat from the boiler room were also retracted and sealed. It was perhaps a prophetic omen that the first of the class to be accepted into service almost changed the course of history in a serious way. The future King George VI, then a youthful naval officer in the Grand Fleet, was having a personal demonstration run in the vessel when the boat went into an uncontrolled dive, and ended up bow down on the muddy bottom in 40m/131ft 3in of water off Portsmouth. It took 20 minutes of delicate manoeuvres before Commander Leir managed to extricate his boat from the mud and return the future king to safety.

K6 also hit problems during her diving trials. Having submerged during tests at Devonport, the boat simply refused to return to the surface after the ballast tanks had been blown. The 50 men on board were trapped for two hours before the trouble was traced to a fault in the compressed-air system. Next, *K4* ran aground at Walney Island during surface trials, and then *K11* suffered generator failure when she too shipped water through the funnel intakes during trials in heavy seas.

On January 29, 1917, *K13* set off from the Clyde heading for Gare Loch with a crew of 53 complemented on this day by civilian passengers, mostly VIPs from the shipbuilders, 82 people in all. Barely had the boat reached the dive depth when the boiler room began to flood. *K13* dropped to the bottom with a bump. As the captain picked up the voice-pipe to give the order to stop engines, water spurted out, which meant the engine room was totally flooded. Then flames erupted on the

ABOVE: *K22* (ex-*K13*) lowering her steam-turbine funnels prior to diving, a procedure that took up to five minutes. She sank on her maiden voyage with 82 crew and civilians aboard. Only 47 survived. BELOW: *K6* also sank on her diving trials, and went to the bottom where she stubbornly remained for two hours until a fault was traced.

THE "JINX" ON THE K BOATS

ABOVE LEFT: *K2* suffered an explosion in the engine room just after she submerged and only the quick thinking of skipper Lt Commander Noel Laurence in surfacing immediately saved her from disaster. ABOVE: **K-class ratings were confronted with endless problems and dangers in these boats. Many of their colleagues did not survive.**

control switchboard, which the men beat out with their bare hands. The boat was immovable, the flooding was becoming more serious by the second and there was no means of contacting the surface. Two men courageously went out through the conning tower to raise the alarm, one of whom died in the attempt. Several hours passed before a rescue operation could be mounted. A head-count of survivors on the boat revealed that 31 on board were already dead.

Further deaths occurred before air pipes were fed into the boat from the surface after 35 hours, but it was another 22 hours before wire ropes had been looped under the bows to raise the boat and holes were cut through the hulls with oxyacetylene equipment to free the remaining 47 still alive on board. A subsequent court of inquiry heard that an inspection had revealed that the ventilator doors were open and that the instruments showed it. The boat was salvaged and was quickly recommissioned as *K22*.

Further dramas were soon to follow, including one of the most horrific accidents in naval history. On February 1, 1918, two submarine flotillas, the 12th and 13th, made up entirely of K-class boats, nine in all, were assigned for exercises with the fleet in the Firth of Forth. As they approached the estuary, the 13th Flotilla had to take avoiding action when a flotilla of destroyers crossed their path. *K14* was rammed by *K22* (the salvaged *K13*). Both submarines were damaged, and as she battled to stay afloat with flooding problems *K22* was hit squarely by the battlecruiser *Inflexible* and had to be taken under tow.

In the chaos that developed, *K17* was rammed and it vanished within seven minutes. Miraculously, all 57 crew managed to escape and were splashing about in the water waiting to be rescued when three destroyers steamed directly towards them unaware of their presence and ran over them. Only eight survived. In the continuing confusion, *K6* rammed *K4*, which sank instantly, and her entire crew of 55 went down with her. The misfortunes of these magnificent boats continued and, in all, 16 were involved in major accidents, and eight finished up on the bottom of the sea before the class was scrapped in 1932. Over 300 men lost their lives in K-class or converted K-class boats – not one of them to enemy action.

BELOW: **The K class was in fact an imposing looking vessel, but designed in haste during World War I, when naval intelligence learned that the Germans had launched a U-boat capable of 20 knots on the surface. The K boats were capable of 23 knots.**
RIGHT: **The familiar bulbous nose of *K12*, one of the lucky ones of the class, surviving a near-miss during exercises with the fleet.**

279

Big guns and aircraft carriers

Innovation in the design and use of submarines has been constant over the years, and none more so than in the early days when experimentation and high-risk projects were quickly coming off the ideas boards. Two in particular dominated the thoughts of many design enthusiasts in the British Naval hierarchy, especially during the war years in Europe, when competitive military might became the mother of invention.

The first aircraft to be used as bombers, for example, instantly caught the imagination of many. Apart from the obvious notion of surface carriers, the prospect of aircraft launched from submarines became an immediate prospect, as indeed did the use of big guns in the style of surface warships. In August 1915, Admiral Sir John "Jackie" Fisher, the instigator of the Dreadnought class of battleship, voiced his theory of having a submarine equivalent with a big gun that could surface amid flotillas of enemy vessels, perform untold damage and vanish again.

Four boats from the K class, *18*, *19*, *20* and *21* were selected for conversion into M class to be reconfigured with revolutionary features that were to make them more like submersible battleships. They were to be armed with a 60-tonne/59.1 tons, 305mm/12in gun, which had a much greater range than any torpedo but could be fired only from a depth of 6m/19ft 8in, hardly a concealed position, and reloading had to be carried out on the surface. Although approval was given for the conversion in 1916, delays and Navy red tape meant none was ready in time for war service and only three were completed. They became *M1*, *M2* and *M3* and looked exceedingly menacing but never fired a shot in anger. They were rendered obsolete by the 1921 Washington Disarmament Treaty, which limited the size of submarine-mounted guns to 216mm/8.5in.

Nor did the change of prefix rid the boats of the jinx of the K class. While submerged, *M1* sank after a collision with a Swedish coaster, SS *Vidar*, off Start Point on November 12,

TOP: A famous image of *M2*, the first British boat to be turned into an aircraft carrier, although ambition proved more hopeful than reality in their use, and the jinx of the K class, from which they were converted, continued. She was lost with all hands. ABOVE: The speed of take-off had to be brisk with the engine racing, as demonstrated here, to achieve lift to avoid dumping into the sea, as often happened.

1925, with the loss of her crew of 68. The wreck was found in 1999 by a sport diver 35 miles south-east of Plymouth.

M2, meanwhile, had a hangar fitted with a gantry to lift a light seaplane, the Parnell Peto, with an endurance of two hours, aboard to become Britain's first submarine aircraft carrier. She too suffered the K-fate. On January 26, 1932, the boat was seen to nose-dive at an angle of about 45 degrees by a passing cargo steamer whose captain did not know anything about submarines and did not realize the significance of such a dive. Only when newspapers carried the reports of a missing submarines did he come forward, but by then the 67 crew and two RAF airmen had already perished. Before long, the submariners who knew of the K-class stories were pointing out that *M2* was commissioned exactly 13 years earlier.

Only *M3* saved the reputation of the class, operating as an experimental minelayer stowing 100 mines on rails inside a free-flooding casing. The mines were laid out over her stern by means of a chain conveyor belt.

The death of *M2* finally brought an end to British attempts to launch an effective submarine aircraft carrier, the Royal Navy

BIG GUNS AND AIRCRAFT CARRIERS

ABOVE: **The Americans' *S1* submarine became the experimental platform for their hull-mounted collapsible seaplane, here the XS-2 all-metal version. After surfacing, the aircraft could be rolled out of its pod, quickly assembled, and launched by balancing the submarine until the deck was awash.**
LEFT: **The Japanese produced some of the best examples of submarine aircraft carriers, notably the *I400* with a hangar carrying three catapult-launched Aichi M6A seaplanes.** BELOW: **The Japanese submarine-launched plane E14Y, the only aircraft to drop bombs on the United States mainland in World War II.**
BOTTOM: **Britain's *M3* which was converted to carry a 305mm/12in gun, and later became a minesweeper.**

constructors having failed in earlier attempts using Sopwith Schneider floatplanes attached to a modified *E22*. This submarine was converted in 1916, with the intention of intercepting German airships over the North Sea. The distinct disadvantage of this first carrier was the boat could not submerge with the aircraft aboard. Only one successful trial was carried out before the submarine sank.

Other navies continued with the carrier experiments. France, Italy and America all produced submarine carriers but none matched the extensive work in this area carried out by the Japanese who began building aircraft-carrying submarines in 1925. Most of their early boats were classified as scouting submarines, *B1* Type, of the I15 class, displacing 2,626 tonnes/2,584 tons submerged and 108.5m/356ft in length. Powered by twin diesel engines and electric motors driving two propeller shafts, the *B1* type boats had a cruising range of more than 22,530km/14,000 miles. They were also heavily armed, and thus doubled as attack boats, carrying 17 torpedoes and sporting a 140mm/5.5in deck gun. The crews were comprised of 97 officers and enlisted men.

The floatplane carried by the *B1* model was collapsed into a water-tight hangar installed forward of the conning tower. Two launching rails extended from the hangar to the bow, from which the reassembled aircraft would be catapulted into the air by compressed air. The returning aircraft had to land on the sea and was recovered using a retractable crane. The Uokosuka E14Y aircraft had an operating range of about 322km/200 miles.

The United States Navy, like the Royal Navy, had no such success with their attempts to launch a submarine aircraft carrier. Their experiments began in 1923, using an S-class submarine with an MS-1 seaplane on deck. The aircraft was to be stowed, disassembled, in a cylinder on deck while the submarine was submerged. It proved to be a totally impractical idea and was abandoned in 1926. Meanwhile, the Japanese proceeded to enhance and advance their own technology in this area, and by World War II they had 47 boats capable of carrying seaplanes. *I14*, for example, was fitted with a hangar capable of housing two aircraft, and the gigantic I400-class boats could carry three. All were at sea preparing for an attack on the US fleet anchorage at Ulithi Atoll, when the Japanese surrendered.

Giants of the deep

By the mid-1920s, it was clear that Britain had made a rod for her own back with rapid developments of submarine technology matched and copied by other nations, now sharing the benefits of the technology gleaned from captured U-boats. Having come through the devastating experience of having so much of the nation's merchant fleet wiped out, the British naval chiefs went through a reappraisal of their own and many reverted to the original thoughts of the traditionalists – that submarines were a cursed invention. In attending the 1921 post-war Washington conference of the five naval powers – the others being France, the United States, Italy and Japan – the British representatives shocked everyone by proposing an international ban on submarines.

The idea was rejected out of hand by the other nations, understandably since most – especially America and Japan – were already embarking on a massive submarine development programme. What the British and the Germans had produced during the war years, however, amounted to a catalogue of designs and ideas that would provide base plans for the construction of bigger, faster, more potent vessels.

The designs of the two senior combatant nations set the standard for progressive and bold experiments that resulted in the production of the world's largest ever submarine, *X1*. The road to that development emerged directly from the fear of what Germany possessed, and vice versa. The British move towards "bigger and better" began first with the production of the V class, which was noted for its increased hull strength,

TOP: **The giant, USS *Nautilus*, one of the *Narwhal*-class submarines, the fifth ship of the US Navy to bear that name, although she was designated *V-6*. Commissioned in 1930, she won a presidential citation for aggressive patrolling and 14 battle stars in World War II.**
ABOVE: ***Nautilus* under construction.**

achieved by external framing between the inner and outer hulls. This allowed the submarine to dive to 45m/147ft 8in, as opposed to the norm of 30m/98ft 5in. Next in the pursuit of the ultimate diving machine came the *Nautilus*, later renamed *N1*, which was built over a four-year period at Vickers shipyards, went through various changes of design and cost £203,850. She was a sleek, fine-looking boat which, at 79m/259ft 2in in length, was at the time of her original design work almost twice the size of any existing submarine. The boat was regarded by many as a failure and never saw service of any description other than for training purposes and as a depot ship. However, that was indeed a short-sighted view. It was first and foremost an experimental boat, an early footprint on the road to the giants of the deep that were to follow. The next major development – outside of Germany's own fast and deep cruiser submarines, already discussed – came the one and only *X1*, which was another milestone in every way. She was a cruiser submarine of 3,600 tonnes/3,543 tons submerged – in no uncertain terms a true submersible cruiser, she could travel at 18.5 knots on the surface, was 110m/360ft 11in in length, and carried four 132mm/5.2in guns in twin turrets. Although conceived in 1915 – when Germany was already producing her cruiser boats – *X1* was not completed until 1925 and successfully passed a rigorous trials procedure. The trouble was, now there was no role for her in the British fleet, and the colossus was finally scrapped in 1937.

Other nations began to pursue the theme of giants of the deep. America produced its own *Nautilus* in 1930, following on from *Narwhal*, first introduced in 1927. Both were still effective and well used in World War II. They were massive boats – 113m/370ft 9in long, sleek in design and excellent to handle.

Elsewhere, other giants had emerged. The Japanese hired German technicians and began a programme of building submarines that went to the extremes of range and size, from midget subs to the largest cruisers, some capable of travelling 31,187km/20,000 miles and with an endurance of more than 100 days. The French also appreciated that size mattered and introduced the *Surcouf*, 110m/360ft 11in in length and 3,357 tonnes/3,304 tons, armed with two 203mm/8in guns and a light aircraft. Such was the fear and loathing of submarine warfare – loathing by the politicians because of the cost – that in 1930, Britain, America and Japan agreed to limit tonnage and impose armament limitations for all future cruisers, destroyers and submarines, with no new capital ships to be laid down until 1937. Neither France nor Italy agreed to sign, and in any event, the whole deal collapsed within three years because of developments in Germany.

ABOVE: **USS *Narwhal*** (originally designated *V5*) was the lead ship in her class, commissioned in 1930, and was one of five submarines docked in Pearl Harbor when the Japanese attacked. Her gunners were quickly in action and shot down two of the torpedo bombers. BELOW: The one and only *X1*, the British cruiser submarine that led the field in the development of these underwater giants when built in 1925.

LEFT: **USS *Barracuda***, (originally *V1*) was the first of the American V boats, commissioned in 1925, but at 2,032 tonnes/2,000 tons was considerably smaller than the giants that followed in the V-designation. She was recommissioned for service in 1942 to patrol the American Pacific coast. ABOVE: The pride of France, *Surcouf*, with a surface displacement of 3,302 tonnes/3,250 tons, was the largest submarine in the world when launched in 1929. She was lost with all 130 crew, supposedly sunk in the Gulf of Mexico in November 1942 amid accusations that she was spying for Hitler.

The inter-war years

While the maritime nations experimented with the *Nautilus* and similar boats, the main area of development in the 1930s was concentrated on building new workhorses for the various national submarine fleets. Britain had particular difficulty in achieving the aspirations of her admirals because of the country's parlous financial state, which was one of the reasons the government was so keen on maintaining international agreements curbing the arms race. However, in this regard, she was in danger of being left behind.

While Japan, Italy, France and Russia were now all focusing heavily on submarine manufacture, Britain had to rely on old stock well into the third decade of the century for the bulk of the service's work. The only new models apart from the experimental classes to appear beyond those ordered up during World War I were eight 1,524 tonne/1,500 ton O class and six slightly larger P class. They were excellent boats, designed for overseas patrols around the far-flung Empire, and especially the Far East. Nevertheless, they had a limited capability and also, by then, America, Japan, France and even Russia all possessed more submarines than Britain. Added to this was soon to be a new fear that would change the complexion of everything.

Adolf Hitler came to power in Germany, and secretly began to re-equip his military. Plans for the rebirth of the U-boat were already underway by 1934 when the Nazis issued bold statements repudiating the Treaty of Versailles, and in March 1935 demanded renegotiation of the permitted level of their armed forces. Britain's appeasement of Hitler in these times through the creation of the Anglo-German Naval Agreement allowed him to begin rebuilding the German Navy, supposedly to be kept within 35 per cent of the tonnage of the Royal Navy.

The single exception to this was in the dispensation for a new U-boat force, under the command of Admiral Karl Dönitz, which was allowed a tonnage 45 per cent of Britain's. The figures were both meaningless and unenforceable. Hitler made it clear that he would no longer be bound by a 20-year-old treaty and was already on the way to creating a new navy, although his plans for it were still far from complete when World War II began. Indeed, Dönitz himself had proclaimed in 1938 that it would take six years to rebuild Germany's U-boat force. In fact, as history now shows, the power house of the new Nazi machine achieved remarkable output and very soon the U-boats were back in business.

ABOVE: **Salute to the U-boats. These were Hitler's greatest sea-borne asset at the onset of World War II and throughout the conflict, given that Germany had been prevented from rebuilding the naval fleet that the nation was forced to surrender in 1918.** LEFT: **An early casualty in the undersea war: the British *Starfish*, commissioned as the third boat in the new S class in 1933, was depth-charged by German minesweeper *M7* in Heligoland Bight in January 1940. She was forced to surface and her crew went into captivity.**

ABOVE: **USS *Cachalot*,** lead ship in the class bearing her name and another version of the V boats, lay in Pearl Harbor when the Japanese attacked. One of her men was wounded, but the submarine suffered no damage. Work on her was completed at a furious pace, and just one month later she sailed on her first war patrol and eight weeks later returned with vital intelligence of Japanese bases.

Coincidence or not – but certainly by good fortune – the Royal Navy had begun its own modernization programme for the submarine service by ordering the building of a smaller boat specifically designed for operating in the North Sea and other confined theatres such as the Mediterranean. The boat to fill this role was another brilliant model, the S class, just 66m/216ft 6in long and displacing 886 tonnes/872 tons. In the fullness of time – and especially during World War II – the S class would prove to be one of the most important of all the Royal Navy submarines, with a total of 62 constructed over a 15-year period from 1935. This was to be quickly followed by the introduction of the T class, another exceptional boat particularly noted for the simplicity of its design. Approval for the build was given in 1935, and the first, *Triton*, came out for trials in 1938 to become the first of the 21 boats of this class built between 1937 and 1941. They were the largest class of ocean-going submarines to have been built by the Royal Navy, displacing 1,348 tonnes/1,327 tons surfaced and 83m/272ft in length, but only a handful were anywhere near ready by the outbreak of World War II.

The Americans, meanwhile, continued to be slow in their construction of new submarines. They were held back to some extent by their own financial depression, and also the fact that some in the US administration were of the same view of many naval traditionalists in Britain who still questioned the morality of submarine warfare and would have preferred the 1930 curtailment to have held.

However, with Hitler casting off the shackles of Versailles, Japan setting her sights across the Pacific and Mussolini already on a mission to build the New Roman Empire, the US Navy was forced to begin a rapid building programme, principally to meet the Japanese threat. By 1940, the American submarine force had answered its fundamental strategic questions and was rapidly enhancing its capability.

ABOVE: **The gathering storm.** Hitler's submarine force was presented with a new flag when the swastika became the official emblem of the German nation in 1934. BELOW: An early workhorse of the US submarine fleet on America's entry into the war, USS *Sturgeon*, a 1,472-tonne/1,449-ton *Salmon*-class boat, was commissioned in 1938. She was operating in Hawaiian waters until December 1941 when she switched to war patrols in the Far East. One of the most notable events in her log occurred after her attack on a nine-ship Japanese convoy in 1943, when, in response, she was dived under a barrage of 196 depth charges and aerial bombs and survived to return safely home.

The Japanese story

Japan, more than any other nation, benefited from the era when Germany was prevented from reviving the U-boat force. Under the terms of international treaties to which the Japanese were signatories, their engineers – like those of Britain, American and France – were able to take apart surrendered U-boats and copy German technology. However, they went one better. They shrewdly hired more than 1,000 German technicians and designers who had built the U-boats in the first place – a move that no other nation had felt inclined to do. The Japanese government approved massive bounty payments to encourage the employment of German expertise, which even included former naval officers who had themselves commanded U-boats. They were offered five-year contracts, some with an annual salary of $12,000 plus bonuses, which was a huge amount of money at the time.

Armed with this double dose of technological know-how, Japan set about building a massive new submarine fleet. As early as 1928, American Intelligence reports noted with some alarm that Japanese efforts, based upon this German input was reaching worrying proportions. "Furthermore," one report stated, "as various submarines were completed, Japanese engineers gradually took over the entire production, from design to completion until finally a distinctly Japanese type of submarine gradually emerged." Indeed, by the mid-1930s Japan was in the final stages of creating the most versatile submarine fleet of any nation in World War II.

Even so, similarities to the U-boats were very evident in three main classes of submarine. The I class, for example, was the Japanese version of the fast and potent German

TOP: Japanese enthusiasm for submarine construction was already evident in the early 1920s, with *RO60*, which was one of nine L4 type medium series submarines, commissioned in 1923, with a surface displacement of 1,012 tonnes/ 996 tons. ABOVE: Early Japanese boats had many of the characteristics of U-boats, not unnaturally perhaps, since they took apart surrendered World War I German submarines and then hired many U-boat engineers and designers.

cruiser submarine. It was the ultimate fleet boat, which Britain and America had also tried to perfect. It was also produced in several versions, including aircraft carriers and submarines that could carry multiple bombers; seaplane tenders; cargo ships; and some as submarine support vessels for the military. Next came the RO class, similar to but not as capable as the German coastal boats, and finally the HA class, which were smaller and intended for local defence and special missions, again sometimes attached to support ground forces. The most notable of the HA class, however, included midget submarines, one of the number of purpose-built boats developed in utmost secrecy by the Japanese in the late 1930s. They also built submarines large enough to transport the midget boats into

LEFT: **Another useful Japanese boat, the *HA101*, lead ship of the 376 tonne/370 ton SS type of small transport submarines, entered service late in the war but was well thought of, and closely examined when surrendered with the Japanese Navy's other surviving warships.** ABOVE: **Torpedo technology was also well advanced: these tubes housed the Type 95 torpedo that was based on the formidable Long Lance design, air launched and, some experts have claimed, was the best torpedo of the war.**

combat or enemy coastal areas where they would be released in swarms to attack – as it transpired – American warships. In fact, every aspect of Japanese technology throughout these years – obviously with an eye on the massive journeys involved in any future action in the boundless space of the Pacific – was geared to extremes in endurance and capability. They had the largest submarines in the world, the only boats with more than 5,080 tonnes/5,000 tons submerged displacement, or submarines over 121.9m/400ft in length – an achievement that was not matched until the arrival of nuclear-powered boats. They were said to have a range of 60,350km/37,500 miles at 14 knots, an achievement unmatched by any other diesel-electric submarine. These giants could carry three floatplane bombers, the only submarines ever built with such a capability.

Of the 56 submarines greater than 3,048 tonnes/3,000 tons built for action by the nations engaged in World War II, at least 50 were Japanese. They also led the field in diesel-electric submarines with 7457kW/10,000hp, and also in diesel-electric submarines capable of more than 23 knots surface speed – unmatched by any other nation.

Japanese boats also came equipped with some of the best torpedoes available. One significant development in this field was a torpedo known as the Long Lance, a submarine version of which, Mk95, was built with a 408kg/900lb warhead driven by an oxygen-fuelled turbine that left no wake, and was capable of travelling a full five miles at 40 knots. It was operative at the start of World War II and was well ahead of anything comparable built by the Allies at the time.

The Mk95 also carried the largest warhead of any submarine torpedo, initially 405kg/893lb, which was increased to 549kg/1,210lb in the final stages of the war. Another vital innovation in the Mk95 was the use of a simple contact

ABOVE: **The *I52* was a Type C-3 cargo boat, known as Japan's Golden Submarine because she was carrying £25 million in gold to Germany as payment for war material when she was sunk by a US Task Force. In 2006, attempts were made to raise the treasure by diver Paul Tidwell.** BELOW: **The sleek lines of the *I21*, a member of the elite Japanese Sixth Fleet, and the boat that famously shelled Australian cities in 1942, presumed lost with all hands in December 1943 while tracking an American convoy in the Pacific.**

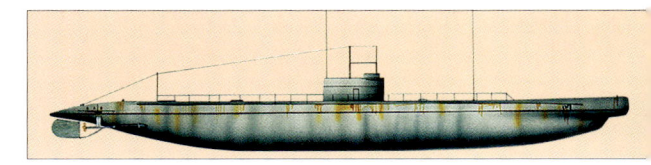

exploder, which was far more reliable than the American counterpart, the Mark 14, although the latter was improved early in 1944. Although there was no denying the sheer fire-power and versatility of the Japanese submarine fleet developed between the wars, and during the conflict itself, it has to be said that overall, Japan's submarine warfare – as will be seen – was not as effective as her masters expected.

LEFT: A defining moment in submarine history, the arrival on the surface of the first men to be saved from a stricken boat using the experimental McCann Rescue Chamber, following the sinking of USS *Squalus,* which failed to surface after the final crash dive test in her last sea trials. She sank in 73.2m/240ft of water, and the surviving 33 crew waited in total darkness and without power for more than 24 hours before the rescue attempt began. BELOW: The *Squalus* badge, although when the boat was recovered, she was given a new name.

The sinking and recovery of USS *Squalus*

In the months leading up to World War II, two notable and tragic events occurred, both of which highlighted the perils faced by submariners of the participant navies in the coming months and years, and drew attention to the rescue possibilities from stricken boats. The two events, involving the US submarine *Squalus* and, across the Atlantic, the British boat *Thetis*, were remarkably similar in detail, but the outcomes were drastically different.

The *Squalus* left the Portsmouth Navy Yard, New Hampshire at 07:30 hours on May 23, 1939, for its 19th test dive under the command of Lt Oliver Naquin with 59 men on board — five officers, 51 enlisted men and three civilian inspectors. The exercise, part of a rigorous series of performance tests to which all boats were subjected, was to perform an emergency dive while cruising at 16 knots, diving to 15.24m/50ft within 60 seconds in order to avoid enemy attack. The dive was to be carried out just south-east of the Isles of Shoals where there was an average depth of 76.2m/250ft. When the order to dive was given at about 08:45 hours, the boat initially refused to respond, but within just a few minutes had settled gently on the bottom at 74.06m/243ft with the bow raised by 11 degrees.

The catastrophe had been caused by flooding of the aft section, and immediate action was taken to isolate the individual compartments to prevent total flooding, a procedure largely completed during the sinking. However, lighting had failed and only a few hand lanterns were available to relieve the darkness as the commander began the process of checking his situation. Of the 59 people who sailed that morning, 23 were in the control room and 10 in the forward torpedo room. It was likely that everyone in the after battery room and both engine rooms had died. No contact was made with the after torpedo room. The possibility of survivors there remained, but communications with the control room had failed.

Saltwater was leaking into the forward battery and if it infiltrated the battery acid, chlorine gas might be released, or it could short-circuit the cells and cause a fire. This meant that the forward battery compartment, which was located between the two occupied spaces, would have to be left vacant. Meanwhile, a communications buoy attached to *Squalus* was released and surfaced soon after the sinking. Rockets were also fired from time to time and the sixth launched after four hours on the bottom was by chance spotted by a lookout on the sister submarine USS *Sculpin*, which rushed immediately to the scene and located the communications buoy to establish contact. Just two minutes later, however, the connecting cable snapped. By mid-afternoon, two ships had arrived at the scene, one with an oscillator that enabled Morse code transmissions. As wives and families awaited news, a part-read message from *Squalus* transcribed as "condition satisfactory but cold" was taken to offer more hope than was the case.

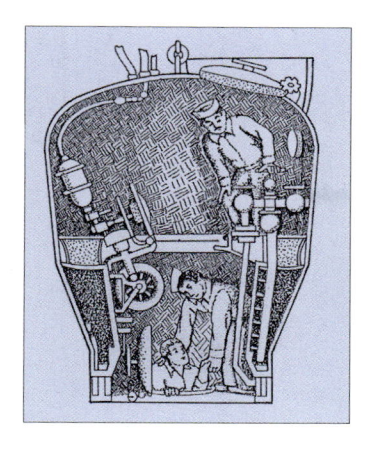

In fact, by that time there were only 33 survivors, and their lives were at risk as the atmosphere in the boat reached twice the normal pressure. The US Navy's attempts to rescue the survivors went through various stages of discussion. The first, to pump out the flooded compartments to bring the *Squalus* to the surface was dismissed as too risky, because the reasons for the sinking were unknown.

Finally, on the morning of May 24, the submarine rescue vessel USS *Falcon* arrived above the submarine with a team of divers and a McCann Rescue Chamber to begin a dramatic rescue attempt that was to last a full ten hours. The divers were commanded by Lt Commander Charles Momsen, who had invented both the Momsen Lung and the diving bell. The latter would be attached to an escape hatch over the forward torpedo room allowing survivors to be drawn to the surface by cable. The theory was fine, and well rehearsed in training conditions, but in practice this was to be an historic, drama-filled mission. By 10:07 hours, divers had managed to get the diving bell over the escape hatch and the crew inside the *Squalus* banged out a welcome on the hull. However, this was merely the beginning of a long and exhausting process, as the bell with its two operators for the motors, ballast, air pressure and communications sought to make the connection to begin the first evacuation, a task that overall would take two hours or more from leaving the mother ship to returning with survivors, with a maximum of eight men at a time. All went smoothly until the last trip, the one carrying Commander Naquin and the last seven of his crew. They were safely aboard the diving bell by 19:50 hours to begin the ascent when the cable attached to the *Falcon* fouled and frayed. It took four and a half hours to bring the chamber to the surface. Nevertheless, all 33 survivors of the original accident were safe.

The boat was salvaged in the summer of 1939, and after repair was recommissioned as USS *Sailfish*. She went on to survive World War II, sinking 40,642 tonnes/40,000 tons of enemy shipping.

ABOVE LEFT: **The internal lay-out of the McCann diving bell, which could extract crew through the escape hatch and return to the surface carrying up to eight passengers on each trip.** ABOVE: **During a three-month salvage effort by the US Navy using air tanks on the surface, the bodies of those who died were removed and the *Squalus* finally returned to the surface.** LEFT: **The salvaged submarine in a sorry state. She was immediately sent to the shipyards for repairs and was recommissioned to serve for the duration of World War II under her new name, USS *Sailfish*.**

The tragic loss of the *Thetis*

Barely a week after the *Squalus* tragedy, an accidental sinking bearing incredible similarities occurred off the coast of Wales where a brand-new British submarine went to the bottom, with totally catastrophic results. It was indeed a disastrous event for the Royal Navy with so much riding on the new T-class submarines just weeks before the outbreak of World War II. HMS *Thetis* was the third of the T boats scheduled for commissioning, and after months of rigorous tests since her launch in 1938, she was to begin final acceptance trials in late May 1939. Her captain, Lt Commander Guy Bolus, had stood by her during her fitting out and, with a crew of five other officers and 48 ratings, left the yard at Merseyside for trial runs in the Clyde estuary during May. There were a few problems to be ironed out, which was not unusual with a new boat, and *Thetis* returned to Cammell Laird yards for adjustments. The final diving trial was postponed until June 1, in Liverpool Bay.

Thetis sailed from Birkenhead soon after 09:00 hours that day with an unusually large number of people on board. In addition to the crew, there were officers from the flotilla *Thetis* was to join when she was fully commissioned, civilian observers from the Admiralty, 26 employees of shipbuilders Cammell Laird, five from other shipbuilding firms who would be building T-class boats, two members of staff from City Caterers of Liverpool, who were supplying the luncheon, and a Mersey pilot: 103 men in all. The weather was fine, the sea was calm with only a touch of an easterly wind. Everyone on board was looking forward to an interesting trip, and for the non-sailors it was an adventure to be enjoyed with perhaps a touch of apprehension. Accompanying *Thetis* during the initial stages of the trial was the *Grebecock*, a two-year-old steam tug manned by a crew of seven and laid on by Cammell Laird as part of their contract with the navy. On board was a navy observer and submariner, Lt Dick Coltart, whose task it was to keep a general watch and to warn any ships that might sail into the diving area. The *Grebecock* was also to stand by to take off any civilian passengers from *Thetis* who might wish to disembark after lunch, but none chose to do so. Then came a signal from *Thetis* that she would be diving for three hours. Coltart watched as Lt Commander Bolus left the bridge and the conning tower hatch was closed. At precisely 14:00 hours, Bolus gave the order to dive. But *Thetis* stubbornly refused to budge. Minutes later, she disappeared beneath the waves very quickly, and it was assumed that all was now going to plan.

Unfortunately it was not. The 533mm/21in wide No. 5 torpedo tube was open to the sea and the internal rear door of No. 5 tube had also been opened because a faulty test drain pipe showed empty when, in fact, the tube was full. Therefore, the door was open and *Thetis* sank. The situation was critical. As time passed, Coltart became convinced the submarine was in trouble and sent a carefully worded signal to the submarine base at Fort Blockhouse. Unfortunately, the telegraph delivery boy's bike got a puncture en route and the message was

LEFT: **HMS** *Thetis*, one of the new British T boats, launched into her acceptance trials in May 1939 in the Clyde estuary before finally beginning diving trials in Liverpool Bay on June 1. On that day, she had a full crew of 54 officers and ratings aboard, along with shipbuilders, civilian observers and other guests, 103 men in all, when disaster struck.
ABOVE: The *Thetis* badge that was never operationally used.

THE TRAGIC LOSS OF THE *THETIS*

ABOVE LEFT: **Pristine again after the dramas below, the *Thetis* was recovered and recommissioned as *Thunderbolt* to enter service in World War II.**
ABOVE RIGHT: **As *Thetis*, she went upside down and stuck firm in the mud when on her pre-acceptance trails. Although rescue ships reached her after some delay, they could not gain access before she finally sank to the bottom with great loss of life.** LEFT: **The salvage boats hover as the recovery begins.**
BELOW: **The *Thetis* is brought to the surface and dragged ashore for repairs and renewal.**

delayed. When it did arrive, fast destroyers were ordered to the scene and the RAF sent a flight of four Ansons, conducting low-level fly-bys until dusk closed in. A salvage vessel, *Valiant* sailed from Liverpool but by then it was almost eight hours since any word had been heard from *Thetis*.

Three hours later, searching over a wider arc, a crewman on the destroyer *Brazen* spotted something in the distance, and as the ship headed towards it, an incredible sight became visible – 5.5m/18ft of the stern of the 83.5m/274ft-long *Thetis* was protruding from the sea. She lay at an angle, nose down in 45m/147ft 8in of water 24km/15 miles off the North Wales coast. Inside the boat, conditions were desperate. The air was foul and rapidly running out. Bolus decided that the only solution was to make an attempt to leave the boat, using the David Submerged Escape Apparatus (DSEA), although few men were fully trained in the procedure. Volunteers stepped forward. Captain Joe Oram, officer commanding the 5th Flotilla, and Lt Woods were selected and successfully made their escape, popping to the surface within seconds. They were picked up by *Brazen* and proceeded to give details of the situation below.

Four more men escaped later, but after that, no further exit attempts were made, for unknown reasons. By then, *Brazen* had been joined by six destroyers, five tugs, the Llandudno lifeboat and the salvage vessel *Vigilant*, all strewn in an arc around the stricken submarine.

One final hope remained: to cut a hole in the side of *Thetis* with oxyacetylene gear, for which that section of the boat had to be raised above the surface. At 15:10 hours on June 2, as efforts were being made to achieve this, the wire rope snapped and *Thetis* plunged back to the bottom, taken all remaining 99 personnel with her. After further attempts to reach the boat failed, the rescue efforts were abandoned the following day amid a critical uproar from relatives. An inquiry did nothing to satisfy the relatives and trade unions, and a long and bitter legal action ended six and a half years later in the House of Lords, where claims for negligence were finally rejected on the grounds that there was no proof of liability.

Thetis was raised three months after she sank. Human remains still on board were retrieved for burial. The boat was repaired and went back to sea under the name of *Thunderbolt*, and had a successful campaign in the Mediterranean before being depth-charged north of Sicily on March 14, 1943, sinking for the second and last time.

The action begins, and *Athenia* goes down

Just after 11:15 hours on September 3, 1939, Royal Navy ships and submarines received the signal: "Commence hostilities with German forthwith." Four minutes later, the submarine *Spearfish* commanded by Lt J.H. Eden delivered a torpedo towards a German U-boat in the North Sea. It missed the target but established the first confrontation with the enemy. The Nazi High Command gave similar instructions to its U-boats that afternoon and before the day was out, Germany had launched into a controversy that matched its World War I attack on the passenger liner, *Lusitania*. This time, the victim was the 13,717 tonne/13,500-ton passenger liner, *Athenia* carrying 1,103 civilians, including more than 300 Americans attempting to escape the war in Europe. She became the first British ship sunk by a German U-boat in World War II.

The *Athenia* had already sailed from Glasgow en route to Montreal when war was official declared, and that afternoon as she steamed 402km/250 miles north-west of Inishtrahull, Northern Ireland, she was spotted by *U30* under the command of Lt Fritz-Julius Lemp. Regardless of the fact that German U-boats were supposed to be operating under prize regulations that obliged them to stop and search any potential targets, Lemp ordered his crew to open fire without giving any prior warning.

In the controversy that followed, and which remained an issue to be considered in the Nuremberg War Crimes trials, it was passed off as a case of mistaken identity. Lemp stated that he believed the *Athenia* was an armed merchant cruiser, and fired two torpedoes. The ship sank quickly with the loss of 112 passengers and crew, including 28 Americans, although

TOP: A photograph of the *Athenia* in the final throes of her sinking, apparently taken from the one of the rescue boats that rushed to the scene after the alert of the attack upon her by the *U30*. Three British destroyers and three merchant ships aided the rescue, which saved 90 per cent of the 1,103 civilians aboard.
ABOVE: The majestic liner in all her glory, a ship that the U-boat commander who ordered the sinking claimed he mistook for an armed merchant cruiser. Few believed him.

that did not prevent President Franklin D. Roosevelt continuing with his plans to declare America's neutrality in the war. Some of the passengers claimed they were attacked again when they were at sea, escaping in lifeboats.

Lemp later offered an explanation. He stated that having received three radio messages sent to all Kriegsmarine vessels stating that war existed between Britain and Germany, he spotted the ship heading away from Britain in a north-westerly direction. Having ordered his boat to dive to periscope depth, he

THE ACTION BEGINS, AND *ATHENIA* GOES DOWN

FAR LEFT: **Fritz-Julius Lemp,** captain of *U30* in the controversial sinking of the *Athenia*. He later sank a total of 17 ships in the same submarine, becoming the seventh U-boat commander to be awarded the Knights Cross at the age of 26. He met his match in May 1941: he was killed in action when the British captured his new submarine, *U110*, with its vital Enigma machine.

ABOVE: The killer blow to the *Athenia* may well have been struck by this torpedo, one of 11 that the Type VIIA *U30* could stow on each mission, a task made easier on July 7, 1940, when the boat became the first German submarine to make use of the newly captured French bases, docking in Lorient.
BELOW: *U30*, one of the busiest in early exchanges of the war and, as the front boat in Germany's 2nd Flotilla, completed eight patrols before she became a training submarine. BOTTOM: The British submarine *Oxley* lost off the coast of Norway after being mistaken for a U-boat and torpedoed by companion submarine *Triton* in September 1939.

saw that the ship was blacked out and came to the conclusion that she was an armed merchant cruiser, and therefore a legitimate target. He fired two torpedoes, the first striking the ship squarely, and the other missing. He claimed he dived to avoid the possibility of being hit by the second torpedo and, returning to periscope depth, fired a third because the ship did not seem to be sinking. This too missed, but undoubtedly ran towards the escaping passengers. At this point, Lemp checked his Lloyd's Register and discovered his mistake.

Soon afterwards, *U30* intercepted a plain-language transmission from the stricken ship identifying itself as the *Athenia*, but even then he did not attempt to aid survivors, as Prize Rules required, and maintained radio silence throughout. Thus, in an instant the memories of Germany's U-boat campaign of unrestricted warfare in World War I were revived.

In fact, the effect worldwide was such that Hitler himself decreed that all such accusations would be dealt with by categorical denial and Goebels even put out a statement accusing Britain of deliberately sinking the *Athenia* to stop Roosevelt declaring neutrality. The Nazis even went to the extent of falsifying records to show that *U30* was at least 322km/200 miles from the *Athenia* at the time. The truth, however, was confirmed at Nuremberg by Adolf Schmidt, a member of Lemp's crew who had been wounded in a later action and was left in Iceland, where he became a prisoner of war. Even so, the international outcry did have immediate repercussions when Hitler signed an order to prevent further attacks on passenger ships, regardless of the nation of origin.

The British, meanwhile, also proved that accidents could happen in this electrifying turmoil at the start of the war. On September 10, an old O-class submarine, *Oxley,* set off on her first major patrol off the coast of Norway. In heavy seas, at night and in poor visibility, she was spotted in the distance by one of her companion submarines, *Triton*. She failed to make the correct recognition signal. As a result, she was mistaken for a U-boat and torpedoed, and became the first submarine loss of World War II. Of the 54 crew, only her captain, Lt Commander H.G. Bowerman, and one other survived.

293

LEFT: The explosion caused by depth charges is violent and dramatic, and Lt Sheldon H. Kinney, Commander, USS *Bronstein* described them as "having a magnificent laxative effect on a submariner". They were used by ships or aircraft to attack submerged submarines and were first developed by the British for use against German submarines in World War I but were substantially improved by 1939. BELOW: Firing depth charges from the deck of a ship.

Mines, depth charges and leaky boats

Heligoland Bight and Skagerrak once again became the early scene of battles between British submarines and their German opponents, and Sir Max Horton, hero of great actions in World War I and whom the Germans had called a "pirate", was now directing operations under the personal eye of his good friend and First Lord of the Admiralty, Winston Churchill. As the battles began in earnest, they identified a particular target for the submarines in the unhindered supply of iron ore, which was being turned into ships and aircraft, coming down into Germany from northern Sweden – exactly the same problem that first emerged in 1914. The ore was being trans-shipped through the ice-free port of Narvik in northern Norway, still a neutral country.

On the same day, the British War Cabinet pronounced that British submarines could and would henceforth sink transport ships in the region on sight, and two days later it extended that order to cover any ship sighted within 16km/10 miles of the Norwegian coast. Max Horton had committed virtually his entire force to the Norwegian campaign a week earlier and although the British force would stay well away from the Baltic, where Horton had made his name, he dispatched every available submarine to join those already on patrol to cover all the German exits from Heligoland Bight, Skagerrak and the Kattegat.

The Skagerrak strait, between the southern coast of Norway and the Jutland peninsula of Denmark, was a vital seaway. Together with the Kattegat strait, it connects the North Sea with the Baltic Sea. About 214km/150 miles long and from 121km/75 to 145km/90 miles wide, the Skagerrak is shallow near Jutland but deepens near the Norwegian coast. It was in these treacherous waters that Max Horton placed an arc of submarines at the beginning of 1940. These were supplemented by others laying 50 mines apiece on each trip, and in the first half of the year there was probably not a single home-based submarine commander who did not see service there. Several would never return.

The extent of their activity is demonstrated by the amount of shipping sunk by the submarine service in the month between April 8 and May 4: close on 35 assorted vessels, of almost 90,000 tonnes/88,579 tons, with the loss of four British submarines. It was a dangerous time, particularly for the less experienced submariners, because it was the first time in history that efficient depth charges were used in abundance, in addition to the normal hazard of mines.

MINES, DEPTH CHARGES AND LEAKY BOATS

ABOVE LEFT: **Destroyer Escorts accompanying shipping movements routinely carried a heavy load of 100 or more depth charges to ward off enemy submarines or preferably kill them off completely. To be fully effective, they had to be fired with extreme accuracy.** ABOVE RIGHT: **An even greater threat to both surface ships and submarines alike was the greatly improved technology for creating minefields. The toll was heavy on both sides.** LEFT: **The British submarine minelayer,** *Porpoise*, **who made her name helping to break the blockade of Malta with food and fuel stacked on her mine deck. She subsequently fell victim to either mines or depth charges while on minelaying patrols in the Far East.** BELOW: **The jubilant crew of the British boat** *Truant*, **which was forced to remain on the bottom for a long period to escape the retribution of depth charges after torpedoing the German cruiser** *Karlsruhe*.

Depth charges first came into use during World War I. The early forms of the weapon consisted of large cylinders containing TNT, which were rolled or catapulted from the stern of a ship. In the intervening years, depth charges and machinery for launching them had improved dramatically, and experimental work on new designs was ongoing and came into use in the early stages of World War II. The use of a new and more powerful explosive called Torpex, a mixture of RDX, TNT and aluminium, substantially reduced the size of depth charges. The casings were also streamlined to make them sink faster and thus more difficult to avoid. To have literally dozens of these sinking towards your boat and exploding all around as the commander looked worryingly at his depth gauge was one of the most frightening experiences imaginable.

The T boat *Tetrarch*, under the command of Captain Roland Mills, took the record for staying submerged for the longest known period to date of 43 hours while under heavy counter-attack by depth charges. When he finally came up for air, his crew were literally falling as if drunk. He confessed in a memoir: "The effects of successive long spells under water, accompanied by depth-charge attacks, could have untoward effects, especially when the charges were poured into the sea by a posse of marauding destroyers, angry because the submarine had just fatally damaged one of Germany's brand-new cruisers."

That is exactly what happened to Admiral C.H. Hutchinson, then a Lt Commander of another of the early T boats, *Truant*. He had carried out a number of successful patrols in the North Sea during the Norwegian campaign, when in April 1940 he, along with other boats, was to provide protection and diversion for what proved to be the ill-fated Allied landings of troops at Narvik to counter the German invasion. One evening his attention was drawn to propeller noises, very faint, to the north. The sounds gradually got louder, and eventually he saw through the periscope a German cruiser dead ahead, screened by an escort of four small destroyers. He fired a large salvo of torpedoes and raised his periscope to take a look. He could see nothing but a very enlarged after-part of a destroyer which was right on top of him.

Unbeknown to Hutchinson at the time, he had torpedoed the famous German cruiser *Karlsruhe,* which was homeward bound from Oslo. The Germans were naturally furious. The cruiser was abandoned and was so badly damaged that Berlin ordered that she should be scuttled immediately.

Heroic work in the Mediterranean

The Norwegian campaign was followed quickly by the Battle of Britain, and the Royal Navy and the submarine force played its own part defending the potentially vulnerable eastern sea board as the threat of invasion mounted in the summer of 1940. It also provided cover for the massive operation to rescue the British Expeditionary force from France, while at the same time confronting the rising tide of U-boat activity in the Atlantic, soon to be facilitated by the use of France's Atlantic ports. But even as the demands of this new menace grew, a fresh area of conflict at sea opened up in the Mediterranean when Mussolini joined forces with Hitler and decided to rebuild the Roman Empire out of British possessions in North Africa and the Suez Canal in particular. One of the keys to this operation was his intention to capture the island of Malta, where defences were woefully meagre.

From the beginning, British resources were stretched to the limit, especially for the submarine flotillas, such as they were. Overnight, traditional British supply routes to its eastern outposts were closed down. The British had to send their ships on the long journey, lasting two or three months, around the Cape of Good Hope for all supplies, other than those borne by special convoys with major fleet escort operations, which the Royal Navy could ill afford. With the lack of very serious competition, the Italian Navy put up a very worthwhile case for supremacy in the Mediterranean, fielding five capital ships, 25 cruisers, 90 destroyers and 90 excellent submarines under a very capable command structure. They had back-up from 2,000 front-line aircraft and were undoubtedly leading the West in the diversity of experiments with mini-subs, human torpedoes, underwater chariots for frogmen and exploding motorboats. When Mussolini entered the war, the British had no real naval force between Gibraltar and the Italian fleet ports. The British base at Malta possessed a puny collection of just six submarines. Three of them, the minelayer *Grampus* and *Odin* and *Orpheus*, were lost in the first week after Mussolini

ABOVE: **British submarine *Upholder* sank or damaged 22 enemy ships, which earned her skipper, Lt Commander Malcolm Wanklyn, the award of a Victoria Cross, though sadly he and his boat did not survive the war.** INSET: **The badge of HMS *Upholder* linked by the crest as a tribute to the original Wanklyn boat when a new British diesel electric submarine was launched in 1987.** BELOW: **Submarines of the 10th Flotilla based at Lazaretto, Malta, went into maritime history for their exploits. They included *Upright* (second from right) which sank Mussolini's cruiser *Armando Diaz*.**

HEROIC WORK IN THE MEDITERRANEAN

signed his pact with Hitler. It was believed that they were all sunk with no survivors by deeply laid Italian mines.

Very soon, however, the British submariners began to show their mettle. Substantial totals of enemy shipping were sunk, and none better than that achieved by the brand new *Upholder*, under the command of Lt Commander Malcolm Wanklyn. He became the most successful submarine commander in World War II in spite of what would prove to be a relatively short career. *Upholder* arrived for duty in the Mediterranean on January 12, 1941. On her first patrol, she sank a 5,000-tonne/ 4,921-ton cargo vessel in one of the Axis convoys just off Tripoli, and in almost the same spot two days later sank an 8,000-tonne/ 7,874-ton supply ship. This time, *Upholder* was counter-attacked and took the brunt of 32 depth charges before escaping. After a brief lay-off, *Upholder* returned to the fray and in April sank three separate targets in a single convoy: a destroyer, a 4,000-tonne/3,937-ton supply ship and a 10,000-tonne/9.842-ton supply ship. On May 24, Wanklyn sighted a troopship, the Italian liner *Conte Rosso* of 17,800 tonnes/17,519 tons, carrying 4,000 troops, with an escort of three cruisers and several destroyers. He launched two torpedoes, which both scored direct hits amidships. The liner sank rapidly, killing 1,500 of the men on board. Wanklyn was awarded the DSO for this attack.

However, it was not all good news. During those vital months, the British submarine force in the Mediterranean lost four of its own boats in quick succession. *Usk* struck a mine at Cape Bon, *Undaunted* and *Union* were both depth-charged off Tripoli and the minelaying submarine *Cachalot* was rammed by an Italian torpedo boat. Malcolm Wanklyn and his fellow commanders began to take greater risks and shorter breaks. In September 1941, as Wanklyn set out on his fourteenth patrol, he joined up with *Unbeaten, Upright* and *Ursula* for a prearranged joint-assault to intercept a troop-carrying convoy leaving the southern Italian port of Taranto bound for Tunisia.

ABOVE: The minelayer *Grampus*, lead boat of her class, built in 1935, was deployed off the coast of Sicily in June 1940, when she was spotted by a group of Italian torpedo boats and torpedoed. There were no survivors. BELOW: The *Undine*-class submarine *Ursula*, also in the Mediterranean flotilla, was noted earlier in action near the *Elbe*, when her captain, Lt Commander G.C. Phillips, courageously dived beneath a screen of six destroyers to sink the German cruiser *Leipzig* at a range so close that the *Ursula* herself was badly shaken by the explosion.

Two torpedoes from *Upholder* hit the transport *Neptunia*, which sank in eight minutes. Wanklyn's third torpedo hit *Oceania* and ripped away her stern. The third transport, *Vulcania*, was hit by *Ursula* from long range, and *Utmost* finished her off as she tried to limp away. Meanwhile, *Utmost* now sighted three Italian cruisers and several destroyers and promptly sank one of the cruisers. As a result of his latest exploits, Malcolm Wanklyn was awarded the Victoria Cross in December 1941. On April 6, 1942, *Upholder* sailed out of the base for her twenty-fifth and last patrol before heading home for a refit, but she never made it back. On April 14, *Upholder* was depth-charged and sunk by the Italian torpedo boat *Pegaso* north-east of Tripoli. Wanklyn's was a remarkable record. In 16 months, *Upholder* had sunk or damaged 22 enemy ships, including three U-boats, two destroyers and one cruiser as well as 120,910 tonnes/119,000 tons of supply ships.

"Finest work" by British submarines

ABOVE: A classic shot of the periscope in operation in the control room, and without which the submarine would be useless. The skills of the operators in judging the distance, heading and speed of the target were imperative when firing a torpedo.

Much action remained, and more VCs were to be won in the continuing saga of the battle for the Mediterranean. Among them was an incident involving *Thrasher*. She had been in the Mediterranean only a couple of months and in February 1942 was operating off northern Crete. There, on February 16, she penetrated an escort screen of five destroyers in broad daylight and torpedoed and sank a large Axis supply ship off Suda Bay. The destroyers gave chase, and as she crash-dived they remained overhead for an hour or more, sending down more than 30 depth charges. She surfaced after dark and headed off towards the Gulf of Taranto, but very soon banging noises were heard on the casing. Two unexploded bombs had become lodged on the submarine.

Lt Peter Roberts and Petty Officer Tommy Gould volunteered to go out and recover the bombs. The first bomb was located and gently removed, wrapped in sacking and dropped over the stern. The second was lodged in a narrow space and they had to lay full length in complete darkness, pushing and dragging the bomb for a distance of some 6.1m/20ft until it could be lowered over the side, a task which took more than half an hour. There was a very great chance that the submarine might have to crash-dive while they were under the casing. Had this happened, they would have been drowned. Robert and Gould deservedly won the VC for their heroic action.

Throughout this period, there were many acts of great gallantry and daring among the submarine flotillas in the Mediterranean, many of which resulted in their final demise. In March 1942, the *Torbay* won particular attention and a Victoria Cross for her captain, Lt Commander Anthony Miers. He sighted a north-bound convoy of four ships too far distant for him to attack initially, and he decided to follow in the hope of catching them in Corfu harbour. During the night, *Torbay* approached undetected up the channel and remained on the surface charging her battery. Unfortunately, the convoy passed straight through the channel, but on the morning of March 5, in glassy sea conditions, Miers successfully attacked two store ships and then brought *Torbay* safely back to the open sea. The submarine endured 40 depth charges and had been in closely patrolled enemy waters for 17 hours.

Turbulent also had numerous successes recorded against her name and represented a remarkable achievement which eventually brought the award of a Victoria Cross for the "great valour" of her captain, Commander John Wallace "Tubby" Linton, at the end of what was ultimately a tragic journey. In March 1943, Linton had already been hailed as one of the greats in the submarine hall of fame, but his was not simply a story of "big hits" in the Mediterranean. It went well beyond that, in terms

"FINEST WORK" BY BRITISH SUBMARINES

of courage, daring and dedication to duty in the face of great adversity, as recorded in the citation for the VC he was awarded: "From the outbreak of war until *Turbulent's* last patrol, Commander Linton was constantly in command of submarines, and during that time inflicted great damage on the enemy."

The journey for Linton and his crew was drawing to a close in February 1943, when they sailed from Algiers for a patrol in the Tyrrhenian Sea. On March 1, she attacked and sank the Italian steamship *Vincenz.* On March 11, she torpedoed the mail and supply ship *Mafalda*. She was herself attacked the following morning by the anti-submarine trawler *Teti II* but escaped, only to hit a mine off Maddalena, Sardinia, on March 23. The discovery of her wreck many years later confirmed the irony of her last voyage.

The part played by the submarines of the 1st and 10th flotillas has not always been fully recognized by historians, although Commander F.W. Lipscomb was moved to record: "There is no doubt that the whole Mediterranean offensive can be regarded as the finest work ever accomplished by British submarines." In the crucial two years between January 1941 and December 1942, the Italians lost 171 ships in the Mediterranean, totalling well over half a million tonnes/492,103 tons, a large proportion of which were sunk by the submarine flotillas. On the debit side at that time, Britain lost 14 submarines in the Mediterranean, with 70 officers and 720 ratings.

TOP LEFT: **HMS** *Thunderbolt*, **the salvaged and recommissioned** *Thetis* **which re-emerged in October 1940, later adapted to carry Britain's "human torpedoes", known as Chariots, before she was lost again, this time sunk by an Italian corvette in March 1943.** TOP RIGHT: *Sokol*, **of the Polish Navy, in Malta Harbour, flying the Jolly Roger to denote her successes. She was previously HMS** *Urchin*, **loaned to the Poles after the loss of their own submarines.**
ABOVE LEFT: **Survivors of a U-boat rescued by Allied vessels in 1943, the year in which the Germans saw their highest number of losses, with 242 boats sunk.**
ABOVE RIGHT: **The uncommon sight of a U-boat in the Mediterranean: only 62 German boats passed through the Straits of Gibraltar throughout the war and none of them returned: all being sunk, severely damaged or scuttled.**
BELOW: **A memorial tribute in Valetta to the British and Allied submarine forces for their efforts during the war.**

TO COMMEMORATE THE CLOSE TIES FORGED BETWEEN THE PEOPLE OF MALTA G.C. AND THE OFFICERS AND MEN OF THE BRITISH AND ALLIED SUBMARINES BASED IN MALTA IN H.M.S. TALBOT, LAZARETTO MANOEL ISLAND IN TIME OF WAR, 1939-1945

THE HISTORY OF SUBMARINES

U-boat war in the Atlantic

In World War I, U-boats operating in the Atlantic almost brought Britain to her knees. The same procedure was attempted by Admiral Karl Dönitz, head of the German submarine service, by attacking Allied shipping at its weakest point – merchant vessels – with what was, at the time, a comparatively small fleet of U-boats. The aim was to harass the movement of essential British troop convoys to the Mediterranean and beyond, and cut Britain's vital seaborne supply routes. This developed into what Churchill christened the Battle of the Atlantic.

Restrictions placed on Germany's re-armament during the inter-war years meant that Hitler began his war with just 46 operational vessels, of which just over half were submarines. Dönitz ensured this state of affairs was quickly rectified as German shipyards began turning out the new-era U-boats at an incredible rate. Notwithstanding the *Athenia* debacle, the U-boats opened their account against the British with spectacular results very early in the war.

U29, under the command of Kapitän-Leutnant Otto Schuhart, sank HMS *Courageous*, one of Britain's four aircraft carriers, off the coast of Ireland on September 17, 1939. The ship went down in 20 minutes, taking with her 518 of her 1,200 crew. On October 13, a U-boat adventurer, Kapitän-Leutnant Günther Prien, commanding *U47*, set course for Scapa Flow, the Royal Navy's northern anchorage, hoping to do some damage. The fleet was out, but the fine old battleship *Royal Oak* was standing guard and Prien promptly dispatched her to the deep with his torpedoes. In all, 833 men lost their lives, and many of the 396 survivors suffered severe burns and life-threatening injuries.

TOP: **A rare shot of battlecruiser *Gneisenau* and *U47* together. The latter, having entered the supposedly impregnable Royal Navy base at Scapa Flow in October 1939, sank the battleship *Royal Oak*, with the loss of 833 men. *Gneisenau*, operating with her sister ship *Scharnhorst*, infamously sank the carrier *Glorious* and two escort destroyers, leaving 3,000 men floundering in the ice-cold waters of the North Atlantic. Only 36 survived.** ABOVE: **A view of an Atlantic convoy of merchantmen from one of the many destroyers that screened their journeys across the Atlantic carrying vital supplies.**

By repeating their tactics of World War I, the Germans – having failed to invade – hoped to subdue the British by starving the nation of food and equipment. Germany's main naval weapon was to be the U-boat, and control of the French Biscay ports provided bases from which they could sally forth into the Atlantic without having to pass either through the Channel or around the north of the British Isles at the end of every patrol. The convoy system of bringing in supplies was operated from the outset and in the first full two years of the

U-BOAT WAR IN THE ATLANTIC

FAR LEFT: **The popular wartime poster expressing the heartfelt feelings of many: "Let 'em have it!" Similar poster art was also rife in Germany.** LEFT: **Admiral Karl Dönitz, naval strategist, was a mastermind of the U-boat campaign and briefly Hitler's successor after the Führer committed suicide.** ABOVE: **The Kriegsmarine U-boat golden badge of honour.**

BELOW: **U-boat wolf-packs made a direct course for the American Liberty ships in the Atlantic convoys. More than 2,750 such ships were built in the US to mass-produced design, each in about 70 days at a cost of less than $2 million per vessel. They could cross the Atlantic at an average speed of 11 knots, carrying over 9,144 tonnes/9,000 tons of cargo in the five holds, plus airplanes, tanks and locomotives lashed to the deck. A Liberty could carry 2,840 jeeps, 440 tanks, or 230 million rounds of rifle ammunition.**

war, 12,057 ships arrived at British ports in 900 convoys. The convoys grew in size: eventually between 40 and 60 ships would steam in columns with 3.2km/2 miles between each column and 0.53km/0.33 miles between each ship. A 12-column convoy would extend almost 11.1km/6 nautical miles in length and almost two miles deep. They needed massive protection: escorts of surface ships, destroyers, submarines and aircraft, when in range, would accompany convoys at various stages en route.

However, the U-boats gradually built their devastating campaign against Allied ships, supplemented by mines, aircraft and surface ships, and by the end of 1940 alone, 3,048,141 tonnes/3,000,000 tons of Allied shipping were lost, and the tonnage escalated dramatically when Dönitz introduced the infamous wolf-pack tactics and night surface attacks. The admiral often directed wolf-pack operations himself. A group of U-boats would patrol in lines scouting for convoys and once spotted, one boat would act as the shadow, reporting its heading and speed to U-boat headquarters. Other boats would be directed to form around the convoy, and at a given time, when all were gathered and in position, launch a combined attack, usually on the surface at night, thus greatly reducing the effectiveness of ASDIC.

A number of German U-boat commanders made their name as wolf-pack specialists, notably Günther Prien, whose *U47* sank 31 ships and damaged eight others before he and his crew were lost when their boat went down in battle on March 7, 1941. Prien, then just 33 years old, was one of the most highly decorated U-boat commanders, and the first to be awarded the Knight's Cross – a feat mentioned in the post-war writings of Winston Churchill. Another famous wolf-pack expert was Otto Kretschmer, who was 28 years old in 1940 and in command of *U99*. He sank almost 304,814 tonnes/ 300,000 tons of shipping and, like Prien, was awarded the Knight's Cross with Oak Leaves, and later the Knight's Cross with Oak Leaves and Swords. He survived the war and lived to the age of 86.

Almost 140 U-boat wolf-packs were assembled during 1940–43. Their operations were meticulously recorded, some fast and effective, others lasting ten days or more. The number of U-boats in each pack ranged from a minimum of three to around 20 in the biggest groups. This phase of the war became known among the Germans as the "happy time", a constant wearing down of merchant shipping that, in fact, became a far greater threat than the possibility of invasion. Eventually, however, brilliant work by scientists and all branches of the armed forces combined to bring an end to this devastating instrument of attrition.

301

THE HISTORY OF SUBMARINES

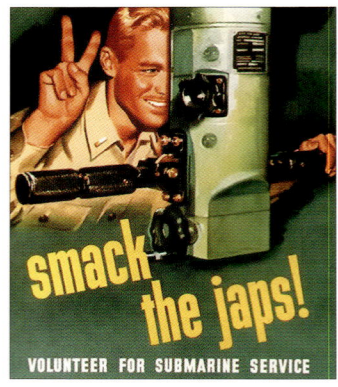

LEFT: USS *Pompano*, one of the *Perch*-class of American submarines, built in the mid-1930s, which saw great service against the Japanese. She was also one of the many losses, having left Midway in August 1943 bound for the coasts of Hokkaido and Honshu. She sank two ships in early September, but was never heard from again, presumed lost to a mine.
ABOVE: Poster art in America, blunt and to the point.

Pacific encounters of America and Japan

American naval experts are the first to admit that prior to their nation's entry into World War II in December 1941, their submarine capability was faulty and neglected. This was due in part to the numerous international treaties that the US had supported on the banning of unrestricted submarine warfare, and due also to the general malaise about getting involved in the war. There were other vital flaws in America's somewhat archaic peacetime submarine strategy in that many considered it to be an unduly hazardous occupation, and suicidal if operating within range of an enemy air base. Thus, the Silent Service amounted to little more than one per cent of the total resources of the US Navy at the beginning of the 1940s. Also on the debit side was the fact that American torpedoes were not always effective, a fact which was not fully corrected until well into the war.

The U-boat campaigns in the Atlantic changed many minds: suicidal or not, an effective submarine force was a necessary evil to be embraced by the US, a fact which was finally confirmed by the Japanese attack on Pearl Harbor on December 7, 1941. The Japanese had been powering ahead: from the late 1920s, submarine development had become an intrinsic element of their growing front-line naval capability.

While the Navy struggled to recover from the Pearl Harbor attack, the submarine force took the war to the enemy. Operating from Pearl Harbor, and Australian bases at Fremantle and Brisbane, and eventually employing the reliable new Gato, Balao and Tench classes, the submariners began to fight back in some style. By the late summer

ABOVE: USS *Plunger*, sister submarine of *Pompano*, survived the war and members of the crew display her battle-flag, while the sailor seated in the centre is wearing a Japanese sailor's hat. The photograph was dated June 21, 1943, following *Plunger's* sixth war patrol.

of 1942, the scorecard was beginning to show signs of improvement but the Japanese still held the upper hand by far, and were inflicting heavy losses on the US Navy. In August, the aircraft carrier *Saratoga* was torpedoed and knocked out of the war for months. Three weeks later, the Japanese submarine *I-19* sank the aircraft carrier *Wasp* and seriously damaged *North Carolina*, America's newest and most powerful battleship. *Wasp's* sister carrier *Hornet* was hit in October, a crippling blow at the time when the Battle of Guadalcanal hung in the balance.

302

Apart from the hasty building programme, the Americans also had to make considerable readjustments to methods of attack, given that most training and operational work had been planned around the principal role of coastal defence. Across America, too, scientists and mathematicians were working around the clock to produce new technology for submarine detection.

One of the leaders in new methods of tactical warfare that became common practice emerged among submarines operating from the Brisbane base, under the command of Admiral James Fife. He suggested a trial of a new command and control system in USS *Wahoo* under Lt Commander Dudley W. Morton. Executive Officer, Lt Richard O'Kane, manned the periscope leaving Morton free to evaluate the entire combat situation. On her next patrol, *Wahoo* sank 32,402 tonnes/31,890 tons of Japanese shipping. Morton received the first of four Navy Crosses and his ship took home a Presidential Unit Citation. Later in the war, as commanding officer of USS *Tang*, O'Kane received the Congressional Medal of Honour and became the Submarine Force's leading ace of the war, credited with destroying 31 ships totalling 227,800 tonnes/224,202 tons.

Similar initiatives were introduced at the Fremantle base under Admiral Charles Lockwood. He totally revamped tactics employed by the newer submarines and towards the year's end, America's submariners slowly began to turn the tide, and ended 1942 with 180 Japanese ships sunk, totalling 725,000 tonnes/713,550 tons. In fact, it was a meagre tonnage compared to the U-boat tally for the same year – 1,160 Allied ships of more than 6 million tonnes/5,905,239 tons sunk.

The impetus continued apace as the new American submarines piled into the region, and after the recapture of Guam in August 1944, boats based there and at Saipan succeeded in imposing a virtual blockade against Japan, causing massive shortages in oil, raw materials and food. By the autumn of 1944, Japan's remaining five fleet carriers had been sunk, and the sea war in the region was as good as settled.

TOP: **A typical scene in the control area of a US submarine before the action gets hot, but the apparent calmness belies the fact that at any moment chaos and confusion may ensue. This was especially so when the US submarine chiefs raised the stakes early in 1943 by totally overhauling tactics, and continued to do so as the war progressed. They employed more aggressive daytime submerged and night-time surface attacks, partly enabled by improving technology, which resulted in considerable damage to the Japanese fleet.** ABOVE: **A periscope view of the carnage on the surface after a successful attack upon enemy shipping, indicating whether it was safe to surface.** LEFT: **The crews of all American boats kept track of progress with their battle flags, this one from USS *Besugo*, a *Balao*-class submarine, circa early 1944.**

303

THE HISTORY OF SUBMARINES

Clandestine travellers aboard

Submarines in all theatres of World War II were used by all sides for many special operations. The Germans landed agents in Britain, America and elsewhere. The British did the same across Europe and the Far East, and to the last, submarines were in continuous use for clandestine operations. Indeed, some of the most famous exploits of particular heroism, which resulted in many a post-war movie, were launched from submarines, including sabotage operations by the Special Boat Service, assault operations by Commando units, the famed but ill-fated Cockleshell heroes and members of the Special Operation Executive. Submariners were also the carriers of a top secret organization whose very existence was denied for 15 years after the war because of ongoing operations on sensitive coastlines – that of the Combined Operations Pilotage Parties (COPPS). This was formed in great secrecy in September 1942 for harbour and beach reconnaissance prior to landings of Allied forces in virtually every theatre of war, operations which still exist today in the shape of Special Forces the world over.

More than 40 Royal Navy submarines were involved in clandestine operations in World War II, and several of them, including the T boats in the Mediterranean and the brand new S-class boat of Lt Norman "Bill" Jewell, commissioned in 1942, were used repeatedly for the service. The British submarine service was a forerunner of these operations and gained early practice in 1940, carrying Commandos to the German-held Norwegian coastline, bristling with all kinds of anti-submarine vessels, mines and air attacks. Lt Commander A.C. Hutchinson and the crew of *Truant* experienced the fiercest and most sustained attacks by depth charges ever known by a British submarine up to that point of the war while carrying his Commando passengers.

Next, the early exploits of the fledgling SBS began in the Mediterranean, when teams were carried around by submarines to be landed clandestinely on Italian shores to blow up railway lines, viaducts, water supplies and bridges. The most famous duo of Lt Robert "Tug" Wilson, an architect from Leamington Spa, and his partner, Marine Wally Hughes, led the way, hitching rides in *Urge* with Lt Commander Tommy Tomkinson. They would be floated off the casing of the boat in their canoe, perhaps 4.8km/3 miles offshore. They would then paddle their little craft ashore, loaded with explosives, where the two men would carry their load to the designated target, set the charges and make a hasty exit. They would lay up until the appointed time, when their host submarine would (hopefully) reappear to pick them up, mission completed.

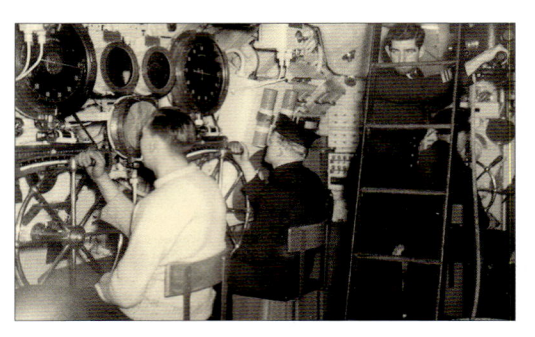

There were many, many dangerous moments when these operations were interrupted by German and Italian aircraft or surface ships. In one ill-fated operation in November 1941, two T boats, *Talisman* and *Torbay*, were put at great risk to insert 56 Commandos on to a beach 322km/200 miles inside enemy lines on a most dangerous mission. Shortly before British forces launched an all-out attack to gain control of the North African coast from German and Italian forces, they were assigned to assassinate Field Marshal Erwin Rommel, then

ABOVE: **The control room of HMS *Tuna*, with Lt Norman at the periscope of the boat that launched "The Cockleshell Heroes", 12 Royal Marines who made their famed canoe-borne attempt to blow up German ships in the Gironde estuary.**
LEFT: **The Anzio landings, part of the Allied invasion of Italy. The beaches had been presurveyed by members of the top-secret Royal Navy Combined Operations Pilotage Parties in their canoes, and clandestinely delivered by submarine.**

CLANDESTINE TRAVELLERS ABOARD

FAR LEFT: **The T-class submarine *Triumph* that delivered many of the secret operatives of organizations such as the Special Boat Squadron or the Special Operations Executive to their destinations on dangerous missions behind enemy lines.** LEFT: **Folboats or canoes used by the SBS and Navy frogmen were stowed aboard the submarines and unloaded near the target coastline.** BELOW: **The canoeists would then paddle their way into shore, and then, in most cases, the submarine would return at a pre-determined time to collect the saboteurs.**

ABOVE: **The American Navy paid particular interest to early British successes in clandestine operations and set up their own units. Although hardly invisible, the USS *Nautilus* was used on early missions, and sailing with submarine *Argonaut*, carried Marines of the 2nd Raider Battalion to stage diversionary attacks on Japanese-held territory.**

commander in chief of Axis forces, who was supposed to be at his inland villa. In very rough seas, *Torbay* and *Talisman* were heaving as the inflatable boats were launched towards the shore. It was so choppy that only 45 made it off the submarines. It was a heroic but ultimately unsuccessful mission. Rommel, it turned out, was not at the villa but in Rome. The Commando force met heavy resistance, and the submarine commanders risked their own safety in waiting around at the rendezvous to pick up the men who, in fact, never returned. Only four Commandos survived the mission and only evaded capture by walking back to their base across a hostile landscape, a journey that took 40 days.

One of them was Bombadier Brittlebank of the Royal Artillery, who subsequently replaced Marine Hughes, who was ill, as Tug Wilson's partner for further missions off the Italian coastline. Their exploits were, however, to be curtailed. The danger of these operations to the submarines was demonstrated by the fate of *Triumph*, under Lt Commander W.J.W. Woods. She carried out a number of special operations, landing commando teams all around the Italian coastline until she was assigned to land a unit near Athens, sailing from Alexandria on December 26, 1941. Four days later

Lt Commander Woods sent a signal confirming the landing of the party, and *Triumph* was due to return to pick up the commandos two weeks later, but failed to make the rendezvous. Nothing further was heard of the submarine.

Another of the famous submarine-launched sabotage groups were the canoeists of Operation Frankton, more commonly known as The Cockleshell Heroes, the brainchild of Lt Colonel H.G. "Blondie" Hasler. Pairs of men were carried by the submarine *Tuna* to the mouth of the river Gironde, on the west coast of France. Five pairs then paddled 113km/70 miles upstream by night to attack 12 German ships lying in the supposed safe haven in the Bassens-Bordeaux area. However, only one pair, Hasler and his colleague Ned Sparks, survived the mission. Of the remaining eight men involved, six were captured and shot as saboteurs by the Germans and the remaining two were lost, presumed drowned.

305

"The most important capture of the war"

Kapitänleutnant Fritz-Julius Lemp, the U-boat captain who sank the *Athenia* on the first day of the war, had been a busy man, commanding *U30*, the lead boat in the 2nd U-boat Flotilla. By May 1941, he was a holder of the Knight's Cross and commander of *U110* in the wolf-packs scouring the Atlantic for their prey, operating in partnership with *U201*. On May 9, Lemp sank two ships totalling 10,000 tonnes/ 9,842 tons, but when he came up to confirm his final "kill", he left his periscope aloft too long and was spotted by the convoy escort, the corvette HMS *Aubretia*. The escort gave the alert to other ships while she herself unloaded a massive bombardment of depth charges.

Aubretia was joined by the destroyers *Bulldog* and *Broadway*, and their attack was delivered with such force that Lemp was forced to surface. As he came up, a dozen men on *U110* rushed to man the guns but were themselves shot by the waiting British ships. Lemp also discovered that *Bulldog* was already lined up for a ramming operation, which her commander Commander Joe Baker-Creswell had no intention of carrying out, having already considered the possibility of a capture. Lemp, expecting the ramming to arrive any time soon, ordered his men to abandon ship, apparently assuming that once his boat was sunk, her secrets would go to the bottom with her. This boat did, indeed, contain secrets – none other than one of the famous Enigma cipher machines, as well as a vital codebook on how to use it.

TOP: **HMS *Bulldog*, the most famous of the seven Royal Navy ships to bear the name, was a Class B destroyer launched in 1930, and she remained in service until 1946 when she was scrapped. The heroic actions of her crew in capturing the first Enigma machine undoubtedly helped change the course of the war.**
ABOVE: **The submarine from which the Enigma machine was extracted, *U110* was captained by Fritz-Julius Lemp, a commander of some notoriety, notably for sinking the liner *Athenia*.**

So, over the side went the surviving members of the crew, Lemp with them, but he never made it to the British ships which picked up the survivors. Many said after the war that he was shot in the water by a British officer who led the boarding party from *Bulldog* to take possession of *U110*. David Balme, the man accused of this act by a German author after the war, denies this categorically in his memoir held in the Imperial War Museum's Sound Archive, and said Lemp died in some other way. The speculation was that realizing his boat, a IXB class, was not going to sink, he either tried to swim back to save the secrets aboard and drowned, or committed suicide, realizing his cardinal sin of failing to scuttle his boat.

Bulldog's crew, meanwhile, had pulled alongside the U-boat and began stripping her of everything they could carry. David Balme recalled: "I was in the control room when our telegraphist called me over and said '*Look* at this, sir,' pointing to what appeared to be an old typewriter. We both thought it looked interesting, and that we'd better take it over. And that is how we discovered the Enigma cipher on board *U110*."

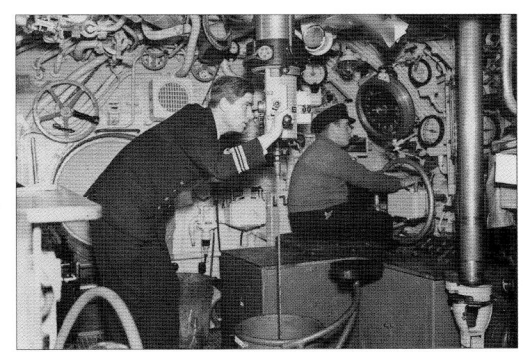

"THE MOST IMPORTANT CAPTURE OF THE WAR"

ABOVE LEFT: **Another Enigma-carrying boat, *U505* was captured by the Americans exactly three years after *U110* was taken by the crew of HMS *Bulldog*, but because the British government had ordered a clampdown, which remained in force for 30 years, it was widely believed that *U505* was the first to be captured – a belief wrongly portrayed in a Hollywood movie.** ABOVE: **U-boat pens provided a safe haven for the German submarine fleet around the French coast as well as in Germany. These were especially vital at the time of the Battle for the Atlantic.** LEFT: **A typical interior of the boats operating during that era.** BELOW: **The Enigma machine, whose mysteries were unlocked at Bletchley Park, thus providing the British with an incredible insight into forthcoming Nazi operations.**

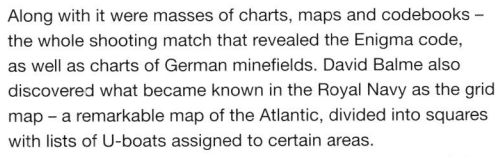

Along with it were masses of charts, maps and codebooks – the whole shooting match that revealed the Enigma code, as well as charts of German minefields. David Balme also discovered what became known in the Royal Navy as the grid map – a remarkable map of the Atlantic, divided into squares with lists of U-boats assigned to certain areas.

It took hours to ferry the material back to *Bulldog* and then Baker-Creswell took the boat under tow. However, as soon as the Admiralty received a description of what had been found, they ordered the boat to be scuttled at once, and all the prisoners taken to Iceland, where they would be interned. The whole operation was now very cloak and dagger to ensure that no one – especially not the German High Command – should know the U-boat and her secrets were in British hands.

An expert from Bletchley Park met *Bulldog* when she arrived in Scapa Flow and took the Enigma machine and the books away. Every man on board the ship was sworn to secrecy. The find was enormously significant and helped the Ultra code-breakers to read top secret communications between Hitler and the German High Command for months ahead, a fact that Churchill did not reveal even to Roosevelt until the end of 1942.

The capture of *U110* was one to become one of the best kept secrets of the war, and indeed was not publicly revealed until 30 years later. That is why the American Navy put into printed history the claim that it captured the first U-boat containing dramatic secrets. How were they to know the British had already done it! Their capture came in May 1944 when US Navy Task Group 22.3 sailed from Norfolk, Virginia, for an anti-submarine patrol near the Canary Islands. On June 4, USS *Chatelain* reported a sonar contact with a submerged submarine. Two fighter planes from the USS *Guadalcanal* were called down to fire their guns into the water to help mark the location of the submerged *U505*. The USS *Chatelain* then fired a pattern of 14 depth charges, forcing *U505* to surface. While the USS *Chatelain* and the USS *Jenks* picked up survivors, the USS *Pillsbury* sent its whaleboat to the *U505*, where Lt Albert L. David led a nine-man boarding party to capture the submarine.

307

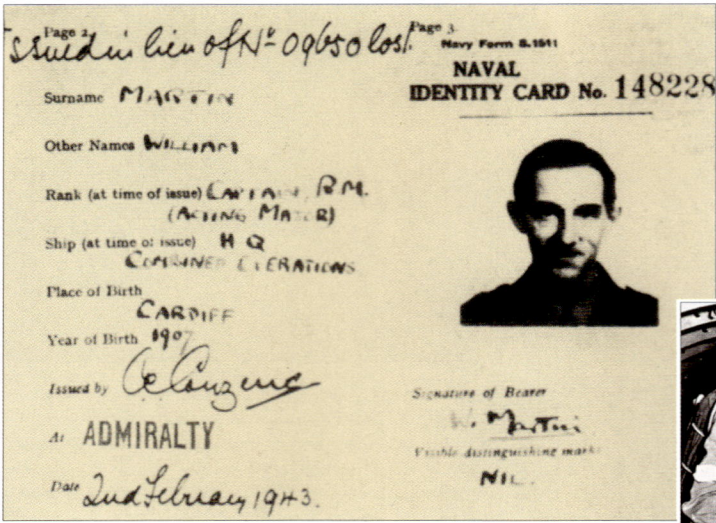

LEFT: The fake identity documents secreted in the pockets of "Major Martin", which helped persuade German intelligence into accepting that he carried genuine details of plans for an Allied invasion of the southern coastline of Greece when, in fact, they were to descend upon Sicily. BELOW: US Paratroops join the Allied invasion of Sicily, a task greatly facilitated by the fake documents found on the body launched from HMS *Seraph*.

Operation Mincemeat (or "The Man Who Never Was")

Lt Commander Norman Jewell had already carried out numerous special operations along the coast of North Africa since taking delivery of the new S-class submarine *Seraph*, including the covert delivery of US General Mark Clark to Algeria in October 1942 to try to persuade the Vichy French to support the planned North African landings. A month later, Jewell and his crew provided the transport for the rescue of French General Henri Giraud off the south coast of France after he had escaped from a German prison camp. It was a dangerous episode because the general's arrival was delayed for almost a week, but *Seraph* had to remain on station, diving and surfacing in hostile waters, ready to pick up her passenger.

The most famous of *Seraph's* secret exploits subsequently became popularly known as "The Man Who Never Was": a cunning scheme codenamed Operation Mincemet, aimed at fooling the Axis powers into thinking that the Allied landings in Sicily would, in fact, take place elsewhere. Norman Jewell tells the story personally, in his memoir for the Imperial War Museum sound archive:

"I was told to report to naval intelligence and there met up with a team concocting an incredible scheme…A body was to be washed up on the coast of Spain which would carry in an attaché case secret papers, a letter for Eisenhower, the Commander-in-Chief in North Africa, saying that rather than going for Sicily the invasion would be on the south coast of Greece.

"My knowledge was limited exactly to that which I needed to know in order to carry out my part of the plan. However, we spent a good deal of time building up a background for this body, who was to be called Major Martin, providing him with a life, a girlfriend, and in his pockets theatre tickets, restaurant receipts, a letter and so on. They knew it would be checked out by German spies in London. Then (when the time came), the body of Major Martin was placed in a canister about the size of a torpedo.

"The body was packed in ice so that it would be the right age when washed up. We were given clear passage down to

LEFT: The fictitious Major William Martin – "The Man Who Never Was" – being cast into the sea off the coast of Spain.

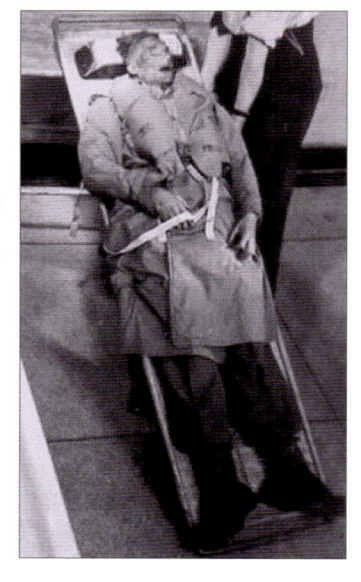

LEFT: **HMS *Seraph* was one of the improved British S-class boats, commissioned in 1942.** BELOW LEFT: **One of the restaurant bills found in the pockets of the dead man that also helped convince the Germans as to his authenticity.**
BELOW: **On their way to the true target, the massive task force of British and American troops join the invasion of Sicily by sea and air.**

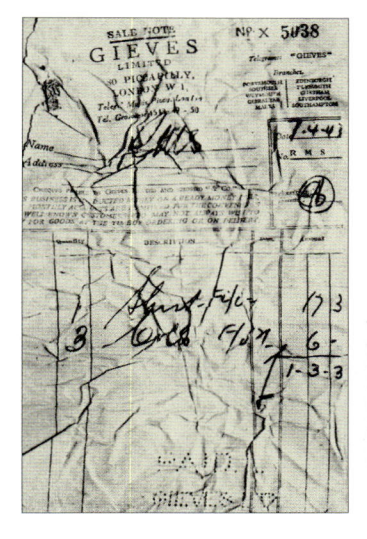

the coast of Spain, which meant that the RAF was aware of our presence. We were also told that we would not be required to attack anything en route because our mission was too important. However, we were taken out of our safe passage line to attack some shipping going to Bordeaux. We never saw them, but thanks to that instruction we were then bombed three times by the RAF. We eventually arrived off the coast of Spain at the point where Spain joins Portugal. Until that point, no one on board – apart from myself – knew that the canister contained a body.

"The cover story was that it was carrying meteorological equipment to fill in the reporting gap for the Meteorological Office in London. But now, the body was to be retrieved from the canister to be put over the side. I had to tell the officers because I could not do the whole thing on my own. I did not give details of the plan, but in any event I had to swear them to secrecy. They were surprised; some were shocked…dispatching the body of an unknown man into the sea in this manner. We took off the end of the canister and brought the body out. It was the first time I had seen it. We made a final check to make sure that his papers and attaché case containing the secret 'invasion' plans were intact and attached to his wrist, and then slid him over the side. We went full astern on the motor so that he would be pushed on his way. We said a few words as a funeral service over him and then secured the canister on the casing and dived. At daybreak we surfaced to try to get rid of the canister

and we had a hell of a time. It had been so designed to keep the ice from melting that it had air pockets all the way around it, and even though we had put about 200 bullet holes through it from a machine-gun nothing happened at all. We then had to go alongside it again and put some plastic explosives inside and outside and then withdrew while it blew up. It then disappeared finally. We then went on to Gibraltar, arriving the next evening. As we arrived, someone came over the gangway carrying a telegram for me, which said the parcel had been received: so the body had arrived safely.

"As would be discovered later, the Germans went to great lengths to discover the background of Major Martin through their spies in London and could not discredit the information that we had placed about him. In due course, the Germans withdrew an armoured division and sent it through Italy and down the other side towards Greece. They were at least a division less in Sicily when the landings eventually took place."

In fact, the ploy was so successful that the Germans thought Sardinia and Greece were the intended objectives until well after the landings in Sicily had begun. As for the "body" that became Major Martin, it was reported in 1997 that it was that of a homeless alcoholic from Wales named Glyndwr Michael, although even that claim has since been challenged. Whoever it was, the body was buried in Heluva, Spain, with a gravestone in the name of Martin.

THE HISTORY OF SUBMARINES

LEFT: The Italians were masters of the human torpedoes and Chariots and had produced a working prototype, which was tested at La Spezia in 1936. This ultimately led to the construction of submarine-borne containers to deliver them to the target area.

BELOW: The British quickly caught on and introduced their own charioteers, here in rehearsal for the invasion of Sicily.

The chariots of stealth

The Japanese, Italians and latterly the British all had specialist teams working on the development of underwater guerrilla warfare. The Axis navies were well ahead of the field when war came as a result of experimental work in the 1930s. After the exploits of the SBS and the Cockleshell Heroes, Lord Mountbatten, as head of Combined Operations, sent a memo to the Chiefs of Staff, pointing out that the men's determination and courage demonstrated a good example of the successful use of limpeteers.

He already had a report which indicated that Italian underwater activity was "filled with ideas involving gadgetry and motorisation and experimentation". In fact, the Italians were well ahead of everyone in their perfection of a number of devices and submarine attack apparatus that would become the model for the future. These included effective breathing apparatus for underwater swimmers, double limpets, human torpedoes, piloted torpedoes, miniature torpedoes and exploding attack boats. Teams of dedicated and highly trained men were inspired by the famous Commander Belloni and the infamous Prince Julio Valerie Borghese from the 10th Light Flotilla of the Italian Navy.

This particular skill of the Italians really began to worry the Allies in 1941, at a time when the British fleet was reduced to two battleships in the Mediterranean, HMS *Valiant* and the brand new HMS *Queen Elizabeth*, which lay sheltered behind torpedo nets at Alexandria. At 03:30 hours on December 19, two Italians were discovered clinging to the anchor buoy of *Valiant*. They surrendered immediately and were taken ashore for interrogation and then, to their dismay, back to *Valiant*, where they confessed that the battleship was about to blow up.

The crew was mustered on deck and the watertight doors were closed, but shortly after 06:00 hours the ship rocked and shuddered as the charge set by the two Italians blasted a large hole in her stern. Soon afterwards, *Queen Elizabeth* reared up from two explosions from charges attached below the water line, and both ships were temporarily out of the war.

It soon emerged that they had been attacked by three human torpedoes known as Maiali (sea pigs) driven by a team of six men from the 10th Light Flotilla, trained to remain under water for miles wearing flexible rubber suits, breathing gear and fins. They had been launched from Prince Borghese's submarine *Sciré* off Alexandria, two astride each of the human torpedoes. The operation even drew praise from Churchill as an example of "extraordinary courage and ingenuity".

Mountbatten drew together a number of eminent military and scientific experts to look at new weapons and methods for his men to "study, coordinate and develop all forms of stealthy seaborne attack by small parties and pay particular attention to attacking ships in harbour". Among the projects launched immediately was the Chariot, a hefty torpedo-shaped submersible which was a copy of the two-man Maiali used by the Italians (one had been captured off Crete). Its crew,

310

equipped with breathing sets that would allow six hours of diving, sat in the open astride the Chariot, which could travel at about 16 knots and carried one 272kg/600lb charge. They were hazardous and slow. The first torpedo force came into operation in September 1942, under the auspices of the submarine service, in a plan to attack *Tirpitz*, the largest and strongest warship ever built in Germany, at 53,000 tonnes/ 52,163 tons.

She was even more powerful than her elder sister, *Bismarck*, and was based in occupied Norway from January 1942. From there, she and her supporting ships would sally forth to attack Allied shipping.

The British began to consider every scheme to destroy the German monster, and in October 1942, an audacious plan was launched to sink her using the Chariots. Two of the Chariots were hidden in a double bulkhead of a Norwegian fishing trawler which would then proceed to Trondheim; there, they would be released with crews to attack *Tirpitz* in her berth behind anti-submarine nets in a fjord north of Trondheim. Although the trawler managed to get through three German checkpoints, the expedition was hit by a sudden change in the weather as the Chariots were being launched. They had to be abandoned, and the crews swam ashore and escaped into Sweden. No further attempts could be launched because of the low temperatures that year.

More than 50 Chariots were built, and their crews experienced mixed fortunes. Their best results were in the Mediterranean, although they were never really considered a success. Operation Principal, for example, was an attack on Palermo harbour on January 3, 1943. Five Chariots were used. Each, with a crew of two, was embarked on the deck in watertight containers in the submarines *Trooper* and *Thunderbolt* (ex-*Thetis*). *Unruffled* took part as the recovery boat after the operation was complete. One Chariot sank the Italian cruiser *Ulpio Traiano*, and another damaged the liner *Viminale,* which sank later in the year. Of the remaining three, one broke down en route and was picked up by *Unruffled* six hours later, a second sank through unknown causes, and on the third, the driver ripped his diving suit negotiating harbour defences and drowned.

ABOVE LEFT: **Luigi de la Penne, one of the pioneers of Italian charioteers, was one of a team of six that attacked British ships in Alexandria harbour in December 1941, causing damage to two British battleships,** *Queen Elizabeth* **and** *Valiant***. He was captured but he refused to inform the ship's captain of the mines attached to the ships' hull until a few minutes before detonation, thus allowing the British to evacuate. Although imprisoned, he worked for the British as a frogman after the Italian surrender.** ABOVE RIGHT: **The British version of the charioteers, whose operations came to the fore at the time of the Allied invasion of Sicily and elsewhere in the Mediterranean.** LEFT: **A British Chariot being unloaded for operations.** BELOW: **The altogether more successful Italian version of charioteering.**

Giant tasks for midget submarines

While Chariots were something of a haphazard affair, midget submarines were a different story altogether. Various nations had experimented with the small boats that could be transported and utilized in situations that their giant sisters would have little chance of even approaching, let alone manoeuvring into position for an operation. The Japanese and the Italians were well ahead of the field in design and numbers, the former producing several dozen in different classes and sizes. By the beginning of the war, the Japanese were already well advanced in their use, also with several dozen in operation, beginning with the A class, 23.9m/78ft 6in long and displacing 46.7 tonnes/46 tons submerged, and capable of a tidy 23 knots on the surface and an incredible 19 knots submerged.

They were originally intended to be carried by larger submarines or surface vessels and deployed to attack an enemy fleet, but they discovered that the midgets were particularly useful for special operations against ships in enemy harbours, where they could be transported and released in packs. Five of the A-class boats took part in the attack on Pearl Harbor and were evident again in May 1942 in raids on Sydney, Australia, and Diego Suarez in the Indian Ocean. Notably, however, they were well used against American ships at Guadalcanal in 1942–43. Japanese midgets in the A, B and C classes were in continual production, ending with the Type D boat, *HA-77*, completed in January 1945. Some 115 units had been completed when Japan capitulated in August 1945, and nearly 500 more were under construction.

Japan also produced some special attack midget submarines which were actually manned torpedoes. The highly successful Type 93 Long Lance torpedo was lengthened and adapted by inserting a central cockpit for the pilot. They became the Kaiten midget submarine that could reach speeds of up to 35.4kph/22mph, and up to six could be piggy-backed on conventional submarines for delivery to the attack area.

Meanwhile, the Italians were in production with a stylish-looking craft in their CB class as the war began, and it was this model that provided additional tips for both the British and the Germans, who took possession of a couple of their boats operating in the Mediterranean. In fact, the British, the

ABOVE: The Japanese Navy was first in action with midget submarines, launching five Type A models in the Pearl Harbor raid of December 7, 1941, transporting them piggy-back on larger submarines and launching the night before the attack, and thereafter throughout the war. LEFT: The British X-craft, which had a varied, terrifying but VC-winning history of high-profile operations, including an attack on the German battleship *Tirpitz*.

GIANT TASKS FOR MIDGET SUBMARINES

LEFT: **In mid-1944, the Japanese Navy developed the Koryu Type D midget coastal defence submarine for a five-man crew, two more than in the Type C.**
ABOVE: **Although classed as a human torpedo, this version of a Japanese *Kaiten* was more of a mini-submarine, with a large conning station attached.**

Americans and the Germans both came late to this field of development, the latter eventually launching a massive programme of midget development, building six different classes, ranging from one-man torpedoes to seven-man midgets. In all, the Germans had planned to produce over 1,700 of such craft, the first appearing early in 1944, but the war ended before many of that number were actually commissioned.

The Royal Navy's own prototype X-craft was laid down in 1939, when intelligence reports gave inspiring accounts of foreign developments, but the British and the Americans had already experienced attacks from midget craft at Pearl Harbor and in the Mediterranean before the British version was commissioned in October 1942. It was classed as *X3* (the first two Xs were already taken: *X1* was an experimental boat built in 1925, and *X2* was a captured Italian submarine which had given the British a few extra pointers). A second prototype vessel, *X4*, was constructed and based on the first British boat and the Italian version. Thereafter, rapid production began with six X-craft (*X5* to *X10*) being built by Vickers, initially for deployment in European waters. The British midgets made their name in some spectacular special missions and, later in the war, when they were used for risky surveillance and mapping of landing sites on hostile coastlines.

Their most famous mission was the attack on the German battleship *Tirpitz*, with which Churchill had an obsession. This magnificent and powerful vessel represented a major threat to British shipping and he wanted it out of the war. The Germans, well aware of British intentions, kept the ship Altenfjord, Norway, out of harm's way, which was also the berth of the Germans' other heavy weapons, the battleship *Scharnhorst* and the pocket battleship *Lützow*. They were the targets in September 1943 when six X5-class submarines, each crewed by four highly trained operatives, set out on a mission that is today a classic point in submarine warfare.

The X-craft, unlike the high-speed Japanese models, had electric motors that generated just 30hp and a 12-knot top

ABOVE: **The German *Neger* consisted of two linked G7e torpedoes, the upper with the warhead removed and a transparent driver cockpit installed; the bottom torpedo would be released.** BELOW: **The 11.2 tonne/11 ton one-man German Molch midgets were all electric, designed for submerged coastal operations, with a range of 64.4km/40 miles, carrying two torpedoes. Around 390 were built.**

speed when submerged. So they had to be towed towards their quarry by regular-sized submarines. Even so, the outward journey to Norway of 1,770km/1,100 miles took eight days in often heavy seas. En route, *X9* (which had been detailed to attack *Scharnhorst*) sank and *X8* (heading for *Lützow*) had to be scuttled, leaving the four remaining X-craft to cover the last 80.5km/50 miles under their own power through the treacherous fjords, mine fields and anti-submarine nets that were in place on the approach to the *Tirpitz*.

313

On September 22, 1943, X6 (under the command of Lt Donald Cameron) and X7 (under Lt Basil Place) followed an old freighter through this obstacle course and reached their target. X6 was spotted, and was under heavy fire from the surface. When Cameron attempted to make his escape, he became caught in the nets but still did not give up. As he surfaced, he dropped two explosive charges and then managed to scuttle the boat before leading his crew to surrender. X7 also released two charges beneath Tirpitz but ironically was damaged when the explosives left by X6 detonated, and Basil Place also had to surrender. Two of his crew did not survive.

Meanwhile, X10 under the command of Lt K.R. Hudspeth also managed to sneak into the inner fjord, only to be hit by mechanical trouble. Rather than give up and possibly alert the Germans to the presence of a larger force, he remained hidden

ABOVE: **The aft portion of the Kaiten (Return to Heaven) Type 1, of which 300 were produced. It became the first Japanese Special Attack weapon whose operational use involved the certain death of the crew and preceded the Kamikaze aircraft.**
BELOW LEFT: **The Biber (Beaver), the smallest German submarine built to attack coastal shipping ahead of the Allied invasion of Europe.**

for five days before he could return to the towing ship. The boat had to be scuttled on the return journey to England. A third submarine, probably X5, was sighted by Cameron close to its target but came under heavy fire and was never seen again.

In spite of this set-back, the raid on Tirpitz herself was successful, and that was the key object of the exercise. Although the explosive charges left by the midget did not have the power to sink her, they did sufficient damage for the vessel to be put out of the war temporarily, and had to be towed south for repairs. Apart from an actual sinking, this could not have been a better result because Tirpitz was now in the range of RAF and Fleet Air Arm bombers and over the coming months, after several attempts, she was finally blown apart when her own ammunition store was hit by British bombers. Fewer than 90 of her 1,000 crew survived. The role played by the midget submarines in crippling Tirpitz was recognized in 1944, when Basil Place and Donald Cameron were awarded the Victoria Cross.

Meanwhile, new versions of the British midgets were coming off the production line, beginning with the XE class which carried out a number of successful raids around Europe, including that of XE3 under the command of Lt Ian Fraser, which put a large floating dock at Bergen out of action for the rest of the war. As targets began to become fewer, six of the XE-class boats were shipped for operations in the Far East for what turned out to be the final months of the war. They were earmarked to carry out raids against the Japanese at a number of locations, including Singapore and Hong Kong. Again, a

LEFT: An aerial view of the German battleship *Tirpitz*, which was damaged in an attack by the British X-craft midget submarines. This allowed British bombers to sink her. ABOVE: One of the most successful German miniature submarines was the Seehund Type 127, of which the Kriegsmarine had planned to build over 1,000 from 1944. They had a crew of two, carried two under-slung G7e torpedoes and had a range of 300km/186 miles at 7 knots.

number of successes were chalked up, including that of *XE4* under the command of Lt M.H. Shean, of the Royal Australian Navy Volunteer Reserve, whose team managed to cut the Hong Kong to Saigon cable and the Saigon to Singapore cable.

The most famous of the missions, however, was reserved for Ian Fraser's *XE3*. His mission was a *Tirpitz*-style raid on the Japanese heavy cruiser *Takao*, moored in the Johore Strait, Singapore. Once again, the X-craft was towed towards its target location, and then continued on under her own steam. They reached the *Takao* without incident and settled beneath her to get to work. Leading seaman James Magennis, the diver, went out and attached six limpet mines to the hull of the ship, a task which took forty minutes because he had to scrape each position free of mud and barnacles. He returned aboard exhausted. A further problem occurred as Fraser attempted to turn away and escape before the explosion. To his horror, the boat would not budge because, while working on the explosives, the tide had gone down and the boat had become stuck in a very narrow hole. Only by going ahead and then full astern for several minutes did he manage to escape, only to encounter a further problem: an empty limpet container had jammed, preventing the side cargoes of explosives from being jettisoned, which gave the submarine an uncontrollable list. Magennis volunteered to go back outside, and spent 15 minutes freeing the load. *XE3* eventually made her escape and, while returning to base unscathed, the charges detonated to put the 11,177-tonne/11,000-ton cruiser on the bottom. Lt Fraser and Leading Seaman Magennis were both awarded the Victoria Cross for their bravery in performing this operation.

Although disliked by some, the X-craft had performed a number of exceedingly useful tasks, including their use by the top-secret group Combined Operations Pilotage Parties (Copps) in preliminary surveys ahead of troop landings and, notably, to mark the invasion beaches for the D-Day invasions.

ABOVE: The Kairyu (Sea Dragon) was another Kamikaze midget submarine for a two-man crew and was fitted with an internal warhead for suicide missions. Designed at the beginning of 1945 to meet the anticipated approach of invading American naval forces, 200 had been built by the time of Japan's surrender. RIGHT: Various methods were tried to disguise the tell-tale periscope of midget boats; this was the Beaver camouflage.

315

LEFT: **The forlorn sight of U-boats in Hamburg harbour as Germany capitulated, a reflection of the final days of the once-mighty Kriegsmarine.** BELOW: **The experimental** *U3008*, **an XXI submarine, known as the electro-boats, which provided technology for the Allies to plunder. Transferred to Portsmouth, New Hampshire, she was commissioned into the US Navy.** BOTTOM: **Having the distinction of being the first German submarine to surrender at the war's end, the crew of** *U249* **come ashore at Weymouth having shown the white flag to HMS** *Magpie* **off the Cornish coast.**

The cost and the legacy

For the second time in the 20th century, the final reckoning of submarine warfare produced a devastating catalogue of destruction of hardware and human life, as well as a record of many thousands of incidents of great heroism and skill, regardless of the flag under which the men were fighting. The U-boat force was undoubtedly the greatest in the world in terms of quality and innovation. It also suffered the highest proportion of casualties. A total of 1,154 diverse and versatile U-boats were commissioned prior to or during World War II, not counting the 135 still under construction at the end of the war and excluding the midget submarines. However, the toll had been relentless: 727 U-boats manned by crews totalling 26,918 were lost, the majority sunk by Allied surface ships and shore-based aircraft. The progression of those U-boat losses paints a mini-portrait of the way the fortune of war proceeded: 1939: 9 lost with 204 crew. 1940: 24 lost; 643 crew. 1941: 34 lost; 887 crew. 1942: 85 lost; 3,277 crew. 1943: 235 lost; 10,081 crew. 1944: 219 lost; 8,020 crew. 1945: 121 lost; 3,806 crew. The human cost was enormous, and the final figures showed that Germany lost an astonishing two-thirds of the men who served in the submarine force.

The British, with far fewer submarines, lost 74 boats during the war years, manned by crews totalling 341 officers and 2,801 ratings. In addition, 50 officers and 309 ratings became prisoners of war. America lost 52 submarines and of the 16,000 men serving in the US submarine force, 375 officers and 3,332 men did not survive. For all her productive pre-war promise, Japan's submarine service did not perform as well as her enemies'. Excluding midgets, Japan started the war with 63 ocean-going submarines and completed 111 during the war, giving a total of 174, of which 128 were lost during the conflict. Japan's emphasis on size proved to be a disadvantage, in that the huge boats were easy to sight and target. They were slow to dive, hard to manoeuvre underwater, easy to track, and easy to hit, especially by the US Air Force. Japanese submarines also had no radar until the first sets were installed in June 1944. Russia had 272 submarines in operation during the war and lost 108. Details of their operations are scant because Soviet submarines were rarely on patrol. However, it is known that one of their boats caused the greatest disaster in maritime history, in sinking the German liner *Wilhelm Gustloff* on March 30, 1945. The liner was moving more than 6,000 German troops and up to 2,000 civilians from Poland ahead of advancing Russian forces. She was sunk soon after leaving the port of Gotenhafen (Gdynia), and fewer than 1,000 people were rescued.

THE COST AND THE LEGACY

LEFT: **Surrendered VIIC boats, the mainstay of the German force from 1941 and still in production at the end of the war. They bore the brunt of the Allied anti-submarine onslaught from late 1943 onwards. One of them, *U96*, was featured in the film *Das Boot*.**
BELOW: **The revolutionary snorkel fitted to the XXI types that could have won the war, had they been in production earlier.**

At the end of it all, as in World War I, the victors picked over the spoils. There had been a resurgence of successful U-boat activity towards the autumn of 1944, when freshly launched German submarines were fitted with an important new invention: the snorkel ventilating tube. First tested by the Dutch Navy and picked up by German scientists, the retractable device contained air-intake and exhaust pipes for the engines and general ventilation. The telescopic tube fed air into the diesel engine and carried off exhaust gases. A U-boat equipped with the snorkel could run submerged on her diesel engine while also charging her batteries; while the boat could do so only at a slow speed and at shallow depth, the chances of being picked up by radar were greatly reduced. When they heard of it, Allied naval commanders breathed a sigh of relief that its development had not arrived earlier in the war.

It was one of a number of significant developments in German U-boat technology which were about to come on stream as the war reached the final stages. By then, it was already clear that submarine technology was on the threshold of dramatic developments. The Allies made a dash for the German U-boats and their accompanying manuals, which were to provide some inspiration for a new breed of submarines built on both sides of the Iron Curtain after it had slammed down at the start of the Cold War.

The Walther engine, used in four U-boats built before the war ended, was put under the microscope. It was a steam-generating power plant of a kind that had eluded British and American submarine engineers for years. It worked on the principle that hydrogen peroxide, when passed over a catalyst, produced oxygen and water. The oxygen and water were fed into a combustion chamber, sprayed with fuel, and the resulting mixture generated steam that powered a turbine. Walther had been working on the engine for four years, but because of its revolutionary principles there was little chance of proving it at the time of increasing pressure on the U-boat command.

One of the Walther boats commissioned in March 1945 was scuttled at the German port of Cuxhaven on 5 May 1945. The British had already learned of its existence and raised the boat by the end of the month. It was recovered, towed back to England, rebuilt and commissioned as *Meteorite* for evaluation. By then, the two big powers – picking over the bones of German technology – were on the threshold of a new era. Nuclear power was in sight.

BELOW: **Sections of the Type XXI, the first real combat submarines whose technology the Allies could not wait to get their hands on. Perhaps this type could have won the Battle for the Atlantic, had she arrived earlier.**

317

Unfinished business: surviving a sinking

With so much loss of life due to submarines lost during the war, a special committee formed in 1939 after the *Thetis* disaster was reactivated under the chairmanship of Rear-Admiral P. Ruck-Keene, and was able to draw on a vast wealth of experience. He was given a large team of experts to assist him, and they began by taking detailed statements from survivors of 32 submarine incidents involving British, American, Norwegian and German vessels. All past methods of escape were examined, and new ideas were brought forward, extended training programmes drawn up and a better system for rescue response recommended and acted upon.

The immediate outcome of the early testimony was to improve escape training for crews. For this a 30m/98ft 5in water-filled tower, 5.5m/18ft in diameter, was built at the submarine school at Fort Blockhouse, although it was not completed until 1952. The rescue alerts for submarines in distress, with particular attention to reaction times, were also overhauled as part of the two systems called Subsmash and Subsunk. Some of the modifications to submarine safety and rescue procedures were thus to be tested sooner than anyone could possibly imagine. Less than five years after the end of the war, Britain suffered two major submarine disasters.

On January 12, 1950, the World War II submarine *Truculent* spent the day at sea off the Thames Estuary carrying out trials, following a long refit in Chatham dockyard. On board was her crew of 59, plus 18 civilian dockyard technicians who were to check the final performance before officially handing her back to the Royal Navy. As *Truculent* made her way back to Sheerness, she was in collision with a tanker with ice-breaking bows, *Dvina,* on passage from Purfleet bound for Sweden with a cargo of paraffin. Sixty-seven men made a near-perfect escape from the sunken submarine and, apart from one or two problems with untrained technicians, the Davis gate saw everyone get to the surface alive. However, in the end, only 11 men were picked up alive. The remainder died of the cold or were swept away by the tide.

At the subsequent inquiry, it was observed that had the men remained inside the submarine for 20 or 30 minutes longer, the rescue ships sent under the Subsunk alert would have arrived over *Truculent* to save them. By the same token, it was also pointed out that because of the flooding and the closure of all but the after-compartments of the submarine, the 67 men on board were already beginning to feel the effects of carbon dioxide poisoning when the first officer made the decision to get them to the surface. He had little choice. If he had delayed, they might have been in no state to make the attempt, as had been the case in so many previous incidents examined in recent times. *Truculent* was salvaged on March 14, 1950, and

ABOVE LEFT: **The salvage operation to raise HMS *Truculent*, which sank after a collision. Even though almost all aboard escaped, only 11 survived on the surface.** ABOVE: **U-boat crews were well advanced in their training to escape a catastrophe.** LEFT: **HMS *Affray*, which was lost on a patrol exercise in 1951. The search for her kept the British nation agonizingly enthralled for days.**

beached at Cheney Spit. The wreck was moved inshore the following day, where ten bodies were recovered. She was refloated on March 23, 1950, and towed into Sheerness Dockyard. A subsequent inquiry attributed blame both to *Truculent* and to a lesser extent *Dvina*. The loss led to the introduction of the "Truculent light", an extra steaming all-round white light on the bow of British submarines.

The *Truculent* disaster was comparatively fresh in the memories of submariners when a second post-war tragedy struck, with further implications. At 16:30 hours on the afternoon of Monday, April 16, 1951, the six-year-old A-class submarine *Affray* left Portsmouth for a war patrol exercise with an unusually large number of men on board. Under the command of Lt John Blackburn, she carried his team of four officers and 55 ratings. There were also 23 young sub-lieutenants in training, who came along to observe a simulated war patrol, and a party of four marines. Blackburn's orders were to proceed down the Channel to the Western Approaches, carry out dummy attacks for three days to give experience to the junior officers and then land the marines at a bay on the Cornish coast.

At 20:56 hours, Blackburn signalled from the Isle of Wight that he intended to dive and proceed westwards up the Channel. He would surface at 08:00 hours the next morning. No surfacing signal was received, and at 09:00 hours on the 17th a Subsunk operation was launched. By midday, forty ships, eight submarines, various aircraft from the RAF and Fleet Air Arm and a flotilla of US destroyers visiting Plymouth were all engaged in the search for *Affray*.

But after 46 hours, the massive search operation was stood down. The task of locating her was handed over to a smaller team, consisting of four frigates and three minesweepers equipped with all the special electronics available for underwater location. It was an epic search lasting 59 days, covering 37,013km/23,000 miles and involving the investigation of 161 shipwrecks in the search area before the submarine was found. Navy divers discovered the snort mast had broken off, but that probably occurred when the sub hit the bottom. Suggestions of a battery explosion were also evaluated, but in truth the cause of the sinking could not be ascertained. What was brought home once again, however, was that dramatic new escape systems were needed. The *Affray* was the last British submarine to be lost with all hands.

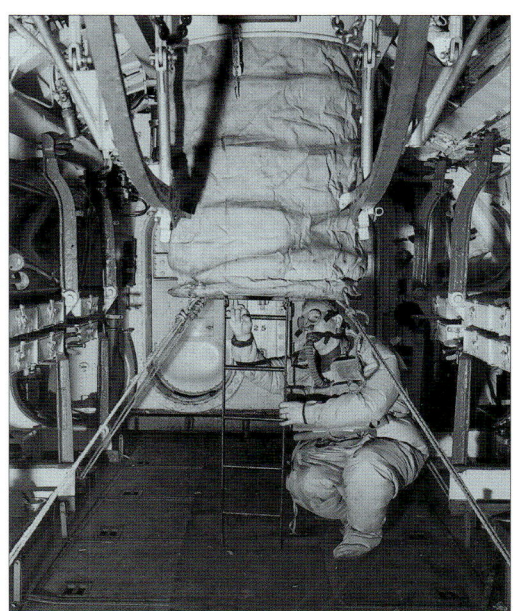

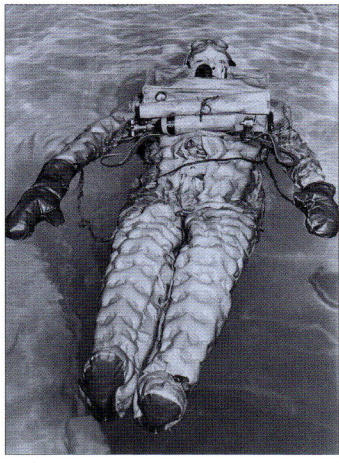

ABOVE: **Immediately after the war, when so many recent experiences could be recalled, the safety issues for the escape and rescue of personnel from a stricken submarine were the subject of numerous studies and experiments, including a large tank for training purposes with breathing apparatus.**
LEFT: **Other training methods and equipment were tried, but survival remained something of a haphazard affair.** ABOVE: **Immersion suits and life jackets were also tested, although their suitability for escaping from a submarine – as opposed to surviving an accident or the sinking of a surface ship – proved to require many more years of trial and error before satisfactory solutions to catastrophe beneath the waves were found. Meanwhile, the accidents and tragedies continued to occur.**

The Cold War: teardrops and Guppies

After World War II, the beginning of an undersea warfare revolution brought the United States and the Soviet Union into a confrontation in which they were the only two serious players – and it was the submarine forces of the two nations on which the naval developments were stridently focused. Building on the advanced German XXI submarines – the United States, Russia and Britain took possession of one apiece – the US Navy anticipated submarines of the future going deeper, staying there longer, and moving much faster. However, they weren't alone in these endeavours, of course, and naval and civilian advisers warned that in exploiting the XXI type, the Soviet Union presented "the most potent post-war naval threat to the United States".

It was known that the Soviets, still repairing the devastating effects of the war, lagged behind the Americans. They publicly boasted a potential force of 300 Soviet Type XXI equivalents by 1950, but it was not until 1949 that the first post-war Soviet submarine designs went to sea. Two classes were deployed: the Whiskey and the Zulu. The Zulu was a true Type XXI, equipped with a snorkel, capable of 16 knots submerged. But only 21 Zulus were commissioned between 1949 and 1958. During the same period, 236 Whiskeys were commissioned. They were smaller, shorter range boats, designed more for European littoral operations.

Technology was still in its infancy and intelligence gathering tended to be of the manual kind. US submariners were on round-the-clock front-line positions to gather clues as to Russian advances. In August 1949, for instance, submarines *Cochino* and *Tusk* were deployed to the waters off Norway 161km/100 miles from the Soviet Northern Fleet's bases at Murmansk and Polyarnyy to learn what they could about Soviet missile testing. Without warning, batteries in *Cochino* exploded and badly burned one officer. Fire and noxious gases released

TOP: **Initially, the Soviet Union lagged behind the West. Their largest class of new boats was the Whiskey class, of which 236 were built between 1949 and 1958, all of conventional shape.** ABOVE: **USS *Albacore* changed everything. Her design became the model for the teardrop hull adopted in all modern submarines across the world, and was critical in the race for the development of superior submarines.**

by this and subsequent blasts spread throughout the submarine, endangering the entire crew. Two *Cochino* men, trying to bring help from nearby *Tusk* while maintaining radio silence, were pitched into the bitterly cold water when their rubber boat overturned. Without hesitation, men from *Tusk* jumped in to help rescue their fellow sailors. Several men drowned in the attempt and their bodies drifted silently off into the northern waters. Finally, after heroic efforts by everyone, the surviving crewmen of both submarines gathered safely on board *Tusk*, and as they prepared to set sail for home, the *Cochino*, gutted by fire and explosion, vanished beneath the waves.

This was one of the last occasions that such primitive cloak and dagger work was undertaken. The Guppies made sure of that. This was the name given to the boats produced for the sole purpose of "Greater Underwater Propulsive Power". They were developed in the United States, and followed by the

THE COLD WAR: TEARDROPS AND GUPPIES

ABOVE: **USS *Cochino*,** a *Balao*-class submarine, commissioned in 1946, was transformed into one of the world's most modern submarines with the Guppy conversion. She sank after a severe battery explosion in stormy seas off northern Norway, though the crew was rescued by USS *Tusk*.

ABOVE RIGHT: **USS *Pickerel*,** a *Tench*-class submarine, was another boat converted to Guppy, and in 1950 she made a record 8,369km/5,200 miles submerged trans-Pacific voyage. RIGHT: **USS *Blueback*,** commissioned in 1959, was the first US submarine built specifically to the Guppy configuration (as opposed to a conversion) and was also the last non-nuclear boat to take her place in the US Navy. Key features included removing the deck guns, streamlining the outer hull, replacing the conning tower with a sail, installing more air conditioning and a snorkel, and doubling the battery capacity. She can be seen in the Sean Connery movie *The Hunt for Red October* in the role of USS *Dallas*.

Soviets both using features borrowed from the XXI. The star elements of the Guppy design consisted of the removal of the deck guns, streamlining of the outer hull, installing new propellers for submerged operations and – most distinctively of all – replacing the conning tower with a sail. Initially, existing boats were converted to take the new developments, and instantly underwater speeds were almost doubled. The first Guppy sent to the Far East, *Pickerel* made the entire trip back from Hong Kong to Pearl Harbor on snorkel – 8,359km/ 5,194 miles in 21 days submerged, a record that was held until 1958. In the new boats that were to get these innovations as standard, the Tang class first commissioned in 1951 led the field in this development. The *Tang* was the first truly new post-war construction that represented the first step towards greater speed and endurance below the surface.

There was one other innovation that was to change the look of submarines forever. American researchers and designers had been drawing new shapes on their board since 1944. In 1950, the one that grabbed the eye of everyone was an attractive hydrodynamic hull shape that became known as the teardrop.

A prototype was built and extensively tested in wind tunnels, subsequently leading to a $20 million development budget out of which came the *Albacore*: the first teardrop submarine, fast and whale-like with a sail distinctively positioned a third of the overall length from the bow.

She was commissioned in December 1953, and initial trials showed that she was faster submerged than the designers had anticipated. The attractive design set the standard, and was adopted in due course by most navies of the world.

BELOW: **USS *Tang*** was the first of the American new breed to be designed post-war and as such was the first of six that incorporated the Guppy (snorkel) configuration into the design, as well as being test platforms for the first nuclear submarines.

THE HISTORY OF SUBMARINES

LEFT: USS *Nautilus*, the sixth American ship to carry that name, was the world's first operational nuclear-powered submarine. Heading south for her shakedown cruise, she travelled 2,100km/1,300 miles from New London to San Juan, Puerto Rico, in less than 90 hours, which was the longest ever submerged cruise by a submarine and at the highest sustained speed ever recorded. Later, she became the first vessel to complete a submerged transit across the North Pole. By February 4, 1957, *Nautilus* had logged 111,120km/60,000 nautical miles, matching the endurance of the fictional *Nautilus* in Jules Verne's *Twenty Thousand Leagues under the Sea*. INSET: The badge of SSN-571, the first nuclear-powered attack submarine.

Nautilus, the first true submarine

And so to the vessel that Jules Verne predicted in his 1870 novel, *Twenty Thousand Leagues under the Sea*: a true submarine that could travel the globe without ever surfacing, a fictional construction that bore many similarities to the reality that finally emerged in 1955. Even the name was the same: *Nautilus*. It all began in the mid-1940s, when Captain Hyman Rickover, a brilliant naval engineer and experienced submariner, was burning the midnight oil, working on his own theories for such a boat. Without any great enthusiasm from more senior naval figures, Dr Ross Gunn of the US Naval Research Laboratory and Dr Philip Abelson of the Carnegie Institute joined Hyman in 1948. Both had been working on similar themes that would bring about a revolution in submarine propulsion on similar lines to the Walther boat, and indeed their eventual product bore a number of similarities. The difference was that unlike Walther who used highly concentrated hydrogen peroxide, Gunn proposed the use of nuclear fission.

In the simplest terms, a reactor would generate steam, which would drive the turbine. For the next two years they struggled with the theory of a nuclear-powered submarine while at the same time fighting a relentless rearguard action against formidable opponents. Early in 1950, Rickover's team produced designs for a land-based nuclear reactor as a prototype for one that could power a substantial submarine. They demonstrated how a single power plant could provide the propulsion for unlimited surface and submerged travel. A small quantity of enriched uranium would produce enough power to run for years, and the nuclear submarine would be able to

ABOVE: All eyes on the monitors as *Nautilus* travels under the North Pole. The main Control Room was located directly below the Attack Centre, accommodating the instruments and controls for diving, surfacing and steering the ship. The Diving Officer of the Watch was in charge of this space and received orders for depth, course and speed from the Officer of the Deck in the Attack Centre.

operate at high speed, completely and indefinitely submerged and restricted only by human endurance.

Rickover drew the comparison against even the most modern conventional diesel-electric submarines, in which the submerged approach to a target had to be made at a very low speed of no more than three knots, to avoid wasting battery power, and whose ability to stay submerged was limited to the state of on-board batteries. As every submarine commander well knew, this was critical in any attack situation because sufficient power always had to be husbanded in case of counter-attack and the possibility of having to sit on the bottom

NAUTILUS, THE FIRST TRUE SUBMARINE

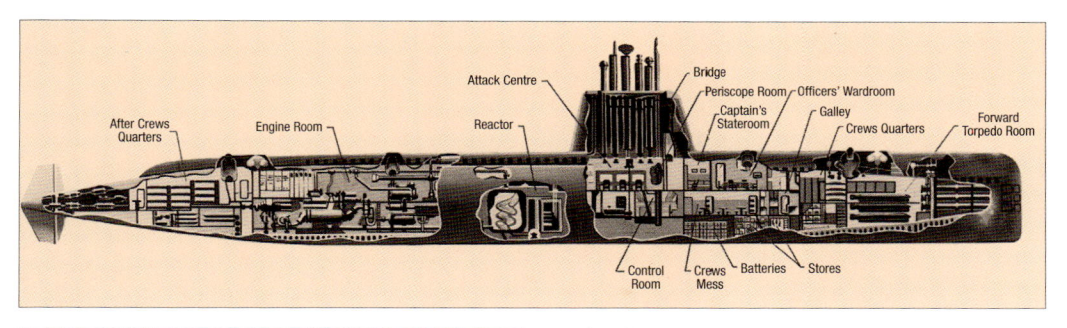

ABOVE: Apart from the historic nature of the submarine's development, great emphasis was placed on interior design, as is evident from this compartmentalized view of the various operational stations. LEFT: A fine starboard view of SSN-571 *Nautilus* at sea. BELOW: A view of the Torpedo Room, which held six tubes, initially for Mk 14 torpedoes as displayed above, as well as stowage racks for 24 torpedoes. Directly aft of the Torpedo Room was a small berthing area with 10 bunks, toilets, shower and sinks for the weapons crew.

until the danger had passed. The need to conserve battery power had always meant that submarines had to be cautious about engaging fast surface warships. Nuclear submarines, said Rickover, would end all those problems overnight. They would be fast, they could travel at top speed without ever having to surface and they could remain submerged for great distances. The size of the nuclear reactor and its shielding meant that the submarine had to be 97m/318ft 3in long and displace 3,539 tonnes/3,483 tons on the surface, which was more or less the size of a modern cruiser.

Many were unconvinced by these claims; some were even scared by them. Even so, the US Congress approved a $30 million budget to build the world's first nuclear-powered submarine, and her keel was laid down by President Harry Truman at the Electric Boat Company shipyard – the same company that had produced the first Hollands at the turn of the century – in Groton, Connecticut, on June 14, 1952. On the morning of January 17, 1955, the first commanding officer, Commander Eugene P. Wilkinson, ordered all lines cast off and signalled the historic message: "Under way on nuclear power."

Very soon, *Nautilus* began to shatter all speed and distance records, and in August 1958, then under Commander Bill Anderson and with 116 men on board, she left Pearl Harbor under top secret orders to commence Operation Sunshine – the first crossing of the North Pole by a ship, a mission that many said was impossible. The achievement became known to the world when, on August 3, *Nautilus* reached the geographic North Pole 90 degrees north and Anderson signalled a message that would be echoed by the moon landing team a few years later, he said: "For the world, our country and the navy – the North Pole."

These developments came at a time of mounting East-West tension and, we now know, were to have a profound effect on the race for nuclear domination by the superpowers.

Skipjack sets the standard

Now the Americans had nuclear power in a relatively conventionally shaped boat, *Nautilus*, and the teardrop design of *Albacore*, which had proved exceptionally fast, even with conventional power. Next, the two technologies were merged to create the Skipjack class, combining the endurance of nuclear propulsion with the streamlined hull that at a stroke would produce the world's fastest submarine, said to be capable of an incredible 30 knots dived. The American team had also created the design base for all future US submarines.

In 1955, five Skipjacks were ordered, and were subsequently commissioned between 1959 and 1961. They were essentially attack submarines in support of the American anti-submarine warfare programme, codenamed SOS-US, which came into effect after US intelligence surmised that any atom-bomb attack on the United States would most likely be carried by submarines.

This was extrapolated from the fact that both sides were already working on the development of ballistic missiles, again based initially on the German technology of the V1 and V2 rockets that had caused so much devastation in wartime London. From that one assessment, the whole development of attack submarines subsequently began to take on a new complexion, as indeed did America's own anti-submarine protection. From the late 1950s, a detection system revealing the advance of any submarine towards the American east coast was installed along the entire coastline, from north to south, and later extended to cover the west coast and Hawaii.

Skipjack was also unique in that it was the first nuclear submarine with a single shaft. Placement of the bow planes on the sail greatly reduced flow noise at the bow-mounted sonar. The deep-diving and high speed capabilities of the class were the result a new reactor design, the S5Ws, that became the US Navy's standard until the Los Angeles class joined the fleet in the mid-1970s.

Further developments focused on reducing the noise levels of the Skipjacks, which were easy to detect even at extreme range. For this, the designers turned to the smaller *Tullibee*, which had been designed specifically as an Anti-Submarine Warfare (ASW) weapon. These boats were noted in US submarine history as the quietest nuclear submarine with turbo-electric drive, the first with a sonar suite that included a low-frequency passive array for long-range detection and

LEFT: **USS *Shark*, a *Skipjack*-class submarine commissioned in 1961, later joined the Sixth Fleet in the Mediterranean, the first such deployment for a nuclear submarine. In 1964, she was awarded a commendation for "achieving results of great importance in the field of anti-submarine warfare". She was decommissioned in 1986.**
ABOVE: **The Soviet *Hotel*-class ballistic missile submarine was put into service in 1959, designed to carry the D-2 launch system. This version, from the 1969 era, with a NATO reporting name of Hotel III, had been lengthened to test R-29 missiles.**

LEFT: **USS *Tullibee*,** commissioned in 1960, was something of a test platform, with innovative designs. She was nicknamed the "boat of firsts" – the first designed for anti-submarine warfare, the first to be equipped with a new series of sonar equipment, the first with torpedo tubes amidships and the first to use turbo-electric propulsion.
ABOVE: The Russian November class was also a boat of firsts – the first Soviet nuclear-powered submarine in 1958, the first to traverse the North Pole (four years after the Americans) and the first to carry ballistic weapons when the class was modified.

LEFT: **USS *George Washington*** was already under construction when the nuclear arms race opened up, and was cut in two for the installation of a ballistic missile compartment, to become America's first ballistic boomer.
ABOVE: **USS *Scamp*,** a *Skipjack*-class submarine, was among the early nuclear boats later converted to receive SubSafe, whereby every component and every action is intensively managed. The system added significant cost, but no submarine certified by SubSafe has ever been lost.

a spherical array for approach and attack, and the first submarine with torpedo tubes amidships. This step was a further milestone in the history of nuclear boats, which signalled the development of the multipurpose SSN that combined the speed of *Skipjack* and the ASW capability of *Tullibee* into one boat. This became the *Thresher* from which all future US submarine classes derived. The acoustic advantages were hailed as dramatic, and the new boats were in a class of their own when compared with the fleet that the Russians were in the process of building. These were colloquially known as the Soviet HENS, standing for the initials of the Red Navy's principal classes, Hotel (SSBN), Echo (SSGN) and November (SSN), which began deploying alongside the Threshers in the early 1960s as these great monsters jostled for position and supremacy.

However, there was yet to be one more crucial development based on the *Skipjack* model. Since the end of the war, both nations had been experimenting with submarine-launched ballistic missiles, and *Skipjack* proved to be an ideal platform for that purpose. It was the beginning of the true era of potential nuclear annihilation launched from beneath the waves. Unlike easily targeted land-based missiles, submarines carrying strategic ballistic missiles (SSBNs) were constantly on the move, lurking deep in the ocean, with almost unlimited staying power. They were regarded as being capable of reaching almost any target in the world, and after the successful trials of the Polaris A1, *Scorpion*, an SSN of the Skipjack class, was sliced in two for a 39.6m/130ft missile section to be inserted to create the first nuclear-powered ballistic missile carrier. *Scorpion* was renamed *George Washington*, thereby establishing a new class of submarine. This giant weighed in at 5,900 tonnes/5,807 tons, was 116.4m/382ft long and carried 16 Polaris missiles with a range of 2,222km/1,200 nautical miles. They were to be matched and bettered, at least in terms of size, by the Soviet Union's 8,128-tonne/8,000-ton Yankee class, which eventually packed in an armoury of 16 SS-N-6 missiles with a range of 2,408km/1,300 nautical miles.

LEFT: **Britain's first nuclear powered submarine, *Dreadnought*,** whose endurance and versatility demonstrated the limitations of the rest of Britain's submarine fleet, especially when she travelled from Rosyth to Singapore and back in 1969. Later, she became the first British submarine to surface at the North Pole. BELOW: **The modernity of the control room was,** at the time, an eye-opening experience for all newcomers to an era of nuclear-powered travel, which of course also required a new elite at all levels of submarine manpower.

Life aboard the *Dreadnought*

Britain, once the greatest sea power in the world, could not even begin to contemplate anything more than a tag-along role to the United States in the two-horse race for supremacy in submarine warfare. Her shipyards were still very capable of producing world-class boats, of course, but the nation's submarine capability at the start of the 1960s would barely raise a blip on the radar screen. Her only nuclear deterrents were the RAF's V-bomber force and land-based missiles strung down the east coast pointing towards the Soviet Union. However, Lord Louis Mountbatten, as First Sea Lord and later as Chief of Defence Staff, was an ardent campaigner for Britain's own nuclear submarines and eventually persuaded the British government to provide the finance to begin the process of turning the nation's submarine force into an all-nuclear complement, a process that would take several years.

It began with the building of Britain's first nuclear powered submarine with a power plant bought from the Americans. She was to be christened *Dreadnought,* the ninth ship in British naval history to carry that most famous name and in a subliminal way this perhaps demonstrated that the Admiralty had finally acknowledged that the submarine had graduated to capital ship. She was launched by the Queen at Barrow-in-Furness on Trafalgar Day, October 21, 1960, by which time, incidentally, the United States had stopped building conventional submarines altogether.

Dreadnought was a proud bearer of a bit of British face-saving in a world where submarine power was assuming astronomical proportions. She had a surface displacement of 3,500 tonnes/3,445 tons and 4,000 tonnes/3,937 tons submerged. She was 78m/256ft long, had a beam of 10m/32ft 10in, could travel effortlessly at 28 knots submerged and had a crew of 88. She was classed as a hunter-killer fleet submarine, armed with six conventional bow torpedoes. She was to be the prototype for the creation of Britain's nuclear submarine force, which from now on would be built entirely by British scientists, engineers and shipbuilders, with more planned for the immediate future, to form the Valiant class. The price the First

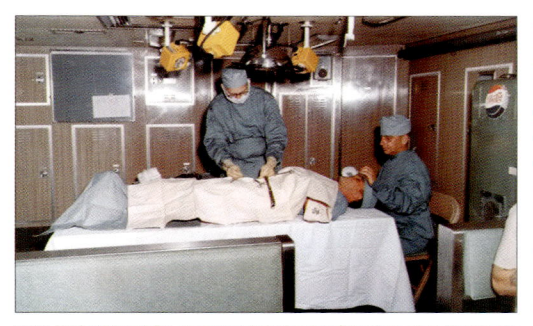

LIFE ABOARD THE *DREADNOUGHT*

ABOVE: **Nuclear propulsion also presented other considerations, given the greater length of time spent submerged. The medics on the 1969-built USS *Andrew* had to perform an emergency operation on a makeshift table in the mess room, although by then newer ships were already being fitted with full medical suites.** BELOW: **An image demonstrating the sleek lines of HMS *Dreadnought*, which rightly instilled pride among the British submarine community.**

ABOVE: **Catering was also to become a major new consideration for submarines of the nuclear age with enough chefs to prepare meals for several sittings in pleasant, clean and hygienic surroundings, carrying enough stores for extended journeys at sea, and with a varied and healthy diet of fine quality fruit, vegetables and meat.** BELOW: **The mess halls on the nuclear submarines also took on the air of a relaxing, spacious restaurant with modern accoutrements.**

Sea Lord had to pay for that agreement from the government was a halt on the building of further diesel-electric submarines, which in turn left Britain very short of boats a decade later.

Dreadnought delivered the long-awaited revolution to the British submarine force. She was new in every regard, handled by telemotor controls using a joystick and a dazzling array of dials that made up the elaborate instrument panel. For the crew going aboard for the first time, it was a jaw-dropping experience, with accommodation to a standard they had never seen before, even in surface vessels. Apart from an efficient air-conditioning and purification system, there were numerous luxuries, such as showers, washing facilities, a laundry, and a large galley equipped for serving decent meals. There were also separate messes for junior and senior ratings, well-furnished recreational spaces and a range of leisure facilities, such as a cinema, a library and other features to relieve the monotony of long periods submerged.

By then, the British government had approved the building of *Valiant*-class boats, for which *Dreadnought* was the prototype. Five were to be laid down for construction between 1962 and 1970, and with that approval came a major operation in recruitment and retraining to prepare the crews and shore bases to take control of these revolutionary boats. Nor was it simply a question of training. As had been discovered in the United States, the unique qualities of life aboard a nuclear submarine required commanders of outstanding leadership skills and crews capable of withstanding the particular pressures that came with long periods of life beneath the waves. There was no precedent to the experience. The whole

point of nuclear boats was that they would submerge as soon as they left their base and, if necessary, remain submerged for the duration of their patrol. From the very beginning, crews might go for weeks without seeing daylight or having any contact whatsoever with the outside world. Most on board would not have the slightest inclination of their whereabouts, the time zone they were in or even whether it was night or day.

Two, three or four month patrols submerged became commonplace, and the aspects of crew welfare necessarily became a priority in both selection and training. The fact of life that had faced all submariners since the beginning – the confined and restricted nature of travelling in a boat tight for space and packed with dangerous gear – was no less pronounced in the comparatively palatial surroundings of the nuclear boats. If anything, they were heightened by the longer periods of time spent submerged in what was still a confining, if not confined, space. Greater studies would follow, but from the early American experience, repeated in Britain, it was immediately evident that prospective crews needed careful screening for temperament, intelligence and fitness. Selection and training of commanders, officers and senior ratings in turn became perhaps the most crucial elements of all. In their hands rested the responsibility for all elements, human and mechanical, in these highly sophisticated war machines.

Two lost submarines jolt the US nuclear team

American leaders had called USS *Thresher* the most advanced submarine in the world in the new era of hunter-killer submarines. She was in fact a star, capable of speeds and depths never before achieved, and early in 1963 her manoeuvres off Charleston had been watched and applauded by the US Naval Antisubmarine Warfare Council. However, during her return to port she was accidentally struck by a tug, sustaining slight damage to one of her ballast tanks, and she went off to Groton, Connecticut for repairs at the Electric Boat Company. On completion, she underwent further trials with dockyard technicians aboard before her final release, 322km/200 miles off the coast of New England.

There, on April 10, she put to sea for deep-diving exercises with 16 officers, 96 enlisted men and 17 civilian technicians aboard. She had an escort vessel, *Skylark*, on the surface equipped with monitoring and underwater telephonic equipment, maintaining contact throughout the dive. Then, the submarine reported she was in difficulties. Transmissions became unclear and garbled.

Subsequently, investigators concluded that a seawater pipe in the aft engine spaces had broken, spraying water into the engine room and shorting one of the main electrical bus boards. The sub lost electrical power and couldn't operate the reactor. Darkness, a sea mist and sheer terror inhibited the crew from manually actuating the valves. The aft part of the sub filled up with water and tilted down. With no power to get back on line, the sub drifted down below 1,676m/5,500ft, to crush depth and

ABOVE: When the USS *Thresher* went down with all hands, the US Navy vowed that such a tragedy should never occur again. A Presidential Deep Submergence Review Group initiated a study and initiated the Deep Submergence Rescue System: the *Mystic* (DSRV 1) and *Avalon* (DSRV 2), pictured here, became the genesis of that programme.
RIGHT: The newly honed emblem of the Deep Submergence Unit.

imploded. A ghastly death for an entire crew, and one whose impact on the whole submarine community, as well as the nation, brought the US Navy to declare that it would never happen again.

Lessons learned from the *Thresher* tragedy led to the formation of the American SubSafe Programme, which called for checks on every submarine in the US fleet and every pressure-related part within their systems. In future, they could not move without certification that the systems were completely safe. The Deep Submergence Rescue System was developed from a special Presidential Deep Submergence Review Group in the mid-1960s. The deep submergence rescue vehicles *Mystic* (DSRV 1) and *Avalon* (DSRV 2) were constructed, and over the years they progressively improved.

Despite these measures, America lost a second nuclear submarine five years later. *Scorpion*, which had assumed the

ABOVE: The USS *Scorpion*, lost in May 1968, is reported to be resting on a sandy seabed 3,048m/10,000ft down in the Atlantic, approximately 644km/400 miles south-west of the Azores. The US Navy acknowledged that it periodically visited the site to conduct testing for the release of nuclear materials from the nuclear reactor or the two nuclear weapons aboard her.

ABOVE: The loss of USS *Thresher* with military and civilian technicians aboard stunned the nation: the boat was the best of the newest, built at the Portsmouth Naval Shipyard and was the first of a new class of submarine, designed for optimum performance of sonar and weapons systems. LEFT: The high-tech sail of USS *Scorpion*.

name from the earlier boat which was converted to the SSBN *George Washington*, was reported missing. Although overdue for a major overhaul because of budget concerns and tight operational schedules, in April 1968 she was operating with the Sixth Fleet on anti-submarine warfare exercises in the Mediterranean, until she was suddenly pulled out and ordered to the Canaries. It was reported later that her mission was to check on some curious activity involving large balloons by Soviet ships and submarines. Crew on the *Scorpion* spent two or three days monitoring the situation and photographing activity among the Soviet group but in fact reported nothing unusual, and she was ordered back to her home port on May 21. Six days later, it was reported that she was overdue at Norfolk and that all contact had been lost. A massive search was mounted, but on June 5 it was conceded that *Scorpion* and her crew of 99 officers and men were presumed lost.

Various causes were surmised, not least rumours of a clash with the Soviets. However, the search continued using the same techniques employed to find a missing H-Bomb that had fallen out of a B-52 off the coast of Spain after the aircraft had collided with its fuel tanker. At the end of October, a Navy oceanographic research ship located the hull of *Scorpion* in more than 3,048m/10,000ft of water 644km/400 miles south-west of the Azores. Deep submergence vehicles were sent down to record the scene, and found that the boat had made a huge gash in the ocean floor, her back was broken and the two portions of the hull were held together by mere slivers of metal. A Court of Inquiry concluded that her loss could not be determined with any certainty but conjectured that the most probable cause was the accidental activation of the battery of a Mark 37 torpedo during an inspection, causing a live "hot run" within the tube. If it had been released from the tube, the torpedo, fully armed, would have engaged its nearest target, *Scorpion*. Alternative theories suggested that the torpedo may have exploded in the tube or that there was an explosion in the battery well. Monitoring stations did record a "loud acoustic event" coinciding with the loss of the boat.

In 1969, when the Court of Inquiry resumed to consider its final verdict, it found that there was no "incontrovertible proof" of the exact cause, and that the loss of *Scorpion* remained a mystery. Further investigations using the deep submergence vehicles showed that the battery well had been destroyed, the torpedo room remained intact and there was no external evidence of being hit by a torpedo. No further inquiry was initiated, but the media did reveal that one of the crew had written to his parents complaining that internally the submarine was in constant need of running repairs, and that another had written to demand his transfer from "USS *Scrap Iron*". Meanwhile, as with any nuclear accident, the navy had to monitor the area of the sinking for any possible effects on the environment.

The ballistic boomers

One fact underlines the great race between the superpowers to equip themselves with submarines packed with ballistic missiles: In any one of their boats, the total nuclear armoury was more powerful than all the bombs dropped in World War II by all sides put together. Such a situation began when the need for a hidden second-strike nuclear force arose in the contemplation of a nuclear conflict – this at a time when the two superpowers already had their H-bombers constantly in the air. Then came MAD – Mutually Assured Destruction – which was promised by Eisenhower in the event of an attack by the Soviet Union. This "madness" was pursued year upon year with bigger and more powerful nuclear ballistic submarines, some military advisers concluding that when an optimum level of destructive capability was reached by both sides, an effective stalemate would be achieved and further weapons, as Winston Churchill laconically put it, would merely "make the rubble bounce".

However, the Americans, shocked by the event of Sputnik 1 being delivered into the earth's orbit, decided to maintain the principle of being able to strike or retaliate with hugely destructive power. Thus, as already noted, USS *George Washington* conducted the world's first submarine launch of a strategic ballistic missile on June 28, 1960, and the floodgates opened for the great "boomers", as ballistic missile submarines became known. The boomers moved out into the areas of potential confrontation, often surrounded by "minders", the new breed of nuclear hunter-killer submarines.

ABOVE: **USS *James K. Polk*, of the Benjamin Franklin class, was originally completed with the Polaris A3, but was refitted with the Poseidon missile in the 1970s. In 1994, as the Cold War began to scale down, she converted from missile carrier to an attack-mission submarine to operate with US special forces.**
BELOW: **The badge of the USS-645 *James K. Polk*.**

ABOVE: **Poseidon was the second US Navy ballistic missile system and had improved accuracy compared with the Polaris A3, along with 14 W68 multiple independently targetable re-entry vehicles.**

The Soviet Union was never far behind in the race, and indeed aimed to outnumber the US boat for boat, promising a fleet of at least 300. Their *Yankee*-class submarines were

THE BALLISTIC BOOMERS

FAR LEFT: The *Ohio*, lead ship of the class that bore her name, led the American modernization programme to replace the ageing ballistic missile submarines of the 1960s, and was far more capable. These submarines could carry 24 ballistic missiles which could be accurately delivered to selected targets from almost anywhere in the world's oceans. In 2005, *Ohio* was converted to an SSGN – a guided missile carrier. ABOVE: The corridors are long and spooky in the ballistic boats, especially in the huge missile compartment, as here aboard the USS *Ohio*. INSET: The missile tubes of an SSBN.

the first Soviet ballistic missile carriers with firepower comparable to that of their US counterparts, and their arrival signalled the first step in the Soviet leadership's avowed intention to defend the homeland.

The Yankees were significantly quieter than any other previous Russian boats, due to their smoother hull shape, propeller design, exterior sound-deadening coatings and other modifications. They were also the base model for the Delta class of Russian SSBNs, which became the mainstay of the Soviet sea-launched deterrent, having been laid down in 1969 and maintaining a presence in the fleet until the beginning of the 21st century.

The *Delta*-class submarines could deploy on alert patrols in the Soviet arctic and the Norwegian and Barents seas. Consequently, unlike their predecessors, they no longer needed to pass through Western SOSUS sonar sound detection barriers to come within range of their targets. Deployed close to home, they could be protected in "bastions" by the rest of the Soviet Navy.

The submerged firing of the missiles could be conducted in a single salvo while the submarine moved at a speed of 5 knots. A high degree of automation allowed a significant reduction in the time required for pre-launch preparations in comparison with the Yankee class.

THE HISTORY OF SUBMARINES

LEFT: There is great ceremony for the christening of submarines and the names often have poignancy too, even if somewhat obscure. The *Mariano G. Vallejo* was named after a 19th century Mexican who helped bring about the annexation of California by the United States. The boat that bore his name began the routine of all ballistic boomers in 1965 and continued for the next 30 years before being decommissioned to join the growing graveyard of old nuclear boats in the recycling programme. ABOVE: A pre-launch photograph of the *Lafayette*-class ballistic missile submarine *Thomas A. Edison*.

The Soviets also began building the world's biggest ballistic submarine, the massive *Typhoon*, 175.3m/575ft in length and 22.9m/75ft wide (compared to *George Washington*, 116m/382ft and 10m/33ft respectively). The design was based on a multi-hulled construction that bore a resemblance to a catamaran. The submarine had two separate pressure hulls with a diameter of 7.3m/24ft each, five inner habitable hulls and 19 compartments.

The *Typhoon* was introduced with a specific role in mind when she was laid down in 1977, a much feared vehicle capable of carrying 20 long-range ballistic missiles with up to 200 nuclear warheads that were once aimed at the United States. Like the Americans, the Soviet leadership determined that they must have the capability to maintain a massive and ever-ready retaliatory position by putting the Typhoons on permanent patrol beneath the Arctic Ocean, only to come out of hiding if and when a strike back became necessary. With hulls of ultra-strength, they would supposedly then crash their way to the surface through an ice-cap up to 3.7m/12ft thick and make their attack.

The six boats of the class were the ultimate in largesse, with a crew of 150. They were also expensive to operate and proved less than satisfactory in service. However, the last of the breed remained in service until 1994 when the Americans promised cash and technical aid to decommission them, which in itself was also a problem of gigantic proportions.

Next in this progression to annihilation, if it ever came to the crunch, came the American's Lafayette and Benjamin Franklin classes, which were a prelude to the *Ohio*, laid down

332

THE BALLISTIC BOOMERS

RIGHT: **The distinctive look of a Soviet nuclear submarine, always with a slightly dishevelled appearance and perhaps all the more menacing for it, like the rough kid on the block. The *Yankee*-class boats were the first Soviet boomers with firepower comparable to that of their US counterparts. In 1986, a missile fuel leak on *K219* caused an explosion, and the resulting fire killed four people. The ship sank off the east coast of America. By 2005, all but two had been taken out of service.**

LEFT: **The dramatic spectacle of a Trident 1 C4 missile MIRV warhead re-entry. Every line represents the path of a warhead which, were it live, would detonate with an explosive power 25 times greater than the atom bomb dropped on Hiroshima in 1945.**

RIGHT: **The *Trident II D-5* missile is the sixth generation member of the US Navy's Fleet Ballistic Missile programme. It is a three-stage inertia-guided FBM with a range of more than 7,408km/ 4,000 nautical miles and has a significantly greater payload than its predecessor.**

in 1976, and which came with the tag of possessing the "world's most powerful weapons platform". The Ohio class became the principal workhorse of the US boomer fleet, with 18 of the boats launched between 1979 and 1996, eventually with the Trident strategic ballistic missile system. The US Navy gives the range of the Trident II missile as "greater than 7,360km" and it could be up to 12,000km/7,456 miles. Trident II was capable of carrying up to 12 MIRVs (multiple independent re-entry vehicles), each with a yield of 100 kilotons, although the SALT treaty between the superpowers limited this number to eight per missile.

Lower down the scale of possible contributors to a nuclear Armageddon came the British SSBN fleet, for which Prime Minister Harold Macmillan persuaded President John F. Kennedy to supply the latest Polaris A3P ballistic missiles at a historic meeting in the Bahamas. This decision, which aroused great controversy in Britain at the time, enabled the Royal Navy to build its own Resolution class, four submarines built in pairs at the Vickers Armstrong yard in Barrow-in Furness. These were later to be replaced with the Vanguard class, to carry the Trident missile in the 1990s. China, France and Australia were the only other nations to operate SSBNs, albeit on a limited scale.

333

LEFT: **The 1980s British *Trafalgar*-class boats were designed as hunter-killers for Cold War operations in the North Atlantic, and were on constant patrols with dual crews. But cracks were discovered in one of them in August 2000, and it was found that only one of the seven boats could remain operational until repairs had been carried out. They were also fitted with Tomahawk land attack cruise missiles and used them in the 2001 attack on Afghanistan in the action to oust the Taliban.**
BELOW: **Control room action.**

Fast and versatile: the hunter-killers

While the boomers of both sides played out their role of maintaining a "hidden and survivable retaliatory strike capability", fully loaded for a nuclear strike, the fast attack submarines (SSNs), commonly known as "hunter-killers", were established from the outset as multi-functional boats, in the "do anything, go anywhere" mode. They are, of course, also widely used by nations of the world who do not possess SSBNs, although there principally were and still are only two major nuclear submarine forces, with the United Kingdom in third place following the arrival of her *Resolution*-class SSBN fleet and the supporting *Trafalgar*-class SSNs.

They are designed to operate in the truer role of the submarine, so often demonstrated in World War II: operating alone in anti-submarine or anti-surface missions, surveillance and intelligence-gathering or with submarine battle groups or Joint Task Force operations with surface vessels. Most Cold War operations remain classified, but the very few that have been revealed demonstrate how it all works. In the 1970s, USS *Guardfish* was tracking a Soviet cruise missile submarine (SSGN), which, in turn, was following US aircraft carriers off Vietnam, ready to pounce should the Soviet sub launch her missile. In 1978, USS *Batfish* (SSN) tracked a Soviet ballistic missile submarine sailing off the east coast of America, thus learning Soviet SSBN patrol areas and operating patterns, to provide early indications of any potential attack on the US.

In modern times, their stealth and virtually unlimited endurance allowed the SSNs to operate in the most sensitive of regions, or as one US commander put it "up close and personal with the Russians", who were doing exactly the same thing. The SSNs can reach their target or areas of operations at a high rate of knots, independently and undetected.

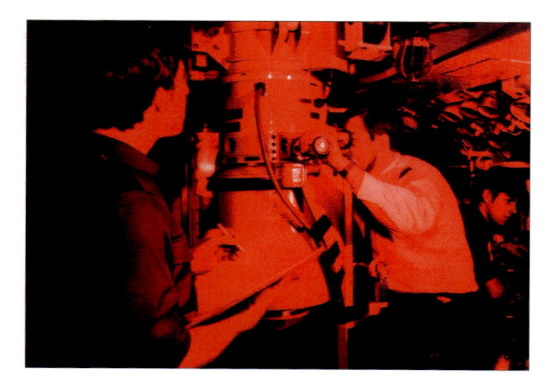

Now bristling with a highly efficient torpedo armoury (SSN) and/or cruise missiles (SSGN), they are lethal against enemy submarines, surface ships and targets ashore. The latter has been spectacularly demonstrated in recent times in the conflicts of Kosovo, Afghanistan and the two Gulf Wars. Nevertheless, at the height of the Cold War, the principal role of the attack boats was in anti-submarine warfare, and in that regard, the scientists and designers strove to produce the fastest, quietest and generally most capable fast attack vessel, and each class that arrived significantly improved upon its predecessor.

FAST AND VERSATILE: THE HUNTER-KILLERS

LEFT: The French submarine *Rubis*, an *Amethyste*-class hunter-killer nuclear boat, serves with the Toulon-based *Escadrille des Sous-marins Nucléaires d'Attaque* (ESNA) or nuclear submarine attack squadron. Modern upgrades provided additional firepower when she was re-equipped to carry both anti-surface and anti-submarine weaponry, with a mixed load of 14 missiles and torpedoes. The record of long patrols by *Rubis* included operations with the coalition forces during the first Gulf War and Operation Trident, the 1999 NATO bombing campaign over Yugoslavia. ABOVE: In 2002, *Rubis* took part in the naval bombardment of Afghanistan, using Exocet SM39 missiles.

The key element for both sides during that period, however, was the survivability of strategic assets – the SSBNs. This became a key role in the work of the SSNs of both sides, who each had around 80 operational boats of various classes. Eleven of the American SSNs were specially equipped to perform the sole task of locating and following Soviet submarines without the enemy counter-detecting their presence, day and night, 365 days a year. Soviet missions matched that capability. The anti-submarine missions of the SSNs, therefore had two major roles: to get into a position to sink the opposing SSBNs before they could launch a pre-emptive attack, and second, to destroy the opposition's SSNs or cruise missile submarines (SSGNs) to protect carrier battle groups. Therefore, for almost four decades, opposing teams roamed the oceans looking for each other. Quietness and stealth became the absolute keynote of all progressive technology surrounding the building of fast attack boats.

Overall, the SSNs operated under a much wider brief, as part a complete naval battle scenario involving the capital ships of the national sides, the US Carrier Battle Groups and the Soviet Surface Action Groups fighting it out for control of the sea. By the 1980s, however, the emphasis shifted heavily towards submarines as the attackers, being assigned to "take out" the heavy surface vessels. The days of a head-to-head Battle of Jutland-style surface shooting match between capital ships were finally put to rest. From that point on, the two sides concentrated heavily on improving their SSNs and SSGNs, and that situation continues in the post-Cold War environment. Indeed, far-ahead projections from both sides see the retention of a strong force of fast attack submarines.

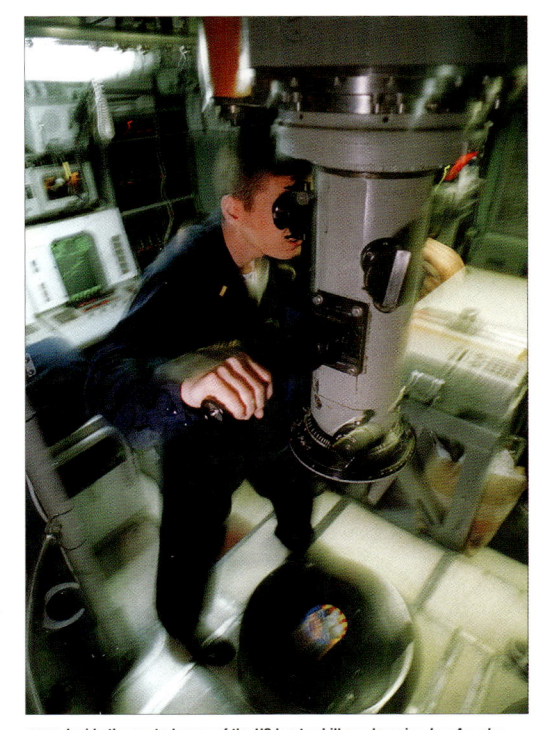

ABOVE: Inside the control room of the US hunter-killer submarine *Los Angeles*, a key element in the American SSN fleet for more than two decades.

335

The boats of both sides were designed for a life span of 20 or 30 years, but technology rapidly caught up with them. The American Thresher class of 14 boats was quickly overtaken by the Sturgeon class, of which 38 were built from the mid-1960s. However, the Los Angeles class, which arrived in the mid-1970s and was built through to 1996, was the absolute workhorse of the US SSN fleet. Initially designed as an escort for the carrier battle groups and for attacks on Soviet surface battle groups, the class went through over 20 years in production with continual updates and improvement. They were fast, quiet, and could launch Mk48 and Advanced Capability (ADCAP) torpedoes, Harpoon anti-ship missiles, and both land attack and anti-ship Tomahawk cruise missiles. The newer submarines in the class showed another step improvement in quieting, perhaps the most competitive element between the main protagonists, and an increase in operating speed.

Escort duties regularly included conducting ASW sweeps of hundreds of miles ahead of the carrier group and conducting surveillance and attacks against the Soviet surface actions groups, the *Kirov*-class Soviet cruiser being a particular target. It was fitted with state-of-the art surface-to-air missiles, surface-to-surface missiles and anti-cruise missile defences. While operating in concert with a surface group, the *Kirov* was reckoned to be an almost unreachable target, but in fact particular studies carried out by the Americans showed that, with the exception of the helicopters she carried, her ASW defences were minimal. Therefore, each time the *Kirov* was encountered, particular boats were assigned the sole task of preparing to sink her if it became necessary.

TOP: **The US Navy has long collected its formations into battle groups, each one deployed as a unique combination of ships or submarines. Naturally, whenever these groups were on the move, Soviet submarines would be close at hand, keeping watch, and vice versa.** ABOVE: **The fast Akula SSNs of the Soviet fleet were spy boats, introduced in 1986 and constantly upgraded since.**

The final SSN in the American repertoire is the *Seawolf*, a magnificent state-of-the-art vessel commissioned in 1997, which claims to be the fastest, quietest and most heavily armed submarine in existence, carrying 50 torpedoes or 100 mines. At the time of writing, two others were listed in the class, *Connecticut*, commissioned in 1998, and *Jimmy Carter*, due to begin operations in 2006.

Against this, the Soviets lined up a greater range of SSNs, if less technologically sound boats. The range began with the November class, introduced in 1959, which provided *K3*, the first Soviet submarine to reach the North Pole in 1962. Twelve boats were built for patrols in the North Atlantic, Pacific and Mediterranean, primarily targeted at surface battle groups, although their greatest disadvantage was that of noise. The Russians' principal anti-submarine warfare boats arrived with the long-running Victor class, which was produced in three versions from 1967 to 1984, operating in the classic role of hunters for enemy SSBNs, while protecting the Red Navy's own SSBNs and surface groups from the Americans. During the Cold War, Victors were operational around the globe. Far less successful was the Alfa class, which initially promised much as a highly automated, high speed submarine noted for its high acceleration rate. The hull was constructed from titanium alloy to achieve greater diving depth, with the intention of negating some of the acoustic advantages of Western submarines. Sadly for the Soviets, however, it was an expensive boat to build and maintain, and ultimately unreliable. The first of the class, *K64*, had so many problems it was decommissioned after only two years of service. A dozen were eventually built to a new design standard and remained in service throughout the Cold War. Another of the long serving classes in the Soviet fleet was the Akula class, designed as multipurpose attack submarines to take over from the Viktors in ASW operations and shadowing American battle groups. The class became a workhorse of the Russian fleet and went through three major developments, adding an improved version and the Akula II, remaining in production until the late 1990s.

Most of the Russian SSNs were larger than their US counterparts, and it took years for their designers to come close to matching the Americans in terms of noise and acoustics. Surprisingly to Western observers, it was achieved with the Oscar class, a massive boat, 154m/505ft in length with a 18.3m/60ft beam, with a dived displacement of 18,594 tonnes/18,300 tons. The Oscar II version was hugely armed, with 24 Shipwreck surface-to-surface missiles with nuclear warheads or 40 torpedoes and 200 depth charges. Eleven Oscar IIs were built, with four apiece being constantly deployed with the Pacific and Northern fleets. Among them was the ill-fated *Kursk*, which sank in the Barents Sea with the loss of all hands.

ABOVE: **HMS *Talent*, one of the *Trafalgar*-class submarines, which in spite of problems with cracks in one of their systems in 2000, remained the Royal Navy's most advanced SSN until the arrival of the Astute class.**

SECOND FROM TOP: **Soviet *Victor*-class SSNs were designed to protect Soviet surface fleets and attack American ballistic missile boats, should the need arise. When the Soviet spy network discovered that the Americans could easily track *Victor II*-class submarines, production was halted to design *Victor III* (pictured).** ABOVE: **The US trackers might well have been this crew, in the control room of the US *Los Angeles* SSN.** LEFT: *Los Angeles,* **lead boat in her class, undergoing trials. Sixty-two were built.**

337

Sink the *Belgrano*!

The invasion of the Falkland Islands by Argentina in 1982 brought the British submarine service into immediate action, and it was the first to get the alert, presenting the real possibility that they would fire their first shots in anger since World War II. The SSN *Splendid*, from the UK's Swiftsure class, was chasing a Russian submarine, when she was called off by Northwood and ordered to go quickly to Faslane and fill the boat with stores and torpedoes. The order came on March 30, 1982, two days before the invasion. It was a top-secret move and no telephone calls could be made to relatives by the crew, in spite of the fact that *Splendid* had already been at sea for ten weeks. At that point, the crew had no idea of the plan of action, and the politicians probably didn't either.

For years, submarines had been used for a spot of old-fashioned gunboat diplomacy in British-linked hot spots, but this time it was altogether more serious. Sure enough, on April 1, Argentine troops began pouring into the Falklands, and the token British force of Royal Marines was taken prisoner. Argentinian photographers flashed around the world a photograph of them being marched away with their hands over their heads. British Prime Minister Margaret Thatcher was furious, and immediately announced she was sending a task force of 40 warships and a very large contingent of her finest soldiers, including Commandos, Gurkhas, Paras and a large special forces contingent from the SBS and SAS, to take the islands back.

She also announced a 322km/200-mile Maritime Exclusion Zone around the Falklands and that any ships entering that zone did so at their peril. The fast nuclear boats were dispatched immediately to enforce the order. *Spartan* completed the 10,461km/6,500-mile journey to her designated patrol area in less than ten days, a speed of advance of around 26 knots, which, allowing for navigational checks and going to shallow depth to receive messages, was virtually flat out. *Splendid* and *Conqueror* were not far behind, although a long way back came the diesel-engined Oberon boat, *Onyx,* which had a submerged speed of just eight knots. She arrived three weeks after the nuclear boats. Information on Argentina for the submarine commander was sparse, to say the least. *Jane's* provided the best intelligence. Whitehall and the Ministry of Defence had little to offer in the way of up-to-date information about the Argentine fleet and what kind of opposition or anti-submarine operations the British boats might expect.

Splendid, commanded by Commander Roger Lane-Nott, arrived on station 11 days after leaving Faslane, her journey down utilized for a heavy training programme that involved a great deal of effort on the part of every member of the crew. Commander Jim Taylor in *Spartan* had already begun his

TOP RIGHT: **HMS *Splendid*, a hunter-killer SSN of the Swiftsure class, was one of the British submarines on patrol at the time of the Falklands war, providing vital reconnaissance for the Royal Navy Task Force.** ABOVE: **The ill-fated Argentine ship *General Belgrano*, sunk by conventional torpedoes fired from the submarine HMS *Conquerer*, which had tracked her for 30 hours.** RIGHT: **HMS *Sheffield* sank after being hit by Exocet missiles fired by a French-made Dassault Super Etendard aircraft belonging to the Argentine Navy.**

LEFT: **Coming home to controversy and flying the Jolly Roger, a customary act of Royal Navy submarines after a "kill", HMS** *Conqueror*, **the** *Churchill*-**class boat that went into the history books as the only British nuclear-powered submarine to sink an enemy ship with torpedoes since World War II.** NEAR LEFT: **Survivors come ashore after the Falklands bombing of British troop-landing ship,** *Sir Galahad*, **which had been hit by a 453.6kg/1,000lb bomb that did not detonate. She was later hit again by two or three bombs while unloading soldiers from the 1st Welsh Guards, of whom 48 were killed in the explosions and subsequent fire.** BELOW: **The image that made the front pages: the** *Belgrano* **going down, with the loss of 368 lives.**

patrol, but both commanders were short of information. They were eventually tasked by submarine HQ to locate and observe a suspected movement of Argentine ships towards the Falkland Islands, including the aircraft carrier *25 de Mayo* and the cruiser *General Belgrano*. It was a slow process because they had no idea where they were. They did know, however, that the Argentinians had a US-built *Guppy*-class diesel submarine transmitting somewhere around the Falklands.

Splendid was then moved to patrol the northern end of the Falkland Sound, since there was a great fear that the *25 de Mayo* would get into that area before the British task force arrived so that she could extend the range of her aircraft armed with Exocet missiles. Diplomatic efforts were still proceeding, and the rules of engagement were still changing from "sink" to "do not sink Argentinian ships".

On April 26, *Splendid* reported to Northwood that she had sighted an Argentine task group composed of two Type 42 destroyers together with Exocet-armed frigates moving south along the coast. However, although *Splendid*'s commander had had the destroyers in his periscope sights, he did not have rules of engagement and could not fire. Instead, he was ordered to break off and join the hunt elsewhere when concern now switched to the activities of the cruiser *General Belgrano*, thought to be moving towards the exclusion zone. *Splendid* went north with *Spartan* between Argentina and the task force,

while *Conqueror* searched to the south. The rules of engagement had started to become specific, and the British made known their intention to order the sinking of anything within the 322km/200-mile exclusion zone.

On May 1, however, *Conqueror*'s CO, Chris Wreford-Brown, found *General Belgrano* in his sights. His submarine's nuclear power allowed him to track the cruiser for 30 hours and choose the moment for attack when authorized to do so. The "sink her" command came from London, and he fired a salvo of three ancient Mark VIII torpedoes from 1,100m/1,203yd. They were straight-running, non-homing torpedoes of 1940s vintage, travelling at 45 knots, and two of them struck on a right-angle track. The cruiser sank fast, with the loss of 368 lives. The question arose immediately as to whether the ship was inside or outside the exclusion zone. As it transpired, it was outside and had been for six hours. However this question, as far as the three submarine commanders were concerned, was immaterial. Orders came from on high. If the cruiser had been allowed to get through, the submariners would have been castigated because the ship would have posed an immediate threat to the British ships.

The question of the location and intentions of the *Belgrano* did not go away, and the submariners became caught up in the politics of the affair, although the sinking and the loss of life did bear heavily on some members of the crew.

339

Submarine TLAMs rain on Iraq, Belgrade and Afghanistan

The commissioning of *Seawolf*, the latest in America's long line of hunter-killer submarines, was notable for a specific inclusion: whereas all US SSNs carry Tomahawk land attack missiles (TLAMs), *Seawolf* can carry 50 torpedo tube-launched TLAMs, the very latest in subsonic, all-weather cruise missiles with a range of 1,111km/600 nautical miles. Most recently, the TLAMs were very evident in the war in Iraq to oust Saddam Hussein and indeed have featured in all of the major areas of conflict of modern times. Another feature of their use is that they have, without exception, been used in joint operations with the British, with Royal Navy submarines also firing the missiles. This somewhat new feature to American foreign policy caused some observers to ponder the motives behind the two-handed firing of such weapons, given that almost all were originally created with the annihilation of the Soviet Union in mind.

The submarine programmes the missile flight profile from the launch point to landfall, and thereafter a pre-stored flight plan is followed. According to the Americans who manufacture the TLAMs, high accuracy in hitting the target was assured by the use of a Global Positioning System receiver, inertial and terrain contour matching guidance, and a Digital Scene

TOP: **USS *Minneapolis–Saint Paul*, the 26th member of the Los Angeles class, became the first submarine to carry Tomahawk land attack missiles, specifically designated for use in strikes against Iraq during the Gulf War.** ABOVE: **General Tommy Franks, commander of the US forces in the Gulf, inspects TLAM damage in Baghdad after the 2003 bombardment.**

Matching Area Correlation system. However, there was considerable comment in the media about the number of TLAMs that appeared to miss their targets in the first Gulf War. However, the systems have been modernized, particularly those in the brand new Seawolf class, which was launched under the tag of "the most advanced and most capable submarine fleet in the world". There is, however, no doubt that competition with the Soviet Union in the final stages of the Cold War played its part in forging continued improvements to the systems and boats of both sides.

The Tomahawk missile was long ago judged by the American scenario planners to be an integral part of future submarine operations, and so it was to be proved. Tomahawk was used extensively during Operation Desert Storm in 1991 and again in Iraq in January and June 1993 during air

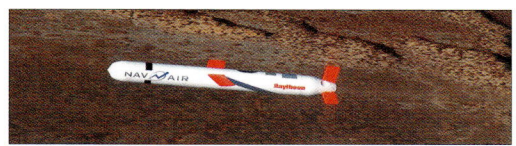

SUBMARINE TLAMS RAIN ON IRAQ, BELGRADE AND AFGHANISTAN

RIGHT: **The Regulus guided cruise missile was successfully developed into America's sea-going deterrent, first deployed on the heavy cruiser USS *Los Angeles* in 1955 – and after successful trials five submarines were also fitted to carry and launch the missile, thus to become America's principal deterrent force of that era.**
MIDDLE RIGHT: **The Tomahawk cruise missile became the much-used and most feared arm of the British and US land attack suite: 600 were fired by the US in the first six days of the 2003 attack on Iraqi targets.** BELOW: **HMS *Triumph* which launched Tomahawk missiles during Operation Veritas on targets inside Afghanistan and returned home after operations had ended flying the Jolly Roger to indicate "kills" during a successful patrol.** BELOW RIGHT: **Another of the targets, an alleged terrorist training camp inside Iraq.**

operations against Saddam Hussein. They were used again in Bosnia (Deliberate Force) in 1995 and in Iraq (Desert Strike) in 1996. Four hundred Block II and Block III missiles were fired on five separate occasions.

This and improvements in subsequent operations was taken as fair evidence that long-range missiles fired from hidden submarines could carry out some of the missions of strike aircraft and reduce the risk of pilot and aircraft losses. It was following these operations that British submarines were also equipped with Tomahawks, and they were first introduced in 1998 and used operationally the following year during the Kosovo crisis. During the 78-day NATO bombing campaign, the British submarine *Splendid* was among the launchers of TLAMs that slammed into Belgrade. According to a summary of the cruise attacks published in *Jane's Defence Weekly*, *Splendid* fired 20 Tomahawk cruise missiles during the war, 17 of which hit their targets. US ships and submarines fired 218 cruise missiles at 66 targets, and 181 reached their "intended aim-points" according to US naval officers. The attack on a television building, in which 16 civilians were killed, was strongly criticized by US human rights groups and Amnesty International. However, NATO's supreme commander at the time, General Wesley Clark, and his British counterparts insisted that the building was a legitimate military target because it was used to pass information to Serbian military units in Kosovo and to promote Serbian propaganda.

The use of *Splendid* in the bombing campaign was a significant departure from the established pattern of patrols and surveillance. It also gave a pointer to the future and the kind of situations that might engage the British submarine service in its more global approach. Warning signs of possible future trouble spots were already evident at the dawn of the new millennium and after 9/11 when the Americans, with British support, decided to unseat the Taliban regime in Afghanistan.

A Royal Navy surface fleet, along with the SSNs *Superb*, *Trafalgar* and *Triumph*, were in the Indian Ocean in support of air operations against the land-locked nation. The two T boats carried out the cruise missile attacks. British submarines kept up the vigil all year long, and another T boat, *Turbulent,* had just finished her tour of duty at Christmas 2002, having been at sea for a full six months without a break, when she was placed on alert to go to the Gulf. Before she was done, *Turbulent* played a full part in the "shock and awe" bombing campaign over Baghdad. When she was finally released from this duty, she had travelled 85,295km/53,000 miles during a single deployment lasting ten months.

341

THE HISTORY OF SUBMARINES

LEFT: The wreck of the *Kursk* is discovered, and spotlights reveal catastrophic damage to the submarine of a nature and extent that would have rapidly enveloped the whole structure.
BELOW: A memorial plaque to the lost submarine and her crew.

The tragedy of the *Kursk*

On August 12, 2000, scientists at the Norwegian Seismic Institute recorded two explosions, the second registering 3.4 on the Richter scale, which would have required the massive power of 2,032kg/2 tons of explosives to create such a reaction. A "thundering boom" was also picked up by an American spy ship, USS *Loyal* which, at the time, was listening into transmissions from one of the giant Russian submarines of the Oscar II class, *Kursk*, as she participated in a major naval exercise 322km/200 miles away. The Americans knew that the sound could only mean one thing. The submarine had suffered a major catastrophe. As word got out that one of the most technically advanced boats in the Russian fleet was in trouble, the official word from Moscow was initially quite different.

First, they admitted there was a problem and the vessel had been allowed to drift to the bottom in about 103.6m/340ft of water until technicians had resolved the issue. They could not bring themselves to admit – or perhaps believe – that the showpiece of the Russian submarine fleet displacing 18,594 tonnes/18,300 tons submerged was in dire straits. Therefore, in the style of the Soviet Union of old, they tried to pass it off as a minor incident and rejected offers of help from the West.

However, there was more to it than that. The boat was packed with technology the West knew little about, including her brand new armoury pack – 24 SS-N-19 Shipwreck missiles with either a 500-kilotonne nuclear warhead or 350kg/772lb of high explosives – which in total added up to the equivalent of about two Hiroshima bombs. Also, fitted to the bulbous bow of the 153.9m/505ft long boat was a top-secret target detection sonar which up to that point had never been outside a Russian naval base. It was no wonder, then, that the Russians stalled when the other side offered to send in their deep sea rescue craft.

Thus began what developed into a horrendous saga that gripped the world for days as the Russians tried unsuccessfully to retrieve the 118 men aboard the stricken sub. As relatives began their vigil on the dockside, those who had followed the Russian catalogue of costly mishaps with their submarines, dating back through the decades, feared the worst, regardless of the spin and contradictory stories. As the Russians alone pressed on with their rescue attempt, conflicting stories came out of Moscow suggesting the damage resulted from

ABOVE: USS *Loyal*, an American intelligence ship, was among those in the area monitoring the Russian exercises, along with submarines USS *Memphis*, USS *Toledo* and HMS *Splendid*.

342

THE TRAGEDY OF THE *KURSK*

LEFT: **The massive surface profile of the stricken submarine *Kursk*, which was on "routine exercises" in the Barents Sea, a region that had seen no fewer than 25 reported accidents or collisions between opposing submarines in the previous three decades of the Cold War. The theory that the *Kursk* had been bumped by an opposing submarine monitoring her movements was propagated in Russia, but proved to be false.**
BELOW: **Damaged: the aft escape hatch of the *Kursk*, photographed by rescuers.**

a collision with another submarine. The deputy prime minister told the media that it had been hit by a "very large tonnage". It was also pointed out that British and American submarines were in the area at the time, monitoring Russian exercises. Some websites to this day still support such allegations, though long ago disproved.

Analysts in the West worked out a probable scenario. The Russians' use of cheap but dangerous liquid hydrogen peroxide fuel to power their torpedoes had triggered an explosion so powerful that it ripped through the first four or five compartments of the boat. Day after day, Russian attempts to get into the boat failed, despite assurances from the government that no foreign help was needed. By Day 7 of the crisis a multi-national team aboard a Norwegian rescue ship was finally invited in. On August 20, they wrenched the after escape hatch free, only to discover the boat was totally besieged.

It took another two months before the Russians were able to set up a mission to retrieve the bodies, during which notes written by members of the crew were found. They poignantly demonstrated the hell they had experienced in the pitch black of the boat before they were eventually overwhelmed by the water. The task of raising the *Kursk* took many months and she was finally brought to the surface by a Dutch contractor in 2001, when it was discovered that the whole of the forward section of the boat had been blown apart. It took another two years for the Russian authorities to admit that there was no collision, that no other boat was involved, and that the cause was, just as Western analysts had surmised, some sort of malfunction in the torpedo room that caused the hydrogen peroxide to ignite while the *Kursk* was practising torpedo firings.

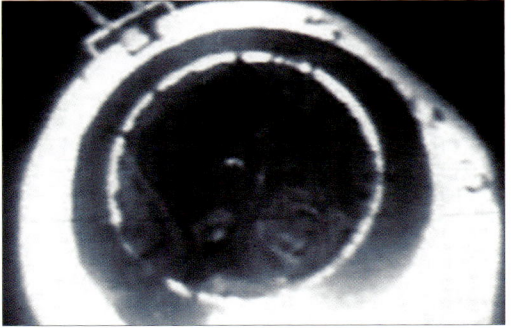

ABOVE: **A Russian photograph showing two submarine personnel in training for underwater escape and rescue missions.**

International rescue: deep sea survival teams

Although submarine accidents of a life-threatening nature are becoming less frequent, the development of more sophisticated tools for the deep sea rescue of stranded crews is ongoing. In June 2004, Britain, France and Norway placed a contract with Rolls-Royce for the development of a totally new rescue platform, the NATO Submarine Rescue System (NSRS) which will replace existing models. The system will consist of an unmanned remotely operated vehicle to locate the submarine, check for signs of life and provide emergency supplies, and a three-person Submarine Rescue Vehicle which will be able to dive to depths down to 600m/1,968ft and rescue survivors, in groups of up to 15 at a time.

A UK-based company Kongsberg Maritime Ltd, of Waterlooville, is involved in development of the navigation and communication systems, and the NSRS will be headquartered at the Royal Navy base on the Clyde upon entering service in 2006. Thereafter the equipment will be available for emergency calls for any nation within the NATO alliance. Meanwhile, the UK Submarine Rescue Headquarters continues to operate from its own base at Renfrew in Glasgow, Scotland. The service, managed by the Royal Navy, has a permanent operational team of pilots, engineers and technicians, employed by Rumic Ltd, to maintain and upgrade the system.

Their equipment features a remotely-operated submersible vehicle, *Scorpio 45*, which investigates a rescue scene, and the LR5 submersible vehicle (one of the systems used in the *Kursk* rescue attempt), which can operate at depths up to 500m/1,640ft, carrying divers to a disabled submarine and returning with survivors. The service, like any emergency crew, is on a 24-hour standby and can be ready to travel to any rescue site worldwide within 12 hours. Where the incident is outside the range of the UK rescue ships, a remarkable international rescue effort, well-practised and ready for any emergency, swings into action.

It requires speed, efficiency and the co-operation of many people around the globe, including major shipping concerns, to enable the fast deployment of the crew and their gear to the scene of the submarine. The process begins with an assessment of ships capable of hosting the rescue craft at sea in the area of the distress call. This is achieved by means of an international register which can provide up-to-the-minute locations of potential mother ships. They are usually diving vessels or similar ships that have sufficient deck space and

TOP: **International submarine rescue efforts are co-ordinated by NATO. In one of the largest-ever rescue exercises in the wake of *Kursk*, the Italian SRV-300 vehicle was deployed from the mother ship *Anteo* and successfully rehearsed docking procedures with the Italian submarine *Prini*. Two sailors from *Prini* were evacuated to a Turkish ship, using a McCann rescue bell.**

ABOVE: **The *Scorpio* ROV (remotely operated deep submergence vehicle) which was used in an attempt to save *Kursk*'s crew, shown here recovering the flight recorder. It is commonly used in the offshore oil industry.**

344

INTERNATIONAL RESCUE: DEEP SEA SURVIVAL TEAMS

necessary machinery to launch and retrieve the rescue vehicle, as well as adequate facilities to accommodate the rescue team and survivors. At the same time, the host ship must have the speed to travel quickly to the nearest port to pick up the 11-strong rescue team of divers and technical officers, together with the rescue submersible and ancillary equipment, and carry them to the rescue site.

The submersible, manned by a crew of three, is manoeuvred into position to make a watertight connection to the submarine's escape hatch to allow technicians and medical staff to enter, and then to bring out crew members. Under normal conditions, the LR5 could make up to eight trips to evacuate the submarine before its batteries needed recharging, a time-frame sufficient to bring out up to 120 personnel. On the surface, portable decompression chambers will have been installed on the mother ship to treat survivors where necessary.

The NSRS replacement will come with a complete back-up of supporting equipment, operating in much the same manner as its predecessor. The 10m/32ft 10in, 27-tonne/26.6-ton submarine will be partnered by an unmanned craft which will locate the sunken submarine and provide decompression chambers, medical facilities and other support equipment. It is described by the Ministry of Defence as the most effective submarine rescue system available, and is expected to have a life of 25 years.

In the United States, the US Navy is equipped with Deep Submergence Rescue Vehicles (DSRVs) which were developed as a matter of urgency in the 1960s in the wake of the loss of the *Thresher*. They also operate on a ready-to-move basis similar to the British team, to deploy for accidents involving their own submarines or those of any other navies. The rescue work knows no international barriers. The DSRV is larger than the British version, at 15m/49ft in length with a displacement of 38 tonnes/37.4 tons, and can work at depths down to 1,500m/ 4,921ft. With a crew of four, it is also capable of transferring up to 24 personnel to the surface at a time.

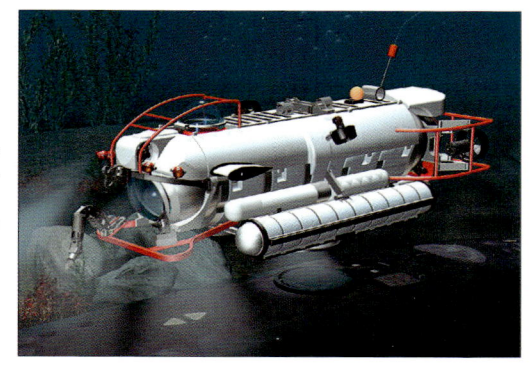

ABOVE: **An impression of a future remotely operated submersible vehicle being developed under the auspices of NATO.**

ABOVE: **The *Scorpio* ROV was called to assist the Russians again, on August 4, 2005, to join an international effort to free the AS-28 mini-sub *Priz* – itself a rescue vehicle – which had become trapped deep in the Pacific, near the Kamchatka peninsula, with seven submariners trapped on board and oxygen supplies dwindling. The *Scorpio* craft had to cut the vessel free from the debris pinning it to the seabed.** LEFT: **The Russian SS-750 rescue vehicle, with a 66-tonne/65-ton heavy lift gantry at the stern, was built as a very large mooring tender and reclassified in 1995 to serve as a submersible support and transport submarine. A similar craft was unsuccessful in the effort to reach the *Kursk* crew.** BELOW: **An underwater photograph of attempts to drag the *Priz* free.**

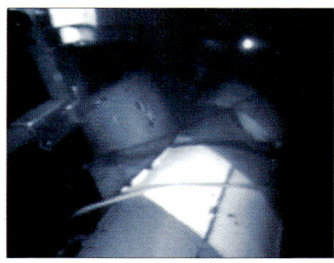

345

Shaping the future

Submarine warfare is on the brink of transformation, with new boats, new concepts and an overall leaning towards the demands of diversity in modern operational requirements. Brand new boats, such as the Virginia class produced in America and the Astute class for the UK, herald the coming of fast, powerful attack submarines designed for the 21st century. Additionally, alongside them will emerge a "new for old" conversion, which will introduce a totally fresh *modus operandi* for some of the older ballistic boomers that still have a life of 20 or more years left in them, but whose original role in the Cold War has long since diminished. Now, it is planned to re-deploy these successful boats to make use of their incredible payload, stealth, and endurance in a new deterrent role.

It will be recalled that the very first SSBN carrier in the US submarine service was quickly constructed by cutting the attack submarine *Scorpion* in two and inserting the missile section. The boat re-emerged two years later as *George Washington*, America's first "boomer" carrying a very large pod of doomsday weaponry. Now, the reverse situation is underway that will transform submarine warfare of the future. *Ohio*-class ballistic missile submarines are being converted to bring forward a totally new concept, although in many ways it harks back to the heyday of British submariners in World

TOP: **USS *Virginia*, SSN-774, under construction in 2003. It became the first US submarine designed to meeting the requirements of the post-Cold War era, capable of deep ocean anti-submarine warfare and shallow water operations.**
ABOVE: **The *Astute*, Britain's 21st-century entry into the multi-functional world of SSN boats, carrying a weapon load 50 per cent greater than the Trafalgar class, which includes Spearfish torpedoes and Tomahawk cruise missiles.**

War II, when they undertook many varied tasks, such as clandestine insertion of special forces, in addition to their main role as attack boats.

The concept emerged in discussions following the end of the Cold War, which subsequently became conjoined with the events of 9/11 and all that came in its wake. Urgent studies were initiated by governments and military study groups around the globe on how future threats could be faced effectively. Initially, the role of submarines in this scenario was not immediately clear, but the pointers were already there, in history and in fact, the US Navy had the model ready to bring forward. Their plan was to introduce a new class of SSGN boats: nuclear-powered submarines carrying guided missiles based on the boomers, whose numbers were already being culled as the Cold War faded into history. The converted boats would carry an armoury of missiles with tremendous fire power, but also include operational possibilities that would revolutionize submarine activity.

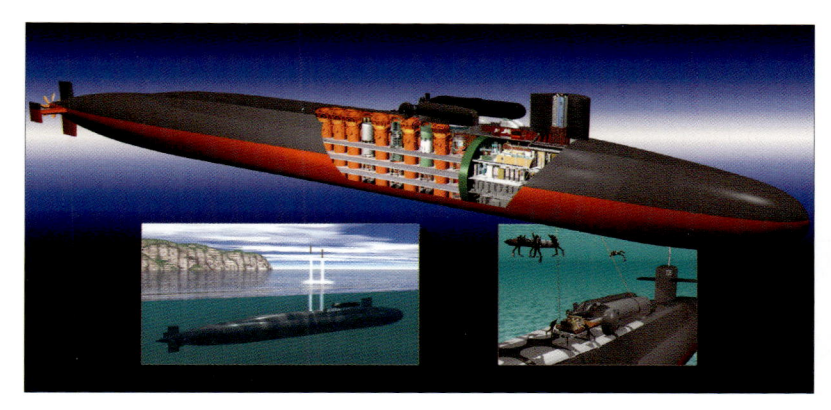

In conjunction with designers from the Electric Boat Company, they produced conversion designs for the insertion of vertical launch systems that provide the SSGNs with a massive firepower of 154 Tomahawk cruise missiles – more than the total complement of a normal US Navy battle group. They will also have the facilities to carry up to 70 special forces personnel, keep them aboard far longer than the SSN boats and have the equipment to send them ashore wherever they are required. As the concept develops, new additions will further transform submarine operations when the boats are equipped with large manned and unmanned undersea vehicles for special operations, unmanned aerial vehicles and off-board sensors all capable of submerged operations, although at the time of writing no details of their design and appearance has been released.

ABOVE LEFT: **A cutaway of USS *Ohio*, one of four strategic missile carriers converted to carry Tomahawk cruise missiles. *Ohio* also allowed the installation of lockin-lockout chambers for up to 100 Special Forces personnel and equipment. This was achieved by utilizing 22 of the 24 tubes for the Vertical Launch System canisters, which could stow six conventional land attack missiles per tube.**

ABOVE RIGHT: **USS *Florida* launches a Tomahawk cruise missile on the firing range off the coast of the Bahamas as part of the trials for the conversion work.**

These developments have been heralded by submarine warfare analysts as the most innovative since the arrival of nuclear-powered, nuclear-armed boats. The project began when the oldest US Trident ballistic missile submarine, *Ohio*, arrived at the Electric Boat Company's Puget Sound Naval Shipyard in Bremerton, Washington, in 2003, where the conversion work would take place at the same time as her mid-life refuelling. She was to be followed in the conversion at other shipyards by three other Trident boats, *Florida*, *Michigan* and *Georgia*. All were back in operation by 2008.

RIGHT: **USS *Ohio* returning to Puget Sound Naval Shipyard in December 2005 after sea trials to test the functions of the conversion, which was completed in less than three years. Three other *Ohio*-class Trident boats – *Michigan*, *Florida* and *Georgia* – had similar surgery at a total cost of $1.4 billion, and the four will also test new weapons systems, sensors and littoral operational concepts that will transform naval warfare by carrying large unmanned undersea vehicles.**

Notably, the transformation work will include the installation of advanced equipment such as sensors and surveillance systems. Specifically, the new boats will bring a rapid precision strike capability against land-based targets and assure access to hostile or denied areas. These decisions were taken before the Iraq war, although doubtless such a possibility was already in the minds of members of the Bush administration. Having established the conversion programme, all aspects of the joint capabilities were put under the microscope and key aspects to emerge were as follows:

• Stealth, power, reliability and versatility of the converted boats, with more than 20 years of service life remaining for each SSGN, plus the operation of two crews so that each boat would be available for continuous operations.

• Large-volume precision strike, with up to 154 Tomahawk and Tactical Tomahawk cruise missiles aboard, 20 times larger than the payload of the SSNs.

• Sustained special forces operations, to include insertion from the SSGN, extraction and continued support while in action. Also planned is the use of unmanned vehicles that can deliver weapons and communications equipment to the surface from a submerged submarine, for a "dry" landing with the troops.

• Operating as a command centre for mission planning and execution, with capacity for conducting other missions normally carried out by the SSN fleet, including intelligence gathering, surveillance, reconnaissance and targeting, anti-submarine warfare, anti-surface warfare and mine warfare. With the boat able to function as a dedicated command centre, on-board personnel will be able to control a special forces campaign over a period of months from her covert position. Special forces would deploy from the submerged boat or in the Advanced SEAL Delivery System (ASDS) mini-subs, which

TOP LEFT: **Special Forces and submarines go together, as proved here by a SEAL Delivery Vehicle (SDV) team fast-roping from a Seahawk helicopter to the deck of USS *Toledo* of the Improved Los Angeles attack class.** ABOVE LEFT: **US Navy SEALs seize a beach during a training mission after exiting a submarine.** TOP: **The dexterity of submarine-based forces is demonstrated here by an SDV team being launched in their vehicle from the back of another *Los Angeles*-class boat, USS *Philadelphia*, sending them underwater and undetected towards enemy targets ashore.** ABOVE: **The US Navy Special Warfare Trident insignia worn by qualified SEALs, whose expansion in terms of numbers and ability is being matched by most major seafaring nations.**

enable the SEALs to travel to locations 231.5km/125 nautical miles away in a dry environment. It will become, says the Navy, "the most advanced covert special forces platform ever".

As already noted, these developments come alongside the much anticipated arrival of two spectacular new boats in the international inventory, the Virginia class in the US and the

BELOW: **As littoral operations become more vital, so does the training, as shown here with two US SEALs on a rigorous Combat Swim.**

SHAPING THE FUTURE

LEFT: USS *Greeneville* was one of the first *Los Angeles*-class submarines to be converted to accommodate and install systems for the Deep Submergence Rescue Vehicle and/or the Advanced SEAL Delivery System, completing trials in 1993. BELOW LEFT: A Tactical Tomahawk cruise missile, photographed during a controlled test flight from a vertical submerged launch in 2002, hitting its target 1255km/780 miles away. The next generation was capable of being reprogrammed in flight. BELOW: Members of a SEAL Delivery Vehicle team inside a flooded Dry Deck shelter aboard USS *Philadelphia*, from which they are launched on missions while the submarine remains submerged.

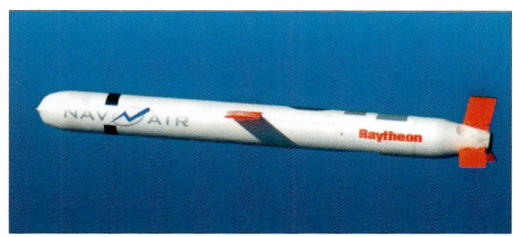

Astute in Britain. Indeed, some of the technology of the Virginia class will be included in the SSGN conversions, inasmuch as the *Virginia* – the newest of the US Navy's fast attack boats – is fully loaded with the designs and intentions to keep it in business for the next 20 years or more.

Again, the emphasis in the creation of the class, of which four will be built initially, has been to extend the capability of the SSN into multi-purpose functions. The whole concept of submarine warfare is rolled into a massive package of what the Americans claim "will surpass the performance of any current projected threat submarine, ensuring US dominance well into the 21st century".

The Royal Navy is also laying claim to a share of that dominance with the launch of their brand new *Astute*, with an extravagant description as the "biggest and most powerful attack submarine to be built for the Royal Navy", yet it will have a much smaller ship's company. HMS *Astute* will displace 7,800 tonnes/7,677 tons dived and is 97m/318ft long and fully equipped for cruise missiles. Construction of the second submarine of the class, *Ambush*, began in October 2003, with the third, *Artful*, laid down in March 2005.

Meanwhile, the Royal Navy also recognizes that the needs of the modern navy are changing rapidly, particularly in submarine operations. The Navy has set in motion what it describes as a decisive break away from the Cold War emphasis on anti-submarine warfare, to embrace an operational concept aligned to Joint Operations. This in turn will call for training up to meet a range of tasks in direct support of surface forces. The transformation of submarine operations across the board is underway.

ABOVE: The versatile USS *Seawolf* fast attack submarine was built to achieve the lowest noise levels while achieving the highest tactical speed.

349

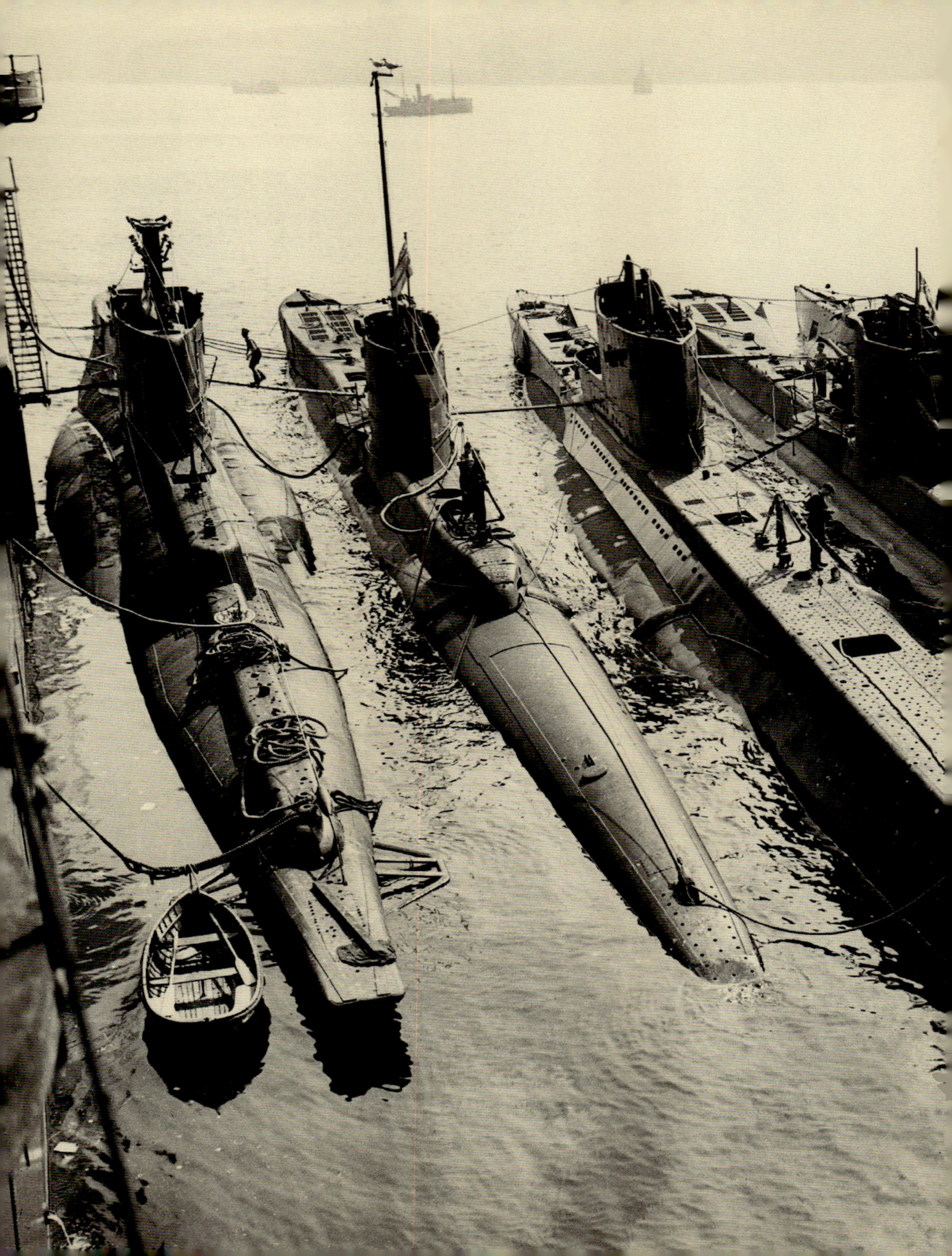

Directory of Submarines

1900–45

In 1900, the Royal Navy did not possess a single submarine. In fact, Britain was the only major maritime power not to have even the beginnings of a submarine flotilla. The United States Navy was trialling her own *Holland I*, and the Royal Navy followed the US lead in 1901. Thereafter it became a race to produce boats of ever-increasing endurance and sophistication.

By the outbreak of World War I, the unimaginable was already happening: submarines could actually take on the mighty surface ships – and win. Between the wars, design emphasis switched to diesel-electric boats, and considerable advances had been made by the onset of World War II. With the outbreak of hostilities, Germany turned to her submarines to take the war to the Allies at sea, using their boats as submersible destroyers.

Britain relied on her new O, S, T and U-class boats, but was forced to begin with older stock. The Japanese had begun producing giant boats, while the Americans went into mass production with a number of major classes, such as Gato, Balao and Tench, that were to become the workhorses of the US submarine fleet.

LEFT: **British submarines of the 10th Flotilla based at Lazaretto, Malta, included** *Upright* **(second from right), which sank Mussolini's cruiser** *Armando Diaz* **on February 25, 1941.**

LEFT: With no room on top, the crowded state of the early submarines meant a wet start to the day for the inexperienced, and it was even more crowded down below. BELOW: The classic shape of the *Holland* boat, repeated in magnified proportions more than half a century later.

The *Holland*

After much deliberation, submarines formally became part of the US Navy's inventory in 1899 when a series of trials of the *Holland* convinced the Navy Board that they should go ahead. It had been a long and difficult journey for her creator, J.P. Holland, who had won a competition staged by the Navy 11 years earlier to build a torpedo-firing submarine that could "travel submerged for two hours at eight knots at depths up to 150 feet".

Although he won the competition, Holland did not receive a contract to build his boat, and it took several more unsuccessful attempts that saw him slide into near bankruptcy before the US Navy finally came up with a $165,000 contract for *Holland VI*.

Launched on May 17, 1897, at Elizabethport, New Jersey, it was equipped with a 37.3kW/50hp petrol engine for surface propulsion, for which a range of 1,609km/1,000 miles was claimed. The US Navy was impressed during trials when the boat managed to get within 91.4m/100 yards of the US battleship *Kearsage*, whereupon a light was flashed to demonstrate that the ship could have been sunk with the submarine's 450mm/17.7in Whitehead torpedoes.

The *Holland* was built under her designer's supervision at the Crescent Shipyard at Elizabethport, New Jersey, and was noted for her sleek lines in the likeness of a porpoise. In reality, however, she travelled low in the water when on the surface, making it precarious for her crew to work on deck, especially when operating the Zalinski dynamite gun mounted on the bow, which was subsequently removed. The Navy contracted for the building of five boats, although there were serious doubts as to their viability among those who still had to be convinced of the usefulness of submarines. Not least among these were some of the sailors who were destined to man the new contraptions. The boat's stability on the surface left much to be desired and the internal arrangements were spartan and dangerous.

Inside the boat, the slightest malfunction of the exhaust system from the petrol-driven engine could kill the entire crew by carbon monoxide poisoning. Even a minor fuel leak might cause an explosion, as could battery problems, which plagued submarines for years hence. The *Holland* did not see any serious service, and was used mainly for training as the first new boats of an improved Holland design came on stream.

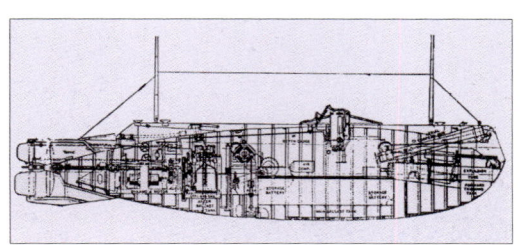

LEFT: The original *Holland* drawings for his boat, more or less adhered to by the US Navy designers.

Holland

Displacement: 62.98 tonnes/62 tons (surfaced); 72.83 tonnes/71.7 tons (submerged)
Length: 16.18m/53ft
Beam: 3.13m/10ft 3in
Armament: 1 x 457mm/18in bow tube, 2 x torpedoes
Propulsion: 33.6kW/45hp petrol; 41kW/55hp electric
Speed: 8.0 knots (surfaced); 5.0 knots (dived)
Complement: 9 men

UNITED STATES

LEFT: **USS *Porpoise* (which became *A6*) and *Shark* (*A7*) were the last two boats of the A class. Both were eventually loaded aboard a collier and transported to the Philippines for local patrols.**
BELOW: **The safest way to keep watch, since periscopes were yet to be invented.**

A class

The seven boats of this class entered service in the first three years of the new century, all based upon an enlarged version of the *Holland I*, although confusingly the first boat in the class, originally named *Plunger*, was classified as *A1* on the creation of the class. However when all US submarines were given the SS classification in 1920, she became *SS2*, the first Holland to enter service becoming *SS1*.

The *Plunger* and the rest of the A class saw considerable service in those early years, and despite all problems concerning human habitation inside the boats, remained in service well into the second decade of the century. Three were reconditioned for coastal work and training in the early years of World War I. *Plunger* also went into history as being the first submarine to have a President of the United States aboard. She was conducting trials at Oyster Bay, close to the home of Theodore Roosevelt, in the summer of 1905. The crew had been given advance warning, giving them time to paint the outside of the boat before the president stepped aboard on August 22, 1905.

He spent almost three hours on board, and was given a full demonstration and experienced a number of dives, an event that of course captured the interest of the media and public, many of whom were still somewhat sceptical about the safety of these underwater creatures. Roosevelt took note of the reaction, and later wrote, "I went down in it chiefly because I did not like to have the officers and enlisted men think I wanted them to try things I was reluctant to try myself. I believe a good deal can be done with these submarines, although there is always the danger of people getting carried away with the idea and thinking that they can be of more use than they possibly could be".

Later, *Plunger* hosted another figure of subsequent fame: Chester W. Nimitz became her skipper in May 1909, the first command of the man who would rise to become Fleet Admiral. Although at the time Nimitz said he considered submarines "a cross between a Jules Verne fantasy and a humpbacked whale", he later became one of America's most distinguished naval figures. The experience on board *Plunger* and others of the early classes, however, was unforgettable. A Navy Medical Officer's report at the time was scathing about conditions on the boats, with the crew sleeping, cooking, eating, and answering the calls of nature in such a confined space. He said even in moderate seas, the boat rolled and pitched so that practically the whole crew was seasick. Food had to be packed in crates and the cooked meats soon spoiled and, coupled with the use of the open toilet, the air was foul.

RIGHT: **Assigned to the Naval Torpedo Station at Newport, Rhode Island, *Plunger* operated locally for the first two years.**

A class

Displacement: 105.30 tonnes/103.6 tons (surfaced); 121 tonnes/119.1 tons (submerged)
Length: 19.24m/63ft 1in
Beam: 3.6m/11ft 10in
Armament: 1 x 457mm/18in tube, 5 x torpedoes
Propulsion: 119kW/160hp petrol; 111.9kW/150hp electric
Speed: 8.0 knots (surfaced); 7.0 knots (dived)
Complement: 7 men

353

B class

Three boats of this class, *Viper*, *Cuttlefish* and *Tarantula* (*B1*, *B2* and *B3*), commissioned in 1907, saw the final stage of development in the Holland single-screw design and introduced a more extensive superstructure for sea keeping. On the original plans, *Viper* had only the single periscope let into the conning tower; however a second periscope was added later. Air compressors and the main bilge pumps were driven from the main shaft via noisy clutches and gears. The boats were altogether more substantial in appearance, and length, stability and conditions aboard were better, but still very cramped. A reload torpedo in the B class, for example, left little space in the hull. Even so, this class saw considerable service in the Atlantic Torpedo Boat Fleet and in April 1914 was posted for an assignment in distant waters.

B1 was towed to Norfolk to be loaded on board USS *Hector* to be carried to the Philippine Islands, arriving at Luzon in March 1915 to be recommissioned into the Submarine Division 1, Torpedo Flotilla, Asiatic Fleet. She remained in the Philippines throughout the rest of her working life before being decommissioned in 1921. *B2* and *B3* had a similar history to the first-born of the class.

B3, for example, operated along the Atlantic coast with the 1st and 2nd Submarine Flotillas on training and experimental exercises until going into reserve at Charleston Navy Yard on November 6, 1909.

She came back into service when she was recommissioned on April 15, 1910, and served with the Atlantic Torpedo Fleet until assigned to the Reserve Torpedo Group on May 9, 1911, and placed out of commission again in December 1912. Two days later, she was towed to Norfolk and loaded on board *Ajax* for transfer to the Asiatic Station. Arriving at Cavite, Philippine Islands on April 30, 1913, *B3* was launched from *Ajax* on May 12. She remained in the Philippines, where she served with Submarine Division 4, Torpedo Flotilla, Asiatic Fleet until she was decommissioned in July 1921, and subsequently used as a target.

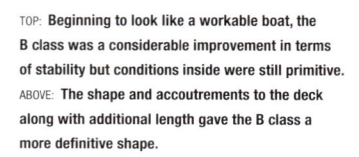

TOP: **Beginning to look like a workable boat, the B class was a considerable improvement in terms of stability but conditions inside were still primitive.**

ABOVE: **The shape and accoutrements to the deck along with additional length gave the B class a more definitive shape.**

LEFT: **For the first decade, US submarines were attached to the Torpedo Fleet, until finally they were accepted as permanent, and the name was changed to Submarine Flotillas.**

B class

Displacement: 142 tonnes/140 tons (surfaced); 170 tonnes/167 tons (submerged)
Length: 25.15m/82ft 6in
Beam: 3.85m/12ft 8in
Armament: 2 x 457mm/18in tube, 4 x torpedoes
Propulsion: 186.4kW/250hp petrol; 44.7kW/60hp electric
Speed: 9.0 knots (surfaced); 8.0 knots (dived)
Complement: 10 men

UNITED STATES

LEFT AND ABOVE: **Although subs had been around for a decade or more, there were still many doubters in the hierarchy of the US Navy, but these boats of the C class, *Octopus* (*C1*)** (LEFT) **and *Tarpon* (*C3*)** (ABOVE) **at last turned a few heads.**

C class

With the entry of *C1*, originally christened *Octopus*, US submarines were beginning to be taken seriously by naval aficionados. Even so, the boats of the equivalent British class were already much larger – almost one third longer and with 447kW/600hp engines, compared with the 373kW/500hp for the US C class. The debate in the United States over the true value of submarines in warfare was probably still weighted towards the doubters, but the new designs were beginning to change minds.

In that regard, *Octopus* had the distinction of introducing what was to become the recognizable stern design of the Electric Boat Company, and was the first boat designed by L.Y. Spear following the departure of J.P. Holland from the company. It was also the first of the US boats that came with an air-operated bell for underwater signalling, which was then fitted to all earlier submarines. By the time *C5* (*Snapper*) was commissioned in 1911, further improvements were under way and this boat was also used for experiments with radio, signalling apparatus, alternative batteries types and a number of other innovations which eventually became standard. With war clouds gathering in Europe, the C class was also used in the first major trials in operations with warships, and later with aircraft with the advent of naval aviation. Lt Chester Nimitz wrote an interesting observation about *C5*:

"*Her Craig gasoline engines were built in Jersey City by James Craig an extraordinarily wise and capable builder. Craig was a self-taught engineer who began as a draftsman in the Machinery Division of the New York Navy Yard and who started his Machine & Engine Works in Jersey City at a later date. C5's engines were excellent as were the Craig diesel engines he built for a subsequent submarine. These engines were designed and built by Craig and I have never forgotten his Foreword to the pamphlet of Operating Instructions which read briefly somewhat like this: 'No matter what the designer and the builder may have planned for these engines and no matter what the operator may try to do with them the Laws of Nature will prevail in the End'. How True!*" Five C class were built.

ABOVE: **C-class submarines in the Gatun Locks, Panama Canal, just prior to World War I. The submarines in the line-up were *C1*, *C2*, *C3*, *C4* and *C5*.**

C class

Displacement: 234.25 tonnes/230.6 tons (surfaced); 270 tonnes/265.7 tons (submerged)
Length: 32.12m/105ft 5in
Beam: 4.25m/14ft
Armament: 1 x 457mm/18in forward tube, 5 x torpedoes
Propulsion: 372.8kW/500hp petrol; 111.9kW/150hp electric
Speed: 10.5 knots (surfaced); 9.0 knots (dived)
Complement: 15 men

355

LEFT: **Getting visibly larger, a starboard-side view of *Grayling (D2)*, circa 1914, thought to be in the harbour of Newport, Rhode Island.**
ABOVE: **The somewhat spartan control panel.**

D class

The experiences among all submariner nations gradually drew the emphasis in design and development towards greater safety for crew members in the event of a catastrophe. In conjunction with US Navy engineers, designers at the Electric Boat Company came up with some ingenious techniques first tried with *D1*, originally launched in 1908. She became the first US boat to be compartmentally divided specifically for survivability. Each compartment was defined by closely positioned bulkheads so that the submarine (surfaced) could survive flooding.

In fact, the layout proved to be difficult in terms of the complicated internal access because of the closeness of the bulkheads. The US Navy ordered a hasty re-design for *D3* that actually reversed the overall safety ideal that had been the original aim. As a result she had only two bulkheads, one at the after end of the torpedo room and one at the fore-end of the engine room. By pushing out the bulkheads, space in the control room was greatly increased, but the resulting compartments were so large that the boat was unlikely to survive if one of them was flooded.

This re-adjustment was considered by some analysts to be the cause of a number of US submarine losses in the 1920s, especially after collisions.

There were other experimental features with *D3* that led to further development, including placing the two periscopes very close to each other, which made it possible to brace both against vibration, a very serious problem with these boats. The object of the forward periscope was to act as a ventilator. The original drawings for *D3* also showed an improved temporary bridge, with a portable canopy frame and external ladder, protected by a trunk. Three D-class submarines were built.

LEFT: ***Grayling*, moored prior to a Presidential Review of the fleet in North River, New York.**

D class

Displacement: 234.23 tonnes/230.5 tons (surfaced); 270 tonnes/265.7 tons (submerged)
Length: 32.10m/105ft 4in
Beam: 4.26m/14ft
Armament: 2 x 457mm/18in tubes, 4 x torpedoes
Propulsion: 186.4kW/250hp petrol; 111.9kW/150hp electric
Speed: 10.5 knots (surfaced); 9 knots (dived)
Complement: 15 men

UNITED STATES

E and F classes

These boats represented a substantial step forward in looks, style and design over their predecessors and were also the carriers of a number of US innovations. *E1* (laid down under the name of *Skipjack*) was commissioned in February 1912 under Lt Chester Nimitz, who also took command of the US Atlantic Submarine Flotilla before coming ashore in 1913 to continue his outstanding career in the big ships. *E1* was used to pioneer a number of major innovations, including the first ballistic gyro compass, invented by Elmer A. Sperry.

E1 was also used to trial submerged radio transmission and other major experiments initially under Nimitz. During his time with the boat, he was awarded a Silver Medal for his heroic action in saving W.J. Walsh, fireman second class, from drowning. A strong tide was running and Walsh was rapidly being swept away from his ship. Nimitz dived into the water and kept Walsh afloat until both were picked up by a small boat.

In December 1917, *E1* left Newport for the Azores to begin patrols against U-boats, and at the end of the war, *E1* resumed her role in experimental work, conducting trials with undersea listening equipment.

The F-class boats were launched around the same time as the E class. The first, *F1*, was commissioned in June 1912 and was assigned to the 1st Submarine Group, Pacific Torpedo Flotilla, operating along the US west coast between San Diego and San Pedro until 1915, when the Flotilla moved to Honolulu for development operations in the Hawaiian Islands. Later, she returned to San Pedro to begin surface and submerged trials in the development of submarine tactics. On December 17, 1917, while manoeuvring in exercises at sea, *F1* and *F3* collided, the former sinking in

TOP AND ABOVE: **Commissioned in 1912, *Skipjack* (*E1*) had the distinction of being fitted with the first Sperry gyro compass in submarines, for which she became a pioneer underwater test ship.**

10 seconds, her port side torn forward of the engine room. Nineteen of her men were lost, while the others were rescued by the submarines with whom they were operating. Two E-class and four F-class submarines were built.

E1

Displacement: 282 tonnes/277.5 tons (surfaced); 336 tonnes/330.7 tons (submerged)
Length: 41.24m/135ft 4in
Beam: 4.5m/14ft 9in
Armament: 4 x 457mm/18in tubes; 4 x torpedoes
Propulsion: 522kW/700hp diesel; 447.4kW/600hp electric
Speed: 13.5 knots (surfaced); 11.5 knots (dived)
Complement: 20 men

F1

Displacement: 324 tonnes/318.9 tons (surfaced); 394 tonnes/387.8 tons (submerged)
Length: 43.50m/142ft 9in
Beam: 4.70m/15ft 5in
Armament: 4 x 457mm/18in tubes, 4 x torpedoes
Propulsion: 581.6kW/780hp diesel; 462.3kW/620hp electric
Speed: 13.5 knots (surfaced); 11.5 knots (dived)
Complement: 22 men

357

LEFT: Simon Lake's *Seal (F1)* saw major advances in submarine technology in many ways, with innovations to improve comfort and safety. ABOVE: The launching of *Turbot (G3)* on December 27, 1913.

G class

G1 has the distinction of being the first submarine designed for the US Navy by Simon Lake, the brilliant engineer from Pleasantville, New Jersey, whose submarine *Argonaut* had lost out to John Holland in the competition to build America's first boat. Rejected by his own country, he was poached by the Russians, then at war with Japan. He went on to build boats for several other nations. The American Navy chiefs thereafter shut him out of the competition for contracts until 1908 when, realizing the error of their ways, they finally approached him to build USS *Seal*, the first boat in G class.

It proved to be one of the most important developments in American naval history. Given virtually a free hand, Lake produced a revolutionary design for *Seal (G1)* in that it was the first-ever even keel submarine to be built by the United States Navy, and it was particularly noted for its sleek lines. However, it was only the beginning. Lake went on to initiate the introduction of many innovations in a long career producing boats for the United States, and his designs would influence submarine development well into the atomic age. It was only a pity that his enormous contribution was not formally recognized until after his death, in 1945.

G1 joined the Atlantic Torpedo Flotilla and made a record dive of 78m/256ft in Long Island Sound. In October 1915, she began a new career as a submarine designated for experimental tests and instructional purposes. The G class thus became established in the important role of school ships for the newly established Submarine Base and Submarine School at New London. This was much needed as the submarine service expanded to meet the demands of World War I.

G1 was also used to test new detector devices for the US Navy Experiment Board, off Provincetown, and played a similar role in the development and use of sound detection. Notably, she spent two four-day periscope and listening patrols against U-boats thought to be operating in the vicinity of Nantucket.

After the war, she resumed her role as a schooling boat for student submariners of the Listener and Hydrophone School, at New London, until January 13, 1920, when *G1* was towed to the Philadelphia Navy Yard. It was decommissioned on March 6, 1920.

She ended her days as a target for depth charge experiments by the Bureau of Ordnance before finally sinking on June 21, 1921 following a bombardment of eight attacks using experimental bombs.

LEFT: A starboard side view of *Turbot (G3)*, looking aft at the Lake Torpedo Boat Company shipyard, Bridgeport, Connecticut, 1915. Four G class were built.

G class

Displacement: 393 tonnes/387.8 tons (surfaced); 507 tonnes/499 tons (submerged)
Length: 49m/160ft 9in
Beam: 3.9m/12ft 10in
Armament: 6 x 457mm/18in tubes, (including two deck firing tubes), 6 x torpedoes
Propulsion: 894.8kW/1,200hp petrol; 387.8kW/520hp electric
Speed: 14 knots (surfaced); 10 knots (dived)
Complement: 24 men

H class

H1, commissioned as *Seawolf*, was attached to the 2nd Torpedo Flotilla, Pacific Fleet, principally used for patrols along the west coast of America, as were other members of the class, operating out of San Pedro. When America entered World War I, the H boats were shifted to the east coast. *H1* completed the journey to New London 22 days later via Acapulco, Balboa, Key West, Charleston and Philadelphia. She remained on the east coast, patrolling Long Island Sound for the duration, often with officer students from the submarine school on board. *H1* and *H2* (originally named *Nautilus*) returned to San Pedro in 1920 via the Panama Canal but on March 12, *H1* ran aground on a sandbank off Santa Margarita Island, California. *H2* stood by and sent rescue and search parties for survivors, helping to save all but four of her sister ship's crew. Those killed included the commanding officer, Lt Commander James R. Webb. A salvage ship dragged her clear only to see her sink in 18.3m/60ft of water.

A similar misfortune hit *H3*. While engaged in patrolling the Californian coast, near Eureka, she ran aground in heavy fog on December 16, 1916. The crew was rescued by Coast Guard breeches buoy, but the cruiser *Milwaukee* was also stranded trying to pull the submarine off the beach, and the Navy was forced to call in a commercial salvage firm. Their job was made all the more difficult because *H3* was marooned on a high sandbank surrounded by quicksand, and at low tide she was 22.9m/75ft from the water, but at high tide the ocean reached almost 76.2m/250ft beyond her. Eventually, after a month of trying, she was pulled on to giant log rollers and taken overland to the sea.

Six other H-class submarines originally built by the Electric Boat Company for the Imperial Russian Government also came into the US inventory under the H4 class title. Their shipment was held up pending the outcome of the Russian Revolution, and the boats were stored in knockdown condition at Vancouver, B.C. All six were eventually purchased by the Navy on May 20, 1918, and assembled at Puget Sound Navy Yard. The first went into service in November 1918, and were engaged in extensive battle and training exercises out of San Pedro, varying this routine with patrols off Santa Catalina Island, but by then, of course, the Armistice had been signed. They were decommissioned in the early 1920s and eventually sold for scrap.

ABOVE: USS *Garfish* (*H3*) in dry dock at the Mare Island Navy Yard, California, in 1915, to repair damage following a recent grounding, evident on the bilge keel.
LEFT: *H2*, the first US submarine to bear the name *Nautilus*.

LEFT: USS *Sea Wolf* (*H1*) was the prototype for a class that attracted considerable orders from overseas, yet only three were built for the US Navy. Most were destined for Britain in the latter stages of World War I.

H class

Displacement: 352 tonnes/346.4 tons (surfaced); 459 tonnes/451.8 tons (submerged)
Length: 45.82m/150ft 4in
Beam: 4.84m/15ft 11in
Armament: 4 x 457mm/18in tubes, 8 x torpedoes
Propulsion: kW/950hp diesel; kW/600hp electric
Speed: 14 knots (surfaced); 10.5 knots (dived)
Complement: 25 men

K class

K1, commissioned as *Haddock*, and her sister ships continued the emerging theme in US submarine design: to increase and improve space, conditions and safety inside the boats without a massively increased overall displacement or length. This class was no exception, increasing the complement to 28 men with the addition of little more than 30 tonnes/29.5 tons surface displacement. The K boats were deployed on both the east and west coasts of America, mostly in almost continual trials in underwater manoeuvres, diving and torpedo-firing practice. The techniques learned from these experiments were soon to prove useful when U-boats began their attacks on Allied shipping bound for Europe.

Five of the K boats were among the first US submarines assigned to duties in World War I and saw service off the Azores, conducting patrol cruises and protecting shipping from surface attack. Some boats were modified for these operations, including the introduction of passive sound gear forward, a permanent chariot bridge and housing periscopes. These vital patrols continued almost to Armistice Day, by which time they returned to North America to resume coastal operations. They were then assigned to naval exercises and trials of new technology that contributed much to the improvements that lay ahead.

The K-class boats were especially engaged in experimental work, notably in the areas of listening devices, storage batteries and torpedoes, and the *Dictionary of American Naval Fighting Ships* states that this work "greatly accelerated" the technology learned from these experiments. The boats were gradually decommissioned in the early 1920s. Eight K-class boats were built.

TOP: **The US Navy dropped the practice of naming their boats in the K class, retaining the class number and boat number, in this case** *K8* **and** *SS39*, **here dry-docked at Honolulu.**

ABOVE: *K5* **underway on a 1919 cruise down the Mississippi River.**

LEFT: *K2* **off Pensacola, Florida, in April, 1916, in a new "zebra" camouflage.**

K class

Displacement: 385 tonnes/378.9 tons (surfaced); 512 tonnes/503.9 tons (submerged)
Length: 46.8m/153ft 6in
Beam: 5.07m/16ft 8in
Armament: 4 x 457mm/18in torpedo tubes, 8 x torpedoes
Propulsion: 708.4kW/950hp diesel; 507.1kW/680hp electric
Speed: 14 knots (surfaced); 10.5 knots (dived)
Complement: 28 men

L class

L1 was christened as *SS40* when the new numbering classification replaced the tradition of naming the boats came into effect with the last three of the K boats. This was to last until names, as well as numbers, were introduced with the Barracuda class in the early 1920s. Again, displacement and length were further extended, and wartime modifications to the class included the installation of a retractable mount for the 76mm/3in gun, and sound gear as well as a permanent sheltered bridge. The retractable gun mount was an idea inspired by a version seen on board a pre-war U-boat.

The L boats were also the first to use independent torpedo tube shutters, which replaced a single-rotating bow cap. A further interesting aspect of the Ls was the difference between those designed and built by the Electric Boat Company and those developed by Simon Lake. The latter's boats were more compartmentalized in terms of the mechanics of the boat than the Electric Boat Company vessels, providing separate engine and motor rooms aft, and concentrating pumps and other auxiliary tools into the large space beneath the control room.

For their war service, L boats crossed the Atlantic after brief service around the Azores and operated from Bantry Bay, Ireland, where they began patrols in support of Allied shipping and hunting U-boats. In July 1918, a large explosion rocked *L2* while patrolling in the Irish Sea. A periscope was sighted and the *L2* submerged and tried to ram the submarine, but the U-boat had superior underwater speed. Later, it was suspected that a U-boat had fired on the *L2*, but another U-boat, the *U65*, was in the way and was badly damaged and sank. Some time later, when the *L2* was dry-docked, her hull plating was noted to be heavily dented from the proximity of the explosion. The *U65* never returned to port.

Meanwhile, in the US, one of the Lake boats, *L8*, was seconded to a top secret mission initiated in 1918 to lure U-boats into a trap. The boat joined forces with the schooner USS *Charles Whittemore*, which was to act as a decoy in the hope of prompting an attack from a pair of enemy submarines menacing the Atlantic coast. The *Whittemore* towed the submerged *L8* to avoid the submarine's detection, while at the same time acting as mother ship, carrying supplies, fuel and torpedoes. In the event, the war ended while the pair was on patrol without firing a shot. Eleven L boats were built and they were decommissioned progressively in the mid-1920s.

ABOVE: **A profile of the L class, the first of which began operations in the US in 1916. It became the largest class of American submarines to date, with 11 being built for service in World War I.**

ABOVE: **Submarine bridges of the day were small to limit underwater drag. *L3* had an enlarged chariot bridge, in contrast to the more streamlined *L9*.**

LEFT: ***L10* arrived in the British Isles in January 1918 with other submarines of the Atlantic Division to take part in operations hampering U-boat activity.**

L class

Displacement: 443 tonnes/436 tons (surfaced); 539 tonnes/530.5 tons (submerged)
Length: 51m/167ft 4in
Beam: 5.3m/17ft 5in
Armament: 4 x 457mm/18in tubes, 8 x torpedoes, 1 x 76mm/3in (23 calibres) deck gun
Propulsion: 671.1kW/900hp diesel; 507.1kW/680hp electric
Speed: 14 knots (surfaced); 10.5 knots (dived)
Complement: 28 men

M class

M1 was something of an experimental boat, and as only one of the class was built, it was generally assumed that there were flaws that prevented further orders. Doubtless there were flaws, but she was rightly in a class of her own. *M1* was the longest boat built to that point in time (1918) and was the Electric Boat Company's first US double-hull submarine. The company had already designed larger double-hull boats for Russia, which were a match for the cruiser-style boats coming out of Germany. In her trials, she was promoted as being the embodiment of all the newest technology in submarine construction and design. Her battery was to have solved some of the past difficulties in submarine battery design and operation.

With a stern described as being honed to a vertical chisel shape, much like contemporary cruiser sterns, she was an impressive sight. Inside, there was decent – if somewhat crowded – accommodation for the crew. Indeed, a Royal Navy observer, Stanley Goodall, later knighted as head of British naval construction, noted that facilities were very presentable, with bunks stacked three high that were light and easily stowed. An additional luxury was that the boat was heated and had an ice tank for food storage.

Even so, *M1* had a short life of barely four years' active service post-war, before being decommissioned and scrapped.

LEFT: *M1* was the Electric Boat Company's first US double-hull submarine, although the company had already designed a larger double-hull boat for Russia. This submarine also had a number of internal innovations, including an efficient heating system and an ice box/refrigerator.

M class

Displacement: 480 tonnes/472.4 tons (surfaced); 665 tonnes/654.5 tons (submerged)
Length: 58.75m/192ft 9in
Beam: 4.49m/14ft 9in
Armament: 4 x 457mm/18in tubes, 8 x torpedoes, 1 x 76mm/3in (23 calibres) deck gun
Propulsion: 626.4kW/840hp diesel; 507.1kW/680hp electric
Speed: 14 knots (surfaced); 10.5 knots (dived)
Complement: 28 men

N class

These boats were at the other end of the spectrum compared to *M1*, being relatively small and intended largely for harbour defence and even inland waterway patrols. *N3* became one of the first submarines to navigate the St Lawrence River and the Great Lakes and visited Halifax, Quebec, Montreal, and Port Dalhousie before arriving at Toledo on June 25, 1921.

At most stopping points, she went on public display and took visitors aboard. Rushed into being towards the end of World War I to meet production targets, none saw any challenging duties in the few remaining months of the conflict.

Thereafter the N-class boats were used extensively as training platforms, given the absence of any serious threats in the intended role. Like the M class, they too had a short life. Seven of the class were built, but virtually all were decommissioned by the mid-1920s.

LEFT: After war service patrolling the New England coast of America, *N2* served as a training ship for the Submarine School and in 1921 became a test platform for experimental Navy weapons, such as a radio controlled torpedo.

N class

Displacement: 342 tonnes/336.6 tons (surfaced); 407 tonnes/400.6 tons (submerged)
Length: 44.85m/147ft 2in
Beam: 4.8m/15ft 9in
Armament: 4 x 457mm/18in tubes, 8 x torpedoes
Propulsion: 357.9kW/480hp diesel; 208.8kW/280hp electric
Speed: 13 knots (surfaced); 11 knots (dived)
Complement: 25 men

O class

After the small harbour protectors came the O-class boats, 500 tonnes/492 tons or more in surface displacement. These were laid down before America's involvement in World War I in sufficient numbers to provide a failsafe position should the worst happen – as, indeed, it did. It was in many ways rather ironic that the O boats began rolling off the production lines, along with the even more advanced R class, providing some satisfaction for the public and the media clamouring for new ships and submarines. In the event, the boats of this class saw little or no war service – at least not in the way they were intended. On November 2, 1918, a number of the Os were included in a 20-boat contingent that set out for European waters to take on the U-boats, but the Armistice was signed before the ships reached the Azores, and they returned to the United States without firing a single torpedo in anger.

It was a remarkable fact that, while many boats were disposed of during the 1920s and early 30s for scrapping – some in connection with the international agreements to limit submarine construction — eight of the O class were mothballed. These were brought back

ABOVE: **The O-class side view.** RIGHT: **After 12 years' service in her duties for the US Navy, *O12* was converted for use on the Sir Hubert Wilkins Arctic Expedition of geophysical investigation, for which she was given the temporary name of *Nautilus*. After being returned to the Navy, she ended up in a Norwegian fjord, where she sank in 1931.**

into service following the Japanese attack on Pearl Harbor in 1941, to become the oldest boats in the US submarine fleet to participate in World War II. Most survived the war, remaining in service throughout, fulfilling operational and training purposes, with two still in business in 1946.

There was one casualty among them, occurring in the months prior to America entering World War II. Recommissioned in April 1941, *O9* left New London with others of her class on June 19 for trials off the Isles of Shoals, 24km/15 miles off Portsmouth, New Hampshire. The following day, after sister ships *O6* and *O10* had successful completed their trials, *O9* hit trouble during deep submergence tests and slipped well below her depth limit of 60.9m/200ft. She was crushed by the pressure of the water and sank. Search operations were launched immediately by the sister ships and one of the newer submarines, *Triton*, along with the submarine rescue vessel, *Falcon*, but they found no trace.

After two days, divers eventually located her in 134m/440ft of water in the same area where *Squalus* had been lost in 1939. The depth meant they could only stay down for a brief time and salvage operations were considered too risky. All further efforts to raise her were cancelled and the crew of 33 was declared lost.

ABOVE: **The starboard diesel engine of the O class, which was upgraded as the building of the O boats progressed to the last of that configuration, *O16*, which had Busch Sulzer Brothers diesels to provide 745.7kW/1,000hp driving a single propeller.**

O class

Displacement: 513 tonnes/504.9 tons (surfaced); 619 tonnes/609.2 tons (submerged)
Length: 52.41m/171ft 11in
Beam: 5.5m/18ft 1in
Armament: 4 x 457mm/18in tubes, 8 x torpedoes, 1 x 76mm/3in (23 calibres) deck gun
Propulsion: 656.2kW/880hp diesel; 551.8kW/740hp electric
Speed: 14 knots (surfaced); 10.5 knots (dived)
Complement: 29 men

R class

The R class had a very similar story to that of the O boats, whose relatively short working life in the 1920s was also reactivated for World War II. This class also came into being as World War I was ending, with no fewer than 27 having been laid down in 1917 for commissioning by the end of 1918. At that time, plans for the much larger new S class were also on the drawing board. By then the emergency was over, and with such a surfeit of submarines available to the United States as the much larger S class also came into being, many of the R boats were laid up by the mid-1920s, and all had been decommissioned by 1931 in the wake of international agreements on undersea warfare.

The R class was built by three different submarine yards to achieve prompt delivery in case the war dragged on, and there were some differences in the final build, in terms of compartments and even overall length and weight. The first years of service for the class leader *R1* and many of her sister boats were spent on patrol, training crews and developing submarine tactics before being laid up. She was brought back to life in 1940 and, after a refit, was transferred to Squadron 7 to hunt U-boats on a patrol line 402km/ 250 miles north-east of Bermuda, a task which continued through World War II. From 1944, she and several sister ships were tasked exclusively with anti-submarine work.

The rest of the R-class boats followed much the same pattern, and suffered only two losses. *R12*, which was recommissioned in October 1940, spent much of her time patrolling the region around the entrance to the Panama Canal, operating primarily from Guantanamo Bay. However, on

ABOVE LEFT AND ABOVE: **Six R boats and two S class boats nestled together off New York City, in May 1920, alongside a submarine tender. All of the R boats have gun platforms, but guns are fitted only on *R10* and *R3*.**

June 12, 1943 while conducting torpedo practice with Brazilian observers on board, the forward battery compartment flooded as she prepared to dive. She sank in less than half a minute taking the 42 officers, crew and visitors with her. None escaped.

The demise of *R1*, on the other hand, was down to a case of mistaken identity. She was among the boats transferred to the Royal Navy under a lend-lease programme in 1942 and reclassified as *P514*. Unfortunately, she was rammed by HMCS *Georgian* on June 21, 1942 in the western Atlantic. The Canadians thought she was a U-boat. She sank in minutes with all hands.

ABOVE: ***R2*, like many of her class of 27 boats, took a long layoff from duty for much of the 1930s, having been decommissioned only to be brought back into service in the period immediately prior to World War II.**

R class

Displacement: 560 tonnes/551.2 tons (surfaced); 669 tonnes/658.4 tons (submerged)
Length: 56.7m/186ft
Beam: 5.5m/18ft 1in
Armament: 4 x 533mm/21in tubes forward, 8 x torpedoes, 1 x 76mm/3in (50 calibres) deck gun
Propulsion: 894.8kW/1,200hhp diesel; 745.7kW/1,000hp electric
Speed: 13.5 knots (surfaced); 10.5 knots (dived)
Complement: 29 men

UNITED STATES

LEFT: *S40* was typical of many of her class in that they were excellent submarines built for work in the 1930s but not quite robust enough for what was to follow in the 1940s. Even so, collectively they had a fine record, *S40* completing nine war patrols, operating out of the East Indies and Australia.
BELOW: An impressive "sharp end" view of *S4* exiting the repair bay.

S class

S boats were built in three types in the 1920s under the same general specifications but with varying designs. However, as an overall mass-production class, it was the largest class ever undertaken by the US Navy, in every respect. Fifty-one boats of this class were built and, becoming America's most successful submarine to date, they were operational in each of the following three decades. The first, *S1* – known as the Holland type — saw the culmination of the Electric Boat Company's single-hull design for the US Navy. *S2* was known as the Lake-type and *S3* as the Government-type. All three versions undertook experimental duties of varying kinds in the decade of their manufacture, which greatly contributed to future US submarine developments. One of particular note fell to *S1* in that she became the experimental platform for the US Navy's first submarine aircraft carrier. This would also be tried by other countries, notably Britain, Italy and Japan, but only the latter continued the experiments into wartime operational use of any magnitude.

S1 was given a cylindrical capsule mounted to the rear of the conning tower to house a collapsible Martin MS-1 seaplane, first built of wood and fabric and later in two metal types. On the surface, the aircraft would be rolled out, assembled and launched from the deck by partially submerging the submarine. The first trials that took the operations through all phases, from loading the disassembled aircraft into its pod through to reconstruction at sea, launching and eventual retrieval were conducted in July 1926 on the Thames River at New London.

S1 then went on to become a divisional flagship operating in the Panama Canal Zone and later took up duties based at Pearl Harbor and in other home ports. By then, a fairly active peacetime training cycle had been established across the board so all boats took up rotational postings around all areas of operation. These preparations did not stop the Japanese attack on the Pearl Harbor base, but did however prepare the S boats for a staunch and versatile involvement in World War II, from defensive and offensive positions.

Six of the S boats became casualties: *S5* sank after an accidental intake of water soon after being commissioned, but miraculously all aboard escaped through a hole cut in the hull. *S26* sank after a collision in the Gulf of Panama in December 1941, with the loss of 46 men; three survived. On September 25, 1925, *S51* was rammed and sunk off Block Island, New York, by a merchant steamer, with only three survivors. *S28* was lost at sea with all hands in July 1944. *S39* became a victim of accidental grounding in 1942 after heroic action against the Japanese, but the entire crew was evacuated to safety. *S44* was the victim of heavy enemy bombardment while stranded through mechanical problems on the surface in October 1943. Only two of the crew survived. They spent the rest of the war in a Japanese slave labour camp.

LEFT: The S-class profile, which remained virtually the same for all of its 51 boats.

S class

Displacement: 840 tonnes/826.7 tons (surfaced); 1,045 tonnes/1,028.5 tons (submerged)
Length: 66.75m/219ft
Beam: 6.35m/20ft 10in
Armament: 4 x 533mm/21in tubes, 12 x torpedoes, 1 x 102mm/4in (50 calibres) deck gun
Propulsion: 1,342.2kW/1,800hp diesel; 1,118.6kW/1500hp electric
Speed: 14.5 knots (surfaced); 11 knots (dived)
Complement: 38 men

LEFT: **By now, the US Navy had reverted to names rather than numbers, and** Skipjack **came in the Salmon class, a strong class that showed influences from the recent trials with larger submarines such as the V boats** Barracuda, Argonaut **and** Narwhal. ABOVE: **The** Skipjack **badge.**

Salmon class

In the 1930s, the classification of new submarines in the US Navy reverted to the name of the lead boat, in this case *Salmon*, commissioned in 1938. This class was one of the new generation of huge submarines that had begun rolling out of the US shipyards in the wake of experimental fleet and cruiser submarines of the late 1920s, such as *Argonaut*, *Narwhal* and *Nautilus*, originally commissioned under the V classification. Indeed, from the mid-1930s and beyond, a massive production schedule was imposed upon the shipbuilders as the US government embarked upon a programme of submarine construction matched at that time only by the Japanese. *Salmon*, laid down in April 1936 by the Electric Boat Company at Groton, Connecticut, was commissioned 23 months later, and was joined over the coming months by five others in her class, names which became famous in the annals of US submarine history – *Seal*, *Skipjack*, *Snapper*, *Stingray* and *Sturgeon*.

After coastal trials from Nova Scotia to the West Indies, *Salmon* became flagship of Submarine Division 15, Squadron 6 of the Submarine Force, US Fleet, at Portsmouth, operating along the Atlantic coast for a year. She then transferred to the west coast to bolster the submarine presence prior to transferring to the Asiatic station in Manila, along with submarine tender *Holland* and three other boats, to strengthen defences around the Philippines in response to growing tension with Japan. *Salmon* had been leading defensive patrols from Manila when the Japanese attacked Pearl Harbor on December 7, 1941, and, like US submarines everywhere, was placed on an immediate offensive alert and a few days later fired her first shots in anger, sending a spread of torpedoes against Japanese destroyers to scatter their attack.

As the opposition became fierce in the region, the submarine base was moved out of Manila to Exmouth Gulf, Australia, from where sorties into the Java Sea were launched. In March, *Salmon* moved to the US submarine base at Fremantle, Australia, from where patrols were being organized and established along the south coast of Java to intercept Japanese shipping. On May 3, she torpedoed and sank the 11,625-tonne/11,441-ton repair ship *Asahi*, and on the 28th, sank the 4,452-tonne/4,382-ton passenger-cargo vessel, *Ganges Maru*. These operations were merely the beginning of a busy wartime career operating from both Australia and Peal Harbour, for which she was awarded nine battle stars for Asiatic and Pacific operations.

ABOVE: **A bow view of USS** Snapper **in dry dock in 1939. It was a fortuitous refit for what lay ahead, which in this boat's case amounted to 11 busy war patrols, for which she was awarded six battle stars.**

Salmon class

Displacement: 1,426 tonnes/1,403.5 tons (surfaced); 2,163 tonnes/2,128.8 tons (submerged)
Length: 93.8m/307ft 9in
Beam: 7.9m/25ft 11in
Armament: 8 x 533mm/21in tubes, 24 x torpedoes, 1 x 76mm/3in (50 calibres) deck gun, 2 x 12.7mm/0.50 calibre machine-guns, 2 x 7.62mm/0.30 calibre machine-guns.
Propulsion: 4,101.3kW/5,500hp diesel; 4 x electric motors developing 2,460.8kW/3,300hp
Speed: 21 knots (surfaced); 9 knots (dived)
Complement: 55 men

UNITED STATES

LEFT: The launch of *Spearfish*, third of the ten-boat Sargo class, all of which were in for a busy war. Apart from aggressive patrolling, *Spearfish* was also engaged on dangerous reconnaissance work, winning ten battle stars. ABOVE: Sister ship *Swordfish*, launched in 1939. BELOW: The war is over in this photograph, which includes class leader *Sargo* with *Spearfish* and *Saury*. The mothballing process is underway with the preservative cocoons around the deck guns that would never again be fired in anger.

Sargo class

Ten boats from this class were commissioned progressively from February 1939 to become the first of the principal classes in the US Navy's submarine fleet amassed before and during World War II – a force which amounted to more than 400 boats in addition to another 100 from the classes listed previously. *Sargo* went straight to business with a war patrol off French Indochina and to the Dutch East Indies, delivering eight separate attacks on enemy shipping. However, her Mark 14 torpedoes malfunctioned, and her targets escaped. Later that year (1942), she temporarily took on the role of transport, offloading her remaining torpedoes and 76mm/3in ammunition to stow a million rounds of 7.62mm/0.30 calibre ammunition desperately needed by Allied forces in the Philippines, and thereafter took up station at Fremantle.

The welcome she received was somewhat unfortunate. As the first Sargo class in the region, she was mistaken for a Japanese vessel and attacked by an Allied aircraft. Fortunately, the damage was not excessive and she went on to participate fully in the war effort with ten patrols, receiving the Philippine Presidential Unit Citation for her work in that area.

However, another blue-on-blue incident had a devastating effect on another in the Sargo class. *Sculpin* was scheduled to lead a co-ordinated group attack on enemy shipping located near the Eniwetok islands in the Pacific. During the raid, *Sculpin*, already at her depth limit, was blasted by 18 depth charges and with her pressure hull distorted, the boat leaking and diving plane gear damaged, Captain Fred Cromwell had no option but to surface. As her executive officers came on to the bridge, they were killed by shellfire, some of which went through the main induction. Cromwell could do nothing more, and ordered his submarine to be scuttled and all hands to abandon ship.

About 12 men "rode the ship down" according to an account in the *Dictionary of American Naval Fighting Ships*. Captain Fred Cromwell stayed aboard, determined to go down with his submarine, because he alone possessed secret intelligence of US Fleet movements and specific attack plans. He feared that he would be forced to reveal this information under Japanese torture or use of drugs, an action for which he was posthumously awarded the Congressional Medal of Honour.

In all, 42 men were taken prisoner by the Japanese destroyer. The group was split up, 21 in the carrier *Chuyo* and 20 in another ship, bound for captivity. Now, an ironic twist of fate took hold: en route to Japan, *Chuyo* was torpedoed and sunk by another Sargo-class boat, *Sailfish*, on December 31, 1943.

Sargo class

Displacement: 1,427 tonnes/1,1404.5 tons (surfaced); 2,312 tonnes/2,275.5 tons (submerged)
Length: 94.5m/310ft
Beam: 8.25m/27ft
Armament: 8 x 533mm/21in tubes, 24 x torpedoes, 1 x 76mm/3in (50 calibres) deck gun, 2 x 12.7mm/0.50 calibre machine-guns, 2 x 7.72mm/0.30 calibre machine-guns
Propulsion: 4,101.3kW/5,500hp diesel; 2,043.2kW/2,740hp electric
Speed: 20 knots (surfaced); 7.75 knots (dived)
Complement: 55 men

367

Gato class

Gato had a baptism of fire as one of the boats commissioned in December 1941 soon after the Japanese attack on Pearl Harbor. She was the first of 74 boats in this class, one of three main types that became the workhorses of the American effort in World War II. Developed towards the end of the 1930s, and employing the round-the-clock capacity of every major submarine builder in the United States, the new submarines were coming off the production lines at an incredible rate, a state of affairs that was to continue well into 1943.

Given that the surface fleet was being similarly enhanced, this represented an outstanding effort by the shipbuilders, who were producing brilliant boats that incorporated numerous technological advances covering every aspect of submarine activity. These boats bristled with new and heavy deck armoury and carried a substantial stock of torpedoes to match their increasing endurance. The 1,500-tonne/1,476-ton (surfaced) Gato class could stay out on patrol for 74 days, and cruise 17,703km/11,000 miles surfaced at 10 knots, although the boats were capable of a top speed of 20 knots.

It was also a great credit to their designers, engineers and shipwrights that, unlike the many submarines produced up to that point in time, whose life expectancy was often quite limited, the Gato class led the way to longevity. Along with the other newer classes that followed, many boats were

ABOVE: **Larger still, in class and size, *Raton* is photographed here in post-war mode as a Radar Picket submarine, with a slightly different configuration, circa 1953–60.** LEFT: **The famous *Wahoo*, one of the US Submarine Force's most successful boats, whose exploits under Commander "Mush" Morton were legendary. During just six patrols she sank 27 ships, totalling 121,011 tonnes/ 119,100 tons, and damaged two more, making 25,300 tonnes/ 24,900 tons before her own luck ran out on October 11, 1943, when she was lost with all 79 hands.**

still in service in the 1970s, some of which were converted into the post-war classification of hunter-killers in the Guppy configuration.

Despite their increasing size, the versatility of submarines was also being extended to the full, especially in the areas of intelligence-gathering and combined operations with special forces. *Gato* herself, for example, did some fine work landing Australian commandos in Japanese-held territory while at the same time transporting evacuees to safety. In fact, the submarine survived 13 war patrols, her last a particularly dangerous mission, rescuing downed Army aviators after waves of air strikes off the eastern coast of Honshu. It was there that she received the signal "Cease Fire" on August 15, 1945, and then steamed into Tokyo Bay. She remained there for the signing of surrender documents on board USS *Missouri* on September 2, before setting off for home to receive the Presidential Unit Citation in recognition of daring exploits, and 13 battle stars for service in World War II.

In all, the *Gato*-class boats won more than 700 battle stars, although the cost was high, with the loss of 19 boats and more than 1,100 men to wartime action. The casualties included a particular, but not especially uncommon, misfortune that befell the last of the class, *Tullibee*, which occurred in 1943 while the boat was patrolling off the Philippines. She had fired a volley of torpedoes towards an enemy passenger ship and two destroyers, at least two of which were hit. Minutes later an explosion rocked the submarine and Gunner's Mate C.W. Kukyendall – on the bridge at the time – was knocked unconscious and thrown into the water. When he regained consciousness, the submarine was gone. One of her own torpedoes had apparently turned full circle and hit her. Kukyendall was the only survivor.

LEFT: **The patches for class leader USS *Dace* and USS *Gato*. Both boats survived the war with commendations for meritorious service.**

BELOW: **USS *Barb* had a busy after-life following her war service, first undergoing a Guppy conversion and later on being loaned to Italy in 1955, where she served under the name of *Enrico Tazzoli* until 1975.** BOTTOM: **A slightly cramped-looking control room in USS *Cero*, one of a large number of boats laid up in reserve after the war.**

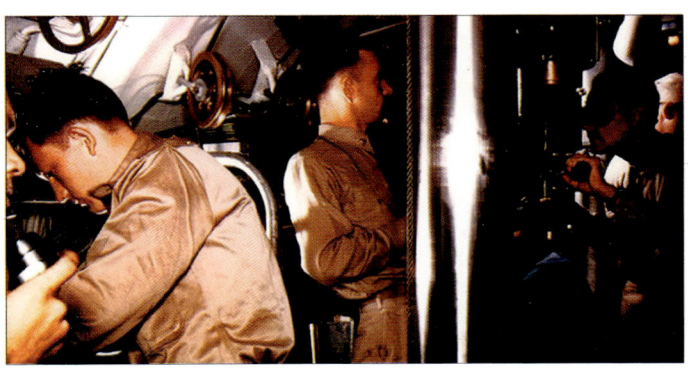

Gato class

Displacement: 1,501 tonnes/1,477.3 tons (surfaced); 2,386 tonnes/2,348.3 tons (submerged)
Length: 95m/311ft 8in
Beam: 8.3m/27ft 3in
Armament: 10 x 533mm/21in tubes, 6 x forward, 4 x aft, 24 x torpedoes, 1 x 76mm/3in (50 calibres) deck gun, 2 x 12.7mm/0.50 calibre machine-guns, 2 x 7.63mm/0.30 calibre machine-guns
Propulsion: 4,026.8kW/5,400hp diesel; 2,043.2kW/2,740hp electric
Speed: 20.25 knots (surfaced); 8.75 knots (dived)
Complement: 60 men

LEFT: More big boats and a big history in the Balao class, this one being *Pampanito*, noted for her role in the American submarine service's own wolf-pack operations in the South China Sea, although she had to temporarily retire for repairs after a severe depth charge attack.

Balao class

This was the largest class of submarines ever produced by the US Navy, in terms of numbers, with a total of 131 earmarked for production during World War II. Ten were subsequently cancelled towards the end of the production cycle, by which time the war's end was in sight. From first to last in production – *Balao* to *Tiru* – was a three-year span from the point in April 1942 when the class leader was laid down, to 1947 when the last was commissioned. *Balao*'s own war operations spanned a period from July 1943 until the end of August 1945. During this period, she completed ten war patrols and ended her war effort with a fine record, having sunk seven Japanese ships totalling 32,623 tonnes/32,108 tons, in addition to sinking 11,177 tonnes/11,000 tons of miscellaneous enemy small craft by gunfire.

As a whole, the Balao class, with the largest number of submarines afloat during the final 18 months of the war, undertook many successful patrols in all regions of the conflict. However, the cost was high. Nine boats and almost 600 men were lost to enemy action. Throughout the submarine stories, there were many examples of heroism and survival that provided dramatic true-life scenarios for numerous movies. One such event was recognized in 2004 with the erection of a plaque at the Damage Control Training Centre at Pearl Harbor, a story from November 1943 aboard *Balao*-class *Billfish* that led to extensive research in damage limitation. The submarine became riddled with leaks after being inundated with depth charges during an attack by the Japanese that incapacitated the boat's commander and senior officers.

As the attack continued, Lt Charles Rush, then 23, took charge and risked diving the boat to 51.8m/170ft below test depth for 12 hours. Meanwhile Chief Electrician's Mate John D. Rendernick gathered a team for emergency repairs to reduce the heavy flooding through the stern tubes by pumping grease into the worst leaking tube. He then used six men and a hydraulic jack to reposition the port main motor, which had been knocked off its foundation. When the increasing heat reached the limit of the crew's tolerance, Rendernick told them to wrap wet towels around their heads. These actions and Rush's coolheaded command in the face of continuing explosions around the boat, saved it from destruction – and the lives of the entire crew. Crucially, he also turned his boat to regain a previous position to sit under an oil slick, thus fooling the Japanese destroyers above into thinking the boat had been destroyed.

After the war, many of the surviving Balao class underwent substantial remodelling, both internally and in the superstructure to keep them operational for years to come. *Balao* was among a number of boats sold to Turkey under a Security Assistance Program in 1970, and under the new name of *Burak Reis*, she remained on the Turkish naval register until 1996.

LEFT: USS *Blackfin*, one of nine Balao submarines converted to the Guppy 1A configuration between 1947 and 1951. This was a less drastic remodelling than the costly Guppy II programme, an interim measure in the developing Cold War providing boats with streamlined sail and superstructure, new masts, snorkel and equipment, and greater underwater propulsion.

Balao class

Displacement: 1,501 tonnes/1,477.3 tons (surfaced); 2,375 tonnes/2,337.5 tons (submerged)
Length: 95m/311ft 8in
Beam: 8.32m/27ft 4in
Armament: 10 x 533mm/21in tubes, 6 x forward, 4 x aft, 24 x torpedoes, 1 x 102mm/4in (50 calibres) deck gun, 1 x 40mm/1.57in gun, 2 x 12.7mm/0.50 calibre machine-guns
Propulsion: 4,026.8kW/5,400hp diesel; 2,043.2kW/2,740hp electric
Speed: 20.25 knots (surfaced); 8.75 knots (dived)
Complement: 66 men

UNITED STATES

LEFT: **USS *Pickerel*,** one of the Tench class which arrived too late for war service, was among 24 boats selected for the Guppy II conversion and later went into Guppy III mode. ABOVE: This is what *Pickerel* could do after that: surfacing at a 48-degree up angle, from a depth of 45.7m/150ft during tests off the coast of Hawaii, March 1, 1952.

Tench class

The Tench boats came late to World War II, the first of the class not being laid down until July 1944, but she was speedily built and commissioned on October 6. Even though the build time was very swift indeed, only 31 of a planned 128 boats in this class were commissioned before the end of the war came into view and the remainder were cancelled. Those that did participate came at time when the Japanese were in desperate straits, and had long ago given up any semblance of adherence to the international agreements on the rights and safety of prisoners of war. Consequently, many of the US boats, and indeed surface vessels, were almost daily engaged in the recovery of downed air crews, attempting to snatch them to safety before they could be picked up by enemy ships and submarines.

Allied submarine tactics were by then also well developed, tried and practised, helped by the inclusion of the latest technological aids, particularly in the fields of communication and surveillance. Another development that had successfully been employed by the US submarine command for many months was the utilization of the wolf-pack system of submarine deployment, used to great effect by the Germans. Thus, when *Tench* became the first of her class into battle, she did so in the company of *Balao*, *Sea Devil* and *Grouper* in what were by then described as "co-ordinated attack groups".

The patrol area to which they were assigned encompassed a region of the East China Sea south-west of Kyushu and extended north into the Yellow Sea. Their tasks ranged through rotational patrols, weather reporting, photographic reconnaissance and lifeguard duties. The latter could be extremely hazardous for a submarine, often requiring these massive boats to be manoeuvred close to the shoreline and in the shallows. If trouble came in overhead, there was no place to dive, as *Tench* discovered during her lifeguard stint in support of the 5th Fleet air raids on Nagasaki. Dyes were used to mark the position of downed pilots, and spotter planes kept up a round-the-clock watch. When pilots were spotted, rescue submarines moved in with F6F Hellcat fighters providing cover overhead. On this occasion, the dye was no more than a reflection, and while *Tench* was searching, a flight of bombers appeared out of the sun, but due to the water depth the submarine could not dive. She was a sitting duck. However, the aircraft were friendly and *Tench* escaped unharmed. Further war patrols kept the submarine busy right up to the last, but that was by no means the end of *Tench*'s journey.

In 1950, she and others in her class were converted to Guppy 1A submarines, which involved considerable modifications in almost every department. Thus equipped, she was recommissioned and remained in service until the early 1970s, along with others who had undergone the same modifications.

LEFT: **USS *Argonaut*,** also of the wartime Tench class, was reassigned to Submarine Squadron 6 at Norfolk, Virginia. In 1947 she received some of the Guppy modernizations to become one of the first guided missile submarines armed with the new Regulus I missile.

Tench class

Displacement: 1,545 tonnes/1,520.6 tons (surfaced); 2,378 tonnes/2,340.4 tons (submerged)
Length: 95.02m/311ft 9in
Beam: 8.25m/27ft 1in
Armament: 10 x 533mm/21in tubes, 6 x forward, 4 x aft; 24 x torpedoes, 1 x 127mm/5in (25 calibres) deck gun, 1 x 40mm/1.57in gun, 1 x 20mm/0.79in gun, 2 x 12.7mm/0.50 calibre machine-guns
Propulsion: 4,026.8kW/5,400hp diesel; 2,043.2kW/2,740hp electric
Speed: 20.25 knots (surfaced); 8.75 knots (dived)
Complement: 66 men

371

Holland

Britain's very first submarine, the *Holland* launched in 1901, can still be seen. She forms part of the collection at the Royal Navy Submarine Museum in Gosport, Hampshire. Bought for £35,000 and constructed under conditions of great secrecy, she was originally known as HM *Submarine Torpedo Boat No. 1*. Initially, Royal Navy engineers and shipbuilders Vickers had great difficult with the drawings, which had many discrepancies, and the British eventually went their own way and severed contact with Holland and the Electric Boat Company of America.

Unlike today's boats with their conning towers and periscopes, *Holland* looked more like a short fat cigar tube with a hatch or scuttle for the captain's head and shoulders, although an experimental periscope was designed and fitted to a later Holland. Built for the Royal Navy under licence, she was a copy of the US Navy's A-class boats.

Steering was by two vertically mounted rudders above and below the single screw and by a horizontal pair of rudders for when the boat was submerged. This design gave anti-submarine sceptics plenty of ammunition, and the boats were certainly no place for anyone with even a hint of claustrophobia. There were no interior bulkheads, very little ventilation and no real accommodation for sitting or sleeping. The fumes were appalling – a combined stench from the petrol engine and the buckets used for ablutions that could only be emptied when they surfaced.

Notoriously unstable, it took almost a year of trials and modifications to settle it down. When surfaced, the boats were difficult to control, and the captain and coxswain had great difficulty hanging on to masts and wheels while on deck, with water washing around their feet. Submerged, the boat seemed to have a constant "nose-down" attitude, which made it appear to be constantly diving. This unnerved the sailors at first, but underwater control and manoeuvrability were described as good.

ABOVE LEFT: **The Royal Navy customized the *Holland* designs they bought from the American Electric Boat Company; consequently, the British and US versions differed somewhat.** ABOVE: **Length and width remained the same, however, and room on top was still scarce.**

Exhaustive trials of *No. 1* lasted three years with the result that *No. 2* became the first submarine to be commissioned into the Royal Navy on August 1, 1903, quickly followed by four more entering service by the end of that year. Despite the experimental environment and their fragility, they saw a decade of service, and many a complacent warship captain was shocked to hear the clang of a practice torpedo hitting his ship's sides. Although only equipped with a single 356mm/14in tube, they were armed with either three long or five short torpedoes. *Holland 1* sank while taking part in manoeuvres off the Nab Lightship in March 1904. All her crew were rescued.

LEFT: **A pair of *Holland* boats undergoing a clean, probably prior to their display to the public, who were interested in the curious new craft.**

Holland 🇬🇧

Displacement: 114.8 tonnes/113 tons (surfaced); 124 tonnes/122 tons (submerged)
Length: 19.5m/64ft
Beam: 3.58m/11ft 9in
Armament: 1 x 533mm/21in tube (bow); 3 x long or 5 x short torpedoes
Propulsion: 119.3kW/160hp petrol; 55.9kW/75hp electric
Speed: 7.5 knots (surfaced); 5 knots (dived)
Complement: 8 men

UNITED KINGDOM

LEFT: *A4* was one of several boats of this class that came to an unhappy end when the wash from a passing ship sank her, fortunately without loss of life. BELOW: *A13* was the survivor of the class, though not with the longevity of HMS *Victory* in the background.

A class

Developed from the Holland class, the A-class submarines were 50 per cent longer, but still put to sea with the primitive technology of their predecessors. *A1* was originally intended to be the sixth Holland class. However, with a raft of design improvements on the drawing board it was decided this boat would include the majority of them in an enlarged hull, which was increased by 12.2m/40ft. It was then decided to increase the number of torpedo tubes to two from *A2* onwards and this resulted in a further increase in size by almost 0.6m/2ft and was to become the standard for the rest of the class.

However, the improved design and engine power brought little improvement in terms of performance, with the engine speed changing little from the original Hollands. On the surface, speed was slightly quicker, but submerged things were virtually unchanged. *A5* was the first Group 2 boat and was fitted with a 410kW/550bhp 16-cylinder engine, replacing the 12-cylinder unit, but again this was a disappointment.

Speed increased by only half a knot and the engine was much less reliable. On the surface, this class was still powered by petrol engines, and the dangers soon became apparent. In February 1905, five crewmen on *A5* were killed in an explosion caused by a build-up of petrol fumes after refuelling. *A13* was fitted with an experimental heavy-oil-powered MAN engine built under licence by Vickers – what we call a diesel engine today. Although it used a much safer fuel, it was a much heavier engine, and consequently the boat had to carry a reduced amount of fuel.

It was not until the introduction of the D class that the improved diesel engines replaced the dangerous petrol-powered machinery. However, there were several changes that did work and improve safety – the conning tower being one.

It featured two hatches, one leading on to the bridge and a lower one sealing the conning tower from the control room. This prevented water entering the boat from larger waves and enabled it to put to sea in rougher weather. As well as giving better protection to the captain and coxswain when sailing on the surface, it also gave them a better view. *A11* featured an even larger conning tower, and although the lengthened hull gave a better passage than the Hollands while surfaced, overall it was still poor.

As experience was gained it was also found that – using care – the boats could be dived while under way, but with only rudders at the rear, control was difficult. *A7* was therefore fitted with a pair of hydroplanes on her conning tower.

RIGHT: *A2* was the first boat to be upgraded and slightly elongated to take an additional torpedo tube, and the two tubes fitted side by side.

A class

Displacement: 189 tonnes/186 tons (surfaced); 208 tonnes/204.7 tons (submerged)
Length: 32.1m/105ft 4in
Beam: 3.9m/12ft 10in
Armament: 2 x 432mm/17in tubes (bow); 3 x torpedoes
Propulsion: 447.4kW/600hp petrol; 111.9kW/150hp electric
Speed: 11.5 knots (surfaced); 6 knots (dived)
Complement: 11 men

373

B class

The B-class boats were the first Royal Navy submarines to have a casing that gave extra protection to the hull and improved buoyancy on the surface. Additionally, they were also the first British submarines to be fitted with a second pair of hydroplanes near the bow in addition to those astern, enabling them to dive more easily when under way. Although surface speed was better than the A class, submerged it remained similar. With the B class came a giant leap forward for the Royal Navy, with the boats ranging further and further from home waters. To patrol in the Mediterranean, they would be towed there by surface ships before deploying. In spite of these long deployments, soon to be in a war environment, there were still no dividing bulkheads, accommodation space or improved ventilation.

Still rather limited in endurance and meant for defensive purposes, the two 432mm/17in torpedo tubes in this class were angled downwards in the belief that torpedoes would be discharged while the submarine rose to the surface. Two reload torpedoes were carried.

Just before Christmas 1914, it was a B-class boat in which Lt Norman Douglas Holbrook became the first submarine commander to be awarded the Victoria Cross, for a daring operation that resulted in the sinking of a Turkish battleship. Holbrook dived *B11* under five rows of mines and attacked the *Messudieh*, returning the same way, and braved attacks by gunfire and torpedo boats. The boat had been submerged for nine hours. As well as Holbrook's VC, all the crew were decorated for gallantry, each man receiving either a DSO or DSM.

One B-class boat was lost with all hands when run down by a surface ship off Dover, and another was sunk by Austrian aircraft. Other boats became inoperable because of a lack of spares and were modified and used as patrol boats instead of submarines, with their conning towers removed and replaced by wheelhouses.

They were also armed with a 12pdr gun. Eleven of these craft were built, and when the war ended only *B3* was operational, largely because she had mainly been used for trials and training.

ABOVE: *B4* was among the first boats to be taken out of coastal waters and towed to the Mediterranean, opening up vast possibilities for the future.

ABOVE: *B5* demonstrates the relatively unpractised and therefore often hazardous task of taking on torpedoes at sea, which was necessary during operational manoeuvres, especially when far from home. Given that the class carried only two reloads for the two bow tubes, it was a regular occurrence during wartime.

B class

Displacement: 291.59 tonnes/287 tons (surfaced); 321.06 tonnes/316 tons (submerged)
Length: 43.34m/142ft 2in
Beam: 3.88m/12ft 9in
Armament: 2 x 432mm/17in tubes (bow); 4 x torpedoes
Propulsion: 447.4kW/600hp Vickers petrol engine; 149.1kW/200ehp electric
Speed: 12 knots (surfaced); 6.5 knots (dived)
Complement: 15 men

UNITED KINGDOM

LEFT: **On July 6, 1918, a squadron of German seaplanes returning from a daylight raid on Lowestoft caught Harwich-based *C25* on the surface and used her for target practice. Her captain and six crew were killed outright, but the remaining crew, some badly wounded, managed to close up and dive the boat, and eventually reached the safety of their home base.** BELOW: **An interior view of the C class.**

C class

Thirty eight C-class boats were built in total, all but six of these by Vickers and for the first time HM Dockyard at Chatham provided submarines for the Royal Navy by building this last half dozen. They also represented the last of the Holland design, and the last to be powered wholly by petrol engines. Given their limited endurance, the C-class boats made a remarkable contribution to the defence of the UK during World War I. All played a gallant and extremely dangerous role, operating mainly in the coastal regions in the North Sea, with many gallantry decorations won by the crews, although losses were also heavy. Safety was also being taken into account, with four of the boats equipped with airlocks and helmets, which were intended to give crew time to breathe extra air before trying to escape through the torpedo hatch.

As the submarine war became more intense, casualties among submariners began to mount and the C boats were to become involved in a daring plan to hit marauding U-boats, which were finding British North Sea trawlers easy pickings. Decoy trawlers would sail into the fishing fleets towing a submerged C boat until a U-boat had been lured into the trap, at which point the submarine was released. *C27* was involved in one such operation, being towed by the decoy trawler *Princess Louise* off Aberdeen, there to attack and sink *U23*. Another successful pairing was that of *C24* and the trawler *Taranaki* to sink *U40*. But then disaster struck. *C33* vanished, presumed victim of a mine while operating with the trawler *Malta*, and *C29* was lost after her towing trawler *Ariadne* strayed into a minefield in the Humber estuary.

Elsewhere, *C7* successfully attacked and sank *U63* and *U68* in 1917, and *C15* disposed of *U65* in what had developed into the dramatic cut and thrust submarine warfare in the North Sea and English Channel. Other British losses included *C31* and *C34*. Four C-class boats were also deployed to the Baltic Flotilla, tasked with attacking German shipping. In 1917, *C26*, *C27*, *C32* and *C35* were loaded on to barges at Archangel and transported to the Baltic using the Siberian Railway. C boats were also included in the taskforce used to block the U-boat base at Bruges, trapping many of the U-boats inside. Two old boats – *C1* and *C3* – were provided for the mission, with the bow of *C3* being filled with explosives and used to block the entrance channel at Zeebrugge.

LEFT: **A typical view of the C-class boats, this one being *C22*, which had an active but uneventful life compared with some of her 37 sister boats. She was among the 24 in the class scrapped at the turn of the 1920s.**

C class

Displacement: 291.59 tonnes/287 tons (surfaced); 321.06 tonnes/316 tons (submerged)
Length: 43.28 m/142ft
Beam: 4.11m/13ft 6in
Armament: 2 x 457mm/18in tubes (bow); 4 x torpedoes
Propulsion: 447.4kW/600hp petrol; 223.7kW/300ehp electric
Speed: 12 knots (surfaced); 8 knots (dived)
Complement: 16 men

D class

This class saw the arrival of the first diesel-powered submarines of the Royal Navy and the first for which the Admiralty produced the basic design. Twin screws and saddle tanks were introduced along with an enhanced conning tower providing better visibility, and, from *D4* onwards, they were also the first boats equipped with a gun – albeit a paltry 12pdr.

Intended as an effective patrol submarine with overseas potential, the eight D-class boats were meant to undertake patrols in excess of 3,200km/1,988 miles. With better visibility came better manoeuvrability, and the placement of the main water ballast tanks outside the hull in a saddle tank configuration increased space internally. *D4* had its gun in a housing that could be retracted into the conning tower, and it was also fitted with a stern-firing torpedo and a new wireless system that enabled the crew to transmit as well as receive. Mounting the bow torpedo tubes vertically also led to a more streamlined shape. Six of the boats were built by Vickers at Barrow, and the other two at Chatham Dockyard.

At the outbreak of World War I the D boats were stationed along the east coast of Britain, and their role was to support the Grand Fleet and to destroy German warships. *D5* became the first one to fire a torpedo in anger, but the setting used was that for peacetime training and it ran too deep and missed the target. In November 1914 *D3*, *D5* and *E10* were sent to intercept German cruisers bombarding the Norfolk coast, but *D5* was lost after striking a mine.

Shortly afterwards, *D2* was also lost after being hit by a German warship. In 1918, *D3* was sunk accidentally in the English Channel after being bombed by a French airship. *D6* was sunk by a German U-boat off Ireland in 1918, leaving *D7* as the only boat of the class to conduct a successful attack, sinking a U-boat off the north of Ireland in September 1917. Only three boats – *D4*, *D7* and *D8* – survived the war, and they were used for training purposes before being paid off.

ABOVE: **A photograph that puts things into perspective – a D-class boat a few hundred feet from a British battleship. It is easy to see why, in those pioneering days, a submarine could be sunk by the wash of a ship.**

ABOVE: **Launched in May 1910, *D2* became an early victim of World War I when, on November 25, 1914, she was hit and sunk by gunfire from a German patrol vessel in the Ems estuary, The Netherlands.** LEFT: **A profile of the D class.**

D class

Displacement: 490.73 tonnes/483 tons (surfaced); 604.52 tonnes/595 tons (submerged)
Length: 50.16m/164ft 7in
Beam: 6.22m/20ft 5in
Armament: 3 x 457mm/18in tubes, (2 x bow, 1 x stern); 6 x torpedoes
Propulsion: 2 x 447.4kW/600bhp Vickers diesel engines; 206.6kW/277ehp electric motors
Speed: 14 knots (surfaced); 9 knots (dived)
Complement: 25 men

UNITED KINGDOM

LEFT: *E6*, whose class of 56 submarines had a heroic war, ran out of luck on December 26, 1915, while leaving port for her patrol duty. Nearing a sunken light vessel, she was signalled by a patrolling torpedo boat to keep clear. *E6* continued on her course and within minutes struck a mine and disappeared.
BELOW: **The torpedo tubes of an E-class boat.**

E class

The E-class boats were the teeth of the Royal Navy's submarine fleet, carrying out many daring operations throughout World War I and fulfilling both the conventional submarine role and being adapted to work as mine-layers. One was even adapted to carry aircraft in an attempt to counter the threat to London from German airships. Fifty seven of these brilliantly versatile craft were built and 28 were lost. Larger engines were fitted in an attempt to give the boats extra power, and this resulted in an increase in hull size. While a small increase in performance was achieved, the larger hull enabled more fuel and weapons to be carried.

However, with the increase in size came a problem with their manoeuvrability, and it became necessary to position the boat closer to its target in order to fire torpedoes. This gave the enemy an advantage in counter-attack. At one stage, consideration was given to getting rid of the bow torpedo tubes and firing them broadside. Torpedo tubes were introduced in the beam and again the hull had to be increased to accommodate the tubes and loading space.

E class were also the first boats to have watertight bulkheads, which meant compartments could be sealed in emergencies. Previous British submarines had comprised one single compartment. With the bulkheads came other complications in construction, but the boat builders quickly realized the safety benefits and willingly incorporated them in future designs.

Crew comfort was also becoming part of the equation because of the length of time the men were spending aboard. Although it normally took anything from 20 to 30 months to build a submarine, the pressure of war soon began to reduce build-time to around a year, with Vickers completing *E19* in just eight months. This boat went on to become the first Royal Navy submarine to sink a merchant ship, in 1915 in the Baltic, and increased its tally to eight sinkings, including a German light cruiser. *E1* was the first to torpedo a German battleship – attacking the battlecruiser *Moltke* in the Gulf of Riga in August 1915. The boats of the British Baltic submarine flotilla were so successful in their campaign against enemy shipping that the Germans withdrew all major warships from the area.

Six E-class boats were also modified to act as minelayers, with the mines located in chutes in their saddle tanks. An E-class boat – *E3* – also became the first British submarine to be lost in action, when she was attacked by a U-boat in October 1914. Her wreckage was not located until 1997. As well as operating in home waters and the Baltic, the boats carried the war to the enemy in the Dardanelles, braving minefields to carry out their attacks. *E11* sank shipping off Constantinople and sank a Turkish battleship, the *Hayreddin Barbarossa*. Such was the effect of the E boats and the gallantry of their crews that three E boat captains won the Victoria Cross.

E22 was modified to carry a pair of Sopwith Schneider seaplanes on her deck, and trials began with the aim of launching the aircraft in the North Sea to intercept Zeppelin airships attacking London and other cities. However, the aircraft were too frail to operate in anything other than very calm conditions and the trials were abandoned. Twenty-nine E-class boats survived the war and were finally scrapped between 1921 and 1923. The six minelayers laid almost 2,500 mines.

E class

Displacement: 665.48 tonnes/655 tons (surfaced); 808.73 tonnes/796 tons (submerged)
Length: 53.65m/176ft
Beam: 6.86m/29ft 1in
Armament: 4 x 457mm/18in tubes, (1 x bow, 2 x beam, 1 x stern); 8 x torpedoes; 1 gun of various calibres was carried from 1915
Propulsion: 2 x 596.6kW/800bhp Vickers diesel engines; 2 x 313.2kW/420ehp electric motors
Speed: 15 knots (surfaced); 9 knots (dived)
Complement: 30 men

377

DIRECTORY OF SUBMARINES: 1900–45

LEFT: **Alphabetically out of context (using the initial of the manufacturer, Vickers), the early V class was a brave attempt to find the solution to creating the versatile submarine capable of coastal and ocean-going sorties, already being investigated by France, Germany and Japan. In that regard, it was a failure, with a disappointing performance, and the four V boats were relegated to training duties.**

V class (Early)

Four of the V-class boats were built by Vickers to compete with other experimental boats being constructed at other shipyards. They represented Vickers designers' interpretation of a coastal-type boat designed to meet the requirements of the 1912 Submarine Committee on future submarine development. The innovation was in the double hull section in the middle part of the boat, the result of a number of experimental hulls being tested in a tank.

Vickers built their own diesel engines for the V boats, although the battery was considered small for a boat of its size, and was in two of the class only a third larger than A-class batteries. The estimated cost of the four V-class boats was £75,790 each, and was clearly not the answer to the need for an ocean-going boat that was becoming ever more apparent in December 1913, as Germany pressed ahead with their U-boats. In the meantime, the V boats went into service,

V class (Early)

Displacement: 397.26 tonnes/391 tons (surfaced); 464.31 tonnes/457 tons (submerged)
Length: 44.95m/147ft 6in
Beam: 4.95m/16ft 3in
Armament: 2 x 457mm/18in tubes (bow), 4 x torpedoes; 1 x 12pdr gun
Propulsion: 2 x 335.6kW/450bhp Vickers diesel engines; 2 x 141.7kW/190ehp electric motors
Speed: 14 knots (surfaced); 9 knots (dived)
Complement: 20 men

but their performance was disappointing, and they lasted no longer than 1919, when they were paid off.

LEFT: **The pattern of the above V class was utilized for a double-hulled coastal submarine, although with a number of alterations and improvements to the design, including a stern torpedo tube, with no great success, either.**

F class (Early)

Displacement: 368.8 tonnes/363 tons (surfaced); 448.06 tonnes/441 tons (submerged)
Length: 46.02 m/151ft
Beam: 4.88m/16ft
Armament: 3 x 457mm/18in tubes (2 x bow, 1 x stern), 6 x torpedoes
Propulsion: 2 x 335.6kW/450bhp Vickers diesel engines; 2 x 149.1kW/200ehp electric motors
Speed: 14.5knots (surfaced); 8.75 knots (dived)
Complement: 19 men

F class (Early)

The F class were to be compared with other experimental boats, based on the V class and had similar performance. Although said to be less stable, F1 and F3 were equipped with Vickers diesel engines, with a MAN diesel engine installed in the third boat for comparison.

They were also fitted with an additional stern-mounted torpedo tube. The three were built between 1913 and 1917 and, at one time, there were plans for five of them to be built. This was scrapped once war broke out. They were used for local defence patrols and later sent to Portsmouth and Campbeltown to be used for training before being paid off in 1919.

UNITED KINGDOM

LEFT: The *G13* immediately became part of the Royal Navy's 10th Flotilla, based in the Tees, in a class which was the first to be armed with 533mm/21in torpedoes, with which *G13* sank the German *UC43* off Muggle Flugga light house on March 10, 1918. BELOW: The G-class profile, based on an Italian double-hull design.

G class

The G-class boats, of which 13 were built, were supposed to become the British answer to ocean-going submarines to match the U-boats, but didn't quite make it. The design features added to the continuing improvements in overall accommodation, allowing more and better equipment to be installed; however, they cost £125,000 apiece. The crew were better off, with improved living conditions that even included an electric oven. The two eight-cylinder diesels generated a worthwhile 1,193kW/ 1,600bhp, providing a surface speed of 14 knots, but undoubtedly the biggest improvement brought about by early war experience was the upgrade in armaments, which saw the beginning of larger torpedoes as standard. The specification was changed to provide two 457mm/18in bow tubes, two 457mm/18in beam tubes and one 533mm/21in stern tube.

The class also carried one 76mm/3in Quick Firing High Angle (QF HA) gun, which was fitted just forward of the bridge, and a portable 2pdr fixed to a pedestal at the after end of the bridge. In operations the boat is also known for diving to what was described as an exceptional depth of 51.8m/170ft, when being chased in error by three British destroyers.

During World War I, *G7*, *G8* and *G11* were lost on active service through unknown causes, and in September 1917, HMS *Petard* sank *G9* in error off the Norwegian coast after the submarine had attacked the ship – also in error. Of the boats that survived, four were taken out of service at the end of the war, and the remaining six were withdrawn from service in January 1921. They had proved something of a disappointment to many, given that their performance was little better than that of the E class, even with the incorporation of the double-hull concept.

LEFT: The control compartment of the G-class boats demonstrated the rapid pace of improvements aboard the new submarines coming on stream, as beam and length were increasing with each new design.

G class

Displacement: 710.18 tonnes/699 tons (surfaced); 982.47 tonnes/967.9 tons (submerged)
Length: 57.02m/187ft
Beam: 6.86m/22ft 6in
Armament: 4 x 457mm/18in tubes (2 x bow, 2 x beam); 8 x torpedoes; 1 x 533mm/21in tube (stern); 3 x torpedoes; 1 x 76mm/3in gun
Propulsion: 2 x 596.6kW/800bhp Vickers diesel engines; 2 x 313.2kW/420ehp electric motors
Speed: 15 knots (surfaced); 9 knots (dived)
Complement: 30 men

H class

LEFT: **The stylish-looking H class, rushed into service for World War I, was of an American design, with some being built in Britain and Canada. They proved a handy boat with the fastest dive, down in thirty seconds.**
ABOVE: *H23* **photographed in the Kiel Canal.**

As World War I continued to put pressure on British industry to feed the war machine, the country's shipyards were unable to satisfy the Admiralty's demands for more submarines. The Admiralty despatched a delegation to the United States, and 20 single-hulled craft were ordered from the Electric Boat Company.

The boats were to be shipped to the UK for assembly as America had not yet entered the war, but this idea was to fall foul of the US government's neutrality laws. It was then decided to build the first ten at Vickers Canada, with another ten being built by the Electric Boat Company. These, however, were interned at Boston by officials, still fiercely guarding America's neutrality while at the same time selling boatloads of vital supplies to Germany.

Eventually they were released to the Royal Navy, but by then the Canadians had shown the way by sending their boats across the Atlantic – the first such voyage by a submarine – and were in service in 1915. The first four, escorted by a warship, went straight on deployment in the Mediterranean, and the other six sailed to Britain escorted by a cruiser and support freighters.

With their up-to-date accommodation and facilities, these boats were very popular with their crews, and several of them were still serving in various navies in World War II. So successful was the H class that a further batch was ordered. They were to be built by Vickers at Barrow and were to be armed with the bigger 533mm/21in torpedo and fitted with a more powerful radio. Most of the components were shipped from America. A further 22 boats were ordered from various British shipbuilders in 1917, and most were delivered in 1918–19.

This completed a total fleet of 54 H boats in three groups, which until that point in time was only exceeded by the E class, although a number were not completed in time for action, and of those, eight American-built boats were ceded to the Canadian and Chilean Navy, the latter still running them in 1953 before they were scrapped.

LEFT: *H31* **was not completed in time for World War I, but was immediately in action in World War II and sank a U-boat on July 18, 1940. In December, she was involved in operations against the German battleship** *Scharnhorst* **near Brest, from which she failed to return, assumed mined.**

H class 🇬🇧

Displacement: 369.82 tonnes/364 tons (surfaced); 440.94 tonnes/434 tons (submerged)
Length: 45.79m/150ft 3in
Beam: 4.80m/15ft 9in
Armament: 4 x 457mm/18in torpedo tubes (bow); 8 x torpedoes
Propulsion: 313.2kW/420hp diesel; 231.2kW/310hp electric
Speed: 13 knots (surfaced); 10 knots (dived)
Complement: 22 men

J class

The J-class submarine came into being because the Admiralty wanted a craft capable of sailing with the surface ships of the Grand Fleet at a speed of 21 knots on the surface. It was not to be achieved. Because of the extra power needed, the boat's length was increased by more than 50 per cent over the E class that it was intended to replace. An extra shaft and third diesel engine would be needed to try to increase the power. However, all this achieved was a bigger and heavier hull with an increase in speed of just four knots, bringing it up to 19 knots on the surface.

Once this became apparent the Admiralty turned their attention to the even larger K class, which was also under construction, and the J-class boats were reclassified as overseas boats. Eight J-class boats had been ordered in January 1915, but by April two had been cancelled. Another boat had been ordered with a modified design but, again, there was no great improvement in performance.

J7 had a different layout to others of the class, with the control room positioned between the two engine rooms and the conning tower built slightly further back, giving better access space for the bow torpedo tubes.

They operated from their base in Blyth with the Grand Fleet, but because of their insufficient performance saw little action. However, J1 attacked four German warships with a salvo of torpedoes, seriously damaging the battleships *Kronprinz* and *Grosser Kurfurst*. At the end of World War I the six remaining J-class boats were transferred to the Royal Australian Navy.

TOP: **Most of the J-class boats were in action by mid-1916. *J1* had a spectacular initiation under Lt Commander Laurence when, sighting four battleships off Horns Reef, he fired four torpedoes and hit two enemy dreadnoughts.** ABOVE: **A profile of a J boat.** LEFT: ***J6* came to an unhappy end due to friendly fire, having been mistaken for *U6* and sunk by gunfire from the Q ship *Cymric* off Blyth on October 15, 1918. Fifteen survivors were picked up, but 19 other crewmen were killed.**

J class

Displacement: 1,223.26 tonnes/1,204 tons (surfaced); 1,849.12 tonnes/1,820 tons (submerged)
Length: 83.74m/274ft 9in
Beam: 7.16m/23ft 6in
Armament: 6 x 457mm/18in torpedo tubes (4 x bow, 2 x beam); 12 x torpedoes; 1 x 76mm/3in gun, 1 x 12pdr gun, and depth charges
Propulsion: 3 x 894.8 kW/1,200bhp Vickers diesel engines; 3 x 335.6kW/450ehp electric motors
Speed: 19 knots (surfaced); 9.6 knots (dived)
Complement: 44 men

Nautilus

This was the first Royal Navy submarine to be given a name, and in retrospect can be seen as a stepping stone to larger submarines. Designed with a double hull and increase in length, *Nautilus*' sea-keeping qualities, particularly in bad weather, were a great improvement on other submarines. Laid down in March 1913, she had an overall length of almost 79.2m/260ft, and was twice the size of any existing submarine. She was also the most expensive boat hitherto built by the Royal Navy, with costs escalating to almost £250,000.

Even so, there were a number of disappointing factors, especially in her speed, which did not meet the 17 knots on the surface called for in the design specifications. Her weaponry comprised two 457mm/18in bow torpedo tubes, four 457mm/18in beam tubes and two 457mm/18in stern tubes, with a combined load of 16 torpedoes carried. A 76mm/3in High-Angle gun was fitted on the superstructure just forward of the bridge, and this was raised and lowered on a vertical ram.

In the event, *Nautilus* never saw any active service and was used largely as a depot ship and for training purposes. However, there is no doubt that she provided a link in the British shipbuilding industry between the smaller boats and the great developments that followed in the quest for larger submarines.

The Admiralty was spurred on to seek better performances than 17 knots, and although engine performance was generally improving, as engines almost doubled in power during the building of these experimental boats, many difficulties and teething problems lay ahead. As for *Nautilus*, she was paid off in 1919 and sent to the scrap yard three years later.

ABOVE: *Nautilus*, a large experimental boat built during World War I and described by the Royal Navy as an "exceedingly interesting" project, was ultimately a failure. She ended her days charging batteries for other submarines.

Nautilus

Displacement: 1,464.06 tonnes/1,441 tons (surfaced); 2,058.42 tonnes/2,026 tons (submerged)
Length: 78.73m/258ft 4in
Beam: 7.92m/26ft
Armament: 8 x 457mm/18in tubes (2x bow, 4 x beam, 2 x stern), 16 x torpedoes; 1 x 76mm/3in deck gun
Propulsion: 2 x 1379.5kW/1,850bhp Vickers diesel engines; 2 x 372.8kW/500ehp electric motors
Speed: 17 knots (surfaced); 9 knots (dived)
Complement: 42 men

LEFT: The first of two boats named *Swordfish*. This one, built in 1916 (the other came with the 1930s S class), was an experimental steam turbine-powered submarine designed for long-range work, a development from the J class and the predecessor of the steam-powered K class.

Swordfish

Displacement: 946.91 tonnes/932 tons (surfaced); 1,493.52 tonnes/1,470 tons (submerged)
Length: 70.48m/231ft 3in
Beam: 6.93m/22ft 9in
Armament: 2 x 533mm/21in tubes (bow), 4 x torpedoes; 4 x 457mm/18in tubes (beam), 8 x torpedoes; 2 x 76mm/3in guns
Propulsion: 2 x 1,491.4kW/2,000shp steam turbines; 2 x 1,044kW/1,400ehp electric motors
Speed: 18 knots (surfaced); 10 knots (dived)
Complement: 42 men

Swordfish

Swordfish was built as part of the Admiralty's ongoing attempt to have submarines which could keep up with the Grand Fleet on the surface at a speed of 21 knots, which was to be achieved by installing a remarkable steam-powered propulsion system, supposedly making her much safer. However, it became very hot inside.

During her trials it was discovered that despite having a mount which meant the gun could be stowed, an exposed gun created less water resistance than had been estimated in theory. The biggest disappointment was that the speed was hardly improved upon, and she had poor manoeuvrability, a dangerous failing when operating in company with the Grand Fleet. Eventually *Swordfish* was converted into a surface patrol boat and fitted with two 12pdr guns.

UNITED KINGDOM

LEFT: **K26** was a new and improved version of the K class completed in 1923, but no others were built. She was noted for completing a successful journey to the Far East via Malta, through the Red Sea to Colombo, Singapore and back.
BELOW: The gunnery tasks on the K class become something of a nightmare, given the length of the boat, with ammunition stored in the bow and stern, thus requiring a long-distance haul by manpower.

K class

The obsession in certain quarters of the Admiralty for a fleet submarine that could operate with the Grand Fleet led to the K class. Designed to travel at 24 knots, it was also a reaction to a rumour around 1914 that the Germans had secretly developed a boat capable of 22 knots. With the current crop of petrol and diesel engines incapable of delivering the power required to drive a boat at that speed, steam power was chosen. As a production class, these were the largest and fastest submarines in the world with firepower to match, and such was the prestige surrounding them that ambitious officers cherished command of one of these boats – until the reality of sailing them hit home.

Initially they were armed with six torpedo tubes in the bow, four in the beam and three guns – but two of the bow tubes soon had to be removed to improve stability, followed by one of the guns. Even with a speed comparable to that of a destroyer, their manoeuvrability was a problem. Their turning circle was more like that of a dreadnought. They were also slow to submerge and once under water difficult to control. Gunnery, too, was a problem as the guns were slow to bring to bear because of poor control and the ammunition being stored in the bow or the stern requiring a lot of men to get the shells to the guns.

Diving could take anything from three to five minutes because of the number of hatches, vents and other equipment which needed to be closed before the 28 ballast tanks could be blown – and this was another operation fraught with danger, to ensure the boat did not end up in a nosedive or submerge with a list. Forty valves had to be operated in a carefully-controlled manner.

It was also discovered that because of the speed at which the boats travelled on the surface with the Grand Fleet, the door shutters of the torpedo tubes were often unable to survive the high water pressure, which left the tubes fouled and inoperable. The crews who operated these boats became increasingly alarmed about their safety because of what they regarded as the vessels' poor seaworthiness.

Their forebodings were to prove correct as 16 major accidents and eight disasters hit the K-class fleet, costing lives and boats. On only one occasion did a K-class boat fire its torpedoes at the enemy when engaging a U-boat, and even then it missed.

K class

Displacement: 2,011.68 tonnes/1,980 tons (surfaced); 2,600.96 tonnes/2,560 tons (submerged)
Length: 103.32m/339ft
Beam: 8.07m/26ft 6in
Armament: 10 x 457mm/18in tubes, (4 x bow, 4 x beam, 2 x casing – later removed); 18 x torpedoes; 2 x 101mm/4in guns, 1 x 76mm/3in anti-aircraft gun
Propulsion: 1,193.1kW/1,600hp diesel; 4 x 536.9kW/720ehp electric motors
Speed: 24 knots (surfaced); 9 knots (dived)
Complement: 59 men

383

L class

Unlike the K-class boats, the first batch of eight L class was developed from the successful E class, had increased speed, better range, and improved armament. They were equipped with six 457mm/18in torpedo tubes, four forward and two beam firing. A second batch of 26 L-class boats was then ordered, but only 18 of them were actually built. These were armed with four 533mm/21in torpedo tubes in the bow, which also necessitated lengthening of the boat. Six were then converted to minelayers, losing their beam tubes and replacing them with vertical chutes capable of launching 16 mines that were located in the saddle tanks.

A further 25 were then ordered, although only seven were delivered. On these craft, the number of bow tubes was increased to six and the beam tubes were done away with altogether. Nearly all were fitted with a 101mm/4in gun, and the last batch had a rear-firing gun located in an enlarged conning tower. In May 1926, during the General Strike, L12 was one of several submarines used as an emergency electricity generator moored at the Royal Victoria and Albert Docks.

Popular with their crews, one of them – L8 – became known as "The Boat That Would Not Sink". Having survived two collisions in 1918, one of them with another L craft, she was towed into the Channel as a target in 1929 after being paid off when trials of new 119mm/4.7in ammunition were being carried out. After being hit several times, she remained afloat and was towed back to Portsmouth for further inspection before being finally scrapped. Although obsolete by the outbreak of World War II, L boats initially served operationally before being transferred to the training role and then taken to Canada to give anti-submarine training to convoy escorts. The last operational boat of this class, L23, was finally paid off in October 1945, and foundered off Nova Scotia while being towed to the breakers yard.

TOP: The first of the L class were among the last to be commissioned in World War I, but they were a popular utility boat that continued on into the 1930s, although most were disposed of by the outbreak of war. ABOVE: The profile of L23, launched in 1919.

LEFT: The firepower varied on the L class, and although they were designed to carry two 76.2mm/3in D/HA guns, most were only fitted with one.

L class

Displacement: 905.26 tonnes/891 tons (surfaced); 1,091.18 tonnes/1,074 tons (submerged)
Length: 70.43m/231ft
Beam: 7.15m/23ft 6in
Armament: 6 x 457mm/18in tubes (4 x bow, 4 x beam),10 x torpedoes; 1 x 76mm/3in gun later replaced by a 101mm/4in gun
Propulsion: 2 x 894.8kW/1,200bhp Vickers diesel engines; 4 x 298.3kW/400ehp electric motors
Speed: 16.5 knots (surfaced); 10 knots (dived)
Complement: 35 men

UNITED KINGDOM

LEFT: *M2*, originally built with a 305mm/12in gun, was converted to carry aircraft by having a hangar installed in the empty space. A gantry was fitted to lift a Parnell Peto spotter plane. But disaster struck when the hangar doors were left open, and the submarine sank, with the loss of 60 men. ABOVE: The profile of the M class with the gun fitted.

M class

Admiral Sir John "Jackie" Fisher, the man who conceived the Dreadnought class of battleships, came up with the idea of a dreadnought submarine. He had little faith in the torpedoes of the day, believing they were incapable of stopping, let alone sinking, a warship.

These submarines would have a 305mm/12in gun forward of the conning tower similar to those fitted to the Majestic battleships. A smaller 76mm/3in gun would also be fitted as an anti-aircraft weapon. The main gun weighed 123.95 tonnes/122 tons, and 40 rounds – weighing a further 29.5 tonnes/29 tons – were stowed. Then there was the gun crew – 11 specialist gunnery ratings plus 16 in the ammunition party for the main gun, plus another six for the anti-aircraft gun. One unexpected bonus was that all the additional weight made the boat very stable.

The gun mount had a non-watertight housing, and the mechanism for loading the shell and charge were inside a watertight tower. The gun had a range of 29,900m/32,699yds, and the boat had to surface to load and fire. Accuracy would be approximate because of the movement of the boat on the sea and the lack of an artillery spotter.

Approaching a target – whether afloat or on the enemy coast – the boat would pop up and down from periscope depth until it got into position. Then it could surface and fire between 30 and 40 seconds before disappearing back to periscope depth in a further 50 seconds. Although Admiral Fisher came up with the proposal in 1915, none of the three M-class boats was to fire its armament in anger. *M1* did not go to sea until 1919 and was joined by *M2* the following year. Although the gun was waterproofed at the muzzle end, it was not made watertight at the breech. Water in the barrel when firing was to prove disastrous, and at least four barrels were burst because of it.

The Washington Disarmament Treaty of 1920 meant that no submarine could have a gun larger than 203mm/8in, so *M2* and *M3* had their guns removed, with *M2* being converted to an aircraft carrier with a hangar constructed where the gun mount had been. She carried a single Parnell Peto aircraft specially designed for the project. She became the first submarine to have a watertight hangar which could be sealed when she was submerged. The boat was able to surface and launch its aircraft in around 12 minutes. However, in January 1932, one of the hatch doors was left open and she sank off Portland Bill, with the loss of her entire crew.

RIGHT: The attractive looking *M1*, leader of the class of three converted K boats was rammed and sunk by a Swedish collier in the English Channel in November 1925, with the loss of 69 crew.

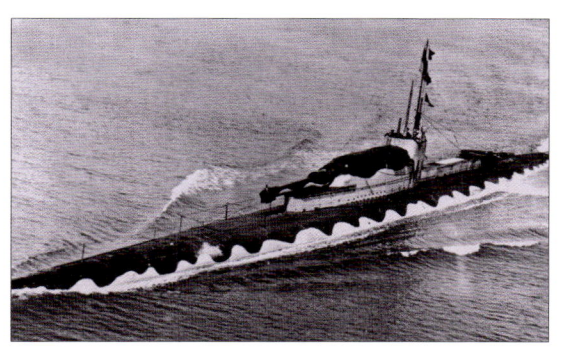

M class

Displacement: 1,635.76 tonnes/1,610 tons (surfaced); 1,977.13 tonnes/1,946 tons (submerged)
Length: 90.14m/295ft 9in
Beam: 7.49m/25ft 7in
Armament: 4 x 483mm/19in tubes (bow), 10 x torpedoes; 1 x 305mm/12in gun, 1 x 76mm/3in anti-aircraft gun
Propulsion: 2 x 894.8kW/1,200bhp Vickers diesel engines; 4 x 596.6kW/800ehp electric motors
Speed: 15 knots (surfaced); 9 knots (dived)
Complement: 64 men

385

R class (Early)

LEFT: **With a streamlined shape, the first R-class boats were built for speed underwater, and this was achieved. However, there were setbacks in other areas of production, and although ten were built at considerable expense, all were scrapped within eight years.**

R class (Early)

Displacement: 421.64 tonnes/415 tons (surfaced); 513.08 tonnes/505 tons (submerged)
Length: 49.91m/163ft 9in
Beam: 4.61m/15ft 1in
Armament: 6 x 457mm/18in tubes (bow), 12 x torpedoes
Propulsion: 1 x 179kW/240bhp American diesel engine; 2 x 894.8kW/1,200bhp electric motors
Speed: 10 knots (surfaced); 15 knots (dived)
Complement: 22 men

These boats were the first anti-submarine submarines, or what today are called hunter-killers. Entering service with the Royal Navy in 1917 they were designed to be quicker submerged than when surfaced. This they achieved with a speed of 15 knots that was not to be bettered until the latter stages of World War II, more than a quarter of a century later. The R class had six 457mm/18in torpedo tubes in the bow, and although it had originally been intended to mount a 101mm/4in gun, this was omitted in order to keep the weight down. The superstructure was as light as possible and ballast tanks were internal to keep the shape streamlined.

This boat also had problems. Although fitted with two powerful 895kW/1,200bhp electric motors, which enabled it to reach 15 knots when submerged, the 179kW/240bhp diesel engine was not strong enough to charge the 220 batteries, and because of this lack of power, it was a difficult craft to steer on the surface. In addition to the periscope, the boats had five primitive hydrophones to assist with detecting enemy submarines.

The boats only ever mounted one attack on a German U-boat, and the torpedo failed to explode. Of the 12 ordered, 10 were built and all were paid off by 1925.

LEFT: **A profile of the twin-turreted *X1* cruiser submarine with six torpedo tubes – a brilliant-looking boat that promised great potential, but was a disappointment in the end.**

X1 class

X1

Displacement: 2,824.48 tonnes/2,779.9 tons (surfaced); 3,657.6 tonnes/3,599.8 tons (submerged)
Length: 106.68m/350ft
Beam: 9.07m/29ft 9in
Armament: 6 x 533mm/21in tubes (bow); 12 x torpedoes; 2 x twin 132mm/5.25in guns
Propulsion: 2 x 2,237.1kW/3,000bhp MAN diesel engines; 2 x 969.4kW/1,300ehp electric motors and 1 x 894.8kW/1,200bhp diesel generator
Speed: 19 knots (surfaced); 9 knots (dived)
Complement: 109 men

Only one X1-class boat was ever built – the biggest submarine in the Royal Navy until the nuclear boats came into service decades later. Although conceived by the Royal Navy Submarine Committee in 1915 as a cruiser submarine armed with big guns as well as torpedoes, she was not laid down until November 1921. Dyed-in-the-wool naval planners still wanted submarines operating as part of the Grand Fleet, but submarine warfare experts wanted her to be able to operate in an independent role – a large, fast boat operating at extended ranges. At 2,824 tonnes/2,779 tons on the surface, she was certainly that. After World War I the navy had time and opportunity to carefully examine captured German submarines, including their cruiser submarines. She would also be the first new boat since the war.

X1 was completed in September 1925, joined the Navy the following spring and was the largest submarine in the world at that time. She was sent on a return trip to Gibraltar but problems arose with her diesel engines, and she was sent back to the RN Dockyard at Chatham for repairs.

The following January she passed all her tests and was assigned to the Mediterranean Fleet, but within a year she again had engine trouble, this time in Malta. There were other niggles, too. Officers claimed that she handled well and that most of her problems were because of crew errors. *X1* was laid up in reserve in 1933 and scrapped three years later – the only Royal Navy submarine built after World War I that did not survive until World War II.

O class

These were long-range submarines based on the L class and designed to operate in Far Eastern waters as concerns grew about Japanese intentions after failure to renew the Anglo–Japanese Alliance in 1922. The first one became *Oberon*, and although 2 knots slower than the L class, the hull was 12m/39ft 4in longer and they could carry double the number of torpedoes. Their range was also nearly double that of their predecessor. In addition, their wireless range was better and diving depth was deeper. The 101mm/4in gun mounted on the front of the conning tower was later modified to be fitted on a revolving mount. *Oberon* was also the first boat to be fitted with the ASDIC submarine detection system, which evolved into today's sonar.

An O-class boat, *Oxley*, became the first Royal Navy submarine to be lost in World War II when another submarine, *Triton*, mistakenly torpedoed her off the Norwegian coast in 1939. It was only when two survivors were plucked from the water that the true horror unfolded. *Triton* had been signalling *Oxley*, but when no recognition signal was received, assumed her to be an enemy U-boat and torpedoed her. With the recovery of the crewmen, they discovered *Oxley* had been returning the signals but her signal lamp was faulty. A full-scale cover-up was ordered, and it was not until the 1950s that the true account of what happened was released. At the time, a cover story was put out that she had suffered an accidental explosion.

Oberon and *Otway* both went on operations in World War II, but were later transferred to a training role. A second batch of six O-class boats were fitted with a more powerful diesel engine that gave them a higher surface speed, and their hydroplanes were moved from the bottom of the pressure hull to the top and hinged so they could be turned in when not in use. Although this increased dive time, it eradicated a lot of the damage they suffered when the boat was submerged for long periods of time.

As the Germans tightened their stranglehold on the strategic Mediterranean island of Malta by sea and air, causing havoc among the convoys trying to supply the beleaguered garrison, the O-class boats – the first to be given names instead of numbers – joined other large submarines to run the gauntlet underwater by ferrying in vital supplies of ammunition, aviation fuel, torpedoes, food and fresh water.

ABOVE: *Otway*, *Oberon* and *Oxley*, a trio of O-class boats built in two groups from the late 1920s, including two that joined the Australian Royal Navy but which returned for wartime duties. LEFT: Chile later bought and modified O-class boats, and renamed them as O'Brien class.

LEFT: *Oberon*, the class leader commissioned in 1927, was rather troublesome, suffering breakdowns that forced her into reserve status until she was brought out for war duty and then scrapped. She gave her name to the Oberon class of the 1960s.

O class

Displacement: 1,513.84 tonnes/1,489.9 tons (surfaced); 1,922.27 tonnes/1,891.9 tons (submerged)
Length: 82.19m/269ft 8in
Beam: 8.53m/28ft
Armament: 8 x 533mm/21in tubes (6 x bow, 2 x stern), 16 x torpedoes; 1 x 101mm/4in gun
Propulsion: 2 x 1,006.7kW/1,350bhp Admiralty diesel engines; 2 x 484.7kW/650ehp electric motors
Speed: 13.5 knots (surfaced); 7.5 knots (dived)
Complement: 53 men

LEFT: *Pandora* was engaged in running supplies to Malta and was unloading when an enemy bombing raid began. Her crew courageously carried on only to receive two direct hits from bombs, and she sank on April 1, 1942. BELOW: HMS *Perseus* was mined off Cephallonia, leaving a sole survivor from the crew of 51 to tell the tale.

Parthian class

Like the O class before them, boats of the Parthian class were prone to leaking fuel from their saddle tanks when submerged, which then left a giveaway smear across the ocean's surface. The leaks were caused by the pressure on the riveted tanks. One of the boats, *Poseidon*, was lost after colliding with a Chinese coaster in the Yellow Sea in June 1931, but 35 of the 57-man crew managed to survive by taking part in the first big escape from a submarine using the Davis Submarine Escape Apparatus.

During the siege of Malta in 1941–42, *Parthian*-class boats *Pandora* and *Parthian* along with other submarines were used as supply craft. A section of their batteries was removed and their spare torpedoes left behind to create additional space for stores for the garrison to be carried. Petrol and other fuels were also ferried in, and fresh water was stored in the ballast tanks.

One of the most remarkable escape and survival stories of World War II involved *Perseus*, which struck an Italian mine in the Ionian Sea. Leading Stoker John Capes and four other survivors were trapped in the submarine at a depth of 52m/171ft. Their only means of escape was the Davis Apparatus. After downing a bottle of rum for courage, they began their escape attempt, but only Capes made it to the surface alive. Exhausted, he managed to struggle a further 8–10km/5–6 miles to the island of Cephalonia, where he was found by locals who looked after him before handing him over to the Resistance. It took 18 months for him to reach home, and he was awarded the British Empire Medal. There were sceptics who did not accept his account of his escape. It was not until 1998 that the wreck of the *Perseus* was located with all the evidence, including the empty rum bottle. Capes went on to become a Chief Petty Officer, but, sadly, he died ten years before the wreck was found and his story verified.

One of the most deadly of the *Parthian*-class boats was *Proteus*, which had spent the pre-war years in the Far East. Deployed to the Mediterranean with other large submarines to help Malta, she was eventually sent back to Britain in 1943, but not before she had damaged or sunk 11 Italian transports.

LEFT: *Parthian* led the P class to China and then to the Mediterranean when war broke out. She is known to have sunk two Italian submarines, the Vichy French submarine *Souffleur* and other Italian vessels before she was herself posted lost, presumed mined in 1943.

Parthian class

Displacement: 1,796.29 tonnes/1,767.9 tons (surfaced); 2,067.56 tonnes/2,034.9 tons (submerged)
Length: 88.13m/289ft 2in
Beam: 9.12m/29ft 11in
Armament: 8 x 533mm/21in tubes (6 x bow, 2 x stern, 14 x torpedoes); 1 x 101mm/4in gun
Propulsion: 2 x 1,730kW/2,320bhp Admiralty diesel engines; 2 x 492.1kW/660ehp electric motors
Speed: 18 knots (surfaced); 8.5 knots (dived)
Complement: 53 men

UNITED KINGDOM

LEFT: **HMS** *Scorcher* **was a late arrival in the large class of more than 60 S-class boats. Classic workhorses of World War II, although many were not commissioned until the latter stages, some, like** *Scorcher***, remained in service for 20 years or more.** BELOW: **A profile of Group III S-class boat,** *Storm***.**

S class

The S boats carried out some of the most daring and dangerous and, at times, most celebrated operations of World War II. With an increased capability in speed, range and depth, they were quicker to dive and were also the first boats to have escape hatches located both fore and aft, something which was to save the lives of many submariners as the war grew in intensity and they operated in some very hostile environments.

Slightly smaller than some other classes, they were able to operate in shallower and more confined waters. The first four boats joined the fleet in 1932–33 and were equipped with a 76mm/3in gun positioned in a forward extension of the conning tower that was stowed before diving. A second batch of eight boats was ordered with the gun mounted on the casing, which meant the conning tower could be reduced in height, although a small extension to the front served as an ammunition bunker. The next tranche of these craft began production at the outbreak of the war, and production continued throughout, with variations to lines and equipment as innovations were discovered. Eventually, instead of being riveted or part-riveted, the hulls were all welded. Air-warning radio direction finders, ASDIC, external stern tubes and more powerful anti-aircraft guns were introduced.

In addition to the German threat, these submarines suffered so-called "friendly fire" attacks from RAF aircraft, other submarines and, occasionally, Royal Navy ships. A lot of the British torpedoes were also found to be faulty, a problem shared by the German U-boat packs. An S-class submarine, *Sturgeon*, carried out the first successful Royal Navy submarine attack of the war when she sank the anti-submarine trawler *V209* off Heligoland in November 1939. In addition, *Salmon* carried out the first successful attack on a U-boat, sinking *U36* three weeks later. Just over a week later, she attacked a formation of German warships, hitting the light cruisers *Leipzig* and *Nurnberg*. *Spearfish* attacked and damaged the German pocket battleship *Lützow*, leaving her helpless with her propellers and steering gear out of action. *Lützow* had to be towed to port and was out of action for a year. However, the success was not one-sided and many brave men were lost with their boats after clashes with U-boats, aircraft and surface craft. Others perished when their boats struck mines.

Seraph was certainly the most famous of these boats, particularly after the war, with two films made about her exploits: the first, *The Man Who Never Was*, and the second, *The Ship With Two Captains*. The boats were also used to gather intelligence about possible landing sites for various operations to liberate Europe from the Germans.

RIGHT: **A quartet of S-class boats,** *Shark***,** *Sunfish***,** *Snapper* **and** *Sealion***, of whom sadly only the latter survived the war.**

S class Group 1

Displacement: 650.24 tonnes/640 tons (surfaced); 941.83 tonnes/927 tons (submerged)
Length: 61.72m/202ft 6in
Beam: 7.31m/24ft
Armament: 6 x 533mm/21in tubes, 12 x torpedoes; 1 x 76mm/3in gun
Propulsion: 2 x 1,156kW/1,550hp diesel, 2 x 969kW/1,300 electric
Speed: 13.5 knots (surfaced); 10 knots (dived)
Complement: 38 men

389

LEFT: "T" for "tremendous". A brilliant class of British boats, the T class came in abundance, saw great war service and continued on for 20 years or more. *Tally Ho*, for example, became the first T-class boat to cross the Atlantic on snorkel. BELOW: Profile of a T-class boat of the 1942 vintage.

T class

The T class were the first British submarines to have their fuel tanks inside the hull, which eradicated the problems caused by leaking fuel leaving a trail across the sea's surface. Intended to replace the O, P and R classes and 406 tonnes/400 tons smaller, they were superior in nearly every respect to those they were succeeding. They had better armament and two more torpedo tubes, and their all-welded hull meant that the boats were much stronger and able to dive deeper to escape attack and counter-attack. The London Naval Treaty of 1935 had placed restrictions on Britain's submarine ambitions, so these craft had to be constructed within the rules laid down.

There was a slight loss of speed, for example, as the size of the submarine was limited by the treaty, so larger engines could not be fitted. A variety of engines were used to try to improve performance, but with the outbreak of war only Admiralty or Vickers diesels were fitted. One batch of this class even featured 11 torpedo tubes plus a 20mm/0.79in anti-aircraft gun and 7.7mm/0.303 machine-guns.

One of the T class, *Thetis*, was at the centre of one of the most tragic episodes in Royal Navy submarine history when she sank while on trials in Liverpool Bay in 1939 with more than 100 people aboard, including shipyard workers, office staff and others there to celebrate the chance to sail in a submarine. Another T-class boat, *Tetrarch*, attacked a large merchantman in the North Sea, whereupon she was the subject of a very hostile counter-attack by the escorts. Forced to dive deep, she reached 120m/394ft and stayed there for 43 hours.

Triton attacked a German convoy taking part in the occupation of Norway, with a salvo of six torpedoes hitting the *Friedenau*, *Wigbert* and *V1507*, killing 900 German troops who were being sent to occupy the country. *Thistle* attacked U-boat *U4* in the North Sea in April 1940 unsuccessfully – but a few days later *U4* caught *Thistle* on the surface and sank her with the loss of all hands. T boats were heavily involved in the Mediterranean and in the Far East, scoring some spectacular results against the Japanese fleet, particularly *Trenchant* which fired a salvo of all eight of her

LEFT: Wartime T-class boats carried a 102mm/4in guns, and later in the war, three machine-guns were added.

UNITED KINGDOM

ABOVE: **A typical T boat patch.** RIGHT: **An impressive whole boat view of HMS *Thorough*, the first Royal Navy submarine to circumnavigate the globe, when she travelled to Australia through the Mediterranean and the Suez Canal and returned via the Panama Canal.**

bow torpedoes at the Japanese heavy cruiser *Ashigara*. Five struck home, blowing away the bows and setting the ship ablaze before she sank.

Truant was the only Royal Navy submarine to sink enemy ships in three different theatres – Home, Mediterranean and Far East – sinking almost 81,284 tonnes/80,000 tons of enemy shipping. Before that, she was returning from a refit in America when she spotted a Norwegian ship acting suspiciously. *Truant's* captain discovered that the ship had already been boarded and was under the command of a German prize crew. As well as this, there were captured British survivors from the SS *Braxby* on board. The British crew were taken aboard *Truant*, along with the captain and his wife, the latter of whom became the first woman to sail in a submarine.

In February 1945, *Tantalus* completed the longest wartime patrol, during which she travelled 18,507km/11,500 miles in 55 days. One of the most bizarre stories surrounding a T-class boat came when *Totem* visited Canada and was in turn visited by members of the Cowichan Indian tribe, who presented the boat with a small totem pole. The sailors were told the totem pole had magic properties provided by the carvings of the thunderbird, grizzly bear, killer whale and Fire God, and while the totem remained on board no harm would come to *Totem*. The boat was transferred to the Israeli Navy and renamed *Dakar* in 1964 and the carved totem placed on display in the Royal Naval Museum in Gosport. In January 1968, *Dakar* was lost in the Mediterranean. In 1957, *Thorough* became the first submarine to circumnavigate the world.

LEFT: ***Thermopylae*** **was among the last of the T boats to be built, thus benefiting from the extensive modifications that were progressively applied to the class, especially in electronics and crew spaces.**

T class

Displacement: 1,326.90 tonnes/1,306 tons (surfaced); 1,597.15 tonnes/1572 tons (submerged)
Length: 84m/275ft 7in
Beam: 8.1m/26ft 7in
Armament: 10 x 457mm/21in tubes (8 x bow, 2 x beam – 5 of them external),16 x torpedoes; 1 x 101mm/4in gun
Propulsion: 2 x 1,864kW/2,500hp diesel, 2 x 1,081kW/1,450 electric
Speed: 16.25 knots (surfaced); 9.25 knots (dived)
Complement: 55 men

U class

FAR LEFT: The British U-class boats were heroes of World War II. They saw extensive action and became the scourge of the Italian Navy in the Mediterranean. LEFT: Naturally, the raising of the Jolly Roger was a common sight at the time, as seen here by *Unbroken*, which torpedoed and damaged the Italian cruisers *Bolzano* and *Muzio Attendolo* on August 13, 1942. INSET: A patch for *Unbroken*.

Originally designed as unarmed target submarines between the two world wars, the Admiralty quickly changed its mind as alarm bells began to sound across Europe, and it was decided to give them torpedo tubes so they could be used for training crews meant to man the much larger T-class boats. Only three of these boats had been completed by the outbreak of World War II, but their design was so simple it was easy to increase production. Moreover, their small size was considered an advantage for operating in difficult coastal waters, and they proved to be highly successful.

At the outset, the boats had six torpedo tubes with two in an external bulbous bow, but this shape caused wake problems, reduced visibility at periscope depth and was changed by removing the extra two tubes in later models. With fuel and ballast within the pressure hull and diesel-electric power, the shaft was driven at all times by the electric motors, with the diesel engine used on the surface to power the generator that, in turn, topped up the batteries and fed the motor.

The first to be commissioned was *Undine*, which was also the first to be lost when she attacked three German minesweepers in the Heligoland Bight. Her salvo missed, but the torpedo trail gave the enemy a fix on her position, and they counter-attacked. *Undine* dived and, after thinking it safe to return to periscope depth, she did so only to be hit by an explosion that wrecked the hydroplanes. Out of control, the crew had little option but to abandon ship, scuttling the boat with an explosive charge as they left.

U-class boats made a significant contribution to the war effort, particularly *Upholder*, commanded by Lt Cdr Malcolm David Wanklyn, VC, DSO, who sank or damaged 22 enemy ships totalling well over 101,605 tonnes/ 100,000 tons.

Another remarkable boat, *Unbroken*, used her last four torpedoes to attack an Italian heavy cruiser and a light cruiser which had been bombarding Allied convoys trying to get supplies to Malta. Attacking from close range, she put both ships out of action for the remainder of the war. The escorting Italian destroyers reacted with fury, unleashing a barrage of more than 100 depth charges to try to hit *Upholder*, who survived the onslaught and quietly slipped away to Malta.

Unbroken was eventually loaned to the Russian Navy, and several other U-class boats were loaned to other Allied navies. As soon as the war in Europe ended, the U class lost their operational role and reverted to being used as training craft.

LEFT: The loading of torpedoes and armaments into *Ursula* prior to another patrol, possibly when she hit the Italian liner *Vulcania*, being used for troop transport in September 1941.

U class

Displacement: 636 tonnes/626 tons (surfaced); 739.65 tonnes/728 tons (submerged)
Length: 58.21m/191ft
Beam: 4.88m/16ft
Armament: 6 x 533mm/21in tubes (bow – 2 x external), 10 torpedoes; 1 x 76mm/3in gun
Propulsion: 2 x 298.3kW/400bhp Davy Paxman diesel engines; 2 x 307.2kW/412ehp General Electric motors
Speed: 12.5 knots (surfaced); 10 knots (dived)
Complement: 30 men

UNITED KINGDOM

LEFT: It was a great tragedy that *Porpoise* became the last British submarine to be sunk in hostile action in World War II, after laying mines in the vicinity of Penang, leaving a tell-tale trail of oil sighted by a Japanese spotter plane.

Porpoise class

Porpoise class

Displacement: 1,792.22 tonnes/1,763.9 tons (surfaced); 2,068.58 tonnes/2,035.9 tons (submerged)
Length: 87.78m/288ft
Beam: 9.12m/29ft 11in
Armament: 6 x 533mm/21in tubes, 12 x torpedoes; 50 x mines (although more could be carried in place of torpedoes); 1 x 101mm/4in gun
Propulsion: 2 x 1,230.4kW/1,650bhp Admiralty diesel engines; 2 x 607.7kW/815ehp electric motors
Speed: 15 knots (surfaced); 8 knots (dived)
Complement: 59 men

These boats, the Royal Navy's submarine minelayers, went about their business in perilous coastal waters which often left them vulnerable to danger from land, sea, air and their own deadly cargo. Of the six built, four were lost and one captured. Founded on the experience gained with *M3*, the boats featured a chain conveyor and rail system atop the pressurized hull that could carry 50 Mk XVI mines. Because of the extra space intended for mine-carrying, the Porpoise boats were pressed into service to carry vital supplies to the beleaguered island of Malta in 1941–42, with fuel, ammunition and other material occupying the space reserved for the mines.

With the development of a special submarine mine which could be launched using the 533mm/21in torpedo tubes, other Porpoise boats were cancelled. *Rorqual* laid minefields in both the North Sea and Mediterranean, and *Seal*, spotted laying a minefield, was attacked by a German aircraft which also alerted anti-submarine craft. However, before they could reach her *Seal* struck a mine and sank, becoming embedded in the mud on the sea floor. After a struggle she freed herself, but as soon as she returned to the surface, she was attacked, forcing the crew to surrender.

By the end of hostilities, the *Porpoise*-class minelayers had laid more than 2,500 mines, with only *Rorqual* surviving to the end of the war.

LEFT: *X25*, one of the last of the midget submarines to be built in Britain, after some challenging operations and an exceedingly creditable history.

X-craft

X-craft

Displacement: 30.48 tonnes/30 tons (surfaced); 33.02 tonnes/32.5 tons (submerged)
Length: 13.26m/43ft 6in
Beam: 2.44m/8ft
Armament: 2 x containers with 1,620kg/3,571.5lb of explosives; Limpet mines
Propulsion: 1 x 31.3kW/42bhp Perkins diesel engine; 1 x 18.6kW/25ehp electric motor
Speed: 6.5 knots (surfaced); 4.5 knots (dived)
Complement: 3–4 men

Initially, when Winston Churchill was First Lord of the Admiralty, he and the Admiralty looked down their noses at the concept of midget submarines. They were dangerous and the sort of power a weaker nation would employ – certainly not the Royal Navy! However, come World War II and the German threat to both British shipping and the country itself, particularly from the massive German warships operating with seeming impunity from the fjords of occupied Norway, the Admirals began hailing midget submarines as the solution.

Built, developed and trialled under conditions of great secrecy, the midget submarines were crewed by a special breed of men, many of whom were to lose their lives in the service of their country as they struck at German capital ships and installations in seemingly impregnable locations.

After World War II, many films and books were made about the gallant men of the X-craft. Not only did they face the dangers of enemy fire, but they also had to brave minefields, anti-submarine nets, acoustic alarms and other perils just to reach their target before dropping their explosives and trying to find their way out again to rendezvous with their escorts.

For their gallantry in wartime, X-craft crews won 4 Victoria Crosses, 11 DSOs, 17 DSCs, 12 DSMs, 6 CGMs, 4 BEMs, 3 CBEs, 1 OBE, 10 MBEs and 27 Mentions in Despatches.

LEFT: *U14* was commissioned in 1912 with the altered specifications introduced with *U13*, but while serving as part of the I Flotilla, she was damaged by gunfire from the armed trawler *Oceanic II* and sank off Peterhead, with one member of crew killed and 27 rescued. BELOW: *U9*, noted for reloading torpedoes while submerged, for the first time in history, and later for sinking three British cruisers, *Aboukir*, *Hogue* and *Cressy* with an hour.

U1 (Early)

German shipbuilders were producing submarines for the Russian Navy a full two years before the first of what would prove to be a long and successful progression of U-boats made her appearance. *U1* was launched from the Germaniaweft yard in August 1906, and commissioned primarily for trials and evaluation by the Imperial German Navy. Already larger than the British and American counterparts of the A and B classes, *U1* did not, however, impress her own Naval chiefs. They complained that her displacement rendered her unfit for operations any distance from the coast, and modifications began immediately. Even so, *U1* was the precursor to 375 U-boats of three principal classes ranging through 29 different types available for World War I. These new offerings also came with the distinct advantage of a heavy oil motor that precluded the internal problems experienced by petrol-driven engines. However, the downside of this development was that the boat billowed smoke and sparks from a rear-mounted upper-deck exhaust system, emissions that were more on a par with a steamer. Thus, any opposition would have no problem in tracking her on the surface.

This was soon to be modified with a development that dramatically changed surface propulsion forever, with the introduction of diesel engines for the bulk of the U-boats built by Germany. *U1* did impress in other areas, however, and notable among her early trials was a 1,087km/587-nautical-mile endurance test from Wilhelmshaven that took her around Denmark and back to Kiel in exceedingly dire conditions. Based upon these findings, Germany initiated a rapid programme of development and innovation, and by 1911, U-boats had progressed from 42.4m/139ft to 57.3m/188ft in length with subsequent upgrades in both speed, endurance and firepower, increasing her torpedo payload from one to four tubes, two bow and two stern. Further types in this series emerged with additional design improvements through to *U18*.

The fortune of war, however, did not favour these early submarines of the Imperial Navy. Four days after the United Kingdom declared war on the German Empire on August 4, 1914, ten boats, *U5*, *U7*, *U8*, *U9*, *U13*, *U14*, *U15*, *U16*, *U17* and *U18* were despatched to launch an audacious attack on the British Grand Fleet at Scapa Flow. Two boats, *U5* and *U9*, had to return to port with engine trouble, *U13* was lost without trace, and *U15* went down with all hands after being rammed by the British cruiser HMS *Birmingham* in the North Sea on August 9,

LEFT: **Loading torpedoes on the World War I training boat *U25*, which survived the war to be surrendered and broken up at Canning Town in 1922.**

LEFT: **A classic silhouette of *U35*, one of the most successful boats of World War I, which, during 17 patrols with the II Flotilla in August 1915, is credited with sinking 224 ships for a total of 548,402 tonnes/539,741 tons, and survived the conflict, to be surrendered and broken up at Blyth.** ABOVE: **An internal view of the engine room.**

1914. This unpromising start was soon to be repealed. On July 16, 1914, the ageing *U9*, commanded by Otto Weddigen, became famous in the German submarine fraternity by performing a torpedo reload while submerged, for the first time in history. Weddigen began drilling his crews in fast reloads by moving members of his crew forward then aft while the ballast was regulated. On September 22, he used this technique to sink three British cruisers in an hour. It was an unique achievement in that after the first strike, the other British ships sailed to assist the stricken vessel thinking that it had hit a mine, unaware of *U9*'s presence. The succession of strikes occurred at 07:20 hours (*Aboukir*), 07:55 hours (*Hogue*) and 08:20 hours (*Cressy*), each one with a single shot, and claiming a total of 1,400 lives. A few days later, *U9* torpedoed another British cruiser, *Hawke*, and in doing so, this one submarine had killed more British sailors than were lost by Lord Nelson in all his battles put together.

As for *U1*, although no wartime patrols are recorded, she survived the conflict and was decommissioned in the post-war surrender of German U-boats to the Allies. She was thereafter sliced in two and retained for posterity in the *Deutsches Museum* in Munich. The improvements achieved in the designs in the first 18 boats prior to the introduction of diesel propulsion can be seen by comparing the specifications below.

U1

Displacement: 234 tonnes/230.3 tons (surfaced); 278 tonnes/273.6 tons (submerged)
Length: 42.39m/139ft
Beam: 3.75m/12ft 4in
Armament: 1 x 450mm/17.7in tube (bow), 3 x torpedoes
Propulsion: 298.3kW/400hp heavy oil; 298.3kW/400hp electric
Speed: 10.8 knots (surfaced); 8.7 knots (dived)
Complement: 12 men (22, then 28 on larger types)

U18

Displacement: 555 tonnes/546.2 tons (surfaced); 680 tonnes/669.3 tons (submerged)
Length: 62.35m/204ft 7in
Beam: 6m/19ft 8in
Armament: 6 x 450mm/17.7in tubes (2 x bow, 2 x stern); 1 x 10.5cm/4.13in deck gun

ABOVE: **A U-boat flotilla (left to right): *U13* was lost with all hands in 1914; *U5* survived the war after 22 patrols; *U11* was a training boat; *U3* was a training boat which surrendered in 1918 but sank on the way to the UK; and *U16* sank ten ships during the war, then sank on the way to surrendering.**

RIGHT: **Impressively sleek for the era and suitably menacing, an array of early German submarines, from left to right in the front row,** *U22, U20, U19* **and** *U21* **pictured at Keil harbour, part of Germany's High Seas Fleet of 20 boats at the beginning of World War I. They were subsequently deployed as a defensive screen in the North Sea.**
ABOVE: **Profile of** *U21*, **the first U-boat to sink a British warship, the cruiser HMS** *Pathfinder.*

U19: diesel

Innovations in U-boat construction continued at a rapid pace with the first four U-boats designed specifically for the ocean-going hunter role, entering service from 1913 with the leader boat of this type, *U19*.

Her commissioning brought another landmark in submarine development in that she was the first to be manufactured with a diesel engine, so-called after the German engineer who invented it. Even so, by 1914 Germany had only 24 boats in service, four others under repair or seconded to a training role and another 17 under construction, representing one of the smallest fleets among the major powers.

However, it had become clear that coming late to submarine warfare had enabled the Germans to learn from the costly lessons experienced by other navies, at least in design if not immediately in operational tactics. This benefit was beginning to show in the development of their first oceanic boats whose clear aim would be to attack merchant ships in wartime.

New targets had been set for endurance and surface speed, and it became evident, not least in the use and placement of deck guns, that these were to become an important element in surface operations against merchant shipping. Some boats of the new class were equipped with top-mounted guns that folded neatly away after operations, thus allowing greater speed.

It was also a noticeable tactic in the first ship attacks that torpedoes were only used on high profile targets. One such target appeared in the periscope vision of *U21* commander Otto Hersing off the Scottish coast on September 5, 1914. He opened fire to become the first submarine to release a torpedo in anger in World War I. The victim was the British light cruiser, *Pathfinder*.

Hersing went on to become one of the most successful U-boat commanders, sinking or disabling almost 40 ships in 21 patrols over the next three years, a run that included Allied battleships while assigned to assist the Turks during the Gallipoli crisis.

More famously, a sister ship in this class, *U20*, torpedoed the Cunard liner *Lusitania* on May 7, 1915, with the loss of nearly 1,200 passengers and crew.

RIGHT: **Given the prolific success record of** *U35*, **the submarine was also leading the league table of torpedoes fired. This series of U-boats carried only six torpedoes, so it required a constant re-supply, often at sea.**

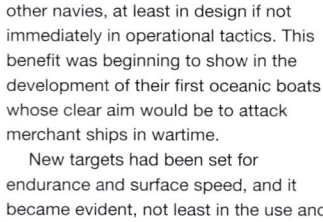

U19

Displacement: 546.25 tonnes/537.6 tons (surfaced); 669.25 tonnes/658.7 tons (submerged)
Length: 62.35m/204ft 7in
Beam: 6.10m/20ft
Armament: 6 x 457mm/18in tubes; 1x 10.5cm/4.13in deck gun
Propulsion: 1,305kW/1,750hp diesel; 894.8kW/1,200hp electric
Speed: 15.4 knots (surfaced); 9.5 knots (dived)
Complement: 35 men

U81

By 1914, Germany's U-boat fleet had numerically reached *U38* but as the war progressed, production doubled and then trebled, along with numerous changes in type, layout and variations of armament. However, the key to German submarine expansion was the drive for longer-range boats, introduced in numerous types built in small classes, which consequently allowed the introduction of new features and capabilities. By 1916, the series of 46 Mittel-type boats that began with *U81* was well underway, providing ever-increasing endurance and firepower, which enabled the expansion of operations outward from European waters into the Atlantic and ultimately in threatening posturing towards the east coast of America.

The capabilities of these boats were geared towards long patrols, packed to the gills with torpedoes. The 813-tonne/800-ton U81 series carried ten torpedoes and a substantial deck armoury to a range of up to 12,070km/7,500 miles, while their successors in the U90 and U100 series could take up to 16 torpedoes, although their endurance was significantly lower.

Given the possibilities for causing huge damage to the British, the Germans declared unrestricted warfare on February 29, 1916, under which enemy armed vessels could be attacked anywhere and merchant ships in the war zone could be attacked without warning. This was curtailed only after strong protests from the Americans following the sinking of passenger vessels and the death of American citizens.

The retraction once again forestalled American entry into the war, but it had little effect on the mounting U-boat toll as the German submarine fleet continued to expand both numerically and in capability. *U81*, for example, sank 31 ships – excluding enemy warships – of 91,444 tonnes/90,000 tons on just four patrols, between October 1916 and May 1917, before she herself was sunk by the British boat *E24* off the west coast of Ireland, while *U90* took down 35 ships in the last year of the war.

ABOVE: **An interesting view of *U117*, a minelayer of the UE2 class of which nine boats were commissioned. Although not operational until March 1918, she sank 24 Allied vessels (warships excluded). She was surrendered to the Americans and was used for exhibitions.**
ABOVE LEFT: **A profile of Type U139, a cruiser merchant class of which three were built.**

ABOVE: **The mechanics of the ocean minelayer *U117*, capable of carrying 42 mines, as well as 14 torpedoes, thus providing not only greater firepower but also endurance at sea.**

U81

Displacement: 795 tonnes/782.4 tons (surfaced); 934 tonnes/919.2 tons (submerged)
Length: 70.06m/229ft 10in
Beam: 6.30m/20ft 8in
Armament: 6 x 508mm/20in tubes (4 x bow, 2 x stern), 16 x torpedoes; 1 x 8.8cm/3.46in and 1 x 10.5cm/4.13in deck guns
Propulsion: 1,789.7kW/2,400hp diesel; 894.8kW/1,200hp electric
Speed: 16.8 knots (surfaced); 9.4 knots (dived)
Complement: 39 men

UB classes I, II and III

LEFT: **Class leader *UB1*.** Built primarily for coastal work, although they did not come into production until the start of the war, they certainly made up for lost time in terms of patrols completed. A total of more than 100 patrols was not uncommon, although the casualty rate was high. BELOW: A profile of a UB-class boat.

While remarkable advances were being achieved by Germany in the construction of larger, long-range boats, there was a yawning gap in the coverage of areas where endurance and range were less critical. With a build time of up to 18 months for ocean-going U-boats, in the interests of sheer expediency, a smaller boat was required to undertake missions closer to home. A solution was quickly instigated under which two new classes of smaller submarines were designed, the UB and UC classes, the former to operate principally in the North Sea and coastal regions and the latter designed specifically as minelayers.

The great advantage of this policy was the dramatic cut in the build time. Initially, the UBIs at 125-tonne/123-ton surface displacement were just a quarter of the size of the newest U-boats and could be built in a fifth of the time by having prefabricated sections constructed in Germany and assembled in Belgium. The overall construction time was cut to 80 days for the first of the UB boats, with the first entering service in the late spring of 1915, thereafter to be built in large numbers through three classes to accommodate ongoing improvements and higher specifications. The fact was the UBI series was underpowered, with a 44.7kW/60hp diesel engine turning a single screw.

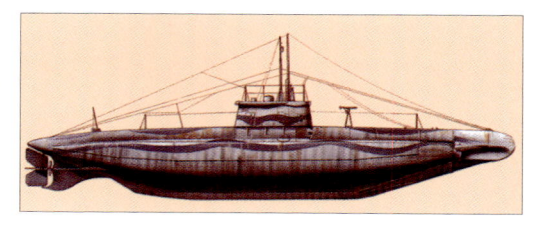

They were slow and difficult to handle, and 17 of the UBI range were built before progressive improvements in almost every area were initiated. UBII was better and was extensively used, but still suffered from the limitation of

LEFT: **The familiar cigar shape of *UB64*, commissioned in 1917 in the UBIII series. It operated in the 5th and 2nd Flotilla respectively and claimed 30 ships sunk (excluding warships) during eight patrols in her 13-month lifespan, prior to being surrendered.**

GERMANY

being underpowered. This was evident from the fact that of the 30 built, only seven survived the war. Of those, *UB29* became famous for two reasons: in March 1916, she torpedoed and sank a French cross-channel steamer, *Sussex*. An international furore ensued when it was learned that among the 80 civilians who died were 25 Americans, although even that did not persuade the US to enter the war. In December the same year, *UB29* became the first boat to be sunk by a depth charge during action in the English Channel.

The final model in this class, UBIII, was a larger improvement on the previous two versions in every respect, but given the risk of the heavily mined areas in which they operated, the mortality was only slightly improved. Even so, of the 95 commissioned, 41 were lost or damaged, more than half of which were mined during coastal patrols.

TOP RIGHT: **A member of the UBIII class, possibly *U127*, which later disappeared, probably mined south of Fair Isle, with the loss of all 34 crew.** ABOVE: **The crew of an unidentified UB-class boat pay considerable interest in a passing *Mittel*-class boat.** BOTTOM: **A meeting at sea – *UB11*, a training boat, pulls alongside *U35*.**

UBI class

Displacement: 125 tonnes/123 tons (surfaced); 140 tonnes/137.8 tons (submerged)
Length: 28.10m/92ft 2in
Beam: 3.15m/10ft 4in
Armament: 2 x 508mm/20in tubes (bow), 4 x torpedoes
Propulsion: 44.7kW/60hp diesel; 89.4kW/120hp electric
Speed: 6.5 knots (surfaced); 5.5 knots (dived)
Complement: 14 men

UBII class

Displacement: 258 tonnes/253.9 tons (surfaced); 287 tonnes/282.5 tons (submerged)
Length: 36.10m/118ft 5in
Beam: 5.80m/19ft
Armament: 4 x 508mm/20in tubes (bow); 1 x 8cm/3.15in deck gun
Propulsion: 179kW/240hp diesel; 164.1kW/220hp electric
Speed: 9.5 knots (surfaced); 5.8 knots (dived)
Complement: 23 men

UBIII class

Displacement: 508 tonnes/500 tons (surfaced); 650 tonnes/639.7 tons (submerged)
Length: 53.30m/174ft 10in
Beam: 5.80m/19ft
Armament: 3 x 508mm/20in tubes (2 x bow, 1 x stern), 16 x torpedoes; 1 x 8cm/3.15in deck gun
Propulsion: 179kW/240hp diesel; 164.1kW/220hp electric
Speed: 13.5 knots (surfaced); 7.8 knots (dived)
Complement: 34 men

DIRECTORY OF SUBMARINES: 1900-45

LEFT: **The *UCI* coastal minelayers, which progressed through three classes, with modifications at each stage and for which 105 boats in total were either commissioned or being built when the war ended. The tally of Allied ships sunk through the mines that they laid was a horrendous total.**
ABOVE: **A profile of a UC-class boat.**

UC class (Minelayers)

Built with similar urgency to the UB boats, this class was a mining specialist destined largely for coastal work. The same problems also occurred with the UC boats in that the first in production were substantially underpowered, with the result that only 15 of the first series, UCI, were completed before UCII boats went into production in June 1915, with an order for round-the-clock manufacture in five shipyards.

A staggering 63 boats of the improved version were commissioned between June 1916 and January 1917 and with hurried training largely carried out on the older boats, the UCIIs took the brunt of the effort in this vital arena. From a German perspective, the UC crews made a courageous contribution.

Minelaying activities around the British Isles and the Mediterranean proved to be one of the most hazardous of all the diverse operations of German submariners. Of the 15 boats in the first class, only one survived to be surrendered in 1918. At least five fell victim to either their own mines or others laid by their own side.

In class II, the toll was equally horrific. Of the 63 UCIIs built, only 15 survived to complete the act of surrender after the Armistice was signed. This fate befell most of the UCIII version, which was introduced with a more powerful motor, but production came too late for the German war effort, and many were still under construction when the war ended.

LEFT: **A mine taken from the coastal minelayer *UC5*, after the boat was grounded on the infamous Shipwash Shoal in the North Sea. She was scuttled, but the charges failed to explode and she fell into Allied hands.**

UCII

Displacement: 410 tonnes/403.5 tons (surfaced); 485 tonnes/477.3 tons (submerged)
Length: 39.47m/129ft 6in
Beam: 5.40m/17ft 9in
Armament: 3 x 508mm/20in tubes (2 x bow, 1 x stern), 16 x torpedoes; 1 x 8.8cm/3.46in deck gun; 18 x mines
Propulsion: 372.8kW/500hp diesel; 313.2kW/420hp electric
Speed: 11.6 knots (surfaced); 7 knots (dived)
Complement: 14 men

400

U151 class

The story of the appearance of a septet of giant and lethal U-cruisers that began to cause havoc among Allied shipping in late 1917 had its beginnings in what was a strangely peaceful mode in June 1916. It was in that month that Britain, and the Americans for that matter, were surprised by the arrival on the other side of the Atlantic of what was heralded as a civilian submarine, a 1,524-tonne/1,500-ton unarmed cargo-carrying boat christened *Deutschland*. The idea was that huge boats would transport cargoes across to the United States and return with much needed raw materials that were in short supply as a result of the British blockade of Germany.

The Americans were happy to accept such arrangements, and *Deutschland* completed the crossing safely and steamed untroubled into Baltimore, Maryland, in July, and unloaded her cargo. She returned unhindered in August, packed with much-needed supplies.

Encouraged, the Germans sent her on a second trip to New London, Connecticut. However, this voyage was less profitable, as the Americans were beginning to get agitated over Germany's application of unrestricted warfare. Consequently, the cargo-carrying mode was abandoned, and *Deutschland* and the rest of her class (*U151–U157*) were promptly converted into attack boats, each manned by 56 submariners and a prize crew of 21.

Outfitted during the summer of 1917, they were rushed into service to become much-feared raiders, literally cruising around the Atlantic for several months at a time. They each carried a relatively light load of 16 torpedoes, given the time they were on patrol, and relied heavily on deck artillery – 15cm/5.9in and 8.8cm/3.46in guns – for surface attacks. They were pointedly put under the command of some of Germany's most experienced and famous U-boat skippers.

Even so, these giants of the deep were difficult to manoeuvre and a nightmare for crews during heavy weather, when they rolled and tossed in a gruesome, uncomfortable manner. In spite of this, the boats scored considerable successes. *Deutschland*, recommissioned as *U155*, stayed out for 105 days on her first patrol, covering almost 16,093km/10,000 miles, sank 19 ships and shelled targets ashore on the Azores. *U151* was notably active along the coastline of America during an eventful 13 week cruise, laying mines and sinking 23 ships. Overall, the six cruisers sank 174 ships for a total of 366,793 tonnes/361,000 tons.

TOP: *U151* was the lead boat in a class of armed merchant cruisers that bore her name, of which seven – including the famous *Deutschland* – were designed and built as large commercial submarines carrying materials to and from locations otherwise denied to German surface ships because of Allied submarine operations. All seven boats were converted to cruisers after the United States entered the war in 1917. ABOVE: A glimpse inside *Deutschland*, or *U155*, as she later became known.

LEFT: The engine room of one of the U-cruisers/merchant boats built early in 1916 and which created much interest when surrendered to the Allies at the end of the war.

U151 class

Displacement: 1,488 tonnes/1,464.5 tons (surfaced); 1,845 tonnes/1,815.9 tons (submerged)
Length: 64.9m/212ft 11in
Beam: 8.93m/29ft 4in
Armament: 2 x 508mm/20in tubes (bow); 20 x torpedoes; 2 x 15cm/5.9in guns
Propulsion: 2 x 298.3kW/400hp diesel engines; 298.3kW/400hp electric motors
Speed: 12.4 knots (surfaced); 5.2 knots (dived)
Complement: 56 men, plus 21 prize crew

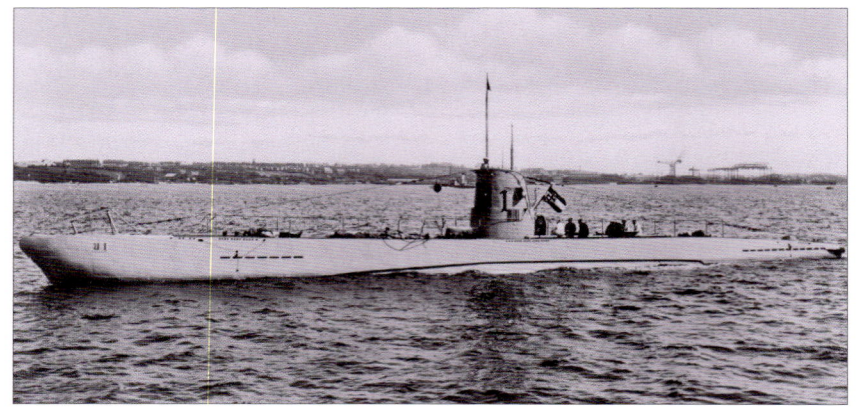

LEFT: *U1*, pristine leader of a brand new breed of U-boats built under the Nazi emblem and commencing with the IIA class. Commissioned in 1935, she lasted only six months into the war before she was lost with all 24 hands, probably to a mine in the North Sea.
BELOW: A bird's-eye view of the tower for surface operations.

U classes (1939) Types IIA, B, C and D

The Treaty of Versailles at the end of World War I saw the U-boat force decimated as the Allied nations took possession of the best of the surrendered submarines to plunder the technology, and destroyed the rest. Germany was also barred from building or possessing any submarines in the tiny navy she was allowed to retain. Even so, the vast storehouse of scientific and engineering acquired during those years could not simply be wiped away. Indeed, when the time came, it would form the backbone of the resurrection of what would become the greatest submarine force the world had seen, bar none.

In the meantime, German submarine crews secretly trained in Russia and Spain and within their own country under the guise of anti-submarine warfare exercises, which were allowed. Nor was Germany prevented from continuing research into submarine development, and by the early 1930s, observers were reporting that a considerable team of scientists and engineers were employed on numerous projects that would prepare the way for the revival of the nation's submarine fleet. Indeed, it was a vital aspect of Hitler's plans when he announced that Germany would no longer be bound by the Versailles Treaty and began to re-arm.

With no navy to speak of, submarines immediately became a crucial element in the Nazi re-armament, and all the pre-planning that had taken place in earlier years now blossomed into reality at an incredible pace. Shipyards across the nation swung into operation, building rapidly during 1934–35, with the first U-boat commissioned on June 29, 1935. This was the date that marked the arrival of the new *U1*, the lead boat of the Type IIA, whose eventful fate was to be lost with all hands, probably due to hitting a mine, in the North Sea on April 6, 1940. Five more boats came in the first wave of the new U-boats, before they were upgraded in size through three additional types, with 20 boats in IIB, 8 in IIC and 16 of IID. In the final reckoning, quite a number of this type survived World War II; however, the fate of a greater number was settled by mines and British ships in the North Sea.

LEFT: The distinctive emblem, displayed here on the tower of *U9*, originally lead boat of the 1st Flotilla, from which position she sank seven Allied merchantmen and two warships before she herself went down in the Black Sea under a hail of bombs from a Soviet aircraft.

U1, Type IIA

Displacement: 240 tonnes/236.2 tons (surfaced); 374.9 tonnes/369 tons (submerged)
Length: 40.90m/134ft 2in
Beam: 3.83m/12ft 7in
Armament: 3 x tubes (2 x bow, 1 x stern), 5 x torpedoes
Propulsion: 522kW/700hp diesel; 233.7kW/300hp electric
Speed: 13 knots (surfaced); 6.9 knots (dived)
Complement: 22–24 men

GERMANY

U-VIIA, B and C

This is the boat that through its three versions became the principal enemy of the Allies for much of the war, especially when operating in wolf-packs. The ocean-going 670-tonne/659-ton Type VIIA, which arrived with *U27* in 1936, was developed from the Finnish Vetehinen design. An improved version came on stream in 1939. These were very efficient machines, agile and popular with their crews. The second version could carry 11 torpedoes or 22 mines, as well as a very effective 8.8cm/3.46in deck gun.

By 1940, the Type VIIC, which became one of the great assets of the German fleet, had overtaken this with more than 600 being built from 1941, beginning with *U69*. Her range was limited to around 10,461km/6,500 miles, but the collapse of France in June 1940 gave the Nazis access to the Atlantic ports, thus providing a haven for 12 U-boat flotillas subsequently to be based in Brest, La Rochelle, La Pallice, St Nazaire, Lorient and Bordeaux, providing access to British waters and the open Atlantic.

A number of the final batch of the VIICs were fitted with the snorkel and another, *U96*, became famous as the U-boat featured in the film *Das Boot*, although the boat was actually sunk by American bombers in Wilhelmshaven in 1945.

The material for the movie resulted from an excursion by Lothar-Günther Buchheim, who was ordered aboard as a war correspondent and artist for propaganda purposes. He took more than 5,000 photographs that survived the war, and his experiences resulted in a best-selling novel.

TOP: **One of Germany's VIIA boats, a new fast attack boat design of which ten were built in the late 1930s. Further improvements in range and firepower were added to the Type VIIB and Type VIIC.** ABOVE: *U251*, **one of the Type VIIC boats that were produced in great numbers from 1941 and became the workhorses of the German U-boat fleet.** BELOW LEFT: **The Type VIIB was given greater fuel-carrying capacity by the addition of external saddle tanks, thus providing a considerable increase in range.**

U-VIIC

Displacement: 755 tonnes/743.1 tons (surfaced); 857 tonnes/843.5 tons (submerged)
Length: 67.10m/220ft 2in
Beam: 6.20m/20ft 4in
Armament: 5 x 533mm/21in tubes (4 x bow, 1 x stern), 14 x torpedoes or 26 mines; 8.8cm/3.46in deck gun
Propulsion: 2,386.2kW/3,200hp diesel; 559.3kW/750hp electric
Speed: 17.8 knots (surfaced); 7.5 knots (dived)
Complement: 44–50 men

403

U-IX

Another major development emanating from the 1935–36 period was the introduction of Type IX, an ocean-going submarine with a range of 19,312km/12,000 miles that could travel, when the time came, well into American waters. With 23 torpedoes on board, these boats carried formidable firepower. They were produced in three versions, and the second subtype, IXB, became the most successful type in U-boat history, with some boats accounting for more than 101,605 tonnes/100,000 tons of shipping. The total losses attributed to IXB amounted to 282 ships, displacing 1,551,006 tonnes/1,526,510 tons.

It was also an IXB boat, *U123*, that led the attack in US waters in early 1942 known as Operation Drumbeat, in which five boats sank nine ships in raids along the east coast of America. The marauding boats remained in the area for almost a month and were kept supplied with fuel by a U-boat tanker circling off the coast near Bermuda, an innovation that in this instance extended their patrol for an incredible eight weeks.

But even as these huge campaigns and wolf-pack operations reached their peak in 1943 – a period known among the U-boat men as "The Happy Time" – new scientific developments and sophisticated anti-submarine tactics by the British were already beginning to deliver the required results. This was especially effective in curtailing the operations of IX types, because they took far longer to replace. With mortality rates rising among U-boats of all types, production had to be stepped up to almost impossible levels to keep pace with losses.

Two areas where the British were scoring the most significant results were in the greater protection of convoys, which involved not only surface ships and submarines, but also aircraft equipped with the latest tracking devices. One of the most dramatic examples occurred in May 1943, when a wolf-pack of 12 U-boats attacked a convoy and lost three quarters of their number. The realization began to dawn that the days of such stunning victories against the convoys were coming to an end and, at the very least, would require a significant overhaul of tactics.

One of the Kriegsmarine's attempts to resolve the problem was the order that the IX boats should be fitted with more anti-aircraft guns to attack incoming aircraft, but the RAF simply introduced their own avoidance tactics of staying out of range until the U-boat was about to dive, thus stowing the guns, and then came in for the attack. The switch in operational tactics by the British brought some stunning results, notably in April and July 1943, when 109 U-boats were lost. Coinciding with declining success at sea, U-boat shipyards and pens were now being successfully and regularly bombed by the Allies. It was a major turning point in the fortunes of the German U-boat campaign, and one that resulted in Hitler's intervention, demanding new and better boats and defences. After all, according to his theory, the war should already have been won. As it was, only one IX boat survived the war.

ABOVE: **Under attack: a Type IX, designed as a long-range ocean-going boat, with five external torpedo containers and space for ten additional torpedoes. As mine-layers, they could carry 44 TMA or 66 TMB mines.** INSET: **A profile of *U123*, Type IXB, the most successful of the IX types, with each boat averaging over 101,605 tonnes/100,000 tons of shipping sunk.**

LEFT: **To counter the Allied radar threat, the Germans perfected a snorkel, enabling a submarine to run its diesel engines and recharge its batteries while operating just below the surface.**

U-IX

Displacement: 1,034.40 tonnes/1,018.1 tons (surfaced); 1,160 tonnes/1,141.7 tons (submerged)
Length: 76.50m/251ft
Beam: 6.70m/22ft
Armament: 6 x 533mm/21in tubes (4 x bow, 2 x stern), 22 x torpedoes or 44 mines; 10.5cm/4.13in (45 calibres) deck gun
Propulsion: 3,281.1kW/4,400hp diesel; 745.7kW/1,000hp electric
Speed: 18.5 knots (surfaced); 7.5 knots (dived)
Complement: 48–56 men

LEFT: *U441*, formerly a VIIC boat rebuilt as *U-Flak1* in 1943, the first of three U-Flak boats, was instantly recognizable by the much larger bridge which accommodated an additional gun platform ahead of the conning tower. BELOW: The Flak boat concept was deemed a failure, and instead the VIIC boats were fitted with new anti-aircraft guns.

U-Flak boats

This most deadly of contraptions emerged in the spring of 1943, when Germany realized that losses of their submarines in the fiery hell of the Bay of Biscay to Allied aircraft was reaching hugely damaging proportions. The boats were being picked off at an alarming rate as they travelled in and out of the U-boat bases of St. Nazaire, Lorient, Brest and Bordeaux. The region had become commonly known as the Valley of Death among U-boat submariners, and the statistics pinpointing their losses in that area show why they were getting exceedingly worried. More than ten per cent of the entire U-boat losses, or 28 boats, had been sustained in the Bay of Biscay in one year alone, and by the end of the war that total had risen to 72.

After much discussion, the Kriegsmarine came up with what they hoped would be a solution, converting a number of their superb VIIC boats into what amounted to floating flak platforms that could deliver massive firepower against incoming aircraft. Seven boats in all were earmarked for conversion, although only three were completed before the project was called off. They were fitted with two rapid-fire four-barrelled cannon, one placed forward of the conning tower with a shield to protect

RIGHT: **A U-boat under attack from the air, ever more common as the RAF extended its anti-submarine operations.**

the gun crew and another located behind the bridge. A further upgrade was to add two heavy machine guns mounted on the bridge. With the additional personnel required for manning the guns and as ammunition handlers, the crew was increased in number from 48 to 69.

Towards the end of May, *U441*, operating under her new name of *U-Flak1*, moved out of Brest to take up her position. Within two days of operations, however, the British realized what was happening and an RAF Sunderland flying boat came over and sent a volley of depth charges that badly damaged the flak boat. Unfortunately, the Sunderland also crashed moments later. *U-Flak1* made an undignified retreat to base but, undaunted, she was hastily repaired and returned to her station in July only to come under almost immediate attack in a pincer movement by three Beaumont aircraft of 248 Squadron, RAF. The boat was again heavily blasted topside, killing ten crew and wounding another 13. The commander had to risk diving with damage to escape total obliteration.

She made it safely back to Brest, but the Kriegsmarine did not give up and ordered three more of the converted flak boats to take up position as the losses in the bay continued to mount. By the middle of August, *U256*, *U271* and *U953* were sent out, but only completed one more patrol before the whole flak-boat concept was abandoned. Instead, the VIIC submarines were fitted with new anti-aircraft guns, and all the flak boats were restored to their former state.

U-Flak1

Displacement: 755 tonnes/743 tons (surfaced); 857 tonnes/843.5 tons (submerged)
Length: 67.10m/220ft 2in
Beam: 6.20m/20ft 4in
Armament: 2 x 2.2cm/0.87in 38/43U four-barrelled cannon; 1 x 3.7cm/1.46in automatic-firing cannon, 2 x MG 42 machine-guns, 8.8cm/3.46in rockets
Propulsion: 2,386.3kW/3,200hp diesel; 559.3kW/750hp electric
Speed: 17.8 knots (surfaced); 7.5 knots (dived)
Complement: 69 men

LEFT: **A sad end for a brilliant boat which was a generation ahead of its time. This is one of the many scuttled or sunk at the time of Germany's surrender and is apparently being recovered. In the years ahead, they were taken apart by the Allies, and the technology purloined.**

XXI

Ironically, Germany already possessed and was developing technology that might well have won them the war at sea, and certainly the Battle of the Atlantic had it been introduced earlier. New engines were being built, such as the Walther propulsion system that attracted so much attention among the Allies. However, the new star of the show would undoubtedly have been the brand new XXI, a deep-diving combat submarine that had enormous potential, as demonstrated after the war when it became the model for the first nuclear boats. The principal advantages were the super-streamlining of the hull, the snorkel and the huge battery capacity for underwater speed and endurance.

In fact some of the technology had been available since the mid-1930s. The Dutch had already produced snorkel-equipped boats, which fell into both British and German hands after the Blitzkrieg. At the time, neither navy saw any value in them. The thinking among Germany's submarine hierarchy was that U-boats performed better and were safer on the surface after dark, and in the first few years of the war this belief was confirmed. As noted above, the greater use of aircraft combined with radar, in which the British were well ahead in anti-submarine warfare, totally altered this conception. There is no doubt the Germans underestimated the British ASW capability, and in the event, daytime surface running became suicidal.

The solution might have been resolved by Dr Helmut Walther's propulsion system that would create the "true submarine" capable using hydrogen peroxide to power a boat that could operate submerged for a greater period of time, but the project had been shelved through cost and shortage of materials. However, he did resurrect the snorkel idea for modern application, and boats were converted in 1943–44. This permitted them to operate slightly submerged to take in fresh air for the diesels and remove engine exhaust. From there, the snorkel was to be used for a totally new boat, the XXI, with extra batteries in place of Walther's original idea of hydrogen peroxide. Now the Germans had the technology to meet the British counter-measures. It would arrive in the shape of the revolutionary new boat, the XXI ocean-going submarine, and the smaller XXIII coastal version.

The XXI would have electric power three times greater than the VIIC, the recharging process was also considerably shorter, and safer, and a new hydraulic torpedo reload system meant that six tubes could be loaded in the time it took to reload one in the VIIC. Furthermore, the facilities for the crew – always a bugbear among submariners – were excellent, with modern amenities such as individual showers and freezers for food storage.

LEFT: **The sleek lines of the tower of an XXI submarine form the background of this scene of formal welcome for a VIP.**

GERMANY

With its streamlined hull and exciting new features for greater submerged speed and overall efficiency, the boat was heralded as the most important development in submarine warfare, as indeed it was. In 1943 when the tide was definitely turning against the U-boats, Hitler demanded the immediate introduction of the XXI. More than 100 were ordered along with 30 XXIIIs.

Dönitz promised the first would be commissioned within six months. It didn't happen, on account of the increased Allied bombing raids over the shipyards, coupled with chronic shortages of raw materials. The Führer's anger was only placated when his trusted architect Albert Speer agreed to take personal control of the project, but by then the Allies were closing in on all fronts and Germany's war at sea was almost played out. Even so, work on the XXI continued to the last. The first one to undergo trials, *U2511*, went to sea just one week before Germany surrendered and performed in an excellent manner. Others lay in the shipyards, ready and waiting for the Allies to share the spoils – and to contemplate their good fortune that the XXI did not arrive earlier.

TOP: **Another boat before its time, a Type XVII with the Walther turbine. This was an experimental research boat, one of which was transported to the United States, the technology dissected and the boat then used for trials by the US Navy.** ABOVE: **A profile of XXI.** BELOW: **A profile of the Type XXIII, *U2326*, which subsequently became the British submarine *N35*. She sank after a collision in Toulon harbour in 1946.**

ABOVE: Commissioned as *U2367* in March 1945, this Type XXIII sank before seeing service, after a collision near Schleimünde. She was raised in 1956 and incorporated into the German Federal Navy under the name of *U-Hecht* with pennant number S171, and remained in service for a further 20 years.

XXI

Displacement: 1,595 tonnes/1,569.8 tons (surfaced); 1,789 tonnes/1,760.7 tons (submerged)
Length: 76.50m/251ft
Beam: 8.0m/26ft 3in
Armament: 6 x 533mm/21in tubes (bow), 23 x torpedoes 12 mines; no deck gun
Propulsion: 2,982.8kW/4,000hp diesel; 3281.1kW/4,400hp electric
Speed: 15.6 knots (surfaced); 17.5 knots (dived)
Complement: 60 men

407

KD classes

The Japanese story in terms of submarines prior to 1945 is one of superlatives and extremes, and thus represents a fascinating array of technology. They produced some of the fastest, largest, longest, widest, heaviest and smallest boats, as well as excelling in aircraft-carrying, long-distance and huge armament, often not exceeded until the arrival of the post-war nuclear fleets. In so many areas their fleets, geared to the vastness of the Pacific Ocean, appeared to have the advantage over any of the other major powers.

Yet, for all that, in the final analysis the Japanese submarine campaign of World War II was widely regarded as an abject failure that even some of their most senior commanders recognized as such. Given the diversity of their fleet and the

ABOVE: **The Japanese Type KD1, built in the inter-war years and based on the surrendered German *U139*, it was used as the prototype for larger I boats (KD2–KD7 types) that came in its wake. A large double-hulled submarine, it was intended to operate with the battle fleet.** BELOW LEFT: **The torpedo tubes of the giant KD3A class.**

spectacular opening of their campaign with the raid on Pearl Harbor supported by 30 submarines, intelligence analysts in the West feared the worst as the Nippon shipyards powered ahead with everything from midget to multi-bomber-carrying boats, and from medium attack boats to giant cruisers. There was also a heavy concentration on endurance, enabling more than 60 of their ocean-going types to travel up to 32,187km/ 20,000 miles or 100 days at sea – a statistic unmatched by any other submarine fleet.

Another remarkable achievement was that of the 56 submarines exceeding 3,048 tonnes/3,000 tons operating in World War II, only four were not Japanese. Yet, tactically they often mystified their opponents, and appeared to be acting in a reconnaissance role to find Allied naval task forces in preparation for the big battles, rather than using their firepower in the hit-and-run role or as wolf-packs, which the British and the Germans in particular mastered so effectively with much smaller boats. Size did matter, and the sheer bulk of these giant craft often proved to be their downfall. They were slow to manoeuvre, sluggish to dive and thus became far easier targets.

JAPAN

The final score card told its own story and indicated the role to which their submarines at large were directed. Japanese submarines were credited with sinking a mere 184 merchant ships throughout the war, compared with the 2,800 claimed by the U-boats. Their losses meanwhile were catastrophic, losing almost three-quarters of her entire fleet, a figure matched only by the U-boats as both those nations faced an onslaught resulting from developments in anti-submarine warfare by the British and Americans. It was also a matter of some satisfaction to the Americans that none of the 30 Japanese submarines identified as having participated in the attack on Pearl Harbor actually survived the war.

The KD classes were among the workhorses of the fleet and had an interesting birth – with a prototype built in 1925, based upon *U139*, which came into the possession of the Japanese after World War I. The KD type progressed through various modifications to the KD7 class over a span of 16 years to 1942. By then a milestone was achieved when the KD6 class produced boats capable of the fastest surface speed of any submarine at the time.

The KD type was moderately successful although there was an early loss of *I70*, sunk by USS *Enterprise* off Oahu on December 10, 1941, in the American strike-back following Pearl Harbor. Overall, the KD classes suffered heavy casualties, with the KD7 class losing all ten boats within a year of coming into service.

TOP: *I176* was one of ten Japanese Type KD7 boats produced by 1942 as attack submarines. They had an outstanding endurance of 75 days and differed significantly from earlier types in that all tubes were sited forward. All were lost by 1944. ABOVE: The Type KD4 which were actually smaller than their predecessors of the KD3 class but were said to be unusually agile for Japanese boats and well liked by their crews. BELOW: The stylish KD6A, with the highest surface speed of any submarines upon their arrival in the 1930s, although this record was beaten by later Japanese boats. In spite of their speed, the whole class was wiped out by enemy action.

LEFT: The KD3A were massive submarines whose design was later revised to enable them to carry a second aircraft. The range of these boats was incredible, but because they were so large, they were easily spotted, slow to dive, easy to track and easy to hit. Consequently losses were also extraordinarily high.

KD7 class

Displacement: 1,804 tonnes/1,775.5 tons (surfaced); 2,560.88 tonnes/2,530.4 tons (submerged)
Length: 105.5m/346ft 2in
Beam: 4.57m/15ft
Armament: 6 x 533mm/21in tubes (bow), 12 x torpedoes
Propulsion: 2 x diesel engines, 5,965.6kW/8,000hp; 1,342.3kW/1,800hp electric
Speed: 23 knots (surfaced); 8 knots (dived)
Complement: 86 men

409

LEFT: Another giant, *I14* was an A-class Modified, the latter to take two Aichi M6A1 seaplanes able to carry a torpedo or an 800kg/1,764lb bomb. Again, the boat had an extensive range but was let down by an indifferent performance underwater.

Type A

Only three boats in this class were built, however they are very worthy of mention as a further development of the KD design, but once again much larger even than their forebear, *J3*. The A boats were among the largest built during the war, weighing almost 3,048 tonnes/3,000 tons surfaced and over 4,064 tonnes/4,000 tons submerged.

They were intended as flagship boats with communications systems that allowed them to have command and control of a submarine group, a more formal arrangement of the wolf-pack system.

The A1 design was also used to carry an aircraft, with the hangar pod opening forward of the conning tower, and for easy loading on to the catapult that would shoot the seaplane into the air while at the same time taking advantage of the forward movement of the ship at the point that the aircraft was launched. This development of submarines as aircraft carriers continued through the war, with some spectacular results.

A variation followed with the introduction of the A2 type in 1944 and two substantially larger Modified A2s that carried two seaplane bombers. Once again, however,

A1

Displacement: 2,872.9 tonnes/2,827.5 tons (surfaced); 4,083.5 tonnes/4,019 tons (submerged)
Length: 113.62m/372ft 9in
Beam: 9.54m/31ft 4in
Armament: 6 x 533mm/21in tubes (bow), 18 x torpedoes; 1 x 14cm/5.5in (50 calibre) deck gun; 1 x seaplane
Propulsion: 2 x diesel engines, 9,246.7kW/12,400hp; 1,789.7kW/2,400hp electric
Speed: 23.5 knots (surfaced); 8 knots (dived)
Complement: 114 men

a complicated diving routine and inert manoeuvrability made these boats an easy target, and none of the class survived more than a couple of years.

LEFT: *I30*, one of the 20 boats of the B class, the largest and busiest group of the Japanese submarine force. Although they were efficient machines, only one survived the war. They were fast and had a forward catapult launch arrangement for their seaplane for a rapid take-off. *I30* was an early victim of Allied mines off Singapore in October 1942.

B1

Displacement: 2,543 tonnes/2,502.8 tons (surfaced); 3,596 tonnes/3,539.2 tons (submerged)
Length: 108.66m/356ft 6in
Beam: 9.2m/30ft 2in
Armament: 6 x 533mm/21in tubes (forward), 17 torpedoes; 1 x 14cm/5.5in (50 calibre) deck gun; 1 x seaplane
Propulsion: 2 x diesel engines, 9,246.7kW/12,400hp; 1,491.4kW/2,000hp electric
Speed: 23.5 knots (surfaced); 8 knots (dived)
Complement: 95 men

Type B

A busy general-purpose group and numerically one of the largest of the Japanese classes, the B1, B2 and B3 classes were also among the most successful, sinking almost a third of all the merchant ships claimed by Japan during the war, as well as a lion's share of warships. However, in time, they also suffered badly, with a 95 per cent loss rate.

Not quite a monster of the deep compared with others built around the same time, these boats were relatively fast, quicker to react and capable of an impressive range of around 24,140km/15,000 miles at 16 knots. They also had a seaplane tucked away for catapult launching, but on this class the aircraft was aft-mounted. Later in the war, some of the aircraft were removed to provide space for more effective deck armaments, and in early 1945 two of the B3s – *I56* and *I58* – were converted to carry four Kaiten human torpedoes for special operations.

The B boats recorded a number of high profile successes. Of particular note was an action by *I19* in September 1942 when a salvo of six torpedoes sank two American warships and damaged another. She fired the salvo at the aircraft carrier USS *Wasp*. Two struck the giant ship forward and hit the fuel storage tanks, which exploded upon impact. The rest of the torpedoes sallied forth for a further 3,200m/3,500yd into the midst of another US carrier group, this time sinking a destroyer with one shot and causing sufficient damage to the battleship *North Carolina* for her to be withdrawn for major repairs.

The most infamous of the B boat attacks, however, came in early November 1942, when a number of US warships were limping away from the first naval battle of the Guadalcanal campaign. Among them was the light cruiser USS *Juneau* that had been torpedoed on her port side near the forward fire room. The shock wave from the explosion buckled the deck, shattered the fire control computers, and knocked out power. On November 12, however, the wounded American ships were being shadowed by the B type submarine *I26*. At 11:01 hours, the submarine fired a three-torpedo salvo at the cruiser *San Francisco*. None hit that target, but one passed beyond and struck *Juneau* close to her previous damage. The magazine exploded and blew the cruiser in two. She sank within minutes, although 115 of *Juneau*'s crew survived the explosion. However, because of uncertainty about the number of Japanese ships in the area, rescue efforts did not begin for several days.

Exposure, exhaustion and shark attacks whittled down the survivors, and only ten men were subsequently rescued from the water eight days after the sinking. The casualties included five members of one family, now written into US naval history as the Tragedy of the Sullivan Brothers. Many memorials have since honoured the brothers and caused the US Navy to review its policy of allowing family members to serve together at sea.

Thereafter, the fortunes of the B boats began to fade as the US Navy hunted them down. Between August and November 1943, 15 were sunk and others went in early 1944. By the end of the war, there was only one survivor of the B-type boats.

Type C

The Japanese built a large number of midget submarines between 1936–38, and the C boats, originating from the Type KD6 design, were among the classes capable of carrying them. They were active in that role from the outset, delivering five midgets to participate in the attack on Pearl Harbor. Only one of the midget-carrying boats actually entered the harbour, and that was promptly sunk after she had fired her two torpedoes, which missed their target.

Numerous attacks followed, and in many instances the success rate was less than encouraging for the Japanese Navy. At the end of May 1942, for example, *I16*, *I18* and *I20* spearheaded an attack in which midgets were unloaded for an attack on a British base at Diego Suarez, Madagascar. Only two of the three midgets made it to the attack zone, and torpedoes from one of them hit both of their targets, damaging the battleship HMS *Ramillies* and sinking a tanker. However, in the return fire, both midgets were sunk, and the crews were killed as they attempted to escape to shore. Later that month, five midgets were launched in an attack on Sydney Harbour but failed to score a hit, and all were lost. A similar result came when using midgets despatched from *I16*, *I20*, and *I24* on November 7, 1942, at Guadalcanal. The net result was all five midgets lost in return for damage to one US destroyer.

None of the midget-carrying C1 Type boats survived the war, most falling victim to US warships.

ABOVE: *I16* was one the key players in the transportation of midget craft into attack zones, including Pearl Harbor, and was among the most successful of all the large Japanese submarines in conventional battle. With *I19*, she sank the carrier USS *Wasp* and the destroyer *O'Brien*. *I16* was herself lost in 1944.

ABOVE: HMS *Ramillies* was damaged by torpedoes from midget submarines carried by the Japanese submarine *I16* during the bombardment by British warships of Diego Suarez, Madagascar, in May 1942.

C1 Type

Displacement: 2,513 tonnes/2,473.3 tons (surfaced); 3,540 tonnes/3,484.1 tons (submerged)
Length: 117.5m/385ft 6in
Beam: 9.44m/31ft
Armament: 8 x 533mm/21in tubes (forward), 20 x torpedoes; 1 x 14cm/5.5in (50 calibre) deck gun
Propulsion: 2 x diesel engines, 9,246.7kW/12,400hp; 1,491.4kW/2,000hp electric
Speed: 23.5 knots (surfaced); 8 knots (dived)
Complement: 102 men

Type J

LEFT: *I3*, one of the J1 type built in the 1920s, was already tired by the time of their entry into the war, although the class had been fitted with German-supplied diesel engines which provided a higher degree of reliability but no great speed. Consequently, after early battles, they were converted into supply boats, but none survived the conflict. ABOVE: A profile of the J3 boat. Altogether more reliable, these were the largest submarines built by the Japanese prior to the war. Two boats, *I7* and *I8*, were intended as squadron flagships.

The J boats, produced through three classes – J1, J2 and J3 – had a heritage dating back to *U139*, and subsequently the prototype of the KD classes, with one big difference – they were much larger. Although the first were launched in the mid-1920s, they were still active in World War II, as can be noted by the naming/numbering system adopted in the same style as U-boats, and the J types were all early numbers. They also represented an early example of the Japanese penchant for monsters of *junsen*, or cruiser, boats that could turn their hand to a number of disciplines.

Even the earliest of the boats had substantial endurance of around 65–70 days and around 40,234km/ 25,000 miles, although they were inevitably very slow when dived. The diesel engines came from Germany, as did a number of technicians and scientists hired by the Japanese Navy to bring their World War I expertise into their new breed of submarines.

Although deployed in a combat role at the start of World War II, the older boats were converted to cargo vessels and were especially used in the latter stages to ferry supplies to starving Japanese troops in far-flung theatres. Their guns were removed to provide accommodation for a barge used to shift their load to the hungry multitudes ashore.

The earliest of the boats, *I1*, became one such carrier but went into history for a totally different reason. While on a supply run to Guadalcanal, she was set upon by a pair of New Zealand frigates and sank less than a mile offshore. The escaping crew managed to scramble to safety with some of the boat's logs and codes, but left behind the past and future codes. However, the boat did not go under. Her bow was protruding above the water, and repeated attempts by Japanese ships to blow her out of the water failed. The Americans arrived on the scene and managed to salvage a vast hoard of codes and charts, amounting to over 150,000 pages. It provided the intelligence for the American Navy to carry out a series of raids that sent more Japanese submarines to the bottom.

Only two of the last class, J3, were built, utilizing more of the design features of the latest KD types during construction in 1938. They were also the largest submarines completed by Japan before the war, and intended as squadron flagships.

Both carried a seaplane, which were known to have completed intelligence sorties over Pearl Harbor 11 days after the Japanese attack. The Americans sank the two submarines in 1944 and 1945 and indeed none of the J class survived the war.

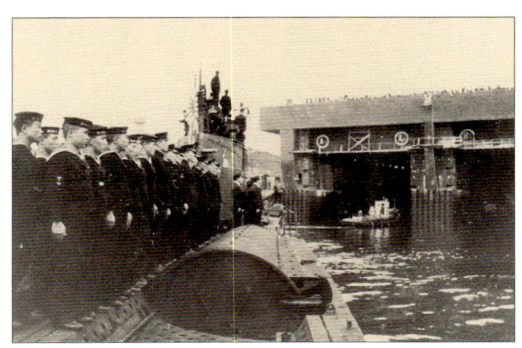

LEFT: A ceremonial line-up: the J3-class boat *I8* enters German-occupied Brest harbour in 1943. She was later converted to carry the Kaiten human torpedoes, and was sunk off Okinawa in March 1945 by two US destroyers.

J3 class

Displacement: 2,484 tonnes/2,444.8 tons (surfaced); 3,526 tonnes/3470.3 tons (submerged)
Length: 109m/357ft 7in
Beam: 9m/29ft 6in
Armament: 6 x 533mm/21in tubes (bow), 21 x torpedoes; 1 x 14cm/5.5in (50 calibre) deck gun; 1 x seaplane
Propulsion: 2 x diesel engines, 8,351.8kW/ 11,200hp; 2,088kW/2,800hp electric
Speed: 23 knots (surfaced); 8 knots (dived)
Complement: 102 men

JAPAN

Type Sen Taka

The Sen Taka I200-class submarine took its name from an abbreviation of the Japanese words for "submarine" and "fast", and it certainly lived up to that christening. It was the only World War II submarine that was easily a match for the German U-boat XXI and was superior to it in the three key areas of power, speed and weaponry.

The Sen Taka stood out among the Japanese boats, which had something of a reputation for slow manoeuvrability and diving. The two 2,051kW/2,750hp

BELOW: A profile of the medium-sized Sen Taka I201 class, the only World War II boat comparable with the German ground-breaking Type XXI, with a streamlined double hull. She was faster submerged than on the surface, and had a snorkel fitted that allowed underwater recharging. Only three were built before Japan's surrender, and none saw service.

engines and streamlined welded hulls provided around 17 knots on the surface, but even more impressive was the coupling with heavy-duty battery cells supplying an impressive 3,728kW/5,000hp electric motor capable of achieving 20 knots – double the speed achieved by contemporary American designs. They were equipped with a snorkel, which allowed for underwater diesel operation while recharging batteries.

Eight boats were laid down, but only three were completed before the end of the war, and the commissioning came too late to see any operational activity. The submarines were designed for mass production, which is why the incoming Americans made sure they kept the Sen Taka secrets to themselves. They took possession of two of the boats and were among the convoy of four Japanese

ABOVE: One of the Sen Taka Sho type submarines, unusually small for the Japanese and designed for fast reaction in the defence of coastal regions. Two dozen boats of this type were planned, the later models with snorkels, but only ten were completed before the war's end, and none became operational.

submarines, including two Sen Tokus, which were sailed to Hawaii for inspection by American engineers and designers. Once the inspection was complete, the boats were taken out to deep water near Oahu, torpedoed and sunk by the US submarine *Cabezon* on May 31, 1946, thwarting demands by the Russians to be allowed to examine the boats.

Sen Taka class

Displacement: 1,270 tonnes/1,249.9 tons (surfaced); 1,427 tonnes/1,404.5 tons (submerged)
Length: 79m/259ft 2in
Beam: 5.8m/19ft
Armament: 4 x 533mm/21in tubes (forward), 10 x torpedoes; 2 x 25mm/0.98in machine-guns
Propulsion: 2 x diesel engines, 2,050.7kW/ 2,750hp; 3,728.5kW/5,000hp electric
Speed: 16 knots (surfaced); 19 knots (dived)
Complement: 31 men

Type Sen Toku

LEFT: A giant, *I402* was one of three Sen Toku boats that were more than 50 per cent larger than the biggest American submarine of that era and with almost twice the range. The three mono-winged aircraft carried by these boats could carry one aerial torpedo or a bomb.

ABOVE: The open door of the Sen Toku aircraft pod.

These huge submarines are really a postscript to World War II in that only three of a projected 16 were built before the war ended, and none saw any action. However, they must be noted for their sheer size, power and potential. At the time, they were the largest submarines ever built anywhere in the world, and more than half as big again as the largest American boat of that era, USS *Argonaut*. They were equipped with a snorkel and the latest radar and also had an incredible range of 59,546km/ 37,000 miles, almost twice that of the American giant, and were specifically designed to bomb the Panama Canal and west coast American cities. However, there were other major differences between the American and Japanese boats, mainly in the hidden added extra that the Japanese had included that, given any further extension of the war, might well have had dire consequences.

As well as a formidable torpedo load, each of the submarines, numbered *I400*, *I401* and *I402*, was equipped to carry three very efficient mono-winged bombers. They were the collapsible Aichi M6A1 Seiran floatplanes that could be stowed in a 36.6m/120ft hangar that would be opened forward to link to the catapult. They could be unpacked, armed and prepared for launch in 45 minutes. The aircraft payload was either one aerial torpedo or an 800kg/1,764lb bomb and claimed a range of up to 1,158km/625 nautical miles and a top speed of 475kph/ 295mph. The submarine carried enough stock for up to 20 flying missions.

Meanwhile, the submarines carried massive on-board anti-aircraft protection with 11 25mm/0.98in anti-aircraft cannon.

For all that, the Sen Toku came too late. They did not come into service until July 1945, and at the end of the month, the first two – *I400* and *I401* — set out on a mission to launch their aircraft in a joint attack with submarines carrying the Kaiten human torpedoes against an American naval anchorage off Ulithi, scheduled for the third week of August. Hostilities ended before they reached the target area, and the attack force returned to base to hoist the white flag.

Two of the boats were subsequently taken to the United States for a detailed examination and were subsequently scuttled in the Pacific a year later.

RIGHT: Two Sen Toku boats, *I400* and *I401*, were en route to launch their aircraft in kamikaze attacks on the American fleet anchorage at Ulithi on July 26, 1945, when hostilities ceased.

Sen Toku class

Displacement: 5,140 tonnes/5,058.8 tons (surfaced); 6,456 tonnes/6354 tons (submerged)
Length: 121.92m/400ft
Beam: 11.9m/39ft
Armament: 8 x 533mm/21in tubes (forward), 20 x torpedoes; 1 x 14cm/5.5in (50 calibre) deck gun
Propulsion: 4 x diesel engines, 6,338.4kW/ 8,500hp; 1,491.4kW/2,000hp electric
Speed: 18.5 knots (surfaced); 6.5 knots (dived)
Complement: 145 men

JAPAN/FRANCE

LEFT: **The great *Surcouf* was a one-off – the world's largest boat – and her mysterious sinking in World War II gave her an unsurpassed record for the largest loss of life in a single submarine accident.** BELOW: **A view of the boat in all her glory, with the twin gun turret – a powerful design feature.**

Surcouf

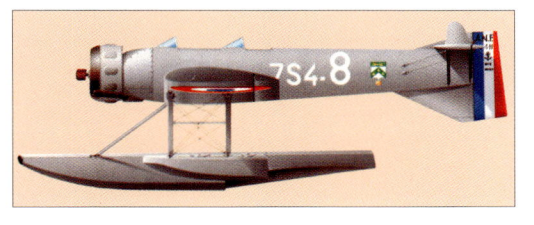

The single boat known as *Surcouf* was literally in a class of her own. Construction dated to 1929, when the French Navy won approval to build what was then the largest and most costly submarine the world had ever seen – and one to which the Japanese would soon pay homage by capping that title. *Surcouf* was commissioned in 1934, there to begin a controversial career and wartime escapades that might have been a plot for a James Bond thriller. She was designed and built as an underwater cruiser to fulfil France's avowed intention of keeping her coastline well defended.

For that mission, the boat carried a hangar for a floatplane, designed primarily for observation. The idea was that the submarine would cruise the coastline unseen, and in the event of being called into action, the giant would rise through the waves and become a warship. She also had the ability to blast the opposition out of the water with no fewer than ten torpedo tubes, and the floatplane was theoretically capable of directing fire for the boat's big guns, up to a range of 24km/15 miles.

There was also a 4.9m/16ft motorboat, and a cargo compartment below was fitted out to hold prisoners. She had a 90-day endurance, and a range of 18,520km/10,000 nautical miles. When the Germans invaded France in 1940, the submarine was in the process of being refitted at Brest, and was ordered to sail immediately even though she had only one engine in operation. Arrangements were made for her and other boats to cross the English Channel to Portsmouth, where, in due course, her commander was called upon to surrender the boat to the British under the terms of Operation Catapult, launched to seize French ships and submarines to prevent them being used against Britain. He refused, and consequently British forces boarded her at Portsmouth, and placed the submarine under the control of the Free French. A fresh crew was mustered, and she began convoy patrol for a while but was then involved in allegations that she was spying for Vichy France, and the British sent two officers to join the boat to keep watch.

The following year, she was used to carry an admiral of the Free French to Canada, and subsequently took on the role of gunboat with other ships to liberate islands off the coast of Newfoundland, helping to remove the Vichy administration. This caused some difficulty with the United States, which had just concluded a deal with the Vichy Government to maintain neutrality in French possessions in the Western Hemisphere. She sailed again amid rumours she was off to liberate islands in the Caribbean. Others stories suggested she was carrying a cargo of French gold.

However, having called at Bermuda on February 12, 1942, the great *Surcouf* was mysteriously lost with all hands.

ABOVE: **The MB 410 and MB 411 were observation aircraft with a single central float and two small stabilizing floats. They were designed to be carried by *Surcouf* and were easily disassembled for stowage.**

Two theories were proposed, suggesting that she had either been attacked by American bombers, who mistook her for a U-boat, or that she had been accidentally rammed by an American freighter.

Surcouf

Displacement: 3,198 tonnes/3,147.5 tons (surfaced); 4,235 tonnes/4,168.1 tons (submerged)
Length: 110m/360ft 11in
Beam: 9.2m/30ft 2in
Armament: 6 x 550mm/21.7in tubes, 14 x torpedoes; 4 x 400mm/15.75in tubes, 8 x torpedoes; 2 x 203mm/8in twin turret guns, 2 x 37mm/1.46in anti-aircraft cannon, 2 x 13.2mm/0.52in anti-aircraft machine-guns; 1 x MB 411 float plane; 284.5 tonnes/280 tons cargo capacity
Propulsion: 5,667.3kW/7,600hp diesel; 2,982.8kW/4,000hp electric
Speed: 18.4 knots (surfaced); 10 knots (dived)
Complement: 118 men

LEFT: **French submarine *Glorieux* from Series II of the Redoutable class**, whose boats were launched between 1928 and 1937, was among the French boats that escaped the Nazi occupation at Toulon on November 27, 1942. She reached Oran to join the Allied cause, surviving the rest of the war before being sold for scrap in 1952.

BELOW: ***Sfax***, on the other hand, remained faithful to Vichy France but was accidentally torpedoed and sunk by *U37* off Cape Juby, Morocco, in December 1940.

Redoutable class

The French produced some extremely attractive submarines in the inter-war years, with sleek lines that sat well on the surface. However, the diversity of boats listed in a dozen classes, including what was then the world's largest submarine, made it difficult to read French policy. Indeed, there seemed to be no precise pattern of development, unlike British policy where an orderly progression was evident, in spite of the latter's financial constraints.

This was partially due to the carryover from World War I in which the 55 French submarines that participated quickly became obsolete. The aftermath saw disagreement between senior naval officers, government figures and international allies as to future requirements. Those who held sway were of the view that the French should concentrate on an armada of surface ships to protect the coastlines, and, where necessary, deliver gunboat diplomacy to their overseas interests in the Far East, Asia and Africa. In consequence, almost three-quarters of French submarines operational at the outbreak of World War II were of designs dating back to the 1920s. Numerically largest of all the classes – and the designated workhorse – was the Redoutable class, whose leader of that name was a 1,422 tonne/1,400-ton submarine known to be a slow diver in emergency situations.

In the event, the scenario confronting French submarines at the onset of World War II and during the early months of the conflict was like no other. There is hardly a story among the nation's 77 boats that prepared for the outbreak of World War II that can be told in the straightforward manner of service, action and fate, from which may be deduced the performance of the boats. Consequently, unlike in World War I when French submarines joined Britain and Australia in the Dardanelles, their impact on the second war bore no comparison.

It was an unholy mess that resulted in great bitterness and the eventual loss of almost 50 per cent of the French submarine fleet, though not necessarily through operational activity at sea. Some boats fell victim to U-boats prior to the French surrender. Next, Winston Churchill announced that the British would sink or impound the French fleet unless the Navy put them out of commission, and eventually carried out that threat against those who did not conform. In a further development in November 1942, fleet commanders at the French naval base of Toulon scuttled their boats to avoid them falling into British or German hands. In the Redoutable class

FRANCE

LEFT: *Casabianca,* a heroic boat that escaped Nazi clutches at Toulon on November 27, 1942, joined the Allies at Algiers, and there performed sterling work in various intelligence roles, especially in delivering agents into hostile territory.
BELOW: Vichy submarine *Poncelet,* scuttled by her crew in December 1940. HMS *Milford* was blockading Gabon and forced *Poncelet* to the surface with depth charges and then shot off the boat's conning tower. The crew was saved.

BELOW: The profile of *Casabianca,* which was a standard *Redoutable*-class design.

of 17 boats, the situation was as follows: eight were scuttled, six were sunk by British destroyers in various locations, one on foreign service was arrested in the Far East and two rejoined the Allies.

There was a famous and mysterious exception to this tragedy. *Casabianca* under the command of Capitaine de Frégate Jean L'Hérminier was among those who took his boat towards the Allies in North Africa.

She was one of the third series of the Redoutable class of boats built and lost under individual type names such as Redoutable, Agosta and L'Espoire dating from 1924. Of the final overall total for the Redoutable series of 31 boats, two were lost before the war and another 23 sunk or scuttled. *Casabianca* had one of the most notable operational records of any French submarine and was the only third series boat to survive the war, operating for the Free French under General de Gaulle's overall command. Commander L'Hérminier risked constant attack as his boat was employed on secret missions delivering agents and saboteurs into Nazi-held Europe and particularly in running supplies and weapons to Corsica for the French resistance. At the same time, he was fully operational as an attack submarine and achieved a number of successes against German shipping. *Casabianca* thus played a key role in the eventual capture of Corsica by the Allies.

RIGHT: *Conquerant,* a Series II Redoutable of the Agosta type, was launched in 1935 and sunk in November 1942 off Dakhla, Morocco, by two American Catalina aircraft.

Redoutable class

Displacement: 1,360 tonnes/1,338.5 tons (surfaced); 2,047 tonnes/2,014.7 tons (submerged)
Length: 92m/301ft 10in
Beam: 8.75m/28ft 8in
Armament: 9 x 550mm/21.7in bow tubes; 2 x 400mm/15.7in stern tubes; 1 x 99mm/3.9in deck gun; 1 x 37mm/1.46in anti-aircraft gun; 1 x 13mm/0.51in anti-aircraft gun
Propulsion: 4,474kW/6,000hp diesel; 1,491.4kW/2,000hp electric
Speed: 17 knots (surfaced); 10 knots (dived)
Complement: 63 men

417

LEFT: The *Dekabrist* was produced by post-Tsarist Russia, but the shipbuilders of the Soviet Russia had to battle with out-dated technology.

Dekabrist

Displacement: 910 tonnes/895.6 tons (surfaced); 1,190 tonnes/1,171.2 tons (submerged)
Length: 76.5m/251ft
Beam: 6.3m/20ft 8in
Armament: 8 x 533mm/21in tubes (6 x bow, 2 x stern), 5 reloads; 1 x 45mm/1.77in anti-aircraft gun, 500 rounds
Propulsion: 820.3kW/1,100hp diesel; 391.5kW/525hp electric
Speed: 15.5 knots (surfaced); 8 knots (dived)
Complement: 53 men

Dekabrist class

Russia had fully embraced the concept of submarine warfare prior to World War I when the Tsar's Navy acquired almost 50 boats, including five American Hollands, eight from Simon Lake and others from Britain, Germany and France. They were based around the Baltic and the Black Sea as a defensive measure, but given the political turmoil within the country, her submarines had little impact on events of that era.

Towards the end of the 1920s, however, the new regime of the USSR once again sought external help in establishing a new submarine fleet, employing many German designers and engineers in their new production programme. The result was the Dekabrist class, which represented the new Soviet Union's first attempt at fully home-grown submarines.

The boats, said to be wholly Soviet creations, went into production in 1927 and were overseen by the Bureau of Submarine design, headed by engineer Boris Malinin, who designed the Bars class in 1916–17. They were the first Russian boats with watertight bulkheads and were designed for long-range attacks on enemy communications. They were constructed with riveted hulls of high-strength steel, with a 45mm/1.77in AA gun aft of the conning tower.

In fact, the Dekabrist class proved to be very useful boats for Soviet purposes – manoeuvrable and quick-diving – but eventually falling foul of poor maintenance routines in post-Tsarist Russia and subsequently in constant need of repair. Furthermore, the technology was a good 10 years behind that of the West, and the boats required extensive modernization as World War II approached, when, in time, they would see service in the Baltic and Black Sea. Later in the war, the British loaned some technology, providing an ASDIC-129 sonar and a new torpedo launching system for one of the boats.

The Dekabrist class led the Soviet Union into serious submarine construction, and they next produced the Leninec class of six minelaying boats, laid down in 1928 and 1930 based on the same hull. In this class, which entered service in 1933, the two stern torpedo tubes were discarded in favour of tubes for 20 mines.

LEFT: Mini-submarines had been left behind by the major seafaring nations. Not so with the Soviets, who produced this small craft in vast numbers.

Malukta class

Displacement: 153 tonnes/150.6 tons (surfaced); 187 tonnes/184 tons (submerged)
Length: 37.10m/121ft 9in
Beam: 4.15m/13ft 7in
Armament: 2 x 457mm/18in tubes, 2 x torpedoes (4 x tubes, 4 x torpedoes on later versions)
Propulsion: 507.1kW/680hp petrol; 186.4kW/250hp electric
Speed: 13 knots (surfaced); 7.4 knots (dived)
Complement: 18 men (30 for the XV version)

Malutka class

The class name Malutka, meaning "baby", was an apt description. Almost 100 were eventually built, and they were designed primarily as coastal submarines on a mass-production basis, intended largely to defend naval bases or, in times of war, to blockade enemy shipping routes and harbours. However, for the USSR, the Malutkas had a distinct advantage in that they were also fully transportable by rail, thus enabling them to be carried towards any theatre of war across the vast Russian terrain to the nearest sea to begin their patrols – or, in some cases, the nearest lake.

A number of the boats were said to have been transported to Lake Ladogo, near Leningrad, for operations. The M class was built in four versions, each following on from the last with improvements, modifications and lengthening.

LEFT: **The Scuka class was a candidate for mass production in Soviet Russia. By the time of World War II the Soviets had a large number to call upon, but the submarines were nowhere near as efficient as the German U-boats and consequently suffered the consequences.**

Scuka class

Displacement: 558 tonnes/549.2 tons (surfaced); 689 tonnes/678.1 tons (submerged)
Length: 57.50m/188ft 8in
Beam: 7.15m/23ft 6in
Armament: 6 x 533mm/21in tubes (4 x bow, 2 x stern), 12 x torpedoes; 2 x 45mm/1.77in deck guns
Propulsion: 894.8kW/1,200hp petrol; 335.6kW/450hp electric
Speed: 12.5 knots (surfaced); 6.5 knots (dived)
Complement: 50 men

Scuka class

This medium-sized submarine became one of the main workhorses of the Soviet fleet during World War II, passing through three versions, with 91 eventually operational. When originally planned, these boats represented the first major USSR programme of attack submarines designed to be "positioned against closed and defended enemy theatres of war" and, in due course, would be assigned for operations with four principal Soviet Navy fleets in the North, the Pacific, the Black Sea and the Baltic. It was in the latter two stations that they were eventually to suffer the heaviest casualties against the Nazis, where almost 70 per cent of their front-line boats were lost. World War II operational records also include confrontations with the Japanese in the Pacific, where their performance was outstanding.

LEFT: **Ironically emanating from German design work and Dutch engineering, the Soviets began producing what they proudly called the Stalinec class from around 1934 and into the war years. Some boats were still operative in the 1950s.**

Stalinec class

Displacement: 829 tonnes/815.9 tons (surfaced); 988 tonnes/972.4 tons (submerged)
Length: 77.80m/225ft 3in
Beam: 9.85m/32ft 4in
Armament: 6 x 533mm/21in tubes (4 x bow, 2 x stern), 12 x torpedoes; 2 x 45mm/1.77in deck guns
Propulsion: 894.8kW/1,200hp petrol; 335.6kW/450hp electric
Speed: 12.5 knots (surfaced); 6.5 knots (dived)
Complement: 50 men

Stalinec class

This boat was one that emerged in the 1930s as a result of direct co-operation between the USSR and Germany – a partnership that the latter nation subsequently came to regret. The boat emerged from a prototype originally built at Karhatena by a Dutch subsidiary using German designers for the Spanish Navy. When the Spanish subsequently cancelled the order, the Soviet Navy was invited to inspect the boat for possible inclusion in their fleet. An agreement was reached whereby plans and drawings for the boat would be purchased by the USSR. Later, a party of Soviet designers and engineers travelled to Bremen and Karhatena to discuss with the German engineers design changes to accommodate Soviet requirements. Thus, the S class was born, utilizing Soviet parts and machinery, built in five Soviet shipyards.

600 class

The build-up of Italian submarines began in earnest in 1925 under Mussolini and included a number of medium to large boats whose quality may well have been hampered by financial constraints in the aftermath of World War I. However, in the early 1930s, the Italians began a substantial programme of construction following an international disarmament conference in London in 1930 that set limits on the size – but not quantity – of boats built by the naval powers.

The conference was called amid international concern about the growth in submarine fleets, which had arisen since a 1921 conference that placed restrictions on the expansion of naval fleets but excluded submarines. Britain, the United States, Japan and France had already been demonstrating to the world some grandiose projects for international operations in the late 1920s. Thus, in 1930, defining limits were set for coastal and oceanic boats, 610 tonnes/600 tons for the former and 2,032 tonnes/2,000 tons for the latter. The Italian Navy took a somewhat pragmatic approach to the new regulations and responded by introducing what became known as the 600 class. This, in effect, set them on course to build a large number of boats of the coastal classification, which were well suited for their principal area of operations in the Mediterranean, under the generic name of the 600 class.

They were introduced progressively in five types, built to a master drawing with some deviations for each under the names Argonauta (after the first boat of the series), Sirena, Perla, Adua and Platino. The result was that by the time of Italy's entry into World War II, Mussolini was able to deploy a diverse range of modern submarines made up of 50 large, 89 medium, two cargo and assorted midget boats, to which further additions came during the war years.

The 600 class, built with remarkable speed by various shipyards across Italy, was at the heart of the nation's submarine force, and undoubtedly the most successful. Furthermore, the stream of boats emerging through this period was competitive and well managed. Unfortunately, the lead member of the group was not among those who participated. When Mussolini declared war on Britain on June 9,

ABOVE: *Argonauta*, one of the most successful Italian submarines, led the way in the pre-war 600 class, which consisted of a series of five types produced progressively under the names of Argonauta, Sirena, Perla, Adua and Platino. In all, 59 submarines were built by various shipyards, and these differed in their minor detail.

1940, the *Argonauta*, under the command of Lt Vittorino Cavicchia Scalamonti, was one of the 55 boats patrolling the Mediterranean.

Her station was to cover the British naval base of Alexandria and Suez where the Royal Navy was already engaged in anti-submarine activity. Eleven days into the patrol, she took a heavy bombardment of depth charges, and the damage included her periscope. She was forced to return to the Italian base at Tobruk, but there were no facilities for such repairs, and she was sent on to Taranto. Thereafter, nothing more was heard of her, and she was presumed lost with all hands.

LEFT: *Nichelio*, one of the Platino types in the 600 series. The 600-class boats were of a very decent and sleek design that evolved and improved through 59 units.

Argonauta Type

Displacement: 656 tonnes/645.6 tons (surfaced); 797 tonnes/784.4 tons (submerged)
Length: 61.5m/201ft 9in
Beam: 5.65m/18ft 6in
Armament: 6 x 533mm/21in tubes; 1 x 102mm/4in deck gun; 2 x 17.2mm/0.68in anti-aircraft guns
Propulsion: 932.1kW/1,250hp diesel; 596.6kW/800hp electric
Speed: 14.5 knots (surfaced); 8.2 knots (dived)
Complement: 36 men

Marconi class

Among the new classes introduced by the Italian Navy in the 1935–40 period, Marconi boats had a good record in seaworthiness and ease of deployment, although later alterations when they were moved to Bordeaux in support of U-boat operations included enlargements that affected their buoyancy to what some naval specialists regarded as dangerously low levels. Even so, Regia Marina Italiana today maintains that they were "surely among the best vessels produced by Italy". One them, the *Leonardo Da Vinci*, was credited with the highest number of sinkings among Italian submarines, second only to U-boats. Infamously among them (from both points of view) was the sinking on March 14, 1943, of the transatlantic liner *Empress of Canada* with 3,000 British soldiers and 500 Italian prisoners of war aboard. The submarine managed to save only one, a doctor named Vittorio Del Vecchio.

The six submarines of the Marconi class operated in the Atlantic and Indian oceans for the majority of the war, sinking an aggregate total of 38 ships with a total of 219,697 tonnes/216,227 tons and damaging another 17 for a total of 118,558 tonnes/116,686 tons. None of them survived the war, five having been lost with all hands in the Atlantic. The sixth, *Torelli*, had an interesting journey towards her final demise. She was captured by the Japanese in Singapore after Italy's surrender in 1943 and was subsequently handed over to Germany's U-boat command, who renamed her

ABOVE: The *Marcello* was the first one of a series of 11 boats of the successful Italian class of the same name, from which the Marconi design emanated. The six submarines of the Marconi class became renowned for "good seaworthiness and easiness of deployment, especially after the reduction in size of the conning tower displayed on the *Marcello*".

U(IT)25. The boat operated with a German/Italian crew until Germany's own surrender, when she was hastily recovered by Japan, again operating with a mixed crew, including some Italians. The Americans subsequently sank her off the Japanese coast near Kobe.

ABOVE: A profile of the *Leonardo da Vinci* from the Marconi class, credited with the highest number of sinkings among Italian submarines. This sink rate was comparable to U-boat performance and was a higher rate than most of the Allied submarine forces.

Marconi class

Displacement: 1,172 tonnes/1,153.5 tons (surfaced); 1,465 tonnes/1,441.9 tons (submerged)
Length: 70.04m/229ft 9in
Beam: 6.82m/22ft 5in
Armament: 8 x 533mm/21in tubes; 4 x 13.2mm/0.52in anti-aircraft guns
Propulsion: 2 x diesel engines, 2,684.5kW/3,600hp; 2 x electric motors, 1,118.6kW/1,500hp
Speed: 18 knots (surfaced); 8 knots (dived)
Complement: 57 men

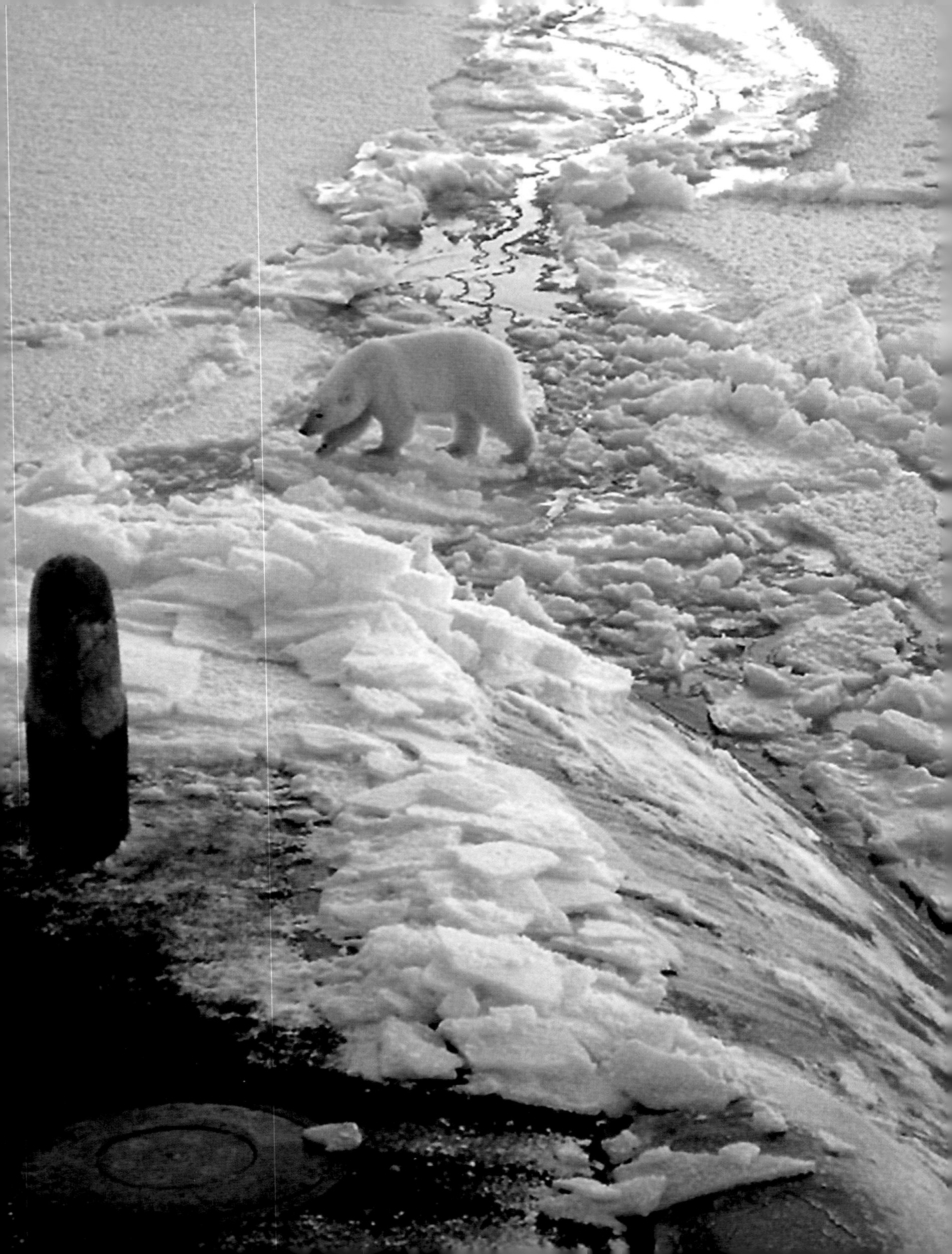

Directory of Submarines

1945 to Date

The defeat of Germany at the end of World War II provided Allied scientists and engineers with access to the Type XXI U-boat and a mass of other material and designs. In 1949, a report by US Naval Intelligence warned that Soviet exploitation of the U-boat technology presented the most potent post-war naval threat to the United States. The Soviets were of the same mind with regard to American intentions. The plain fact was that no warship of the time could effectively detect and track a fast attack submarine like the German Type XXI.

In the US it was USS *Nautilus* that turned the tide when it went to sea propelled by a pressurized water nuclear plant in January 1955. The Soviets developed their own version, beginning a new quest among the two major powers to equip their submarine service with high-speed, nuclear-powered attack submarines. This was soon to be followed by the giant boomers, the ballistic missile carriers that could roam the seas undetected for months. Britain and France launched their own nuclear squadrons, while lesser navies equipped themselves with very effective diesel-electric boats.

LEFT: **By 1983, polar bears were used to nuclear submarines poking their sails through the ice. Here, USS** *Honolulu* **was on a mission to collect scientific data and water samples in 2003.**

LEFT: **USS *Seawolf*, at the beginning of an historic journey in which she would remain submerged for two months, demonstrating that a nuclear-powered submarine could operate completely without support or the need to surface for the length of an average war patrol, a first step towards rapid progression among the major powers.**

Seawolf SSN (Early)

Although *Nautilus* was America's first nuclear-powered submarine, *Seawolf* also had the distinction of being the first SSN in this new era. Although, like *Nautilus*, she was fully armed from the outset, *Seawolf* was essentially an experimental platform whose every detail from performance to crew conditions was to be monitored and analysed so that any discoveries could be dealt with. The build-time was obviously far greater than the production-line efforts of the war years. She was laid down on September 7, 1953, and finally commissioned in March 1957.

Intensive training programmes occupied the crew for almost all of the first year of operations before *Seawolf* went public, steaming across the Atlantic to take part in NATO exercises at a time when the Cold War was already in the deep freeze zone. A number of nuclear firsts were claimed by the Americans during these early stages. Much was made of the fact that *Seawolf* submerged on August 7, 1958, and did not surface again until October 6, having covered 13,780 nautical miles, thus "demonstrating to the world the ability of the nuclear-powered submarine to remain independent of the earth's atmosphere for the period of a normal war patrol".

Thereafter she went through a routine of both independent and fleet operations over the coming years, including a period of service with what the US Navy described as the world's first nuclear task force, consisting of submarines and surface ships equipped with guided missiles.

Seawolf was the only submarine built with a liquid metal nuclear reactor. While the liquid metal (sodium) provided for a more efficient power plant, it also caused several hazards for the ship and crew, including fire potential and highly corrosive effects. After two years of operation, *Seawolf* was converted to a pressurized water reactor because of these concerns.

Her first overhaul and conversion came in 1967, and the following year she was grounded off Maine while conducting sound and weapons systems tests and had to be towed off. No other major incidents were recorded in her 30-year life span, ending her days in the role of what the US Navy described as a "special projects platform", having long ago been overtaken by the vast panoply of nuclear developments that were to come. She was decommissioned in 1987 and stricken from the naval register. She was then stored for ten years before finally being dismantled in the US Navy's Nuclear-Powered Surface Ship and Submarine Recycling Programme.

ABOVE: **President Dwight Eisenhower, the wartime general, pictured inside *Seawolf*, had a special liking for submarines and now "pushed the boat out" to speed up the development of the nuclear era.**

RIGHT: **The portraiture of nuclear submarines has become a fascination for many observers, especially as the whole boat is never visible when on the move. The amount of foam around the boat is the only way of judging its speed and size.**

Seawolf SSN

Displacement: 3,209 tonnes/3,260.5 tons (surfaced); 4,045 tonnes/4,109.9 tons (submerged)
Length: 103m/337ft 11in
Beam: 8.5m/27ft 11in
Armament: 6 x 533mm/21in tubes, 8 x torpedoes
Propulsion: SG2 liquid metal nuclear reactor (later converted)
Speed: 23 knots (surfaced); 19 knots (dived)
Complement: 101 men

Triton SSN

At her commissioning, *Triton* obviously set out to write herself into the history books from the very outset. Having put out to sea on what the US Navy describe as the "shakedown cruise", her maiden voyage on February 15, 1960, she set off submerged for the South Atlantic. She arrived in the middle Atlantic off St Peter and St Paul Rocks on February 24 to commence a history-making voyage. She had remained submerged since leaving the east coast of America, and carried on south towards Cape Horn. She rounded the tip of South America, travelling west into the Pacific, on past the Philippines and the Indonesian archipelago into the Indian Ocean, round the Cape of Good Hope, arriving back off the St Peter and St Paul Rocks on April 10. She had completed the first submerged circumnavigation of the earth in 60 days and 21 hours, although she did break the surface once to transfer a sick sailor to a surface ship off Montevideo on March 5.

If any proof was still needed, the voyage confirmed to the world the great advances that had been achieved in both speed and submerged endurance through nuclear power, not to mention the political dimension in this highly sensitive period. In fact, it was through such developments that the USSR and the United States – as the two key players in the nuclear race – now began the process of playing leapfrog, with each attempting to outdo the other at every turn. Nor was it simply a case of technical achievement. During the voyage, the submarine collected untold oceanographic data, which was not only important at the time but which pointed to the need for further and continual exploration for the future safety of the underwater armadas.

The achievement was recognized with a Presidential Citation for the crew and the award of the Legion of Merit for her commander, Captain Beach. It was no coincidence that international security analysts reported a rising threat as the USSR piled resources into building up their own submarine fleet to "meet and beat" the Americans head on. Consequently, the US Navy made it clear that they needed more nuclear-powered attack submarines with anti-submarine warfare capability. Until that point in time, *Triton* had been a SSNR, which denoted she was part of the US radar picket patrol on the outer rims of the US coastal defences. In 1962, she was converted into an attack submarine to meet the navy's shortfall in numbers and served in that role until 1967. By then, however, new and more modern nuclear boats were arriving and in the pipeline. The escalating costs prompted a thorough review of US naval requirements, and indeed it was quite apparent that a hefty cull of older members of the submarine fleet was required.

Battle planners concluded that it would be utterly useless in modern submarine warfare scenarios to put forward some of the ageing boats in the US fleet. Consequently, *Triton*, along with 60 other vessels, was taken out of service.

TOP: **USS *Triton* began life as one of the nuclear vessels destined to patrol and protect the outer rim of the nation's coastline.** However, she was converted into attack mode during the Cold War, as more submarines were required for what became something of an obsession on both sides – that of the potential for submarine-based warfare. ABOVE LEFT: ***Triton's* hull cylinder, an indication of the massive scale of engineering now involved in submarine manufacture.** ABOVE RIGHT: ***Triton's* internal fit, spectacular at the time but merely a beginning.** INSET: **The patch tradition continues.**

Triton SSN

Displacement: 5,686 tonnes/5,596.2 tons (surfaced); 7,650 tonnes/7,529.2 tons (submerged)
Length: 136m/446ft 2in
Beam: 11.27m/37ft
Armament: 6 x 533mm/21in tubes (4 x forward, 2 x aft)
Propulsion: 2 x S4G nuclear reactors
Speed: 30 knots (surfaced); 27 knots (dived)
Complement: 159 men

LEFT: **Size certainly mattered,** as evidenced by the first major nuclear class of boats anywhere in the world, with its 14 members. USS *Barb* was the fourth, commissioned in 1963 and remaining in business for 26 years. ABOVE: **Taking shape,** the evolving profile of the nuclear boats.

Thresher/Permit-class SSN

The dual name for this class resulted from a disaster that was to befall the *Thresher*, and consequently the mantle passed to *Permit*. *Thresher* was a purpose-built nuclear attack boat to lead in what the Federation of American Scientists describe as "the world's first modern, quiet, deep-diving fast attack submarine". The design integrated such advanced features as a hydro-dynamically shaped hull, a large bow-mounted sonar array, advanced sound-silencing features, and an integrated control/attack centre with the proven S5W reactor plant. In short, the *Thresher/Permit* boats represented a major advance over previous submarine designs, and established the pattern of all successive American attack submarine classes. They were, for example, the first to have hulls constructed of High Yield-80 (HY-80) steel alloy, which allowed operations at substantially greater depths than previous submarines. They were the first submarines to have a large bow-mounted sonar, requiring the installation of torpedo tubes amidships. They were larger than the previous Skipjack class, but with the lighter hull, they were able to use the same nuclear power plant without sacrificing speed. They were designed for prolonged periods submerged, and that certainly proved to be the case. In fact, they were limited only by the amount of food that the boats could carry, and were capable of sustained operation at high speed. The lead boat of the class, *Thresher*, spent the early part of her evaluation year of 1962 testing and participating in the Nuclear Submarine Exercise Programme (Nusubex). This was designed specifically to improve the tactical capabilities of nuclear submarines and anti-submarine warfare training, which was judged to be in need of constant review and overhaul in the face of increasing USSR capability.

She was engaged in operations off Charleston under the observation of the Naval Anti-Submarine Warfare Council before moving on to Florida for further trials. While

RIGHT: **The sheer scale of engineering now becomes apparent** with the first pictorial evidence of the beam width. This photograph shows USS *Plunger* with intrepid submariners atop, beginning a 27-year journey that would be mainly devoted to the perfection of anti-submarine warfare techniques.

426

UNITED STATES

manoeuvring into a berth at Port Canaveral, the submarine was accidentally struck by a tug, damaging one of her ballast tanks. The Electric Boat Company, at Groton, Connecticut, carried out repairs, and *Thresher* then went back to sea for deep-diving exercises. In addition to her 16 officers and 96 enlisted men, 17 civilian technicians remained aboard to record her performance in the company of a surface submarine rescue vessel *Skylark*, which was in constant communication with her during the trials.

Fifteen minutes after reaching her assigned test depth, the submarine communicated with *Skylark* by underwater telephone to report the boat was in trouble, but before the full story could be relayed, the transmission became garbled. Then, the listeners on the surface heard what they would describe as a noise like "air rushing into an air tank" and then nothing. The line went dead. As all hope of re-establishing communications vanished, a rescue group was hurriedly assembled and the submarine rescue ship *ASR-43* recovered items of clothing and debris, which indicated that *Thresher* has suffered a catastrophic failure. This was confirmed by photographs that showed that the submarine had broken up in 2,560m/1,400 fathoms of water, taking all on board to their deaths some 354km/220 miles east of Boston. *Thresher* was officially declared lost in April 1963.

The subsequent investigation into the disaster identified that the primary cause of the sinking was the failure of a seawater pipe in the aft engine spaces, which in turn caused a total loss of electrical power. In dire straits, the crew failed to operate the valves manually, which could have saved the submarine before they were overcome. With no power, the boat simply drifted down to the crush depth, where her structural integrity failed, resulting in a terrible death for the remaining crew members. The US Navy was stunned by the loss and vowed never to let such a tragedy happen again.

Consequently, the SubSafe Programme was developed from the lessons learned. This includes more rigorous manufacturing standards and operating procedures, and the relocation of safety equipment. SubSafe guarantees that every submarine in the US Fleet and every pressure-related part is certified as being 100 per cent safe for use on a submarine, and it ensures that the integrity of the material used on the ship can operate at design test depth. It was believed that this would provide for a situation in which disaster threatened the ship and its crew.

Other controls were also set in place as a result of the SubSafe programme, to ensure that when an emergency arose aboard a submarine, all vital equipment which sailors would need quick access to was clearly marked and accessible, even in gloomy conditions. Further, an operator should only be one second away from flipping the emergency main ballast tanks to vent, so the boat can rise to the surface. Further recommendations of a special Presidential Deep Submergence Review Group resulted in the creation of the Deep Submergence Rescue System, which was developed in the mid-1960s, and which initiated the development of the modern rescue vehicles *Mystic* (DSRV 1) and *Avalon* (DSRV 2) of the US Deep Submergence Unit.

ABOVE: **USS *Tinosa*, eighth boat launched in the Thresher class, spent the 28 years of her life on assignments and patrols throughout the world, undergoing two major overhauls, during one of which she received submarine safety improvements designed in the wake of the loss of USS *Thresher* in 1963.**
BELOW LEFT: **A declassified photograph of a test and evaluation firing of a SUBROC missile in 1963, USS *Permit* (SSN-594) becoming the first submarine to fire one.**
BELOW RIGHT: **USS *Dace*, from which 16 crew members were taken off at Roosevelt Roads Naval Station in critical condition from heat stroke after a cooling water pump seized up and the temperature in one part of the boat reached 85°C/185°F. The boat was on her way to dry dock for an overhaul at the time.**

Permit

Displacement: 3,484 tonnes/3,429 tons (surfaced); 4,133 tonnes/4,067.7 tons (submerged)
Length: 84.9m/278ft 7in
Beam: 9.7m/31ft 10in
Armament: 4 x 533mm/21in tubes (forward), Mk 48 torpedoes, Harpoon missiles, Mk 57 deep water mines, Mk 60 CAPTOR mines
Propulsion: S5W nuclear reactor
Speed: 22 knots (surfaced); 20 knots (dived)
Complement: 143 men

FAR LEFT: **An historic event in the development of submarine warfare, the construction of USS *George Washington*, America's first ballistic missile carrier, which was hurriedly created and put into service by cutting the SSN *Scorpion* in two and inserting the missile compartment.** ABOVE: **The *George Washington* underway. She did not need to refuel for four years from commissioning, having then completed an incredible 160,934km/100,000 miles.** INSET: **The badge of the first SSBN of the United States Navy.**

George Washington SSBN

George Washington was the first ever ballistic missile carrier in the United States Navy, but she was not a purpose-built SSBN. In a previous life, she was the SSN *Scorpion* and had been reborn by being cut in two and having a 39.6m/130ft missile compartment inserted to accommodate the arrival of the much-vaunted Polaris ballistic missiles. According to the Federation of American Scientists (FAS), she became "the submarine that most influenced world events in the 20th century. With its entry into service in December 1959 the United States instantly gained the most powerful deterrent force imaginable – a stealth platform with enormous nuclear firepower."

She re-emerged from the Electric Boat Company yards in June 1960 as the lead boat in a new class bearing her name, and sailed to Cape Canaveral, Florida, to be equipped with two solid-propellant missiles for trials. She then went to the US Atlantic Missile Test Range with officials of the Polaris Submarine programme and on July 20, 1960, completed the historic event of launching the first Polaris missile from a submerged submarine, although it was unarmed. The launch was confirmed at 12:39 hours in a message sent by *George Washington*'s commanding officer to President Eisenhower: "Polaris – from out of the deep to target. Perfect."

A further missile was launched from the submerged submarine an hour later, travelling 1,770km/1,100 miles down the firing range to hit the target area. Two weeks later she duplicated the test firing before finally travelling to Charleston to take on board her full load of 16 Polaris missiles and as already noted in these pages, was thus equipped with a greater power than all the bombs dropped by all sides in World War II. The submarine completed her first patrol after 66 days of submerged running on January 21, and there began her lifelong series of patrols as part of America's nuclear deterrent programme, operations which today remain classified. The voyage over the next four years covered 160,934km/100,000 miles before she put in for a refuel, and of course that was just a beginning.

It is also noteworthy that the third member of the George Washington class, *Theodore Roosevelt*, was also something of a hybrid when she was rushed into service in 1961. Components initially assembled for the *Skipjack*-class nuclear attack submarine *Scamp* were diverted and used to speed up her construction.

Five days after commissioning, the submarine set off, bound for the east coast, and en route set another precedent by become the first fleet ballistic missile submarine to transit the Panama Canal.

ABOVE: **Same boat, different staff in the missile control room of the *George Washington*, who were thankfully never called upon to press the button in 25 years of dramatic service.**

Four days later, she arrived at Cape Canaveral to test-fire her first Polaris A1 missile before heading off to the American base at Holy Loch, Scotland, to begin the first of many years of patrolling. It was during her second tour of duty that the submarine ran aground off the western coast of Scotland while returning from her 21st patrol from the Holy Loch base. She was hauled into dry dock for temporary repairs before returning to the United States.

George Washington SSBN

Displacement: 5,512 tonnes/5,424.9 tons (surfaced); 6,424 tonnes/6,322.5 tons (submerged)
Length: 116.43m/382ft
Beam: 10m/32ft 10in
Armament: 16 Polaris missiles
Propulsion: S5W nuclear reactor
Speed: 20 knots (surfaced); 24 knots (dived)
Complement: 120 men

UNITED STATES

Ethan Allen SSBN/SSN

Ethan Allen led her class into production, thus becoming the sixth SSBN submarine in the American fleet, and on May 6, 1962, she also took her place in history by test-firing the only nuclear-armed Polaris missile ever launched. The A1 missile was fired from the *Ethan Allen* while submerged in the Pacific, and the nuclear warhead was detonated over the South Pacific at the end of the programmed flight.

It was the only complete proof test of a US strategic missile, prior to an international ban on atmospheric testing. Later, this class became the first to be equipped with the A2 series missiles, and subsequently the A3 version in the 1970s. All five of the Ethan Allen boats were eventually reclassified as attack submarines under the Strategic Arms Limitation Treaty (SALT).

After almost two decades of service as SSBNs, their missile sections were decommissioned in 1981 in compliance with the SALT I treaty. The missile fire control systems were removed, and cement blocks were placed in the missile tubes to assume the role of SSNs, although a number of the SSBNs from this and other classes were retained merely for training purposes or anti-submarine warfare duties. *Sam Houston* of the Lafayette class was also converted again for use during the 1980s as a transport and landing vehicle for US Special forces and remained as such for some years. Most, however, were gradually called in for decommissioning and subsequent entry into the recycling programme in the 1990s.

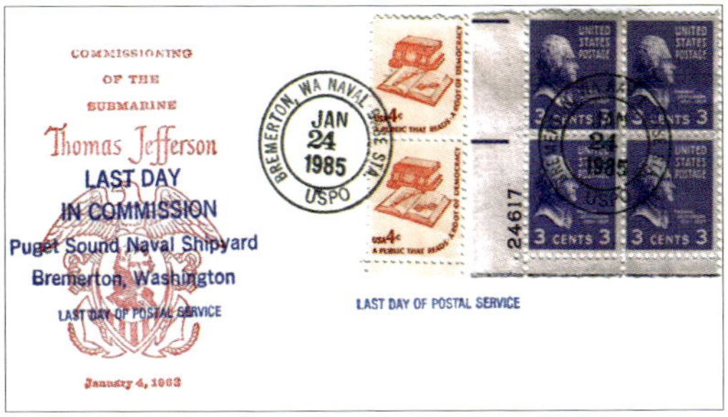

TOP LEFT: **Class leader *Ethan Allen* also found her place in history for two reasons, firstly for firing a Polaris missile and then almost 20 years later, in being stripped of her nuclear armament completely as part of the scaling down of the nuclear arms race under the SALT I agreement.**

TOP RIGHT: **In the same class, the *Thomas A. Edison* was similarly converted to an attack submarine through the procedure of having cement blocks placed in the missile tubes.** ABOVE: **A Last Day cover to mark the retirement of *Thomas Jefferson*, which was converted in 1981 and ended her service completely on January 24, 1985.**

ABOVE: **Considering the mass of superstructure below, the Ethan Allen class kept a relatively low profile on the surface, as aptly demonstrated here by the second of the class, USS *Sam Houston*, which spent 20 years up close and personal against the USSR fleet before being reclassified as an SSN.** INSET: **The badge of the fourth and last member of the Ethan Allen Class, USS *Thomas Jefferson*.**

Ethan Allen SSBN

Displacement: 6,790 tonnes/6,682.8 tons (surfaced); 7,873 tonnes/7,748.7 tons (submerged)
Length: 125m/410ft 1in
Beam: 10m/32ft 10in
Armament: 16 Polaris missiles; 4 x 533mm/21in tubes
Propulsion: S5W nuclear reactor
Speed: 22 knots (surfaced); 25 knots (dived)
Complement: 110 men

Lafayette-class SSBN

The 19 boats of the Lafayette class added a further dimension to the expanding US ballistic missile capability and were known as fleet ballistic missile carriers. They were commissioned with some speed over an 18-month period from early 1963, and the leader of the class, *Lafayette*, was operational from January 4, 1964, destined for her first deterrent patrol operating out of Rota, Spain. Over the course of the next three years, she carried out 15 such patrols, a typical workload for a member of the Polaris fleet, demonstrated by the fact that Lafayette's 15th actually marked the 400th patrol carried out by the Polaris-carrying fleet. The following year, she was called into Newport News Dry Dock Company for a refit, lasting almost a year, before returning to her deterrent operations.

Another boat of the same class, *James Monroe*, completed her overhaul around the same time and became the first submarine with Polaris A2s to be called in to be upgraded to the A3 capability. At that time, the ballistic boats were scheduled for refits after four years and a major overhaul after seven years, the latter taking the boat off line for around two years, a fact of life that could seriously limit the US Navy's ability to meet the SSBN patrols they were now expected to carry out. In 1974, they therefore introduced an SSBN Extended Refit Programme to provide additional preventive or corrective maintenance at the mini-refit stage, thus enabling them to extend the major overhaul to ten years. Another of the Lafayette class, *James Madison*, was the first SSBN to undergo the extended refit, which was conducted at Holy Loch, Scotland in September 1974.

A further important development for the Lafayette class arrived in the same year when the Trident I ballistic missile programme was authorized, although the boats that would carry it – the new *Ohio*-class submarines – would not be available until 1979. Six of the Lafayettes were therefore selected for what was termed a "backfit" programme to take the Tridents. The class was therefore engaged in fleet SSBN deterrent operations over three decades, until decommissioning of the class began in the late 1980s and continued to 1994. One, *Sam Rayburn*, was taken out in 1985 to conform to the SALT II agreements and converted into a training ship with her missile tubes filled with concrete.

It is worth noting that the 12 boats of the Benjamin Franklin class that followed the Lafayettes were largely similar, except that they had new and quieter machinery and were thus considered a separate class. Two of them, *Kamehameha* and *James K. Polk*, were later converted to attack submarines exclusively for operations with SEAL special warfare forces, a role they performed for many years.

ABOVE LEFT: The *Lafayette*-class *Woodrow Wilson* SSBN arrived at the Panama Canal on her maiden cruise in January 1964 to be met by violent anti-American demonstrations over an unconnected incident. The submarine was forced to transit the canal in a record 7 hours and 10 minutes while combat-ready Marines and soldiers guarded the locks. ABOVE: The USS *Sam Rayburn*, with her 16 Polaris missile tubes open, was converted into a training platform in 1986.

ABOVE: The USS *James Monroe* became the first submarine with Polaris A2 missiles to enter overhaul, and on January 9, 1968, she became the first to receive Polaris A3 capability.

Lafayette-class SSBN

Displacement (standard version): 7,135 tonnes/ 7,022.3 tons (surfaced); 8,110 tonnes/ 7,981.9 tons (submerged)
Length: 129.6m/425ft 2in
Beam: 10.06m/33ft
Armament: 16 x missile tubes for Polaris or Poseidon; 4 x 533mm/21 torpedo tubes (forward); Mk4/16 anti-ship torpedo; Mk 37 anti-submarine torpedo; Mk 45 Astor nuclear torpedo; Mk 48 anti-submarine torpedo
Propulsion: S5W nuclear reactor; 2 x geared steam turbines, 11,185.5kW/15,000shp
Speed: 20 knots (surfaced); 25 knots (dived)
Complement: 143 men

UNITED STATES

Sturgeon-class SSN

A major class of 39 submarines built specifically for anti-submarine warfare in the late 1960s and 70s, the Sturgeon boats became the highly flexible workhorses of the American fleet through some of the most tense and difficult times covering a span of more than 20 very active years. In using the same propulsion power pack as the smaller Thresher/Permit classes, the Sturgeons sacrificed speed for more efficient and versatile combat capabilities that, in fact, did not prove to be a handicap. Their versatility also took on another dimension when six of the boats were also modified to carry the SEAL Dry Deck Shelter (DDS) for "special operations", of which the class history is littered with references, without delving into great detail. Those that received this configuration were primarily used for the covert insertion of special forces from the DDS, a submersible launch hangar attached to the submarine's Weapon Shipping Hatch. This provided the most effective method of SEAL delivery because of its position on the ship.

The weaponry initially used by the Sturgeon boats was the Harpoon missile system and later the Tomahawk cruise missile, along with Mk 48 torpedoes with the tubes sited amidships to allow for the bow-mounted sonar. The class was also equipped with sail-mounted dive planes that rotated to a vertical position for breaking through the ice while surfacing in Arctic regions. The last ten of the class were also given an extended hull, with 3m/10ft added specifically to provide greater working and living space on long patrols.

The Federation of American Scientists noted in their summary of this class that, while the boats achieved little publicity during their heyday, this class of ship was "the platform of choice for many of the Cold War missions for which submarines are now famous". The Sturgeons were also subjected to a five-year study that resulted in their working life being extended from 20 years to 30 years, with a possible extension to 33 years on a case-by-case basis. In the event, many boats of this class were retired as the Cold War eased, to avoid expensive reactor refuelling.

TOP RIGHT: **An experience longed for and achieved by many submariners, as attack submarine USS *Pogy*, of the Sturgeon class of SSNs surfaces through 0.46m/18in of Arctic ice in November 1996. Perched high on the sail of the boat as lookout is Radioman Second Class Mark Sisson scanning the horizon for any inquisitive polar bears.** MIDDLE RIGHT: **With her smooth lines clearly evident, another of the *Sturgeon*-class boats, *Pintado*, was one of the most advanced submarines in the fleet when commissioned in 1971.** LEFT: **A starboard view of *Seahorse*, from the same class which was also able to boast of Arctic experience.**

Sturgeon-class SSN

Displacement: 4,183 tonnes/4,116.9 tons (surfaced); 4,704 tonnes/4,629.7 tons (submerged)
Length: 89m/292ft
Beam: 9.75m/32ft
Armament: 4x 533mm/21in tubes, Mk 48 torpedoes; Harpoon missiles; Mk 57 deep water mines; Mk 60 Captor mines
Propulsion: S5W nuclear reactor, 2 x steam turbines, 11,185.5kW/15,000shp
Speed: 20 knots (surfaced); 25 knots (dived)
Complement: 110 men

LEFT: The renowned *Los Angeles*, leader of the largest class of SSNs produced by the US Navy, a brilliant boat much loved by those who sailed in her. She was also historically important as the submarine whose target assignments included ASW against Soviet submarines assigned to sink US carriers, and ASUW against capital ships in the Soviet surface action groups.

Los Angeles-class SSN

The Los Angeles class was numerically the largest post-war group built by the US Navy, with 62 boats commissioned between 1976 and 1996, costing $900,000 million apiece at 1990 prices. They had a projected lifespan of 30 years, although some of their makers predicted that the improved version introduced in 1988 could still be in full operational condition 40 to 45 years from their date of birth. The range was designed and introduced specifically for anti-submarine warfare operations against Soviet submarines, which in turn were targeting US battlegroups.

The early Los Angeles boats were primarily concerned therefore with Carrier Battlegroup protection. They were fast and exceedingly quiet, features that were improved even further as the class progressed through the 1980s and 90s. Initially, they were equipped with Harpoon anti-ship missiles and anti-ship Tomahawk cruise missiles. Later, as the Cold War faded, many were fitted with Tomahawk land attack missiles in support of the military in hotspots such as the Balkans and the Persian Gulf.

In the principal role for which they were designed, they were at the sharp end of the little known Cold War beneath the waves in which US submarines and those of their British

ABOVE: An interesting perspective on size, with the *Los Angeles*-class boat *Scranton* surfacing in the North Arabian Sea while aircraft carrier *George Washington* cruises in the background.

allies performed their duties with aplomb. This brought them into close contact with the opposition, with some scary shunts, bumps and close encounters given that the Russians were doing exactly the same thing, and both sides were conducting sweeps literally hundreds of miles ahead of their battle groups and strike boats.

To meet these requirements, the *Los Angeles*-class boats were progressively updated and consequently were the most advanced attack submarines in the world. However, as time and conditions moved on, and the Cold War gradually receded, these boats were versatile enough to move along with the times and modern requirements. Unlike the SSBNs, great monoliths for which there was a shortage of alternative occupations, the fast attack submarines of Los Angeles class possessed the stealth, speed and endurance to match the requirements of the modern political climate. These 110m/361ft boats became the epitome of the true submarine driven by a brilliant power pack, highly accurate sensors, sophisticated weapons control systems and central computer monitoring.

They were built in three variants, first comprising the original Los Angeles class for the first 30 boats. The next 30 had an upgraded reactor core and 12 vertical tubes for Tomahawk cruise missiles. The last 23 came with an advanced BSY-1 sonar suite combat system and the ability to lay mines from their torpedo tubes. They were also adapted for under-ice operations by moving the diving planes from the sail structure to the bow, and the sail was strengthened for breaking through ice.

One great feature of the Los Angeles boats has been the constant upgrading of communications systems for use both within the boat and externally. The interior phones on the modern boats, for example, operate on sound powered circuits without electrical power and were thoroughly reliable in battle situations. The possible need to stay submerged for long periods at a time also provided the impetus to ensure the crew

UNITED STATES

were well catered for both in terms of atmospheric comfort and off-duty relaxation, and the configuration of these boats allowed a situation where work and rest were physically divided. Considerable thought had clearly gone into the boat's architecture, providing for two watertight compartments. All the living and rest-and-relaxation accommodation is housed forward, along with control centres, sonar and the computer suite. The after compartment houses the nuclear reactor and the ship's propulsion equipment.

Although some of the first-edition boats have been retired, a five-year study was carried out to evaluate potential life span of the class. It was discovered that after 30 years' service, a major overhaul would equipment them for a further 10-year operating cycle. It was assessed that at 2001 prices, the additional overhaul would cost $400 million. Every option is being considered given that Department of Defense studies have projected a need for 68 attack submarines by 2015 and 76 by 2025. The refuelling of a number of *Los Angeles*-class submarines previously earmarked for retirement at a certain age seems a strong possibility. In the meantime, it is also interesting to note the major difference between first and last in this class, from *Los Angeles* to *Cheyenne*, that of the Submarine Advanced Combat System AN/BSY-1, which is the latest in technology, combining the Sonar and Fire Control Systems. The Combat Systems Department is divided into four distinct divisions: Torpedo, Fire Control, Sonar and Deck. The personnel in each of these divisions are responsible for ensuring that the Weapons System is always maintained in a condition of maximum readiness.

As the Federation of American Scientists (FAS) points out, the Sonar portion, utilizing advanced array systems, can detect, classify, and track multiple contacts at extreme ranges under adverse conditions. The Fire Control portion provides weapons orders, as well as targeting information to the ship's four torpedo and 12 vertical launch tubes.

The *Cheyenne* carries the latest variety of advanced submarine weaponry, including the Mk 48 Advanced Capability torpedo, the Harpoon anti-ship missile and the Tomahawk cruise missile. The Torpedo Division is manned by machinists, who stand their watch in the Torpedo Room.

LEFT: **Down the hatch – an aerial resupply operation aboard the *Los Angeles*-class boat, *Scranton*, deployed as part of the USS *Kearsarge* Expeditionary Strike Group participating in two major joint exercises, Caya Green, a bilateral US/Israel exercise, and Inspired Siren, with the Pakistani Navy in the summer of 2005.**

BELOW: **Balloons fly as the *Los Angeles*-class submarine *Newport News* slides down the launch-way at Newport News Shipbuilding and Drydock Co., Newport News, Virginia, on March 15, 1986.**

ABOVE: **The control room of USS *Toledo* has the appearance of an executive office suite.**

LEFT: **USS *Greeneville* dry-docked at the Pearl Harbor Naval Shipyard to perform necessary repairs following a collision at sea with the Japanese fishing vessel *Ehime Maru* off the coast of Honolulu, Hawaii.**

Los Angeles-class SSN

Displacement: 6,210 tonnes/6,111.9 tons (surfaced – variable depending on age); 6,750 tonnes/6,643.4 tons (submerged)
Length: 109.73m/360ft
Beam: 10m/32ft 10in
Armament: Harpoon and Tomahawk ASM/LAM missiles; 4 x 533mm/21in tubes (forward), Mk 48 torpedoes
Propulsion: S6G reactor; 1 x shaft, 26,099.5kW/35,000shp
Speed: 23 knots (surfaced); 30–32 knots (dived)
Complement: 129 men

FAR LEFT: **The broad back of USS Pennsylvania, of the Ohio class.**
LEFT: **The first firing of a C-4 Trident I missile was staged at Cape Canaveral and later from a member of the *Ohio*-class ballistic fleet. Eight boats of the class were initially assigned to the Pacific, armed with Trident. The Ohio submarines were also fitted with 24 missile tubes as opposed to the 16 of earlier boomers.**

Ohio-class SSBN

In 1981 when the *Ohio*-class submarines were making their debut in what was planned as a long-running production schedule, few would have put money on an early end to the Cold War. Quite the reverse, and so the emphasis on strategic deterrence by way of a massively armed ballistic fleet remained unswerving and generally unopposed politically in spite of the enormous costs involved. Deterrence had been the sole reason to maintain a ballistic fleet since inception in 1960. Furthermore, because of the latter element, much work had been done in the meantime to keep the boats effective and at work for as long as possible in terms of life and as busy as possible in terms of the cycle of deployment.

The optimum level for SSBN operations was achieved in the late 1970s and maintained for the Ohio fleet: that they should be at sea at least 66 per cent of their life, and that included downtime for major overhaul periods of 12 months every nine years, although modern design concepts allow the submarines to operate for 15 years between overhauls. At sea, a standard patrol would last 70 days, although this might be extended in exceptional circumstances, and indeed the Ohio class was designed for extended deterrent patrols. A 25-day period was then allowed for maintenance, reloading of munitions and supplies, and change of crew.

The Ohio class, first introduced in the 1980s, progressively replaced the older fleet ballistic missile submarines, whose working life was coming to an end, and they were fully up to date with the latest technology and internal comforts. The streamlining of the outer hull also allowed the boats to move with considerable stealth and to increase cruising speed when submerged. A rate of 25 knots was comfortably achieved at depths in excess of 243.8m/800ft.

The final member of the class, *Louisiana*, commissioned in 1997,

LEFT: **The loading of the most powerful weapons on earth into one of the *Ohio*-class submarines, whose larger hulls accommodate more weapons of larger size and greater range, as well as sophisticated computerized electronic equipment for improved weapons guidance and sonar performance.**

completed the fleet of 18 Ohio boats. Ten were assigned to the Atlantic fleet, initially equipped with the D-5 Trident II missile. The remaining eight boats went to work carrying the C-4 Trident I missile, although they were scheduled for upgrading to carry the D-5 by 2005.

Whereas earlier ballistic boats carried 16 missiles, the Ohio class were capable of carrying 24 missiles bearing warheads that could all be launched within one minute and delivered to targets virtually anywhere on the world's surface, while at the same time able to operate at depths where it was possible to avoid detection.

When all 18 boats of Ohio were fully operational, they represented almost half of the total number US strategic warheads. As part of the Navy study on the longevity of boats, the Navy adjusted the lifespan of the Ohio to 42 years, made up of two 20-year cycles separated by a two-year overhaul.

Ohio-class SSBN

Displacement: 16,500 tonnes/16,239.4 tons (surfaced); 18,453 tonnes/18,161.6 tons (submerged)
Length: 170.69m/560ft
Beam: 10.06m/33ft
Armament: 24 missile tubes for Trident I or II; 4 x 533mm/21in tubes, Mk 48 torpedoes
Propulsion: 1 x S8G nuclear reactor
Speed: 20 knots (surfaced); 25 knots (dived)
Complement: 157 men

UNITED STATES

LEFT: USS *Virginia*, the new attack submarine that represents the future. This boat can act as a deployment platform for a wide range of missions and technologies: covert strikes by launching land attack missiles from vertical launchers and torpedo tubes, highly advanced ASW capabilities, Unmanned Undersea Vehicles, an Advanced SEAL Delivery System, plus 38 assorted weapons. BELOW: *Virginia* during her Alpha trials, which included a full range of speed and depth capability assessments, as well as checking all systems essential for the safe operation of the submarine.

Virginia-class SSN

The *Virginia*-class submarine was designed in the late 1990s as the first multi-mission, multi-purpose boat that will carry the US Navy's operations forward for most of the first half of the 21st century. The submarine has been designed entirely by computer to provide maximum flexibility. The keynote features of the design were based on the requirements that the five boats of the Virginia class would be responsive to the changing needs, missions and threats of modern submarine warfare. The principal aim was that the V boats could be redirected to meet any need and updated by inserting new technologies using integrated electronic systems combined with Commercial-Off-The-Shelf (COTS) components. This, in turn, say the submarine's designers, will allow the state-of-the-art technology that is the boat's prime feature to be maintained and updated throughout the life of the Virginia class, thus avoiding obsolescence. Other key features will include:

• A sonar system with much greater signal processing power than any currently existing attack submarine.
• A sail designed for future installation of a "special mission-configurable mast" for enhanced flexibility and war-fighting performance.
• An integral Lock-Out/Lock-In chamber for special operations, combined with the hosting of Special Operations Forces equipped with underwater delivery vehicles.
• A substantial array of weapons encompassing the most advanced heavyweight torpedoes, mines, vertical-launch Tomahawk cruise missiles and Unmanned Undersea Vehicles for horizontal launch.

The US Navy maintains that the *Virginia* will surpass the performance of any current projected threat submarine and will "maintain American undersea dominance well into the 21st century". Much of the thinking surrounding submarine development altered considerably with the end of the Cold War. Significantly, the fundamental focus in preparing the *Virginia* for ASW conflict is to be achieved by combining the under-sea capability with the ability to attack littorals from the sea to influence events ashore. *Virginia*, the Navy maintains, is the boat that will achieve those ambitions.

LEFT: Dressed and ready to go, the Virginia class which is the last word (for the moment) in advanced stealth multi-mission and SEAL delivery submarines but with an important break with the past: no periscope – simply two Photonics masts delivering images of the surrounding area on to large screens.

Virginia-class SSN

Displacement: Not known (surfaced); 6,567 tonnes/6,463.3 tons (submerged)
Length: 115m/377ft 4in
Beam: 10.36m/34ft
Armament: 4 x 533mm/21in tubes, Mk 48 ADCAP heavyweight torpedoes; 12 Vertical Launch System Tubes for Tomahawk cruise missiles, Advanced Mobile Mines, Unmanned Undersea Vehicles, Special Warfare Dry Deck Shelter, Advanced SEAL Delivery System
Propulsion: So far stated as 1 x S9G pressurized water reactor; Improved Performance Machinery Programme Phase III; 1 x secondary propulsion submerged motor; no power output data available
Speed: 20 knots (surfaced); 25 knots (dived)
Complement: 113 men

Seawolf-class SSN

The Seawolf submarines, a fleet of 29 boats each costing billions of dollars, were to become the most expensive submarines ever built, and they would operate autonomously against enemy vessels should the occasion arise. In other words, their sole reason for being afloat was to destroy Soviet ballistic missile submarines before they could attack American targets, in the event of conflagration. When the Seawolf programme was being formulated in the mid-1980s, there was no greater concern among the Reagan administration than to secure total superiority over the USSR's seaborne nuclear capability. American defence analysts were convinced that in such a situation, the SSBNs were the most survivable parts of the Soviet nuclear arsenal, and they would have to be taken out.

ABOVE: **The ultimate in ASW, *Seawolf* can operate 75 per cent faster before being detected than any previous submarine and is said to be quieter at its tactical speed of 25 knots than a *Los Angeles*-class submarine at the pier-side and, according to the USN, is "capable of establishing and maintaining battlespace dominance".** BELOW LEFT: **The obligatory trip to see the polar bears, and vice versa.** BELOW: **Former US President Jimmy Carter visits to discuss the third and last boat in the Seawolf class, which carries his name.**

Consequently, the US government was prepared to write an open cheque to finance the building of what would be billed as the most advanced attack submarine the world had seen, the only one truly capable of destroying the Soviet SSBNs. Work pressed ahead but by the time the lead boat was in production,

UNITED STATES

the Cold War was all but over. Approval for more two more Seawolf boats – to be named *Connecticut* and *Jimmy Carter* – was given by President George Bush, supported by Defence Secretary Dick Cheney, in 1992 at a cost of $2,765,900,000. They were to be the last. The cost of *Seawolf* forced the whole project into public debate, and thus it became the most controversial submarine programme in American history. When the Cold War ended, the Bush (Senior) administration cancelled the entire 29-ship order, except for the lead submarine.

However, the nuclear submarine community, led by Admiral Bruce DeMars, and influential shipyard lobbying forced the US Congress into a change of heart, and it was agreed that two additional boats would be built. With the reduction of the programme to a three-ship class, costs escalated astronomically, with the third boat in the series expected to cost in excess of $3 billion. The Clinton administration confirmed the cancellation of the remaining 26 on the grounds that there was no existing situation that could justify such vast expense against a threat that apparently no longer existed. Even so, the three that were approved were well worth having.

The sea trials of the first boat in 1996 proved that the great sales pitch that was given for them a decade earlier proved to be totally justified, and *Seawolf* was commissioned on July 19, 1997, at Electric Boat Shipyard. In fact, the US Navy claimed that trials had proved the aim that she should have the highest tactical speed of any US submarine. Stealth was the keynote, and proved by the novel additional of being able to put "combat swimmers" into denied areas.

Indeed, the whole concept of increasing the role of the submarine in special forces operations was also to the fore with the *Seawolf* project. A newly designed combat swimmer silo, along with the SEAL Dry Deck Shelter (DDS), would provide these additional facilities. The DDS for use with *Seawolf* is transportable by air and placed piggy-back on the submarine. It can accommodate and launch a swimmer delivery vehicle and combat swimmers. The swimmers' silo is an internal lock-out chamber that can deploy up to eight combat swimmers and their equipment at one time. Inside the boat, the tremendous innovations in virtually every aspect of seaworthiness make this another jewel in the crown of the US submarine service.

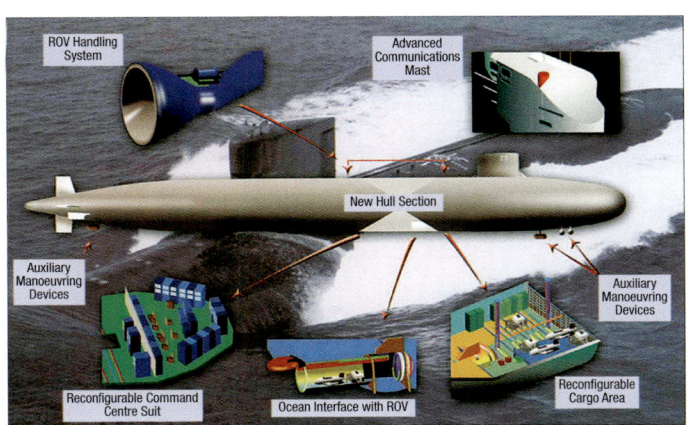

ABOVE LEFT: The control room of *Seawolf*. This crew operates some of the most sophisticated electronics ever produced, providing enhanced indications and warning, surveillance and communications capability. ABOVE: *Seawolf* on her final trials before acceptance into naval service.

ABOVE: When the third boat in the Seawolf class – USS *Jimmy Carter* – was being built, the US government approved an additional spend of $887 million for the development of advanced technology in naval special warfare, tactical surveillance and mine warfare operations.

Seawolf-class SSN

Displacement: 7,432 tonnes/7,314.6 tons (surfaced); 8,992 tonnes/8,850 tons (submerged)
Length: 107.6m/353ft
Beam: 10.67m/35ft
Armament: 8 x 660mm/26in tubes, 50 Mk 48 ADCAP torpedoes or 100 mines, or 50 Tomahawk cruise missiles or 50 Harpoon anti-ship missiles
Propulsion: S6W nuclear reactor delivering 38,776.4kW/52,000shp
Speed: 25 knots (surfaced); 35 knots (maximum – dived)
Complement: 133 men

LEFT: **The Russian Kilo class entered service in the early 1980s. It was designed by the Rubin Central Maritime Design Bureau, St Petersburg. Subsequent developments led to the current production version and, most recently, Type 636.**
ABOVE: **The Kilo diesel electric boat has been a workhorse of the Russian fleet principally in anti-ship and anti-submarine operations. The class has also drawn an ongoing export trade from smaller nations.**

Kilo-class SSK

The Russian Kilo diesel-electric boats have been in constant use since the submarine first entered service in the early 1980s and more recently with the newer versions, the Type 877EKM and the Type 636. Further development of this class ensures that it will be around well into the 21st century with the introduction of the *Lada* (Project 677), which is expected to come into service in 2007. The new model will be based on a new air-independent propulsion (AIP) system that is likely to be retrofitted to earlier boats of this class.

Designed for both anti-submarine and anti-ship warfare, Type 636 is considered to be one of the quietest of all the diesel submarines currently in production. The principal features in the boat's warfare capabilities are significant, and its designers at the St Petersburg shipyards claim she is capable of detecting an enemy submarine at a range three to four times greater than it can be detected itself. That said, the role of the 636 is also highly practicable for general reconnaissance and patrol missions. With six watertight compartments separated by transverse bulkheads in a pressurized double-hull and a good reserve buoyancy, this class has a greater level of survivability if the submarine is holed. The 636 design is an improved development of the 877EKM Kilo class, with an extended hull.

The power of the diesel generators has been increased and the main propulsion shaft speed has been reduced to provide a substantial reduction in the acoustic signature. Conversely, the submarine's combat and command system is equipped with high-speed computers that can rapidly process information from the surveillance equipment and determine submerged and surface targets and calculate firing parameters. Armaments include a launcher for eight surface-to-air missiles or alternatively, the vessels can be fitted with the Novator Club-S (SS-N-27) cruise missile system which delivers an anti-ship missile to a range of 220km/137 miles with a 450kg/992lb high-explosive warhead.

The computer-controlled torpedo system comes with an automated quick-loading device enabling the first salvo to be fired within two minutes and the second within five minutes. The six torpedo tubes are situated in the nose, all loaded, and with 12 reloads. Two of the tubes are designed for firing remote-controlled torpedoes that have a very high accuracy.

LEFT: **A considerably improved version of the Kilo design, which includes a much better noise insulation system and updated combat systems. Although production was eventually suspended for domestic purposes, several variants remained available for export.**

Type 636

Displacement: 2,288 tonnes/2,251.9 tons (surfaced); 3,027 tonnes/2,979.2 tons (submerged)
Length: 73.76m/242ft
Beam: 9.9m/32ft 6in
Armament: 6 x 533mm/21in tubes, 18 x torpedoes; or 24 x mines; SA-N-8 Gimlet SAM
Propulsion: 2 x 1,118.6kW/1,500hp diesel engines; 1 x 4101.3kW/5,500hp electric motor
Speed: 10 knots (surfaced); 19 knots (dived)
Complement: 52 men

USSR

LEFT: The *Victor III* is a substantially upgraded version with improved noise levels and new sonar, sensor and command suites. This unusual image arose from the snagging of a frigate's towed array sonar, the cable for which can be seen looped around the submarine's stern fin. ABOVE: The *Victor II* cuts a sleek figure amid the foam, with rather a sporty look, but the reality was rather different, given that she was a merely a lengthened version of the *Victor I* to take a new ASW missile.

Victor-classes I, II and III SSN

The Victor class is the NATO classification for the Soviet submarine developed under the name Project 671. It was among the earliest of the Russian boats to feature an advanced tear-drop hull design to achieve higher underwater speeds for the primary role of protecting Soviet surface fleets and to attack American SSBNs. The Victor first appeared in 1967, and 15 of the class were built with the capacity for 24 tube-launched weapons or 48 mines. They were later retrofitted to handle the TEST-68 wire-guided torpedo weapons. However, the boats were noisy, and the Victor II class was introduced in 1972 with the hull extended by 6m/20ft to accommodate sound insulation measures and space for additional weapons, including a new generation of heavy torpedoes that required power assistance to handle them in the torpedo room. The noise problem was not resolved, as the Russians discovered through the infamous Walker spy ring, which reported that the Americans could easily track the Victor II through its acoustic design. By then, seven of the Victor IIs had already been built, and work on any further boats was halted to await improvements in the design.

The final version, Victor III, was introduced in 1979, and over the next decade or so, a further 25 boats were built with the outer hull coated with anti-hydroacoustic materials to reduce the possibility of detection. Now generally quieter, they also had further internal alterations to accommodate a more up-to-date weapons stock, allowing for 24 tube-launched weapons or 36 mines on board. The outer hull of the Victor III was built partly from light alloys, and was distinguishable by a high stern fin fitted with a towed array dispenser – the first Soviet submarine to be fitted with a towed array.

LEFT: A Victor III attack submarine with the towed array sonar clearly visible, here in company with a small Soviet ship (middle) and USS *Peterson* (back). This version, built between 1984 and 1992, was gradually withdrawn at the end of the 20th century and replaced by the Akula class. The remaining boats mostly served with the Northern Fleet.

Victor III-class SSN

Displacement: 5,173 tonnes/5,091.3 tons (surfaced); 7,134 tonnes/7,021.3 tons (submerged)
Length: 106m/347ft 9in
Beam: 10.6m/34ft 9in
Armament: 2 x 650mm/25.6in tubes; 4 x 533mm/21in tubes, Type 53 and Type 65 torpedoes; SLCM-SS-N-21 Sampson; A/S: SS-N-15, SS-N-16 missiles
Propulsion: 2 x VM-4 reactors delivering 23,116.7kW/31,000shp
Speed: 18 knots (surfaced); 30 knots (dived)
Complement: 102 men

439

LEFT: **The Yankees were the first class of Soviet submarines whose firepower was comparable to that of the Americans. As the *Yankee* versions progressed from I to III, they also became considerably quieter. Armed with 16 ballistic missiles apiece, they were the Soviet front-line boats, and at least three Yankees were continually positioned in a patrol box east of Bermuda.**
BELOW: **Yankee boats were heavily reduced to meet SALT I requirements, and many were converted to SSNs by having their ballistic missile compartments removed.**

Yankee-class 667A SSBN

The SSBN Project 667A was developed in 1962 as an improved version of a project that began four years earlier and which had suffered a number of problems, especially with the launch system. The result was a submarine unlike any other, in that the horizontal hydroplanes were arranged on the sail. It was designed with specific attention to the contours of the submarine to achieve minimal resistance under water. Similar attention was paid to the reduction of noise and a new type of propeller was designed for that purpose, as well as covering the pressure hull with sound-absorbing rubber and the external hull with an anti-hydroacoustic coating.

The submarine was initially equipped with the Soviet D-5 launch system for 16 R-27 missiles with a range of about 2,400km/1,491 miles, arranged in two rows in the fourth and fifth compartments of the ten-compartment boat. They could be launched from a depth of up to 50m/164ft and fired in four salvos each comprising four missiles at intervals of eight seconds per missile. The first four 667A Yankee submarines employed the Sigma navigation system, whereas the follow-on ships were equipped with the Tobol, the first Soviet navigational system that used a satellite navigation system that was shown to be especially reliable in the Arctic region, one of the main Soviet areas of operation. The first 667A Yankee submarine completed sea trials at the end of 1967, and it was introduced into the Northern Fleet between 1967 and 1974, with a total of 34 strategic submarines of the class being built. The early boats were all upgraded with the D-5U launch systems and R-27U missiles in the late 1970s and early 80s, which provided a greater range, estimated at up to 3,000km/1,864 miles.

The Yankee class initially formed part of the important Northern Fleet as part of the 31st Division of Soviet strategic submarines based at Sayda. At the end of the 1960s, the 19th division of strategic submarines was also equipped with 667A submarines. Both divisions were a vital part of the Soviet strategic submarine coverage and consisted of 12 squadrons, which later became the 3rd Flotilla. In October 1986, considerable international concern was voiced when one of the Yankee boats, *K219*, suffered an explosion and a serious fire on board while operating to the east of Bermuda, in which four crew were killed. Attempts were made to put the boat

USSR

LEFT: A Yankee II conversion, one of the boats reconstructed for special duties which resulted in various new configurations when the ballistics equipment was removed. One, nicknamed the Yankee Sidecar, became a cruise missile carrier with 12 SS-NX-24 missiles as well as six tubes for Type 53 torpedoes, while another appeared in 1983 as a trial boat known as the Yankee Pod. BELOW: A depiction of an underwater release of missiles from a Yankee conversion. BOTTOM: Another conversion of a Yankee I, known as the Yankee Notch, an attack submarine that had six launch tubes for up to 20 missiles in addition to six torpedo tubes.

under tow, but eventually the task was aborted and she was scuttled into a depth of 5,500m/18,045ft. Subsequently a book and a television film appeared in the US about the incident and in the aftermath, the United States Navy categorically denied that any of their submarines was in collision with *K219*, or was in any way involved in the incident.

The ageing Yankee submarines were gradually removed from operational service between 1985 and 1994, and their missile compartments were taken out to comply with arms limitation agreements. Nevertheless, they had given good service, with two versions of the boat, 667A and 667AM, completing 590 patrols in most of the world's oceans. Several were also converted to perform special missions; most notable was the so-called Yankee Stretch, which was elongated to carry the new Soviet mini-submarines used for ocean research and intelligence. This was achieved by replacing the missile compartment with an extended hull so that the boat could serve as a mother ship for the very small special operations submarine AS-35 *Paltus*. The system was similar to that adopted by the Americans, utilizing the Dry Dock Shelter system for SEAL and other missions. These developments in both Russia and the United States, and to a lesser degree the UK, reflected the need to meet new challenges in 21st century submarine operations. Another conversion, called the Yankee Pod, was equipped with radio equipment and a towed hydroacoustic station. Both of these versions were said to be still active in 2004.

Yankee-class 667A SSBN

Displacement: 7,760 tonnes/7,637.4 tons (surfaced); 9,600 tonnes/9,448.4 tons (submerged)
Length: 132m/433ft
Beam: 11.6m/38ft 1in
Armament: 4 x 533mm/21in tubes; 667A: D-5 launch system with 16 x R-27 missiles; 667AU: D-5U launch system with 16 x R-27U missiles
Propulsion: 2 x pressurized water reactors; 2 x steam turbines, 38,776.4kW/52,000hp each
Speed: 12 knots (surfaced); 25 knots (dived)
Complement: 130–140 men

441

LEFT: Accidental clashes at sea between the principal players during the Cold War were not uncommon. An Echo II surfaces after a run-in with a *Garcia*-class frigate, USS *Voge*, which was conducting ASW exercises en route home from her German base. The submarine was subjected to "hold down" tactics by the frigate, for which the latter was awarded the US Meritorious Unit Commendation. BELOW: An Echo II submarine is kept under observation by a British Nimrod surveillance plane.

Echo-classes I and II SSN

Project 659 Echo was a boat on which old hands of the Russian Navy did not wish to serve. There was an inherent problem with the boats of this class in that it took at least 20 minutes for a trouble-free launching of the missiles, an operation which had to be conducted on the surface. Consequently, the boats were considered sitting ducks for the opposition. The five Echo I nuclear-powered cruise-missile submarines were designed to launch the land attack version SS-N-3c Shaddock missiles in erectable launch tubes mounted in pairs above the pressure hull on both sides of the sail. The Echo I boats were converted to attack submarines in the early 1970s. Some were decommissioned completely in the late 1980s, and others were taken out of service in the 1990s.

Twenty-nine Project 675 Echo II class were built from the mid-1960s, designed primarily to perform anti-ship duties at a time when the Americans had their carriers bristling with A3 Skywarrior aircraft capable of nuclear strikes against the Soviet Union. Echo II series boats were later modified to enable them to launch the anti-shipping version of the Shaddock. These were primarily anti-carrier weapons, intended to respond to nuclear strikes against the Soviet Union by carrier-based aircraft. As such, their SS-N-3s came in both nuclear and conventional versions. A total of eight missiles were carried, two more than on the Echo I, and the hull was lengthened by 5m/16ft 5in to accommodate the extra pair of launchers.

To fire its missiles the submarine surfaced, deployed and activated tracking radar, and remained on the surface, linked to the high altitude cruise missile in flight via datalink, providing guidance commands based on the submarine radar's tracking data. The submarine itself was highly vulnerable to attack while on the surface operating its radar. A total of 29 Echo IIs were constructed between 1962 and 1968, of which a dozen were converted to carry the improved SS-N-12 by the mid-1980s. All had been decommissioned by the mid-1990s.

At least four Echo submarines suffered serious accidents. In August 1980 a fire in an Echo II off Japan killed at least nine crew members. On June 26, 1989, a fire erupted in the two reactor compartments on an Echo II submarine of the Northern Fleet. The reactor had to be shut down, and the submarine surfaced to return to Murmansk under auxiliary diesel power. Several crew members were injured, but none were killed in the incident.

Echo II-class SSN

Displacement: 4,710 tonnes/4,635.6 tons (surfaced); 5,905 tonnes/5,811.7 tons (submerged)
Length: 115m/377ft 4in
Beam: 9m/29ft 6in
Armament: 6 x 533mm/21in tubes (forward), 4 x 406mm/16in tubes (aft); 8 x SS-N-3 or 8 x SS-N-12 missiles
Propulsion: 2 x pressurized-water nuclear reactors delivering 22,371kw/30,000shp
Speed: 20 knots (surfaced); 23 knots (dived)
Complement: 92 men

LEFT: Echo II cruise-missile submarines were modified to carry a series of radars to launch anti-ship weapons, intended originally as a response to nuclear strikes against the Soviet Union by carrier-based aircraft.

LEFT AND ABOVE: The *Alfa*-class hunter-killer submarines were considered to be part of the Soviets' "demonstration of power", in which planned numbers and ability were exaggerated. They were very much experimental platforms to test innovations supposedly for a new generation of submarines, but although the Alfa boats were exceedingly fast and deep diving, they were also very noisy.

Alfa-class SSN

Project 705 Alfa class was undoubtedly the fastest and deepest diving submarine of her age when she made her appearance in the late 1960s. Originally designed for the specific purpose of attacking American carrier battle groups, the first in this series was capable of 40 knots, a speed unmatched anywhere in the world for a 1,524-tonne/1,500-ton boat. This was largely achieved by the first-ever use of a titanium alloy, which meant the thickness and weight ratio of the hull to the power plant was substantially reduced against comparable boats of that era. The design of the submarine also included substantial automation.

The ability to travel at such speeds was increased further when the design was revised in 1963. At that time, the displacement was also increased to around 2,337 tonnes/2,300 tons when the size of the crew was also doubled, and internal compartments increased from three to six. The outcome was a relatively small, fast submarine capable of 44 knots, an ability that caused great concern to American observers. It was wrongly assumed that the boat would lead the Soviet submarines in to a new era of development, although that proved not to be the case.

Even though she was eventually to be billed as a strong competitor to the US Los Angeles class, the claims were exaggerated. The submarine proved to be exceedingly noisy at the high speeds and turned out to be somewhat unreliable and poorly armed. The lightweight hull was also suspect in the event of a torpedo attack. Even so, the Americans were sufficiently alarmed by the potential of a fast, deep-diving boat that they were provoked into a substantial investment in ASW weapons, especially in what has been described as a "dramatic improvement" in the Mk 46 and Mk 48 torpedoes.

Meanwhile, the Project 705 boats suffered a number of casualties as demands on them increased in the 1970s, and the programme was eventually ended in 1983. Four were lost due to reactor failures, one was retired in 1987, and four others were decommissioned in 1990–92. Even so, the Soviets felt they had served a useful strategic role.

ABOVE: The *Alfa*-class submarine operated up close and personal against the American submarine force. This provoked a massive US investment in anti-submarine warfare.

Alfa-class SSN

Displacement: 2,264–2,854 tonnes/2,228.2–2,828.9 tons (surfaced); 3,579–4,251 tonnes/3,522.5–4,183.9 tons (submerged)
Length: 79.5–81.4m/260ft 10in–267ft 1in
Beam: 9.5m/31ft 2in
Armament: 6 x 533mm/21in tubes (bow); 18 x 53-65K, SET-65 torpedoes or 20 x VA-111 torpedoes or 24 x mines; 21 x 81R (SS-N-15) missiles or 12 x Vodopad (SS-N-16)
Propulsion: 1 x liquid metal reactor; 2 x steam turbines, 29,828–35,048kW/40–47,000shp
Speed: 14 knots (surfaced); 43–45 knots (dived)
Complement: 31–45 men

Delta-classes I, II, III and IV SSBN

A cruiser submarine continuing the Soviet penchant for largesse, the four versions of the Delta series became the mainstay of the Red ballistic fleet over the most vital period of the Cold War. Eighteen boats were built in the first series, the first completed in 1972. Based on the old Yankee class, they saw hefty service, with the last two being finally withdrawn in 2000. The Delta II boats added only an inertial navigational system before major advances were introduced in the Delta III SSBN class, which entered service in 1976.

ABOVE: Big, bold and ugly: a Delta IV submarine, last of the nuclear missile-carrying boats placed together with Delta I, II and III under the NATO classification system, although the Russians' own classification put them as three different submarines, designed to attack cities, military and industrial installations.

Fourteen of the boats were added to the Delta fleet over the next six years, with an anticipated lifespan of up to 25 years, and went straight into service, half with the Northern and the others with the Pacific fleets. The further improved Delta IVs, complete with sports complex and spa, brought another seven boats to the arena, all assigned to the Northern Fleet during their period of commissioning over a ten-year span, from 1982.

However, when the START-I treaty was signed in 1991, 25 older *Delta*-class, five *Typhoon*-class, and one *Yankee*-class ballistic missile submarines capable of launching over 400 missiles with over 1,700 warheads were due to be culled by 2005. It was an unlikely prospect given the large number of nuclear submarines around the world waiting patiently in line for the recycling experts to come along.

In 1999, the Russian Navy began a refit and overhaul programme for the remaining Deltas, which observers took to mean that there would be ongoing delays with the introduction

LEFT: The Delta III carried a number of innovations: it was the first submarine that could launch any number of missiles in a single salvo, and it was the first that was capable of carrying ballistic missiles with multiple independently-targeted re-entry vehicles.

USSR

LEFT AND ABOVE: **Although the Delta IV strategic missile submarine was classed in the West as a follow-on from the III-series whose design it resembles, the Soviets saw it as a separate development. Seven of the vessels were built between 1981 and 1992, with a propulsion system that provided speeds of 24 knots submerged.**

of the heralded replacement, the Borei class, which was due in 2002, but at the time of writing had not materialized.

The Delta name therefore remains a potent force in the 21st century. The boats are capable of launching the Novator SS-N-15 Starfish anti-ship missile or Mk 40 anti-ship torpedoes. Starfish is armed with a 200kT nuclear warhead and has a range of up to 45km/30 miles. The submarine has four 533mm/21in torpedo tubes capable of launching all types of torpedoes, including anti-submarine torpedoes.

Given that the first Delta IV submarine was launched in January 1985 and was introduced into the Northern Fleet between 1985 and 1990, there is still plenty of life left in later members of the class. The seven boats would have an operational life estimated at 20–30 years, although a major overhaul would have to be performed every 7–8 years, otherwise the life expectancy is dramatically reduced. The latter is more likely to be the case.

LEFT: **An interesting starboard overhead view of the Delta III version. This is now the only way of viewing submarines of this class at sea, because every one of them is thought to have been taken out of service through a combination of arms limitation agreements and a lack of funding to keep them afloat.**

Delta IV-class SSBN

Displacement: 11,554 tonnes/11,371.5 tons (surfaced); 17,912 tonnes/17,629.1 tons (submerged – full load)
Length: 167m/547ft 11in
Beam: 11.7m/38ft 5in
Armament: 4 x 533mm/21in tubes; 18 x Type 40 torpedoes or SS-N-15 Starfish ASW weapon with 200Kt depth charge; 16 x SS-N-23 Skiff SL ballistic missiles, 4–10 MIRVed 100kT warheads
Propulsion: 2PWR nuclear reactor
Speed: 14 knots (surfaced); 24 knots (dived)
Complement: 135 men

445

LEFT: At the time of its arrival in 1972, the Sierra class represented what Russian warfare analysts *Warfare.RU* described as the apex of Soviet attack submarine design. These boats were intended to be the primary Soviet attack weapon, "incorporating a variety of new sensors, silencing equipment, command systems and countermeasures".
ABOVE: A profile of the Sierra design. BELOW: A starboard bow overhead view of the Sierra II.

Sierra-class SSN

The Sierra series was introduced as a successor to the Alfa, again with the primary objective of attacking surface task forces, with a secondary commitment of launching cruise missiles against land-based objectives. Described in the Russian Arms Catalogue as the apex of Soviet attack submarine design when the class was developed in 1972, the Sierra boats became the first division of Soviet attack submarines of their time. Their eventual appearance in the early 1980s saw them generally accepted as being comparable in performance to early American *Los Angeles*-class vessels.

Noise levels, which had been a problem with the Alfa boats, were reduced by the addition of Cluster Guard anechoic tiles on the outer hull which, also like the Alfa, was constructed of titanium alloy for deep diving, while making the Sierra more difficult to detect. The double hull reduced possible damage to the inner hull's six compartments, and there was also a crew escape chamber said to be capable of bringing up the entire crew from a depth of 1,500m/4,921ft. However, the cost of the titanium hulls made them expensive to produce, and consequently only limited numbers were built.

Even so, the boat performed well and a larger version, Sierra II, was introduced in the late 1980s. This boat was almost 6m/19ft 8in longer and contained an additional compartment, providing better accommodation for the crew, as well as a second crew escape chamber. Further silencing measures were also added, along with a new American-style spherical bow sonar. The expensive nature of the boat, however, was clearly causing concern in the Soviet naval hierarchy. As early as 1976, when the first submarines of the class were being built, it became evident that the titanium hulls were not suited to mass production.

As a result, construction was slower and in the end failed to meet the force requirements. In due course, production of the Sierra class was cancelled before completion of the required numbers, in favour of the less expensive Akula class. The last of the Sierra II boats were commissioned into Russia's Northern Fleet in the early 1990s.

Sierra II-class SSN

Displacement: 7,479 tonnes/7,360.9 tons (surfaced); 8,956 tonnes/8,814.6 tons (submerged)
Length: 111m/364ft 2in
Beam: 14.2m/46ft 7in
Armament: 4 x 650mm/25.6in tubes; 4 x 533mm/21in tubes, 90kg/198lb HE Type 40 torpedoes; SS-N-15 Starfish anti-submarine weapon; SS-N-21 Sampson SLCM with 200kT nuclear warhead
Propulsion: 1 x OK-650 190mW/254,794hp pressurized-water nuclear reactor
Speed: 10 knots (surfaced); 32 knots (dived)
Complement: 59–61 men

ABOVE: A distinctive shape of the two-thirds submerged Sierra II boat, but not for long; only three were built before they were overtaken by the development of the Akula class.

USSR

Akula-classes I and II SSN

This general purpose submarine, better known in the Soviet Union as the Bars (Snow Leopard) class, was constructed from low magnetic steel with a double hull noted for the substantial gap between the outer and inner hulls, thus reducing the threat of internal damage. The use of the hull was authorized in 1976, when the expensive titanium structures were ruled out for future use. Visually, the submarine was also different, with a distinctive high aft fin.

The first of eight boats was laid down in 1979 and in service by the mid-1980s. An improved version was introduced for the last three boats of Series I, and thereafter Series II took over in the 1990s, with 3m/9ft 10in added to the length, although that programme was curtailed after two boats were built, the last being commissioned in June 2000.

Throughout the building of the two designs, the Akula boats were constantly being upgraded and improved and eventually became one of the quietest Russian submarine classes, a vital improvement since the class was to function in various roles, principally as an attack boat against hostile battlegroups and against coastal installations.

The low acoustic signature was apparently achieved by, among other things, the installation of active noise cancellation techniques, some of which were unsurprisingly similar to Western commercial techniques, thus increasing the survivability potential while at the same time improving the sensitivity of the on-board sonar in detecting hostile weapons or boats. The weaponry was substantial, and included 12 Granat submarine-launched cruise missiles capable of carrying a 200kT warhead to a range of over 3,000km/1,864 miles.

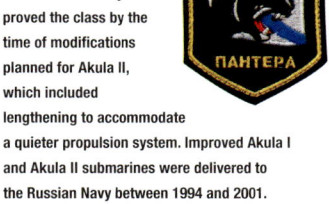

ABOVE LEFT: Project 971 submarines, known in the West as the *Akula*-class nuclear-powered attack submarines (SSN), were deployed to the Pacific region in multi-purpose roles, being capable of strikes against groups of hostile ships and against coastal installations. Akula I had already proved the class by the time of modifications planned for Akula II, which included lengthening to accommodate a quieter propulsion system. Improved Akula I and Akula II submarines were delivered to the Russian Navy between 1994 and 2001. ABOVE: The retractable masts viewed from bow to stern are the periscopes, radar antennae, radio and satellite communications and navigation masts. INSET: The badge of Akula K317 Pantera.

Akula I class

Displacement: 7,381 tonnes/7,264.4 tons (surfaced); 8,956 tonnes/8,814.6 tons (submerged)
Length: 108m/354ft 4in
Beam: 14m/45ft 11in
Armament: 4 x 650mm/25.6in tubes; 4 x 533mm/21in tubes; 90kg/198lb HE Type 40 torpedoes; SS-N-15 Starfish anti-submarine weapon, SS-N-21 Sampson SLCM with 200kT nuclear warhead
Propulsion: 1 x pressurized-water reactor 190mW/254,794hp; 2 X 750hp emergency motors
Speed: 10 knots (surfaced); 28 knots (dived)
Complement: 62 men

ABOVE: The last Akula II submarine equipped with the best that the Russian shipbuilders could provide was commissioned into Russia's 24th Division, Northern Fleet, on December 4, 2001. President Putin described this as "an event of special national importance".

Oscar II-class SSGN

This massive 14,225-tonne/14,000-ton boat that could dive to 304.8m/1,000ft was a brilliant construction with a blot on its copybook – the *Kursk* disaster. Again lining up in the Soviet armoury as a giant whose sole mission in life was to attack battlegroups of the North Atlantic Treaty Organization, the Oscar boats were at the epicentre of Soviet battle plans for two and a half decades. They came equipped with a strong stable of surface-to-surface weapons, with 24 missiles in two banks of 12. These were set in pairs on an incline of 40 degrees outside the 8.53m/28ft pressure hull. This in turn created a gap of 3.5m/11ft 6in between the inner and outer shell, resulting in a huge, unheard-of 18m/59ft beam that, in turn, made it possible to withstand moderate battle damage.

ABOVE: A portrait of Oscar II, or to give this one a name, *Veronesh*, first of the Oscar II SSGN, Type 9489A, whose eight sisters in this class included the ill-fated *Kursk*. As can be seen from this classic shot against the mountainous background, they were indeed massive submarines and were said to be slow to dive and tough to manoeuvre, though they are also credited with a submerged speed of about 30 knots, easily adequate to keep pace with their targets. BELOW LEFT: A close-up of the sail and missile hatch area of the Oscar II. At the stern, all have a tube on the rudder fin as in Delta IV, which is used for dispensing a thin line-towed sonar array.

It also came with numerous optional extras which were entirely fitting for a boat of this nature. They included a reinforced rounded cover of the sail to break through the Arctic ice cap. The two periscopes, radio-sextant and radar masts were sited in the retractable devices area, where there was a floating antenna buoy to receive radio messages, target designation data and satellite navigation signals at a great depth and under the ice. Although said to be slow divers and difficult to manoeuvre, down and in a straight line they could achieve in excess of 30 knots, which was more than sufficient to shadow their targets.

The firepower on board was 24 SS-N-19 Granat (which NATO codenamed Shipwreck) cruise missiles with a range of 550km/342 miles, with a 1,000kg/2,205lb warhead. Under the START treaty, however, high explosives replaced the nuclear warheads. The tubes opened in pairs with a single hatch covering each pair. The torpedo tubes, meanwhile, were capable of firing both torpedoes and shorter range anti-ship missiles. Consequently, a combination of 24 weapons was

USSR

carried, as well as a Type 40 torpedo. It was a Type 65 high test peroxide 650mmm/25.6in torpedo that was found to have caused the sinking of the *Kursk* on August 12, 2000, with the loss of all 118 crew. The blast triggered a further explosion in the weapons compartment that caused the vessel to sink. The blast was caused by highly volatile torpedo propellant that leaked and came in contact with kerosene and metal. The Russians completed several new submarines of the third generation Oscar II, 11 of which were the larger Oscar II boats, built between 1985 and 2001.

ABOVE: Despite the billions spent in dollars, pounds and roubles, it happens to them all in the end, and sometimes in an unsophisticated manner: this Oscar submarine is shown in a breaker's yard with its nuclear fuel and reactors detached and embalmed for safe disposal. The nuclear fuel is removed from the reactor and sent to a processing plant, while the nuclear reactor compartments are cut out, carefully sealed and taken to an approved disposal site. INSET: The badge of the Oscar II submarine *Omsk*.

LEFT: The exceptionally wide beam of the Oscar II version accommodates the surface-to-surface missile (SSM) tubes, which are in banks of 12 on either side and external to the 8.5m/27ft-diameter pressure hull. The tubes are inclined at a 40-degree angle, with one hatch covering each pair.

Oscar II-class SSGN

Displacement: 13,680 tonnes/13,464 tons (surfaced); 18,010 tonnes/17,726 tons (submerged)
Length: 153.9m/504ft 11in
Beam: 18.19m/56ft 8in
Armament: 4 x 533mm/21in tubes; 4 x 650mm25.6in tubes, Type 45 torpedo; SSM – 24 x SS-N-19 Shipwreck; A/S: SS-N-15 fired from 533mm/21in tubes, SS-N-16 fired from 650mm/25.6in tubes
Propulsion: 2 x VM-5 190mW/254,794hp pressurized-water nuclear reactors (OK-650b); 2 x steam turbines, 67,113kW/90,000shp
Speed: 15 knots (surfaced); 28 knots (dived)
Complement: 107 men

449

Typhoon-class SSBN

The Typhoon submarines were the largest ever built and truly a defining feature of the Cold War. The sheer size, capability and destructive power of these boats was awesome, as was the fact that they could stay submerged for months if need demanded it. They operated principally in the waters of the North Atlantic, with each boat capable of carrying 20 long-range ballistic missiles with up to 200 nuclear warheads that were once aimed specifically at cities of the United States. Indeed, one of the principal roles of this boat was that in the event of nuclear exchanges, the Typhoon would sit it out beneath the Arctic ocean to maintain a "survivable nuclear retaliatory strike capability" for the Soviet leadership. From the outset, the boats had been fully equipped for under-ice operations with a fin strengthened and contoured to break through an ice cap up to 3.7m/12ft thick. This, of course, was one of the reasons that American and British submarines were, over the years, to be found making highly publicized and well photographed sorties to the Arctic, showing their own capacity for rising up through the ice.

The Typhoons were originally built at the Severodvinsk Shipyard on the White Sea near Archangel, and six were delivered to the Soviet Navy between 1981 and 1989 for service with the Northern Fleet. They were hugely expensive to run but even so, three remained in operation into the 21st century, with one converted to a training vessel. The rest are waiting to be scrapped and recycled with assistance from the United States under the Co-operative Threat Reduction

ABOVE: The Typhoon class was developed under Project 941 as the Russian Akula class – Akula meaning "shark", which was confusing in the West because Akula was the name NATO used to designate the Russian Project 971-class attack submarines. Typhoon submarines became one of the quietest sea vessels in operation at this time, being more silent and yet more manoeuvrable than their predecessors.

BELOW: Inside the control room of a *Typhoon*-class submarine. Speed is 12 knots when surfaced and 25 knots when submerged, and the submarine is capable of spending 120 days at sea.

BELOW: The Typhoon carried intercontinental, three-stage solid propellant ballistic missiles, each missile consisting of ten independently targetable multiple re-entry vehicles, each with a 100kT nuclear warhead with a range of 8,300km/5,157 miles.

USSR

FAR LEFT: **A bow-facing overhead view of the Typhoon, showing the area of the missile housing: two rows of ten launch tubes are situated in front of the sail between the main hulls.**

ABOVE: **A profile of the Typhoon class, which is now being decommissioned through US-funded processing facilities and converted into forms suitable for long-term storage or re-use; Britain has also agreed to assist.**

an electronics suite that was unlike anything the Russians had previously produced in terms of its spaceship-style appearance. At the time of construction, there were also a number of interesting innovations, including an advanced stern fin with horizontal retractable hydroplane. The system also included two periscopes, radar, radio communications, navigation and direction finder masts. They were all housed within the sail guard.

The submarine's main arsenal was 20 RSM-52 intercontinental three-stage solid propellant ballistic missiles located in two rows of missile launch tubes in front of the sail between the main hulls. Each missile consisted of ten independently targetable re-entry vehicles (MIRVs), each with a 100kT nuclear warhead. The missiles had a range of 8,208km/5,100 miles, putting large portions of the Western Hemisphere into the attack zone without the submarine even leaving port.

The submarine's main machinery consists of two nuclear water reactors and two turbogear assemblies comprising a steam turbine and gearbox. One reactor and one turbogear assembly are fitted in each main hull. Each nuclear water reactor produced 190mW/254,794hp driving 37,285kW/50,000hp steam turbines and four 3,200kW/4,291hp turbogenerators. Two 800kW/1.073hp diesel generators served as standby propulsion units coupled to the shaft line. The two propellers are seven-blade, fixed-pitch shrouded. The built-in thrusters on the bow and stern are two telescopic turning screw rudders and are powered by a 750kW/1,005hp motor.

Programme. Britain has also joined the disposal effort, and along with all nations who possess nuclear boats, there is now a worldwide strategy for processing these old nuclear reactors, and converting them into a state for recycling or long-term storage. There remains considerable international disquiet over the safety of the rotting hulls.

Even so, the Typhoon submarine was an incredible engineering feat, being a multi-hulled boat with five inner hulls within a superstructure of two parallel main hulls. Nineteen separate compartments within the boat included a strengthened module housing a vast control room and

RIGHT: **A *Typhoon*-class submarine showing the sail with its retractable masts. The design also includes features for travelling under ice and equipment for breaking through it. Maximum diving depth is 400m/1312ft.**

Typhoon-class SSBN

Displacement: 23,265 tonnes/22,897.6 tons (surfaced); 33,787 tonnes/33,253.4 tons (submerged)
Length: 172m/564ft 4in
Beam: 23m/75ft 6in
Armament: 4 x 711mm/28in tubes; 2 x 533mm/21in tubes; 22 x anti-ship missiles and torpedoes; 20 RSM-52 ballistic missiles and 20 launchers
Propulsion: 2 x mW190/254,794hp nuclear water reactors; 2 x steam turbines, 74,570kW/100,000shp
Speed: 20 knots (surfaced); 25 knots (dived)
Complement: 160 men

A-class SSK

Work began in 1942 to produce a boat with superior speed, range and crew conditions, designed especially for use in the Far East. Based on the T class, but incorporating the lessons learned in war conditions, and even including air conditioning, the boats represented a leap forward. With fully welded hulls and a heavy armament of six forward-firing torpedoes and four firing aft, coupled with an air-warning radar which worked while the boat was submerged, they were a vast technological improvement. They also had the "Snort" breathing capability.

The Admiralty ordered 46 A-class boats with the first, *Amphion*, launched in August 1944. *Astute* was next and these were the only two delivered before hostilities ceased. At first they were unstable, but an extra buoyancy tank cured the problem. When Japan surrendered, 30 of the A-class boats were cancelled. But a new type of war – the Cold War – faced the world, and the 16 A-class boats were fully deployed in improving submarine warfare by undergoing strenuous trials and deployments. *Alliance* and *Ambush* were used to carry out exercises in endurance underwater as they stayed submerged for long periods. *Alliance* sailed submerged for 30 days, and in February 1948, *Ambush* sailed from Rothesay on a submerged patrol that was to last six weeks.

Other craft were submerged – unmanned – to see how deep they could go before the hull failed. *Andrew* sailed submerged for 4,023 km/2,500 miles from Bermuda to England in 15 days, the first submerged trans-Atlantic passage. She was also the last Royal Navy submarine to be fitted with a permanent deck gun.

LEFT: HMS *Artful*, one of the A-class boats that were the backbone of the British submarine fleet in the immediate post-war years.

A-class SSK

Displacement: 1,497.16 tonnes/1,473.5 tons (surfaced); 1,645.92 tonnes/1,619.9 tons (submerged)
Length: 85.85m/281ft 8in
Beam: 6.78m/22ft 3in
Armament: 10 x 533mm/21in tubes (6 x bow – 2 x external, 4 x stern – 2 x external), 20 x torpedoes or 26 mines; 1 x 101mm/4in gun, 1 x 20mm/0.79in anti-aircraft gun
Propulsion: 2 x 3206.5kW/4,300bhp Admiralty or Vickers diesel engines; 2 x 932.1kW/1,250ehp English Electric electric motors
Speed: 18.5 knots (surfaced); 8 knots (dived)
Complement: 60 men

Porpoise class (Late)

If the A class was considered a leap forward, the Porpoise was a giant one. As the first post-World War II designed boat to enter service, it was capable of high underwater speed, very deep diving and was very quiet. It was fitted with very large batteries to store the power required, and with its advanced snort and replenishment systems could operate independently without support anywhere in the world for months – exactly what the old time submariners had dreamed of decades earlier.

Porpoise had both air and surface warning radar which could operate at periscope level and while on the surface, as well as an advanced snort system which allowed maximum charging even in rough seas. A bonus was that this provided adequate air conditioning for the boats to operate in Arctic or tropical environments and kept it dry internally.

Periods of six weeks underwater were also made possible because of its oxygen replenishment system and the carbon dioxide eliminators. As well as being equipped to distil fresh water from seawater, they had enough space to carry substantial stores to enable them to operate far from home and far from support for long periods.

In general, they were excellent, seaworthy boats superbly manufactured. However, they were already out of date, at least in terms of Britain's ambitions towards being a nuclear power, and these diesel boats began to take a back seat.

LEFT: HMS *Walrus*, of the Porpoise class, noted for its clean welded hulls and for being fast and silent underwater, undoubtedly among the best conventional boats in the world at the time.

Porpoise class (Late)

Displacement: 2,062.48 tonnes/2,029.9 tons (surfaced); 2,443.48 tonnes/2,404.9 tons (submerged)
Length: 89.99m/295ft 3in
Beam: 8.08m/26ft 6in
Armament: 8 x 533mm/21in tubes (6 bow, 2 stern), 30 x torpedoes
Propulsion: 2 x 1,230.4kW/1,650hp Admiralty Standard Range diesel engines; 2 x 3,728.5kW/5,000ehp electric motors
Speed: 12 knots (surfaced); 17 knots (dived)
Complement: 71 men

UNITED KINGDOM

LEFT AND BELOW LEFT:
HMS *Explorer* was an experimental boat, but initially had so many problems that her first captain was never able to take her to sea. The issues were eventually resolved, but the boat was scrapped.

Explorer class

Displacement: 1,117.6 tonnes/1,099.9 tons (surfaced); 1,216.15 tonnes/1,196.9 tons (submerged)
Length: 68.74m/225ft 6in
Beam: 4.76m/15ft 7in
Armament: Nil
Propulsion: 11,185.5kW/15,000shp Vickers Armstrong hydrogen peroxide plant; 2 x diesel engines; 2 x electric motors
Speed: 15 knots (surfaced); 25 knots (dived)
Complement: 41 men

Explorer class

Designed to trial a new diesel-electric powerplant that incorporated hydrogen peroxide in its fuels, these were believed to be the fastest submarines in the world at the time. The main propulsion was provided by turbines powered with steam and carbon dioxide, which enabled the boat to produce full power while submerged, independent of any external air source. In addition, the *Explorer*-class boats were fitted with conventional diesel engines for use on the surface and battery-powered electric motors for underwater operations.

Only two boats in this class were built. With retractable fittings improving their already streamlined shape, they had excellent manoeuvrability combined with a high submerged speed. However the fuel was highly unstable, and there were several explosions. As the boats were purely experimental, they were unarmed, and their crews were accommodated in converted minesweepers for safety reasons. Capable of 25 knots submerged, they were very fast. But once the Americans succeeded in building a nuclear reactor for a submarine, the project with the Explorers was quickly terminated.

LEFT: **HMS *Orpheus* of the Oberon class was Britain's first major step into modern design, with improved detection equipment and the ability to fire homing torpedoes. Known for their reliability and quietness, many Oberons were sold to overseas buyers.**

Oberon class

Displacement: 2,062.48 tonnes/2,029.9 tons (surfaced); 2,448.56 tonnes/2,409.9 tons (submerged)
Length: 89.99m/295ft 3in
Beam: 8.08m/26ft 6in
Armament: 8 x 533mm/21in tubes, Mk 8 torpedo, Tigerfish torpedo; Sub-Harpoon anti-ship missiles
Propulsion: 2 x 2,237.1kW/3,000bhp Admiralty Standard Range diesels; 2 x 1,280kw/1,716.5hp electric motors
Speed: 12 knots (surfaced); 17 knots (dived)
Complement: 71 men

Oberon class

Although almost identical to the Porpoise class, the Oberons were fitted with improved detection equipment and were equipped with homing torpedoes. In addition, for the first time in a Royal Navy submarine, plastic was used and glass fibre was incorporated on part of the bridge superstructure and casing. *Oberon*, the first of the class, was launched in 1959. In 1970, during trials in the Mediterranean with a submarine escape-team, a world record was established when the men "escaped" from *Osiris* while she was moving at a depth of 182.9m/600ft.

Only one *Oberon*-class boat – *Onyx* – saw active service when she was the only diesel submarine sent to the Falklands as part of Operation Corporate, and Historic Warships now preserve her at Birkenhead.

In the 1980s, the fitting of sonar and the capability to fire Tigerfish torpedoes and Harpoon anti-ship missiles enhanced the performance of Oberon boats, and the submarines had the ability to guide two torpedoes simultaneously. *Otus* also took part in a series of trials in a Norwegian fjord to determine at which depth submariners could safely expect to escape from a stricken submarine. Two sailors managed to "escape" from 182.9m/600ft yet again. A number of the boats were eventually leased and then sold to Canada.

453

Dreadnought SSN

Britain's own nuclear reactor for submarines was still under development at the newly-formed naval section of the Atomic Research Station at Harwell when the decision was made to proceed with the building of Britain's first nuclear-powered submarine, *Dreadnought*. Consequently, with Cold War tensions rising by the day, American expertise was called upon in utilizing the new teardrop design of USS *Albacore* for the hull design, and the purchase of the nuclear reactor. She was laid down in June 1959, launched by the Queen on Trafalgar Day 1960 and commissioned in April 1963 in the role of hunter-killer.

It was the beginning of a long and successful British involvement in nuclear submarine production. *Dreadnought*, meanwhile, was soon displaying her mettle, when in 1967 she travelled from Rosyth to Singapore and back, travelling 7,467km/4,640 miles surfaced and 4,271km/2,654 miles submerged. In 1971, she became the first British submarine to surface through the ice at the North Pole.

Such events were, of course, soon to become commonplace, but at the time they were momentous and a great achievement by the crews, who had to adapt to a whole new way of life. With long periods submerged without a glimmer of daylight or fresh air, accommodation and facilities were of an unprecedented standard. Particular attention was paid to the decoration and furnishing of living quarters and recreational spaces, which include cinema equipment, a library and tape recordings to relieve the monotony associated with prolonged voyages.

Her early operations included the Royal Navy's first annual Group Deployment in 1977, designed to demonstrate to the world the fighting efficiency of British warships and submarines. In the same year, *Dreadnought* joined a secret task force to the South Atlantic with frigates *Alacrity* and *Phoebe* and auxiliaries *Resource* and *Olwen*, at a time when Argentina appeared to be taking an aggressive stance over her claim to possession of the Falkland Islands. The Argentine military junta backed away, but the threat remained and within five years, *Dreadnought*'s sister submarines of the newer classes were called into action in those unforgiving waters.

As with the first nuclear boats of other nations, and the USSR in particular, *Dreadnought* was small and noisy compared with the later arrivals. Moreover, as the leader of what was, in effect, an experimental project, *Dreadnought* began to suffer from a number of technical problems. She was subsequently withdrawn from service under the 1981 Defence Review and moved to Rothsyth for her retirement.

ABOVE LEFT: *Dreadnought* represented Britain's entry into the world of nuclear-powered submarines in 1962, completing her first dive in Ramsden Dock in January 1963, thus equipping the nation with one of the most potent attack submarines, albeit of an experimental nature, in the world at that time.
ABOVE: **A close-up bow view of the *Dreadnought* sail.**

LEFT: **The launch of *Dreadnought* brought a new era of life at sea for the submariner, whose accommodation was of an unprecedented standard in terms of ablutions, living quarters and recreational areas, which included a cinema and library. This would help them as they faced the prospect of long voyages underwater.**

Dreadnought SSN

- **Displacement:** 3,448 tonnes/3,393.5 tons (surfaced); 3,937 tonnes/3,874.8 tons (submerged)
- **Length:** 81m/265ft 9in
- **Beam:** 9.8m/32ft 2in
- **Armament:** 6 x 533mm/21in tubes, 24 x torpedoes
- **Propulsion:** Rolls-Royce-Westinghouse S5W nuclear reactor driving 2 x steam turbines, 11,185.5kW/15,000shp
- **Speed:** 25 knots (surfaced); 30 knots (dived)
- **Complement:** 113 men

UNITED KINGDOM

LEFT AND ABOVE: **A view of *Warspite*, of the Valiant class, similar in almost every respect to the *Dreadnought*. The Valiant boats were, however, significantly quieter than their predecessor and equipped with a diesel-electric generator that could be used for silent running in emergencies.**
INSET: **The badge of HMS *Valiant*, depicting a proud fighting cockerel.**

Valiant-class SSN

Valiant and sister ship *Warspite* led the all-British technology programme with a nuclear reactor developed at Dounreay, Scotland, by Rolls-Royce and the Atomic Energy Authority. Although *Dreadnought* was still under construction when *Valiant* was laid down in 1960, there was still sufficient time to take note of lessons learned, and consequently, noise levels rather than speed became the first priority with the new class ahead of *Valiant*'s commissioning in July 1966. She joined the Third Submarine Squadron at Faslane and, like *Dreadnought*, one of her early tasks was to undertake the run from the United Kingdom to Singapore. *Valiant* went one better than her predecessor on this mission, completing the 19,312km/12,000-mile journey in 28 days, during which she was submerged throughout. This was a record for any British vessel at the time, although it would soon be broken again and again.

In the 1970s, *Valiant* and her sister *Warspite* remained in constant service and set a number of endurance records for British boats, which to some extent was due to the delay in the arrival of further British SSNs when all resources were deployed on the construction of the nation's first Polaris-carrying SSBNs of the Resolution class. As a result, *Valiant* remained in service longer than any of the early British nuclear boats, recording a total of 1,068,148km/576,754 nautical miles and 53,840 hours (2,243 days) at sea during her career. Not unsurprisingly for such a workhorse, *Valiant* developed engine problems in June 1994 while returning from America. One month later, she was sent into retirement and laid up at Devonport, where she was occasionally open for public inspection.

Warspite, commissioned in April 1967, was also in almost constant operational mode but in May 1976 suffered a fire which put her out of commission for two years for repairs and refitting. On her return to duty, she was part of the British Task force sent to the South Atlantic at the time of the Falklands War. She remained active for another nine years before she was taken out of service following the discovery of hairline cracks in the primary coolant circuit during a refit, and was laid up two years earlier than *Valiant*.

LEFT: **Leader of the class, HMS *Valiant*, after her much-vaunted launch following completion at the Vickers Barrow-in-Furness yards to begin 18 years of continuous and successful service. This inspired her use as the template for Britain's *Resolution*-class ballistic submarine and subsequent fleet submarines.**

Valiant-class SSN

Displacement: 4,232 tonnes/4,165.2 tons (surfaced); 4,800 tonnes/4,724.2 tons (submerged)
Length: 86.9m/285ft 1in
Beam: 10.1m/33ft 2in
Armament: 6 x 533mm/21in tubes (bow), 24 torpedoes
Propulsion: 1 x Rolls-Royce Pressurized Water Reactor (2 x English Electric steam turbines, 11,185.5kW/15,000hp); 1 x Paxman diesel-electric generator
Speed: 20 knots (surfaced); 28 knots (dived)
Complement: 116 men

LEFT: **A giant of their own, but with American nuclear weapons, HMS *Resolution* heralded Britain's arrival in this exclusive club of ballistic boomers in which membership was expensive, beginning at £40 million for the first of the class and rising.** BELOW: **The American-supplied Polaris ballistic missile for the Resolution class underwent a British-designed life-extension programme called Chevaline, which reduced the number of warheads and added defensive countermeasures. It replaced Britain's own Blue Streak and Skybolt missiles, which were cancelled because of their cost.**
BELOW LEFT: **The badge of *Resolution*.**

Resolution-class SSBN

The *Resolution*-class submarines were the first British strategic ballistic missile submarines to carry Polaris missiles. Five boats were originally planned, but the order was cut to four by the incoming Labour government in 1964. That their arrival marked the era of the submarine as a capital ship was recognized by naming the four boats after great British capital ships of the past, *Resolution*, *Repulse*, *Renown* and *Revenge*. Their arrival also marked an important milestone in Britain's overall capability as a nuclear power, two previous missile programmes having been aborted. The boats would each carry 16 US Polaris A3 missiles and consequently, the bow and stern were constructed separately to be assembled later with the American-designed missile compartment. The missiles measured 9.4m/31ft long and had a range of 4630km/2,500 nautical miles.

By then, the United States and the Soviet Union were already head to head in the era of using a submarine-based nuclear deterrent, where weapons could be hidden beneath the waves and launched from virtually anywhere in the world to reach virtually any position. At the same time, being nuclear powered, the submarines could and would roam the oceans unhindered for months on end without the need to surface.

Resolution was commissioned in 1967 and then pursued a year of training and sea trials before she took off for Cape Kennedy for the test firing of a Polaris missile. Five months later, in June 1968, *Resolution* commenced her first operational patrol, thereby embarking on a journey that was to last 28 years of Polaris patrols. At the time, the *Daily Telegraph* recorded in a leader article: "The *Resolution* in making her first dive of her patrol into the waters of a troubled world will be taking out on behalf of the nation the best insurance policy it has ever had".

LEFT: **Deliveries of supplies or personnel, or extractions of sick submariners unable to be treated at sea (as seen here), were often made by Sea King helicopters flown from a surface vessel. These helicopters were also extensively deployed on anti-submarine warfare operations by the Royal Navy, as well as in search-and-rescue and airborne early-warning missions.**

UNITED KINGDOM

FAR LEFT: **The loading of the Polaris ballistic missiles into a *Resolution*-class submarine, thus enabling Britain to move a survivable nuclear system within range of enemy targets. Although the submarine was not capable of destroying hardened targets, it would have been effective against population centres, a targeting decision that would ultimately rest with the government.** LEFT: **A busy day at the office. For the most part, a smart dress code was adhered to in the control centres of the ballistic submarines, and indeed in all modern boats.**

The new boats had a similarity in size and appearance with the US Los Angeles class, although like all British submarines, the hydroplanes were located on the bow rather than the fin. At the beginning of their assigned patrols, the Polaris boats would leave Faslane, submerge and remain submerged on a course and location unknown to all but the highest ranking officers among the 156 men aboard. The Royal Navy operated a system similar to the both the Americans and the Russians whereby each submarine had two crews – known as Port and Starboard in Britain – with one on leave or training, while the other was at sea. Living conditions onboard were even better than on the new SSNs and they needed to be, given the length of time the crews would be on patrol.

In the early 1980s, the British government forged an agreement to take the new American Trident missile system, for which four new boats of the Vanguard class would be needed. In the meantime, the existing Polaris system was upgraded with a new warhead codenamed Chevaline, and fitted to the four Resolution boats over a period of four years. This would keep the British nuclear capability afloat until the early 1990s, when the changeover was due to take place.

Revenge was paid off in May 1992, followed by *Resolution* six months later. *Renown* remained in service until 1995 and *Repulse* the following year, by which time the four Trident boats were operational.

The Resolutions left behind a remarkable record, having conducted an unbroken sequence of 229 patrols in which, fortunately, they were never called upon to fire in anger. Their record was marked by a monument to the Polaris submarines that recognized not only the contribution of the crews who took them on patrol, but also those on shore, and the control, command and maintenance teams, all of whose work was equally vital.

LEFT: **A view of the sail and missile compartment of *Resolution*, where 16 Polaris A3s were carried in two rows of eight. There was also an emergency diesel generator and six 533mm/21in torpedo tubes located at the bow, capable of firing Tigerfish wire-guided homing torpedoes.**

Resolution-class SSBN

Displacement: 7,381 tonnes/7,264.4 tons (surfaced); 8,267 tonnes/8,136.4 tons (submerged)
Length: 130m/426ft 6in
Beam: 10.1m/33ft 2in
Armament: 6 x 533mm/21in tubes (bow); 16 x A3 SLBM Polaris ballistic missiles
Propulsion: Rolls-Royce PRW1 nuclear reactor (2 x English Electric steam turbines producing 11,185.5kW/15,000shp); 1 x back-up diesel generator 2982.8kW/4,000bhp
Speed: 20 knots (surfaced); 25 knots (dived)
Complement: 156 men (two crews)

DIRECTORY OF SUBMARINES: 1945 TO DATE

LEFT: **Class leader HMS *Churchill* took the British attack-submarine contingent to the next level with a trio of boats. Sister ships *Courageous* and *Conqueror*, along with *Valiant*, became the first British submarines to be placed on war alert since 1945 – for the Falklands conflict in 1982.** BELOW: ***Courageous* also became the first British submarine to carry the Sub-Harpoon missile.**

Churchill-class SSN

This class represented the resumption of work on the Valiant class, which had been suspended to place all British resources into the Resolution ballistic missile submarines. Now, three more boats, *Churchill* and *Courageous* at Vickers and *Conqueror* at Cammell Laird were built to begin what would become almost 60 years of combined service. The class leader was, of course, named after one of Britain's great heroes, who himself was a foremost advocate of submarine development when he was First Lord of the Admiralty prior to World War I. It was a fitting tribute since it was he who had insisted that submarines be named rather than carry a number.

With the benefit of *Dreadnought* and *Valiant*-class experience, the Churchills included a number of improvements, especially in weaponry. *Churchill* was selected to evaluate both the American Mk 48 torpedo and the Sub-Harpoon anti-ship missile, although only the latter was selected for use and was fitted first to the sister ship *Courageous*. In terms of operational activity, the Churchills remained busy through their lifespan with *Conqueror*, under the command of Christopher Wreford-Brown (who was later awarded the DSO), famously sinking the Argentine ship *General Belgrano* during the Falklands conflict, an act which cost 368 seamen their lives.

Controversially *Conqueror*'s crew flew the Jolly Roger as she returned to Faslane, a customary act of Royal Navy submarines after a mission on which a "kill" has been achieved. Even so, she was the first nuclear-powered submarine to fire in anger, and by 2005 she remained the only one to engage and sink an enemy ship with torpedoes. *Conqueror* and *Churchill* remained in service until 1990. *Courageous*, which also served in the Falklands, was paid off in 1992.

LEFT: ***Conqueror* receiving her load of Tigerfish wire-guided homing torpedoes, although when she achieved the distinction of being the only nuclear-powered submarine to have sunk a surface warship in anger, the Argentine ship *General Belgrano*, she was using conventional Mk 8 torpedoes.**

LEFT: **The badge of HMS *Churchill*. She was taken out of service and laid up in the early 1990s for mothballing before finally being scrapped.**

Churchill-class SSN

Displacement: 4,133 tonnes/4,067.7 tons (surfaced); 4,822 tonnes/4,745.8 tons (submerged)
Length: 86.9m/285ft 1in
Beam: 10.10m/33ft 2in
Armament: 6 x 533mm/21in tubes (bow), 26 x torpedoes and/or mines
Propulsion: Rolls-Royce PWR nuclear reactor driving 2 x English Electric steam turbines, 11,185.5kW/15,000shp; 1 x Paxman diesel generator also fitted
Speed: 22 knots (surfaced); 28 knots (dived)
Complement: 103 men

UNITED KINGDOM

LEFT: **The Swiftsure boats took the British capability to a new level and ensured that a busy submarine workload could be safely met well into the 21st century. They were also the first to receive the Tomahawk land attack missiles (TLAMs).**
ABOVE: **HMS** *Splendid* **pictured in dry dock was the busiest of boats, firing her TLAMs in the first Gulf War, the Kosovo crisis and the post-9/11 action against Afghanistan.**

Swiftsure-class SSN

This class followed on from the Valiant and Churchill boats and with updates and improvements, including what was described as a cylindrical hull and improved sonar. The boats also showed an improvement on their predecessors in a number of operational areas in that they were quieter, faster to submerge and could dive to greater depths. The first boats came on the scene in the late 1970s, and indeed two of them – *Splendid* and *Spartan* – saw almost immediate action in the Falklands, operating at the time *Conqueror* was shadowing the *Belgrano*. At the same time, *Splendid* and *Spartan* were on the lookout for an Argentinian aircraft carrier which was reportedly heading towards the Falklands, but the vessel turned back prior to the *Belgrano* sinking, apparently through intelligence that the British nuclear submarines were operating in the area.

The Swiftsure boats went on to have long careers, and were chosen to lead the Royal Navy into the conversion to Tomahawk cruise missiles. *Splendid* became the first Royal Navy submarine to be equipped with such a capability, having been retrofitted with the equipment in 1998. Her initial target practice was a small building in the United States 644km/400 miles inland, which she hit with perfection. *Splendid* then went on to become the first British submarine to fire a shot in anger since the Falklands and the first to launch an attack using cruise missiles when she joined the Americans in the bombing campaign against Serbian targets during the Kosovo crisis of 1999. Later, she and others were extensively used in cruise missile attacks on land-based targets in Afghanistan and the Persian Gulf. Between 1987 and 1993 *Spartan*, *Splendid* and *Sceptre* were fitted with improved nuclear reactor cores, but the leader of the class, *Swiftsure* was decommissioned in 1992, well short of her anticipated life, due to technical problems.

In 1997, the new Labour Government ordered a review of defence spending and, coupled with the need for a new SSN class within ten years, agreed to go ahead with the Astute programme if the overall number of attack boats was cut from 12 boats to 10 boats. This was to be achieved by the decommissioning of *Splendid* in 2003 and *Spartan* in 2006, which would leave *Sovereign*, *Superb* and *Sceptre* still operational.

LEFT: **HMS** *Superb*, **the last of the Swiftsure class, during the much-photographed event of bursting through the ice at the North Pole.**

Swiftsure-class SSN

Displacement: 4,445 tonnes/4,374.8 tons (surfaced); 4,900 tonnes/4,822.6 tons (submerged)
Length: 82.9m/272ft
Beam: 8.9m/29ft 2in
Armament: 5 x tubes capable of firing Spearfish torpedoes, RN Sub-Harpoon missiles, Tomahawk missiles
Propulsion: 1 PWR reactor; 2 x General Electric Steam Turbines, 11,185.5kW/15,000shp; 2 x Paxman diesels, 2982.8kW/4,000shp
Speed: 24 knots (surfaced); 30 knots (dived)
Complement: 116 men

Trafalgar-class SSN

The T boats, as they became known after their World War II namesakes, represented the largest number in a single class of nuclear boats built by the Royal Navy. Seven boats were constructed and represented major improvements on the Swiftsure class, which was in turn a derivative of the Churchill class. The submarines *Trafalgar*, *Turbulent*, *Tireless*, *Torbay*, *Trenchant*, *Talent* and *Triumph* would ostensibly become the Royal Navy's most advanced nuclear fleet submarine until the planned introduction of the Astute class, scheduled for 2006/7.

The T boats, whose design literature came a full six years after that of the Swiftsures, arrived into commission over a ten-year period from 1983. They were heralded with publicity regarding their major improvements, which include a new reactor core and the Type 2020 sonar. Even so, internal layout was nearly identical to the *Swiftsure*, and they were only 2.5m/8ft 2in longer.

Once again the emphasis was on quietening processes, and instead of the seven-bladed propeller on the Swiftsures, *Trafalgar*-class submarines used pump-jet propulsion, which was a low-revolution propeller which is much quieter but much heavier than conventional propeller designs, although it was not available in time for the commissioning of the first boat,

ABOVE: The famously named boats of the *Trafalgar*-class hunter-killers such as HMS *Tireless* used a high-pitch, low-revolution propeller which was much quieter than earlier designs. The hull was also covered in anechoic tiles designed to absorb sound. There were a number of other innovations, including a strengthened fin and retractable hydroplanes, allowing them to surface through thick ice. There was also a new record set in 1993, when *Triumph* sailed to Australia, covering a distance of 66,000km/41,000 miles while submerged and without any forward support. This represented the longest solo deployment by any nuclear submarine. LEFT: A typical control room of the Trafalgar class. INSET: The badge of the lead boat.

UNITED KINGDOM

LEFT AND BELOW: **Two views of the Trafalgar boats, showing the retractable sail attachments and missile areas. The Sub-Harpoon long-range anti-ship missile, with a range of 110kms/68.35 miles, became the principal anti-surface ship weapon in these submarines. They were also armed with homing torpedoes that can be used against other submarines or surface vessels.**

Trafalgar. Despite these advances, there were problems that brought some boats in this class a good deal of publicity for the wrong reasons and resulted in them being laid up with reactor malfunction. This also resulted in checks being made on all members of the class. The first was *Tireless*, on which a coolant leak in the reactor caused her to interrupt a world cruise and limp into Gibraltar, where local inhabitants were none too happy.

Other boats were also laid up, some tested for what became known as The Tireless Fault. Several went through long refits in the early 2000s, and were all back in action and destined to remain so through the first decade of the 21st century.

ABOVE: **An excellent port view providing an overall look at the Trafalgar class.**
BELOW LEFT: **The long endurance and sophisticated weapon systems of the Trafalgar boats made them formidable adversaries and of course required fully trained teams at every control centre and computer screen. Although there were three decks, the emphasis on technology meant that, while space was restricted, living conditions were comfortable.**

Trafalgar-class SSN

Displacement: 4,650 tonnes/4,576.6 tons (surfaced); 5,200 tonnes/5,117.9 tons (submerged)
Length: 85.4m/280ft 2in
Beam: 9.8m/32ft 2in
Armament: 5 x tubes capable of firing Spearfish torpedoes, RN Sub-Harpoon missiles, Tomahawk missiles
Propulsion: 1PWR nuclear reactor, 11,185.5kW/15,000shp
Speed: 25 knots (surfaced); 30 knots (dived)
Complement: 130 men

Vanguard-class SSBN

According to some naval analysts, the arrival of Britain's new SSBN *Vanguard* represented a masterclass in submarine building. Some 14 years after the start of the Trident project, the first submarine entered service on time, in December 1994. The remaining three – *Victorious*, *Vigilant* and *Vengeance* – repeated the performance at yearly intervals to form a squadron of purpose-built boats carrying the only remaining nuclear weapon system in the employ of the United Kingdom – the much-vaunted Trident D5.

At over 150m/492ft in length and 16,000 tonnes/15,747 tons displacement, they have almost twice the displacement of the Polaris carriers of the Resolution class. The 16-tube missile compartment is based on the design of the 24-tube system used in the American *Ohio*-class Trident submarines. Other than that, Vanguard is all British, designed and built by Vickers Shipbuilding and Engineering Limited at Barrow-in-Furness and, by a significant margin, the largest ever manufactured in the United Kingdom and the third largest vessel in the Royal Navy as a whole. In fact, a special manufacturing facility, the Devonshire Dock Hall, had to be purpose-built at Barrow for

TOP: The Royal Navy was justly proud to take delivery of the Vanguard submarines, impressively deadly and as capable as any other submarines in the world.
ABOVE: Every picture tells a story. The Vanguard Trident ballistic missile carriers are Britain's largest ever submarines and in terms of design, style, accommodation and engineering, they are, without doubt, magnificent boats, notwithstanding that they carried the power to annihilate a large number of the world's population, perhaps in collaboration with their American counterparts, the *Ohio*-class submarines. ABOVE RIGHT: The *Vanguard* badge, which every member of the crews who alternately sail in her is proud to possess.

UNITED KINGDOM

LEFT: **Shadows of the night.** *Vanguard* arrived at Devonport Naval Base in 2002 for a two-year refit, which was completed in January 2005. Following sea trials, which included test launching of Trident II D5 ballistic missiles, the vessel returned to the fleet. HMS *Victorious* began its refit in January 2005. ABOVE: A profile of the *Vanguard*, which gives an idea of proportions.

ABOVE: **A test firing of the Trident II missile,** of which the *Vanguard* has the capacity to carry 16. Each missile can carry up to 12 warheads, giving a potential of 192 warheads in each boat. However, in line with arms limitation agreements, the British government has agreed that each of the D5 missiles carried by the Vanguard class would contain a maximum of four warheads, and that each vessel would therefore carry a maximum of 48 warheads.

their construction. Even so, with greater automation, the crew of a *Vanguard*-class boat is smaller at 132 officers and men compared to a Polaris submarine's crew of 149.

The *Vanguard*-class boats include a number of improvements over previous British submarines, including a new design of nuclear propulsion system and a new tactical weapon system for self-defence purposes both before and after missile launch. Although each *Vanguard*-class submarine is capable of carrying 192 warheads, the boats will in fact deploy no more than 96, and possibly significantly fewer. Since January 1995, British Trident submarines have taken on a secondary "sub-strategic" role in the international scheme of things since the Cold War ended, with a number of Trident missiles carrying only one nuclear warhead. The submarines in reserve may be armed with 11 missiles, each with eight warheads, four missiles with one warhead on each, plus an Active Inert Missile during trials.

Although the threat of a nuclear conflagration has subsided, most naval analysts consider that the £12.57 billion cost of acquiring the Trident fleet was money well spent, as is the annual operating costs, running at around £200 million a year over an estimated 30-year in-service life. There is also a fair body of opinion, however, that disagrees.

ABOVE: **All above-water sensors on the *Vanguard*-class boats were combined into self-protection masts in the fin. The submarines were fitted with the CK51 search periscope and the CH91 attack periscope from Pilkington Optronics, which also included a television camera and thermal imager.**

Vanguard-class SSBN

Displacement: 15,130 tonnes/14,891 tons (surfaced); 16,000 tonnes/15,747.3 tons (submerged)
Length: 149.9m/491ft 10in
Beam: 12.8m/42ft
Armament: 4 x 533mm/21in tubes, 18 x Spearfish torpedoes; Trident D5 Weapons system
Propulsion: 1 x Rolls-Royce PWR-2, 20,507kW/27,500shp
Speed: 20 knots (surfaced); 25 knots (dived)
Complement: 132 men

LEFT: An artist's impression of the new British *Astute* attack submarine, which was the result of a 1986 feasibility study by the Royal Navy. Already committed to billions of pounds on the Trident boats, the British government nonetheless agreed further massive expenditure on the new SSN class, which will comprise Britain's largest-ever nuclear-powered attack submarines, the first of which was due into service in 2006. However, original ambitions for seven Astute boats were scaled back to three, to replace five Swiftsure and two Trafalgar boats. ABOVE: The first *Astute* under construction. BELOW: At the screens of the *Astute* combat management system.

Astute-class SSN

With the *Vanguard* build underway, the Royal Navy's department of future requirements turned its attention to a replacement for the ageing Swiftsure attack submarines. A programme of studies costing an estimated £6million was approved in 1991, which led to the issue of an invitation to tender for the design and build three submarines in the new Astute class. The process of design selection, affordability and a whole raft of other procedures had to be negotiated before a successful outcome was achieved six years later, when the prime contractor, GEC-Marconi (now BAE Systems), undertook to build the three boats, with an option for a further two.

The first of class, *Astute*, was laid down in January 2000, the centenary year of the Royal Navy's Submarine Service. Her arrival was anticipated with great interest and expectation, given that the design called for a truly multi-role submarine meeting today's requirements, with a growing emphasis towards possible rogue and terrorist seaborne activity as well as traditional forms of deployment. *Astute* is reckoned to match all requirements and at almost 7,000 tonnes/ 6,889 tons will be the largest and most capable class of attack submarine, with Tomahawk cruise missiles as standard. She will also be armed with six torpedo tubes, able to fire

UNITED KINGDOM

ABOVE AND BELOW: Views of the new submarine on early test trials. The *Astute* will be equipped with Tomahawk Block IV cruise missiles fired from 533mm/21in torpedo tubes. Guidance is by the Navstar Global Positioning System, and the Block IV deal includes a two-way satellite link that allows reprogramming of the missile in flight and transmission of Battle Damage Indication imagery.

ABOVE: Work in progress: the massive construction task confronting BAE Systems Astute Class Ltd, prime contractor for the project, with the submarines being built at BAE Systems Marine Barrow shipyard. The next two Astute ships are to be named *Ambush* and *Artful*. The government will then build three more as the Trafalgar boats are progressively retired.

advanced weapons, including the Spearfish guided torpedo, and, with a larger torpedo room than *Virginia*, she can carry up to 36 torpedoes.

Astute was launched in 2004 and is due to enter service in 2006. Two other boats of this class – *Ambush* and *Artful* – are also being built at Barrow, and overall the project has employed around 5,000 people with the main contractor, sub-contractors and supply chain at the peak of production work.

Astute-class SSN

Displacement: 6,200 tonnes/6,102.1 tons (surfaced); 6,692 tonnes/6,586.3 tons (submerged)
Length: 91.7m/300ft 10in
Beam: 10.8m/35ft 5in
Armament: 6 x tubes for Spearfish torpedoes, Royal Navy Sub-Harpoon anti-ship missiles and Tomahawk land attack missiles; 38 weapon capacity
Propulsion: Not known
Speed: Not known (surfaced); 32 knots (dived)
Complement: 100 men

Rubis-Améthyste-class SSN

The French Navy operates six Rubis-Améthyste-class nuclear attack submarines from the naval base in Toulon, four of them originally commissioned as first generation nuclear attack boats in the 1980s. At that time, they were deployed in an anti-surface ship role in the Rubis class. However, a substantial modern upgrade for the first four boats in 1992 re-equipped them to carry both anti-surface and anti-submarine weaponry for what was called the Améthyste configuration. The two names were joined for the purpose of creating a useful class of attack boats without the expense of building new boats and enabling the older submarine to carry a mixed load of 14 missiles and torpedoes.

Indeed, there was already a great affection in the French Navy for Rubis, which was named after a distinguished World War II boat. The record of long patrols by the modern Rubis included operations with the Coalition Forces during the time of the first Gulf War, operating between September 1992 and July 1993. In July 1993, she undertook a major refit for the Améthyste missile upgrade. Rubis also took part in Operation Trident, the 1999 NATO bombing campaign over Yugoslavia.

Her role was to offer protection to the naval aviation group and later, with Améthyste, to keep the Serbian Navy out of the Koton Straits while gathering intelligence at the same time. In 2002, Rubis performed a similar role with Task Force 473 in the Indian Ocean, during Operation Hercules, the naval participation in the overthrow of the Taliban in Afghanistan. The others in the class are Saphir, Emeraude and Casabianca, commissioned with Rubis in the 1980s, and Perle, the 1990s sister of Améthyste.

TOP: **Rubis** is affectionately viewed in France for the link to her World War II namesake, although she was originally christened *Provence*. She was renamed *Rubis* in December 1980. *Rubis* was alleged to have entered the Pacific Ocean in 1985 in support of an operation that ended in the sinking of the Greenpeace ship *Rainbow Warrior*. ABOVE: An inside view of the weaponry, for which these submarines have the capacity to carry 14 Exocet missiles and torpedoes in a mixed load. The missiles are also launched from the torpedo tubes.

FRANCE

More of a general-purpose boat than exclusively an attack craft, the Améthyste class, which incorporated the Rubis class, has proved its value to the French Navy in many ways. The development into littoral anti-submarine operations was only part of the new equation. Many additional features that came as a follow-on to the Rubis class specifically included a much quieter power system, to meet the requirements of the type of operations they were now to undertake. The boats were thus subsequently utilized in a variety of situations, and given a fairly wide brief that covers reconnaissance and intelligence gathering, as well as adopting the anti-shipping and power projection capabilities that the Rubis boats brought with them.

The improvements were noticeable in virtually every department, with a longer hull, far better accommodation, modern electronics suites and modern sonar. The major innovation in terms of weaponry was the introduction of the Exocet missile, which has proved to be a shudderingly effective ship killer. This was famously demonstrated against the Royal Navy by the Argentine naval aviation forces in the Falklands War in 1982 with devastating effect and great loss of life. The missile skims the surface of the sea in its approach to the target to avoid detection. It is armed with 165kg/364lb of high explosive and is guided by target range and bearing data downloaded into the Exocet's onboard computer.

TOP: **A torpedo handler for the Rubis-Améthyste boats. Generally up to 14 F17 Model 2 torpedoes may be carried, although the armaments compartment is versatile enough to take Exocet missiles in a combination of weapons.**

ABOVE: **Inside the control room of the Rubis-Améthyste boats, from where the armaments are fired.**

ABOVE: *Améthyste* **became a lead partner in the class title by virtue of the fact that she brought innovations to this series of boats when commissioned in 1992.**
RIGHT: **She was followed soon after by** *Perle***, pictured here at the Golden Jubilee celebration of Queen Elizabeth II. The four earlier boats were then re-equipped to the same standard as the later submarines for both anti-surface and anti-submarine warfare.**

Rubis

Displacement: 2,362 tonnes/2,324.7 tons (surfaced); 2,558 tonnes/2,517.6 tons (submerged)
Length: 72.1m/236ft 7in
Beam: 7.6m/24ft 11in
Armament: 4 x 533mm/21in tubes, F17 Mod 2 torpedoes; 14 x Exocet SM39
Propulsion: Pressurized water K48 nuclear reactor, 48mW/64,369hp
Speed: 20 knots (surfaced); 26 knots (dived)
Complement: 70 men

Améthyste

Displacement: 2,730 tonnes/2,686.9 tons (surfaced); 2,812 tonnes/2,767.6 tons (submerged)
Length: 73.6m/241ft 6in
Beam: 7.6m/24ft 11in
Armament: 4 x 533mm/21in tubes, F17 Mod 2 torpedoes; 14 x Exocet SM39
Propulsion: Nuclear reactor, 7,084.1kW/ 9,500shp
Speed: 22 knots (surfaced); 25 knots (dived)
Complement: 70 men

DIRECTORY OF SUBMARINES: 1945 TO DATE

LEFT: *L'Inflexible*, one of four French ballistic missile submarines whose origins dated to the 1960s–70s, but which remained in business through extensive upgrades and streamlining in the 1980s, including an improved reactor core and the back-fitting of the M4 missile. The massive cost of the overhaul, however, was deemed insufficient to keep them all operational until France's new generation of SSBNs arrived. ABOVE: The nuclear reactor core is lowered into the reactor room during the overhaul.

L'Inflexible-class SSBN

This class was previously known as Le Redoutable after France's first ballistic missile-carrying submarine. However, after 20 years of service, she was decommissioned in 1991 and the class was renamed L'Inflexible after the youngster of the class, but even she was already an old lady of similar age and no doubt due for retirement before long. The class had certainly been a good servant of the French Navy, although its patrol programme over those years did not match the activity of the American and British SSBNs.

Indeed, while co-operating under the auspices of NATO, the French maintained singular independence in terms of operational strategy and always retained as the sole right of their Government the order for the launching and targeting of France's nuclear weapons. The reality was never likely to have brought about a situation in which France acted alone in any international nuclear exchange; the French submarine-launched nuclear weapons nevertheless remained under the trigger-finger of the French President, whereas the British, through their 1962 agreement with America, were bound to take response and targeting parameters from the US.

L'Inflexible and the four remaining submarines of this class underwent a two-year modernization refit and overhaul in the 1980s to allow continued commitment to France's Strategic Oceanic Force until their replacement boats of the Le Triomphant class began to be commissioned. Even so, they

LEFT: **The loading of a French M4 intermediate-range submarine-launched ballistic missile that is similar to the US Polaris. These entered service in the French SSBN fleet in the mid-1980s, although the missile has since been upgraded.**

have given good service, and their hefty refit provided them with M4 missiles, a new missile launch system, new reactor cores, an updated sonar suite and some noise abatement measures. However, delays in the arrival of the new SSBNs meant that two of the L'Inflexible boats stayed in business far longer than was originally intended by the French Navy.

Consequently, the class remained active well into the 21st century, although three other boats, *Terrible*, *Foudroyant* and *Tonnant* also went into retirement in the late 1990s, leaving *L'Inflexible* and *Indomptable* to carry the flag until their own retirement, scheduled for 2004–06.

L'Inflexible-class SSBN

Displacement: 9,000 tonnes/8,857.9 tons (surfaced); 9,842 tonnes/9,686.6 tons (submerged)
Length: 128m/419ft 11in
Beam: 10.5m/34ft 5in
Armament: 4 x 533mm/21in tubes; Exocet SM39 missiles, 16 x M4 SLBM
Propulsion: Nuclear reactor, 11,931kW/16,000shp
Speed: 20 knots (surfaced); 25 knots (dived)
Complement: 130 men

Agosta-class 90B SSK

The Agosta-class submarine has proved a popular export model for the French, as well as with their own navy. From the stable of DCN of France, variations of the class are currently in service with the French, Spanish and Pakistani navies. The 90B is an improved version of the original and equally popular 1970 boat, now featuring higher performance and a propulsion system that provides a submerged endurance three times longer than earlier versions. Another feature is a substantially increased level of automation, which in turn enabled a reduction in crew from 54 to 36.

The submarine has a choice of propulsion systems: a French diesel-electric combination providing 2,685kW/3,600hp and a 2,200kW/2,950hp electric motor driving a single propeller is offered as standard. However, the latest versions of the Agosta class are being equipped with the MESMA Air Independent Propulsion System (AIP), which consists of a turbine receiving high-pressure steam from a combustion chamber, burning a gaseous mixture of ethanol and liquid oxygen. While a diesel-electric submarine has to surface to periscope depth to recharge the batteries, thus risking detection, with the MESMA AIP system, a submarine can remain submerged three times longer. The Agosta 90B's length was extended by 9m/29ft 6in to accommodate the AIP system.

Additional upgrades put the new improved Agosta well ahead in terms of electronic warfare, equipped with the Thales DR-3000U radar warning receiver, which uses a masthead antenna array with omni-directional and monopulse directional antennae and a separate periscope warning antenna. The weaponry is also updated to include a mixed load of up to 16 torpedoes and missiles. They will carry the wire-guided ECAN F17 Mod 2 torpedo that delivers a 250kg/551lb warhead to a depth of 600m/1,968ft. The Exocet SM39 missile, with a target range of over 50km/31 miles, is also launched via the torpedo tubes and has a 165kg/364lb high-explosive shaped-charge warhead.

LEFT: **The refloating procedure in the dry dock.**
ABOVE: **A full-on bow view of the popular 90B *Agosta* attack submarine produced by France for both domestic use and export, with a choice of propulsion systems, currently in service with the French, Spanish and Pakistani navies. The 90B is a direct derivative of the successful 1970s version and contains a greater level of automation, resulting in the ship's crew being reduced from 54 to 36. There are four bow torpedo tubes and a capacity to carry a mixed load of up to 16 torpedoes and missiles.** BELOW LEFT: **Cutaway images showing a comparison of internal layouts.**

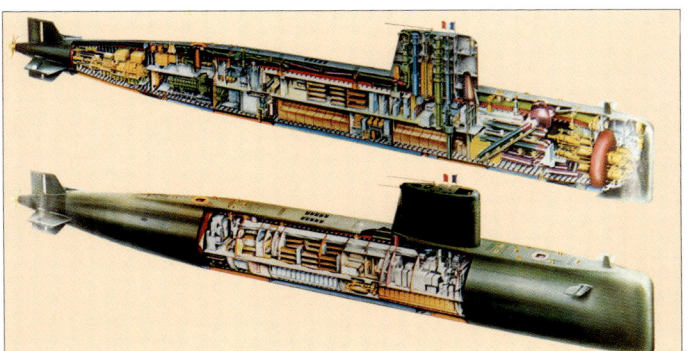

Agosta-class 90B SSK

Displacement: 1,486 tonnes/1,462.5 tons (surfaced); 1,732 tonnes/1,704.6 tons (submerged)
Length: 67m/219ft 10in
Beam: 5.4m/17ft 9in
Armament: 6 x 533mm/21in tubes, mixed parcel F17 Mod 2/ Exocet SM39 submarine-launched anti-ship missiles
Propulsion: Diesel-electric, 2684.5kW/3,600hp or Mesma AIP
Speed: 15 knots (surfaced); 17 knots (dived)
Complement: 36/41 men

Le Triomphant-class SSBN

Le Triomphant became the new standard bearer of the French Navy's ballistic missile fleet in 1998, the first of four boats in this class to be delivered progressively through to 2008. This submarine was designed and built at Direction des Constructions et Armes Navales (DCN), Cherbourg shipyard, and the first-of-class entered service in 1997.

The new boat carries 16 vertically launched M54 ballistic missiles each with a warhead of six multiple re-entry vehicles (MRVs). The explosive power of such weapons, indicated variously through this directory, can once again be demonstrated by the French figure: each MVR possessed the equivalent of 147,638 tonnes/145,306 tons of TNT – ten times greater than the atomic bomb dropped on Hiroshima in 1945.

A new warhead due into service in 2008 will extend that power in the French boats even further with a warhead with 12 multiple independently targetable re-entry vehicles with

ABOVE: **The pride of France, *Le Vigilant*, commissioned in 2004, is the third of four new submarines in the French Le Triomphant class which became the French Navy's ballistic missile carriers succeeding the L'Inflexible class. The first-of-class submarine, *Le Triomphant*, entered service in 1997.**

LEFT: **Against the floodlit backdrop of its home base, *Le Vigilant* brings to the international scene France's own propulsion design, a nuclear turbo-electric system based on a Type K15 Pressure Water Reactor with an auxiliary diesel electric back-up. *Le Triomphant*-class boats have a submerged speed in excess of 25 knots and a surface speed of 20 knots, a diving depth of more than 300m/984ft and an endurance in excess of 60 days.**

LEFT AND ABOVE: The second of the new French ballistic submarines, *Le Temeraire* entered service in 2000 followed by *Le Vigilant* in 2005, with the last member of the group, *Le Terrible*, scheduled for 2008/9. These submarines carry 16 vertically launched M45 ballistic missiles supplied by EADS Space Transportation, based in Les Mureaux, France. The missile's propulsion system consists of a three-stage solid-fuel rocket motor producing hypersonic speed and carries a thermonuclear warhead, developed by the *Commissariat à l'Energie Atomique*, with six Multiple Re-entry Vehicles, each of 150kT in the TN-71 warhead. The range is 6,000km/3,728 miles. In spite of the re-evaluation of nuclear requirements in recent times, the French will introduce a more powerful M51 missile, due to enter service in 2010 and retro-fitted to all boats. It will carry a warhead with 12 MIRVS, and have an increased range of 8,000km/4,971 miles. BELOW: A profile of a *Le Triomphant*-class submarine.

an increased range extending to 8,047km/5,000 miles. It is noticeable that France has continued to proceed with this, one of the most costly areas of naval defence, while other nations are substantially curtailing their expenditure. The French Navy's continued endeavours in this area coincide with the arrival of the British Royal Navy's Vanguard fleet.

The second of the French boats, *Le Temeraire*, entered service in January 2000, *Le Vigilant* was commissioned in 2005 and the fourth, *Le Terrible*, is scheduled for commissioning in 2008. The submarine has four 533mm/21in torpedo tubes and has the capacity to carry a mixed load of torpedoes and Exocet missiles. The Triomphant class of strategic missile boats are being introduced into service to provide the sea-based component of the French nuclear deterrent with the M45-SLBM.

ABOVE: The leader of the class, *Le Triomphant*, at sea. Apart from her nuclear capability, the submarine and her sisters have four 533mm/21in torpedo tubes and the ability to carry a mixed load of 18 ECAN L5/III torpedoes and Exocet missiles. The torpedo, armed with a 150kg/331lb warhead, is equipped with both active and passive homing and has a range of 9km/5.5 miles.

Le Triomphant-class SSBN

Displacement: 12,440 tonnes/12,243.5 tons (surfaced); 14,108 tonnes/13,885.2 tons (submerged)
Length: 184m/603ft 8in
Beam: 12.5m/41ft
Armament: Nuclear: 4 x 533mm/21in tubes, 18 ECAN L5 Mod 3 torpedoes and Exocet missiles; 16 M45 SLBM missiles with TNT75 warheads
Propulsion: 1 x GWC PAR K15 nuclear reactor; 1x steam turbine, 30947kW/41,500shp
Speed: 22 knots (surfaced); 25 knots (dived)
Complement: 65 men

Xia-class SSBN

The People's Republic Army Navy has operated a single ballistic missile submarine since it was commissioned in 1987 and upgraded in 1995. However, it apparently seldom ventures out of territorial waters, apparently in dire need of replacement. The boat is considered so noisy to underwater detection gear that its chances of surviving an attack in ocean waters would be minimal. The home-built Xia experienced persistent problems through virtually every phase – construction, commissioning and sea trials. It was also three years after commissioning before the first successful firing of its JL-1 missile was achieved.

Undaunted and with some help from Russia and France, China announced plans for a new SSBN, Type 094 with a projected commissioning by 2005, but again the project has been plagued by problems and delays. In 2004, the US Defence Intelligence Agency reported that the boat was in fact under construction but estimated that it would be at least 2010 before it would be deployed.

Both the Xia and the new 094-class submarine will eventually carry the underwater-launched version of China's new DF-31 missile, according to US defence analysts whose intelligence on the project suggests that when the problems have been overcome, China will have her first truly intercontinental strategic nuclear delivery system. The US analysts also believed that there were early problems with the JL-2 missile programme when a test flight of the missile failed, but this appeared to have been resolved by 2003.

Richard Fisher, of the Washington-based International Assessment and Strategy Centre, admitted that the launch of the new missile submarine was "an astounding development". He said that in the near future, China would have a second-strike nuclear attack capability

TOP AND ABOVE: **The Xia SSBN boat was heralded as a great advance in the Chinese Navy's defence capabilities against any potential enemy equipped with nuclear surface forces, although the creation and running of the nation's sole vessel has not been without its problems.**

that it could use as a threat "to deter the United States from aiding Taiwan after an attack by the People's Liberation Army". Fisher also maintained that the new submarine would make it more difficult for the US military to become unilaterally involved in the defence of Taiwan because of the threat of nuclear retaliation.

ABOVE: **The Xia class was initially armed with this home-built JL-1, which was considered a major achievement. It is being replaced by the much improved JL-2 SLBM system in China's new SSBN.**

Xia-class SSBN

Displacement: Not known (surfaced); 6,397 tonnes/6,296 tons (submerged)
Length: 120m/393ft 8in
Beam: 10m/32ft 10in
Armament: 6 x 533mm/21in tubes (bow), Set-65E torpedoes; 12 x Ju Lang-1 SLBM with 1 x single 250kT warhead and range of 1770km/1,100 miles
Propulsion: 1 x PWR nuclear reactor; 1 auxiliary diesel; power output not known
Speed: 20 knots (surfaced); 22 knots (dived)
Complement: 140 men

Han-class Type 091 SSN

China's Type 091 attack submarine was generally regarded as being well past its sell-by date by the early 2000s and a new Type 093, already under construction, was awaited with interest. Meanwhile, the 091 has served China well, although as with their SSBN experience, the Chinese surmounted a series of problems bringing this class into production. Six submarines of this class were built during the 1970s and 80s to provide the Chinese Navy with the experience of operating nuclear-powered submarines.

On the way, and again with some help and input from Soviet and French technicians, the class has been upgraded and modernized, including from the third boat, a lengthening of the hull to accommodate an anti-ship missile system, and modifications were made to the nuclear reactor to reduce noise and achieve greater reliability. A new French-designed intercept sonar set and the obsolete Soviet ESM suite were also replaced with a new French design. A further refit in the 1990s provided three of the boats with wire-guided torpedoes and the capability to launch YJ-82 missiles from a 533mm/21in torpedo tube, however by 2001 two were reported to be out of commission.

By then, the building of the next generation of China's nuclear attack submarines of Type 093 was reportedly well underway, although few details have been released. However, intelligence reports published in the USA suggest that they will perform on the lines of the Soviet Victor III class. Meanwhile, the Chinese Navy has announced ambitious plans for modernization elsewhere in their 57-strong submarine fleet, which is packed with ageing diesel boats of such vintage as to be completely outmoded. The most modern are eight of the Russian *Kilo*-class boats, purchased in 1993. Again, there are reports that China had also embarked on a building programme for a new class of diesel boats. These developments at the time of writing were naturally giving the Americans even more cause for concern in relation to Taiwan, which has significantly failed to put together a submarine force capable of any impact.

TOP AND ABOVE: The newest addition to the Chinese fleet is the non-nuclear Type 039A. It is thought to be of Chinese indigenous design with Russian influence, with six 533mm/21in bow torpedo tubes which can launch a range of Chinese indigenous or Russian homing torpedoes, as well as the 80km/50-mile-range YJ-82 anti-ship missile.

ABOVE: An artist's impression of the long-awaited Type 093, the next generation of China's nuclear attack submarine, which was scheduled for an appearance in the early years of the 21st century, but at the time of writing was still nowhere in sight.

091

Displacement: 4,423 tonnes/4,353.1 tons (surfaced); 5,413 tonnes/5,327.5 tons (submerged)
Length: 98m/321ft 6in or 106m/347ft 9in
Beam: 10m/ft in
Armament: 6 x 533mm/21in tubes; YJ-82 anti-ship missiles
Propulsion: Nuclear reactor; power output not known
Speed: 12 knots (surfaced); 25 knots (dived)
Complement: 65 men

LEFT: **HDW, the principal German builder of this highy regarded submarine, notched up a notable record, becoming the first shipyard in the world to offer a fuel cell propulsion system ready for series production.**

Type 212A-class SSK

Germany's shipbuilders, whose production of fine submarines is written into history, are today perhaps best known for serving a thriving export market, with nations around the globe anxious to acquire their diesel-electric boats, which have all the features and high-tech accoutrements that made the original U-boats so respected. The 212A is the latest in a long line of such vessels, capable of long-distance submerged passage to the area of operation. The German Navy has ordered four of the submarines, which are being built by HDW shipbuilders of Kiel and Thyssen Nordseewerke of Enden.

HDW were to build the bow sections and TNSW the stern section, and then each builder alternately assembled the vessels. *U31*, the first of class, began sea trials in April 2003 and was due for commissioning at the end of 2005 with the remainder following in 2006 and 2007. Two Type 212A submarines are also being built in a link-up with Italian shipbuilders Fincantieri for the Italian Navy. The first, *Salvatore Todaro*, was due to enter service by the end of 2005 and the second, *Sciré*, in 2006.

The Type 212A is equipped with a highly integrated command and weapons control system that interfaces with sensors, weapons and navigation systems. This much-vaunted system is being supplied by Kongsberg Defence and Aerospace of Norway. The counter-measures for the Type 212A include an ultra-efficient electronic warfare system developed under a contract awarded to EADS Systems & Defence Electronics and Thales Defence Ltd and will be included in the German and Italian versions of the submarines.

The counter-measures hardware includes the development of the TAU 2000 torpedo system, which has four launch containers, each with up to ten discharge tubes with a remarkable addition known as effectors – small underwater vehicles, similar in appearance to a torpedo. The effectors are jammers and decoys with hydrophones and acoustic emitters. Multiple effectors are deployed in order to counter torpedoes in re-attack mode.

The propulsion system combines a conventional system consisting of a diesel generator with a lead acid battery, and an air-independent propulsion. The submarine can thus operate at high speed on diesel power or switch to the AIP system for silent slow cruising, staying submerged for up to three weeks.

LEFT: **The efficiently compartmentalized 212A is constructed in the manner of Airbus aircraft: different sections of the submarines are constructed at the two sites involved and then shipped to the respective other yard, so that both HDW and Thyssen Nordseewerke assemble two complete submarines each.**

Type 212A-class SSK

Displacement: 1,500 tonnes/1,476.3 tons (surfaced); 1,797 tonnes/1,768.6 tons (submerged)
Length: 57m/187ft
Beam: 7m/23ft
Armament: 6 x 533mm/21in tubes, 24 x stn Atlas Electronik DM2A4 torpedoes
Propulsion: 2 x MTU 16V 396 diesel generators; Permasyn electric motor, 600–900V battery, 3,164kW/4,243shp
Speed: 12 knots (surfaced); 20 knots (dived)
Complement: 32 men

GERMANY

Type 206A-class SSK

Type 206A-class SSK

Displacement: 442 tonnes/435 tons (surfaced); 490 tonnes/482.3 tons (submerged)
Length: 48.6m/159ft 5in
Beam: 4.6m/15ft 1in
Armament: 8 x 533mm/21in tubes (bow), 12 AEG Seeschlenge Type 206 torpedoes
Propulsion: 2 x MTU 16V 396 diesel generators; Permasyn electric motor, 600–900V battery, 3,164kW/4,243shp
Speed: 10 knots (surfaced); 17 knots (dived)
Complement: 22 men

Germany operated one of the smallest and, for its size, most successful and enduring attack boats anywhere in the world, with a surface displacement of just 457 tonnes/450 tons. The Type 206 first went into production in the early 1970s, when 17 were built, followed by 14 of the improved Type 206A.

A dozen of the first type went through a substantial upgrade in the early 1990s to bring them to "A" standard, and they continued to give excellent service in the primary role of anti-surface warfare, with capability for anti-submarine warfare, mine-laying and reconnaissance. Because of their size, they were especially suitable for operations in shallow water, with a tolerance of a mere 20m/65ft 7in in minimum depth.

As the new millennium approached, the German submarine flotilla still had 14 of the two types in operation. However, further decommissioning followed when two flotillas were merged, although as of 2003, 12 of the 206A were still in use. Curiously enough,

ABOVE LEFT: **The 206A proved to be a reliable workhorse of the 1980s and 90s. Although Germany began decommissioning, they remained in use elsewhere in the world.**

however, the area of operations was extended around that time, extending from the Baltic Sea to the Atlantic Ocean and from the Norwegian Sea to the Mediterranean.

Some of the early 206s are still operative elsewhere in the world, five being purchased by Indonesia in 1998.

Type 214 class

A further development on the Type 212 by HDW is the Type 214 submarine, which has again attracted attention from around the world. The Greek Navy has ordered three for delivery in 2006. Hellenic Shipyards, acquired by HDW in 2002, will build the second (*Pipinos S121*) and third (*Matrozos 122*) vessels at Skaramanga, for commissioning in 2008–09. South Korea also ordered three Type 214s, to enter service in 2007, 2008 and 2009. These will be built by Hyundai Heavy Industries.

The Type 214 will have an improved pressure hull that will give an increased diving depth of over 400m/1,312ft 4in. Four of the eight torpedo tubes will also be capable of firing missiles. Type 214 submarines for the Hellenic Navy will be armed with the WASS Black Shark heavyweight torpedo, a dual purpose, wire-guided torpedo that is fitted with an Astra active/passive acoustic head and a multi-target guidance-and-control unit incorporating a counter-countermeasures system.

Performance of the propulsion system has been increased with two Siemens fuel cells that produce 120kW/161hp per module and will give

Type 214 class

Displacement: 1,700 tonnes/1,673.2 tons (surfaced); 1,859 tonnes/1,830 tons (submerged)
Length: 24m/78ft 9in
Beam: 6.30m/20ft 8in
Armament: 8 x 533mm/21in tubes, WASS Black Shark heavyweight torpedoes
Propulsion: 2 x MTU 16V 396 diesel generators; Permasyn electric motor, 600–900V battery, 3,164kW/4,243shp
Speed: 12 knots (surface); 15 knots (dived)
Complement: 30 men

ABOVE: **The German export market was clearly impressed by the hull of the 214, with its low-noise propeller, both of which decreased the submarine's acoustic signature.**

the submarine an underwater endurance of at least two weeks. A hull shape that has been further optimized for hydrodynamic and stealth characteristics and a low-noise propeller combine to decrease the submarine's acoustic signature. The submarine has an exceptional mission endurance of 12 weeks, of which three weeks may be spent submerged without snorkelling.

475

Victoria-class SSK

Having had years of service from their fleet of British diesel-electric *Oberon*-class submarines during unrelenting anti-submarine warfare activities in the North Atlantic, the Canadian Royal Navy switched to another British boat for their new era of post-Cold War operations. They continued in the diesel mode with the purchase of four boats from the Royal Navy's Upholder class. These were built in the 1980s and 90s, but were withdrawn from UK service following a defence review in 1994.

The Canadians renamed the group as the Victoria class, and recommissioning work on the first, *Victoria*, was completed in December 2000. The remaining three were to be progressively taken into service by the end of 2004. However, the Canadians' delight on obtaining these boats was marred after work on the last of the four, HMCS *Chicoutimi*,

ABOVE: The Canadian *Corner Brook*, one of the highly regarded Victoria class, also known as the Type 2400, which are the renamed boats of the British Upholder class. These originally made their appearance in the in the late 1970s as a back-up to the UK nuclear attack submarines and are still regarded as among the best diesel-electric boats in the world. BELOW: A view of the Victoria type, which fulfils the principal role in both the Canadian Contingency Task Group, on 10 days' readiness to deploy, and the National Task Group, at 60 days' readiness.

CANADA

was completed in September 2004. The vessel was handed over to the Canadian Navy at Faslane Naval Base, Scotland, in October 2004, but while sailing home to its base in Halifax, Nova Scotia, a serious electrical fire broke out on the vessel, in which one Canadian crew member died and others were seriously affected by the heat and smoke.

The submarine was foundering when a Royal Navy Type 23 frigate, HMS *Montrose*, arrived to take the boat under tow back to Faslane. Subsequently, *Chicoutimi* was loaded on to a Norwegian sealift vessel in January 2005, bound for Halifax for repairs. In the meantime, the Canadians confined the Victoria class to port pending an inquiry. Some modifications were carried out and *Victoria* and *Windsor* were cleared for duty. The others would follow later.

They are relatively modern boats, quiet and stealthy, and well suited for Canada's current naval defence roles, which include patrols connected to fisheries, immigration, law enforcement and environmental monitoring. It is also intended that *Victoria* will join the west coast fleet as part of Maritime Forces Pacific, thus re-establishing a permanent Canadian Pacific submarine presence, lost in 1974 when *Rainbow* (formerly USS *Argonaut*) was paid off.

ABOVE: **HMCS *Victoria*, leader of the class, was assigned to operate in the Maritime Forces Pacific (MARPAC) fleet, which has a base at Esquimalt, near Victoria, in British Columbia. The hull is of a classic teardrop design, and the main sail houses a five-man lockout chamber.** BELOW: **An internal cutaway showing the compartmentalized layout of the Victoria submarines.**

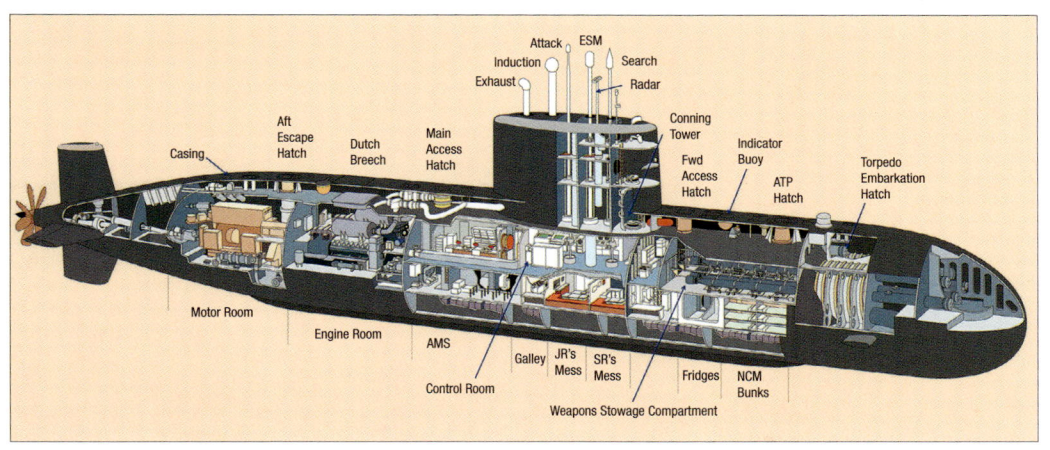

LEFT: **An alternative view of *Corner Brook*, patrol-ready. She has an endurance of 54 days, and a cruising capability of 12 knots surfaced and 20 knots submerged. In snorting mode, at periscope depth, the range at an 8-knot snorting speed is 12,872km/ 8,000 miles.**

Victoria-class SSK

Displacement: 2,150 tonnes/2,116 tons (surfaced); 2,416 tonnes/2,377.8 tons (submerged)
Length: 70.3m/230ft 8in
Beam: 7.6m/24ft 11in
Armament: 6 x 533mm/21in tubes, 18 x Gould Mk 48 heavyweight torpedoes
Propulsion: 2 x Paxman Valenta 16SZ diesel engines, 2.7mW/3620.8hp each; 2 x 2.5mW/3352.6hp Alsthom alternators; Alsthom motor, 4mW/5364.1hp
Speed: 12 knots (surfaced); 20 knots (dived)
Complement: 48 men

LEFT AND ABOVE: **The Yushio class were the mainstay of the Japanese fleet in the 1970s, first with the Type 575 and later with Type 576, a succession that has provided excellent vessels for the maintenance of that nation's highly efficient submarine force. These have been regularly updated and improved, including the ability to launch the Harpoon missile.**

Yushio-class SSK

From the late 1960s, the Japanese maintained a submarine force of around 16 boats, and this remained pretty much the norm through the rest of the century. In that time, they acknowledged and experimented with improving designs and technology but, perhaps not unnaturally, were not tempted by the nuclear-powered creations of other nations. As a result they have remained aligned to the diesel-electric ideal and have produced some fine boats in the process. One of the largest was the Yushio class, introduced in 1975 and of the teardrop design.

They were produced over a number of years, and numerous refinements and upgrades were added as the class progressed through the building of six boats. This was clearly demonstrated by the fact that the cost of the first boat was 23,724,000,000 Yen, while the final one cost 31,950,000,000 Yen.

Improvements included the ability to launch the Harpoon missile, and in later units the control navigation system was improved. Quietening measures included a novel solution of fitting a propeller of seven blades rather than five for the screw. Overall, the wide-ranging modernizations meant an increase of displacement of almost 406 tonnes/400 tons, compared with the earliest versions. The Yushio boats which came in to service through the 1970s and 80s remained in commission until towards the end of the century, when they were gradually transferred to training duties.

ABOVE: **Broaching, or breaking, the surface at some speed is a spectacular event, as demonstrated here by one of the Yushio boats.**

Yushio-class SSK

Displacement: 2,463 tonnes/2,424.1 tons (surfaced); 2,830 tonnes/2,785.3 tons (submerged)
Length: 76m/249ft 4in
Beam: 9.9m/32ft 6in
Armament: 6 x HU-603 torpedo tubes; (dual use with Harpoon USM)
Propulsion: 2,535.4kW/3,400hp diesel; 5369kW/7,200hp electric
Speed: 12 knots (surfaced); 20 knots (dived)
Complement: 75 men

JAPAN

LEFT: *Asashio*, the last ship of the Harushio class, was transferred to the training wing of the Japanese Navy with the designation of TSS rather than SS. This is in accordance with Japan's practice of providing boats for that purpose, which are equipped with the latest technology and therefore enable a high level of training for new recruits in a modern environment.

Harushio class

Displacement: 2,410 tonnes/2,371.9 tons (surfaced); 2,460 tonnes/2,421.1 tons (submerged)
Length: 77m/252ft 7in
Beam: 10m/32ft 10in
Armament: 6 x HU-603 torpedo tubes, Type 89 torpedo (dual use with Harpoon USM)
Propulsion: 2 x Kawasaki 12V25/25S diesel engines, 5,369kW/7,200hp
Speed: 12 knots (surfaced); 20 knots (dived)
Complement: 75 men

Harushio class

An improved and slightly larger version of the Yushio, from which it was derived, the Harushio was easily recognizable by a projecting fin over the countermeasure intelligence sonar. The class was built with a high-strength steel pressure-resistant boat hull for an increased operating depth thought to be in excess of 300m/984ft, although the Japanese Navy makes a point of keeping such details to itself. The rows of noughts on the budget figures again looks mind-boggling to those in the West without a calculator to hand. The budget for the Harushio boats was estimated at 38,673,000,000 Yen (equivalent to about $333 million), but construction expenses increased substantially, to 44,266,000,000 Yen (about $381 million).

The last of the six boats in this class, the *Asashio*, initiated a new practice introduced by the Japanese Maritime Self Defence Force. The *Asashio* was redesignated as a training boat and was specially modified for the role. This rather sensible move was to give the new recruits the experience of a modern boat, with modern techniques and equipment, rather than providing training experience in older ships where virtually every aspect of submarine life might well be so old as to be unrecognizable in a modern boat. Instead, the hierarchy decreed that where possible training should henceforth be carried out in boats with equipment as near as possible to newly built submarines.

LEFT: **SS *Narushio*** of the Oyashio class, a series that saw a departure from what has become the traditional teardrop hull form, opting instead for what is known as a "leaf coil" hull shape. It is the newest and most powerful of the Japanese attack boats.

Oyashio-class SSK

Displacement: 2,706 tonnes/2,663.3 tons (surfaced); 2,986 tonnes/2,938.8 tons (submerged)
Length: 82m/269ft
Beam: 8.9m/29ft 2in
Armament: 6 x 533mm/21in tubes, (4 x bow, 2 x stern); 24 x stn Atlas Elektronik DM2A4 torpedoes
Propulsion: 2 x Kawasaki 12V25/25S diesel engines, 5369kW/7,200hp
Speed: 12 knots (surfaced); 20 knots (dived)
Complement: 68 men

Oyashio-class SSK

The brand new Oyashio class, the most powerful that Japan has built since the war, is something of a departure from previous submarine stock in that her naval designers in the Maritime Self Defence Force this time opted not for the classic teardrop hull but a form called the leaf-coil type. It has a revolutionary form of hull, part single, part double, the whole having been produced from an unusual design approach, in which the arrangement of the sensors was considered first and the layout of the entire boat was built around that concept. Previously the sonar was mounted in the bow, but this new model designates the entire hull as the sensor, equipped with a sonar arrangement on the hull to provide improved detection efficiency.

A state-of-the-art combat intelligence processing system is also new, and this brings the boat's attack capability to one of high order. Further, the positioning of the torpedo tubes differs from conventional types, with the bow tube placement decided after the arrangement of the sensor. The acoustic stealth efficiency of the hull is improved by installing sound-absorbing rubber tiles. There is also a relatively small crew, compared with submarines of a similar size run by other countries. However, such technology does not come cheap. The *Oyashio*-class submarines cost around half a billion dollars each.

Collins-class SSK

Like Canada, Australia had relied on the British Oberons for many years, until finally they were forced to invest in new boats to replace their ageing workhorses. With a workload that alternates between coastal patrols and domestic surveillance work to long endurance operations in the Pacific, the Indian Ocean and the Antarctic, there were numerous design requirements to be considered. In the end, the Australian Government approved the purchase of six *Collins*-class Type 471 diesel-electric boats, designed by Swedish shipbuilders Kockums especially for the Royal Australian Navy.

ABOVE: Mostly home grown, the impressive Type 471 class, led by HMAS *Collins*, began the commissioning process in 1996, and delivery of six submarines was completed by 2003. Armaments include the Boeing Sub-Harpoon anti-ship missile. BELOW LEFT: HMAS *Waller* takes on its load, which now includes up to 22 Mk 48 Mod 4 heavyweight torpedoes.

Construction was in part carried out in Sweden, although the bulk of the work was completed by the Australian Submarine Company of Adelaide. The first of class was commissioned in 1996 and the remainder were delivered by 2003. The lines were distinctive, with the single hull carrying a prominent sonar pod above the bows and a set of hydroplanes mounted halfway up the fin. However, in the years between the original design and final construction, certain elements of the boat were believed to have been overtaken by modern technology coming on stream at an ever more rapid pace, and there were problems that had to be attended to before they could become fully operational.

A Government inquiry initiated an upgrade programme to the weapon systems, sonar and noise reduction, and this was carried out in 2004. More fundamental upgrades are also in the pipeline over the longer term, and the Royal Australian Navy

AUSTRALIA

LEFT: **With a large crowd of shipyard workers looking on, a Collins boats is rolled out for the final fitting out process at the Australian Submarine Corporation in Adelaide.** ABOVE: **Under way and looking good.** BELOW: **HMAS** *Sheean*, **fifth of the Collins boats, commissioned in 2000.**

signed an agreement with the US Navy for the development of a new Combat Control System based on that being fitted to the United States' latest state-of-the-art boat, *Virginia*. The Mk 48 Mod 7 ADCAP (Advanced Capability) torpedo is also a probability for 2006 under an Armaments Co-operation Project with the US Navy. In fact, the first of the AN/BYG-1 Combat Control Systems was delivered in January 2006, and the installation work was started immediately on HMAS *Waller*, the first of the Collins submarines to be upgraded with the system and the new heavyweight torpedoes. First trials at sea were scheduled to begin in 2007, and the upgrade programme is scheduled for completion in 2010. These and other upgrades will doubtless keep the Collins boats in gainful employment for many years hence.

Collins-class SSK

Displacement: 3,002 tonnes/2,954.6 tons (surfaced); 3,300 tonnes/3,247.9 tons (submerged)
Length: 78m/255ft 11in
Beam: 8m/26ft 3in
Armament: 6 x 533mm/21in tubes for Harpoon missiles and Gould Mk 48 torpedoes – total of 22 carried or up to 44 mines in place of torpedoes
Propulsion: 3 x V18B/14 diesel engines, 1,475kW/1,978hp each
Speed: 10 knots (surfaced); 20 knots (dived)
Complement: 42 men

Sauro-class SSK

The Sauro class has in recent times constituted the entire submarine fleet of the Italian Navy although, as noted above, the Italian and German governments reached agreement for the supply of two new Type 212As. The Sauros were built in the shipyards of Fincantieri of Monfalcone and replaced the ageing Toti class, which was not only worn out, but had a bad reputation among the crews for cramped conditions. The Sauro dated back to 1967, when the first two were ordered, but financial constraints forced the Italian government to cancel and re-order in the 1970s. Even then, completion was delayed by defective batteries, which were subsequently replaced with Swedish units.

Once all of these problems had been resolved, the Sauros were delivered in four batches with modifications in size and updating as and when required. Subsequently eight submarines in three classes were built for the Italian submarine fleet over the following two decades, the last batch commissioned in 1993 under the name of the lead submarine *Primo Longobardo* having the advantage of more modern technology. In 2000 six of the eight boats began to go through the workshops again for further upgrades and refits to extend their life further, the Italian Ministry of Defence having ruled that they must remain in service for the foreseeable future, given the expenditure already committed on the two new Type 212As. The upgrades included combat data and control systems, silencing measures and ship control systems.

The addition of a new weapons system with wire-guided torpedoes completed the modernization to provide both anti-ship and anti-submarine capabilities. The improvements were adjudged to be "remarkable" among the senior officers of the boats, with the addition of cutting-edge instruments. The upgrades to the six boats, combined with the two more modern versions, thus gave Italy an as-good-as-new fleet without the crippling expenditure that comes with new constructions for the 21st century.

TOP AND ABOVE: **Between the *Nazario Sauro*, leader of the class built in 1980, and the *Gianfranco Gazzana Prairoggia*, which slipped down the launch-way in 1995, numerous upgrades and improvements were applauded by submariners and analysts alike.**

LEFT: **The Sauro class benefits from the ongoing process of improvements; further upgrades are scheduled to include new combat data and control systems for the more modern of the Sauro boats.**

Sauro-class SSK

Displacement: 1,452 tonnes/1,429.1 tons (surfaced); 1,635 tonnes/1,609.2 tons (submerged)
Length: 64.36m/211ft 2in
Beam: 6.83m/22ft 5in
Armament: 6 x 533mm/21in tubes, 12 x torpedoes
Propulsion: 3 x diesel engines, 3,184kW/4,270shp; 1 x electric motor, 2,394kW/3,210shp
Speed: 11 knots (surfaced); 20 knots (dived)
Complement: 55 men

ITALY

LEFT AND BELOW: **The *Salvatore Todaro*, based on the German Type 212A but built under licence in Italy, was commissioned in 2005, and her sister *Sciré* was to follow in 2007. Two more Italian Type 212s are planned, all modified to include a number of Italy's home-grown technologies.**

Salvatore Todaro-class SSK

This new Italian class of two diesel-electric boats, the first of which was due to be commissioned in 2005, will represent the full extent of the Italian Navy's spending on its submarine fleet for the foreseeable future, apart from the general maintenance and upgrading costs of its existing boats.

The new class taking the name of the first built, *Salvatore Todaro*, is based on the German Type 212A, and the boats were to be built under licence by the Italians at the Fincantieri shipbuilders at their Monfalcone yards. Although the overall specifications are similar, there are a number of significant differences in the final Italian version compared with that of the German builder. The Italians ordered a re-design of the interiors to allow for additional escape systems to be installed.

The German design allowed for individual escape mechanisms, whereas the Italians have installed a more efficient system allowing for collective rather than individual escape. Elsewhere, however, the state-of-the-art technology that has impressed so many foreign buyers remains unchanged from the original German manifesto. The boats are also considered ideal for the Italians' principal area of operations around the Mediterranean and Adriatic, both now requiring round-the-clock naval patrols in view of the amount of illegal traffic reaching Italian shores, both in terms of immigration and criminal activity in drugs, contraband and people-smuggling.

LEFT: **A cutaway illustration of the Italian version of the Type 212A.**

Salvatore Todaro-class SSK

Displacement: 1,610 tonnes/1,584.6 tons (surfaced); 1,830 tonnes/1,801.1 tons (submerged)
Length: 57m/187ft
Beam: 7m/23ft
Armament: 6 x 533mm/21in tubes, 24 x stn Atlas Electronik DM2A4 torpedoes
Propulsion: Diesel-electric AIP, 3,164kW/4,243shp
Speed: 12 knots (surfaced); 20 knots (dived)
Complement: 24 men

Delfin-class SSK

The Spanish Navy has maintained a modest submarine force for over 30 years, effectively patrolling coastal waters. They are not and never have been really interested in the serious end of submarine warfare with all the responsibilities and finance that such an undertaking entails. However, they have participated fully with NATO in providing port facilities for the Atlantic patrols of American boats. For many years, theirs has been a more domestic requirement that falls within the general auspices of guarding shores. However, in recent times in which few European nations have escaped infiltration by terrorist cells, the Spanish along with others have been reconsidering their commitment to submarines.

For years, the Spanish Navy has relied on its good relationship with the French to provide submarines, and since the early 1970s has been running Delfin-class boats, which are a derivative of the French-designed Daphne class, dating back to the 1950s but built under licence in Spain. Other nations with a more aggressive submarine defence policy than Spain's also equipped with these boats at the time because they were attack submarines, and at 1,000 tonnes, were substantial boats. Nevertheless, they had their limitations, not least because of the age of the actual design.

Over the years, they have been refitted and upgraded, but not to any exceptional degree, and it is a credit to the Spanish Navy that they have kept the flag flying with boats that some would now regard as old tubs – indeed the more elderly ones did look just like that towards the end of their service. They were fairly straightforward boats when originally designed, even down to the somewhat old-fashioned notion of aft-facing torpedo tubes for protection while escaping. However, that hardly mattered for the type of role for which the boats were employed by Spain.

ABOVE: Four boats of the Delphin class, a derivative of the French Daphne, have given the Spanish Navy years of service, but they have reached the point where they are no longer viable in terms of upgrading.

Even so, however lightly used, the sheer weight of miles covered over such a lifespan took its toll, and reinforced by the need for more effective units to face the dangers of the times, the Spanish Navy began phasing out the Delphins in the 1990s, with the last one due to be decommissioned in 2006–07.

Delfin-class SSK

Displacement: 943 tonnes/928.1 tons (surfaced); 1,043 tonnes/1,026.5 tons (submerged)
Length: 57.9m/190ft
Beam: 6.7m/22ft
Armament: 4 x 533mm/21in tubes, 12 x torpedoes or mines
Propulsion: Diesel-electric, 1,491.4kW/2,000shp
Speed: 13 knots (surfaced); 14 knots (dived)
Complement: 56 men

SPAIN

LEFT: **A familiar boat among the continental nations, the Spanish Galerna class originated from the French Agosta design. The Spanish built four at the turn of the 1980s which remained operational into the 21st century, focusing their equipment on littoral operations.**

Galerna-class SSK

Displacement: 1,582 tonnes/1,557 tons (surfaced); 1,767 tonnes/1,739 tons (submerged)
Length: 67.7m/222ft 1in
Beam: 6.8m/22ft 4in
Armament: 6 x 533mm/21in tubes; mixed parcel of torpedoes and Exocet missiles
Propulsion: Diesel-electric AIP, 3430.2kW/ 4,600shp
Speed: 18 knots (surfaced); 22 knots (dived)
Complement: 54 men

Galerna-class SSK

The four boats of this class also became stalwarts of the Spanish submarine fleet as they came into service from 1984, and remained active 20 years later. The class originated from the French *Agosta* design but again were built under licence by the Spanish ENB Cartega Company with substantially modified electric systems. These became the Galerna class that were required specifically for coastal patrols and therefore lacked some of the deepwater specifications of the *Agosta*. The Spanish versions did, however, carry an impressive array of weapons with a heavy leaning towards littoral operations.

Scorpene-class SSK

The effects of terrorist infiltration into national territories has become a number one security issue with regard to policing borders and coastlines, and submarines have an increasing role to play in such issues, both in their national deployment and international responsibilities. Spain was already considering its course of action long before experiencing a major terrorist atrocity, and one of the decisions the government took, upon the recommendation of the Spanish Navy, was to immediately bolster its submarine force and bring it into the 21st century.

Once again, the Spanish turned to the French when the decision was made to replace the old Delphins. The result was an agreement to purchase five of the new Scorpene class designed by the French shipbuilders, DCN, for export but with the promise that they would include the latest technologies that are built-in features of the French SSBN and SSK fleets.

Once again, much of the build will be in the hands of the Spanish Izar Cartagena Shipbuilding Company, and the first off the lines was due to be

LEFT: **Under construction, the Spanish version of another French design, created as the Scorpene class. The first of class was due to enter service in 2006 to replace the Delphins.**

Scorpene-class SSK

Displacement: 1,460 tonnes/1,436.9 tons (surfaced); 1,565 tonnes/1,540.3 tons (submerged)
Length: 66.4m/217ft 10in
Beam: 6.2m/20ft 4in
Armament: 6 x 533mm/21in tubes (bow), 18 x torpedoes; SSM; SUBTICS combat system
Propulsion: Diesel-electric AIP, 2,833.7kW/ 3,800shp
Speed: 18 knots (surfaced); 20 knots (dived)
Complement: 33 men

commissioned in 2005. It will, of course, be chalk and cheese compared to the old Delphins, a third larger but more importantly a versatile boat bristling with the latest technology, including the very effective Air Independent Propulsion system and an assortment of weaponry to match all possibilities, including surface-to-surface missiles. The design and equipment are also strongly geared to the intelligence role as well as being fully equipped for special operations.

LEFT AND BELOW: **Unlike the Vastergotland class that they succeeded, Sweden's new *Sodermanland*-class submarines are constructed to undertake missions in warmer and more saline waters than the familiar seas around the Swedish coastline. In replacing the refrigeration system, analysts have assumed it is destined to join international peacekeeping missions in warmer climes now that the Soviet threat has diminished.**

Sodermanland-class SSK

The hunter-killer reputation of Swedish submarines has been impressive, given that they have the task of operating in regions that brought them up close and personal with the operations of the Soviet submarine force during some of the periods of great intensity in the Cold War. The Sodermanland class, named after a Baltic Sea port, was introduced as Sweden's prime attack vessel from its launch in the mid-1980s and commissioned in the early 1990s. By that time, international tensions had eased somewhat, but Sweden continued with its submarine construction programme, which would see the introduction of some fine new boats over the next decade that would carry them forward well into the 21st century.

The Sodermanland class was an upgraded and improved version of the slightly earlier Vastergotland class first introduced in 1988, and the two models would operate side by side, although in time they would all be outshone by the new Gotland.

In fact, the final two boats of the Vastergotland class became the Sodermanland class by virtue of their relaunch after having been refitted with some of the latest technology and a propulsion system designed for the new Gotland class. This was a substantial undertaking that required the two boats to be sliced in two immediately aft of the tower and lengthened with the insertion of the Stirling AIP propulsion compartment, which added another 12m/39ft 4in to the length of the boat.

The section was built and completely outfitted prior to installation as a complete unit, creating the *Sodermanland* in 2003 and the *Ostermanland* in 2004. The two boats were also equipped and designed for international peacekeeping duties and received conversion of their filtration systems and cooling apparatus to operate in warmer and less saline waters.

Meanwhile, the sister submarines of the Vastergotland class, although overtaken by the technology of the latest Swedish boats, remained a very capable weapons platform. They were retained for operations in the region for which they were originally designed: the cold, deep theatres of the North Atlantic, the Baltic and the North Sea.

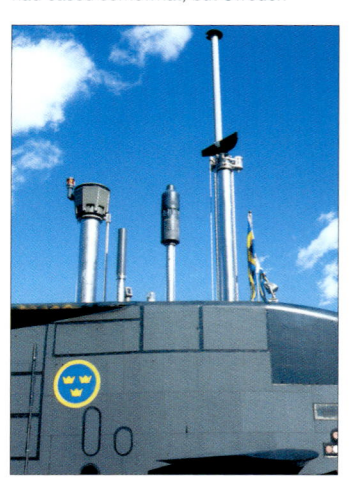

LEFT: **The array of retractable antennae on the sail of the Sodermanland boats.**

Sodermanland

Displacement: 1,385 tonnes/1,363.1 tons (surfaced); 1,446 tonnes/1,423.1 tons (submerged)
Length: 60.5m/198ft 6in
Beam: 6.1m/20ft
Armament: 6 x 533mm/21in tubes (bow); 3 x 406mm/16in tubes (aft); mixed package of Type 613 heavy torpedoes, Type 431/451 lightweight torpedoes and SSM
Propulsion: Stirling AIP, 1,342.3kW/1,800shp
Speed: 20 knots (surfaced); 24 knots (dived)
Complement: 30 men

Gotland-class (Type A19) SSK

LEFT: **HMS** *Gotland*, first of the class of the fine Swedish boats bearing her name which came into service progressively in the late 1990s and which were to be upgraded in 2005 with a new combat system called SESUB 960, along with improvements to navigation, sensor management and weapon handling systems.

ABOVE: The submarine is fitted with a Kollmorgen search-and-attack periscope and a Terma Scanter navigation radar, and includes a surveillance-and-warning system for the identification of hostile radar threats.

Sweden's *Gotland*-class submarines, commissioned in the late 1990s, have an excellent reputation and are noted for the fact that they are packed with first-class home-grown electronics and technology from the likes of Saab Industries, although the shipbuilder, Kockums, is actually part of the German HDW conglomerate.

The combined input of up-to-the-minute operational systems was doubtless one of the reasons why the US Navy selected the Gotland to take part in a modern "battle" scenario. In November 2004, the Swedish Government gave the go-ahead for the first of class and her crew to be leased to the Americans for a year to take part in naval exercises. Gotland arrived at the San Diego Naval Air Station in June 2005 to operate as part of the "enemy" force pitted against US submarines and surface vessels.

The *Gotland*-class boats have a combat management system known as 9SCS Mark 3 from Saabtech Vectronics, an extended version of which is used in Swedish surface vessels. The fire control system can control a number of torpedoes in the water simultaneously. The submarines are fitted with four 533mm/21in tubes and two 400mm/15.75in tubes. Type 613 heavy-weight anti-surface ship torpedoes, fired from the larger tubes, come with wire guidance and passive homing, delivering a warhead of 240kg/529lb, while the smaller tubes fire the Saab Bofors Type 43 lightweight anti-submarine torpedo.

However, a modification of the combat system will include a brand new heavyweight torpedo developed by Saab for the Swedish Navy, the Model 2000. It has both anti-submarine and anti-surface capability with a fast 40 knots delivery rate.

A similar modification is planned for the lightweight torpedo range, with a Saab Bofors Type 43x2, a wire-guided torpedo with improved tracking. The Gotland boats also have the capacity to carry 48 mines externally fitted in a girdle arrangement. The Kockums V4-275R Stirling Air Independent Propulsion diesel engines provide an endurance of two weeks at a speed of 5 knots without snorting.

BELOW: **A cutaway illustration showing the internal layout of the *Gotland*.**

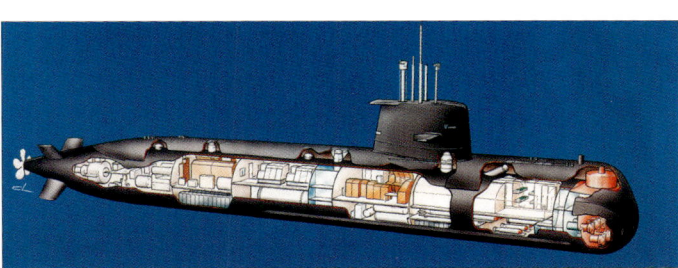

Gotland-class (Type A19) SSK

Displacement: 1,168 tonnes/1,149.6 tons (surfaced); 1,466 tonnes/1,442.8 tons (submerged)
Length: 61m/200ft 2in
Beam: 6m/19ft 8in
Armament: 4 x 533mm/21in tubes; 2 x 400mm/15.75in tubes; 16 x torpedoes; 48 x mines
Propulsion: 2 x MTU diesels; 2 x Kockums V4-275r air independent units
Speed: 11 knots (surfaced); 20 knots (dived)
Complement: 33 men

Khalid-class SSK

The often tense political situation between Pakistan and India since the British pulled out in 1947 resulted in both sides arming themselves to the fullest extent, each with a counterweight to the other's armoury. Suppliers of such machinery seemed unconcerned as to their potential use, and both nations built up an effective naval force which included submarines.

In this case the supplier was DCN, makers of the popular Agosta class in service with several smaller navies around the world. Two boats were supplied in the late 1970s, apparently part of an order originally intended for South Africa but which was diverted to Pakistan instead. The boats received an extensive refit a decade later, with the addition of the famed Exocet missile, which represented a serious threat to the Indian Navy. More potent, however, was the agreement in the mid-1990s for DCN to supply three of the new *Agosta 90B*-class boats to Pakistan, the first built at DCN's Cherbourg shipyard during the late 1990s for commissioning in time for the new century. The remaining two were to be assembled at the Pakistani Naval Dockyard at Karachi with the assistance of French engineers; both boats were expected to be in service by 2004. This proved to be a particularly useful agreement for the Pakistanis, both in regard to the government's ambitions to increase the nation's submarine capability as well as expanding its own industrial base in shipbuilding technology.

However, the latter objective hit a serious snag. Completion of the third submarine at Karachi was halted by a terrorist attack in 2002 in which more than 40 workers were killed or injured. Eleven French engineers were among the fatalities. The damage and subsequent delay meant that the third boat would not be in service before 2006, and a programme of further modernization of earlier models was instigated. Despite this, the French were sufficiently impressed by the skills of the Pakistani workforce to grant the country's shipbuilders a licence by DCN to offer commercial production of the submarines.

ABOVE LEFT AND ABOVE: **In settling a deal with the French, the Pakistani Navy has acquired these classic SSKs of proven ability and whose weaponry consists of torpedoes, mines and the renowned anti-ship SM-39 Exocet missiles. The submarine is fitted with the most modern command and control systems and can dive below 300m/984ft.**

ABOVE: It is no wonder that it is with national pride the Pakistani Navy displays their latest acquisition, a boat they call the *Khalid*, which will be the star of their submarine force and also the model for its shipbuilders to manufacture.

Khalid-class SSK

Displacement: 1,486 tonnes/1,462.5 tons (surfaced); 1,732 tonnes/1,707.6 tons (submerged)
Length: 67m/219ft 10in
Beam: 5.4m/17ft 9in
Armament: 6 x 533mm/21in tubes, mixed parcel F17 Mod 2/Exocet SM39 submarine-launched anti-ship missiles
Propulsion: Diesel-electric, 2,684.5kW/3,600hp
Speed: 15 knots (surfaced); 17 knots (dived)
Complement: 36 men

PAKISTAN/INDIA

LEFT: **Like the Pakistani Navy, the Indian Navy also chose a submarine of well proven ability and with good service back-up, in the form of ten custom-tailored units from the Russian Kilo class. These were supplied under contract with the Indian government and renamed the Sindhu class, the last being delivered at the turn of the 21st century.**

BELOW LEFT: **An interesting and seldom seen shot of torpedoes being loaded into the bow tubes.**

Sindhu-class SSK

Pakistani ambitions towards an effective submarine force were, of course, no match for their neighbours. Picking up from the naval tradition that the British brought to India, the newly-independent nation acquired substantial assets which became the foundations for what is today the world's seventh largest navy. Submarines were very much a part of that force, especially in the purchase of ten diesel-powered Soviet Project 877 Kilo submarines, known in India as the EKM or Sindhu class.

They were built under a contract between the Russians and the Indian Ministry of Defence, with the last unit delivered to India in 2000, and all equipped with some well-proven electronics and modern weaponry. The final boat, for example, was fitted with the Klab ZM-54E (SS-N-27) anti-ship cruise missiles, with a range of 220km/137 miles. The older boats will no doubt benefit from a back fit of upgrades in due course, although the Indian Navy already possesses a number of imported cruise missile systems in its arsenal, as well as systems of its own already in service or currently under development. The Sagarika (Oceanic) submarine-launched cruise missile has been in development for some years. It is said to have a range of around 500km/311 miles and was planned to be in service by the end of 2005.

Additionally, India bought four Type 209 diesel-electric submarines from *Howaldtswerke Deutsche Werft* (HDW) of Germany in the late 1980s and has also delved into the arena of nuclear-powered boats. In January 1988, her government reached agreement with the Soviet Union to lease a nuclear-powered attack submarine of the 670A Skat series with eight Ametist (SS-N-7 Starbright) anti-ship missile launchers. In the Indian Navy, the submarine was re-christened *Chakra*, and was manned by a Russian crew to train Indian seamen.

Upon expiration of the three-year leasing term in 1991, the submarine was returned to Russia and decommissioned from the Russian Navy. However, India did not abandon the idea of a nuclear-powered fleet, and according to some accounts, the navy is already at an advanced stage in the design and construction of her own nuclear submarines. The Indian nuclear-powered attack submarine design is said to have a 4,064-tonne/4,000-ton displacement and a single-shaft nuclear power plant of Indian origin.

Sindhu-class SSK

Displacement: 2,180 tonnes/2,145.6 tons (surfaced); 2,400 tonnes/2,362.1 tons (submerged)
Length: 92m/301ft 10in
Beam: 8.6m/28ft 3in
Armament: 6 x 533mm/21in tubes (forward), 4 x 533mm/21in tubes (aft), 22 x torpedoes or 44 x mines; missile package
Propulsion: Diesel-electric; 2 x shafts, 3,952.2kW/5,300shp
Speed: 15.5 knots (surfaced); 19 knots (dived)
Complement: 75 men

DIRECTORY OF SUBMARINES: 1945 TO DATE

Walrus II class

The Royal Netherlands Navy has enjoyed a long love affair with submarines and so they should, given that their countryman Cornelius Drebbel played such a large part in bringing undersea boats into fruition. During World War I, they began the production of the K class built for service around the Dutch colonies, followed by the O (for *Onderzeeboot*) boats for coastal operations. There were a number of noteworthy developments, and especially significant was O19, regarded in many quarters as the first submarine class in the world to be equipped with a diesel "snort system" that was much copied later on. Post-war, the Dutch Royal Navy received the loan of a decommissioned member of the US *Balao*-class wartime submarines, *Icefish*. Following a refit to produce a Guppy configuration, she was rechristened *Walrus* I and saw many years of uninterrupted service. This was achieved under a post-war arrangement with the Americans called Mutual Defence Assistance in which a number of ageing US vessels were received on loan by grateful European nations whose finances were tied up elsewhere, rebuilding the devastation of the war.

Upon her retirement, the name was continued with the introduction the Walrus II class, the diesel attack submarine that brought the Dutch Navy up to date with modern requirements in the 1980s, an event seriously delayed by a devastating fire in the first-of-class submarine during the latter stages of construction. Consequently, the lead boat had the embarrassment of being beaten into commissioning by the second of her class, *Zeeleeu II*. *Walrus II* was finally relaunched in April 1987, more than a decade after she was originally laid down. The Walrus II class replaced the ageing Dutch trio of the Zwardvis class, built between 1964 and 1972 and which gave good service over almost two decades.

In Walrus II, the Dutch had built a fast general-purpose boat, principally an attack submarine for operations in the Eastern Atlantic, the North Sea and the Norwegian Sea, often under the auspices of NATO while participating in both exercises and active service roles. The Dutch – like the British – are dedicated users of their submarines in support of special forces operations and in

ABOVE LEFT AND ABOVE: **Another relatively small but brilliant European submarine of strong pedigree is the Dutch Walrus II class, successor to the Zwaardvis. Although slightly larger, a high degree of automation has enabled a reduction in the crew from 67 to 49 men. They are popular submarines, especially with NATO who have used them extensively for operations, especially those involving special forces.** BELOW LEFT: **A profile and cutaway view of the *Walrus* II.**

intelligence-gathering. The Walrus II class, along with other RNLN boats of the new Zwaardvis II class, are recognized among NATO commanders as highly useful boats in these operations, and in both anti-surface and anti-submarine operations. As such, these boats took part in anti-terrorist missions as part of Operation Enduring Freedom, in which the US-led forces wrested control of Afghanistan from the Taliban.

Walrus II class

Displacement: 2,560 tonnes/2,519.6 tons (surfaced); 2,800 tonnes/2,755.8 tons (submerged)
Length: 67.7m/222ft 1in
Beam: 8.4m/27ft 7in
Armament: 6 x 533mm/21in tubes, 12 x torpedoes; mines
Propulsion: Diesel-electric, 4623.3kW/6,200shp
Speed: 18 knots (surfaced); 21 knots (dived)
Complement: 33 men

NETHERLANDS/BRAZIL

Type 209-class SSK

This popular German-designed submarine is the mainstay of small submarine forces around the world and has been built in substantial numbers over many years, almost entirely for the export market, by *Howaldtswerke Deutsche Werft* (HDW) at Kiel.

The Brazilian Navy, for example, won government approval to upgrade its submarine force in the late 1980s, initially taking delivery of the German-built Type 209 but with agreement from the supplier to continue indigenous manufacture in their own shipyards, all taking the name of the first-of-class submarine, *Tupi*. This was built in HDW shipyards in Germany and commissioned into the Brazilian Navy in 1989.

Thereafter, three more boats of the class were built at the *Arsenal de Marinha* naval shipyard in Rio de Janeiro over the next ten years. The Brazilian Navy then contracted to buy two further boats of the improved Type 204/1400 series, the first scheduled for completion in 2005 and the second the following year. They came with the latest in electronics suites, including two Mod 76 periscopes supplied by Kollmorgen, the Calypso III I-band navigation radar from Thales, and the submarine's hull-mounted sonar, the CSU-83/1, from STN Atlas Electronik.

Elsewhere in South America, and across the globe, Type 209 was appearing as the principle brand for a diverse range of nations and requirements. Over two decades, orders were placed for boats with a variety of mission profiles for operations in the Atlantic, the Caribbean, the Indian Ocean and the Far East. Virtually every customer required their own design in terms of internal arrangements and equipment to meet the needs of the varying tasks, range, diving depth and climate. These requirements led to the Type 209 being produced in three series, and by the beginning of the 21st century the following nations were equipped with 209s:

ABOVE LEFT AND ABOVE: **The theme of the general-purpose boat re-appears in various parts of the world, and is instrumental in recording the submarine acquisitions of the Brazilian Navy. It relies on the German 209, which has been exported to more than a dozen nations around the globe. In Brazil, it is known as the Tupi class.**

Argentina (2 submarines, Type 209/1200), Peru (6, Type 209/1200), Colombia (2, Type 209/1200), Venezuela (2, Type 209/1200), Ecuador (2, Type 209/1200), Indonesia (2, Type 209/1200), Chile (2, Type 209/1400), India (4, Type 209/1400), Brazil (3, Type 209/1400), South Korea (9, Type 209/1200), Turkey (6, Type 209/1200, 4, Type 209/1400), and Greece (4, Type 209/1100, 4, Type 209/1200).

The Type 209 will begin to be replaced by the new Type 212 following a successful commissioning into the German Navy in 2003 and with the Italian Navy in 2004.

LEFT: **The Type 209 diesel-electric became one of the world's most popular submarines in the 1960s, and remains so into the 21st century. It is pictured here in Chile where, like in Brazil and several other South American nations, the navy has long relied on the German boats.**

Brazilian Tupi class (Type 109/1400)

Displacement: 1,462 tonnes/1,438.9 tons (surfaced); 1,560 tonnes/1,535.4 tons (submerged)
Length: 61m/200ft 2in
Beam: 6.2m/20ft 4in
Armament: 8 x 533mm/ 21in tubes, 14 x torpedoes/mines
Propulsion: Diesel-electric, 1789.7kW/2,400shp and 2610kW/3,500shp
Speed: 13 knots (surfaced); 22 knots (dived)
Complement: 33 men

DIRECTORY OF SUBMARINES: 1945 TO DATE

LEFT: **The Norwegian *Ula*-class boats are recognized as being among the most silent and manoeuvrable submarines in the world, which when combined with their relatively small size, makes them difficult to detect from surface vessels and ideal for operations in coastal areas and intelligence work.**
ABOVE: **Systems operatives aboard the *Ula*.**

Ula-class SSK

For almost 40 years, Norway was precariously placed in the midst of Cold War activity as the Soviet Union transformed the Kola peninsula into a base for its formidable Northern Fleet, which at its height consisted of more than 150 nuclear-powered and nuclear-armed submarines and a similar number of surface vessels. Once described as the most complex and concentrated naval base in history, this vast array of boats needed to traverse the Norwegian Sea to reach the Atlantic Ocean.

Norway was therefore in a front-line position in the event of conflagration, and from the late 1970s a series of agreements involving allied support for reinforcing the defence of northern Norway were put in place and constantly reviewed along with a massive conglomeration of early-warning systems, both on land and at sea.

Radar stations in Norway, Iceland and Greenland continually oversaw the whole area while permanent listening devices for the purpose of monitoring the movement of the Soviet submarines were placed at strategic points under the Norwegian Sea, and NATO's Standing Force, Atlantic took responsibility for sea patrols. In the event of military action, allied reinforcements were on a permanent ready-to-move footing through Allied Command Europe under the Rapid Reinforcement Plan established in 1982.

So immense was the weight of submarine forces pitted against each other in this era of incredible tension that any serious involvement was simply beyond the capability of such a small nation. However, the Royal Norwegian Navy has maintained an efficient submarine force which latterly consisted of six improved *Kobben*-class and six *Ula*-class submarines. Both classes were no more than patrol boats designed for littoral operations. The Royal Norwegian Navy, nevertheless, played a full part both in the efforts of self-protection and by involvement in the wider brief of supporting NATO operations and exercises.

The Norwegians, however, were always well aware of the reality that, in the event of war, their role could only be that of a lesser participant alongside their NATO allies, to which end the bulk of their training and operational activity was geared. Having said that, there is no denying that the Ula class was especially effective in intelligence gathering and had the ability to lay mines or attack the opposing forces if the event ever arose.

LEFT: **Norway played a vital role in NATO security exercises during the Cold War, and still does, lately linked to joint operations with helicopter units.**

Ula-class SSK

Displacement: 1,150 tonnes/1,131.8 tons (surfaced); 1,350 tonnes/1,328.7 tons (submerged)
Length: 59m/193ft 7in
Beam: 5.4m/17ft 9in
Armament: 4 x 533mm/21in tubes, 12 x torpedoes/mines
Propulsion: Diesel-electric, 1,416.8kW/1,900shp
Speed: 18 knots (surfaced); 23 knots (dived)
Complement: 21 men

492

NORWAY/TAIWAN

LEFT AND ABOVE: **The Taiwanese Hai Hu** *Sea Tiger* immaculately turned out, as are the crew lining the deck, but behind this impressive façade is a submarine service deeply concerned about its future. ABOVE: **Another of the Taiwanese boats,** *Sea Dragon* **of the Dutch-built Hai Lung class.**

Hai Hu/Hai Lung class

The government of Taiwan has long been attempting to put together a viable submarine force to provide some protection from the ambitions of China to bring the nation back into the fold. In 2001, President George W. Bush said the United States was considering selling the Taiwanese eight diesel submarines for $4 billion, but internally there was much discussion about the implications with regard to China, which was clearly opposed to the idea. Skeptics pointed out that the United States hadn't built a conventional submarine for more than 40 years.

In the event, the US quote was far higher than Taiwan had anticipated because America would have had the boats built in foreign shipyards. Most of the world's major submarine-building nations, including Germany, the Netherlands, Sweden and Australia, have also ruled out providing Taiwan with submarines or the use of their designs for fear of antagonizing Beijing.

In the summer of 2005, the attempts were continuing. Taiwan's Minister of National Defence, Lee Jye, re-affirmed his nation's intention to acquire more submarines, warning that "China's Navy is building a force with a long range war capability that will pose a serious threat to Taiwan by 2020". By then, if speculation proves correct, China will have built a force approaching 80 submarines, and given that Taiwan relies almost entirely on the freedom of her sea lanes for trade and daily materials, a Chinese blockade – or worse – would have severe consequences that might reverberate around the world.

Taiwan may yet build submarines if she is not able to acquire them from other countries. According to the Federation of American Scientists, Taiwan's state-run China Shipbuilding Corporation, in co-operation with Taiwan's Chungshan Institute of Technology, could build six to ten of the submarines for military service, starting in 2006. Taiwan's China Steel Company has developed HY submarine steel; China Shipbuilding Company has also begun studying and developing the design and build process of submarine hulls on the basis of its experience in submarine servicing; and the development of heavy wire-guided anti-submarine torpedoes is underway at Chung Shan Academy of Scientific Research. However, key technologies for the submarine, including the torpedo fire control system and electronic radar system, still have to be obtained through the arms sale channel. Taiwan is currently exploring obtaining the parts to build submarines from other countries in the face of strict regulations on the export of submarine parts.

So Taiwan continues the quest and for the time being is relying on a fleet of just four submarines, two of which are almost too old for operational roles. They are diesel-electric boats with a fairly versatile remit, with capability for patrolling and attack, and powerful enough to discourage hostile action.

LEFT: **In dry dock for running repairs and upgrades, one of Taiwan's remaining Hai Lung submarines. Although these vessels put on a brave front in the head-to-head with the Chinese, they do require attention to the problems associated with old age.**

Hai Hu class

Displacement: 2,360 tonnes/2,322.7 tons (surfaced); 2,660 tonnes/2,618 tons (submerged)
Length: 66.9m/219ft 6in
Beam: 8.4m/27ft 7in
Armament: 6 x 533mm/21in tubes, 10 x torpedoes; surface-to-surface missiles
Propulsion: Diesel-electric, 3,803kW/5,100shp
Speed: 17 knots (surfaced); 20 knots (dived)
Complement: 67 men

493

Glossary

A

AA Anti-Aircraft (deck guns).
AS Anti-Submarine.
abaft Toward the stern of a boat.
ACINT Acoustic Intelligence.
acoustic Torpedo that detects its target by means of sound, and uses that sound to steer along its path.
active sonar The type of sonar most commonly referred to in movies about submarines, in which the "ping" sound is emitted and targets are detected by echolocation. There are disadvantages to the system, since it may also give away the position and identity of the transmitting platform, rendering it vulnerable to attack. Furthermore, false targets may arise from the transmissions. *See also* passive sonar.
aft Rear or the rear extremity.
after trim Ballast tank used to adjust a submarine's weight and tilting movement.
AIO Action Information Organization. A station in all modern submarines that receives inputs from the sonars and other equipment to formulate a tactical picture around the submarine and ultimately to perform Target Motion Analysis of activity within an area up to 241km/150 miles from submarine.
AIP Air-Independent Propulsion.
Aphrodite German anti-radar device which gave out reflecting impulses.
ASDIC British Anti-Submarine Detection Investigation Committee, 1917, whose initials were used for the name given to a device that detected the presence of submerged submarines.
Asdic Early British term for Sonar.
ASM Air-to-Surface Missile.
ASROC Anti-Submarine Rocket. American stand-off weapon.
ASSW Anti-Surface Ship Warfare.
ASW Anti-Submarine Warfare; Anti-Submarine Work.
awash When a submarine is in a position whereby the sea is flowing over the superstructure.

B

ballast Material taken aboard to improve or correct draught, trim, stability or ship motion.
ballast tanks Located between the pressure hull and the outer hull, and saddle tanks within the torpedo room. These are blown to provide positive buoyancy when the submarine is surfaced and completely flooded to give neutral buoyancy when submerged.
battle surface Surfacing manoeuvre to ensure the boat arrives flat, or nearly flat enabling quick deployment of gun crews.
BdU *Befehlshaber der Unterseeboote*, Commander-in-Chief for German submarines, Karl Dönitz, 1939–45.
beam In this book, the maximum width of the hull at the waterline at standard displacement. With flare, a ship may be wider at higher levels.
bearing Defining a course from a particular point.
belt Vertical armour protection of a ship's hull. Rare in smaller ships.
bhp Brake horsepower. The power output of a (usually) internal combustion engine.
bilgekeel Longitudinal fin attached at the turns of the bilge to dampen rolling.
bistatic Overt active sonar illuminating a target for a covert, remote passive sonar.
boiler Original US slang name for a submarine (as well as pigboat or sewer pipe).
Bold A device used by U-boats to confuse ASDIC.
boomer Ballistic missile submarine.
bow Forward end of a vessel.
bow, stern planes Guiding fins that determine the submarine's angle of dive and permit the submarine to stay at any desired depth under water.
broach Breaking through the surface and rising out of the water. Also known as porpoising.
bulkhead Internal partitions of a submarine to compartmentalize the various functions within the submarine; many early boats were of single-compartment design, within which every activity was conducted, including the calls of nature. Later, as water-tight bulkheads were introduced, they became vital to a damaged submarine's survival.
bunkers Compartments for the stowage of fuel. May refer loosely to the fuel itself.

C

CAP Combat Air Patrol.
caisson A self-contained, buoyant gate for a dry dock.
calibre Bore diameter of a gun barrel. Also measure of barrel length, e.g. a 3in 70 will be of 3 x 70 = 210in length.
camber Athwartships convex curvature to a ship's deck.
casing Outer skin of light plating which encloses the ballast tanks and pressure hull.
catapult Device to accelerate aircraft to take-off velocity.
cavitation Visible tracks on the surface caused by a submarine propeller, a long-standing problem even when submerged and easily detectable either by sound devices or aerial reconnaissance.
centre of buoyancy The point through which the resultant of all upward, or buoyant, forces act. It is directly below the centre of gravity in a surface ship.
centre of gravity The point through which the resultant of all downward, or weight-related, forces act.
Chidori Japanese anti-submarine vessel; a type of torpedo boat.
C-in-C Commander-in-Chief.
CIWS Close-In Weapons System. Self-contained, fully-automatic, "last-ditch" defensive system, typically comprising several high rate-of-fire cannon and/or short-range SAMs.
CODAG Combined Diesel And Gas.
CODOG Combined Diesel Or Gas.
COGAG Combined Gas And Gas.
COGOG Combined Gas Or Gas.
COSAG Combined Steam And Gas.
commission Point at which a new submarine officially enters service.
COMSUBLANT Commander, Submarine Forces, US Atlantic Fleet.
COMSUBPAC Commander, Submarine Forces, US Pacific Fleet.
conning tower Heavily armoured horizontal hull over the control room and below the bridge, which developed into the control centre of all operations.

GLOSSARY

contra-rotating propellers Propellers, as in a torpedo, mounted on coaxial shafts and rotated in opposite directions to nullify side forces.

control room Usually amidships, the compartment housing all diving and communications controls as well as the ship's gyrocompass and radio room.

Controller Earlier, Comptroller. In the British Board of Admiralty, the Third Sea Lord, responsible for the design, provision and upkeep of HM warships.

crank Lacking initial stability and easily inclined by external forces, such as wind and sea.

crash dive Emergency dive by a submarine.

CVE Escort carrier. Usually converted from mercantile hull.

D

DASH Drone Anti-Submarine Helicopter.
DDK General Purpose Destroyer.
DE Destroyer Escort.
DEG Destroyer Escort with an anti-aircraft missile system.
DESRON In the US Navy, a Destroyer Squadron.
dipping sonar Small sonar lowered by cable from a hovering helicopter. Sometimes "dunking sonar".
displacement (fl) Full load, or deep, displacement of a ship which is fully equipped, stored and fuelled.
displacement (std) Standard displacement. Actual weight of a ship less fuel and other deductions allowed by treaty.
Division Boat In Imperial German Navy, a larger type of Torpedo Boat, equivalent to a flotilla leader.
DP Dual-Purpose, i.e. a gun suitable for engaging both aerial or surface targets.
Dräger Tauchretter Underwater escape apparatus for U-boat crewmen.
draught (or "draft") Mean depth of water in which a ship may float freely. In frigates particularly, mean draught (quoted) may be considerably less than that over protruding sonars.
DSRV Deep Submergence Rescue Vehicle.

E

echo sounder Navigation or position-finding device to determine depth by measuring the time taken for a pulse of high-frequency sound to reach the sea bed or a submerged object and for the echo to return.
ECM Electronic Counter Measures.
escape hatch Hatch positioned for an escape from a stricken submarine.

escape pod Many new submarines are now equipped with small pods which can be used to evacuate some of the crew.
ER Extended Range.
ESM Electronic Support Measures.

F

fan A spread of torpedoes.
FAT Fedapparat Torpedo, developed by Germany for U-boat attacks on convoys, the torpedo travelling in a pre-determined straight line then zigzagged.
fin The conning tower of the submarine, which contains the masts.
fire control The operation of directing action against the enemy.
Flak Anti-aircraft gun
flare Outward curvature or angle of hull plating.
flood down To fill tanks until the decks are awash.
flotilla Standard operational unit of destroyers or frigates, particularly in the Royal Navy.
forefoot Junction of stem with keel line.
Foxer A British noisemaker towed behind ships to fool German acoustic torpedoes.
FRAM Fleet Re-habilitation And Modernization. An updating programme applied to many US destroyers.
freeboard In a warship, the vertical distance between the water to any particular point on the weather deck. Unlike merchant ships, warships do not have a designated freeboard deck.

G

GM Guided Missile.
GNAT The name given by the Allies to the German T5 acoustic torpedo.
Grand Fleet Title carried by the British battle fleet during World War I.
gross registered tons (grt) Measure of the volumetric capacity of a merchant ship. One gross ton equals 100ft^3 (2.83m^3) of reckonable space.
ground tackle General term for anchors and associated equipment.

gunhouse A relatively light, enclosed containment for guns, usually not extending more than one deck below. In contradistinction to a *turret*, a usually protected containment located atop a barbette or deep armoured trunk.

GUPPY The Greater Underwater Propulsion Power Program was launched in the US in 1945 to combine captured German technology with American developments. Since GUPPP didn't sound quite right, the third P was dropped and a Y added, to be named after the fish. To coincide with this development, all US submarines were for the time being named after undersea life.

gyroscope A rapidly spinning mass, which stabilizes by virtue of its inertia or resistance to displacement of it axis of rotation.

H

HA High Angle. Usually with reference to a gun's elevation.
HA/LA High Angle/Low Angle.
hard-lying A reference to the spartan conditions inseparable from early destroyers and escorts. Recognized (sometimes) by a supplement of "hard-lying money".
head A somewhat complicated toilet on board submarines
Hedgehog Forward-firing AS weapon of World War II, in the form of a spigot mortar projecting 12 or 24 fast-sinking bombs in an elliptical pattern.
High Sea(s) Fleet Title carried by German Battle Fleet during World War I.
horsepower Unit of power equal to 746 Watts.
Huff-Duff Popular term for HF/DF, or High Frequency Direction Finding, used by Allied AS forces to obtain bearings of a transmitting U-boat.
hunter-killer Attack submarine, or (in US) anti-submarine operation by surface ships and/or air units to hunt out and destroy submarines.
hydrophone An underwater sound detection device.

IJK

ihp Indicated horsepower. The power delivered by the pistons of a reciprocating steam engine.
IR Infra-Red.
Jeune École Late 19th-century French naval movement espousing the ideas of Admiral Théophile Aube, who advocated torpedo platforms as a counter to a battle fleet.
kite balloon Aerostat deployed by ships for observation or spotting.
Kriegsmarine The German Navy 1935–45.

495

GLOSSARY

L

LAMPS Light Airborne Multi-Purpose System.
L/B Length-to-Breadth.
LCA Landing Craft, Assault. Large enough to carry an equipped platoon; small enough to be carried under davits.
LCPR Landing Craft, Personnel, Ramped.
LCT Landing Craft, Tank.
length (bp) Length between perpendiculars. Customarily the distance between forward extremity of waterline at standard displacement and the forward side of the rudder post. For American warships, lengths on design waterline and between perpendiculars are synonymous.
length (oa) Length overall.
length (wl) Length on waterline at standard displacement.
Limbo British triple-barrelled AS mortar, designed to supersede Squid.
littoral ops Using modern digital technology, modern submarines approach a coastline in shallow water to make a significant contribution to the intelligence collection effort prior to any subsequent maritime or land action.
locomotive boiler Early form of boiler in which hot products of combustion were forced through tubes to heat a surrounding water mass.
LSM Landing Ship, Medium.
LST Landing Ship, Tank.

M

masts Modern submarine masts carry a plethora of technology that covers many functions, including periscopes, navigation, radar, communications and electronic detection masts.
MCM Mine Counter-Measure groups have become the renewed focus of most submarine forces around the world, as terrorist threats to coastal waters and estuaries escalate. The latest equipment, such as Sonar 2193 (S2193) and NAUTIS3, employs mine-hunting sonar, utilizing state-of-the-art techniques to meet the emerging possibilities of modern mines.
metacentric height Vertical distance between the centre of gravity and the (usually) transverse metacentre. An indicator of the degree of transverse stability.
MR Medium-Range.

N

NATO North Atlantic Treaty Organization. Effectively a counter to the Warsaw Pact.
NBCD Nuclear, Biological and Chemical Defence.
neutrally buoyant Having density identical with that of surrounding water, tending neither to sink nor to float.
NSRS NATO Submarine Rescue System, currently a small team based in Abbey Wood, Bristol, UK, managing a single international co-operative procurement project. The UK is acting as Host Nation on behalf of three participant nations, France, Norway and the UK.
nuclear reactor A sealed unit that is the source of power and electrical requirements on board modern nuclear submarines, and has a lifespan that can outlive the boat itself.

P

paravane A kite-like device, streamed from either bow, whose lines deflect those of moored mines, preventing the ship from striking them.
passive sonar The covert nature and long-range capability of the passive systems (as opposed to active sonar) made this system more popular for much of the second half of the 20th century. They pick up sound radiated (usually involuntarily) by the target. In this case, only one-way transmission is involved, and the system centres around the hydrophone array (*see* Towed Array Sonar). However, the advent of much quieter submarines brought a renewed interest in active sonar.
PDMS Point-Defence Missile System.
periscope (or scope) A tube-like optical instrument containing an arrangement of prisms, mirrors and lenses that enabled vision of the sea above while the submarine was submerged.
PF In US Navy, a Patrol Frigate. Category for British River-class frigates built in the United States.
phased-array radar A radar whose beam depends not upon a rotating antenna but upon sequential switching of a matrix of fixed, radiating elements.

Plan "Orange" American war plan for potential use against Japan.
Poseidon Russian deep submergence rescue vehicle.
pressure hull The inner hull and conning tower, built to withstand sea pressure at a stipulated depth.
protection In this book, usually described as "nominal", comprising only patches of splinter-proof, or radiation-proof, plating covering essential areas may be of "plastic", e.g. Kevlar, or of sandwich construction.
protective deck Either flat, or incorporating side slopes or pronounced curvature, it shields spaces beneath from projectiles or fragments.

QR

QF Quick-Firing. Applied to guns with "fixed" ammunition with projectile and charge combined.
RAS Replenishment-At-Sea.
RCN Royal Canadian Navy.
rudder Rudders and planes used to steer the submarine and as an aid to the diving and surfacing process, along with the flooding or emptying of ballast tanks.

S

SACCS Submarine Automated Communications Control System.
SAM Surface-to-Air-Missile.
SAR Search and Rescue, defined as the use of aircraft, ships and submarines with specialized rescue teams and equipment to search for and rescue personnel in distress, noted for a most comprehensive radio fit to support multi-agency communications.
SARR Submarine Automated Radio Room.
scantlings A scale of dimensions governing the size of all structural parts incorporated in a ship.
schnorkel (or "snort") A hollow mast enabling a submerged submarine to ingest atmospheric air and exhaust engine gases.
screws Propellers.
scuttle Deliberately sinking a vessel.
seakeeping/seakindliness/seaworthiness All applicable to a ship's ability to cope with weather conditions in discharging her functions as an efficient, but habitable, weapons platform.
sheer Curvature of deck line in fore-and-aft direction, usually upward toward either end.
shell plating General term for all outer plating of a hull.

496

GLOSSARY

shp Shaft horsepower. Power measured at point in shaft ahead of the stern gland. Does not include losses incurred in stern gland and A-bracket, if fitted.

sided Situated toward the sides of a ship, usually as opposed to a centreline location.

SLAB Submarine Locator Acoustic Beacon, an electronic device used by submarines in distress, for emitting a repetitive sonic pulse underwater.

SLBM Submarine-Launched Ballistic Missile.

SLMM Submarine-Launched Mobile Mine.

sonar Sound Navigation and Ranging device for locating objects underwater by emitting vibrations similar to sound and measuring the time taken for those vibrations to bounce back from anything in their path. Originally, the US equivalent to British ASDIC.

spar torpedo Warhead mounted on long spar protruding ahead of a small, fast launch. Operated by ramming target.

"Specials" Within the envelope of a class specification, the British Admiralty allowed key builders to incorporate non-standard features worth evaluation.

squat Tendency to trim by the stern at speed. Particularly noticeable in shallow water.

Squid British triple-barrelled, ahead-firing AS mortar. Precursor to Limbo. Designed to supersede the Hedgehog but not adopted by the US Navy.

SS The initials denoting conventionally powered submarines.

SSB Conventionally powered submarine that carries nuclear-tipped ballistic missiles.

SSBN Nuclear-powered submarine that carries nuclear ballistic missiles as its primary weapons system.

SSG A conventionally powered submarine that carries guided missiles as its primary means of attack.

SSGN Nuclear-powered submarine that carries guided missiles.

SSIXS Submarine Satellite Information Exchange System Surveillance. This modern technology enhances the classic capability of the submarine in surveillance of opposition forces and to monitor their operations and movements while remaining undetected. This surveillance can include underwater photography, sometimes of surface warships, which will almost certainly be unaware of the submarine's presence.

SSK Non-nuclear hunter-killer submarine, specifically designed to hunt other submarines rather than surface ships.

SSM Surface-to-Surface Missile.

SSN Nuclear-powered submarine, also known as a Fast Attack Submarine. Primary tasks involve supporting SSBN submarines, anti-submarine and anti-ship warfare, surveillance/intelligence gathering, task group operations, land attack and special operations.

stability range The range through which a ship may list while still maintaining a positive righting moment. If exceeded, capsize will follow.

stiffness The measure of the resistance of a ship to list under the action of external forces. "Stiff" is effectively the opposite to "crank".

superimposition If a gun is "superimposed" on another, i.e. located at a higher level, it is said to "superfire" it.

T

TACAN Tactical Air Navigation.

TBD Torpedo Boat Destroyer.

TCM Torpedo Counter Measures, an ongoing aspect of submarine warfare, which in the UK consists of a multi-discipline team whose purpose is to provide a comprehensive Torpedo Defence capability for the Royal Navy to counter current and future threats. All British submarines are being fitted with a defensive countermeasures system.

tender Tending to be "crank", but not so extreme.

TGB Torpedo Gun Boat.

TLAM Tomahawk Land Attack Missile, in this context a submarine-launched, long-range precision-strike weapon designed to hit strategic targets with the minimum of collateral damage, capable of travelling subsonically at low or high altitude to deliver a 454kg/1,000lb warhead over a range of around 1,609km/1,000 miles with pinpoint accuracy.

ton As an imperial unit of weight, equal to 2,240lb.

tonne Metric unit of weight, equal to 1,000kg, or approximately 0.982 tons.

tophamper Commonly, all structure above the weather deck. More specifically, masting.

torpedo room Used for the firing of torpedoes, although in modern times will control an armoury of wire-guided torpedoes, anti-ship missiles and cruise missiles.

Towed Array Sonar Used to listen to the target sounds. These arrays are towed behind the submarine and may be greater than 500m/1640ft long, usually in the form of a flexible, neutrally buoyant pipe, with many low-frequency passive sonars along its length.

trim Balancing of a submarine's weight and equilibrium underwater.

trim down Reducing buoyancy until the boat is running virtually awash.

turbo-electric Propulsion system in which a steam turbine drives an electrical generator. This supplies energy via cable to a propulsion motor coupled to the propeller shaft.

UV

Ultra Codeword applied to high-grade intelligence derived from Enigma signals decrypts.

uptake Conduit conducting products of combustion to the funnel.

VDS Variable Depth Sonar.

VLS Vertical Launch System.

volume critical Of a ship whose design is driven by needs of space rather than weight, e.g. aircraft carrier.

WXYZ

Warsaw Pact Defunct Eastern military bloc, essentially a counter to NATO.

water-tube boiler Boiler in which water is carried in tubes surrounded by hot products of combustion. Effectively a reverse, and more efficient, concept to that of the earlier Locomotive Boiler.

Weapon "Able" (Alfa) US Navy's post-war successor to Hedgehog. Trainable stabilized mounting to fire 12 rounds per minute.

weight critical Of a ship whose design is driven by considerations of weight rather than volume, e.g. a heavily armoured battleship.

Y Gun US anti-submarine gun used to launch depth charges.

Class lists of destroyers and frigates

Page 66 Early torpedo boats: Numbered TB.1–T117 inclusive.
Page 67 27-knotters/"A" class: *Ardent, Banshee Boxer, Bruiser, Charger, Conflict, Contest, Dasher, Dragon, Fervent, Handy, Hardy, Hasty, Hart, Haughty, Hunter, Janus, Lightning, Opossum, Porcupine, Ranger, Rocket, Salmon, Shark, Snapper, Spitfire, Starfish, Sturgeon, Sunfish, Surly, Swordfish, Teazer, Wizard, Zebra, Zephyr.*
Page 68 30-knotters/"B" class: *Albacore, Bonetta, Earnest, Griffon, Kangaroo, Lively, Locust, Myrmidon, Orwell, Panther, Peterel, Quail, Seal, Sparrowhawk, Spiteful, Sprightly, Success, Syren, Thrasher, Virago, Wolf,* "C" class: *Avon, Bat, Bittern, Brazen, Bullfinch, Chamois, Cheerful, Crane, Dove, Electra, Fairy, Falcon, Fawn, Flirt, Flying Fish, Gipsy, Greyhound, Kestrel, Lee, Leopard, Leven, Mermaid, Osprey, Ostrich, Otter, Racehorse, Recruit, Roebuck, Star, Sylvia, Thorn, Tiger, Vigilent, Violet, Vixen, Vulture, Whiting.* "D" class: *Angler, Ariel, Coquette, Cygnet, Cynthia, Desperate, Fame, Foam, Mallard, Stag.*
Page 69 River/"E" class: *Arun, Balckwater, Boyne, Chelmer, Cherwell, Colne, Dee, Derwent, Doon, Eden, Erne, Ettrick, Exe, Foyle, Gala, Garry, Itchen, Jed, Kale, Kennet, Liffey, Moy, Ness, Nith, Ouse, Ribble, Rother, Stour, Swale, Test, Teviot, Ure, Usk, Velox, Waveney, Wear, Welland.*
Page 70–71 Beagle/"G" class: *Basilisk, Beagle, Bulldog, Foxhound, Grampus Grasshopper, Harpy, Mosquito, Pincher, Racoon, Rattlesnake, Renard, Savage, Scorpion, Scourge, Wolverine.* Acorn/"H" class: *Acorn, Alarm, Brisk, Cameleon, Comet, Fury, Goldfinch, Hope, Larne, Lyra, Martin, Minstrel, Nemesis, Nereide, Nymphe, Radpole, Rifleman, Ruby, Scheldrake, Staunch.* Modified Acorn/"I" class: *Acheron, Archer, Ariel, Attack, Badger, Beaver, Defender, Druid, Ferret, Firedrake, Forester, Goshawk, Hind, Hornet, Hydra, Jackal, Lapwing, Lizard, Lurcher, Oak, Phoenix, Sandfly, Tigress.*
Page 72 Tribal/"F" class: *Afridi, Amazon, Cossack, Crusader, Ghurka, Maori, Mowhawk, Nubian, Saracen, Tartar, Viking, Zulu.*
Page 73 Acasta/"K" class: *Acasta, Achates, Ambuscade, Ardent, Christopher, Cockatrice, Contest, Fortune, Garland, Hardy, Lynx, Midge, Owl, Paragon, Porpoise, Shark, Sparrowhawk, Spitfire, Unity, Victor.*
Page 74 Laforey/"L" class: *Laertes, Laforey, Lance, Landrail, Lark, Laurel, Laverock, Lawford, Legion, Lennox, Leonidas, Liberty, Linnet, Llewellyn, Lookout, Louis, Loyal Lucifer, Lydiard, Lysander.*
Page 75 "M" class: *Manly, Mansfield, Mastiff, Matchless, Mentor, Meteor, Milne, Minos, Miranda, Moorsom, Morris, Murray, Myngs.*
Page 76 Leaders/Lightfoots: *Abdiel, Gabriel, Ithuriel, Kempenfelt, Lightfoot, Marksman, Nimrod.* Leaders/1916/17: *Anzac, Grenville, Hoste, Parker, Saumarez, Seymour.*
Page 77 Emergency "M" class Group 1: *Maenad, Magic, Mandate, Manners, Marmion, Marne, Martial, Mary Rose, Menace, Michael, Milbrook, Minion, Mons, Moresby, Munster, Mystic.* Group 2: *Mameluke, Marvel, Mindful, Mischief, Negro, Nepean, Nereus, Nerissa, Nessus, Nonsuch.* Group 3: *Nestor, Nizam, Noble, Nomad, Nonpareil, Norman, North Star, Northesk, Nugent, Obdurate, Obedient, Octavia, Onslaught, Onslow, Opal, Ophelia, Opportune, Oracle, Orestes, Orford, Orpheus, Ossary.* Group 4: *Napier, Narborough, Narwhal, Nicator, Norseman, Oberon, Observer, Offa, Orcadia, Oriana, Oriole, Osiris, Paladin, Parthian, Partridge, Pasley, Patrician, Patriot.* Group 5: *Medina, Medway, Pelican, Pellew, Penn, Peregrine, Petard, Peyton, Pheasant, Phoebe, Pigeon, Plover, Plucky, Portia, Prince, Pylades, Rapid, Ready, Relentless, Rival.*
Page 78 "R" Class, Group 6: *Radiant, Radstock, Raider, Recruit, Redgantlet, Redoubt, Restless, Retriever, Rigorous, Rob Roy, Rocket, Romola, Rosalind, Rowena, Sable, Sabrina, Salmon, Sarpedon, Sceptre, Setter, Sorceress, Strongbow, Sturgeon, Surprise, Sylph.* Group 7: *Satyr, Sharpshooter, Simoon, Skate, Skilful, Springbok, Starfish, Stork, Taurus, Teazer.* Group 8: *Tancred, Tarpon, Telemachus, Tempest, Tenacious, Tetrarch, Thisbe, Thruster, Tormentor, Tornado, Torrent, Torrid, Truculent, Tyrant, Ulleswater.* Modified "R" class: *Tirade, Tower, Trenchant, Tristram, Ulster, Ulysses, Umpire, Undine, Urchin, Ursa, Ursula.*
Page 79 "S" class. Group 11: *Sabre, Saladin, Scimitar, Scotsman, Scout, Senator, Sepoy, Serpah, Shamrock, Shark, Shikari, Sikj, Simoon, Sirdar, Somme, Sparrowhawk, Speedy, Splendid, Steadfast, Sterling, Success, Swallow, Swordsman, Tobago, Tomahawk, Torch, Tribune, Trinidad, Tryphon, Tumult, Turquoise, Tuscan, Tyrian.* Group 12: *Sardonyx, Scythe, Seabear, Seafire, Searcher, Seawolf, Serapis, Serene, Sesame, Spear, Spindrift, Sportive, Stalwart, Stonehenge, Stormcloud, Strenuous, Stronghold, Sturdy, Tactician, Tara, Tasmania, Tattoo, Tenedos, Thanet, Thracian, Tilbury, Tintagel, Torbay, Toreador, Tourmaline, Trojan, Truant, Trusty, Turbulent.*
Pages 80–81 V & W classes Group 9: *Vancouver, Vanessa, Vanity, Vanoc, Vanquisher, Vectis, Vega, Vehement, Velox, Vendetta, Venetia, Venturous, Verdun, Versatile, Verulam, Vesper, Viceroy, Vidette, Vimiera, Violent, Viscount, Vittoria. Vivacious, Vivien, Vortigen.* Group 10: *Voyager, Wakeful, Walker, Walpole, Walrus, Warwick, Watchman, Waterhen, Wessex, Westcott, Westminster, Whirlwind, Whitley, Winchelsea, Winchester, Windsor, Wolfhound, Wolsey, Woolston, Wrestler, Wryneck.* Modified V & W class. Group 13: *Vansittart, Venomous, Verity, Volunteer, Wanderer, Whitehall, Wishart, Witch, Wren.* Group 14: *Veteran, Whitshed, Wild Swan, Witherington, Wivern, Wolverine, Worcester.*
Page 82 Early torpedo boats. Schichau-built: S.7–23, S.24–31, S.32, S.33–41, S.42, S.43–57, S.58–65, S.66, S.67–73, S.74, S.75–81, S.82–87.
Page 83 *Divisionsboote*. Schichau-built: D.1–2, D.3–4, D.5–6. D.7–8, D.9.
Page 84 *Grosse Torpedoboote*. Schichau/Germania–built: S.90–96, S.97, S.98–101, S.102–107, G.108–113, S.114–119, S.120–124, S.125, S.126–131, G.132–136, G.137.
Page 85 *Grosse Torpedoboote*. Schichau-Germania/Vulcan-built: S.138–149, V.150–160, V.161, V.162–164, S.165–168, G.169–172, G.173, G.174–175, S.176–179, V.180–185, V.186–191, G.192–197.
Page 86–87 V.25–30, S.31–36, G.37–40, G.41–41, V.43–46, V.47–48, S.49–52, S.53–66, V.67–84, G.85–95.
Page 88 G.101–104.
Page 89 S.113–115, V.116–118, G.119–121, B.122–124.
Page 90 Early Torpedo boats: *Cushing, Ericsson, Foote, Rodgers, Winslow, Porter, Dupont, Rowan, Dahlgren, Craven, Farragut, Davis, Fox, Morris, Talbot, Gwin, Mackenzie, McKee, Stringham, Goldsborough, Bailey, Somers, Manley, Bagley, Barney, Biddle, Blakeley, DeLong, Nicholson, O'Brien, Shubrick, Stockton, Thornton, Tingey, Wilkes.* (TB.1–35 inclusive).
Page 91 Bainbridge class: *Bainbridge, Barry, Chauncey, Dale, Decatur, Paul Jones, Perry, Preble, Stewart.* Near sisters: *Hopkins, Hull, Truxtun, Whipple, Worden, Lawrence, MacDonough.*
Page 92 Smith class: *Flusser, Lamson, Preston, Reid, Smith,* Paulding class: *Ammen, Beale, Burrows, Drayton, Fanning, Henley, Jarvis, Jenkins, Jouett, McCall, Mayrant, Monaghan, Patterson, Paulding, Perkins, Roe, Sterett, Terry, Trippe, Walke, Warrington.*
Page 93 Cassin Class: *Aylwin, Balch, Benham, Cassin, Cummings, Cushing, Downes, Duncan, Ericsson, McDougal, Nicholson, O'Brien, Parker, Winslow.* Tucker Class: *Allen, Conyngham, Davis, Jacob Jones, Porter, Rowan, Sampson, Shaw, Tucker, Wadsworth, Wainwright, Wilkes.*
Pages 94–95 Flush-deckers. Caldwell class: *Caldwell, Conner, Craven, Gwin, Manley, Stockton.* Wickes class: *Aaron Ward, Abbot, Anthony, Babbitt, Badger, Bagley, Barney, Bell, Bernadon, Biddle, Blakeley, Boggs, Breckinridge, Breese, Buchanan, Burns, Bush, Champlin, Crew, Claxton, Cole, Colhoun, Cowell, Crane, Crosby, Crowninshield, DeLong, Dent, Dickerson, Dorsey, Dupont, Dyer, Elliot, Ellis, Evans, Fairfax, Foote, Gamble, Greer, Gregory, Gridley, Hale, Hamilton, Haraden, Harding, Hart, Hazelwood, Herbert, Hogan, Hopewell, Howard, Ingraham, Israel, J. Fred Talbott, Jacob Jones, Kalk, Kennison, Kitty, Kimberley, Lamberton, Landsdale, Lea, Leary, Little, Luce, Ludlow, Mackenzie, McKean, McKee, Maddox, Mahan, Maury, Meredith, Montgomery, Mugford, Murray, O'Bannon, Palmer, Philip, Radford, Ramsay, Rathburne, Renshaw, Ringgold, Rizal, Robinson, Roper, Schenck, Schley, Sigourney, Sproston, Stansbury, Stevens, Stribling, Stringham, Talbot, Tarbell, Tattnall, Taylor, Thatcher, Thomas, Tillman, Twiggs, Upshur, Walker, Ward, Waters, Wickes, Williams, Wooley, Yarnall.* Clemson class: *Abel P. Upshur, Alden, Aulick, Bailey, Bainbridge, Ballard, Bancroft, Barker, Barry, Belknap, Billingsley, Borie, Branch, Breck, Brooks, Broome, Bruce, Bulmer, Case, Chandler, Charles Ausburn, Chase, Chauncey, Childs, Clemson, Coghlan, Converse, Corry, Dahlgren, Dale, Dallas, Decatur, Delphy, Doyen, Edsall, Edwards,*

Farenholt, Farquhar, Farragut, Flusser, Ford, Fox, Fuller, George E. Badger, Gillis, Gilmer, Goff, Goldsborough, Graham, Greens, Hatfield, Henshaw, Herndon, Hopkins, Hovey, Hulbert, Hull, Humphreys, Hunt, Isherwood, James K. Paulding, John D. Edwards, John Francis Burnes, Kane, Kennedy, Kidder, King, La Vallette, Lamson, Lardner, Lamb, Lawrence, Litchfield, Long, McCalla, McCawley, McCook, McCormick, McDermut, McDonough, McFarland, McLanahan, MacLeish, Marcus, Mason, Meade, Melvin, Mervine, Meyer, Moody, Morris, Mullany, Nicholas, Noa, Osborne, Osmond Ingram, Overton, Parrott, Paul Hamilton, Paul Jones, Peary, Percival, Perry, Pillsbury, Pope, Preble, Preston, Pruitt, Putnam, Reid, Reno, Reuben James, Robert Smith, Rodgers, S. P. Lee, Sands, Satterlee, Selfridge, Semmes, Sharkey, Shirk, Shubrick, Sicard, Simpson, Sinclair, Sloat, Smith Thompson, Somers, Southard, Stewart, Stoddart, Sturtevant, Sumner, Swasey, Thompson, Thornton, Tingey, Toncey, Tracy, Trever, Truxtun, Turner, Wasmuth, Welborn C. Wood, Welles, Whipple, William B. Preston, William Jones, Williamson, Wood, Woodbury, Worden, Yarborough, Young, Zane, Zeillin.

Page 96 Torpedo cruisers: *Tripoli, Confienza, Goito, Montebello, Monzambano, Aretusa, Calatafimi, Caprera, Euridice, Iride, Minerva, Partenope, Urania.*

Page 97 High Seas Torpedo Boats. Safo class: *Saffo, Sagittario, Scorpione, Serpente, Sirio, Spica,* Perseo class: *Pallade, Pegaso, Perseo, Procione.* Cigno class: *Calipso. Calliope, Canopo, Cassiopea, Centauro, Cigno, Climene, Clio.* Alcione class: *Airone, Albatros, Alcione, Ardea, Arpia, Astore.* Orione class: *Olimpia, Orfeo, Orione, Orsa.*

Page 98 Coastal torpedo boats: *Condore, Pellicano, Gabbiano,* 1PN–12PN, 33PN–38PN, 130S–240S, 25AS–32AS, 39RM, 40PN–45PN, 460S–510S, 52AS–57AS, 580L–630L, 64PN–69PN, 700LT–750LT, 76CP–79CP.

Page 99 Lampo class: *Dardo, Euro, Lampo, Ostro, Strale.*
Page 100 Nembo class: *Aquilone, Borea, Espero, Nembo, Turbine, Zeffira.*
Page 101 Soldati class. Group 1: *Artigliere, Bersagliere, Corazziere, Garibaldino, Granatiere, Lanciere.* Group 2: *Alpino, Carabiniere, Fuciliere, Pontiere.*
Page 102 Indomito class: *Impavido, Impetuoso, Indomito, Insidioso, Intrepido, Irrequieto.* Ardito class: *Ardente, Ardito.* Animoso class: *Animoso, Audace.*
Page 103 Sirtori class: *Francesco Stocco, Giovanni Acerbi, Giuseppe Sirtori, Vincenzo Giordano Orsini.* La Masa class: *Agostino Bertani, Angelo Bassini, Benedetto Cairolo, Giacinto Carini, Giacomo Medici, Giuseppe la Farina, Giuseppe la Masa, Nicola Fabrizi.*
Page 104 Early torpedo boats. Cyclone class: *Audacieux, Borée, Bourrasque, Cyclone, Mistral, Rafale, Simoun, Siroco, Tramontane, Trombe, Typhon.* Second-class torpedo boats: Numbered 1–369.
Page 105 Arquebuse class: *Arbalete, Arc, Baliste, Belier, Bombarde, Carabine, Catapulte, Dard, Epieu, Francisque, Fronde, Harpon, Javeline, Mousquet, Mousqueton, Pistolet, Sabre, Sagaie, Sarbacane.* Claymore class: *Carquois, Claymore, Cognée, Coutelas, Fleuret, Hache, Massue, Mortier, Obusier, Pierrier, Stylet, Trident, Tromblon.* Branlebas class: *Branlebas, Etendard, Fanfare, Fanion, Gabion, Glaive, Oriflamme, Poignard, Sabretagne, Sape.*
Page 106 Saphi class: *Aspirant, Herber, Carabinier, Enseigne Henry, Hussard, Lansquenet, Mameluk, Saphi.* Voltigeur class: *Tirailleur, Voltigeur.* Chasseur class: *Cavalier, Chasseur, Lieutenant, Fantassin, Janissaire.*
Page 107 Bouclier class: *Bouclier, Boutefeu, Capitaine Mehl, Casque, Cimeterre, Commandant Bory, Commandant Rivière, Dague, Dehorter, Faulx, Fourche, Francis Garnier.* Bisson class: *Bisson, Commandant Lucas, Magon, Mangini, Protet, Renaudin.*
Page 108 Arabe class: *Algérien, Annamite, Arabe, Bambara, Hova, Kabyle, Marocain, Sakalave, Sénégalais, Somali, Tonkinois, Touareg.*
Page 109 Early torpedo boats: Numbered 1–75. Various builders.
Page 110 Harusame class: *Arare, Ariake, Asagiri, Fubuki, Harasame, Hayatori, Murasame.* Asakaze class: *Asakaze, Asatsuyu, Ayanami, Harakaze, Hatsuharu, Hatsushima, Hatsuyuki, Hayate, Hibiki, Isonami, Kamikaze, Kikuzuki, Kisaragi, Matsukaze, Mikazuki, Minazuki, Nagatsuki, Nenohi, Nowake, Oite, Shiqure, Shiratsuyu, Shirayuki, Shirotae, Uranami, Ushio, Uzuki, Wakaba, Yayoi, Yudachi, Yugure, Yunagi.*
Page 111 Kaba class: *Kaba, Kaede, Kashiwa, Katsura, Kiri, Kusunoki, Matsu, Sakaki, Sugi, Ume.* Momo class: *Hinoki, Kashi, Momo, Yanagi.* Enoki class: *Enoki, Kawa, Keyaki, Maki, Nara, Tsubaki.*

Page 114 "A" class: *Acasta, Achates, Acheron, Active, Antelope, Anthony, Ardent, Arrow.* "B" class: *Basilisk, Beagle, Blanche, Boadicea, Boreas, Brazen, Brilliant, Bulldog.* "C" class: *Comet, Crescent, Crusader, Cynet.* "D" class: *Dainty, Daring, Decoy, Defender, Delight, Diamond, Diana, Duchess.* "E" class: *Echo, Eclipse, Electra, Encounter, Escapade, Escort, Esk, Express.* "F" class: *Fame, Fearless, Firedrake, Foresight, Forester, Fortune, Foxhound, Fury.* "G" class: *Gallant, Garland, Gipsy, Glowworm, Grafton, Grenade, Greyhound, Griffin.* "H" class: *Hasty, Havock, Hereward, Hero, Hostile, Hotspur, Hunter, Hyperion.* "I" class: *Icarus, Ilex, Imogen, Imperial, Impulsive, Intrepid, Isis, Wanhoe.*
Page 115 Tribal class: *Afridi, Ashanti, Bedouin, Cossack, Eskimo, Gurkha, Maori, Mashona, Matabele, Mohawk, Nubian, Punjabi, Sikh, Somali, Tartar, Zulu.*
Page 116 "J" class: *Jacak, Jaguar, Janus, Javelin, Jersey, Jervis, Juno, Jupiter.* "K" class: *Kandahar, Kashmir, Kelly, Kelvin, Khartoum, Kimberley, Kingston, Kipling.* "N" class: *Napier, Nepal, Nerissa, Nestor, Nizam, Noble, Nonpareil, Norman.* "L" class: *Laforey, Lance, Larne, Legion, Lightening, Lively, Lookout, Loyal.* "M" class: *Mahratta, Marne, Martin, Matchless, Meteor, Milne, Muskateer, Myrmidon.*
Page 117 "O" class: *Obdurate, Obedient, Offa, Onslaught, Onslow, Opportune, Oribi, Orwell.* "P" class: *Packenham, Paladin, Panther, Partridge, Pathfinder, Penn, Petard, Porcupine.*
Page 118 "Q" class: *Quadrant, Quail, Qualify, Queenborough, Quentin, Quiberon, Quickmatch, Quilliam,* "R" class: *Racehorse, Raider, Rapid, Redoubt, Relentless, Rocket, Roebuck, Rotherham,* "S" class: *Saumarez, Savage, Scorpion, Scourge, Serapis, Shark, Success, Swift.* "T" class: *Teazer, Tenacious, Termagent, Terpsichore, Troubridge, Tumult, Tuscan, Tyrian.* "U" class: *Grenville, Ulster, Ulysses, Undaunted, Undine, Urania, Urchin, Ursa.* "V" class: *Hardy, Valentine, Venus, Verulam, Vigilent, Virago, Vixen, Volage.* "W" class: *Kempenfelt, Wager, Wakeful, Wessex, Whelp, Whirlwind, Wizard, Wrangler.* "Z" class: *Myngs, Zambesi, Zealous, Zebra, Zenith, Zephyr, Zest, Zodiac.* "Ca" class: *Caesar, Cambrian, Caprice, Carron, Carysfort, Casandra, Cavalier, Cavendish.* "Ch" class: *Chaplet, Charity, Chequers, Cheviot, Chevron, Chieftain, Childers, Chivalrous.* "Co" class: *Cockade, Comet, Comus, Concord, Consrot, Constance, Contest, Cossack.* "Cr" class: *Creole, Crescent, Crispin, Cromwell, Crown, Croziers, Crusader, Crystal.*
Page 119 Weapon class: *Battleaxe, Broadsword, Crossbow, Scorpion.*
Page 120 Battle class: *Agincourt, Aisne, Alamein, Armada, Barfleur, Barrosa, Cadiz, Camperdown, Corunna, Dunkirk, Finisterre, Gabbard, Gravelines, Hogue, Jutland, Lagos, Matapan, St. Kitts, St. James, Saintes, Sluys, Solebay, Trafalagar, Vigo.*
Page 121 Daring class: *Dainty, Daring, Decoy, Defender, Delight, Diamond, Diana, Duchess.*
Page 122 County class: *Antrim, Devonshire, Fife, Glamorgan, Hampshire, Kent, London, Norfolk.*
Page 123 Type 82: *Bristol.*
Page 124 Type 42: *Birmingham, Cardiff, Exeter, Glasgow, Liverpool, Newcastle, Nottingham, Southampton.* "Stretched Type 42": *Edinburgh, Gloucester, Manchester, York.*
Page 125 Type 45: *Daring, Dauntless, Defender, Diamond, Dragon, Duncan.*
Page 126 Farragut class: *Aylwin, Dale, Dewey, Farragut, Hull, MacDonough, Monaghan.*
Page 127 Porter class: *Balch, Clark, McDougal, Moffett, Phelps, Porter, Selfridge, Winslow.* Somers class: *Davis, Jouett, Sampson, Somers, Warrington.*
Page 128 Mahan class: *Case, Cassin, Conyngham, Cummings, Cushing, Downes, Drayton, Dunlap, Fanning, Flusser, Lamson, Mahan, Perkins, Preston, Reid, Shaw, Smith, Tucker.* Craven class: *Bagley, Benham, Blue,*

Worden, Bainbridge class

499

CLASS LISTS OF DESTROYERS AND FRIGATES

Neuva Esparta, Battle class

Craven, Ellet, Gridley, Helm, Henley, Jarvis, Lang, McCall, Maury, Mayrant, Mugford, Patterson, Ralph Talbot, Rhind, Rowan, Stack, Sterrett, Trippe, Wilson. Sims class: Anderson, Buck, Hammann, Hughes, Morris, Mustin, O'Brien, Roe, Russell, Sims, Walke, Wainwright.

Page 129 Benson class: Bailey, Bancroft, Barton, Benson, Boyle, Caldwell, Champlin, Charles F. Hughes, Coglan, Farenholt, Frazier, Gansevoort, Gillespie Hilary P. Jones, Hobby, Kalk, Kendrick, Laffey, Lansdale, Laub, Mackenzie, McLanahan, Madison, Mayo, Meade, Murphy, Nibleck, Nields, Ordronaux, Parker, Woodworth. Livermore class: Aaron Ward, Baldwin, Beatty, Bristol, Buchanan, Butler, Carmick, Corry, Cowie, Davison, Doran, Doyle, Duncan, Forrest, Frankford, Gherardi, Glennon, Grayson, Gwin, Hambleton, Harding, Herndon, Hobson, Ingraham, Jeffers, Kearny, Knight, Lansdowne, Lardner, Livermore, Ludlow, McCalla, McCook, Macomb, Maddox, Meredith, Mervine, Monsson, Nelson, Nicholson, Plunkett, Quick, Rodman, Satterlee, Shubrick, Stevenson, Stockton, Swanson, Thompson, Thorn, Tillman, Turner, Welles, Wilkes, Woolsey.

Page 130 Fletcher class: Abbot, Abner Read, Albert W. Grant, Ammen, Anthony, Aulick, Bache, Beale, Bearss, Bell, Benham, Bell, Benham, Bennett, Bennison, Black, Boyd, Bradford, Braine, Brown, Brownson, Bryant, Bullard, Burns, Bush, Callaghan, Caperton, Capps, Cassin Young, Charles Ausburne, Charles J. Badger, Charrette, Chauncey, Chevalier, Clarence K. Bronson, Claxton, Cogswell, Colahan, Colhoun, Connor, Converse, Conway, Cony, Cotton, Cowell, Cushing, Daly, Dashiell, David W. Taylor, De Haven, Dortch, Dyson, Eaton, Erben, Evans, Fletcher, Foote, Franks, Fullam, Gatling, Gregory, Guest, Haggard, Hailey, Hale, Halford, Hall, Halligan, Halsey Powell, Haraden, Harrison, Hart, Hazelwood, Healy, Heermann, Heywood L. Edwards, Hickox, Hoel, Hopewell, Howorth, Hudson, Hunt, Hutchins, Ingersoll, Irwin, Isherwood, Izard, Jarvis, Jenkins, John D. Henley, John Hood, John Rodgers, Johnston, Kidd, Killen, Kimberly, Knapp, La Vallette, Laws, Leutze, Lewis Hancock, Little, Longshaw, Luce, McCord, McDermut, McGowan, McKee, McNair, Marshall, Melvin, Mertz, Metcalfe, Miller, Monssen, Morrison, Mullany, Murray, Newcomb, Nicholas, Norman Scott, O'Bannon, Owen, Paul Hamilton, Philip, Picking, Porter, Porterfield, Preston, Prichett, Pringle, Radford, Remey, Renshaw, Richard P. Leary, Ringgold, Robinson, Rooks, Ross, Rowe, Saufley, Schroeder, Shields, Sigourney, Sigsbee, Smalley, Spence, Sproston, Stanly, Stembel, Stephen Potter, Stevens, Stevenson, Stockham, Stockton, Stoddard, Strong, Taylor, Terry, Thatcher, The Sullivans, Thorn, Tingey, Trathen, Turner, Twiggs, Twining, Uhlmann, Van Valkenburgh, Wadleigh, Wadsworth, Walker, Waller, Wedderburn, Wicks, Wiley, William D. Porter, Wren, Yarnall, Young.

Page 131 Sumner class: Alfred A. Cunningham, Allen M. Sumner, Ault, Barton, Beatty, Blue, Borie, Bristol, Brush, Buck, Charles S. Sperry, Collett, Compton, Cooper, DeHaven, Douglas H. Fox, Drexler, English, Frank E. Evans, Gainard, Hank, Harlan R. Dickson, Harry E. Hubbard, Hugh Purvis, Hugh W. Hadley, Haynsworth, Hyman, Ingraham, James C. Owens, John A. Bole, John R. Pierce, John W. Thomason, John W. Weeks, Laffey, Lofberg, Lowry, Lyman K. Swenson, Maddox, Mannert L. Abele, Mansfield, Massey, Meredith, Moale, O'Brien, Purdy, Putnam, Robert K. Huntington, Samuel N. Moore, Soley, Stormes, Strong, Taussig, Waldron, Wallace L. Lind, Walke, Willard Keith.

Page 132 Gearing class: Abner Read, Agerholm, Arnold J. Isbell, Basilone, Baussell, Benner, Bordelon, Brinkley Bass, Brownson, Carpenter, Castle, Charles H. Roan, Charles P. Cecil, Charles R. Ware, Chevalier, Cone, Corry, Damato, Dennis J. Buckley, Duncan, Dyess, Epperson, Ernest G. Small, Eugene A. Greene, Everett F. Larson, Eversole, Fechteler, Fiske, Floyd B. Parks, Forrest Royal, Frank Knox, Fred. T. Berry, Furse, Gearing, George K. Mackenzie, Glennon, Goodrich, Gurke, Gyatt, Hamner, Hanson, Harold J. Ellison, Harwood, Hawkins, Henderson, Henry W. Tucker, Herbert J. Thomas, Higbee, Hoel, Holder, Hollister, James E. Kyes, John R. Craig, Johnston, Joseph P. Kennedy Jnr., Kenneth D. Bailey, Keppler, Lansdale,

Leary, Leonard F. Mason, Lloyd Thomas, McCaffery, McKeen, Meredith, Myles C. Fox, New, Newman K. Perry, Noa, Norris, O'Hare, Orleck, Ozbourne, Perkins, Perry, Power, Rich, Richard B. Anderson, Richard E. Kraus, Robert A. Owens, Robert H. McCard, Robert L. Wilson, Rogers, Rowan, Rupertus, Samuel B. Roberts, Sarsfield, Seaman, Seymour D. Owens, Shelton, Southerland, Steinacker, Stickell, Stribling, Theodore E. Chandler, Timmerman, Turner, Vesole, Vogelgesang, Warrington, William C. Lawe, William M. Wood, William R. Rush, Wiltsie, Witek, Woodrow R. Thompson.

Page 133 Forrest Sherman class: Barry, Bigelow, Blandy, Davis, Decatur, Du Pont, Edson, Forrest Sherman, Hull, John Paul Jones, Jonas Ingram, Manley, Morton, Mullinnix, Parsons, Richard S. Edwards, Somers, Turner Joy.

Page 134 Charles F. Adams class: Barney, Benjamin Stoddert, Berkeley, Buchanan, Charles F. Adams, Claude V. Ricketts, Cochrane, Conyngham, Goldsborough, Henry B. Wilson, Hoel, John King, Joseph Strauss, Lawrence, Lynde, McCormick, Richard E. Byrd, Robinson, Sampson, Sellers, Semmes, Tattnall, Towers, Waddell.

Page 135 Coontz class: Coontz, Dahlgren, Dewey, Farragut, King, Luce, Macdonough, Mahan, Preble, William V. Pratt.

Page 136 Belknap class: Belknap, Biddle, Fox, Horne, Josephus Daniels, Jouett, Sterett, Wainwright, William H. Stanley. Leahy class: Dale, England, Gridley, Halsey, Harry E. Yarnell, Leahy, Reeves, Richmond K. Turner, Worden.

Page 137 Spruance class: Arthur W. Radford, Briscoe, Caron, Comte de Grasse, Conolly, Cushing, David R. Ray, Deyo, Elliot, Fife, Fletcher, Harry W. Hill, Hayler, Hewitt, Ingersoll, John Hancock, John Rodgers, John Young, Kinkaid, Leftwich, Merrill, Moosbrugger, Nicholson, O'Bannon, O'Brien, Oldendorf, Paul F. Foster, Peterson, Spruance, Stump, Thorn. Kidd class: Callaghan, Chandler, Kidd, Scott.

Page 138 Ticonderoga class: Antietam, Anzio, Bunker Hill, Cape St. George, Chancellorsville, Chosin, Cowpens, Gettysburg, Hue City, Lake Champlain, Lake Erie, Leyte Gulf, Mobile Bay, Monterey, Normandy, Philippine Sea, Port Royal, Princeton, San Jacinto, Shiloh, Thomas S. Gates, Ticonderoga, Valley Forge, Vella Gulf, Vicksburg, Yorktown.

Page 139 Arleigh Burke class (Flight I): Arleigh Burke, Barry, Benfold, Carney, Cole, Curtis Wilbur, Fitzgerald, Gonzalez, Hopper, John Paul Jones, John S. McCain, Laboon, Milius, Mitscher, Paul Hamilton, Ramage, Ross, Russell, Stethem, Stout, The Sullivans. Arleigh Burke class (Flight II): Decatur, Donald Cook, Higgins, McFaul, Mahan, O'Kane, Porter. Arleigh Burke class (Flight II A): Bainbridge, Bulkeley, Chafee, Chung-Hoon, Dewey, Farragut, Forrest Sherman, Gridley, Halsey, Howard, James E. Williams, Kidd, Lassen, McCampbell, Mason, Momsen, Mustin, Nitze, Oscar Austin, Pinckney, Prebel, Roosevelt, Sampson, Shoup, Sterrett, Truxtun, Wayne E. Meyer, Winston S. Churchill.

Page 140 Momi class: Hasu, Kaya, Kuri, Momi, Nashi, Tsuga, Warabi. Wakatake class: Asagao, Basho, Botan, Huyo, Karukaya, Kijiko, Kuretake, Nadeshiko, Omadaka, Sanae, Sawarabi, Wakatake.

Page 141 Minekaze class: Akikaze, Hakaze, Hokaze, Minekaze, Namikaze, Nokaze, Numakaze, Okikaze, Sawakaze, Shiokaze, Tachikaze, Yakaze. Yukaze. Kamikaze class: Asakaze, Asanagi, Harukaze, Hatakaze, Hayate, Kamikaze, Matsukaze, Oite, Yunagi. Mutsuki class: Fumitsuki, Kikutsuki, Kisaragi, Mikatsuki, Minatsuki, Mochitsuki, Mutsuki, Nagatsuki, Satsuki, Uzuki, Yayoi, Yuzuki.

Page 142 Fubuki class: Akebono, Amagiri, Asagiri, Ayanami, Fubuki, Hatsuyuki, Isonami, Miyuki, Murakumo, Oboro, Sagiri, Sazanami, Shikinami, Shinonome, Shirakumo, Shirayuki, Uranami, Ushio, Usugumo, Yugiri. Akatsuki class: Akatsuki, Hibiki, Ikazuchi, Inadzuma.

Page 143 Hatsuharu class: Ariake, Hatsuharu, Hatsushimo, Nenohi, Wakaba, Yugure. Shiratsuyu class: Harusame, Kawakaze, Murasame, Samidare, Shigure, Shiratsuyu, Suzukaze, Umikaze, Yamakaze, Yudachi.

Page 144 Asashio class: Arare, Arashio, Asagumo, Asashio, Kasumi, Michishio, Minegumo, Natsugumo, Ooshio, Yamagumo.

Page 145 Kagero class: Amatsukaze, Arashi, Hagikaze, Hamakaze, Hatsukaze, Hayashio, Isokaze, Kagero, Kuroshio, Maikaze, Natsushio, Nowake, Oyashio, Shiranuhi, Tanikaze, Tokitsukaze, Urakaze, Yakikaze. Yugumo class: Akigumo, Akishimo, Asashimo, Fujinami, Hamanami, Hayanami, Hayashimo Kawagiri, Kazegumo, Kishinami, Kiyokaze, Kyonami, Kiyoshimo, Makigumo, Makinami, Murakze, Naganami, Okinami, Onami, Satokaze, Suzunami, Taekaze, Takanami, Tamanami, Tanigiri, Umigiri, Yamagiri, Yugumo.

Page 146 Akitsuki class: Akitsuki, Fuyutsuki, Hanatsuki, Harutsuki, Hatsutsuki, Hazuki, Kiyotsuki, Michitsuki, Natsusuki, Niitsuki, Ootsuki, Shimotsuki, Suzutsuki, Terutsuki, Wakatsuki, Yoitsuki.

CLASS LISTS OF DESTROYERS AND FRIGATES

Page 147 Yamagumo class: *Akigumo, Aokumo, Asagumo, Makigumo, Yamagumo, Yugumo.* Minegumo class: *Minegumo, Murakumo, Natsugumo.*
Page 148 Takatsuki class: *Kikizuki, Mochizuki, Nagatsuki, Takatsuki.*
Page 149 Shirane class: *Kurama, Shirane.* Haruna class: *Haruna, Hiei.*
Page 150 Tachikaze class: *Asakaze, Sawakaze, Tachikaze.* Hatakaze class: *Hatakaze, Shimakaze.*
Page 151 Hatsuyuki class: *Asayuki, Hamayuki, Haruyuki, Hatsuyuki, Isoyuki, Matsuyuki, Mineyuki, Sawayuki, Setoyuki, Shimayuki, Shirayuki, Yamayuki.* Asagiri class: *Amagiri, Asagiri, Hamagiri, Sawagiri, Setogiri, Umigiri, Yamagiri, Yungiri.*
Page 152 Takaname class: *Makinami, Onami, Sazanami, Takaname* (plus 2). Murazame class: *Akebono, Ariake, Harusame, Ikazuchi, Inazuma, Kirisame, Murasame, Samidare, Yadachi.*
Page 153 Kongo class: *Chokai, Kirishima, Kongo, Myoko.* Atago class: *Atago, Ashigara.*
Page 154 Bourrasque class: *Bourrasque, Cyclone, Mistral, Orage, Ouragan, Simoun, Siroco, Tempéte, Tornade, Tramontane, Trombe, Typhon.*
Page 155 L'Adroit class: *L'Adroite, L'Alcyon, Basque, Bordelais, Boulonnaise, Brestois, Forbin, Le Fortuné, Foudroyant, Fougueux, Frondeur, Le Mars, La Palme, La Railleuse.*
Page 156 Le Hardi class: *L'Adroite, L'Aventurier, Bison, Casque, Le Cyclone, Foudroyant, Le Hardi, L'Intrepide, Mameluke, L'Opiniâtre, Siroco, Le Temeraire.*
Page 157 Chacal class: *Chacal, Jaguar, Léopard, Lynx, Panthère, Tigre.*
Page 158 Guépard class: *Bison, Guépard, Lion, Vauban, Verdun, Valmy.*
Page 159 Aigle class: *Aigle, Albatros, Epervier, Gerfaut, Milan, Vautour.* Vauquelin class: *Cassard, Chevalier Paul, Kersaint, Maillé, Brezé, Tartu, Vauquelin.*
Page 160 Le Fantasque class: *L'Audacieux, Le Fantasque, L'Indomptable, Le Malin, Le Terrible, Le Triomphant.* Mogador class: *Desaix, Hoche, Kléber, Marceau, Mogador, Volta.*
Page 161 Surcouf class: *Bouvet, Casabianca, Cassard, Chevalier Paul, D'Estrées, Du Chayla, Dupetit Thouars, Guépratte, Kersaint, Maillé Brezé, Surcouf, Vauquelin.* Duperré class: *La Bourdonnais, Duperré, Forbin, Jauréguiberry, Tartu.*
Page 162 Suffren class: *Duquesne, Suffren.*
Page 163 Tourville class: *De Grasse, Duguay-Trouin, Tourville.*
Page 164 Georges Leygues class: *Dupleix, Georges Leygues, Jean de Vienne, La Motte-Picquet, Latouche-Tréville, Montcalm.* Cassard class: *Cassard, Jean Bart.*
Page 165 Sella class: *Francesco Crispi, Quintino Sella.* Sauro class: *Cesare Battisti, Daniele Manin, Francesco Nullo, Nazario Sauro.*
Page 166 Turbine class: *Aquilone, Borea, Espero, Euro, Nembo, Ostro, Turbine.*
Page 167 Leone class: *Leone, Pantera, Tigre.* Navigatore class: *Alvise de Mosto, Antonio da Noli, Nicoloso da Recco, Giovanni da Verazzano, Lanzerotto, Malocello, Leone Pancaldo, Emanuele Pessagno, Antonio Pigafetta, Luca Tarigo, Antoniotto Usodimare, Ugolino Vivaldi, Nicoló Zeno.*
Page 168 Dardo class: *Dardo, Freccia, Saetta, Strale.* Folgore class: *Baleno, Folgore, Fulmine, Lampo.*
Page 169 Maestrale class: *Grecale, Libeccio, Maestrale, Scirocco.* Oriani class: *Vittorio Alfieri, Giosue Carducci, Vincenzo Gioberti, Alfredo Oriani.*
Page 170 Soldati class, Group I: *Alpino, Artigliere, Ascari, Aviere, Bersagliere, Camicia Nera, Carabiniere, Corazziere, Fuciliere, Geniere, Granatiere, Lanciere.* Soldati class Group II: *Bombardiere, Carrista, Corsaro, Legionario, Mitragliere, Squadrista, Velite.*
Page 171 Imparvido class: *Impavido, Intrepido.*
Page 172 Ardito class: *Ardito, Audace.*
Page 173 Mimbelli class: *Francesco Mimbelli, Luigi Durand de la Penne.*
Page 174 Skoryi class: About 75 in class. Names not certain.
Page 175 Kotlin class: About 18 in class. Names not certain.
Page 176 Kildin class: Four in class. Names not certain.
Page 177 Krupnyi class: *Gnevny, Gordy.*
Page 178 Kanin class: *Boyky, Derzky, Gnevny, Gordy, Gremyashchy, Uporny, Zhguchy, Zorky.*
Page 179 Kashin class: *Komsomolets Ikrainyi, Krasnyi, Kavkaz, Krasnyi Krym, Obraztsovyi, Odarennyi, Reshitelnyi, Skoryi, Smetlivyi, Soobrazitel'nyi, Sposobnyi, Steregushchiy, Strogiy.* Modified Kashin class: *Ognevoy, Sderzhannyi, Slavnyi, Smel'yi, Smyshlennyi, Stroyni.*

Page 180 Sovremennyi class: *Admiral Ushakov, Aleksandr Nevskyi, Bespokoynyi, Bezboyaznennyi, Bezuderzhanyi, Bezuprechniyi, Boyevoy, Burnyi, Bystryi, Gremyashchiy, Nastoychivyi, Okrylennyi, Osmotritel'nyi, Otchayannyi, Otlichnyi, Rastoropnyi, Sovremennyi, Stroikiy, Yekaterinburg.*
Page 181 Udaloy class: *Admiral Kharlamov, Admiral Levchenko, Admiral Panteleyev, Admiral Tributs, Admiral Vinogradov, Marshal Shaposhnikov, Marshal Vasil'yevskiy, Severomorsck, Vitse-Admiral Kulakov.*
Page 182 Maass class: *Bernd von Arnim, Bruno Heinemann, Erich Giese, Rich Koellner, Erich Steinbrinck, Friedrich Eckoldt, Friedrich Ihn, Georg Thiele, Hans Lody, Hermann Schoemann, Leberecht Maass, Max Schultz, Paul Jacobi, Richard Beitzen, Theordor Riedel, Wolfgang Zenker.* Von Roeder class: *Anton Schmitt, Diether von Roeder, Hermann Kunne, Hans Ludemann, Karl Galster, Wilhelm Heidkamp.*
Page 183 Z23–34, Z35–36, Z37–39.
Page 184 Hamburg class: *Bayern, Hamburg, Hessen, Schleswig-Holstein.*
Page 185 Groningen class: *Amsterdam, Drenthe, Friesland, Groningen, Limburg, Overijssel, Rotterdam, Utrecht.* Holland class: *Gelderland, Holland, Noord Brabant, Zeeland.*
Page 186 Ölland class: *Ölland, Uppland.*
Page 187 Östergötland class: *Gästrikland, Hälsingland, Östergötland, Södermanland.* Halland class: *Halland, Smaland.*
Page 190 Black Swan class: *Black Swan, Erne, Flamingo, Ibis, Whimbrel, Wild Goose, Woodcock, Woodpecker, Wren.* Modified Black Swan class: *Actaeon, Alacrity, Amethyst, Chanticlear, Crane, Cygnet, Hart, Hind, Kite, Lapwing, Lark, Magpie, Mermaid, Modeste, Nereide, Opossum, Peacock, Pheasant, Redpole, Snipe, Sparrow, Starling.*
Page 191 Hunt class Type I: *Atherstone, Berkeley, Cattistock, Cleveland, Cotswold, Cottesmore, Eglinton, Exmoor, Fernie, Garth, Hambledon, Holderness, Mendip, Meynell, Pytchley, Quantock, Southdown, Tynedale, Whaddon.* Type II: *AvonVale, Badsworth, Beaufort, Bicester, Blackmore, Blankney, Blencathra, Brocklesby, Calpe, Chiddingfold, Cowdray, Croome, Dulverton, Eridge, Farndale, Grove, Heythrop, Hurworth, Lamerton, Lauderdale, Ledbury, Liddesdale, Middleton, Puckeridge, Southwold, Tetcott, Oakley, Wheatland, Wilton, Zetland.* Type III: *Airedale, Albrighton, Aldenham, Belvoir, Blean, Bleasdale, Derwent, Easton, Eggesford, Goathland, Haydon, Holcombe, Limbourne, Melbreak, Penylan, Rockwood, Stevenstone, Talybont, Tanatside, Wensleydale.* Type IV: *Brecon, Brissenden.*
Page 192 Flower class UK-built, 1939 Programme: *Anemone, Arbutus, Asphodel, Aubretia, Auricula, Begonia, Bluebell, Campanula, Candytuft, Carnation, Celandine, Clematis, Columbine, Convolvulus, Coreopsis, Crocus, Cyclamen, Dianella, Dahlia, Delphinium, Dianthus, Gardenia, Geranium, Gladiolus, Godetia, Heliotrope, Hollyhock, Honeysuckle, Hydrangea, Jasmine, Jonquil, Larkspur, Lavender, Lobelia, Marguerite, Marigold, Mignonette, Mimosa, Myosotis, Narcissus, Nigella, Penstemon, Polyanthus, Primrose, Salvia, Snapdragon, Snowdrop, Sunflower, Tulip, Verbena, Veronica, Wallflower, Zinnia.* UK-built, 1939 Emergency Programme: *Acanthus, Aconite, Alyssum, Amaranthus, Arabis, Bellwort, Borage, Burdock, Calendula, Camellia, Campion, Clarkia, Clover, Coriander, Coltsfoot, Erica, Fleur de Lys, Freesia, Gentian, Gloxinia, Heartsease, Heather, Hybiscus, Hyacinth, Kingcup, La Malouine, Loosestrife, Lotus, (I), Lotus (II), Mallow, Meadowsweet, Nasturtium, Orchis, Oxlip, Pennywort, Peony, Periwinkle, Petunia, Picotee, Pimpernel, Renunculus, Rhododendron, Rockrose, Rose, Samphire, Saxifrage, Spiraea, Starwort, Stonecrop, Sundew, Violet.* UK-built, 1940 Programme: *Abelia, Alisma, Anchusa, Armeria, Aster, Bergamot, Bryony, Buttercup, Chrysanthemum, Cowslip, Eglantine, Fritillary, Genista, Vervain, Vetch.* Supplementary Programmes: *Arrowhead, Balsam, Bittersweet, Eyebright, Fennel, Godetia, (II), Hepatica, Hyderabad, Mayflower, Monkshood, Montbretia, Pink, Poppy, Potentilla, Quesnel, Snowberry, Sorrel, Spikenard, Sweetbriar, Tamarisk, Thyme, Trillium, Windflower.* UK-built Modified Flower class, 1941–42: *Arabis, Arbutus, Betony, Buddleia, Bugloss, Bulrush, Burnet, Candytuft, Ceanothus, Charlock.* Canadian-built, Flower class, 1939–40 Programme: *Agassiz, Alberni, Algoma, Amherst, Arrowhead, Arvida, Baddeck, Barrie, Battleford, Brandon, Buctouche, Camrose, Chambly, Chicoutimi, Chilliwack, Cobalt, Collingwood, Dauphin, Dawson, Drumheller, Dunvegan, Edmondston, Galt, Kamloops, Kamsack, Kenogami, Lethbridge, Levis, Louisburg, Lunenburg, Matapedia, Moncton, Moosejaw, Morden, Nanaimo, Napanee, Oakville, Orillia, Pikton, Prescott, Quesnel, Rimouski, Rosthern, Sackville, Saskatoon, Shawinigan, Shediac, Sherbrooke, Sorel, Subbury,*

Summerside, The Pas, Wetaskiwin, Weyburn. Revised Canadian Flower class 1941–42 Programme: *Calgary, Charlottetown, Dundas, Fredericton, Halifax, La Malbaie, Port Arthur, Regina, Ville de Quebec, Woodstock.* 1942–43 Programme: *Athol, Coburg, Fergus, Frontenac, Guelph, Hawksbury, Lindsay, Norsyd, North Bay, Owen Sound, Rivière du Loup, St. Lambert, Trentonian, Whitby.* 1943–44 Programme: *Asbestos, Beauharnois, Bellville, Lachute, Merrittonia, Parry Sound, Peterborough, Smith's Falls, Stellaton, Strathroy, Thorlock, West, York.* Canadian-built for USN: *Comfrey, Cornel, Flax, Mandrake, Milfoil, Musk, Nepeta, Privet.* Canadian-built to RN via USN: *Dittany, Honesty, Linaria, Rosebay, Smilax, Statice, Willowherb.*

Page 193 River class 1940 Programme: *Balinderry, Bann, Chelmer, Dart, Derg, Ettrick, Exe, Itchen, Jed, Kale, Lagan, Moyola, Ness, Nith, Rother, Spey, Strule, Swale, Tay, Test, Teviot, Trent, Tweed, Waveney, Wear.* 1941 Programme: *Aire, Braid, Cam, Deveron, Dovey, Fal, Frome, Helford, Helmsdale, Meon, Nene, Plym, Ribble, Tavy, Tees, Torridge, Towy, Usk, Windrush, Wye.* 1942 Programme: *Avon, Awe, Halladale, Lochy, Mourne, Nadder, Odzani, Taff.* Canadian-built for RN: *Barle, Cuckmere, Evenlode, Findhorn, Inver, Lossie, Parret, Shiel.* Canadian-built River class 1942–43 Programme: *Beacon Hill, Cap de la Madeleine, Cape Breton, Charlottetown, Chebogue, Dunver, Eastview, Gron, Joliette, Jonquière, Kirkland Lake, Kokanee, La Hulloise, Longuenil, Magog, Matane, Montreal, New Glasgow, New Waterford, Orkney, Outremont, Port Colborne, Prince Rupert, St. Catherines, St. John, Springhill, Stettler, Stormont, Swansea, Thetford Mines, Valleyfield, Waskesiu, Wentworth.* 1943–44 Programme: *Antigonish, Buckingham, Capilano, Carlplace, Coaticook, Fort Erie, Glace Bay, Hallowell, Inch Arran, Lanark, Lasalle, Levis, Penetang, Poundmaker, Prestonian, Royal Mount, Runnymede, St. Pierre, St. Stephan, Ste. Thérèse, Seacliff, Stonetown, Strathadam, Sussexvale, Toronto, Victoriaville.*

Page 194 Castle Class. 1942 Programme: *Allington Castle, Bamborough C., Caistor C., Denbigh C., Farnham C., Hadleigh C., Hedingham C., Hurst C., Kenilworth C., Lancaster C., Oakham C.* 1943 Programme: *Alnwick Castle, Amberley C., Berkeley C., Carisbrooke C., Dumbarton C., Flint C., Knaresborough C., Launceston C., Leeds C., Morpeth C., Oxford C., Pevensey C., Portchester C., Rushen C., Tintagel C.* Transferred to RCN: *Guildford Castle., Hedingham C., Hever C., Norham C., Nunnery C., Pembroke C., Rising C., Sandgate C., Sherborne C., Tamworth C., Walmer C., Wolvesey C.* Transferred to Norway: *Shrewsbury Castle.*

Page 195 Bay class: *Bigbury Bay, Burghead Bay, Cardigan Bay, Carnarvon Bay, Cawsand B, Enard B., Largo Bay, Morecambe B., Mounts B., Padstow B., Porlock B., St. Bride's B., St. Austell B., Start B., Tremadoc B., Veryan B., Whitesand B., Widemouth B., Wigtown Bay.* Loch class, 1942 Programme: *Loch Achanalt, Loch Dunvegan, Loch Eck, Loch Fada.* 1943 Programme: *Loch Achray, L. Alvie, L. Arkaig, L. Craggie, L. Fyne, L. Glendhu, L. Gorm, L. Insh, L. Katrine, L. Killin, L. Killisport, L. Lomond, L. More, L. Morlich, L. Quoich, L. Ruthwen, L. Scavaig, L. Shin, L. Tarbert, L. Tralaig, Loch Veyatie.* Transferred to RCN: *Loch Achanalt, L. Alvie, L. Morlich.* Transferred to South Africa: *Loch Ard, L. Boisdale, L. Cree.*

Page 196 Type 15 conversions: *Rapid, Relentless, Rocket,. Roebuck, Troubridge, Grenville, Ulster, Ulysses, Undaunted, Undine, Urania, Urchin, Ursa, Venus, Verulam, Vigilant, Virago, Volage, Wakeful, Whirlwind, Wizard, Zest.* Type 16 conversions: *Orwell, Paladin, Petard, Teazer, Tenacious, Termagent, Terpsichore, Tumult, Tuscan, Tyrian.*

Page 197 Type 14: *Blackwood, Duncan, Dundas, Exmouth, Grafton, Hardy, Keppel, Malcolm, Murray, Palliser, Pellew, Russell.*

Page 198 Type 41: *Jaguar, Leopard, Lynx, Puma.* Type 61: *Chichester, Lincoln, Llandaff, Salisbury.*

Page 199 Type 12: *Berwick, Blackpool, Brighton, Eastbourne, Falmouth, Londonderry, Lowestoft, Plymouth, Rhyl, Rothesay, Torquay, Whitby, Yarmouth.* Leander class: *Ajax, Arethusa, Argonaut, Aurora, Cleopatra, Danae, Euryalus, Galatea, Juno, Leander, Minerva, Naiad, Penelope, Phoebe, Sirius.* Improved Leander class: *Achilles, Andromeda, Apollo, Ariadne, Bacchante, Charybdis, Diomede, Hermione, Jupiter, Scylla.*

Page 200 Type 21: *Active, Alacrity, Amazon, Ambuscade, Antelope, Ardent, Arrow, Avenger.*

Page 201 Type 22: *Battleaxe, Brazen, Brilliant, Broadsword.* Batch II: *Beaver, Boxer, Brave, Coventry, London, Sheffield.* Batch III: *Campbeltown, Chatham, Cornwall, Cumberland.*

Page 202 Type 23: *Argyll, Grafton, Iron Duke, Kent, Lancaster,*
Marlborough, Monmouth, Montrose, Norfolk, Northumberland, Portland, Richmond, St. Albans, Somerset, Sutherland, Westminster.

Page 203 Le Corse class: *Le Bordelais, Le Boulonnais, Le Brestois, Le Corse.* Le Normand class: *L'Agenais, l'Alsacien, Le Basque, Le Béarnais, Le Bourguignon, Le Breton, Le Champenois, Le Gascon, Le Lorrain, Le Normand, Le Picard, Le Provençal, Le Savoyard, Le Vendéen.*

Page 204 Commandant Rivière class: *Amiral Charner, Balny, Commandant Bory, Commandant Bourdais, Commandant Rivière, Doudart de la Grée, Enseigne Henry, Protet, Victor Schoelcher.*

Page 205 *Aconit.*

Page 206 D'Estienne d'Orves class: *Amyot d'Invilles, Commandant Birot, Commandant Blaison, Commandant Bouan, Commandant de Pimodan, Commandant Ducuing, Commandant l'Herminier, D'Estienne d'Orves, Detroyat, Drogou, Enseigne de Vaisseau Jacoubet, Jean Moulin, Lieutenant de Vaisseau Lavallée, Lieutenant de Vaisseau le Henaff, Premier Maître l'Her, Quartier-Maître Anquetil, Second Maître le Bihan.*

Page 207 Floréal class: *Floréal, Germinal, Nivôse, Prairial, Vendémiaire, Ventôse.*

Page 208 La Fayette class: *Aconit, Courbet, Guépratte, La Fayette, Surcouf.*

Page 209 Shumushu class, *Hachijo, Ishigaki, Kunashiri, Shumushu.* Etorofu class: *Amakusa, Etorofu, Fukue, Hirato, Iki, Kanju, Kasado, Manju, Matsuwa, Mutsure, Oki, Sado, Tsushima, Wakamiya.*

Page 210 Mikura class: *Awagi, Chiburi, Kurahashi, Kusagaki, Mikura, Miyake, Nomi, Yashiro.* Ukuru class: *Aguni, Amani, Chikubu, Daito, Habushi, Habuto, Hiburi, Hodaka, Ikara, Ikino, Ikuna, Inagi, Iwo, Kanawa, Kozu, Kuga, Kume, Mokuto, Murotsu, Oga, Okinawa, Otsu, Sakito, Shiga, Shinnan, Shisaka, Shonan, Takane, Tomoshiri, Uku, Ukuru, Urumi, Yaku.*

Page 211 Kaibokan Type I: Odd numbers 1–235. Kaibokan Type II: Even numbers 2–204. Matsu class: *Azusa, Enoki, Hagi Hatsuyume, Hatsuzakura, Hinoki, Hishi, Kaba, Kaede, Kaki, Kashi, Katsura, Kaya, Keyaki, Kiri, Kusunoki, Kuwa, Kuzu, Maki, Matsu, Momi, Momo, Nara, Nashi, Nire, Odake, Sakaki, Sakura, Shi, Sugi, Sumire, Tachibana, Take, Tochi, Tsubaki, Tsuta, Ume, Wakazakura, Yadake, Yaezkura, Yanagi.*

Page 212 Ikazuchi class: *Ikazuchi, Inazuma.* Isuzu class: *Isuzu, Kitakami, Mogami, Oi.*

Page 213 Chikugo class: *Ayase, Chitose, Chikugo, Iwase, Kumano, Mikuma, Niyodo, Noshiro, Teshio, Tokachi, Yoshino.*

Page 214 Ishikari/Yubari class: *Yubari, Yubetsu.*

Page 215 Abukuma class: *Abukuma, Chikuma, Jintsu, Oyodo, Sendai, Tone.*

Page 216–217 Buckley class: *Ahrens, Alexander J. Luke, Amesbury, Barber, Barr, Bates, Blessman, Borum, Bowers, Buckley, Bull, Bunch, Burke, Charles Lawrence, Chase, Cofer, Coolbaugh, Cronin, Currier, Damon M. Cummings, Daniel T. Griffin, Darby, Donnell, Durik, Earl V. Johnson, Eichenberger, England, Enright, Fechteler, Fieberling, Fogg, Foreman, Foss, Fowler, Frament, Francis M. Robinson, Frybarger, Gantner, Gendreau, George, George W. Ingram, Gillette, Greenwood, Gunason, Haines, Harmon, Hayter, Henry R. Kenyon, Hollis, Holton, Hopping, Ira Jeffery, J. Douglas Blackwood, Jack W. Wilke, James E. Craig, Jenks, Jordon, Joseph C. Hubbard, Joseph E. Campbell, Kephart, Laning, Lee Fox, Liddle, Lloyd, Loeser, Lovelace, Loy, Major, Maloy, Manning, Marsh, Neuendorf, Newman, Osmus, Otter, Paul G. Baker, Raby, Reeves, Reuben James, Rich, Robert I. Paine, Runels, Schmitt, Scott, Scroggins, Sims, Solar, Spangenberg, Spangler, Tatum, Thomason, Underhill, Vanmen, Varian, Weber, Weeden, Whitehurst, William C. Cole, William T. Powell, Willmarth, Wiseman, Witter.* Cannon class: *Acree, Alger, Amick, Atherton, Baker, Baugust, Baron, Booth, Bostwick, Breeman, Bright, Bronstein, Burrows, Cannon, Carroll, Carter, Cates, Christopher, Clarence E. Evans, Coffman, Cooner, Curtis W. Howard, Earl K. Olsen, Ebert, Eisner, Eldridge, Gandy, Garfield Thomas, Gaynier, George M. Campbell, Gustafson, Hemminger, Herzog, Hilbert, John J. van Buren, Kyne, Lamons, Levy, McAnn, McClelland, McConnell, Marts, Micka, Milton Lewis, Muir, Neal A. Scott, O'Neill, Osterhaus, Oswald, Parks, Pennewill, Reybold, Riddle, Rinehart, Roberts, Roche, Russell M. Cox, Samuel S. Miles, Slater, Snyder, Stern, Straub, Sutton, Swearer, Thomas, Thornhill, Tills, Trumpeter, Waterman, Weaver, Wesson, Wingfield.* Edsall class: *Blair, Brister, Brough, Calcaterra, Camp, Chambers, Chatelain, Cockrill, Dale W. Peterson, Daniel, Douglas L. Howard, Durant, Edsall, Falgout, Farguhar, Fessenden, Finch, Fiske, Flaherty, Forster, Frederick C. Davis, Frost, Hammann, Harveson, Haverfield, Herbert C. Jones, Hill, Hissem, Holder, Howard D. Crow, Hurst,*

CLASS LISTS OF DESTROYERS AND FRIGATES

Huse, Inch, J.R.Y. Blakely, J. Richard Ward, Jacob Jones, Janssen, Joyce, Keith, Kirkpatrick, Koiner, Kretchmer, Lansing, Leopold, Lowe, Marchand, Martin H. Ray, Menges, Merrill, Mills, Moore, Mosley, Neunzer, Newell, O'Reilly, Otterstetter, Peterson, Pettit, Pillsburn, Poole, Pople Price, Pride, Ramsden, Rhodes, Richey, Ricketts, Robert E. Peary, Roy O. Hale, Savage, Sellstrom, Sloat, Snowden, Stanton, Stewart, Stockdale, Strickland, Sturtevant, Swasey, Swenning, Thomas L. Gary, Tomich, Vance, Wilhoite, Willis. Evarts class: Andres, Austin, Bebas, Brackett, Brennan, Burden R. Hastings, Cabana, Canfield, Carlson, Charles R. Greer, Cloues, Connolly, Crouter, Crowley, Decker, Deede, Dempsey, Dionne, Dobler, Doherty, Donaldson, Doneff, Duffy, Edgar C. Chase, Edward C. Daly, Eisele, Elden, Emery, Engstrom, Evarts, Fair, Finnegan, Fleming, Halloran, Gilmore, Greiner, Griswold, Harold C. Thomas, Lake, Le Hardy, Lovering, Lyman, Manlove, Martin, Mitchell, Rall, Reynolds, Sanders, Sederstrom, Seid, Smartt, Stadtfeld, Steele, Tisdale, Walter S. Brown, Whitman, Wileman, William C. Millar, Wintle, Wyffels, Wyman. John C. Butler class: Abercrombie, Albert T. Harris, Alvin C. Cockrell, Bivin, Cecil J. Doyle, Charles E. Brannon, Chester T. O'Brien, Conklin, Corbesier, Cross, Dennis, Douglas A. Munro, Doyle C. Barnes, Dufilho, Edmonds, Edward H. Allen Edwin A. Howard, Eversole, Formoe, Francovich, French, Gentry, George E. Davis, Gilligan, Goss, Grady, Haas, Hanna, Henry W. Tucker, Heyliger, Howard F. Clark, Jaccard, Jack Miller, Jesse Rutherford, John C. Butler, John L. Williamson, Johnnie Hutchins, Joseph E. Connolly, Kendall C. Campbell, Kenneth M. Willett, Keppler, Key, Kleinsmith, La Prade, Lawrence C. Taylor, Le Ray Wilson, Leland E. Thomas, Lewis, Lloyd E. Acree, Lloyd Thomas, McCoy Reynolds, McGinty, Mack, Maurice J. Manuel, Melvin R. Nawman, Naifeh, O'Flaherty, Oberrender, Oliver Mitchell, Osberg, Pratt, Presley, Raymond, Richard M. Rowell, Richard S. Bull, Richard W. Suesens, Rizzi, Robert Brazier, Robert F. Keller, Rolf, Rombach, Samuel B. Roberts, Shelton, Silverstein, Stafford, Steinaker, Straus, Tabberer, Thaddeus Parker, Traw, Tweedy, Tulvert M. Moore, Vandivier, Wagner, Walter C. Wann, Walton, Weiss, William C. Lawe, William Sieverling, Williams, Woodrow R. Thompson, Woodson. Rudderrow class: Bray, Chaffee, Charles J. Kimmel, Coates, Daniel A. Joy, Day, DeLong, Eugene E. Elmore, George A. Johnson, Hodges, Holt, Jobb, Leslie L.B. Knox, Lough, McNulty, McTivier, Parle, Peiffer, Riley Rudderow, Thomas F. Nickel, Tinsman.
Page 218 Dealey/Courtney/Claud Jones class: Bauer, Bridget, Charles Berry, Claud Jones, Courtney, Cromwell, Dealey, Evans, Hammerberg, Hartley, Hooper, J.K. Taussig, John R. Perry, John Willis, Lester, McMorris, Van Voorhis.
Page 219 Bronstein class: Bronstein, McCloy, Garcia class: Albert David, Bradley, Brumby, Davidson, Edward McDonnell, Garcia, Koelsch, O'Callaghan Sample, Voge. Brooke class: Brooke, Julius A. Furer, Ramsey, Richard L. Page, Schofield, Talbot.
Page 220 Knox class: Ainsworth, Aylwin, Badger, Bagley, Barbey, Blakeley. Bowen, Brewton, Capodanno, Connole, Cook, Donald B. Beary, Downes, Elmer Montgomery, Fanning, Franic Hammon, Gray, Harold E. Holt, Hepburn, Jesse L. Brown, Joseph Hewes, Kirk, Knox, Lang, Lockwood, McCandless, Marvin Shields, Meyercord, Miller, Moinester, Ouellet, Patterson, Paul, Pharris, Rathburne, Reasoner, Roark, Robert E. Peary, Stein, Thomas C. Hart, Trippe, Truett, Valdez, Vreeland, W.S. Sims, Whipple.
Page 221 Oliver Hazard Perry class: Antrim, Aubrey, Fitch, Boone, Carr, Clark, Clifton Sprague, Copeland, Crommelin, Curts, De Wert, Doyle, Duncan, Elrod, Estocin, Fahrion, Flatley, Ford, Gallery, Gary, George Philip, Halyburton, Hawes, Ingraham, Jack Williams, Jarrett, John A. Moore, John L. Hall, Kauffman, Klakring, Lewis B. Puller, McCluskey, McInerney, Mahlon S. Tisdale, Nicholas, Oliver Hazard Perry, Reid, Rentz, Reuben James, Robert G. Bradley, Rodney M. Davis, Samuel B. Roberts, Samuel Eliot Morison, Sides, Simpson, Stark, Stephen W. Groves, Taylor, Thach, Underwood, Vandegrift, Wadsworth.
Page 222 Spica class: Airone, Alcione, Aldebaran, Altair Andromeda, Antares, Aretusa, Ariel, Calipso, Calliope, Canopo, Cassiopea, Castore, Centauro, Cigno, Circe, Climene, Clio, Libra, Lince, Lira, Lupo, Pallade, Partenope, Perseo, Pleiadi, Polluce, Sagittario, Sirio, Vega.
Page 223 Ariete class: Alabarde, Ariete, Arturo, Auriga, Balestra, Daga, Dragone, Eridano, Fionda, Gladio, Lancia, Pugnale, Rigel, Spada, Spica, Stella Polare.
Page 224 Orsa class: Orione, Orsa, Pegaso, Procione. Animoso class: Aliseo, Animoso, Ardente, Ardimentoso, Ardito, Ciclone, Fortunale,

Ghibli, Groppo, Impavido, Impetuoso, Indomito, Intrepido, Monsone, Tifone, Uragano.
Page 225 Albatros class: Airone, Albatros, Alcione, Aquila. De Cristofaro class: Licio Visintini, Pietro de Cristofaro, Salvatore Todaro, Umberto Grosso.
Page 226 Centauro class: Canopo Centauro, Cigno, Castore.
Page 227 Bergamini class: Carlo Margottini, Luigi Rizzo, Virginio Fasan. Alpini class: Alpini, Carabiniere.
Page 228 Lupo class: Lupo, Orsa, Perseo, Sagittario.
Page 229 Maestrale class: Aliseo, Espero, Euro, Grecale, Libeccio, Maestrale, Scirocco, Zeffiro. Artigliere class: Artigliere, Aviere, Bersagliere, Granatiere.
Page 230 Minerva class: Chimera, Danaide, Driade, Fenice, Minerva, Sfinge, Sibilla, Urania.
Page 231 Kola class: Names uncertain.
Page 232 Riga class: Known names: Astrakhan'skiy Komsomolets, Arkhangel'skiy, Komsomolets, Bars, Barsuk, Bobr, Buyvol, Byk, Gepard, Giena, Komsomolets Litviy, Krasnogarskiy, Komsomolets, Kunitsa, Leopard, Lev, Lisa, Medved, Pantera, Rys, Rosomakha, Shakal, Sovetskiy, Azerbaydzhan, Sovetskiy, Dagestan, Sovetskiy Turkmenistan, Strau, Tigr, Tuman, Volk, Voron, Yaguar.
Page 233 Mirka and Petya classes: Names unconfirmed.
Page 234 Poti class: Names unconfirmed.
Page 235 Grisha classes: Names unconfirmed.
Page 236 Krivak I class: Bditel'nyi, Bezukoriznennyy, Bezzavetnyy, Bodryy, Deyatel'nyy, Doblestnyy, Dostonyy, Druzhnyy, Ladnyy, Leningradskiy Komsomolets, Letuchiy, Poryvistyy, Pylkiy, Razumnyy, Razyashchiy, Restivyy, Sil'nyy, Storozhevoy, Svirepyy, Zadornyy, Zharkyy. Krivak class II: Bessmennyy, Gordelivyy, Gromkiy, Grozyashchiy, Neukrotimyy, Pytlivyy, Razitel'nyy, Revnosnyy, Rezkiy, Rezvyy, Ryanyy. Krivak class III: Anadyr, Dzerzhinskiy, Kedrov, Menzhinskiy, Orel, Pskov, Vorovskiy.
Page 237 Steregushchiy class: Boiky, Soobrziltel'nyy, Steregushchiy, Stoiky.
Page 238 Köln class: Augsburg, Braunschweig, Emden, Karlsruhe, Köln, Lübeck.
Page 239 Thetis class: Hermes, Naiade, Theseus, Thetis, Triton.
Page 240 Bremen class: Augsberg, Bremen, Emden, Karlsruhe, Köln Lübeck, Niedersachsen, Rheinland-Pfalz.
Page 241 Brandenburg class: Bayern, Brandenburg, Mecklesnburg-Vorpommern, Schleswig-Holstein.
Page 242 Sachsen class: Hamburg, Hessen, Sachsen.
Page 243 Braunschweig class: Braunschweig, Erfurt, Magdeburg, Oldenburg.
Page 244 Van Heemskerck class: Jacob van Heemskerck, Witte de With. Kortenaer class: Abraham Crijnssen, Banckert, Bloys van Treslong. Callenburgh, Jan van Brakel, Kortenaer, Philips van Almonde, Piet Heyn, Pieter, Florisz, Van Kinsbergen.
Page 245 De Zeven Provinciën class: De Ruyter, De Zeven Provinciën, Evertsen, Tromp.
Page 246 Karel Doorman class: Abraham van der Hulst, Karel Doorman, Van Amstel, Van Galen, Van Nes, Van Speijk.
Page 247 St Laurent classes Annapolis type: Annapolis, Nipigon. Mackenzie type: Mackenzie, Qu'appelle, Saskatchewan, Yukon. Restigouche type: Chaudière, Columbia, St. Croix. Improved Restigouche type: Gatineau, Kootenay, Restigouche, Terra Nova. St. Laurent type: Assiniboine, Fraser, Margaree, Ottawa, Saguenay, Skeena.
Page 248 Iroquois class: Algonquin, Athabaskan, Huron, Iroquois. Halifax class: Calgary, Charlottetown, Fredericton, Halifax, Montreal, Ottawa, Regina, St. John's,. Toronto, Vancouver, Ville de Quebec, Winnepeg.
Page 249 Anzac class (Australia): Anzac, Arunta, Ballarat, Parramatta, Perth, Stuart, Toowoomba, Warramunga. Anzac class (New Zealand): Te Kaha, Te Mana.

Scarborough, Type 12

503

Index

600 class, 420

A
A class (Destroyer), 67, 114
A class (UK submarine), 260, 261, 262, 276, 319, 373, 374, 394
A class (USA submarine), 262, 353, 372, 394
A class (Midget submarine), 312
A-class SSK, 452
A1 (UK), 260–1, 373
A1 (*Plunger*, SS2, USA), 353
A1 type, 410
A2, 373
A2 type, 410
A4, 373
A5, 373
A6 (*Porpoise*), 353
A7, 373
A7 (*Shark*), 353
A11, 373
A13, 373
Abba, 102
Abdiel, 76
Abraham Crijnssen, 244
Abraham van der Hulst, 246
Abukuma class, 215
Acasta class, 29, 73, 74, 102
Achates, 38, 39, 73
Acheron class, 86
Aconit, 163, 205
Aconit class, 205
Acorn class, 20, 21, 23, 32, 33, 70–1
Active, 200
Adder class, 260
Admiral Chabanenko, 181
Admiral Hipper (*Hipper*), 38, 39
Adua type, 420
AE2, 269, 270
Affray, 318, 319
Agir, 21
Agosta type, 417

Agosta-class 90B SSK, 469, 485, 488
Aigle, 159
Aigle class, 159
Aisne, 120
Akatsuki class, 110, 142
Akebono, 212
Akitsuki class, 146
Akizuki class, 147
Akula I-class (Project 971) SSN, 337, 446, 447, 450
Akula II-class SSN, 337, 447
Albacore (Submarine), 320, 321, 324, 454
Albacore (destroyer), 68
Albatros, 159, 225
Albatros class, 225
Albemarle, 17
Albert David, 219
Alcione class, 97, 222
Aldebaran, 98
Alfa-class (Project 705) SSN, 337, 443, 446
Alfieri, 169
Alfredo Oriani, 169
Algerine class, 47
Algonquin, 248
Aliseo, 224
Allen M. Sumner, 131
Allen M. Sumner class, 131
Alliance SSK, 452
Alligator, 255
Almirante Gago Coutinho, 218
Alpino, 101, 227
Alpino class, 227
Amazon, 72, 114, 200
Amazon class, 30, 88
Ambuscade, 114
Ambush SSK, 452
Ambush SSN 349, 465
Amethyst, 190
Améthyste, 466, 467
Amiral Sénès, 89
Amphion SSK, 452

Amsterdam, 185
Anderson, 128
Andrew, 326
Andrew SSK, 452
Angelo Bassini, 103
Anguilla (Frigate), 48
Anguilla (Submarine), 261
Animoso, 102
Antogonish, 193
Antrim, 122
Anzac, 249
Anzac class, 249
Aotaka class, 109
Aquila, 225
Aquila class, 98
Aquitaine class, 164
Arabe class, 108, 111
Arashio, 144
Ardent, 73
Ardente, 102
Ardito, 102
Argonaut, 305, 366, 413, 477
Argonaut (Simon Lake), 358
Argonaut (Tench class), 371
Argonauta, 420
Argonauta type, 420
Ariete, 223
Ariete class, 223
Arleigh Burke class, 139
Arquebuse class, 105
Artful SSK, 452
Artful SSN, 349,465
Artigliere, 101
Artigliere class, 228
Arturo, 223
Arunta, 115
AS-28 *Priz*, 345
Asagiri class, 151
Asakaze class, 110
Asashio (Destroyer), 145
Asashio (Submarine), 479
Asashio class (Destroyer), 144
Ascaro, 101
Astute SSK, 452
Astute SSN, 337, 346, 349, 459, 464, 465
Astute-class SSN, 346, 349, 464–5
Aspirant Herber, 106
Atago, 153
Athenia, sinking of the, 292–3, 300
Atlantic, battle of, 50–1, 300–1, 406
Audace, 102, 172
Audace class, 172, 173
Audacity, 52, 53
Augsburg, 238
Aukstaitis, 235
Avalon (DSRV 2), 328

Aventurier class, 108
Aviere, 173
Avvoltoio, 98
Awaji, 210
Ayanami class, 147
Ayase, 213
Aylwin, 63, 220

B
B class (Destroyer), 68, 114
B class (UK submarine), 261, 268, 276, 374, 394
B class (USA submarine), 354, 394
B class (Midget submarine), 394
B1 (*Viper*), 354
B1 class, 281, 410
B2 (*Cuttlefish*), 354
B2 class, 410
B3, 374
B3 (*Tarantula*) USA, 354
B3 class, 410
B4, 374
B6, 374
B9, 268
B10, 268
B11, 268, 269, 374
Bainbridge class, 91, 92
Balao, 370, 371
Balao class, 302, 321, 351, 370, 490
Balestra, 223
Balny, 204
Bamborough Castle, 194
Bangor class, 47
Barb, 369
Barb SSN, 426
Barracuda (V1), 283, 366
Barracuda class, 361
Bars class, 418
Batfish SSN, 334
Battle class, 60, 118, 120
Battleaxe, 119
Bay class, 116, 195
Bayern, 184
Beagle class, 23, 70–1
Beatty, Admiral Sir David, 24
Bedovy, 176
Belgrano, sinking of the 338–9
Belier, 105
Belknap, 136
Belknap class, 136
Benham, 93
Benjamin Franklin class, 330, 332, 430
Benson class, 129
Bergamini class, 172
Berkeley, 134
Bersagliere, 101

Minegumo, Minegumo class

504

INDEX

Biber, 314
Billfish, 370
Bison, 158, 159
Bisson class, 107
Bittern class, 47
Black Prince, 24
Black Swan class, 47, 49, 53, 190
Blackfin, 370
Blanco Encalada, 122
Block Island, 54, 55
Blueback, 321
Boadicea class, 76
Bogue, 55
Bonetta, 68
Borea, 100, 166
Borei class, 445
Bostwick class, 216–17
Botha, 27
Bouclier class, 28, 107
Bourrasque, 154
Bourrasque class, 154
Boutefeu, 28
Bouvet, 22
Brandenburg, 241
Brandenburg class, 241
Branlebas class, 105
Braunschweig, 243
Braunschweig class, 243
Brazen, 9, 201
Bremen, 240
Bremen class, 236, 238, 240
Brilliant, 114
Brisbane, 134
Bristol, 123
Broke, 25, 26, 27
Bronstein, 219
Bronstein class, 219
Bronzetti, 102
Brooke class, 219
Buchanan, 34, 35
Buckley class, 216–17
Burak Reis, 370
Burnett, Admiral R.L., 39
Burns, 94
Busugo, 303

C

C class (Destroyer), 50, 68, 114, 118
C class (UK submarine), 261, 264, 276, 375
C class (USA submarine), 355
C class (Midget submarine), 312, 313
C1, 274, 375
C1 (Octopus), 355
C1 class, 411
C2, 355
C3, 274, 275, 375
C3 (Tarpon), 355
C4, 355
C5 (Snapper), 355
C7, 375

C15, 375
C22, 375
C24, 375
C25, 375
C26, 375
C27, 375
C29, 375
C31, 375
C32, 375
C33, 375
C34, 375
C35, 375
Cachalot, 285, 297
Cadiz, 60
Cairoli, 103
Calcaterra, 217
Caldwell, 94
Caldwell class, 94–5
Campbeltown, 34–5
Canopo, 226
Canterbury, 199
Capitaine Mehl, 107
Capitani Romani class, 170
Caprera, 96
Carabiniere, 101, 170, 227
Card, 55
Carducci, 169
Carini, 103
Carlo Bergamini, 227
Carlo Bergamini class, 227
Casabianca, 417
Casabianca SSN, 466
Cassard, 159, 161
Cassard class, 164
Cassin, 128
Cassin class, 93
Cassiopea, 222
Castle class, 49, 57, 194
CB class, 312
Centauro, 226
Centauro class, 226
Cero 369
Cesare Battisti, 165
Cesare Rossarol, 88
Chacal, 157
Chacal class, 157, 167
Chakra, 489
Chandler, 137
Chariots 310–11, 312
Charles F. Adams class, 134
Charlottetown, 248
Chasseur class, 106
Chatfield, Admiral, 44
Cheerful, 68
Chelsea, 35
Cherwell, 69
Chevalier, 104
Chevalier Paul, 159, 164
Cheyenne SSN, 433
Chicoutimi SSK, 477
Chidori, 109
Chikugo, 213
Chikugo class, 213
Chikuma, 215

Chitose, 213
Christopher, 49
Churchill SSN, 458
Churchill-class SSN, 339, 458, 459, 460
Ciclone class, 224
Cigno class, 97
Clare, 35
Claude Jones class, 218
Claus van Bevern, 85
Claymore class, 22, 105
Clemson class, 95
Climene, 47
Climene class, 222
Clio, 98
Cochinio, 320, 321
Collins SSK, 480
Collins-class (Type 471) SSK, 480–1
Combined Operations Pilotage Parties (COPPS), 304, 315
Comet, 50
Commandant Bory, 28, 204
Commandant Ducuing, 206
Commandant Rivière class, 204
Comte de Grasse, 137
Connecticut SSN, 336, 437
Conquerant, 417
Conqueror SSN, 338, 339, 458, 459
Contest, 118
Coontz, 135
Coontz class, 61, 135
Corazziere, 101
Core, 55
Corner Brook SSK, 476, 477
Cornwall, 201
Cossack, 72
County class, 122
Courtney, 218
Courageous, 458
Courtney class, 218
Cowell, 8, 130
Crane, 190
Craven class, 128
Croatan, 55
Crossbow, 119
Crowninshield, 35
CSS *David*, 254
Curtis Wilbur, 139

Curtis Wilbur, Arleigh Burke class

Cushing, 90
Cushing, Lt William B., 17
Cyclone class, 104, 109

D

D class (Destroyer), 68, 114
D class (UK submarine), 261, 264, 476, 373, 376
D class (USA submarine), 356
D1 (UK), 261
D1 (USA), 356
D2, 376
D2 (Grayling), 356
D3 (UK), 376
D3 (USA), 356
D4, 17, 376
D5, 376
D6, 376
D7, 376
D8, 376
Dace, 369
Dace SSN, 427
Dakar, 391
Dainty, 121
Daphne class, 484
Dardanelles, 268–9
Dardanelles campaign, 22–3
Dardo class, 168
Daring, 67, 121, 125
Daring class, 121, 125, 185
de Cristofaro class, 225
de Zeven Provinciën, 245
de Zeven Provinciën class, 245
Dealey class, 218
Découverte, 193
Decoy, 67
Dekabrist class, 418
Delfin-class SSK, 484, 485
Delta I-class SSBN, 331, 444
Delta II-class SSBN, 444
Delta III-class SSBN, 444–5
Delta IV-class SSBN, 444–5, 448
Desperate, 68
d'Estaing, 169
d'Estienne d'Orves, 206
d'Estienne d'Orves class, 206
Destroyer escort (DE) classes, 216–17
Deutschland (*U155*), 272, 273, 401

505

INDEX

Nastoychivyy, Sovremennyy class

Deyo, 9, 137
Diamond, 121, 125
Dixie Arrow, 44
Dobler, 217
Dominica, 53
Dönitz, Admiral, 39, 51, 54, 55, 284, 300, 301
Downes, 128
Dreadnought SSN, 326–7, 454, 455, 458
Duguay-Trouin, 163
Duncan, 197
Duperré, 161
Duperré class, 161
Dupleix, 164
Dupont, 133
Duquesne, 162
Durand de la Penne class, 173
Durandal class, 105

E

E class (Destroyer), 69, 114
E class (UK submarine), 261, 264, 269, 270, 271, 276, 377, 380, 381
E class (USA submarine), 357
E1, 265, 377
E1 (*Skipjack*), 357
E3, 265, 377
E6, 377
E7, 270, 271
E8, 265
E9, 265
E10, 376
E11, 265, 270–1, 377
E12, 270
E14, 269, 270, 271
E15, 269, 270
E19, 265, 377
E22, 377
E24, 397
E32, 265
Echo-class SSGN, 325
Echo I-class (Project 659) SSN, 442
Echo II-class (Project 675) SSN, 442
Eden, 69
Edinburgh, 124
Edsall class, 216–17
EKM, 489
Elbing, 25
Electra, 114
Electric Boat Company, 259, 323, 328, 347, 355, 356, 359, 361, 362, 365, 366, 372
Elrod, 221
Emden, 33, 238
Emperor, 40
Endeavour, 199
England, 136
Enigma, 307
Enoki class, 111
Enrico Tazzoli, 369
Enseigne de Vaisseau Henry, 204
Enseigne Roux class, 107
Epervier, 159
Erfurt, 243
Ericsson, 90
Eskimo, 33
Espero, 100, 166
Estremadura, 241
Ethan Allen SSBN/SSN, 429
Etorofu class, 209
Euro, 99, 166
Evans, Commander Teddy, 27
Evarts class, 216–17
Exeter, 40, 113, 124
Exmouth, 197, 204
Explorer, 59, 453
Explorer class, 453

F

F class (Destroyer), 30, 72, 114
F class (USA submarine), 357
F class (Early, UK submarine), 264, 277, 378
F1 (UK), 378
F1 (USA), 357
F3 (UK), 378
F3 (USA), 357
Fabrizi, 103
Fame, 68
Fanfare, 105
Farenholt, 129
Farragut, 126
Farragut class, 126
Faulknor, 27
Fenian Ram, 258
Ferret, 67

Fife, 122
Fisher, Admiral Sir John (Jackie), 20, 26, 67
Fiske, 132
Fletcher, 130
Fletcher class, 8, 43, 130, 131
Fleuret, 156
Floréal class, 207
Florida SSBN, 347
Flower class, 47, 48, 49, 50, 192
Flying Fish, 68
Folgore, 168
Folgore class, 168
Forbin, 104, 164
Forbin class, 125
Forrest Sherman, 133
Forrest Sherman class, 133
Foudre, 104
Foudroyant, 156
Francesco Crispi, 165
Francesco Mimbelli, 173
Franklin, 42
Fraser, 247
Friesland class, 185
Fubuki class, 142
Fucilliere, 101
Fukuryu, 109
Fulgosi class, 230
Fulmine, 99
Fulton, Robert, 16
Fulton, 259
Fury, 32

G

G class (Destroyer), 23, 70–1, 114, 121
G class (UK submarine), 264, 277, 379
G class (USA submarine), 358
G1 (*Seal*), 358
G3 (*Turbot*), 358
G7, 379
G8, 379
G9, 379
G11, 379
G13, 379
Gabriel, 76
Galerna-class SSK, 485
Gallipoli, 22–3
Garcia class, 219
Garibaldino, 101
Garland, 73
Gato, 369
Gato class, 302, 351, 368–9
Gearing class, 132
Gem class, 76
General Bartolomé Salom, 228
General Belgrano (Cruiser), 338–9, 458, 459
Generale Achille Papa, 47
Generali class, 47
George Washington SSBN, 325, 329, 330, 332, 346, 428

Georges Leygues class, 164
Georgia SSBN, 347
Gerfaut, 159
Gianfranco Gazzana Prairoggia SSK, 482
Giovanni Bausan, 96
Glorieux, 416
Gloucester, 124
Gneisenau, 32
Goito, 96
Gotland SSK, 487
Gotland-class (Type A19), SSK 486, 487
Grampus, 297
Granatiere, 101, 174
Gray, 220
Grecale, 169, 170, 229
Greeneville SSN, 349, 433
Grenville, 59
Gridley, 14
Grimsby class, 47
Grisha class, 235
Grouper, 371
Guadalcanal campaign, 36–7
Guardfish SSN, 334
Guépard, 158, 159
Guépard class, 158, 167
Guppy configuration, 320–1, 339, 369, 370, 371
Gustav Zede, 259, 261
Gyatt, 61, 134

H

H class (Destroyer), 20, 21, 23, 32, 33, 70–1, 114
H class (UK submarine), 264, 277, 380
H class (USA submarine), 359
H1 (*Seawolf*), 359
H2 (*Nautilus*), 359
H3 (*Garfish*), 359
H4 class, 359
H23, 380
H31, 380
HA class, 286
HA-77, 312
HA101, 287
Haddock, 360
Hadleigh Castle, 194
Haguro, 40, 41, 60
Hai Hu class, 493
Hai Lung class, 493
Halcyon class, 47
Halford, 131
Halifax class, 248
Halland, 187
Halland class, 187
Halsey, Admiral William, 36, 43
Hamburg class, 184
Hameenmaa, 232
Hannover, 53
Hans-class Type 091 SSN, 473
Hans Lody, 182
Hans Lüdemann, 182

INDEX

Hardy, 32, 33, 197
Harukaze class, 147
Haruna class, 149
Harusame, 152
Harusame class, 110
Harushio class, 479
Harutsuki, 146
Hassan II, 207
Hatakaze, 150
Hatakaze class, 150
Hatsuharu, 143
Hatsuharu class, 143
Hatsuyuki, 151
Hatsuyuki class, 151
Havock, 20, 21, 32, 33, 67
Hayabusa class, 109
Hessen, 9, 184, 242
Hipper, Admiral, 24
Hipper (Admiral Hipper), 38, 39
Hitler, Adolf, 39
HM *Submarine Torpedo Boat No. 1*, 372
Hobart, 134
Hoche, 106
Holbrook, Lt Norman, 268, 269
Holland UK, 260, 372, 373
Holland 1, 372
Holland 2, 372
Holland I (SS1), 17, 259, 260, 323, 351, 352, 353, 354
Holland class (Destroyer), 185
Holland, John Phillip, 253, 257, 258–9, 352, 355, 358, 372
Hornet, 21, 67
Horton, Admiral Sir Max, 52
Hostile, 32
Hotel-class SSBN, 324, 325
Hotspur, 32, 33
Hunley, 254, 255, 263
Hunt class, 31, 34, 47, 81, 191
Hunter, 33, 67

I

I class (Destroyer), 70–1, 114
I class (Submarine), 286
I1, 412
I3, 412
I7, 412
I8, 412
I14, 281, 410
I15, class 281
I16, 411
I18, 411
I19, 302, 410
I20, 411
I21, 287
I24, 411
I26, 411
I51, 287
I56, 410
I58, 410
I70, 409
I176, 409
I400, 413

I400 class, 281
I401, 413
I402, 413
Icefish, 490
Ikazuchi, 142, 212
Ikazuchi class, 110, 212
Impavido, 171
Impavido class, 171
Improved Kongo class, 153
Inazuma, 212
Independence, 63
Indomito class, 102
Ingham, 43
Insidioso, 102
Intelligent Whale, 256
Intrepido, 171
Iron Duke, 63
Iroquois class, 248
Ishikari, 214
Ishikari class, 214
Isuzu class, 212
Ithuriel, 76
IXB, 404

J

J class (Destroyer), 30, 31, 60, 116
J class (Submarine), 277, 381
J1, 381
J1 class, 412
J2 class, 412
J3 class, 410, 412
J6, 381
J7, 381
Jacob van Heemskerck, 244
Jamaica, 38
James K. Polk SSBN, 330, 430
James Madison SSBN, 430
James Monroe SSBN, 430
Janissaire, 106
Jasmine, 192
Javelin class, 30, 31
Jellicoe, Admiral Sir John, 24, 25, 28
Jimmy Carter SSN, 336, 437
John C. Stennis, 201
Josephus Daniels, 136
Joy, Admiral C. Turner, 42
Jules Verne, 206
Jutland, battle of, 21, 24–5, 28, 39, 46, 87

K

K class (Destroyer), 29, 73, 116
K class (Netherlands), 490
K class (UK submarine), 278–9, 280, 383, 384, 385, 381
K class (USA submarine), 360
K1, 360
K2 (UK), 279
K2 (USA), 360
K3 SSN, 336
K4 278, 279
K5, 360

K6, 278, 279
K8, 360
K11, 278
K12, 279
K13, 278, 279
K14, 279
K17, 279
K18, 280
K19, 280
K20, 280
K21, 280
K22 (*K13*), 279
K26, 383
K64 SSN, 337
K219 SSBN, 333, 440–1
Kaba, 111
Kaba class, 108, 111
Kagero class, 145
Kaibokan class, 211
Kairyu (Sea Dragon), 315
Kaiten, 410, 412, 413
Kaiten (Return to Heaven), 312, 313, 314
Kaki, 140
Kamehameha SSBN, 430
Kamikaze, 40, 41
Kamikaze class, 141
Kanin class, 178
Karel Doorman class, 246
Karlsruhe, 238
Kashin class, 179
Kashmir, 116
Kasodo, 209
Kauffman, 221
Kawakaze, 143
KD classes, 408–9, 410, 411, 412
KD1 class, 408
KD3 class, 409
KD3A class, 408, 409
KD4 class, 409
KD6 class, 409
KD6A class, 409
KD7 class, 409
Kearny, 129
Kempenfelt, 76
Kennington, 73
Kersaint, 159
Khalid-class SSK, 488
Khedive, 40

Kidd class, 137
Kikusuki, 148
Kil class, 46
Kildare, 46
Kildin class, 176
Kilo-class (Project 877EKM) SSK, 438, 473, 489
Kilo-class (Type 636), SSK 438
King, Admiral Ernest, 36
Kirishima, 153
Kiyoshimo, 145
Knox class, 63, 220
Kobben class, 492
Kola class, 231
Köln class, 238
Kongo class, 153
Kortenaer class, 244
Koryu D class, 312, 313
Kosovo crisis, 341, 459
Kotaka, 109
Kotlin class, 175
Krivak class, 236
Krupny class, 177
Kummetz, Admiral Oskar, 38, 39
Kurama, 149
Kursk SSGN 337, 342–3, 344, 345, 448, 449

L

L class (Destroyer), 29, 47, 73, 74, 116
L class (UK submarine), 277, 384, 387
L class (USA submarine), 272, 361
L1, 361
L2, 361
L3, 361
L4 type, 286
L8, 384
L8, 361
L9, 361
L10, 361
L12, 384
L23, 384
la Fayette, 208
la Fayette class, 208
la Galissonnière, 161, 205

Mohammed V, Floréal class

507

INDEX

la Massa class, 103
la Palme, 155
Lada (Project 677) SSK, 438
l'Adroit, 156
l'Adroit class, 155
Lafayette-class SSBN, 332, 429, 430
Laffey, 42–3
Laforey class, 29, 47, 73, 74
Lake, Simon, 253, 257, 358, 361
l'Alcyon, 155
Lampo, 168
Lampo class, 99
Lancaster, 189, 202
Lanciere, 101, 170
Larne, 71
Le Brestois, 203
Le Corse, 203
Le Corse class, 203
Le Fantasque, 160
Le Fantasque class, 160
Le Foudroyant, 468
Le Hardi, 156
Le Hardi class, 156
Le Normand class, 203
Le Picard, 203
Le Redoutable class, 468
Le Temeraire, 471
Le Terrible, 468
Le Terrible (2008), 471
Le Tonnant, 468
Le Triomphant, 470, 471
Le Triomphant-class SSBN France, 468, 470–1
Le Vigilant, 470, 471
Leahy, 136
Leahy class, 130
Leander class, 62, 198, 238
Leavitt, Frank, 17
Leberecht Maass, 31
Leeds Castle, 194
Leninec class, 418
Leone, 167
Leone class, 165, 167
Leonidas, 29, 74
Léopard, 157
L'Espoire type, 417
l'Epeé, 156
Leyte Gulf, 138
Libeccio, 169, 229
Liberty, 74
Libra, 47, 222
Lightfoot, 76
Lightfoot class, 76, 80
Lightning, 18, 66
L'Indomptable, 468
L'Inflexible, 468
L'Inflexible-class SSBN, 468, 470
Lion, 159
Livermore class, 129
Loch Fada, 53, 195
Loch Katrine, 195
Loch Killin, 53
Loch Killisport, 195
Loch More, 57

Loch class, 57, 195
London, 122, 201
Lookout, 116
Lorraine, 27
Los Angeles, SSN 335, 337, 432, 433
Los Angeles-class SSN, 324, 336, 340, 348, 432–3, 443, 446, 457
Louisiana SSBN, 434
Lowestoft, 62
LR5 submersible vehicle, 344, 345
Lübeck, 238, 240
Lübeck, 62
Lucifer, 74
Ludlow, 94
Luigi Durand de la Penne, 9, 173
Luigi Rizzo, 227
Lupo, 229
Lupo class, 228
Luppis, Commander Johann, 16
Lusitania, sinking of the, 266–7, 292
Lütjens, 134
Lützow, 38, 39
Lynx, 67

M

M class (Destroyer), 75, 77, 116
M class (UK submarine), 385
M class (USA submarine), 362
M1 (UK), 280, 385
M1 (USA), 362
M2, 280, 385
M3, 280, 385, 393
Maass class, 182
Maiali (Sea pigs), 310
Malutka class, 418
McCloy, 219
Macdonough, 126
McFaul, 139
Maestrale, 229
Maestrale class, 169, 229
Mahan, 135
Mahan, Admiral Alfred Thayer, 65
Mahan class, 128
Maillé Brézé, 159
Mameluck, 156
Manchester, 124
Manju, 209
Manley, 95
Mansfield, 75
Marcello, 421
Marconi class, 421
Mariano G Vallejo SSBN, 332
Mariscal Antonio José de Sucre, 228
Mariotte, 269
Marksman, 76
Mashona, 114, 115
Massue, 22
Mastiff, 75
Masurca, 162
Matchless, 16
Matrozos S122, 475
Maury, 31

Max Schultz, 31, 182
McCann Rescue Chamber, 288, 289
Memphis SSN, 342
Meteorite, 317
Meynell, 191
Michigan SSBN, 347
Mikura class, 210
Milan, 159
Minegumo, 147
Minegumo class, 147
Minekaze class, 141
Minerva, 230
Minerva class, 230
Minneapolis-Saint Paul SSN, 340
Mirabello class, 165, 167
Mirka class, 233
Missori, 102
Mittel U-boats, 397, 399
Mitscher class, 133
Mobile Bay, 138
Modified Black Swan class, 190
Modified Flower class, 49
Modified Kashin class, 179
Modified R class, 78
Modified Trenchant class, 29
Mogador class, 160
Mogami, 212
Mohammed V, 207
Mohawk, 31
Molch, 313
Mölders, 134
Momi class, 140
Momo class, 111
Monginsidi, 218
Monsone, 224
Moorsom, 75
Mosto, 102
Mounts Bay, 195
Möwe class, 46
Mozambano, 96
Murakumo class, 110
Murasame class, 147, 152
Murray, 75
Mustin, 139
Mutsuki, 37, 141
Mutsuki class, 135

Myoko, 153
Myoko class, 40
Mystic (DSRV 1), 328

N

N class (Destroyer), 116
N class (Submarine), 362
N2, 362
N3, 362
Nachi, 41
Nachi class, 40
Nagatsuki, 148
Naiade class, 261
Najade, 239
Narsturtium, 47
Narushio SSK, 479
Narval, 261
Narvik campaign, 32–3
Narwhal (V5), 283, 366
Narwhal class, 282
Nasmith, Lt Commander Martin, 270, 271
Nassau, 25
Nastoychivyy, 180
NATO Submarine Rescue System (NSRS), 344, 345
Nautilus, 143
Nautilus (1954), 322–3, 324, 423, 424
Nautilus (V6), 282, 283, 284, 305, 366
Nautilus (N1), 282
Nautilus SSN, 326, 380
Navigatori class, 167, 169
Nazario Sauro (Destroyer), 166
Nazario Sauro SSK (Submarine), 482
Neger, 313
Nelson class, 31
Nembo class, 100
Nenohi, 143
Neustrashimy, 63, 175
Neuva Esparta, 120
New Jersey, 220
Newport News SSN, 433
Nibbio, 98
Nichelio, 420
Nicoloso da Recco, 167
Nicotera, 165

Seawolf-class SSN

INDEX

Nievo, 102
Nimitz, Admiral Chester, 55
Nimrod, 76
Norfolk, 122, 133, 202
Normandy, 245
North Cape, battle of, 38–9
Northumberland, 202
November-class SSN, 325, 336
Novik class, 88
Nowaki, 145
Nubian, 72

O

O class (Destroyer), 117
O class (Netherlands submarine), 490
O class (UK submarine), 284, 293, 351, 387, 388, 390
O class (USA submarine), 363, 364
O6, 363
O9, 363
O10, 363
O16, 363
O19, 490
Oakville, 192
O'Bannon, 180
Oberon, 453
Oberon (1927), 387
Oberon class, 338, 453, 476, 480
O'Brien class, 387
Odin, 297
Offa, 117
Ohio SSBN/SSGN, 331, 347
Ohio-class SSBN, 332, 333, 346, 430, 434, 462
Okinawa, battle of, 42–3
Öland, 186
Öland class, 186
Olimpia, 97
Oliver Hazard Perry class, 221
Onslow, 38, 39
Onyx, 338, 453
Opal, 77
Operation Deliberate Force, 341
Operation Desert Storm, 340
Operation Desert Strike, 341
Operation Mincemeat, 308–9
Operation Veritas, 341
Opportune, 117
Oriani class, 169, 170
Orione class, 97
Orpheus, 77
Orpheus (Submarine), 453
Orpheus (1935 submarine), 297
Oscar II-class SSGN 337, 342, 448–9
Osiris, 453
Östergötland, 187
Östergötland class, 187
Ostermanland SSK, 486
Ostro, 166
Osu, 111
Otchayannyy, 180

Otus, 453
Otway, 387
Oxley, 293, 387
Oyashio-class SSK, 479
Oyodo, 215

P

P class, 117
P514, 364
Pampanito, 370
Pandora, 388
Parsons, 133
Partenope, 96
Partenope class, 96
Parthian, 388
Parthian class, 284, 388, 390
Patch, General Alexander, 36
Patrician, 77
Paulding class, 92
Peacock, 190
Pearl Harbor, attack on, 285, 302, 312, 313, 363, 365, 366, 368
Pegaso class, 97, 224
Pegasone, 224
Pembroke Castle, 57
Penelope, 199
Pennsylvania SSBN, 434
Perch class, 302
Perkins, 92
Perla type, 420
Perle, 466
Permit SSN, 426, 427
Perry, 91
Perseus, 388
Perth, 40, 134
Pertuisane class, 105
Petard, 117
Petya class, 233
Phelps, 127
Philadelphia SSN, 348, 349
Pickerel, 321, 371
Pilo, 102
Pilo class, 102
Pincher, 70
Pintado SSN, 431
Pioneer, 255
Pipinos S121, 475
Pique class, 105
Platino type, 420
Plunger, 302
Plunger (1897), 259
Plunger SSN, 426
PN class, 98
Pogy SSN, 431
Polaris missile, 325, 330, 333, 428, 429, 430, 455, 456, 457, 462
Pompano, 302
Pommem, 25
Poncelot, 417
Pontiere, 101
Porpoise (Destroyer), 73
Porpoise (Submarine), 295, 393
Porpoise class (Submarine), 393

Yushio-class SSK

Porpoise class (Late submarine), 452, 453
Porter, 90, 127
Porter class, 127
Poseidon, 388
Poseidon missile, 330
Posen, 25
Poti class, 234
Power, Captain M.L., 40, 41
Prairal, 207
Prebie, 91
Premuda, 89
Primo Longobardo SSK, 482
Prini, 344
Proteus, 388
Puma, 198

Q

Q class, 118

R

R class (Destroyer), 78, 79, 118
R class (USA submarine), 363, 364
R class (Early, UK submarine), 277, 386, 390
R1, 364
R2, 364
R3, 364
R10, 364
R12, 364
Racehorse, 20
Raeder, Grand Admiral, 39
Raider, 78
Rainbow SSK, 477
Rastoropnyy, 180
Rathburne, 94
Raton, 368
Redoutable class, 416–17
Redoutable type, 417
Redpole, 23
Renown SSBN, 456, 457
Repeat Acorn class, 70–5
Repeat W class, 81
Repulse SSBN, 456, 457
Resolution SSBN, 456, 457
Resolution-class SSBN, 333, 334, 455, 456–7, 462
Restigouche, 50, 247
Resurgam, 256, 257

Revenge SSBN, 456, 457
Ricasoli, 165
Riga class, 232
Rio Grande do Norte, 131
River class, 22, 48, 49, 69, 72, 193
RO class, 286
RO60, 286
Roeder class, 182
Rommel, 134
Rorqual, 393
Rostock, 25
Rotoiti, 195
Rotterdam, 185
Rowan, 90, 132
Rubis, 335, 466, 467
Rubis-Améthyste-class SSN, 335, 466–7
Ruchamkin, 217
Rudderow class, 216–17

S

S class (Destroyer), 29, 78, 79, 118
S class (UK submarine), 284, 285, 304, 308, 351, 382, 389
S class (USA submarine), 281, 364, 365
S1, 281, 365
S1 (Holland type), 365
S2 (Lake type), 365
S3 (Government type), 365
S4, 365
S5, 365
S26, 365
S28, 365
S39, 365
S40, 365
S44, 365
S51, 365
Sachsen, 62
Sachsen class, 242
Sackville, 48, 49
Saffo class, 97
Sagittario, 228
Sailfish (Squalus), 289, 367
St. Austell Bay, 195
St. Laurent class, 247
St. Nazaire raid, 34–5
Sakalave, 108

509

INDEX

A4, A class

Sakura, 111
Salisbury, 198
Salmon (Destroyer), 67
Salmon (UK submarine), 389
Salmon (US submarine), 366
Salmon class, 285, 366
Salvatore Todaro, 483
Salvatore Todaro-class SSK, 483
Sam Houston SSBN, 429
Sam Rayburn SSBN, 430
Samidare, 152
San Georgio class, 173
San Jacinto, 138
Santee, 55
Saphir, 269
Saphir SSN, 466
Sardonyx, 79
Sargo, 367
Sargo class, 367
Saumarez, 40, 41
Sauro class (Destroyer), 165, 166
Sauro-class SSK (Submarine), 482
Saury, 367
Savage, 118
Savo Island, battle of, 36
Sawakaze, 150
Scamp SSN, 428
Scarborough, 199
Sceptre SSN, 459
Scharnhorst, 32, 41
Scheer, Admiral, 24, 25
Schleswig-Holstein, 184, 241
Sciré, 310, 474, 483
Scirocco, 169, 170
Scorcher, 389
Scorpene-class SSK, 485
Scorpio ROV 344, 345
Scorpion (George Washington SSBN), 325, 329, 346, 428
Scorpion SSN (1958), 328, 329
Scott class, 28
Scranton SSN, 432, 433
Scuka class, 419
Sculpin, 289, 367
Sea Devil, 371
Sea Dragon, 493
Sea Tiger, 493
Seaflower, 23
Seahorse SSN, 431

Seal (UK), 393
Seal (USA), 366
Seattle, 208
Seawolf SSN, 349, 424, 437
Seawolf-class SSN, 336, 340, 436–7
Seehund (Type 127), 315
Selfridge, 95
Sella, 165
Sella class, 165
Sellstrom, 217
Seraph, 308, 309, 389
Serpente, 97
Sfax, 416
Shaft, 40
Shakespeare class, 80
Shark, 25
Sheean SSK, 481
Sheffield, 38, 39, 124
Sheldrake, 71
Sherbrooke, Captain R. St. V., 38, 39
Shiloh, 153
Shimakaze, 141, 150
Shimayuki, 151
Shirakumo, 110
Shirane, 149
Shirane class, 149
Shiranui, 145
Shirataka, 109
Shiratsuyu class, 22
Shoup, 139
Shubrick class, 90
Shumushu (Shimushu) class, 209
Sierra I-class SSN, 446
Sierra II-class SSN, 446
Sims class, 128
Sindhu-class SSK, 489
Sirena type, 420
Sirio class, 230
Siroco, 154
Sirtori class, 103
Skat-class (670A) SSK, 489
Skipjack, 324, 325, 366
Skipjack-class SSN, 324–5, 426, 428
Skoryi (Skory) class, 174
Smith, 29
Smith class, 8, 29, 92

Snapper, 366
Sodermanland SSK, 486
Sodermanland-class SSK, 486
Sokol, 299
Soldati class, 101, 170
Somers class, 127
Souffleur, 388
South Dakota, 31
Sovereign SSN, 459
Sovremennyy class, 180
Spahi class, 106
Sparrowhawk, 25
Spartan SSN, 338, 339, 459
Sparviero class, 98
Spearfish (UK), 292, 389
Spearfish (USA), 367
Special Boat Service, (SBS) 304, 305
Special Operations Executive (SOE), 304, 305
Spica class, 47, 222
Spiteful, 68
Spitfire, 25
Splendid SSN, 338, 339, 341, 342, 459
Spruance class, 9, 137, 180
Squalus, 288–9, 363
SRV-300, 344
SS type, 287
SS39, 360
SS40, 361
SS-750, rescue vehicle 345
Stalinec class, 419
Starfish, 284
Starling, 52, 53
Steregushchiy, 237
Steregushchiy class, 237
Stingray, 366
Stockton, 94
Stork, 52, 53
Storm, 389
Strale, 99, 168
Strong, 131
Stuart, 28, 29
Sturgeon (UK), 389
Sturgeon (USA), 285, 366
Sturgeon-class SSN, 336, 431
Submarine Rescue Vehicle (SRV), 344
Subsmash, 318
Subsunk, 318, 319
Suffren, 162, 163
Suffren class, 162
The Sullivans, 130
Sumner class, 43
Superb SSN, 341, 459
Surcouf (Frigate), 208
Surcouf (Submarine), 283, 415
Surcouf class, 161
Swale, 193
Swift, 19, 26, 27, 66, 89, 167
Swiftsure SSN, 459
Swiftsure-class SSN, 338, 459, 460, 464

Swordfish (UK), 382
Swordfish (USA), 367

T

T class (Destroyer), 78, 118
T class (Submarine), 285, 290, 295, 304, 305, 351, 390–1, 392, 452
Tachibana, 111
Tachikaze class, 150
Takanami, 152
Takanami class, 152
Takasuki, 152
Takasuki class, 148
Talbot, 219
Talent SSN, 337, 460
Talisman, 304, 305
Tally Ho, 390
Tanaka, Admiral Raizo, 37
Tanatside, 191
Tang, 303, 321
Tang class, 321
Tantalus, 391
Tartar, 72, 115
Tartu, 159
Te Kaha, 249
Tench, 371
Tench class, 302, 321, 351, 371
Termagent, 196
Terra Nova, 247
Terutsuki, 146
Tetrarch, 295, 390
Thetis class, 239
Theodore Roosevelt SSBN, 428
Thermopylae, 391
Thetis, 288, 290–7, 318, 390
Thistle, 390
Thomas J. Gary, 56
Thomas A. Edison SSBN/SSN, 332, 429
Thomas Jefferson, SSBN/SSN 429
Thorn, 68
Thornton, 90
Thorough, 391
Thrasher, 298
Thresher SSN, 328, 329, 345, 426, 427
Thresher/Permit-class SSN, 325, 336, 426, 431
Thunderbolt (Thetis), 291, 299, 311
Thüringen, 24
Ticonderoga class, 138
Tiger, 68
Tigre, 157
Tillsonburg, 57
Ting-Yen, 109
Tinosa SSN, 427
Tipperary, 27
Tirailleur, 106
Tireless SSN, 460, 461
Tirpitz, 34, 35
Tirpitz, Admiral Alfred, 65
Tiru, 370

510

INDEX

Togo, Admiral, 109
Toledo SSN, 342, 348, 433
Torbay (Destroyer), 79
Torbay (Submarine), 298, 304, 305
Torbay SSN (Submarine), 460
Torelli (U(IT)25), 421
Totem, 391
Toti class, 482
Touareg, 216
Tourville, 163
Tourville class, 163
Trafalgar, 120
Trafalgar SSN, 341, 460, 461
Trafalgar-class (T boats) SSN, 334, 337, 341, 460–1, 464, 465
Trenchant, 390
Trenchant SSN, 460
Tribal class, 31, 59, 72, 101, 114
Trident missile, 333, 430, 434, 457, 462, 463
Tripoli, 96
Triton (Frigate), 239
Triton (UK submarine), 285, 293, 387, 390
Triton (USA submarine), 363
Triton SSN (Submarine), 425
Triumph (Submarine), 305
Triumph SSN (Submarine), 341, 460
Trooper, 311
Tromp, 245
Tromp class, 162
Troubridge, 118
Truant, 295, 304, 391
Truculent, 318–19
Truxtun, 91
Tryphon, 79
Tsubaki, 111
Tucker class, 93, 94
Tullibee, 369
Tuna, 304, 305
Tupi SSK, 491
Turbine, 100, 166
Turbine class, 166
Turbulent, 298–9
Turbulent SSN 341, 460
Turpitz (Battleship), 311, 312, 313–14, 315
Turquoise, 46
Turtle, 254
Tusk, 320, 321
Type 093, 473
Type 094, 472
Type 18, 59, 62, 199
Type 20, 197
Type 21, 41, 118, 196
Type 22, 118, 196
Type 27, 200
Type 28, 9, 201
Type 29, 189, 202
Type 47, 198
Type 48, 113, 124

Type 51, 125
Type 67, 198
Type 87, 59
Type 88, 123
Type 128, 240
Type 130, 242
Type 136, 243
Type 206A-class, SSK 475
Type 209-class, SSK 489, 491
Type 212A-class, SSK 474, 475, 482, 483, 491
Type 214 class, 475
Type A, 410
Type B, 410–11
Type C, 411
Type C-3, 287
Type J, 412
Type Sen Taka (I200), 413
Type Sen Toku, 413, 414
Typhoon-class (Project 941) SSBN, 331, 332, 444, 450–1
Tyrant, 78

U

U class (Destroyer), 78
U class (Submarine), 392
U class (1939) Types IIA, IIB, IIC, IID, 402
U1 (1906), 262, 394, 395
U1 (Type IIA), 402
U1 (Early), 394–5
U2, 262
U3, 395
U4, 390
U5, 394, 395
U6, 381
U7, 394
U8, 394
U9, 263, 394, 395
U9, (Type IIA) 402
U11, 395
U13, 394, 395
U14, 394
U15, 262, 394
U16, 394, 395
U17, 261, 277, 394
U18, 263, 394, 395
U19, 396
U20, 266, 396
U21, 263, 396
U22, 396
U23, 375
U24, 267
U25, 394
U27 (UCII), 265
U27 (VIIA), 402
U29, 300
U30, 292, 306
U31, 474
U35, 263, 395, 396, 399
U37, 416
U38, 397
U40, 375
U47, 300, 301

U63, 375
U65, 361
U68, 375
U69, 403
U81, 397
U90, 397
U96, 317, 403
U99, 301
U100, 397
U110, 306–7
U117, 277, 397
U120, 277
U123, 404
U124, 277
U127, 399
U139, 397, 408, 409, 412
U151, 273, 401
U151 class, 401
U155 (Deutschland), 272, 273, 401
U164, 277
U201, 306
U249, 316
U251, 403
U256, 405
U271, 405
U441, 405
U505, 307
U953, 405
U2326 (N35), 407
U2367, 407
U3008, 316
UB1, 398
UB11, 399
UB29, 399
UBI class, 398–9, 400
UBII class, 398–9
UBIII class, 398–9
UC1, 264
UC43, 379
UCI class, 400
UCII class, 400
UCIII class, 400
Ucka, 223
Udaloy class, 181
UE2 class, 397
U-Flak boats, 405
U-Flak1, 405
U-IX, 404
Ukuru, 210
Ukuru class, 210
Ula SSK, 492
Ula-class, SSK 492
Unbeaten, 297
Unbroken, 392
Undaunted, 297
Undine, 392
Undine class, 297
Union, 297
Unity, 73
Unruffled, 311
Upholder, 297, 298, 392
Upholder-class SSK, 476
Uppland, 186

Upright, 296, 297, 350–1
Upshur, 35
Uranami, 142
Urania, 230
Urchin, 299
Urge, 304
Ursula, 297
Usk, 297
Utmost, 297
U-VIIA, 403
U-VIIB, 403
U-VIIC, 317, 403, 407, 408

V

V class (Destroyer), 40, 79, 80–1, 95
V class (Late, UK submarine), 282
V class (USA submarine), 285
V class (Early, UK submarine), 378
Valiant SSN, 455, 458
Valiant-class SSN, 326, 327, 455, 458, 459
Valmy, 158, 159
Van Amstel, 246
van Heemskerck class, 244
Vanguard SSBN, 462, 463
Vanguard-class SSBN, 332, 457, 462, 464, 471
Vastergotland class, 486
Vauban, 159
Vauquelin, 159
Vauquelin class, 159
Vautour, 159
Vengeance SSBN, 462
Venus, 41
Verdun, 80, 158, 159
Veronesh SSGN, 448
Versatile, 80
Verulam, 41
Vetch, 192
Viceroy, 80
Victor I-class (Project 671) SSN, 337, 439
Victor II-class SSN, 337, 439
Victor III-class SSN, 337, 439, 473
Victoria SSK, 476, 477
Victoria-class (Type 2400) SSK, 476–7
Victorious SSBN, 462, 463
Vigilant (Destroyer), 68
Vigilant SSBN (Submarine), 462
Viking, 72
Vincenzo Gioberti, 169
Viper, 21
Virago, 196
Virginia SSN, 346, 349, 435, 465, 481
Virginia-class SSN, 346, 348, 349, 435
Viscount, 80
Voltigeur, 106
Vulcan, 19

511

INDEX/ACKNOWLEDGEMENTS

W

W class, 29, 30, 79, 80–1, 85, 114
Waddell, 134
Wadsworth, 93
Wahoo, 303, 368
Wakatake class, 140
Wakeful, 196
Walke, 131
Walker, Admiral H.T.C., 40
Walker, Commander Frederick (Johnny), 52–3
Waller SSK, 480, 481
Walpole, 81
Walrus, 452
Walrus I, 490
Walrus II, 490
Walrus II class, 490
Wanderer, 81
Wanklyn, Lt Commander Malcolm, 296, 297
Warburton-Lee, Captain B., 32, 33
Ward, 95
Warrington, 127
Warspite (Destroyer), 32, 33
Warspite SSN (Submarine), 455
Watchman, 81
Weapon class, 60, 119
Welland, 69
Wellington, 199
Whirlwind, 81
Whiskey class, 320
White, J. Samuel, 19
White, Lt Commander Geoffrey, 271
Whitehead, Robert, 16
Whiting, 68
Whitworth, Admiral, 33
Wickes class, 95
Wilhelm II, Kaiser, 65
Wilmarth, 216
Windrush, 193
Witte de With, 244
Woodrow Wilson SSBN, 430
Worcester, 81
Worden, 91
Wren, 53

X

X1, 282, 283, 386
X1 (Midget submarine), 313
X1 class, 386
X2, 313
X3, 313
X4, 313
X5, 314
X5, class 313
X6, 314
X7, 314
X8, 313
X9, 313
X10, 314
X25, 393
X-craft, 312, 313–15, 393
XE class, 314
XE3, 314, 315
XE4, 314
Xia-class SSBN, 472
XVII, 407
XXI, 316–7, 320–1, 406–7, 414
XXII, 407
XXIII, 407

Y

Yamagumo, 147
Yamagumo class, 147
Yamakaze, 143
Yankee-class (Project 667A) SSBN, 325, 330, 331, 333, 440, 444
Yarra, 71
Yoitsuki, 146
Yubari class, 214
Yubetsu, 214
Yugumo, 147
Yugumo class, 145
Yushio-class (Type 575/576) SSK, 478, 479

Z

Z23–39, 182
Zeeleeu II, 490
Zeffiro, 166
Zulu class, 320
Zwaardvis, 490
Zwaardvis II, 490

Acknowledgements

Research for the images used to illustrate this book was carried out by Ted Nevill of Cody Images, who supplied the majority of pictures. The publisher and Ted Nevill would like to thank all those who contributed to this research and to the supply of pictures:

AgustaWestland
ArtTech
BAE SYSTEMS
Blohm & Voss
Chrysalis Images
Jeremy Collins
DCN
General Dynamics
Howaldtswerke-Deutsche Werft
James Fisher Defence
Japanese Maritime Self-Defense Force
Kockums
Koninklijke Marine (Royal Netherlands Navy)
Marina Militare, Republica Italiana (Italian Navy)
National Archives & Records Administration, USA
NATO
Naval Historical Center, USA
Naval Photographic Club and Dr Duncan Veasay
Norwegian Ministry of Defence
Photographic Section, Naval Historical Center, Washington, DC, USA
Thomas Reyer
Robert Hunt Library
Royal Navy Submarine Museum
David Saw
Still Pictures, National Archives & Records Administration, College Park, Maryland, DC, USA
Ulis Fleming
US Department of Defense
US Naval Institute
US Navy

Key to flags

For the specification boxes, the flag that was current at the time of the vessel's commissioning and service is shown:

- Australia
- Brazil
- Canada 
- China 
- France 
- Germany: World War I 
- Germany: World War II 
- Germany: post-World War II 
- India 
- Italy: up to 1946 
- Italy: modern
- Japan
- The Netherlands 
- Norway 
- Pakistan 
- Spain 
- Sweden 
- UK 
- USA 
- USSR 

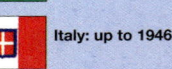

512